Serial Communications Developer's Guide, Second Edition

Serial Communications Developer's Guide,
Second Edition

Mark Nelson

IDG Books Worldwide, Inc.
An International Data Group Company

Foster City, CA ◆ Chicago, IL ◆ Indianapolis, IN ◆ New York, NY

Serial Communications Developer's Guide,
Second Edition
Published by
M&T Books
An Imprint of IDG Books Worldwide, Inc.
919 E. Hillsdale Blvd., Suite 400
Foster City, CA 94404
www.idgbooks.com (IDG Books Worldwide Web site)

Copyright © 2000 IDG Books Worldwide, Inc. All rights reserved. No part of this book, including interior design, cover design, and icons, may be reproduced or transmitted in any form, by any means (electronic, photocopying, recording, or otherwise) without the prior written permission of the publisher.

ISBN: 0-7645-4570-1

Printed in the United States of America

10 9 8 7 6 5 4 3 2 1

1B/RQ/RS/ZZ/FC

Distributed in the United States by IDG Books Worldwide, Inc.

Distributed by CDG Books Canada Inc. for Canada; by Transworld Publishers Limited in the United Kingdom; by IDG Norge Books for Norway; by IDG Sweden Books for Sweden; by IDG Books Australia Publishing Corporation Pty. Ltd. for Australia and New Zealand; by TransQuest Publishers Pte Ltd. for Singapore, Malaysia, Thailand, Indonesia, and Hong Kong; by Gotop Information Inc. for Taiwan; by ICG Muse, Inc. for Japan; by Intersoft for South Africa; by Eyrolles for France; by International Thomson Publishing for Germany, Austria and Switzerland; by Distribuidora Cuspide for Argentina; by LR International for Brazil; by Galileo Libros for Chile; by Ediciones ZETA S.C.R. Ltda. for Peru; by WS Computer Publishing Corporation, Inc., for the Philippines; by Contemporanea de Ediciones for Venezuela; by Express Computer Distributors for the Caribbean and West Indies; by Micronesia Media Distributor, Inc. for Micronesia; by Chips Computadoras S.A. de C.V. for Mexico; by Editorial Norma de Panama S.A. for Panama; by American Bookshops for Finland.

For general information on IDG Books Worldwide's books in the U.S., please call our Consumer Customer Service department at 800-762-2974. For reseller information, including discounts and premium sales, please call our Reseller Customer Service department at 800-434-3422.

For information on where to purchase IDG Books Worldwide's books outside the U.S., please contact our International Sales department at 317-596-5530 or fax 317-596-5692.

For consumer information on foreign language translations, please contact our Customer Service department at 800-434-3422, fax 317-596-5692, or e-mail rights@idgbooks.com.

For information on licensing foreign or domestic rights, please phone +1-650-655-3109.

For sales inquiries and special prices for bulk quantities, please contact our Sales department at 650-655-3200 or write to the address above.

For information on using IDG Books Worldwide's books in the classroom or for ordering examination copies, please contact our Educational Sales department at 800-434-2086 or fax 317-596-5499.

For press review copies, author interviews, or other publicity information, please contact our Public Relations department at 650-655-3000 or fax 650-655-3299.

For authorization to photocopy items for corporate, personal, or educational use, please contact Copyright Clearance Center, 222 Rosewood Drive, Danvers, MA 01923, or fax 978-750-4470.

Library of Congress Cataloging-in-Publication Data

Nelson, Mark, 1958-
  Serial communications developer's guide /Mark Nelson.
     p. cm.
  ISBN 0-7645-4570-1 (alk. paper)
  1. C++ (Computer program language) 2. Application software–Development. 3. Digital communications– Computer programs. I. Title
  QA76.73.C153 N454 2000
  005.7′1262–dc21   99-052733

LIMIT OF LIABILITY/DISCLAIMER OF WARRANTY: THE PUBLISHER AND AUTHOR HAVE USED THEIR BEST EFFORTS IN PREPARING THIS BOOK. THE PUBLISHER AND AUTHOR MAKE NO REPRESENTATIONS OR WARRANTIES WITH RESPECT TO THE ACCURACY OR COMPLETENESS OF THE CONTENTS OF THIS BOOK AND SPECIFICALLY DISCLAIM ANY IMPLIED WARRANTIES OF MERCHANTABILITY OR FITNESS FOR A PARTICULAR PURPOSE. THERE ARE NO WARRANTIES WHICH EXTEND BEYOND THE DESCRIPTIONS CONTAINED IN THIS PARAGRAPH. NO WARRANTY MAY BE CREATED OR EXTENDED BY SALES REPRESENTATIVES OR WRITTEN SALES MATERIALS. THE ACCURACY AND COMPLETENESS OF THE INFORMATION PROVIDED HEREIN AND THE OPINIONS STATED HEREIN ARE NOT GUARANTEED OR WARRANTED TO PRODUCE ANY PARTICULAR RESULTS, AND THE ADVICE AND STRATEGIES CONTAINED HEREIN MAY NOT BE SUITABLE FOR EVERY INDIVIDUAL. NEITHER THE PUBLISHER NOR AUTHOR SHALL BE LIABLE FOR ANY LOSS OF PROFIT OR ANY OTHER COMMERCIAL DAMAGES, INCLUDING BUT NOT LIMITED TO SPECIAL, INCIDENTAL, CONSEQUENTIAL, OR OTHER DAMAGES.

Trademarks: All brand names and product names used in this book are trade names, service marks, trademarks, or registered trademarks of their respective owners. IDG Books Worldwide is not associated with any product or vendor mentioned in this book.

 is a registered trademark or trademark under exclusive license to IDG Books Worldwide, Inc. from International Data Group, Inc. in the United States and/or other countries.

 is a trademark of IDG Books Worldwide, Inc.

ABOUT IDG BOOKS WORLDWIDE

Welcome to the world of IDG Books Worldwide.

IDG Books Worldwide, Inc., is a subsidiary of International Data Group, the world's largest publisher of computer-related information and the leading global provider of information services on information technology. IDG was founded more than 30 years ago by Patrick J. McGovern and now employs more than 9,000 people worldwide. IDG publishes more than 290 computer publications in over 75 countries. More than 90 million people read one or more IDG publications each month.

Launched in 1990, IDG Books Worldwide is today the #1 publisher of best-selling computer books in the United States. We are proud to have received eight awards from the Computer Press Association in recognition of editorial excellence and three from Computer Currents' First Annual Readers' Choice Awards. Our best-selling ...For Dummies® series has more than 50 million copies in print with translations in 31 languages. IDG Books Worldwide, through a joint venture with IDG's Hi-Tech Beijing, became the first U.S. publisher to publish a computer book in the People's Republic of China. In record time, IDG Books Worldwide has become the first choice for millions of readers around the world who want to learn how to better manage their businesses.

Our mission is simple: Every one of our books is designed to bring extra value and skill-building instructions to the reader. Our books are written by experts who understand and care about our readers. The knowledge base of our editorial staff comes from years of experience in publishing, education, and journalism — experience we use to produce books to carry us into the new millennium. In short, we care about books, so we attract the best people. We devote special attention to details such as audience, interior design, use of icons, and illustrations. And because we use an efficient process of authoring, editing, and desktop publishing our books electronically, we can spend more time ensuring superior content and less time on the technicalities of making books.

You can count on our commitment to deliver high-quality books at competitive prices on topics you want to read about. At IDG Books Worldwide, we continue in the IDG tradition of delivering quality for more than 30 years. You'll find no better book on a subject than one from IDG Books Worldwide.

John Kilcullen
Chairman and CEO
IDG Books Worldwide, Inc.

Steven Berkowitz
President and Publisher
IDG Books Worldwide, Inc.

Eighth Annual
Computer Press
Awards ≥1992

Ninth Annual
Computer Press
Awards ≥1993

Tenth Annual
Computer Press
Awards ≥1994

Eleventh Annual
Computer Press
Awards ≥1995

IDG is the world's leading IT media, research and exposition company. Founded in 1964, IDG had 1997 revenues of $2.05 billion and has more than 9,000 employees worldwide. IDG offers the widest range of media options that reach IT buyers in 75 countries representing 95% of worldwide IT spending. IDG's diverse product and services portfolio spans six key areas including print publishing, online publishing, expositions and conferences, market research, education and training, and global marketing services. More than 90 million people read one or more of IDG's 290 magazines and newspapers, including IDG's leading global brands — Computerworld, PC World, Network World, Macworld and the Channel World family of publications. IDG Books Worldwide is one of the fastest-growing computer book publishers in the world, with more than 700 titles in 36 languages. The "...For Dummies®" series alone has more than 50 million copies in print. IDG offers online users the largest network of technology-specific Web sites around the world through IDG.net (http://www.idg.net), which comprises more than 225 targeted Web sites in 55 countries worldwide. International Data Corporation (IDC) is the world's largest provider of information technology data, analysis and consulting, with research centers in over 41 countries and more than 400 research analysts worldwide. IDG World Expo is a leading producer of more than 168 globally branded conferences and expositions in 35 countries including E3 (Electronic Entertainment Expo), Macworld Expo, ComNet, Windows World Expo, ICE (Internet Commerce Expo), Agenda, DEMO, and Spotlight. IDG's training subsidiary, ExecuTrain, is the world's largest computer training company, with more than 230 locations worldwide and 785 training courses. IDG Marketing Services helps industry-leading IT companies build international brand recognition by developing global integrated marketing programs via IDG's print, online and exposition products worldwide. Further information about the company can be found at www.idg.com.   1/24/99

Credits

ACQUISITIONS EDITOR
Greg Croy

DEVELOPMENT EDITORS
Susan Christophersen
Barb Guerra
Terri Varveris

TECHNICAL EDITOR
Tim Kientzle

COPY EDITORS
Susan Christophersen
Mildred Sanchez
Richard H. Adin

PROJECT COORDINATORS
Linda Marousek
Joe Shines

COVER ART
Ron Chapple/FPG

GRAPHICS AND PRODUCTION SPECIALISTS
Mario Amador
Stephanie Hollier
Jude Levinson
Dina Quan
Ramses Ramirez

QUALITY CONTROL SPECIALIST
Chris Weisbart

ILLUSTRATOR
Mary Jo Richards

BOOK DESIGNERS
Jim Donohue
Kurt Krames

PROOFREADING AND INDEXING
York Production Services

About the Author

Mark Nelson is a programmer for Cisco Systems, Inc. in Dallas, Texas. He writes for technical publications such as *Dr. Dobb's Journal* and *C User's Journal,* and is the author of *The Data Compression Book* and *C++ Programmer's Guide to the Standard Template Library.*

This book is dedicated to Bert and Merlin, a pair of originals.

Preface

Welcome to *Serial Communications Developer's Guide, 2nd Edition*. This book teaches programmers how to use C++ to develop flexible communications programs. The sample code is targeted to the IBM PC but, by definition, is easy to port to other machines.

In the past, C programmers developing programs for RS-232 hardware found themselves locked into a "deadly embrace" with particular hardware. While their software may have worked properly in the given environment, changing any one of several variables, such as the hardware platform, the operating system, the C compiler, or the type of serial interface used often required an extensive rewrite of the program. This book shows how to avoid the limitations of serial programming by taking advantage of the strengths of C++.

This book focuses on writing programs that use the RS-232 ports; it doesn't go into detailed discussions of RS-232 hardware, applications software, BBS programs, and so on. Those topics are covered by other books on RS-232. This book covers what the other RS-232 books don't cover – the intricacies involved in developing software to interface computers to RS-232 hardware.

Why I Wrote This Book

RS-232 is still one of the most widespread methods that computers use to communicate with one another. Nearly every desktop PC in existence has one or two serial ports, and they can be used to talk to modems, lab equipment, POS terminals, and so on.

Even though RS-232 is everywhere, when it comes to programming, it suffers from a case of benign neglect. Programming interfaces are under-documented, and device drivers either don't exist or are horribly complicated to use. Programmers attempting to use serial communications on the original IBM PC rightfully thought of this type of programming as a black art.

What's worse, serial communications code tends to be extremely platform specific. The code you write that conforms to the Macintosh API has virtually no chance of being ported to your Win32 system in a reasonable amount of time. While we're used to seeing programs like Excel or Word ported between a wider variety of platforms, serial programs are usually stuck in a particular hardware niche.

But it doesn't have to be this way! With the aid of some carefully designed classes and a little understanding, it is possible to port your program from one platform to another by simply linking in a different driver. This book will show you how to do that.

New to this edition

When the first edition of this book was written in 1992, Windows NT was just beginning to make its presence felt, and Windows 95 was still a few years off. In fact, Windows 3.0 was just beginning to assert its dominance of the destkop. At the time, support for the Win32 Communications API was not a high priority item. Accordingly, the first edition of this book covered the Win16 API in one chapter and did not cover the 32-bit version at all.

Today the 32-bit versions of Windows have a stranglehold on the world's desktop computing, and programmers need to know how to support this platform. For this reason, virtually all of the new material in this second edition is devoted to the 32-bit Windows platform. The new material is as follows:

- ◆ A thorough discussion of the Win32 Communications API is in Chapter 10.

- ◆ The development of a useful and fully featured Win32 port class is covered in Chapter 11.

- ◆ A comprehensive test program for Win32 is covered in Chapter 12.

- ◆ A set of classes used to perform terminal emulation under Win32 is discussed in Chapter 13.

- ◆ A complete chapter, Chapter 15, is dedicated to a discussion of TAPI (Windows Telephony API). TAPI makes including modem support in your programs much easier.

What You Need to Know

This book is not for beginning programmers. To make effective use of this code, you should have a good handle on C programming, and preferably some C++ experience. The code in this book does not make heavy use of C++ features; if you understand the concept of classes and virtual functions you should be fine.

I don't assume that you know much about RS-232 communications. Each chapter builds on the knowledge dispensed in the previous one, but the book starts out with the assumption that you are a novice. The first few chapters go over basic concepts in quite a bit of detail. If you aren't afraid to study a bit and do some hands-on experimenting, you should be able to successfully make it through the material.

What You Need to Have

You need to be able to compile the C++ code in this book. Much of it is 16-bit code designed to run under MS-DOS or 16-bit Windows. This code can be compiled with either Microsoft Visual C++ 1.52 or Borland C++ 4.5 or earlier. Both of these 16-bit compilers are frozen by the manufacturer.

The Win32 code in the book has been compiled with Visual C++ 5.0. You should have either that version of Visual C++ or a later version.

How This Book Is Organized

There are hundreds of ways to organize this material. I decided not to lock the chapters into a structure where they are categorized into "rigid" parts, but I settled on a scheme that allows each chapter to be built upon the previous one. However, the book covers six topical areas that are outlined below. In addition, there is an appendix that explains what is on the accompanying CD-ROM and a glossary at the end of the book.

Chapters 1-2: The Basics

Chapter 1 provides a detailed overview of RS-232. You will learn about the RS-232 standard, its typical implementations, and how to work with it. This covers things like debugging tools, cable making equipment, and so on.

Chapter 2 introduces the RS232 class, which is the base class for all of the interfaces to hardware described in this book. Developing a versatile and easy-to-understand class here is important, because its design directly affects all classes derived from it throughout the book.

Chapters 3-7: 16-Bit DOS Interfaces

These chapters describe some of the most common software and hardware interfaces used to perform serial communications under the 16-bit DOS operating system. This includes classes that talk directly to standard PC comm ports, plus classes that interface with the PC BIOS, multiport boards, or FOSSIL drivers.

Chapters 8 & 13: Terminal Emulation

Terminal emulators provide a convenient way for users to interface with other computers via an RS-232 link. In these chapters, I present two different sample terminal emulator programs that use the standard RS-232 classes created in this book: DOS and Windows. The DOS and Windows terminal emulators are very different in terms of how they look and how the interface to the PC hardware works. But they still use the same body of shared code to talk to the RS-232 ports, as well as to perform terminal emulation internal functions.

Chapters 9-12: Windows Classes

Chapters 9 through 12 cover serial programming for both 16-bit and 32-bit Windows operating systems. Despite the common heritage of these two operating systems, their serial port drivers are quite different. Using the 32-bit driver is particularly difficult, and the use of wrapper classes such as the one presented in this section can be extremely helpful.

The Win16 API and corresponding class is covered completely in Chapter 9. The Win32 API and wrapper class is considerably more complex, and is covered in Chapters 10, 11, and 12.

Chapters 14 and 15: Using Modems

These two chapters show two different ways to interface your programs to standard intelligent modems. Chapter 14 shows the hard way, under MS-DOS, in which you carefully define AT commands that the modem understands, and use them at just the right points in your program.

Chapter 15 shows you how to control modems using TAPI, in which case Windows is tasked with knowing nearly everything important about interfacing with the modem.

Chapter 16: File Transfer Protocols

The final chapter shows how to write a file transfer protocol driver that uses the classes developed in the rest of the book. A sample driver that implements the popular ZMODEM protocol is developed as an example.

About the Companion CD-ROM

All of the source code presented in the book is included on the accompanying CD-ROM. You can build all the samples in the book with this code. For more information about the CD-ROM contents, please refer to the "What's on the CD-ROM?" Appendix.

Reach Out

The publisher and I want your feedback. After you have had a chance to use this book, please take a moment to register this book on the `http://my2cents.idgbooks.com` Web site. (Details are noted in the my2cents page in the back of the book.) Please be honest with your evaluation. Your feedback is the only way I have to know how to better address your needs.

Feel free to send me specific questions regarding the material in this book. I'll do my best to help you out and answer your questions, but I can't guarantee a reply. The best way to reach me is by e-mail:

markn@ieee.org

Also, I invite you to visit my World Wide Web site, which contains additional source material. Despite the massive attempts to make this book completely accurate, it is likely that a few errors have crept into these pages. My Web site also includes a list of any such errors. The URL is:

http://www.dogma.net/markn/

Acknowledgments

No book is the effort of just one person, and this one is certainly no exception. I owe a great debt of gratitude to the editorial staff at IDG Books, including Greg Croy, Barbra Guerra, Susan Christophersen, Terri Varveris, Mildred Sanchez, and Richard H. Adin. Their efforts are greatly appreciated.

I couldn't have finished the project without the understanding of my family. Denise, Kaitlin, and Joey have all been both understanding and forgiving of the inevitable disruptions in our lives that this book has caused. Bronte, true to her species, remained faithful throughout.

Finally, I owe a great debt to the readers of the first edition of this book. Your comments, suggestions, and encouragement made the second edition possible.

Contents at a Glance

Preface ix

Acknowledgments xiv

Chapter 1	RS-232 Overview. 1
Chapter 2	The RS232 Class. 49
Chapter 3	The PC8250 Class. 105
Chapter 4	Shared Interrupt Devices 203
Chapter 5	Intelligent Multiport Boards 219
Chapter 6	The BIOS and EBIOS classes 269
Chapter 7	The FOSSIL Interface 299
Chapter 8	Terminal Emulation 327
Chapter 9	The Win16 Driver 389
Chapter 10	The Win32 Comm API 433
Chapter 11	The Win32Port Class 469
Chapter 12	The Win32Test Program. 509
Chapter 13	Win32 Terminal Emulation 573
Chapter 14	Using Modems Under MS-DOS. 649
Chapter 15	Using Modems Under Win32 – TAPI. 683
Chapter 16	File Transfers and ZMODEM. 765

Appendix: What's on the CD-ROM? 823

Glossary. 829

Index. 835

End-User License Agreement 860

CD-ROM Installation Instructions 864

Contents

Preface ix

Acknowledgments xiv

Chapter 1   RS-232 Overview 1
        The RS-232 Standard 2
        Results of the Omissions from the Standard 3
        ASCII — Another RS-232-C? 3
        Problems with ASCII 5
        DTE and DCE 5
        RS-232: The Physical Interface 6
            Signal Formats 8
            Data lines 10
            Marking and spacing 11
            Control lines 11
            Electrical lines 13
        RS-232-C Specification Limitations 13
        Cabling 14
            The null modem cable 15
            A more rational cable design 16
            RS-232 9- to 25-pin adapters 17
            Home cable making 18
            Macintosh cabling 19
            Cabling recommendations 20
        UARTs 20
            8250 clones 21
            UART (lack of) progress 21
            8250 functionality 22
            Control registers 23
            Status registers 23
            Interrupt functions 23
            The 16550 difference 24
            16550 descendants 25
        Multiport Boards 25
        Intelligent Multiport Boards 26
        Modems 28
            Data rates 28
            Intelligence 31
            Handshaking 33

Contents

Flow Control. 34
    Hardware flow control 34
    Software flow control. 35
    Local versus pass through flow control 36
File Transfers 36
Software and Hardware Tools. 39
    PC software 39
    BBS software 39
    Programming libraries 40
    Tools of the trade 41
    Cable-making equipment 44
What About the Internet? 46

Chapter 2   **The RS232 Class. 49**
Why C++ Is the Language of Choice. 49
    An attempt to get by with C 50
    Problems with this approach 50
    Dispatching with function pointers 51
    Moving function pointers to a structure. 52
    If C can do it, why use C++? 53
Class RS232 55
    A few conventions 58
    Default parameters 61
    Mandatory and optional functions. 62
    Where is the constructor? 62
The RS232 Class, Member by Member 63
    Protected members 63
    Protected member functions. 66
    Public data members 67
    Mandatory virtual functions 68
    Nonvirtual functions 72
    A very short example program. 76
    The optional functions 77
The Code. 86

Chapter 3   **The PC8250 Class. 105**
The 8250 UART 106
    8250 register set 106
    8250 lookalikes 120
    Extensions to the 8250 design 122
    8250 oddities 123
The Standard COM Card 125
    Laptop oddities 126
    How interrupts work on the PC 126
    Hardware basics 127
PC8250 Driver Structure. 129
    The interrupt service routine 129

Contents xix

	The isr_data structure. 133
	The ISR code 137
	PC8250.CPP. 148
	Support Classes. 184
	The Queue package 184
	The interrupt manager package 188
	A Test Program. 197
Chapter 4	**Shared Interrupt Devices** 203
	Multiport Boards. 203
	Interrupt line sharing – the status register 204
	Selecting IRQ lines and addresses. 205
	The Handler Class. 206
	The Digi Classic Board Interrupt Handler 208
	The constructor 208
	The destructor. 211
	CHAPT04.CPP. 213
	Header file inclusion. 213
	Variables and constants 213
	Adding the Classic handler. 214
	Opening ports and windows. 214
	Building and running the program. 215
	Multitasking under MS-DOS. 217
Chapter 5	**Intelligent Multiport Boards** 219
	The Hardware 220
	Design freedom 221
	Control programs. 222
	The Software Interface 222
	The Digi International API 224
	Function 0: initialize port (BIOS compatible) 225
	Function 1: output a single character (BIOS compatible) 226
	Function 2: input a single character (BIOS compatible) 227
	Function 3: read line and modem status (BIOS compatible). 227
	Function 4: extended port initialization (EBIOS compatible) 227
	Function 5: extended port control (EBIOS compatible). 229
	Function 6, Subfunction 0: get port name 229
	Function 6, Subfunction 1: get driver information. 230
	Function 6, Subfunction 2: get board information. 230
	Function 6, Subfunction 0xff: get driver name 231
	Function 7: send break. 232
	Function 8: alternate status check 232
	Function 9: clear a port's buffers 232
	Function 0x0A: input buffer count 233
	Function 0x0B: drop a port's handshake lines 233
	Function 0x0C: get a port's parameters 234

xx Contents

           Function 0x0D: get pointer to character ready flag 235
           Function 0x0E: write a buffer 236
           Function 0x0F: read a buffer 236
           Function 0x10: clear RX buffer 236
           Function 0x11: clear TX buffer 237
           Function 0x12: get free space in the TX buffer 237
           Function 0x13: raise a port's handshake lines 237
           Function 0x14: peek at character. 238
           Function 0x15: get space used in the RX buffer. 238
           Function 0x1B: get buffer sizes and water marks. 238
           Function 0x1C: set handshaking water marks 239
           Function 0x1E: set handshaking 240
           Function 0x20: enable/disable BIOS pacing. 240
           Function 0xFD: get buffer counts. 241
       Summary of INT14 Driver Functions 241
       Configuring Your Intelligent Board. 243
       Configuring the Ports 245
       Implementing the DigiBoard Class 246
       The Code. 246
       CHAPT05.EXE. 265

Chapter 6   **The BIOS and EBIOS Classes. 269**
       BIOS Details 270
           Function 0: initialize port (BIOS) 270
           Function 1: output a single character (BIOS) 271
           Function 2: input a single character (BIOS) 272
           Function 3: read line and modem status (BIOS) 272
           Function 4: extended port initialization (extended BIOS). 272
           Function 5, Subfunction 0: read modem control register
              (extended BIOS). 274
           Function 5, Subfunction 1: write modem control register
              (extended BIOS). 274
       Problems. 275
       The Code. 275
       Inheritance 276
       Testing the BIOS Classes 295

Chapter 7   **The FOSSIL Interface 299**
       History 299
           The solution. 300
       The FOSSIL Specification 301
           Function 0: initialize port (BIOS) 301
           Function 1: transmit a single byte (BIOS). 302
           Function 2: get a received character (BIOS) 302
           Function 3: read status registers (BIOS) 302
           Function 4: open serial port. 303
           Function 5: close port 303

Contents

	Function 6: control DTR.	304
	Function 8: flush the TX buffer	304
	Function 9: purge the input buffer.	305
	Function 0x0A: purge the output buffer	305
	Function 0x0B: transmit with no wait	306
	Function 0x0C: single character peek.	306
	Function 0x0F: select flow control.	306
	Function 0x18: read a buffer	307
	Function 0x19: write a buffer	308
	Function 0x1A: break control	308
	Function 0x1B: get FOSSIL driver information	308
	Sources.	309
	The Source Code	310
	Building CHAPT07.EXE	323
	A Test Run	324
Chapter 8	**Terminal Emulation**	**327**
	How to Create the Test Program	327
	Why Emulate a Terminal?.	327
	Escape Sequences	328
	Terminal intelligence	329
	Tower of babel	329
	ANSI.SYS	330
	ANSI.SYS escape sequences	330
	ANSI.SYS keyboard sequences	335
	A Terminal Class.	337
	A Test Program.	339
	Class AnsiTerminal	341
	Debugging Hooks	360
	The BaseWindow Class	362
	The TextWindow Class	367
	Making the Test Program	386
Chapter 9	**The Win16 Driver**	**389**
	Windows Programming	389
	The Microsoft Windows 16-Bit Device Driver.	390
	The Communications API.	390
	Putting It Together	401
	A Win16 Test Program	422
	Building TEST232W.EXE.	429
Chapter 10	**The Win32 Comm API**	**433**
	Win32 Programming Differences	433
	Comm ports as file objects	433
	Threading a must	434
	The Win32 Device Driver	435
	Data structures.	435
	The communications API	444

Contents

Chapter 11	**The Win32Port Class** **469**	
	The Win32Port Class. 469	
	MTTTY.C – documentation by example 469	
	Threading architecture and conventions. 470	
	The output thread. 472	
	The input thread. 477	
	Notification 482	
	Class member overview 484	
	Helper class – MTDeque 503	
	Helper class – Dcb 504	
	The IdleFunction Under Win32. 505	
Chapter 12	**The Win32Test Program** **509**	
	CHAPT12.EXE. – A Console-Based Test Program 509	
	The dialog-based control panel. 510	
	The customized derived class 516	
	The Source Code 517	
Chapter 13	**Win32 Terminal Emulation** **573**	
	A Terminal Window Class. 573	
	Requirements 574	
	C++ versus Windows 574	
	Class Win32Term – basic internals. 578	
	Class Win32 – Definitions. 580	
	Private classes 580	
	Data members. 581	
	Public code members 587	
	Protected code members. 592	
	Integrating Win32Term with AnsiTerm. 596	
	Class AnsiWinTerm 596	
	AnsiWinTerm and class Win32Port 597	
	AnsiWinTerm RX notification 598	
	AnsiWinTerm and class AnsiTerm 600	
	AnsiWinTerm listings. 600	
	The Chapter 13 Demo Program. 609	
	Menu commands 610	
	The source code 613	
	Suggested Improvements 623	
Chapter 14	**Using Modems Under MS-DOS** **649**	
	Dr. Jekyll and Mr. Modem. 649	
	The hardware standards 650	
	The software standards. 651	
	Today's modems. 657	
	Modem Capabilities 659	
	Creating a capability entry. 662	
	The Modem class 662	

	The public interface 664
	Protected members................................. 667
	A Test Program..................................... 677
	Making TSTMODEM.CPP 681
Chapter 15	**Using Modems Under Win32 – TAPI........... 683**
	The History of TAPI 683
	An Overview of TAPI 684
	TAPI notification methods 684
	Synchronous vs. asynchronous functions 685
	TAPI objects...................................... 685
	TAPI annoyances 686
	TAPI Functions Used in This Chapter 686
	TAPI initialization and shutdown....................... 687
	Line control 688
	Call configuration 692
	Call control 695
	The callback function................................ 699
	The SimpleTapi Class 700
	Class management and status.......................... 701
	Call and line management/configuration 702
	Notification functions................................ 705
	Important internals.................................. 706
	Debugging notes.................................... 708
	Room for improvement – a shortcoming 708
	Class Tapi32Port – the final detail 709
	The Chapter 15 Demo Program...................... 709
	SimpleTapi integration 710
	The source code 711
Chapter 16	**File Transfers and ZMODEM................. 765**
	Protocol History 765
	Enter ZMODEM 766
	Why ZMODEM?.................................... 767
	An Overview of ZMODEM 768
	ZMODEM frame types 768
	Header formats..................................... 773
	Data subpacket formats 775
	Encoding 776
	Odds and ends 777
	A File Transfer 778
	The FileTransfer Class............................ 780
	The Zmodem Class 782
	The Test Program 782
	The CRC Classes 785
	Source Code 788

Appendix: What's on the CD-ROM? 823

Glossary. 829

Index. 835

End-User License Agreement 860

CD-ROM Installation Instructions 864

Chapter 1

RS-232 Overview

IN THIS CHAPTER

- The RS-232 standard and results of the omissions from the standard
- ASCII — another RS-232-C?
- Problems with ASCII
- DTE and DCE
- RS-232: The physical interface
- RS-232-C specification limitations
- Cabling
- UARTs
- Multiport boards and intelligent multiport boards
- Modems
- Flow control and file transfers
- Software and hardware tools
- What about the Internet?

THIS CHAPTER PROVIDES a concentrated overview of RS-232, some of the hardware used in serial communications, and tools of the trade. Many of you may already have a good background in working with RS-232 hardware. If you are comfortable with modems, serial ports, cabling, and so on, you may want to skim this chapter or even skip it entirely for now and come back to it if needed.

By necessity, this chapter skips some of the topics that are tangential to programming. For example, it doesn't discuss the history of electronic communications. It doesn't describe the modulation schemes used by various modems, and it doesn't discuss how to log in to your Internet Service Provider.

Rather, this chapter briefly covers topics that directly affect the creation and testing of the programs in this book. Such topics include the RS-232 standard, connectors and cables, Universal Asynchronous Receiver/Transmitters (UARTs) and serial boards, modems, handshaking, online services, and some basic debugging hardware.

The RS-232 Standard

A well-written standard can become the framework around which developers build useful products. If such products carefully adhere to a standard, users count on them to perform predictably. For C++ programmers, ISO/ANSI C++ is such a standard, spelling out rules that a C++ compiler must follow to conform, as well as the rules a program must follow.

Because of the C++ standard, I can write a program that uses the *iostreams* facility for output with assurance that I'll have that facility in my compiler's library. Thus, I can start to write software that is portable, meaning that it can work with different compilers and even on different types of computers with different operating systems. The C++ standard that was finalized in 1998 will be used whenever possible in this book. (Older 16-bit compilers such as Visual C++ 1.5 are not fully compliant with the standard.)

The RS-232 standard was developed in an attempt to ensure that computer *hardware* shared the same portability characteristics as computer software. In theory, computer equipment that adheres to this standard can communicate with other RS-232 equipment with little or no trouble. The official standard is published by the Electronic Industries Alliance (EIA), a trade organization in Washington, D.C (www.eia.org).

In practice, the RS-232 standard (and its sister standard, ITU Recommendation V.24) can be termed a limited success. The industry developed a de facto standard based on the published standard so that devices adhering to the de facto standard can usually communicate.

The current version of the RS-232 standard is known as EIA-232-F. An earlier version of the standard, EIA-232-C is still the most widely known version of the standard despite the fact that it has been superseded. Whichever version you use, the RS-232 standard can be considered only a limited success because of what it leaves out, rather than what it contains. The standard concentrates on the electrical interface between two different types of equipment: Data Terminal Equipment (DTE) and Data Communications Equipment (DCE). Typically, a desktop computer or terminal is a DTE and a modem is a DCE. The standard spells out which circuits can connect these two pieces of equipment and what the electrical characteristics of these circuits should be.

Nowhere in the RS-232 standard do we find items of major importance, such as the following: the size and shapes of connectors; the format of serial data being exchanged; types of codes used to exchange data; protocols used to exchange data; methods for connecting DTE to DTE or DCE to DCE; or rules regarding when and where particular circuits must be used or can be omitted.

Results of the Omissions from the Standard

Because the EIA left so much open area in the standard, designers of RS-232 equipment have relied on an informal process of evolution to arrive at the de facto standard. Some portions of the specification have jelled very nicely whereas others are still evolving.

The RS-232 connector is a good example of how the lack of definition has brought about duplication. The EIA elected not to define the RS-232 connector in early versions of the specification. Because 25 circuits were defined, designers began using the D-Subminiature 25-pin connector for their RS-232 interfaces. This quickly became part of the de facto standard. However, when IBM introduced the PC-AT in 1984, it used a 9-pin D-Subminiature connector, presumably to save space on its card edges. Because IBM is big enough to set standards on its own, there are now two types of connectors in the de facto standard, and users have to deal with both.

ASCII — Another RS-232-C?

Just as a hardware standard is needed, support of a universal standard for text-based information is required for proper development of serial communications. Without a standard for information interchange (the "II" in "ASCII"), serial communications would be limited to machines of similar architectures, creating an array of information universes that would be unconnected.

Because of ASCII, we can now use RS-232 connections to send files back and forth between UNIX systems, IBM PCs, Macintoshes, and DEC VAX systems. Even recalcitrant systems such as IBM 370s know enough to include conversion software for transportation of data outside their domain. All the code in this book is written with the assumption that ASCII code is used for all transactions. The following table is the official ASCII chart.

0	NUL	30	RS	60	<	90	Z	120	x
1	SOH	31	US	61	=	91	[	121	y
2	STX	32	SP	62	>	92	\	122	z
3	ETX	33	!	63	?	93	]	123	{
4	EOT	34	"	64	@	94	^	124	|
5	ENQ	35	#	65	A	95	_	125	}
6	ACK	36	$	66	B	96	`	126	~
7	BEL	37	%	67	C	97	a	127	DEL
8	BS	38	&	68	D	98	b		
9	HT	39	'	69	E	99	c		
10	LF	40	(	70	F	100	d		
11	VT	41	)	71	G	101	E		
12	FF	42	*	72	H	102	f		
13	CR	43	+	73	I	103	g		
14	SO	44	,	74	J	104	h		
15	SI	45	-	75	K	105	i		
16	DLE	46	.	76	L	106	j		
17	DC1	47	/	77	M	107	k		
18	DC2	48	0	78	N	108	l		
19	DC3	49	1	79	O	109	m		
20	DC4	50	2	80	P	110	n		
21	NAK	51	3	81	Q	111	o		
22	SYN	52	4	82	R	112	p		
23	ETB	53	5	83	S	113	q		
24	CAN	54	6	84	T	114	r		
25	EM	55	7	85	U	115	s		
26	SUB	56	8	86	V	116	t		
27	ESC	57	9	87	W	117	U		
28	FS	58	:	88	X	118	v		
29	GS	59	;	89	Y	119	w		

Problems with ASCII

There is, however, a major problem with 7-bit ASCII that is evident from its name: *American* Standard Code for Information Interchange. Foreign characters with their accents, umlauts, and tildes are not really welcome in the ASCII domain. However, the ASCII standard defines special operations that can be used to transmit some foreign characters.

Despite this provision, the standard still suffers from exactly the same problem as the RS-232 standard. That is, the standard made these features optional rather than required. Thus, the vast majority of devices transferring ASCII data via RS-232 lines are not able to translate alternate character sets.

The Unicode standard, developed by a consortium of companies including IBM, Apple, and a number of UNIX vendors, uses a 16-bit encoding that encompasses all existing national character code standards, including those used in East Asia for ideographic characters. The International Organization for Standardization (ISO) adopted the Unicode standard as a superset of ISO 10646 in June 1992. ISO's adoption of the Unicode standard will encourage programmers worldwide to use a 16-bit encoding, but it will undoubtedly take some time before 16-bit serial transmission is in widespread use.

Most RS-232 communications is done either via transfer of raw binary data (which is generally tied to the architecture of a specific machine) or data encoded in ASCII format.

DTE and DCE

The RS-232 specification wasn't really designed to let computers talk to one another directly. The specification was laid out to let *Data Terminal Equipment* (DTE) talk to *Data Communications Equipment* (DCE.) In the classic definition, Data Terminal Equipment refers to either terminals or PCs acting as terminals (by using terminal emulation software). DCE usually refers to modems that communicate via telephone lines.

Figure 1-1 shows a DTE/DCE session being carried out according to the RS-232 specification. Two DTE devices (in this case, a terminal and a UNIX computer) are communicating via phone lines.

DCE modems move the data long distances over telephone wires. The two DTE devices and the two DCE devices communicate via the RS-232 specification.

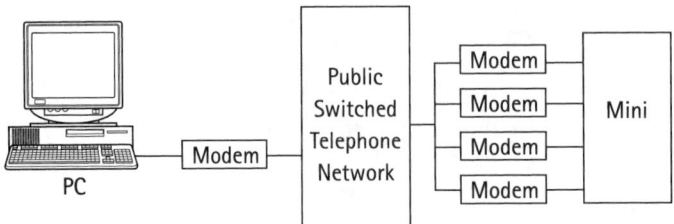

Figure 1-1: A communications session à la RS-232-C

The RS-232 control lines discussed in the next section were all clearly designed for the establishment and control of a communications session using a DTE and a DCE. This is one reason that RS-232 runs into some trouble when trying to communicate between two DTEs, for example. To connect two PCs directly without the use of a modem, you have to resort to such unusual devices as a null modem cable.

RS-232: The Physical Interface

The average user first encounters RS-232 at the mechanical and electrical level. For programmers, having even a basic understanding of RS-232 connections is enough to feel comfortable working with cables, connectors, cards, and wires.

As I mention earlier, the RS-232 standard does not specify a particular connector. Implementers were free to use any type of connector for RS-232 devices. Of course, this sort of freedom leads to the chaos that a good standard should prevent. Manufacturers came to a consensus during the 1970s that led to the acceptance of the D-Subminiature 25-pin connector as the standard RS-232 connector.

Another evolving part of the standard is related to the gender of connectors used in an RS-232 connection. Before the IBM PC, there wasn't much consistency in the use of male and female connectors for RS-232 equipment. IBM began using exclusively male connectors for the RS-232 ports on the PC, thereby implying that DCE equipment should use female connectors. Once again, by sheer power of inertia, most of the industry has followed this convention. Now, regardless of whether a connector is 9-pin or 25-pin, you can reasonably expect that DTE devices such as PCs will have male connectors (with pins), and DCE equipment such as modems will have female connectors (with mating sockets.)

Figure 1-2 shows the pinouts on the standard 25-pin D-Subminiature connector normally used for RS-232 connections. For someone unfamiliar with the interface, even 25 signals can seem like an overwhelming number. All these signals have a purpose, but many are used only rarely. The RS-232 connector is like a Swiss army knife with 25 blades. The user typically relies on just a few blades, and might not even remember what some of the more obscure ones are even designed to do!

Figure 1-3 shows the connectors as they are more commonly seen in the desktop world. The 25 pins used in a standard RS-232-C connection have been reduced to a more manageable nine. Many manufacturers are now using the space-saving 9-pin connector pioneered by IBM.

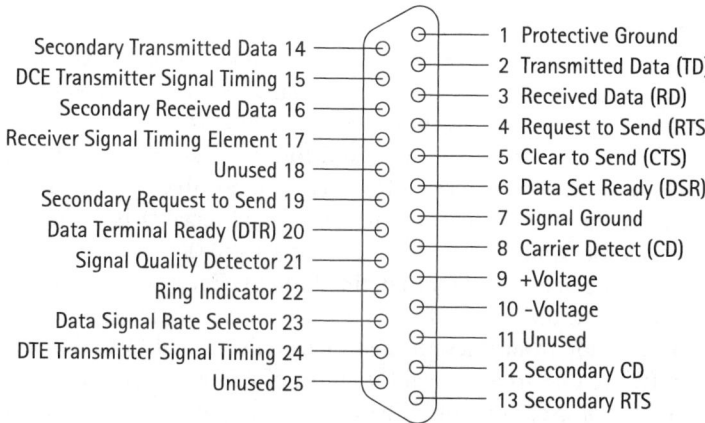

Figure 1-2: Pinouts on a 25-pin connector

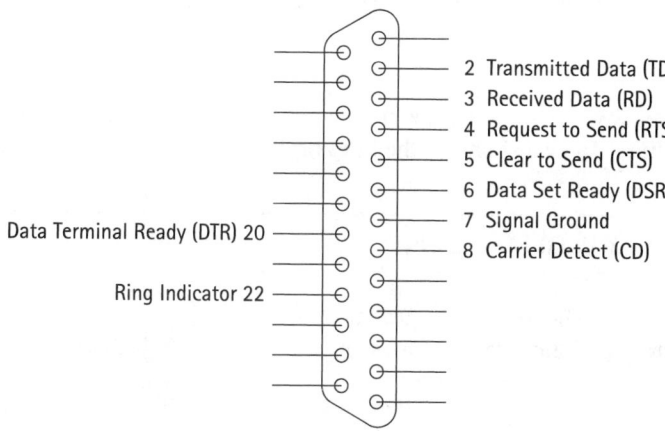

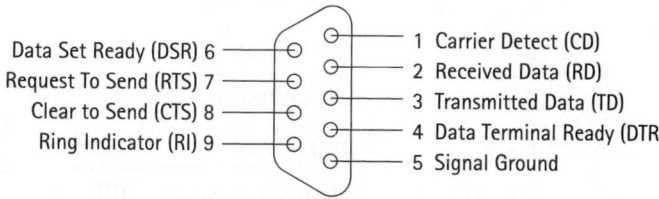

Figure 1-3: Commonly used RS-232 signals (9 and 25 pin)

With the exception of the two ground signals on the connector, all RS-232 connections have the same electrical characteristics. Normally, the digital electronics found in a PC use a single voltage (traditionally 5 volts) as a logical 1, and 0 volts, or ground, as a logical 0. This works fine when the circuit is confined to a well-behaved circuit board with solid copper traces and little or no noise.

RS-232 connections normally can't expect a well-behaved electrical environment. Typical serial connections may be asked to send signals hundreds of feet over noisy lines. The normal 5-volt signals would suffer too much degradation when transmitted over these distances. To assure successful transmission, RS-232 signals must produce outputs that range from +5 to +15 volts for a positive signal, and −5 to −15 volts for a negative signal. A valid input for an RS-232 receiver is defined as +3 volts or greater for a valid 1, and −3 volts or less for a valid 0.

This signaling method is complicated by undefined inputs. Because the standard specifies that input voltages in the range of −3 to +3 volts are undefined, you can't count on any logical behavior from unconnected or heavily loaded lines. For example, I often write software that tries to read the status of a modem via the Carrier Detect (CD) line. If no modem is connected to the CD input pin on my PC, I have no guarantee as to whether I will read in a 1 or a 0 on that line. Under some circumstances, my reading from that input line may frantically jump back and forth between 0 and 1 as noise comes in from other lines.

Signal Formats

The nine commonly used RS-232 lines can be broken down into three groups: data, control, and electrical lines. Table 1-2 shows the lines broken down into this format.

TABLE 1-2 THE COMMONLY USED RS-232 LINES

Category	9-Pin Connector	25-Pin Connector	Signal Name	Abbreviation
Data	3	2	Transmitted Data	TD
	2	3	Received Data	RD
Control	7	4	Request To Send	RTS
	8	5	Clear To Send	CTS
	6	6	Data Set Ready	DSR
	1	8	Carrier Detect	CD
	4	20	Data Terminal Ready	DTR

Category	9-Pin Connector	25-Pin Connector	Signal Name	Abbreviation
	9	22	Ring Indicator	RI
Electrical	5	7	Signal Ground	

Note that signal CD is formally referred to as RLSD, for Received Line Signal Detect. "CD" has come into more common usage, and it will be used consistently in this book.

The communications and control lines used in an RS-232 connection are all unidirectional, meaning that they are output by one side of the connection and input on the other. Each signal has a particular orientation that depends mostly on whether a device is a DCE or DTE. Figure 1-4 shows the normal directions for most of these signals.

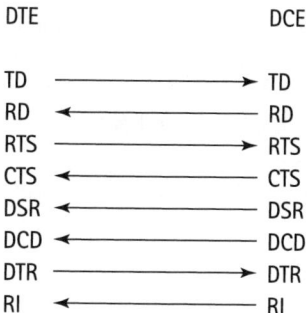

Figure 1-4: Direction of RS-232 Lines

It is difficult to remember the direction of the TD and RD lines. TD has the ambiguous name of Transmitted Data, which could refer to either side of the connection because both are transmitting data. For these lines (and many other RS-232 lines), you should always take the point of view of the DTE device, which is usually the terminal or PC you will be working on. So, TD refers to data that is being *transmitted from* your PC. RD refers to data that is being *received by* your PC.

Data lines

The actual transmission of data between a DTE and a DCE takes place over the two RS-232 communication lines, RD and TD. The TD line handles data being transmitted from the PC (DTE device), and RD handles data being sent from the modem, or DCE device. In the world of desktop systems, TD and RD transmit asynchronous data at a fixed rate using start and stop bits for framing. One oddity associated with RS-232 data is that for the communications lines, a low voltage (less than −3 volts) is considered to be a logic 1 and a high voltage (greater than 3 volts) is considered to be a logic 0. All the RS-232 control lines use the opposite (and more frequent) convention. Fortunately, you don't have to worry about this convention unless you are debugging at the electrical level, with voltmeter and wire strippers.

Figure 1-5 shows the format of the data being transmitted on an RS-232 line. Note that the idle line is held at a logic level 1. The start of a character is signified by the reception of a start bit, which is a normal bit 0 sent at the current baud rate. The start bit is followed by eight (or sometimes fewer) data bits, with the least significant bit first. Finally, one or more stop bits with a logic 1 are sent. (If you are lucky enough to have access to an oscilloscope, you can view this by transmitting a single character in a tight loop and setting your scope to trigger on a positive transition.)

The exact details of the data format are really not crucial to the programmer's ability to write effective communications programs. The interface to the RS-232 line is normally done via a UART, which assembles those bits into a byte to be delivered to the CPU. The UART is usually a single chip that reads and writes serial data like that used by RS-232.

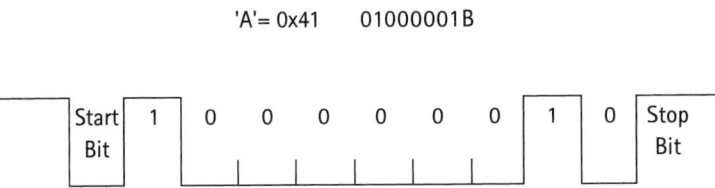

Figure 1-5: A sample character sent via RS-232

The duration of each bit sent across the channel determines the speed of the signal. The unit of speed is commonly referred to as either *bits per second* or *baud*, with the two terms being used interchangeably. Some sticklers for accuracy will point out that "baud" is not interchangeable with "bits per second"; however, for our purposes they are synonymous. The distinction comes into play only if you are an engineer designing modulation schemes for modems; when looking at RS-232 data, you can pretend the terms are identical.

Marking and spacing

When an RS-232 data line is idle, it is said to be in the *marking* state, which corresponds to a logic level of one. When a character is being transmitted, the start bit and any subsequent 0 bits are said to be *spacing*. These two terms date all the way back to the early days of telegraphy, and are still frequently used in discussions of RS-232. For example, in Chapter 2, the description of an RS-232 break is given as an extended period of *spacing* on a data line.

Control lines

Six commonly used control lines are shown in the commonly used subset of RS-232. Physically, these lines are all defined to be true, or logic "1" when a positive RS-232 voltage is asserted, and false, or logic "0" when a negative voltage is present. As I mention previously, an unconnected (or floating) input is undefined, which can cause programmers some trouble.

The six lines discussed here are all supported on the PC by the 8250 family of UARTs, making them the most popular subset of control lines. However, many RS-232 connections are made without these lines, in some cases using only three: Transmit Data, Receive Data, and Signal Ground.

RTS/CTS

In early implementations of RS-232 equipment, these lines were intended for use by half-duplex modems. Now, half-duplex modems are rarely used, and for the most part, RTS and CTS are used almost exclusively to implement hardware handshaking. A device connected to an RS-232 line uses handshaking to indicate when its input buffers are full. For example, if a PC is receiving data from a modem, it may stop reading data RS-232 from an internal buffer while it performs a disk a ccess. As more data comes in, the buffer will continue to receive data while servicing interrupts, placing it in danger of overflowing. The PC alerts the modem of this condition by dropping the RTS line. When the buffer has been emptied, RTS can once again be asserted, which tells the modem the PC is ready to handle more data.

Some devices still emulate the traditional uses for RTS and CTS. For example, the IBM PC BIOS asserts RTS when it sends data out of one of its COM ports, and waits for CTS to be asserted before sending any of its characters. However, this traditional usage is the exception rather than the rule and is usually considered just a slightly less sophisticated form of handshaking.

Most high-speed modems today support handshaking of some sort. The modems' preferred method of handshaking will generally be RTS/CTS. Thus, understanding this sort of handshaking and knowing how to implement it is essential to the development of high-quality communications software.

DTR/DSR

At one time, Data Terminal Ready (DTR) was used to cause a modem to go off hook and to attempt to connect to a remote modem. Data Set Ready (DSR) was used to indicate that the modem had made this connection. DTR would normally be low when the DTE equipment wasn't actually trying to make a connection, and DSR would be low when the modem was idle.

Today's modems generally keep DSR high whenever they are powered up. This is primarily because newer modems can accept commands via the RS-232 connection to the DTE at any time. The DTE device also usually keeps DTR high whenever it actually has an established connection to the modem.

In some cases, DTR is still used as a modem control line. Most modems will hang up when DTR is dropped, which could also indicate that no DTE is hooked up to the modem. Dropping DTR for one or two seconds is still a conventional way to disconnect a modem from a remote line.

To complicate matters even further, the occasional off-beat device will still insist on using DTR/DSR handshaking, although RTS/CTS is really the norm. A programmer developing professional-quality communications software should build in support for both DTR/DSR and RTS/CTS handshaking so as to handle this need when it arises.

To make matters worse, some machines use hybrids of the two forms of handshaking. For example, the Apple Macintosh uses DTR and CTS as its two handshaking lines, which means that you must develop unusual communications software, buy an even more unusual cable, or both.

CD

CD, or Carrier Detect (sometimes referred to as RLSD,) ought to be relatively unambiguous. This line should be asserted by a DCE only when it has established a connection with another DCE, usually over telephone lines. This lets the DTE device know that communications can now take place. Any time this line is low, the modem does not have a valid connection.

CD is frequently used by applications that have to wait for incoming calls. If a modem is programmed to auto-answer an incoming phone line, an application can simply scan the incoming control lines for assertion of CD. If CD goes high on a particular modem, it means a call has been successfully answered.

Unfortunately, before the era of intelligent modems, some terminals or other DTE equipment were designed to treat a modem as unusable without CD. Devices such as these would not send or receive characters to a modem that had CD low. Because of these anachronisms, most modems built today can keep CD high at all times, whether or not a carrier has been established. Because this feature is sometimes the default mode of operation, using CD for accurate detection of carrier presence is somewhat risky. However, most users should be able to configure their modems so as to disable this troublesome behavior.

RI

Ring Indicator (RI) is a signal originating from a DCE and is used solely to indicate that the incoming phone line is ringing. RI should rise and fall in lockstep with the ring cycle, which allows software not only to detect incoming calls but also to count rings. RI is one of the few RS-232 control lines that has remained true to its roots. RI signals still behave much as they did 20 years ago.

In the future, RI may become even more useful. PBX manufacturers have been offering distinctive ringing features for years, and telephone companies are now starting to offer this service for business and residential customers. With these new services, a phone line can serve multiple phone numbers, allowing users to share a single phone line between a FAX and modems, or between several different classes of incoming calls. To differentiate among types of calls, the communications software will have to determine the cadence of the incoming ring by monitoring RI.

Electrical lines

Pin 7 on the 25-pin RS-232 connector is reserved for a signal ground line. Because computers connected using RS-232 links can be physically separated by significant distances, their reference grounds can easily be several volts apart. The sharing of a common signal ground line ensures a common reference point for incoming data and control lines.

RS-232-C Specification Limitations

The RS-232-C specification used by many integrated circuit suppliers recommends that signals be limited to 20,000 bps. At high speeds, it also recommends that cable length not exceed 50 feet. These limitations are routinely ignored by RS-232 users. High-speed modems frequently are connected to PCs at 38.4 Kbps or 57.6 Kbps with little or no problem. And even high-speed signals such as these will sometimes be routed hundreds of feet.

Unfortunately, while the speed and distance limits of RS-232 are routinely broken, it isn't easy to find anyone willing to speculate on what the *real* limitations are. Most manufacturers of driver chips and cables fall back on the standard when asked for recommendations. So for most of us, performance is determined empirically.

To you as the user, it means that you can certainly try to push a signal well beyond what the spec allows, but if problems crop up, you have to be prepared to fall back to lower speeds, lower distances, or both.

Cabling

Over the years, no subject has caused more trouble and frustration for RS-232 users than that of cabling. Every RS-232 connection requires a cable, and every cable has 25 wires that can be routed incorrectly. The odds are against you every time you try to make a connection.

Once again, the IBM PC has helped resolve this problem, strictly because of its massive presence in the market. IBM defined what an RS-232 port was supposed to look like on a PC and what the equivalent connector should look like on a modem. By default, IBM then defined what the cable between the two should be.

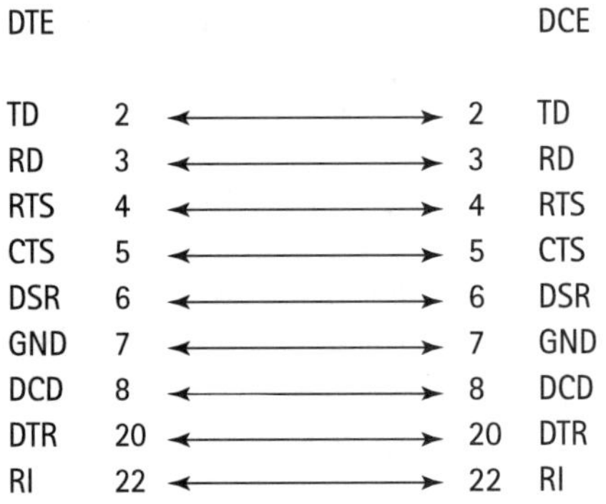

```
DTE                             DCE

TD   2  ◄─────────────►  2   TD
RD   3  ◄─────────────►  3   RD
RTS  4  ◄─────────────►  4   RTS
CTS  5  ◄─────────────►  5   CTS
DSR  6  ◄─────────────►  6   DSR
GND  7  ◄─────────────►  7   GND
DCD  8  ◄─────────────►  8   DCD
DTR  20 ◄─────────────► 20   DTR
RI   22 ◄─────────────► 22   RI
```

Figure 1-6: A "PC-to-modem" cable

Figure 1-6 shows the standard "PC-to-modem" cable. This cable has a male D-Subminiature 25-pin connector on one end and its female equivalent on the other. All the signals are routed straight through, terminating on the same numbered pin where they began. Conceptually, the cable is easier to handle than one whose lines are routed back and forth between various pins. Don't belittle this advantage. Many manuals for older RS-232 devices are filled with different pinout and routing combinations for interfacing to various devices.

In addition to the 25-pin cable, there is also an equivalent cable for routing the 9-pin DTE connection on a PC to a 25-pin DCE device. Thus, even though there are now two "standard" cables, they are difficult to confuse because one is for a 9-pin connector (shown in Figure 1-7) and the other for a 25.

Mass production of molded cables has brought prices down tremendously and increased availability. You can purchase the typical PC/modem cable off the shelf at any computer store for just a few dollars. In 1980, the same cable would likely have had to be custom made and would have cost 10 times as much.

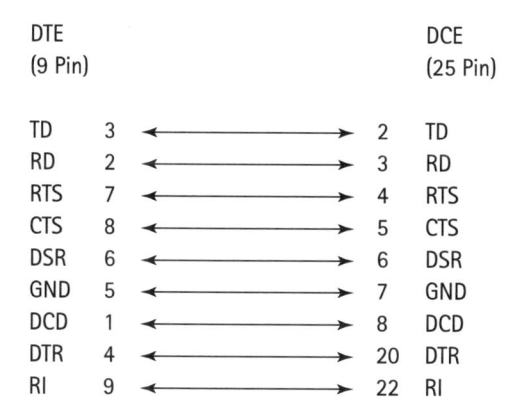

```
DTE                        DCE
(9 Pin)                    (25 Pin)

TD    3   ───────────  2   TD
RD    2   ───────────  3   RD
RTS   7   ───────────  4   RTS
CTS   8   ───────────  5   CTS
DSR   6   ───────────  6   DSR
GND   5   ───────────  7   GND
DCD   1   ───────────  8   DCD
DTR   4   ───────────  20  DTR
RI    9   ───────────  22  RI
```

Figure 1-7: The standard cable for 9-pin connectors

The null modem cable

The PC-to-modem cable is a model of simplicity and doesn't present too many opportunities for wiring errors. You are likely to get into more trouble with cabling when attempting to do something a little more unconventional. One common problem that arises is that the standard modem cable won't work when two PCs are connected via their serial ports. The standard modem cable fails here, for two reasons.

First, the modem cable has a problem with the gender of its connectors. Because both PCs will have male RS-232 connectors, you will need a cable with two female ends. Unfortunately, the standard modem cable has one male end and one female end.

However, solving the gender problem for this cable still won't allow the two PCs to communicate. Because both PCs consider themselves DTE devices, both will transmit on Pin 2 and receive on Pin 3 of their 25-pin connectors. Thus, a cable that routes all signals straight through will be connecting the output from one PC directly to the output of the other PC, and the RD line from one PC will be connected to the RD line of the other. With outputs connected to outputs and inputs connected to inputs, you are guaranteed failed communications.

The solution to this age-old dilemma? The "null modem" cable. *Null modem* refers to the fact that this cable takes the place of the pair of modems that should be connecting the two DTE devices. Remember that traditionally in the RS-232 specification, DTEs communicate only via a connection through DCEs.

If you go back to the neighborhood discount computer store and buy a null modem cable, you will generally get a cable with two female 25-pin connectors wired like the one in Figure 1-8. Probably the first thing you'll notice in the cabling diagram is that this cable doesn't seem to route any control or data lines straight through. Instead, they cross over, bend back on themselves, and generally seem to follow convoluted paths. The lone exception to this is the signal ground pin, which, just as before, is always connected straight through.

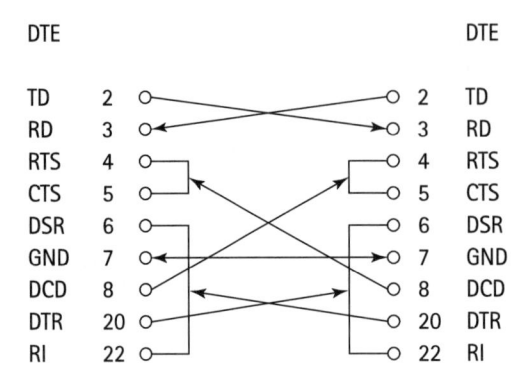

```
DTE                          DTE

TD    2  o────────────o  2   TD
RD    3  o────────────o  3   RD
RTS   4  o──┐      ┌──o  4   RTS
CTS   5  o──┘      └──o  5   CTS
DSR   6  o──┐      ┌──o  6   DSR
GND   7  o──┼──────┼──o  7   GND
DCD   8  o──┘      └──o  8   DCD
DTR   20 o────────────o  20  DTR
RI    22 o────────────o  22  RI
```

Figure 1-8: A traditional null modem cable

It makes sense that the TD and RD lines cross over as shown in Figure 1-8. With this method of wiring, the data output of each PC is connected directly to data input of the other PC, the way things ought to work. By simply crossing wires, you accomplish the same thing that a pair of modems does: routing data to the appropriate lines.

The rest of the connectors are wired as shown for reasons that may be a little more confusing. Each connector has RTS and CTS in a local loopback configuration. If a DTE is using RTS in the traditional fashion, it will automatically receive an assertion on CTS whenever it wants to transmit.

The logic behind the wiring of the remaining pins is even harder to understand. Both the CD and RI lines are routed to dubious destinations on the other side of the connector, presumably to be left on at all times. DTR and DSR are also connected through to the other side using wiring that may not seem logical.

More often than not, this version of a null modem cable accomplishes its purpose. If you write your application to be independent of the state of any control lines in the RS-232 connection, then this cable will work perfectly. Of course, you are giving up some of the functionality of the 9-wire connection, but this isn't usually a problem.

A more rational cable design

If available, a properly designed null-modem cable would offer somewhat more functionality. Figure 1-9 shows the wiring diagram for a cable that attempts to handle the crisscrossing of control lines with a little more reason.

Like the traditional cable, the rational null modem cable simply swaps the TD and RD lines. It really wouldn't make sense to wire these two lines any other way.

The main difference between the traditional and rational cabling is in the way the two pairs of control lines match up. The proper design has RTS and CTS swapped across the cable so that each PC's RTS output is routed in to the CTS input on the other machine. Likewise, DTR and DSR are swapped so that the DTR output of one machine heads straight into the DSR on the other machine.

Such a wiring scheme makes much more sense than the traditional version shown previously in Figure 1-8. Typically, RTS/CTS on modern machines is used for hardware handshaking. Under the traditional cabling scheme, this would not be possible. With the rational cable, RTS/CTS handshaking is wired in directly and should work with no problem.

Likewise, DTR and DSR are typically used to check for a connection between the DTE and DCE. When the DTE opens a port for use, it asserts DTR so that the DCE knows it is being addressed. An active DSR tells the DTE that a DCE is connected. For example, by testing for an active incoming DSR line, communications software can determine that a modem is powered up and ready to communicate. The configuration in Figure 1-9 accomplishes this goal without any problem.

In any null modem cable, you must decide what to do with the RI and CD lines. In this configuration, Ring Indicator doesn't really have an obvious mate. Carrier Detect probably should appear high all the time. So the best thing to do seems to be to connect RI and CD across the line to the DTR line on the remote end. RI could just as easily be disconnected, but leaving it disconnected opens the port to sporadic modem status interrupts that may cause confusion later.

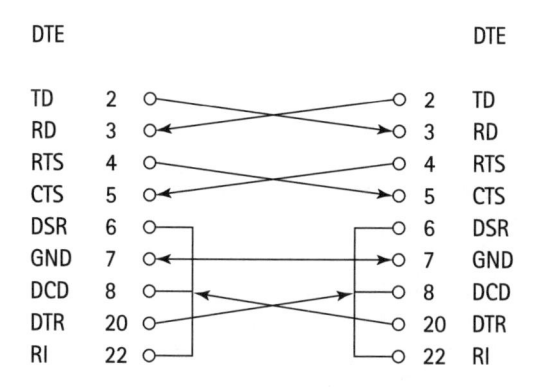

```
DTE                                  DTE

TD    2  o─────────────────o  2   TD
RD    3  o────────────────→o  3   RD
RTS   4  o─────────────────o  4   RTS
CTS   5  o────────────────→o  5   CTS
DSR   6  o──┐            ┌─o  6   DSR
GND   7  o──│────────────│─o  7   GND
DCD   8  o──│─←────────→─│─o  8   DCD
DTR   20 o──│            └─o  20  DTR
RI    22 o──┘              o  22  RI
```

Figure 1-9: The rational null modem cable

There is only one problem with the rational null modem cable: it is nearly impossible to find. This cable, or one nearly like it, is used in commercial communication products such as LapLink, but those cables generally ship with the product. The cables can be custom made by several of the sources listed at the end of this book, but price can be prohibitive. The next section on RS-232 adapters describes my solution.

RS-232 9- to 25-pin adapters

The popularity of the IBM PC architecture led to the availability of inexpensive, molded RS-232 cables, which are relatively easy to find. The advent of the AT architecture ushered in another piece of cabling hardware: the RS-232 9- to 25-pin adapter.

When IBM first introduced the AT, it began using a 9-pin D-Subminiature connector rather than the standard 25-pin connector. Users who bought an AT were now faced with the fact that no existing cables would work with their machines. This problem quickly established a market for the 9- to 25-pin adapter, shown in Figure 1-10.

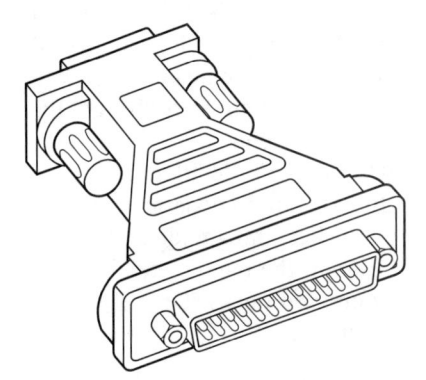

Figure 1-10: The 9- to 25-pin adapter

The 9- to 25-pin adapter is a simple piece of hard-molded plastic with a connector on each end. When attached directly to the 9-pin output of an IBM AT RS-232 port, it immediately made using that port with all existing 25-pin cables possible. Mass production techniques made this cable so inexpensive that it was usually given away with add-on interface cards.

This adapter quickly paved the way for new equipment: gender changers and null modem adapters. A *gender changer* is also a small piece of molded plastic with a 25-pin connector on each end. A cable mismatch can quickly be corrected by the addition of a gender changer. Again, mass production techniques keep the cost of these adapters down to just a few dollars, making them easily affordable for any devoted RS-232 user.

Last but not least is the null modem adapter. It simply performs all the internal wire swapping shown previously in Figure 1-8, which means that two PCs (or other DTE devices) can be directly connected without intervening modems. The low cost of these devices ensures that no wiring diagrams or optional configurations are available. The only way to be sure about a null modem cable like this is to check all connections with a voltmeter.

Home cable making

Despite the lack of availability of the rational style null-modem adapter, all is not lost. Anyone handy with a soldering iron and wire cutters can quickly convert a female-to-male gender changer to an effective null modem cable. In 15 minutes or so, the offending wires can be removed and replaced with more usable connections. The plastic cases for these adapters pop back together easily, leaving an adapter that looks and acts just as good as new.

Macintosh cabling

Although this book concentrates on the IBM architecture for desktop systems, more adventurous readers may want to tackle communications programming for the Macintosh. A couple of interesting problems arise when you use the Macintosh for serial communications. Rather than use RS-232 for an interface, the Mac uses RS-422. As with much on the Mac, RS-422 is a technically superior communications standard that has not yet achieved critical mass in the marketplace. Fortunately, the two standards are electrically similar enough that a special cable can be used to connect a Macintosh to either a modem or a PC.

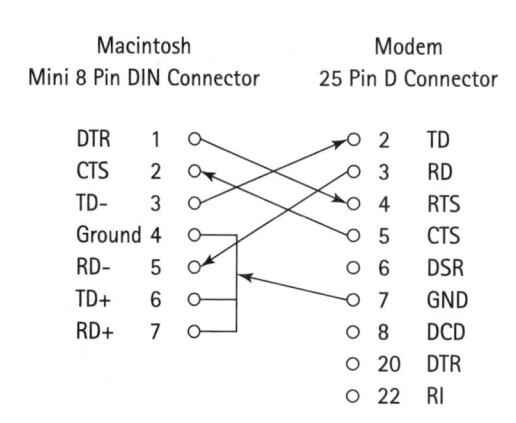

```
Macintosh                    Modem
Mini 8 Pin DIN Connector     25 Pin D Connector

    DTR    1  o----------o  2   TD
    CTS    2  o----------o  3   RD
    TD-    3  o----------o  4   RTS
    Ground 4  o----------o  5   CTS
    RD-    5  o----------o  6   DSR
    TD+    6  o----------o  7   GND
    RD+    7  o----------o  8   DCD
                          o  20  DTR
                          o  22  RI
```

Figure 1-11: Macintosh/modem cables

Figure 1-11 shows a Macintosh/modem cable. A couple of points are worth noting here. First, under RS-422, the TD and RD lines come in balanced pairs. Each data line having its own dual balanced driver lines increases the noise resistance of RS-422, allowing for faster transmission over longer distances. However, RS-232 has only a single line for both directions of data. Remember also that RS-232 transmits its data using an inverted line so that a logical 1 is transmitted as a low voltage. This leads to the strange cabling configuration shown in Figure 1-11.

Figure 1-11 shows the newer Mini 8-pin connector used by Apple. Older Apple equipment used a 9-pin D-Subminiature connector with a slightly different pinout. The primary difference was that the older cable did not have the DTR line connected, which meant that hardware handshaking on older Macs was strictly a one-way affair.

Cabling recommendations

Unfortunately, this section on cabling will be confusing to newcomers. For what it's worth, I have developed a few rules for working with RS-232 cables:

- Never trust a strange cable. Until you have tested it and verified its pinouts, don't assume that it is anything like what you want it to be. When your co-workers tell you that it worked just fine on a computer down the hall, assume that they are mistaken or just having a little fun at your expense. These assumptions will save you a lot of time.

- When you are sure what a cable is, label it and never modify it. A cable you trust is worth its weight in gold.

- Learn to make your own cables. Homemade cables usually aren't as reliable as professionally built ones, and you probably should use them only for testing configurations. But when you need an odd cable at 5:00 on Friday afternoon, having your own cable, crimping tool, hoods, and pins will be a lifesaver.

Later in this chapter, I discuss the ultimate cabling tool: the breakout box.

UARTs

The process of writing data out in a serial bit stream is labor intensive for a computer. Each bit has to be shifted into position, placed into the output stream, and then timed for the proper bit width. Reading input bits is even more difficult. The input stream has to be sampled at a significantly higher rate than the serial bit rate. The processor has to look for start bits, screen out any invalid start bits caused by noise, and then clock in each bit by sampling somewhere near the expected middle of the bit.

Because of the real-time nature of this task, a CPU that is trying to manage a disk-based operating system cannot do it very effectively. So virtually every desktop system performs serial data transfers by passing the work off to a UART chip. For users, the UART is essentially a black box that performs two very important functions. First, it converts bytes to serial data on the RS-232 line. Second, it reads in serial data and converts the data streams into bytes that can be read by the computer. This conversion relieves the computer of all the time-critical jobs of shifting and timing data bits.

8250 clones

There are literally dozens of different chips from different manufacturers being built into PCs every day, but they are virtually all register compatible with the original 8250.

The reason for this compatibility is simply that when IBM and Microsoft collaborated on the design of a BIOS and operating system for the first IBM PCs, they completely left out support for interrupt-driven input from the serial port. By supporting only polled-mode input and output, they limited the functionality of MS-DOS. With polled-mode output, the operating system could handle writing to a serial printer pretty well and that would be about it. Some tightly written programs could manage terminal emulation at 300 baud using only BIOS function calls, but that avenue was closed by the advent of inexpensive 1200 bps modems.

Any programmer wanting to support realistic baud rates for a communications program had to write an interrupt-driven driver for the 8250 UART. This meant programming the chip at the register level, which tied applications software to a particular piece of hardware.

Had IBM and Microsoft been wise enough to offer an interrupt-driven MS-DOS device driver for the 8250 UART (as they do now under OS/2 and all varieties of Windows), things would have been very different. Manufacturers would be free to choose whatever UART they desired for their hardware. By then writing a compatible MS-DOS device driver, they would immediately work with most application programs written for the IBM PC.

Instead, any new serial hardware that goes into a PC must be able to respond properly to commands designed to control an 8250 UART. The serial hardware can be enhanced; it just needs to be downward compatible with the original PC.

UART (lack of) progress

Because of the hardware straightjacket just described, 10 years of progress in CPUs and motherboards has not been matched by similar progress in RS-232 hardware on IBM PCs. Although a wide variety of UARTs are being used on PCs, all are essentially identical to the 8250, with one very minor exception. The 16550 UART (and its close relatives), in use on all new systems since the 486 was introduced, has 16-byte internal buffers for both the transmitter and receiver. Other than that, it is functionally identical to the 8250. Common UART types for the PC come in these variations:

8250: The original PC UART. This part has a few quirks that I cover in Chapter 3. These quirks have all been replicated in later revisions so as not to upset the apple cart of compatibility.

16450:	This version of the PC UART is designed for machines with faster I/O busses, such as the PC/AT. It is functionally identical to the 8250, as far as the communications programmer is concerned.

16550:	This UART family has 16-byte buffers added to the transmit and receive data lines, so as to cut down on the CPU load required to service interrupts.

16560/16570:	These parts have 32- and 64-byte buffers, respectively, and add-on chip handling of RTS/CTS handshaking.

Many books and articles on PC-based communications discuss the difference between these UARTs, how to tell them apart, and so on. Fortunately, the differences are really nothing but window dressing. All five of these UARTs, as well as various clone chips, will respond properly if treated like the base part, the 8250.

> **XREF** In Chapter 3, I present an interrupt-driven interface to the 8250 family UARTs. This driver attempts to determine whether the UART is a 16550, only so that it can take advantage of the 16-byte FIFOs on these parts. Even this is not really necessary, but it offers some low-cost performance enhancements that are hard to pass up.

8250 functionality

The 8250 has most of the functions needed in a UART. In particular, it supports the nine RS-232 lines used in most common RS-232 connections. On the IBM PC, it is addressed via eight consecutive register locations on the I/O bus. On the PC ISA architecture, each UART gets its own interrupt line. The original designers of the PC allocated two interrupt lines for serial ports, effectively limiting the PC to COM1 and COM2.

The 8250 produces an asynchronous output bit stream that looks like that shown in Figure 1-12. Each output byte starts with a start bit and is followed by 5, 6, 7, or 8 data bits. The output data is followed by either 1, 1.5, or 2 stop bits. The output stream can contain as its final bit a parity bit, which can use even, odd, mark, or space parity. Typical PC-based communications applications will use only 7 or 8 data bits and even, odd, or no parity. Usually only one stop bit is used.

'A'= 0x41   01000001B

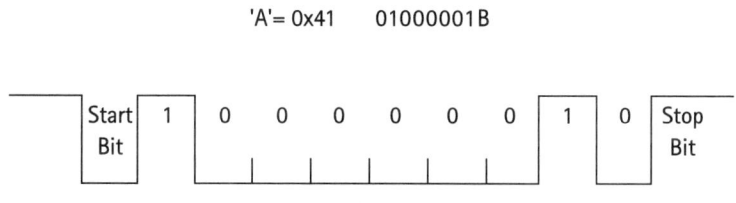

```
     ┌────┐
Start│ 1  │ 0  0  0  0  0  0 ┌─1──┐ 0 ┌Stop
Bit  │    │                  │    │   │Bit
─────┘    └──────────────────┘    └───┘
```

Figure 1-12: The character "A" with 8 bits, no parity

The 8250 has a built-in baud-rate generator, which produces baud rates by dividing an input clock down by an integer. On the IBM PC, the crystal chosen for the baud-rate generator produces a top baud rate of 115.2 Kbps. That base rate can be lowered further by dividing 115,200 by a 16-bit integer ranging from 1 to 65535. Because of the way the 8250 is wired on an IBM COM card, the input and output baud rates must be the same.

The 8250 has single byte-wide registers for both the transmitted and received data. The programmer sends a byte by just writing out to the transmit byte using an output instruction. Likewise, reading in a byte from the Received Data register is all it takes to read in a byte that the UART has assembled from the incoming bit stream. The simplicity of these two operations is the primary reason for having a UART.

Control registers

The 8250 has several control registers. The Line Control Register (LCR) is used to set up the word size, parity, and stop bits used in reading and writing the serial bit stream. The Modem Control Register (MCR) is used to control DTR and RTS, as well as two undedicated lines called OUT1 and OUT2. On the IBM PC, OUT2 is used to gate the UART interrupt line onto the PC bus, which is necessary before interrupts can take place.

Status registers

Just as there are registers to control the modem lines and the serial data stream, there are also a pair of 8250 registers to read the status of the serial data stream and the input modem control lines. The Line Status Register (LSR) is used to read and detect parity, framing, and overrun errors, as well as incoming Break signals. The Modem Status Register (MSR) is used to read the state of the four incoming RS-232 lines: DSR, CTS, RI, and CD.

Interrupt functions

The 8250 can generate interrupts for any one of four different types of events. First, it generates interrupts when a new character is read in from the RS-232 line. It also will generate an interrupt when the transmitter is done sending a character out on the line. The 8250 can generate an interrupt when any one of several status conditions occurs, and it can also generate an interrupt when any of the four incoming modem status lines change. (Details on all these interrupt conditions are found in Chapter 3.)

Each of these four interrupts can be enabled or disabled independently. To achieve just a minimal interrupt-driven interface, you have only to turn on the Received Data interrupt. With this in place, the application program won't have to poll the input register once every millisecond in order to get every incoming data byte. You can then have a reliable and useful communications program.

More sophisticated applications require the use of the other three interrupt systems as well. Having the UART generate interrupts when RS-232 data is output as well as input takes a huge load off the CPU. The alternative to using interrupts is polled-mode output. This method requires you to run in a loop that continually waits for permission to send each character.

Polled-mode output is reliable; you don't have to worry about missing characters. But it is CPU intensive because the processor has to sit in wait loops until the output buffer is ready for another character.

Changes in the incoming RS-232 control lines generate interrupts that allow effective hardware handshaking, and line status interrupts allow finer control over data errors.

> Chapter 3 includes an interrupt service routine and explains in detail how to use such a routine.

The 16550 difference

When the PC was first making its mark in the desktop world, communications applications typically operated at 1200 baud by modem, or perhaps 9600 baud when connected directly. As this book goes to print in 1999, the V.90 modem with V.42*bis* data compression is the desktop standard. The V.90 modem has a top raw data throughput rate of 56 Kbps. V.42*bis* data compression can quadruple that throughput, meaning that to achieve maximum throughput, the RS-232 port has to operate at its peak rate of 224 Kbps. At this data rate, the UART will assemble a new character roughly every 45 microseconds, and the CPU will have to quickly read it in before the next character is done being assembled.

With data coming in at this rate, any operation that locks out interrupts for 45 microseconds or more can cause the CPU to lose at least one incoming byte. One leading candidate for causing this loss of data is mode switching. When an older processor such as the 80286 switches from protected mode to real mode, or vice versa (as it does frequently when running programs like Microsoft Windows), the processor can be prevented from receiving incoming interrupts for as long as 1,000 microseconds. In this length of time, six or seven characters could have been lost. This error is referred to as a "hardware overrun error." Newer processors have made great strides toward reducing this bottleneck but are still vulnerable to interrupt blocks in low-level disk and video drivers.

The 16550 UART has extra hardware built into its chip that is designed to avoid this specific problem. It has a 16-byte buffer on the receiver, which can prevent this overrun error from occurring. If the buffer is enabled, the UART can be programmed to generate an interrupt as soon as a single character is stored in the buffer. The CPU then has 15 more character times to respond before the buffer fills up. This generally eliminates the problem of hardware overrun errors, even at exceptionally high baud rates. Virtually all PCs now being built ship with 16550 family UARTs.

16550 descendants

The 16560 and 16570 up the onboard buffering to 32 and 64 bytes, respectively, which really helps with very high baud rate devices. Even better, they provide on-chip handshaking, which means the UART itself can take care of telling the modem to stop transmitting when the UART buffers are nearly full. This relieves the PC of the responsibility, giving it time to concentrate on more important tasks, such as playing Doom with Internet-based opponents.

You might think that the future is going to bring a succession of UARTs with more and more buffer space, and perhaps better chip features, but this isn't likely to be the case. The architecture of the PC limits standard comm ports to a top speed of 115.2 Kbps, which may prevent modems from operating at their top speed. The new generation of 56 Kbps modems are going to be able to transmit data at speeds well in excess of 115.2 Kbps when compression is enabled.

There are several good approaches to solving the 115 Kbps serial port speed limit. One of the best solutions is adoption of the Universal Serial Bus (USB) as the modem connection to the PC. The USB provides an inexpensive way for multiple devices to talk to the PC at millions of bits per second instead of the thousands of bits per second from the current generation of parts. The USB is included in most new motherboard designs, and has driver support starting in Windows 98. The first USB modems began arriving in 1998, and will eventually be the standard for external modems.

Other options that work well are internal modems that connect directly to the ISA or PCI bus, and modems that connect via the parallel port.

Multiport Boards

Although DOS and the IBM ISA hardware design limit the PC to two standard RS-232 interfaces, some applications need many more ports. To fill this void, a number of third-party manufacturers have developed Shared Interrupt Multiport

Boards. This board takes a number of 8250 family UARTs, usually four or eight, and combines them on a board that contains some additional interrupt management circuitry.

These shared interrupt boards all have one feature in common: interrupt arbitration is done via a status register that indicates to the application which UART on the board needs servicing. The logic on the board takes care of generating an interrupt whenever any of the UARTs requests one, and letting the application software know which UART to service.

Because these boards use conventional 8250 family UARTs, existing programs can easily be modified to support multiple UARTs in this fashion. All that is needed is some "wrapper" code to go around the conventional interrupt service routine. The wrapper code simply sits in a loop, reading in the value from the status register, and then dispatching the interrupt service routine for the correct UART until the status register indicates that no more UARTs need servicing.

Different manufactures such as DigiBoard, Stargate, and Arnet all make these boards, with minor variations on the central theme. However, the shared interrupt boards remain similar enough that designing code that will work with virtually any of them is easy.

The primary disadvantage to these boards is that although they are *nearly* compatible with standard IBM COM ports, they won't work with off-the-shelf 8250 software. So, any application that needs a multiport board will require new code. Most mass-market communications applications don't bother to try to take advantage of this small segment of the market, so popular communications programs don't work with these boards. Because these boards don't work with off the shelf software, they tend to only be used in specialized situations that can justify the expense of custom software.

The good news for multiport board users is that driver support *is* available for most of these boards under Windows 95. Microsoft has added a limited set of drivers, with manufacturers picking up most of the remaining slack. So by leaving the MS-DOS driver-less world of serial communications, programmers can benefit from having a well-defined software interface to all varieties of serial devices.

The other reason that multiport boards don't take the market by storm is more of a horespower issue than anything else. Processing serial port interrupts is still a hardware-intensive task, particularly at the baud rates in use by today's modems. Just reading a continuous data stream from one port uses up a significant portion of a PC's CPU resources. Asking it to handle four or eight streams at one time can be difficult for even the fastest processors.

Intelligent Multiport Boards

The CPU timing requirements on multiport boards can be extremely difficult to manage. As I showed earlier in this chapter, some applications that run at high baud rates already require the CPU to service an interrupt as often as 20,000 times per second. (When the hardware is configured to generate an interrupt for every incoming character.) With a shared interrupt multiport board, that figure can easily be multiplied by 8 under worst-case conditions. Desktop machines simply don't have the power to keep up with that kind of a load. In fact, the whole notion of having a CPU running MS-DOS or Windows and frantically servicing 8250 interrupts at the same time is somewhat ludicrous. It seems wasteful to have an expensive processor spending so much time on such a mundane task. The solution is to move the interrupt servicing chores off the motherboard and onto a dedicated card.

These dedicated cards are called intelligent multiport boards. They are manufactured by the same companies who sell the shared interrupt multiport boards. The market for these boards is healthy because people are designing and building multiuser systems running on Intel x86 platforms, including UNIX variants such as Solaris and Linux. Microsoft and other vendors are even adapting Windows NT to operate as a multiuser system able to run applications over an RS-232 connection. If the main CPUs on systems such as these were performing interrupt servicing, system performance would grow intolerably slow as the number of users increased.

An intelligent board starts off like a shared interrupt multiport board by putting four or eight UARTs on the board. The similarities end there, however. The intelligent board then proceeds to build an entire standalone computer system on the same card. Typically, the intelligent board will contain a processor oriented toward real-time embedded applications, such as an Intel 80186. A control program will be present in EPROM on the board, along with a moderate amount of RAM, usually somewhere between 16KB and 64KB.

The processor on the intelligent board takes care of initializing the UARTs, servicing all their interrupts, reading characters in and sending characters out, dealing with handshaking, and reporting errors. It does all this based on commands it receives from the CPU running on the main machine. Generally, the communication between the main CPU and the intelligent board takes place via a block of shared memory. The main CPU places commands and data in the shared memory block, then lets the intelligent board know that data and commands are ready. Entire blocks of data can be transferred in one command via the shared memory, leading to much more efficient use of the main CPU.

The desktop CPU running UNIX, MS-DOS, or some other system, doesn't ever communicate directly with the UARTs on the intelligent board. Instead it controls the UARTs via a high-level API, much as it would have done had a decent device driver been developed for the comm ports under MS-DOS. Because of this, the board designer has some freedom in hardware design. As long as the command format and the shared memory operation remain the same, any processor can be designed into the intelligent board and any type of UARTS can be in operation there. This is why many other UARTs, besides the conventional 8250 family, reside on intelligent multiport boards. It also means we can expect to see continued improvements in intelligent board hardware with boards becoming more powerful as better and cheaper hardware becomes available.

Intelligent boards work very well for UNIX and Win32 programmers, because their access to serial ports already has to go through a device driver. After you design a good, intelligent board, all you have to do is write a device driver (the serial device driver under UNIX is not particularly difficult to write) and you can start selling your board to every UNIX user of your hardware platform.

MS-DOS is a completely different story. The code written to support the traditional 8250 family of UARTs is completely wasted on these intelligent boards. It usually requires a completely different approach than interrupt-drive RS-232 hardware. One of the reasons for writing this book is to demonstrate how an object-oriented approach can enable the easy implementation of new hardware without having complete rewrites of existing programs. Unfortunately, most real-world software was not written using object-oriented techniques, so intelligent multiport boards are for the most part locked out of the MS-DOS arena.

Modems

When RS-232 was first formulated, the typical modem was a synchronous half-duplex device that operated at fairly slow speeds, perhaps 300 or 1200 bits per second. Half-duplex operation meant that either end of the channel had to specifically request permission to transmit, via the RTS line, and wait for permission to be granted via CTS. After the device received permission to transmit, the remote end of the connection was locked out until the first device was finished.

One obvious implication was that the remote character echo we take for granted when talking to another computer was simply not possible. Today, as I type characters into a local BBS via a modem connection, the BBS transmits my characters back to me as it receives them. This remote echoing lets me see that my data is being properly transmitted. Under the tyranny of the half-duplex regime, however, this wasn't possible. Instead, modems performed the echo function locally, transmitting the characters back to the DTE as they were transmitted. You would see characters echoed to your screen automatically, whether or not the other end was receiving them.

Now modems operate as full-duplex modems, and typically operate at 28.8 or 56 Kbps. With data compression and error control, actual throughputs on these modems can be as high as 224 Kbps. Modem designers feel that 56 Kbps is probably the end of the line for traditional analog modems, so we don't expect any more speed increases for communications over standard dialup phone lines.

Data rates

Historically, progress in modems has proceeded along two paths. First, modems have continually become faster. The data carrier used by most modems in the early 1970s had a capacity ranging from 110 to 300 bps. Today's most advanced modems can transmit up to 33.6 bps. At the same time, modems have grown progressively more intelligent. The 300 bps modems of the 1970s had virtually no intelligence and did nothing more than convert voltage levels to frequency outputs. Today, modems interact locally with the computers they service. They also maintain error-free communications over noisy lines and compress the data streams they transmit.

A brief look at the historical progression of modem transmission schemes follows. Although some have taken the many side branches off the main path, the vast majority of computer users have stayed more or less on this same road. Bear in mind that this synopsis will be current in 1999, but new developments in analog modem technology will soon render it behind the times.

Bell 103: The first standard asynchronous modems to make a big splash in the world of computers were of the Bell 103 family. They were capable of full-duplex communications at data rates ranging from 110 to 300 bps.

Typically, Bell 103 modems were connected to the phone line via an acoustic coupler, a mechanical device that held the handset of a telephone up against the microphone and speaker for the modem.

Bell 212, V.22: The 212 and V.22 standards took a quantum leap forward, quadrupling Bell 103 by increasing throughput on the telephone line to 1200 bps. Most 212-type modems produced also would fall back to supporting a 300-baud connection with older 103 devices, establishing a trend toward downward compatibility that is still with us today.

V.22*bis*: This modem was the first to be truly a worldwide standard. At 2400 bps, this modem doubled the throughput of the previous generation. PC users in the early 1980s looked to this modem as the standard for high-speed communications. After 10 years of telecommunications for IBM users, the 2.4 Kbps modem enjoyed a long reign as the first choice for desktop communications.

V.32: It took many years for the V.32 9600 bps modem standard to be finalized. The technical difficulties involved in developing this new generation of modems were formidable, requiring much research and testing before the final version could be accepted. In the years leading up to V.32, several proprietary high-speed schemes were promulgated by modem manufacturers such as U.S. Robotics and Telebit. Without the backing of worldwide standardization, however, these unique methods were generally viewed as stopgap measures and are slowly falling by the wayside.

V.32*bis*: This standard came close on the heels of the V.32 standard. V.32*bis* is not nearly as big a jump as we have encountered in the past, jumping from 9600 to 14.400 Kbps. However, the 50 percent increase in speed was viewed as relatively easy to accomplish, while still maintaining compatibility with the earlier V.32 standard. Given the public's hunger for ever-increasing bandwidth, this standard was accepted quite quickly.

Hardware manufacturers learned a lot during the development of V.32 modems, which, in turn, has done a lot to lower the cost of V.32*bis* modems. As a result, 14.4 Kbps modems quickly moved into position as the standard for desktop communications applications. Their reign was short lived though, as the next generation of modems appeared on retail shelves after just few short years.

V.34: V.34 modems originally had a throughput rate of 28.8 Kbps, and later made minor changes to increase the rate to 33.6 bps. This basic data rate approaches the theoretical limit of standard dial-up phone lines and at one time was expected to be the end of the road for analog modems. For the past few years, V.34 modems have been a smashing success, quickly achieving price points that destroyed the market for V.32 and slower modems.

V.90: These modems got around the analog limits to standard phone lines by employing a direct digital connection to the phone system at one end of the connection. Internet Service Providers or other customers with many incoming connections could use this direct connection via a T1 or T3 phone line, and hence offer higher-speed communications in one direction only. (The other direction will still transmit at V.34 speeds of 28.8 or 33.6 bps.)

V.90 modems are today the standard for desktop buyers. Although actual throughput rates generally fall well below the maximum allowable 56 Kbps, most users experience rates at least as high as 40 bps. Of course, this is true only when the user connects to a service provider that has a significant investment in digital telephony gear. Connections to another analog modem will be limited to V.34 speeds.

Intelligence

Although modem hardware continued a steady climb towards faster speeds, additional features were being added to the modems. Most of these features were implemented by developing software that ran on embedded microprocessors, which soon became a standard part of the modem hardware.

"Dumb" modems: Although it isn't likely that any manufacturer ever referred to its modems as "dumb," virtually the entire generation of 110 and 300 bps modems have earned this moniker. "Dumb" refers to the fact that these modems don't have any on-board microprocessor to help with dialing, going on and off hook, or controlling the connection after it has been established.

Smart modems: Probably the first widely known "smart" modem (modem with microprocessor) was the Hayes Smartmodem. Hayes first put intelligence in its early 300 bps modems, and then quickly followed with higher speed 1200 and 2400 bps models. These smart modems communicated with the computer through the same RS-232 connection used to communicate with the remote end.

Initially, the smart modems didn't do much more than help set up the phone call. The user could type in a phone number using the now standard "AT" command set. A typical command might be something like `ATD555-1212`, which would cause the modem to go off hook and attempt to make a connection with another modem at 555-1212.

Smart modems have now evolved to the point where they not only establish connections but also store phone numbers, interactively monitor the progress of a phone call, provide help screens, and much more.

MNP-4: Microcom, Inc. developed a protocol referred to as MNP, which provided the next step in the evolution of modem intelligence. MNP is layered in "classes," with each class adding functionality to the modem. MNP features would be virtually impossible without the help of powerful on-board microprocessors.

The first three classes of MNP, MNP-1, -2, and -3, provide for slightly improved use of the phone line. By sending data using a synchronous protocol, these first three levels of MNP eliminate start and stop bits, adding about 20 percent to modem throughput . This feature alone was enough to assure the success of MNP.

But MNP-4 was where the real improvements began. MNP-4 is an error-detecting and correcting protocol that assures the user that the connection between two DTE devices will be 100 percent error free. Two modems connected using MNP-4 will add validation information to data and will retransmit any blocks with errors.

MNP-4 represents an enormous step forward in serial communications. By using MNP-4-class modems, applications programmers can stop worrying about data transmission and spend more time on more important concerns, such as on what to do with the data after it arrives.

MNP-5: MNP-5 offers an even more tangible benefit. It compresses the data stream before transmitting it through the phone lines. MNP-5 uses an adaptive Huffman coding scheme that can compress highly redundant data by a factor of 2:1. This means that the owner of a 2400-baud modem with MNP-5 data compression can perform like a 4800-baud modem if connected to another MNP-5 modem at the remote end.

MNP-5 was an immediate success, although it did have drawbacks. The compression scheme used in MNP-5 actually caused performance to deteriorate if the data had already been compressed using more conventional methods. And MNP was a proprietary protocol. Users who wanted to add MNP protocols to their modem were at the mercy of Microcom, Inc., for licensing. Of course, Microcom acted in enlightened self-interest, realizing that licensing terms had to be attractive enough to help promote the standard. Apparently Microcom found a good balance, judging from the widespread adoption of MNP protocols.

V.42, V.42*bis*: MNP-4 and MNP-5 pioneered the use of error detection and data compression in asynchronous modems. However, just as the AT&T standards for data transmission gave way to CCITT international standards, the Microcom protocols soon gave way as well. The CCITT was reluctant to let a proprietary scheme be used as an international standard. Additionally, some technical improvements over MNP-4 and MNP-5 were suggested and eventually adopted. The result was V.42 and V.42*bis*.

V.42 is a standard that uses one of two methods to detect and retransmit erroneous data. The preferred method for this is to use the Link Access Protocol Method (LAPM). Microcom managed to incorporate MNP-4 as a fallback method for V.42. If a modem that supports V.42 calls an MNP-4 modem, the V.42 side is supposed to fall back to MNP-4 link management.

V.42*bis* is a standard for data compression by the modem. This standard uses an LZW-based data compression algorithm that is considerably more powerful than MNP-5, allowing up to 4:1 data compression ratios for highly redundant data.

Additional proprietary schemes are being used for wireless modems, which have to work considerably harder to maintain an error-free connection. Schemes such as Microcom's MNP-10 have yet to break out of small, proprietary, niche markets.

Handshaking

As I mention earlier in this chapter, one of the consequences of the progression in modems was the steadily increasing speed the modem uses to communicate with the computer. Modem manufacturers today support interface rates even higher than 115.2 Kbps. These high baud rates, combined with error-correcting protocols, have created a basic need for local handshaking in modem communications.

Most high-speed modems now use a "locked DTE" method of communicating with the locally attached computer. This means that regardless of the rate at which a connection is established, the local connection with the computer remains at the same baud rate. For example, a V.34 modem will frequently suggest a connection of 57.6 Kbps with a computer. Even when the modem connects to a V.22*bis* modem at 2400 bps, the local connection remains at 57.6 Kbps. It is up to the modem to convert the 57.6 Kbps data stream coming from the computer to the 2400 bps data stream going out over the telephone line.

Obviously, a few major difficulties can occur here. If the computer continues pumping data as fast as it can at 57.6 Kbps, and the modem is transmitting only at 2400 bps, data is backing up inside the modem at a rapid pace. The modem undoubtedly has to have some internal storage space, but it can't continue indefinitely storing data. The only solution to this problem is to implement flow control.

Flow control has been used in various forms with RS-232 connections since their inception. Flow control is simply an agreed-upon method of letting one end of the connection signal the other end to stop transmission while processing occurs. The two primary methods of flow control used in asynchronous RS-232 connections are RTS/CTS and XON/XOFF.

Flow Control

Flow control is an important part of serial communications. When two computers are connected, there will be many times when one is not able to accept any additional incoming data. This can happen when input buffers are nearly full, or when no process is available to handle the data. When a computer is in this situation, any additional incoming data could easily be lost.

The solution to this is for computers and modems to implement *flow control*. This term applies to any technique by which a device can signal that it can't accept incoming data. There are many different ways to accomplish this, but the important thing is that both parties in a serial conversation agree on a common method.

This section discusses the methods commonly used on desktop PCs today.

Hardware flow control

RTS/CTS flow control is part of the family of flow-control methods collectively referred to as "hardware flow control." Hardware flow-control methods use RS-232 control lines to start and stop the flow of serial data. With RTS/CTS, the computer or other DTE uses RTS to start and stop the flow of data from the modem or other DCE device. The modem uses CTS to start and stop data from the computer.

In theory, RTS/CTS flow control is relatively simple to implement. The modem's input buffer is limited to a certain size. Every time a new character is read in, the modem processor checks to see how full the buffer is. After it passes a certain point, referred to as the "high-water mark," it turns the CTS line off by telling the UART to apply a logic 0 voltage on that pin. When the DTE sees this line drop, it stops transmitting. The DTE generally won't be able to respond to the signal instantly, so there will almost always be a few characters that are transmitted even after the control line drops.

After the control line is brought down and the DTE stops transmitting, the modem can continue pulling characters out of its input buffer and processing them. Eventually, the modem will empty its input buffer past a point referred to as the "low-water mark." At this point, the modem will reassert the CTS line, and the DTE will begin transmitting characters again.

Typical values for the low- and high-water marks would be 25 percent and 75 percent of the buffer capacity. You don't want to put the marks too much lower or higher than that. Setting the low-water mark too low creates the risk of emptying the buffer completely before the DTE resumes transmission, resulting in idle capacity. Setting the high-water mark too high risks input buffer overflow, when the sender doesn't stop transmitting in time.

This discussion of handshaking has concentrated on the modem's restraint of the DTE/computer. This handshaking operation is completely symmetrical and is applied in exactly the reverse fashion when the computer needs to restrain the modem. The computer uses the RTS line to indicate to the modem that it is not ready for incoming data.

Note that although RTS/CTS is a very common method of flow control, there are many variations of hardware flow control, and every modem will offer at least a few. First, other hardware lines can be used besides RTS and CTS, with the second most popular choice being DTR/DSR. Modems traditionally use DTR and DSR for other purposes, but many devices, such as printers, use one of these lines for hardware flow control.

In addition, I have discussed RTS/CTS as if it automatically paired both sides in flow control. This is frequently not the case. Often, the flow control will operate only in a single direction, as just RTS flow control, for example. The computer may not ever need to prevent the modem from transmitting data because it has such a large capacity that the buffer can't become full.

Software flow control

There are plenty of reasons not to like hardware flow control. At the top of the list is the fact that hardware flow control requires a properly configured cable. Many cables don't have RTS and CTS routed through but instead use only TD and RD. This is particularly true of a null-modem cable used to connect two similar devices. If hardware flow control isn't practical or desirable, the alternative is software flow control.

Traditionally, software flow control is implemented via the XON/XOFF protocol. As before, the receiver will have a predetermined high-water mark. When the receiver's input buffer fills beyond this high water mark, it will send an XOFF character to the remote end (Decimal 19 or Control-S). When the remote end receives this character, it knows that it has been requested to stop transmitting, and does so immediately. After the input buffer for the receiver falls below the low-water mark, the receiver sends an XON to the other side (Decimal 17 or Control-Q). This character alerts the remote end to the fact that transmission can resume.

Like hardware flow control, software flow control comes in several varieties. The start and stop characters used by the protocol can vary. There is nothing magical about XON and XOFF; these characters are just traditional. Second, the protocol can be unidirectional, with just one side obeying the flow control characters. In general, however, a link that uses software flow control will almost always use XON/XOFF signaling and will support flow control in both directions.

XON/XOFF has one major disadvantage compared with hardware flow control. When a computer attempts to send raw binary data, the flow control characters will inevitably show up in the data stream. When this happens, the remote end can get very confused. For example, if I am using XON/XOFF flow control with my V.34 modem and I am trying to send a file to the remote end that contains numerous appearances of XON and XOFF, I am going to have a problem. My modem will think those characters are to be used for flow control, and it will strip them out of the data stream and try to respond to them. One of two things will happen: either the file will arrive at the remote end in a corrupted state, or my link will freeze up because the modem has misinterpreted the meaning of the incoming XOFF character.

Local versus pass through flow control

Until now, my discussion of flow control has concentrated on local flow control. This is the flow control between a DTE and a DCE, generally consisting of a modem and a computer directly connected. However, at times I want to exercise end-to-end flow control. For example, I might be using a modem to connect to a remote UNIX system. During the course of my session, I may be typing a file out to the screen. If my modems and computers are set up properly, I may not need local flow control because all four pieces of hardware are keeping up with the data stream. However, my brain can't keep up with the file pouring out on my screen, so I may want to manually stop the flow of data. If I press Ctrl+S on my keyboard, I want that character to go through my modem, pass through the remote modem, and be sent to the UNIX system.

In this scenario, if my modem is using XON/XOFF flow control for my local session, I will immediately run into trouble. My modem will stop transmitting data, but it will not pass the XOFF through to the remote end. So my UNIX system will continue spewing data out to its modem, not knowing that I don't particularly want to see any more. If the two modems don't have a V.42 or MNP-4 connection, the data will continue pouring into my local modem until its internal buffers overflow, resulting in loss of data.

This means that if I want flow control with the far end of my connection, both DTE devices should be set up for XON/XOFF flow control, but neither DCE/modem should have it enabled. If I still need local flow control under these circumstances, I have to obtain it using hardware flow control such as RTS/CTS.

This setup of local versus end-to-end flow control, combined with the differences between hardware and software flow control, has made configuration of modems a subject of consternation among desktop computer users. For one thing, not only do the modems and cables have to be configured properly, but any PC applications software needs to be properly set up as well.

Unfortunately, the problem is not likely to go away soon. I recommend that you *always* set up your local modem connection to use RTS/CTS flow control. It is important when doing this to test your flow control out early, to verify both that your cable works and that your modem has been properly configured. When the hardware flow control is working properly, you can consider adding software flow control for end-to-end handshaking as needed.

File Transfers

After a system has been properly set up with modems and flow control, one of the most common activities a user will want to undertake is that of file transfers. This is another area that once again causes a lot of grief for users of communications software, whether they are novices or experienced users. As with RS-232 cabling, modems, and handshaking, for file transfers to work properly, both computers involved in the transaction have to be set up to do exactly the same thing.

One of the main problems with file transfers is that no clear-cut, definitive standards exist for how to do things. Accordingly, when we want to move files from machine to machine, you have to examine the menu of protocols that are available to both machines. You then look for the protocols common to both machines and try to select the "best" one for the job. Usually, but not always, it is possible to find a match and get the job done.

Following is a brief overview of some of the more well-known protocols. Keep in mind that developing a new software file transfer protocol is much easier than developing a new hardware interface, so new protocols seem to spring up weekly.

- ◆ **XMODEM:** The XMODEM protocol was one of the first file-transfer methods that achieved widespread use on the desktop. XMODEM is a relatively simple protocol that allows a user to perform a binary transfer of a single file. It requires a clear 8-bit channel with no software handshaking, which makes XMODEM somewhat difficult to implement on many mainframe and minicomputer platforms.

  The XMODEM protocol is the lowest common denominator among the online community of electronic bulletin boards and information services. When all else fails, XMODEM can usually be relied on to work for both ends of the connection.

  Many minor variants of XMODEM have sprung up over the years. The most universal is XMODEM-CRC, which uses a 16-bit CRC checksum rather than an 8-bit additive checksum for improved error detection. XMODEM-1K increases the block size from 128 to 1024 bytes, giving greater utilization of connection bandwidth. And XMODEM-1K-G can be used on channels using MNP-4 or V.42, because it assumes an error-free connection and does not require immediate acknowledgment of each packet. Despite its primitive roots, XMODEM-1K-G can transfer files using nearly 100 percent of the available bandwidth. (At great cost, XMODEM-1K-G sacrifices most error correction to gain this speed.)

- ◆ **YMODEM:** YMODEM is an enhancement of the XMODEM file transfer protocol. YMODEM adds a file information packet to the XMODEM protocol so that it can send the filename, size, and date along with the file contents. Because of this extra layer in the protocol, YMODEM can also send batches of files rather than just one file at a time, leading to its often-used alias, "YMODEM-Batch."

  YMODEM is a fairly simple addition to the XMODEM protocol, so it is not too difficult to add to existing software that supports XMODEM. This ease of upgrading has led to the widespread dissemination of this protocol as well.

- **ZMODEM:** XMODEM and YMODEM work well under certain circumstances, but they definitely suffer from limitations. They work only on 8-bit communication lines, and XON/XOFF or other forms of software handshaking give them fits. Packet-switched networks cause XMODEM performance to degrade horribly. Even under the best circumstances, XMODEM and YMODEM don't make very efficient use of their available bandwidth.

    ZMODEM was designed to overcome all of these problems. First of all, ZMODEM was specifically designed to work well on packet-switched networks. ZMODEM is referred to as a "streaming" protocol, meaning that it sends data in a continuous fashion, without waiting for acknowledgment of individual blocks. Instead, ZMODEM expects only to see indications of erroneous data, which will interrupt the current block and cause a retransmission of the bad data.

    ZMODEM was also designed to work in conjunction with software handshaking, such as XON/XOFF. Enhancements to ZMODEM will also allow it to work over 7-bit data channels, which still accounts for a certain amount of electronic data traffic. (Note that the original author of ZMODEM, Chuck Forsberg, claims ownership of many ZMODEM extensions.)

    Public domain ZMODEM source code is now available, so ZMODEM has spread to many different types of systems. Unfortunately, ZMODEM is a relatively complex protocol to implement and, as such, has not spread quite as rapidly as proponents might like.

- **Kermit:** Like ZMODEM, Kermit was developed in an attempt to let machines from various incompatible architectures communicate. Kermit is a carefully designed, well-layered protocol, with a detailed specification and public domain source code available.

    Kermit is a packet-oriented protocol that avoids using characters that could conflict with software handshaking or other protocol characters. It can work on either 8-bit or 7-bit channels and offers built-in data compression and other advanced features.

    Kermit has been implemented on a wider variety of computer systems than any other protocol. The Kermit community also maintains a very strong spirit of communication, with code, ideas, and implementation help being freely distributed.

    As a result of its being ported to so many platforms, one might expect Kermit to be the most widely used protocol. Although protocols such as YMODEM and ZMODEM aren't as easy to work with and implement as Kermit, they are much faster. Kermit has a lot of overhead in both packet formation and acknowledgment.

Enhancements to Kermit have been made to help address efficiency problems. However, these enhancements have generally met with the same fate as enhancements and supersets of other protocols: without mandatory implementation, optional features just aren't used often enough to generate a critical mass of users.

Software and Hardware Tools

This last section of this chapter discusses software and hardware that can be useful to the communications programmer.

PC software

For those just getting started in the world of PC communications, an enormous variety of software is available. For the user, there are quite a few communications programs, ranging from inexpensive shareware programs to popular commercial software, such as Procomm.

Most users first encounter a communications package when they purchase their modems. Most intelligent modems sold today are accompanied by a communications package designed to work properly with that modem. For the most part, these manufacturer-supplied programs are sparse and just barely adequate. Experienced users generally discard them and move on to more powerful commercial and shareware packages.

A good communications package should be able to control your modem; handle all the tasks associated with calling online services and BBSs; have a scripting or macro capability for automating routine chores; and offer upload and download capability for files. Competition among these products has seen vendors going far beyond these basics, with lists of additional features too numerous to detail here.

BBS software

BBS systems started off as simple programs that let users exchange electronic messages and files. The best BBS systems have now moved far beyond that, with networked capability for worldwide messaging, online games and chat features, massive file libraries, and custom "door" software that lets BBS operators develop their own special features.

Before the World Wide Web exploded onto the telecommunications scene in the mid-1990s, the BBS was the connection of choice for PC modem users. Sadly, those days have passed. Although some BBS systems are still alive and doing well in the world, they have been for the most part relegated to a niche service that is way outside the mainstream.

The premiere BBS suppliers of years gone by such as Mustang Software (Wildcat!) or Clark Development (PCBoard) have either moved on to better things or have gone out of business. BBS software can still be found, however, and systems such as Opus and Citadel are still alive and well.

It's difficult to say what the future holds for BBS systems. Much of the traffic that used to take place over BBS systems has moved to the Internet. For example, distribution of commercial software and technical support for computer products are now occurring almost exclusively over the World Wide Web. The BBS community still serves some niches, such as local chat and messaging services. Whether these will survive continued penetration by the Internet remains to be seen.

Programming libraries

This book should teach enough about RS-232 programming to allow you to develop good communications programs. Although this book will start you down the road toward becoming an expert, you might want to take a shortcut. If you decide not to develop your own communications programs from scratch, many excellent C and C++ libraries are available to help.

Regardless of how diligently you apply yourself, you are probably not going to be able to approach the level of testing that goes into one of these commercial libraries. Most have been available for several years and have been purchased and used by hundreds or even thousands of programmers. Thus, they have been tested on a vast number of platforms and operating environments.

The economics of purchasing a library are generally very favorable, *as long as the library is reliable*. If you purchase a buggy product with poor support, you will often end up expending so much time and energy ironing out problems that your initial investment will be dwarfed. Accordingly, my suggestions for evaluating commercial libraries follow:

- ◆ Get working demos of applications built with the library. Most vendors have demo programs available. Test these programs using various hardware and other communications software. This should give you some insight into the quality and flexibility of the library.

- ◆ Talk to the vendor's technical support department about problems you may have had with the demo programs. If you don't experience any problems, try to talk to the technical support person about questions you might have. The ability of the technical support person to help you solve problems quickly will probably be one of the most important factors in deciding whether the library saves you money.

- ◆ Check over the features list of the library, but don't let the number of features be an overwhelming factor in your decision. It is easy to get carried away and make decisions based on the presence or absence of features you don't really need.

- Check the quality of the documentation and source code of the library. If the library doesn't come with source code, think twice before you buy it. To check these items, you may have to purchase the library on an evaluation basis, so this is usually the last part of the evaluation process. Most vendors offer unconditional warranties and will gladly sell you a library on an evaluation basis.

I suggest that you survey the entire market before you make a decision. There are two different sources of information: 1) programming magazines and 2) mail order catalogs. Programming magazines such as *Dr. Dobb's Journal* and the *C/C++ User's Journal* will feature ads from many of the library vendors. A quick call to mail-order software houses such as Programmer's Paradise or Programmer's Connection will usually yield a free catalog listing most of the available libraries.

Several shareware communications libraries are also available. The decision to purchase one of these libraries probably needs to be made for reasons other than those that would factor into choosing a commercial package. You will rarely if ever get the same quality of documentation and support with a shareware library. However, for much less money, you may get access to well-written source code. If you want to learn more about communications programming and incorporate good programming techniques into your own work, these libraries will usually provide good working material.

Tools of the trade

One of the reasons that so many people shy away from communications programming is that it tends to be somewhat hardware intensive. You can feel more confident when faced with all this hardware if you have an adequate supply of tools. Most of these tools are relatively inexpensive, and will often pay for themselves the first time you use them.

BREAKOUT BOXES

Figure 1-13 shows the Blue Box Model 100 (International Data Sciences), a typical breakout box. A *breakout box* is simply a piece of diagnostic hardware that is inserted in line with a cable between two RS-232 devices. Usually, a breakout box will have miniature switches that let you break open or shut individual lines on the 25-conductor cable. In addition, it will usually have some jumper wires so that individual signals can be routed to different destinations. These jumper wires can come in very handy. For example, if you determine that you have two DTE devices trying to talk over a straight cable, you can use two jumper wires to convert the straight cable to a three-wire null-modem cable.

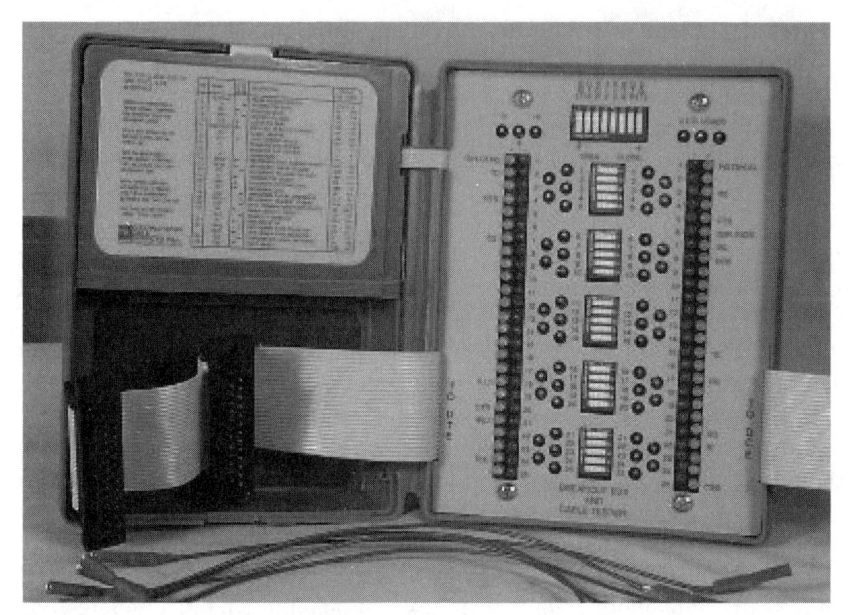

Figure 1-13: A typical breakout box

Perhaps the most useful features on a breakout box are the LEDs attached to most of the commonly used lines. With the aid of these LEDs, you can determine what sort of activity is happening on a given line. For example, if a PC and a modem are using RTS/CTS communications while transmitting, an LED monitor on the RTS and CTS lines should show the lines periodically changing back and forth between two states.

You should try to purchase a breakout box that has dual-state LEDs. Remember that RS-232 signals come in three varieties, not two: low, high, or invalid. A line that is not hooked up to a negative or positive voltage is considered invalid. Unfortunately, a normal red LED can indicate only two states: high or low. It usually can't distinguish between a CTS line that is low and a CTS line that isn't connected.

To solve this problem, better breakout boxes employ an LED that shows three different states: low, high, and off. Usually, red will indicate high, green will indicate low, and no color will indicate no signal. This way, you can tell whether a line is actually disconnected from an RS-232 driver. This information is very valuable when you are dealing with an unknown RS-232 device. For example, with a dual-state LED display, you can quickly determine which of pins 2 and 3 are inputs and which are outputs, thereby helping you properly cable your equipment. Inputs will show up as having no valid RS-232 signal, whereas outputs will always show up as high or low. Another valuable use for dual state LED is to determine when your device is actually transmitting data. At high baud rates, it may not be possible to determine whether a single LED is flickering off for brief periods of time, but if the LED changes color to become slightly more green than before, you will know that the device is actually transmitting data.

As an alternative to an actual dual-state LED, many breakout boxes simply have a pair of LEDs on each line: one green and one red. This accomplishes exactly the same task; it just takes up slightly more space. The Blue Box 100 shown in Figure 1-13 has a pair of LEDs on every signal on both the DTE and DCE sides of the connection. This may seem like overkill, but it is very helpful to never be in doubt as to the state of a given signal.

Breakout box prices can go as high as $300 but you can find very useful units for less than $100. In fact, a fully functional breakout box with 12 dual-state LEDs can be purchased for less than $30. If you are working only on desktop PCs, remember that breakout boxes that have switches and LEDs for all 25 RS-232 lines aren't going to be any more useful than those that have just nine lines. Your PCs will be using only 9 of those 25 signal lines, so there isn't much point to paying for any more. If you are wondering what features are most important, I would look first for dual-state or dual LEDs, second for the ability to jumper every pin.

LINE MONITORS

Breakout boxes do several useful things. They let you examine the state of individual RS-232 lines using an LED. They let you disconnect individual lines using switches, and they let you reconfigure your cable using jumper wires. Breakout boxes also let you observe whether or not data is being transmitted by letting you watch the LEDs attached to the TD and RD lines.

But just seeing whether data is being transmitted often isn't enough to help you debug an application. Sometimes you need to know exactly what data is being transmitted. And most of us aren't skillful enough to decode the actual data by watching LEDs blink on and off several thousand times per second.

Fifteen years ago, this problem would have been solved by the purchase of an RS-232 Data Line Analyzer. This multithousand-dollar piece of equipment would monitor the data and control lines on an RS-232 connection. It would display the actual data being passed in both directions on a screen. It would also log the data for later review, along with accurate time stamps showing when the data was sent. These machines were very nice but, unfortunately, they were also very expensive.

The advent of the inexpensive desktop PC created the possibility for an inexpensive version of the RS-232 Line Analyzer. By combining an existing PC with two serial ports, some custom software, and a special cable, you could have the equivalent of an expensive Line Analyzer for no more than the cost of the software. Today's inexpensive notebook PC prices can even supply an affordable mobile product.

Naturally, once this opportunity existed, several people began making products to take advantage of it. Now there are at least half a dozen PC-based line monitors. They share one characteristic: they require a special cable that taps into an RS-232 connection much like a breakout box and routes the signals found there to two serial ports on the PC. Then they all manage the acquisition, display, and storage of that data via their custom software package. All these packages retail for less than $500, so the cost of an RS-232 Data Line Analyzer has dropped dramatically.

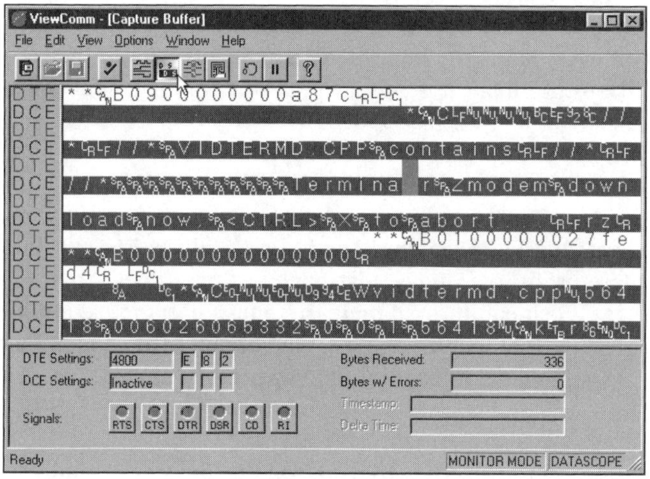

Figure 1-14: An RS-232 monitor screen shot

Figure 1-14 shows a screen shot from a typical monitor program, (Greenleaf Software's ViewComm). The main portion of the screen shows the RS-232 data from both sides of the connection being displayed in real time. The top of the screen has a set of pull-down menus to allow you to analyze the data, save it to disk, or reconfigure the program.

A real-time monitor such as this can prove invaluable when you're debugging RS-232 applications. These products are sold in the same places I recommend earlier in this chapter for C programming libraries.

Cable-making equipment

As I mention earlier in this chapter, RS-232 cables continue to be one of the biggest headaches for programmers working on serial applications. As long as your hardware needs only standard cables with 25-pin connectors, you should not have serious problems. However, anytime your needs stray from this and you require custom cables, life suddenly becomes much more difficult. But there are several simple methods for making your own cables. And I discuss the basic idea behind three fairly simple methods.

One method that is fairly flexible, yet very easy to manage, involves buying premade cabling kits. These kits consist of a 9-conductor wire with connector pins already crimped on to the ends of the wires. All you need to buy in addition to the cables are connectors, hoods, strain reliefs, and an insertion tool. The insertion tool is a simple mechanical device that costs only a few dollars. In addition, you can purchase jumper wires that are used to loop back signals at the connector.

To make a cable using the cabling kit, you simply use the insertion tool to push the crimped pins into the appropriate locations on the connector. After you have inserted all the pins, you complete the end of the cable by connecting the strain relief and the hood. After 5 or 10 minutes, you have a complete cable. This very simple procedure doesn't require any expensive equipment.

Another relatively simple method involves the use of modular connectors. These connectors use RJ-45 8-conductor telephone cable rather than standard unshielded cable to join connectors. As in the previous cable kits, you buy a hood and a connector, and then insert the pins wherever you want. You don't need a strain relief because the RJ-45 connector fastens to the hood to provide strain relief. Perhaps the only major disadvantage to this cabling method is that the RJ-45 cable has only eight conductors, which means that on a standard PC, you have to leave one signal unconnected. This may not be as much of a problem as it sounds. Most applications can probably function quite well with the RI pin disconnected because modems typically send an ASCII message when the phone is ringing. An application can simply watch for the ASCII "RING" message to determine when an incoming ring is detected.

The final method for making cables is completely do-it-yourself. You buy 10- or 12-conductor cable in bulk, then buy connector pins, a crimping tool, connectors, hoods, and strain relief widgets. You cut your own cable to custom sizes, strip the wires, and crimp the pins onto the wires. You then insert the pins into the connectors, attach the hoods and strain relief devices, and you have a cable.

This final method has the most flexibility but comes with two big disadvantages. First, it is labor intensive and will take a fairly long time for a given cable. Second, the crimping tool generally costs about $100 (although cheaper models are available), so the initial outlay is high.

GENDER CHANGERS/ADAPTERS

Along with whatever cabling kits you decide on, you should lay in a supply of several different sorts of adapters (as I discuss earlier in this chapter). An adapter looks like a normal RS-232 connector except that it has pins at both ends and no wire coming out of it. These adapters can be found at prices as low as five dollars.

The adapters you will want to always have on hand are listed as follows:

- 9-pin female to 25-pin male — adapter for AT Serial port
- 25-pin null modem adapter
- 25-pin male-to-female gender changer
- 25-pin female-to-male gender changer

As I mention earlier in this chapter, you might want to get out the soldering iron and modify the null-modem adapter so that its connections are somewhat more useful than those in the pre-assembled connector. Because the adapter costs only a few dollars, you shouldn't feel inhibited about practicing soldering on it.

VOLTMETER

One final piece of equipment that will help you with your RS-232 hardware debugging is a low-cost voltmeter. You will want to use the voltmeter for two different things. First, using it either as an ohmmeter or a continuity checker (if it has that function), you can test cables for internal breaks and shorts. Unknown cables can be checked out for duplication.

If your voltmeter has a continuity setting, you usually can apply it to ends of a piece of wire and determine immediately whether they are connected. If they are, the meter will beep. If your meter doesn't have a continuity setting, you can use the ohmmeter setting. A solid piece of wire should have a very low resistance – less than 100 ohms even if it is very long. An open wire should show a resistance in the Megohms.

Getting voltmeter probes onto RS-232 connectors can try your patience. Two pieces of equipment will help. The first is a set of probes with minihook clips at the end. You can purchase the minihook clips at Radio Shack and just attach them to your voltmeter probes. These clips are small enough that they can attach to a normal RS-232 pin. For getting your probe to make contact with the female connector, there is nothing better than an ordinary paper clip. Just straighten the paper clip out, hook the clip to it, and stick the other end of the paper clip into the socket.

Second, use the voltmeter to check the voltages on RS-232 pins. Remember that a valid RS-232 voltage should be at least plus or minus 3 volts. In practice, unless they're traveling over a very long cable, most RS-232 voltages will be around plus or minus 12 volts, normally standard for the RS-232 driver chips. All voltage measurements on an RS-232 connector should be made relative to pin 7, which is the signal ground. If you fail to connect the black lead of your voltmeter to pin 7, any measurements will be faulty and should be ignored.

What About the Internet?

Most Internet users these days are connecting to their service provider via a PPP connection over standard phone lines. Because of this, you might think that a programming book on serial communications would have extensive coverage of the Internet. However, this isn't the case in this book.

Most Internet programming tasks consists of using high-level protocols to communicate between computers. Protocols such as FTP, HTTP, SMTP, POP3, TELNET, and so on are used to exchange files, mail, message packets, and various other pieces of data. These protocols can operate over computers connected via RS-232, but they work just as well over computers connected via Ethernet, fiber optic lines, or various other methods.

The techniques and strategies you need to use these protocols are certainly a good topic for a book, but they deserve their own book. In particular, users interested in writing code designed to use these protocols don't really need all the other information in this book, such as UART programming, the Windows comm API, and so on. So rather than double the size of this book, Internet programming issues will have to be discussed in their own book.

Summary

This chapter contains all the necessary background information on equipment and compilers for you to become proficient in writing code for RS-232 hardware. Chapter 2, The RS232 Class, provides information specific to programming for RS-232 in C++.

Chapter 2

The RS232 Class

IN THIS CHAPTER

- ◆ Why C++ is the language of choice
- ◆ Class RS232
- ◆ The RS232 class, member by member
- ◆ The code

THE RS232 CLASS IS the base class for all the RS-232 drivers used in this book. This book is intended to be useful for people who are not expert C++ programmers, so some of the explanation of this class will use C terminology. The RS232 class gives a very straightforward and simple example of the reasons for using C++ instead of C, so ideally it will provide a bridge for C programmers to begin working in C++.

Why C++ Is the Language of Choice

The reason for using C++ for the communications code in this book is to take advantage of *virtual functions*. In C terms, a virtual function is simply a function that is called via a pointer rather than directly. To the programmer, the fact that a virtual function is being called via a pointer is for the most part hidden behind C++ syntax.

Writing portable code that can work with various types of hardware means developing a base class called RS232. The base class RS232 contains the definition for a set of virtual functions that are intended to give you complete access to the usable interface to an RS-232 driver. For example, a typical virtual function that you might define for class RS232 might be called Read(). Using C++ syntax, a programmer uses this function to read in a byte from an RS-232 port of some kind. The important fact to remember about Read() is that when you call it, you don't actually call a function named *Read()*. Instead, you call a specific version of Read() that has been written for a particular driver. For example, the Read() coded for an 8250 UART interface on a standard PC will probably be very different from that coded for an intelligent DigiBoard plugged into the same PC. But either one can be called via the Read() virtual function.

49

An attempt to get by with C

To understand why I want to use virtual functions in C++, it might help to see how things would develop if I were to implement function Read() for several different types of hardware in standard C. Remember that the goal is to be able to write applications that make calls to device-independent RS-232 functions. The tried-and-true method for resolving this problem would be to write a routine that dispatches the appropriate version of Read(). This routine would be called directly and would perform some sort of test to see what type of port is being referenced. Then the appropriate function could be invoked.

The code to implement this intelligent dispatcher is similar to code that any experienced programmer has written dozens of times for dozens of different applications. To encapsulate the information about the serial port, I might create a structure called C_RS232. A pointer to this structure would then be passed to all my utility routines that access the port. A simple read function might look like this:

```
int Read( struct C_RS232 *port )
{
  switch( port->type ) {
    case PC8250      : return ReadPC8250( port );
    case INTELLIGENT : return ReadIntelligent( port );
    case NASI        : return ReadNASI( port );
    case FOSSIL      : return ReadFossil( port );
    default          : return RS232_INVALID_PORT_TYPE;
  }
}
```

Problems with this approach

This code is easy to follow and will work reliably. However, as your library of RS-232 drivers is built up over time, a couple of things will become clear. First, your application will be linking in the code for every driver, regardless of whether it is used. So when you try to write a short little program that writes only a couple of bytes out to a PC COM port, you will be dragging along all the code to accomplish the same task over a network, an intelligent board, a FOSSIL driver, and so forth. This could easily double or triple the size of a small application.

Second, you will be paying a small price at runtime for every function call made this way. Every time you make a call to Read(), you have to proceed through the same arbitration process, checking the port type against all the various types before any work is done.

From a programmer's point of view, the maintenance of this code is not that simple. Any time you decide to implement a new driver, you not only have to write all the supported functions for that particular sort of hardware but also implement the hooks in all the dispatcher routines. Doing so effectively doubles the amount of maintenance you have to do, which increases the chances for error.

Dispatching with function pointers

One way to get around the problems of a dispatch function is to use function pointers. It is certainly possible to implement Read() using function pointers rather than direct function calls. This is accomplished by defining Read to be a global function pointer, not the actual function.

When using this approach, you would have a set of global function pointers that talk to your physical RS-232 device. You would have an initialization function that initializes all the function pointers when the port is opened. The pointers would be directed to the appropriate low-level routine, depending on the type of device.

Given that setup, a typical application might end up having a code fragment that looked something like this:

```
int (*Read)( struct C_RS232 *port );

int ReadLine( struct C_RS232 *port )
{
  int c;
  char buffer[ 81 ];

  for ( ; ; ) {
    c = Read( port );
    if ( c == '\r' )
      break;
    .
    .
    .
```

The preceding method for implementing a function pointer works very well with C and is easy to read under ANSI C. The mechanism for calling a function via a pointer is syntactically identical to that for calling a function directly, so the programmer doesn't need to learn anything new.

One problem with the preceding code is that it doesn't really take into account the possibility that different ports in the same program may well need different versions of Read(). For example, in a given program, I might be using COM1, COM2, and four ports from a shared interrupt multiport board. This means that I have two different types of hardware that are accessed by two different versions of a Read() routine. However, there is just one function pointer for that function. How do I resolve this? I explain in the next section.

Moving function pointers to a structure

To manage multiple port types under ANSI C properly, your next step is to have a private set of function pointers for each port that you open. That way, you can open two different types of ports and still call the correct functions for each one in the same program. To support this, you will have to start carrying around these function pointers in a structure. A sample code fragment that defines this structure and then makes use of it might look something like this:

```
struct C_RS232 {
  int (*Read)( struct C_RS232 *port );
  int (*Write)( struct C_RS232 *port, int c );
  .
  .
  .
};

int ReadLine( struct C_RS232 *port )
{
  int c;
  char buffer[ 81 ];

  for ( ; ; ) {
    c = port->Read( port );
    if ( c == '\r' )
      break;
    .
    .
    .

main()
{
    struct C_RS232 *Port;
    int c;

    Port = OpenComPort( COM1, 9600 );
    ReadLine( Port );
    .
    .
    .
```

At this point, two things have happened. First, the functions are now showing a little more flexibility. By allocating the functions on a port-by-port basis, you now have the flexibility you need to use various kinds of ports within the same program via indirect function calls. There is still some overhead associated with each function, but not nearly as much as there was. In this case, it is simply a matter of an extra pointer dereference required to indirectly call the function. With proper function calls to open the port, you won't be dragging in all the different RS-232 drivers to support a program using just one type.

The second interesting thing that has happened is that the C_RS232 structure defined here now looks a lot like a C++ class. The function pointers shown here are acting exactly the way virtual functions behave in C++ (although the implementation of the behavior is slightly different.) This C code would look just like C++ if it weren't for the fact that the C function calls have to pass an explicit pointer to the C_RS232 structure. In C++, this structure is passed implicitly.

If C can do it, why use C++?

The code sample shown previously illustrates that it is possible to implement something very similar to virtual functions without switching to C++. The obvious question then comes up: Why switch to C++?

Virtual functions were designed as part of the C++ language: implementing them in C requires a lot of extra manual labor. In C++, the compiler takes care of most of the work. More important, in C++ the compiler also ensures that the derived classes built from the base class are implemented properly.

The C structure shown earlier had two function pointers defined that pointed to the C code used to read and write bytes. Presumably, a derived "class" (realizing that in ANSI C, there is no such thing) had its own Open() function that set up these function pointers to point to the proper low-level implementations. A driver that communicated with serial ports via BIOS function calls would be opened using a function that looked something like this:

```
struct C_RS232 *OpenBIOSPort( int port_number, int baud_rate )
{
  struct C_RS232 *port;

  port = calloc( 1, sizeof( struct C_RS232 ) );
  if ( port != 0 ) {
    port->Read = ReadBIOS;
    port->Write = WriteBIOS;
    .
    .
    .
```

When writing the code for the preceding routine, inadvertently neglecting to initialize the Write() function pointer would be easy. In that case, when the caller first attempted to call Port->Write(Port, 'A'), the most likely event would be a system lockup, because the function pointer was initialized to a value 0.

When implementing this scheme using true virtual functions under C++, a good compiler would immediately catch an undefined Write() function and generate an error message. When defining a base class, any virtual function that *must* be implemented by a derived class can just be predefined as 0. This makes that function a *pure* function, and the class containing it is therefore an *abstract class*. The abstract class isn't an object in its own right; it merely represents an interface that an object can pledge to implement.

When you derive a class from the abstract base class, in this case RS232, you must define new functions for all the pure virtual functions or the derived class will still be an abstract class. Any attempt to create an object from an abstract class will generate an error message.

A piece of the class definition for class RS232 (the base class used for all the serial classes in this book) looks like this:

```
class RS232
{
protected :
  RS232PortName port_name;
  Settings saved_settings;
  Settings settings;
  RS232Error error_status;
  int debug_line_count;
  virtual int read_buffer( char *buffer,
                           unsigned int count ) = 0;
  virtual int write_buffer( char *buffer,
                            unsigned int count = -1 ) = 0;
  virtual int read_byte( void ) = 0;
  virtual int write_byte( int c ) = 0;
  .
  .
  .
```

Because of the fact that virtual functions have been initialized to 0, the compiler knows that this is an abstract base class and can't be created directly. With this definition of the RS232 class, any program that attempted to create an RS232 object would get an error message from the compiler. For example, Borland C++ gives the following error message:

```
Error TEST.CPP 26: Cannot create instance of abstract class 'RS232'
```

This is exactly what a compiler should do, and only C++ does it. This sort of error checking just wouldn't be possible with standard ANSI C.

C++ provides the added benefit of easing the derivation process when you create new classes. For example, many of the driver programs used to access modems across networks use an expanded version of the PC BIOS interface calls to simulate direct access of a modem. They generally add a few proprietary calls to the existing INT 14H interface, usually to allow more baud rates, block transfers, and the ability to make and break logical connections to modems.

It makes sense to create new classes for each of these interfaces that use an existing BIOS class as a starting place. For example, to use the Novell NASI interface, I would like to be able to derive a NASI class from a BIOS class and just add a couple of new virtual functions. Instead, if I were to try to do this in the C version of the library, I would probably have to take the C code for the BIOS interface, and modify it directly to add my new port open code and to set up function pointers to my new virtual functions. With C++, I can create a new Nasi class that is derived from an existing BIOS class, and count on the compiler to reuse all the existing virtual functions from the BIOS class.

Class RS232

The definition of class RS232 is the core concept in this book. This is the abstract base class that gives birth to all the serial interface classes used in the book. It is also the class used as an interface to all the related functions that work with serial ports, including the modem control, terminal emulation, and file transfer routines. Any code that uses class RS232 objects as parameters will then be portable to all the other drivers developed in this book, as well as to any derived classes you create. The definition for the RS232 class is shown below. Note that the master header file for all the RS232-derived driver classes, RS232.H, contains the class definition.

Initially, you can easily be tempted to include everything but the kitchen sink in a given class. For example, you might like to include a virtual function in class RS232 to enable the synchronous communications capabilities on an Intel 82510 UART. This approach poses two major problems. First, such a large class will eventually become unwieldy. It becomes extremely tedious to derive new classes that must implement all these new functions. Second, the derived classes tend to suffer from "exception-itis" when faced with many calls that they can't support. In every case, a mechanism must be established for handling exceptional functions.

Here is the definition of the RS232 class:

```
class RS232
{
protected :
   RS232PortName port_name;
   Settings saved_settings;
   Settings settings;
   RS232Error error_status;
   int debug_line_count;
// Mandatory protected functions
```

```cpp
        virtual int read_buffer( char *buffer,
                                 unsigned int count ) = 0;
        virtual int write_buffer( char *buffer,
                                  unsigned int count = -1 ) = 0;
        virtual int read_byte( void ) = 0;
        virtual int write_byte( int c ) = 0;

    public :
        unsigned int ByteCount;
        long ElapsedTime;

    //  Mandatory functions. All derived classes must define these.

        virtual RS232Error Set( long baud_rate = UNCHANGED,
                                int parity = UNCHANGED,
                                int word_length = UNCHANGED,
                                int stop_bits = UNCHANGED ) = 0;
        virtual int TXSpaceFree( void ) = 0;
        virtual int RXSpaceUsed( void ) = 0;
        virtual int Cd( void ) = 0;
        virtual int Ri( void ) = 0;
        virtual int Cts( void ) = 0;
        virtual int Dsr( void ) = 0;
        virtual int ParityError( int clear = UNCHANGED ) = 0;
        virtual int BreakDetect( int clear = UNCHANGED ) = 0;
        virtual int FramingError( int clear = UNCHANGED ) = 0;
        virtual int HardwareOverrunError( int clear = UNCHANGED ) = 0;

    // Optional Functions. Derived class are not
    // required to support these.

        virtual ~RS232( void ){ ; }
        virtual int Break( long milliseconds = 300 );
        virtual int SoftwareOverrunError( int clear = UNCHANGED );
        virtual int XonXoffHandshaking( int setting = UNCHANGED );
        virtual int RtsCtsHandshaking( int setting = UNCHANGED );
        virtual int DtrDsrHandshaking( int setting = UNCHANGED );
        virtual int Dtr( int setting = UNCHANGED );
        virtual int Rts( int setting = UNCHANGED );
        virtual int Peek( void *buffer, unsigned int count );
        virtual int RXSpaceFree( void );
        virtual int TXSpaceUsed( void );
        virtual int FlushRXBuffer( void );
        virtual int FlushTXBuffer( void );
```

```
   virtual char *ErrorName( int error );
   virtual int IdleFunction( void );
   virtual int FormatDebugOutput( char *buffer = 0,
                                  int line_number = -1 );

// Non virtual functions. These work the same for all classes.
   int Read( void *buffer,
             unsigned int count,
             long milliseconds = 0 );
   int Read( void *buffer,
             unsigned int count,
             long milliseconds,
             char *terminator );
   int Write( void *buffer,
              unsigned int count = 0,
              long milliseconds = 0,
              char *terminator = 0 );
   int Read( long milliseconds = 0 );
   int Write( int c, long milliseconds = 0 );
   int Peek( void );
   int ReadSettings( Settings &copy )
   {
      copy = settings;
      return RS232_SUCCESS;
   }
   RS232Error ErrorStatus( void ) { return error_status; }
   int DebugLineCount( void ) { return debug_line_count; }
};
```

> **NOTE:** Don't look for a constructor in class RS232. You will never create an RS232 object directly; instead, you will construct objects of classes derived from class RS232. Derived classes will have constructors that you can invoke directly.

The RS232 class is very straightforward. No complex relationships exist between this class and other classes, and no strange constructors or hidden classes. Nearly all the functions are public functions intended to be called by programmers using various RS-232 devices. As stated, this book is not attempting sleight-of-hand using C++. It simply demonstrates a way to improve portability using C++ in place of C. You should be able to tell what most of these functions do just by reading the names.

A few conventions

Classes should always be designed with ease of use as a goal. Such a design goes beyond trying to write fast and efficient code. If a class such as the RS232 class is to be effective, it needs to present a clear, easy to understand, and consistent interface to the programmer. It is usually fairly easy for the original author of a library or program to keep track of a long list of exceptions and oddities associated with his or her work, but pity the programmer who has to take over the project after a corporate reorganization.

FUNCTION/ELEMENT NAMES

One of the best ways to make a library easy to use is to supply it with clear, descriptive names for all the functions, structures, and other objects that appear in the code. In the RS232 class, I try to use multiple word names for all variables and functions. By convention, functions and elements to be used by the programmer mix upper- and lowercase, like this:

```
port.Read( buffer, 20 );
```

Data and functions used internally by the library are defined using all lowercase, with names separated by underscores, like this:

```
port.write_byte( c );
```

Although many people loathe the extra typing necessitated when using "wordy" function names like those used here, I feel that the advantages in terms of code readability overwhelmingly mandate the use of such function names.

FUNCTION RETURN VALUES

Communications libraries always contain some potential for confusion over function returns. C and C++ work best when a function returns a single parameter. Any time multiple pieces of information come back from a function, there is room for confusion. For example, when reading in a buffer full of data from a serial port, you may want to get back the characters, the character count, any error indications, and the elapsed time. Many different strategies can be adopted for this, and each has good and bad points. However, most important is to establish consistent conventions and to stick with them.

With a single exception, all the functions defined in the RS232 class return an integer value. The exception is the ErrorName() function, which always returns a character string. In the case of all the other functions, any error code is returned directly from the function. To determine whether a function has returned with success or an error, see whether the returned value is less than 0. All the standard RS232 error codes are defined as values less than 0, so a function such as Read() will return a positive or zero value if things work properly, or a negative value if an error occurs. C programmers are used to seeing this same convention used in C standard library functions such as getc().

The following code snippet defines the standard class RS232 error codes. The RS232_SUCCESS code is defined as a 0, but all the actual error routines are defined as negative numbers. I have defined the error codes as an enumerated type rather than as constants so that the codes will be more visible during debugging. Note that this list should not be considered to be complete. Derived classes will always be free to define their own error codes, and many of the derived classes in this book will extend the error code list.

```
enum RS232Error {    RS232_SUCCESS                   = 0,

// Warning errors
                     RS232_WARNING                   = -100,
                     RS232_FUNCTION_NOT_SUPPORTED,
                     RS232_TIMEOUT,
                     RS232_ILLEGAL_BAUD_RATE,
                     RS232_ILLEGAL_PARITY_SETTING,
                     RS232_ILLEGAL_WORD_LENGTH,
                     RS232_ILLEGAL_STOP_BITS,
                     RS232_ILLEGAL_LINE_NUMBER,
                     RS232_NO_MODEM_RESPONSE,
                     RS232_NO_TERMINATOR,
                     RS232_DTR_NOT_SUPPORTED,
                     RS232_RTS_NOT_SUPPORTED,
                     RS232_RTS_CTS_NOT_SUPPORTED,
                     RS232_DTR_DSR_NOT_SUPPORTED,
                     RS232_XON_XOFF_NOT_SUPPORTED,
                     RS232_NEXT_FREE_WARNING,

// Fatal Errors
                     RS232_ERROR                     = -200,
                     RS232_IRQ_IN_USE,
                     RS232_PORT_NOT_FOUND,
                     RS232_PORT_IN_USE,
                     RS232_ILLEGAL_IRQ,
                     RS232_MEMORY_ALLOCATION_ERROR,
                     RS232_NEXT_FREE_ERROR };
```

The list of error codes is divided in two. The first section consists of warning errors. When a function generates a warning message, the program should be able to recover and continue operating without much trouble. The second section of error messages are fatal errors. When a port encounters a fatal error, things are in very bad shape and the program probably needs to halt.

When an error occurs in a function, it is returned directly to the programmer via the function return. You can test for it with a simple numeric test, like this:

```
int result;

result = port.Write( buffer, 80 );
if ( result < RS232_SUCCESS )
   cout << "Error, Write Buffer returned %s\n"
        << port.ErrorName( result )
        << "\n";
```

Programmers are frequently annoyed by the boring job of having to check error codes after *every* function call. This can make both reading and writing the code a somewhat unpleasant chore.

To lighten the burdens of error checking, the RS232 class maintains an internal error state at all times. If a fatal error occurs, the protected member error_status will retain that error code. If a subsequent function is called after a fatal error, the program will not crash or lock up. Ideally, it should just check the error state, see that a fatal error has occurred, and return an error code. So, a program can make a few consecutive calls to RS232 functions without your worrying about major catastrophes in the event of an error.

BYTE COUNTS

Two of the functions called here need to return byte counts as well as error codes. For example, when calling the Read() routine with a buffer as the destination argument, the programmer gives a byte count to indicate how many bytes are will be requested from the port. If Read() times out before reading the entire buffer, it returns the RS232_TIMEOUT warning error. It must also return a count of bytes actually read in.

The way this is accomplished by class RS232 member functions is by consistently returning the actual count of bytes transferred in the public element ByteCount. After any function call that transfers data, ByteCount can be checked for an actual count of bytes transferred.

ELAPSED TIME

Finally, the programmer may occasionally want to see the amount of time that has elapsed during the function call. Many of the functions in the RS232 class have time parameters, which indicate how long the function should attempt to read or write before timing out. Occasionally, it is useful to know just how long the function took before it returned. For example, a data collection program might sit in a loop reading in strings while waiting to receive a "CONNECT 28800" message from a modem.

Some of the strings that come back are simply ignored, such as a message like "CONNECT" or "DIALING". By knowing how long each of those messages took to arrive, you can maintain an overall timeout counter.

The `ElapsedTime` member of the `RS232` class takes care of this. `ElapsedTime` will contain a count of the number of milliseconds that elapsed during the reception or transmission of the data. Note that even though the value is in milliseconds, the actual resolution of the timer is dependent on the host system's hardware and software. For MS-DOS, the granularity of the timer is 55 milliseconds. You can perform a few tricks under MS-DOS to get a timer with finer resolution, but most communications applications will work just fine with the 55-millisecond resolution.

Default parameters

The `RS232` class makes extensive use of default parameters in its member functions. Default parameters are another C++ feature that probably don't have much to do with object-oriented programming, but they are nonetheless very useful. The exact use of default parameters varies from function to function, so there isn't a completely consistent pattern. However, there are some general rules to follow:

- ◆ milliseconds: Most of the functions that actually read or write data from the serial port have a time parameter. This parameter indicates how long the function should take to complete its job. If the function is unable to read or write all the bytes requested during the elapsed time, it will return an `RS232_TIMEOUT` error.

  These functions, such as `Read()`, have a default value of 0 for the milliseconds parameter. This means that they will attempt to read or write as many bytes as requested one time, then return.

- ◆ settings: Many of the functions in class `RS232` are used to set port parameters. For example, there is the general `Set()` command, used to set the baud rate, parity, word length, and stop bits. Other functions that set parameters include `Dtr()`, `Rts()`, and `XonXoffHandshaking()`.

  For all these functions, the default value of the settings is the constant `UNCHANGED`. When a function receives a value of `UNCHANGED` for a setting, it leaves that setting alone. This can be particularly useful when you use the `Set()` command. There are probably many times when a programmer just wants to change the baud rate or one of the other parameters. With ANSI C, the function call would require that all the other parameters be set to legitimate values as well (not that you couldn't use the `UNCHANGED` parameter here also). In this case, you can simply call `port.Set( 9600 )` to accomplish the same thing. The remaining three parameters in the function call default to `UNCHANGED`.

- terminator: The `Read( void * )` and `Write( void * )` routines both have an optional string parameter that specifies a string terminator to use for input and output. By default, both of these strings are null pointers, meaning they are not used.

Mandatory and optional functions

Virtual functions help to define which functions are mandatory for a given driver and which are optional. When you declare a virtual function as being pure (by assigning it a value of "0" in the class definition), a derived class *must* implement that function. However, some of the virtual functions are optional. The base class has stubbed versions of the functions that usually do nothing except returning a warning error. These base class implementations mean that a derived class can choose to implement or to ignore the function.

Some functions, such as `read_byte()` and `write_buffer()`, are fundamental to the operation of serial ports. Functions that operate on the base class expect that these have been implemented, so these functions are defined as pure in the class declaration.

Other functions may be difficult or impossible to implement in every derived class, so they are left as optional. For example, the base class has implemented a version of the `XonXoffHandshaking()` function, which means that derived classes are not compelled to implement it. Keep this in mind when you write utility code that operates on the base class.

```
int RS232::XonXoffHandshaking( int )
{
    return RS232_FUNCTION_NOT_SUPPORTED;
}
```

The implementation of this function in the base class is shown in the preceding code. This function doesn't do anything except return the warning message to the calling routine. If a derived class can't make use of this function, it won't define its own version. If that is the case, then any code attempting to use this function with the derived class will revert to the base class implementation and will receive the warning error as its result.

Where is the constructor?

Missing from the class definition for RS232 is a constructor. Generally, a C++ class has a constructor or two for creating objects of that class. In the case of class RS232, however, the only initialization done in the base class is the initialization of a few data members, and those are taken care of by their own constructors.

The derived classes presented later in this book must perform all initializations themselves. This makes sense, because the RS232 class doesn't recognize the hardware being used for the derived class, so its ability to initialize the class is limited.

The RS232 Class, Member by Member

Finally, to make sense of the RS232 class, you must define what each data element and function does. There are quite a few members in the class, but each member has a clearly defined function, so these definitions should serve as a reference.

More important, you should know exactly what job each member performs so that you may create useful derived classes. Although C++ is good at handling the syntax and clerical work associated with deriving classes, the compiler can do nothing to force derived classes to perform as expected. The compiler can ensure that a virtual function takes the right number and type of arguments, and that it returns the right type of data, but it cannot monitor the methods for transforming input to output.

Protected members

Class RS232 has several protected data members. In C++, a protected data element can be accessed only by functions in a few different categories:

- Member functions of the given class
- Member functions of classes derived from the given class
- Member functions of classes declared as friends of the given class

In order to read or modify a protected data element, a function must fit into one of these categories. This provides a nice benefit to the users of classes such as class RS232 because it prevents you from inadvertently modifying a protected data member. This helps avoid careless errors and also clearly stakes out the territory that a class considers to be off limits.

One feature I would have liked to see defined for C++ is the ability to make a data member read-only. This would mean that a nonprivileged function could read the value of a data element, but not change it. You will find in C++ classes lots of one-line functions whose only purpose in life is to return the value of protected data elements to functions outside the class. Fortunately, these functions are usually inline functions, and the compiler can usually optimize them away, but just the fact that the function needs to be created in the first place can be annoying.

The protected members of class RS232 are described in the following sections.

RS232PortName port_name

This data member is of the type `RS232PortName`, an enumerated type that contains COM1, COM2, and so on. When first opened, a serial port is always given a port name, and the value is stored here. The constructor's job is to initialize this value. This data element is protected because it doesn't need to be changed throughout the life of the port.

`Settings saved_settings`

`Settings` is a class defined earlier in the `RS232.H` header file, as shown here. When a port is opened, the base class assumes that all of the settings in the class are available for the port. One of the jobs of the constructor in a derived class is to store all the saved settings in this data member. When the `RS232` object is eventually destroyed, the destructor must restore all the settings in the port to their original states.

```
class Settings
{
public :
  long BaudRate;
  char Parity;
  int WordLength;
  int StopBits;
  int Dtr;
  int Rts;
  int XonXoff;
  int RtsCts;
  int DtrDsr;
  void Adjust( long baud_rate,
               int parity,
               int word_length,
               int stop_bits,
               int dtr,
               int rts,
               int xon_xoff,
               int rts_cts,
               int dtr_dsr );
};
```

One implication of maintaining the `saved_settings` data member is that a derived class is able to change the saved settings of a port. When the `RS232` port object is destroyed, an altered group of settings could be restored to the physical device. This is a useful feature to keep in mind, but it isn't implemented in the base class.

Note that for both `saved_settings` and `settings`, there will be times when the state of a setting is either unknown or illogical. In these cases, all the members of the class that are unknown will be set to −1. The lone exception is the parity character, which will be set to '?'.

Settings settings

This data element contains all of the current settings for the port. Although a derived class may have additional settings to maintain for a port, this data member contains the basic list supported by most RS-232 hardware. The derived class maintains this list of settings. In particular, it must properly initialize the list in the constructor, and then properly modify it upon execution of functions such as Set( ), XonXoffHandshaking( ), and so on.

These settings are sometimes useful to other classes. For example, a file transfer class may need to check the baud rate of a connection in order to properly determine the best packet size. Protocols such as Kermit need to know whether the serial port is operating in 7-bit or 8-bit mode so that they can decide whether to use the special escape codes needed for transmitting 8-bit wide characters on a 7-bit channel.

The data elements in the Settings structure are protected because the settings of the serial port should be modified only via functions in or derived from the RS232 class. However, there are undoubtedly many functions that will want to be able to view these settings, so an access function is defined as a member of this class. The member function ReadSettings( ), which is explored in more detail in this chapter, allows a calling function to obtain a copy of the current settings of the port.

RS232Error error_status

Error handling is an important requirement of a library of functions that talk to hardware. Serial hardware is certainly no exception.

The first line of defense in the RS232 class is the error_status element. This data element keeps track of any fatal error that has occurred somewhere in the life of the RS232 object. After the object has experienced a fatal error, by definition it should no longer be used. Thus, all derived functions should check for this error before doing any serious work. If the value of error_status indicates that a fatal error has been generated, the given function should do nothing but simply return an error condition when called.

Again, the error status is stored away whenever a fatal error occurs, so you don't have to slavishly check the error condition. Instead, you can arrange a program to incorporate error checking so that it takes place at appropriate intervals.

Clearly, you don't want to give easy access to this data element. The error status must be accurately maintained throughout the life of the object. Like so many other protected members, however, you want to let any function read the error status whenever necessary, so the base class also contains an access function called `ErrorStatus()`.

`int debug_line_count`

One of the member functions of class `RS232` is called `FormatDebugOutput()`. This function provides a snapshot of the current state of the port. The programmer calls the function and asks for a line at a time of the debug output. The programmer is then free to do what she or he likes with the output, such as dumping it to a monitor screen or sending it to a file. This is a function that is likely to be used during program development or debugging, not normal operations.

Although you don't *have* to know in advance how many lines can be produced by this virtual function, it can help. When the object is first created, this protected member is initialized with the correct number of lines for its specific class. The application program can then access that number and use it to size windows, buffers, or whatever else is necessary to properly display the debug output.

Because the only function that really can know how many lines this will take is the `FormatDebugOutput()` routine in the derived class, you want this data element to be protected. If you were to inadvertently change it, you might get some scrambled output from the formatting function.

Often, the application program needs to know the value of `debug_line_count`. It does so by calling `FormatDebugOutput()` with a special 0 parameter in place of the buffer where the output is normally directed. The formatting function will then return the number of lines it needs, rather than do its normal formatting job.

Protected member functions

Class `RS232` has four protected virtual functions. These four functions are used to read and write both blocks and individual bytes of data. These low-level virtual functions are called upon by the nonvirtual `Read()` and `Write()` functions to perform the low-level I/O functions.

These four functions are stripped of all the niceties and options found in the nonvirtual public functions used to transfer data. Each of the four attempts to do its task, and returns immediately with a count of bytes transferred, an error status value, and not much else.

These four functions are the worker functions of the derived classes. All of the public I/O functions rely on these worker functions to do the hard work. By properly implementing these four functions, a derived class gets the benefit of all the nonvirtual functions in the base class. So, the developer of a derived class doesn't have to reimplement the logic that reads a buffer with a specific timeout or reads while looking for a specific delimiter.

`int read_buffer( char *buffer, unsigned int count )`

This function reads in as many bytes from the port as it can manage, up to the count specified in the second parameter. If the buffer specified as parameter 1 was filled by the incoming data, a status of `RS232_SUCCESS` is returned, otherwise, `RS232_TIMEOUT` is returned. This function is used by two different versions of the `Read()` function. The buffer has a null terminator appended to it when it returns. The actual count of bytes read in is stored in `ByteCount` before the function returns.

```
int write_buffer( char *buffer, unsigned int count = -1 )
```

This virtual function is used by the various `Write()` functions to send buffers and strings out the port. This function sends as many characters as it can without waiting, and then returns to the calling program with either `RS232_SUCCESS` or `RS232_TIMEOUT`. Note that this function has a default parameter for the count. If no count is specified, the value of –1 signifies that the buffer is actually a string, and the byte count is the length of the string. The actual count of characters transferred is found in the `ByteCount` element after the function returns.

```
int write_byte( int c )
```

This function writes a single byte out if possible. It doesn't have to set the `ByteCount` element because it returns that information to the calling routine by way of the return status, which is either `RS232_SUCCESS` or `RS232_TIMEOUT`. This function is used by the nonvirtual `Write()` functions to perform the virtualized low-level I/O.

```
int read_byte( int c )
```

This function performs the low-level I/O for the nonvirtual `Read()` functions. It also doesn't set the `ByteCount` argument, which can easily be determined by checking the return value.

Public data members

The `RS232` class has two public data members. Any function in the program can access public data members without regard to class or friendship. When designing a class, many object-oriented programming methodologies dictate that data members should *never* be exposed.

I carefully ignore that advice here for one simple reason. The two public data members here are used solely to return additional information upon return from a member function. They don't actually contain any information that is vital to the state of the object. This means that a programmer could modify these members with impunity (although it's hard to imagine why that would be useful), secure in the knowledge that the serial port's state will not be modified in any way.

`unsigned int ByteCount`

Earlier in this chapter, I mention that some of the functions in the `RS232` class need to return multiple pieces of information to the calling program. In particular, `Read()` and `Write()` have to return an actual count of bytes transferred. Both of these functions have options that could cause them to return before the entire buffer is transferred.

`ByteCount` is relatively safe as a public data member. The function calls that modify this member don't depend on it remaining unchanged. They return it from a function after performing a transfer, and then forget about it. Because of this, it is safe to allow public access of this member.

`long ElapsedTime`

All of the input and output functions have the option to be called with a timeout value. If a timeout value is specified, the routine will eventually return to the calling function, even though it has not completed the data transfer. If a complete buffer is transferred, the routines will return earlier. If a routine returns before the timeout value, the `ElapsedTime` data member will contain the amount of time that passed during the transfer. Because many communications applications are time dependent, this feature of the `RS232` class relieves the programmer of the burden of keeping track.

Like the `ByteCount` member, `ElapsedTime` is set by the function before it returns to the caller. After the `RS232` function returns, it doesn't care what happens to the value afterward, so you can safely make this a public data member. `ElapsedTime` is measured in milliseconds, so this value needs to be a C long type. If it were a simple unsigned int, 16-bit programs would be limited to measuring about 60 seconds, which could prove to be a limitation.

All of the timing values used in the `RS232` class are platform dependent, so the values found in `ElapsedTime` will have a granularity that depends on system implementation. For example, under MS-DOS, the granularity of the system clock is roughly 55 milliseconds, so timer values of all kinds will be accurate only to that resolution.

Mandatory virtual functions

The `RS232` class has 11 mandatory public virtual functions. When creating a useful class derived from the `RS232` class, you must create a constructor, 4 private virtual functions, and 11 public virtual functions. (Of course, many classes will probably implement quite a few more functions.)

You need to know which virtual functions are mandatory and which are optional. Later in this book, you can see how to write utility code that operates strictly on objects of the `RS232` class. These general-purpose functions will perform useful jobs such as terminal emulation, modem control, and file transfers. Because utility functions operate on the RS232 class, they cannot know in advance whether a particular driver supports certain virtual functions. Because of this, they need to be able to count on a certain set of functions.

In Chapter 3, you can see a complete implementation of all these functions using the standard 8250 type UART on an IBM-compatible PC. That particular class will probably be the most complex one in the entire book, largely because it has to be built from scratch; there is no operating system or device driver support for class PC8250.

For example, each of the different versions of Microsoft Windows provides a complete RS-232 API. The MS Windows classes just have to implement a simple interface to that driver. Much of the hard work related to making the port operate is handled by the operating system, making the Windows classes close to being wrapper classes. (A *wrapper class* usually is thought of as having little functionality of its own. It simply provides an interface to a set of existing code via an API. The C++ member functions *wrap* up the calls to the API in short snippets of code.)

The best way to get a good handle on how serial communications work in the desktop environment is to understand how these virtual functions work. So, without further ado, here they are.

```
virtual int Set( long baud_rate = UNCHANGED,
                 char parity = UNCHANGED,
                 int word_length = UNCHANGED,
                 int stop_bits = UNCHANGED )
```

This function is used to set the basic transmission parameters for the UART. Note that although this function is mandatory for every driver, the specific baud rates and other parameters supported by the interface can vary among drivers. If an unsupported parameter is passed, one of the following four error messages is returned:

```
RS232_ILLEGAL_BAUD_RATE
RS232_ILLEGAL_PARITY_SETTING
RS232_ILLEGAL_WORD_LENGTH
RS232_ILLEGAL_STOP_BITS
```

Each of the parameters has a default value of UNCHANGED. This special parameter indicates to the Set() function that the specified parameter should be left alone during the set operation. Because of the default parameters, a simple call like this:

```
port.Set( 9600 )
```

can be used to set the baud rate only. Other parameters can be added as necessary.

As another convenience to the programmer, the five parity settings are specified as easy-to-remember characters. For most MS-DOS implementations of serial drivers, the settings are the following:

'N'   No parity

'E'   Even parity

'O'   Odd parity

'S'   Space parity

'M'   Mark parity

In this function call, you can specify the parity parameters in upper- or lowercase. Just as in the baud-rate parameter, various MS-DOS serial drivers will provide different levels of support for these parity settings. In general, every driver will support the first three: None, Even, and Odd. Space and Mark parity are not uniformly supported, so you must be prepared to receive an RS232_ILLEGAL_PARITY_-SETTING response when calling this function.

The word length and stop bit settings are fairly uniform across all MS-DOS serial drivers. The word length can be 5, 6, 7, or 8 bits. Although some hardware supports the 5- and 6-bit settings, they are so rarely used that they are essentially historical oddities. Most hardware supports stop bit settings of 1 and 2.

The four parameters used in this function are also generally used in the constructor for a serial object. Once again, the default value of all four parameters is UNCHANGED.

```
virtual int TXSpaceFree( void )
```

This function improves the operation of a serial driver. A utility routine written for the RS232 class calls this function to determine whether any space is available for transmitting more characters. Without this function, a routine would have to blindly call the Write() routines without knowing in advance that it would succeed. This function helps applications utilities avoid this uncertainty.

It isn't always possible to know exactly how many bytes are free in the output buffer. If this is the case, the virtual implementation of TXSpaceFree() should return a 1 if *any* room is available, and a 0 if no space is free.

```
virtual int RXSpaceUsed( void )
```

Like the previous function, RXSpaceUsed() is an aid to the smooth operation of a serial driver. An application can determine whether any characters are waiting to be read out of the input buffer. This information is often very useful to have in advance of calling the Read() function.

Just as with the previous function, a serial driver can't always know exactly how many bytes are available in the input buffer. This virtual routine should return a 1 if *any* bytes are available, and a 0 if none are. Of course, if an exact count is available, it should be given.

```
virtual int Cd( void )
virtual int Ri( void )
virtual int Cts( void )
virtual int Dsr( void )
```

These four functions all do essentially the same thing, which is to read in the current state of an input modem status line. In many communications programs, all four of these lines are read simultaneously into a bit mask that is returned to the calling function. Although using a single bit mask cuts down on the number of calls in the API, it does require that the programmer learn and remember four equate masks used to extract the individual settings. The form used here eliminates that problem, making your life a little easier.

This family of functions reads in the instantaneous state of the control lines at the point where the function is called. Many times, programmers need more control over these lines than is provided here. For example, it is frequently useful to have a function that not only will read the Carrier Detect line but also report if it has dropped at any time since the previous call. This lets a BBS detect when a caller drops carrier by hanging up the phone line.

Unfortunately, implementation of these features is rather rare for MS-DOS serial interfaces. It doesn't really make sense to add these function calls to the RS232 class set of virtual functions. It's best to add such calls to a derived class and restrict use to that class.

In particular, when you're using an event driven model such as that found under Windows 95 and Windows NT, adding support for these sort of events makes sense, and is done by adding new member functions to the derived class.

```
virtual int ParityError( int clear = UNCHANGED )
virtual int BreakDetect( int clear = UNCHANGED )
virtual int FramingError( int clear = UNCHANGED )
virtual int HardwareOverrunError(  int clear = UNCHANGED )
```

These four functions correspond loosely to the four previous modem status line functions. Once again, these are frequently grouped together in many communications programs, with the individual settings being extracted via masking macros. For ease of programming, the alternate approach is used here.

Unlike the modem status functions, all four of these line status readings remain set after the condition occurs. For example, if an incoming break is detected, the BreakDetect() function will continue to return a true value every time it is called. The true setting will go away only if the optional clear parameter is also set to true. In that case, the function will return the old state of the line status and then clear it.

Under certain circumstances, you might want to implement more sophisticated handling of line status errors. For example, you may want to call a C function in your program the instant the line status error occurs. However, just as with the modem status changes, this sort of functionality is generally not supported in most RS-232 drivers. If the programmer requires this functionality, he or she should develop a derived class with full support for the extended features.

> **XREF** You can see how this is done in Chapters 11 and 12, which present a description of the Win32 comm class.

Nonvirtual functions

There are nine nonvirtual functions defined as part of class `RS232`. These functions all build on virtual functions defined earlier in the program to do their work. In general, derived classes won't implement new versions of these functions. They have been designed to be portable and flexible enough to work with the virtual functions defined by most derived classes.

```
virtual int Read( long milliseconds = 0 )
```

This function is used to read in a byte from the serial interface. Like most of the other functions that perform I/O with a port, it has an optional timing parameter. The timing parameter, named *milliseconds,* gives the amount of time that the function should continue to wait for input before returning empty handed. The default value is 0, which means that the function will return immediately when no input is available. If no data is available, an error message of `RS232_TIMEOUT` is returned to the calling program.

The traditional approach to serial I/O on older operating systems such as UNIX has been for the program to request input of a certain amount of data (1 byte in this case) and then wait indefinitely for input. Options to time out after a certain period were sometimes added, but almost as an afterthought. This sort of programming strategy might have been appropriate when your serial input consisted mostly of keystrokes from alphanumeric terminals, but it is definitely not optimal during file transfers from high-speed modems. Being able to set the time to any value desired is an improvement on this strategy.

If a valid character was input, the return value from this function will be greater than or equal to 0. If the return value from the function is less than 0, an error of some sort occurred and the programmer needs to take action. Note that the `RS232_TIMEOUT` warning can probably be considered benign.

When this function returns, the two other public data members of the `RS232` class will also be set properly. The `ElapsedTime` data member will contain the number of milliseconds that elapsed while in the `Read()` function, and the `ByteCount` member will contain either a 0 or a 1, depending on whether a byte was read in or not.

If the `milliseconds` parameter is nonzero, the `Read()` function may have to wait for input. Under MS-DOS, what a program does while it is waiting for an event is not really important because usually no other programs are competing for system resources. However, under OS/2, MS-Windows, or some other multitasking environment, other processes will want CPU time. This is particularly critical under 16-bit versions of MS-Windows because the operating system will not preempt a process without the process's cooperation.

Because of these considerations, all of the I/O functions that may spend time waiting make a call to an environment-specific virtual function called `IdleFunction()`. The default MS-DOS version of `RS232::IdleFunction()` is found in the file `MSDOS.CPP`. It does absolutely nothing except execute an immediate return. So, while waiting for input, `Read()` sits in a polling loop that consumes all of the CPU time on the system.

Note that if the `milliseconds` parameter is not specified in a function call, it defaults to a value of 0. This means that `Read()` will try one time to read a character in, and if it doesn't receive one, it will return with an `RS232_TIMEOUT` warning message. In addition, there is a special integer parameter called `FOREVER`, which means exactly that. If you specify `FOREVER` for the `milliseconds` parameter, the function will wait forever for an input byte.

This function calls the virtual version of `read_byte()` to actually do the low-level I/O associated with the port.

```
virtual int Read( void *buffer,
                  unsigned int count,
                  long milliseconds = 0 )

virtual int Read( void *buffer,
                  unsigned int count,
                  long milliseconds = 0,
                  char *terminator )
```

The two `Read()` functions are a little bit more complicated than their single-byte relative. Like `Read( long )`, each has a timing parameter indicating how long the function can take to perform the input. The second version of the buffer versions of `Read()` adds a new parameter, `terminator`. The first function reads in a block of fixed length; the second attempts to read in a string with a specific terminator.

These two functions could have been combined into one by using a default parameter for the terminator, but logically, they are quite different. Because they will be implemented separately, it makes sense to have two completely different functions as opposed to one long function that could easily be broken in half.

When not using the terminator, `Read()` does exactly what you might expect, which is to attempt to read in the number of bytes specified in parameter `count`. However, if the terminator parameter is in use, the function will attempt to match it during input. In this mode, the routine reads in bytes until one of three things happens. First, it will terminate if the buffer fills up, returning an `RS232_NO_TERMINATOR` error code. However, if it reads in an exact match for the termination string, it will return an `RS232_SUCCESS` message. In either case, the resulting buffer will be terminated with a '\0' character, meaning that it can be treated as a standard C null terminated string. Finally, it will return if it times out before either of the other two conditions is met.

The two most commonly used terminator parameters are "\r" and "\r\n". When entering input from the keyboard, a user typically terminates lines with a single carriage return, or '\r' character. When data is being received from a computer and is intended for display, it usually ends with a carriage return-line feed pair, which means you would want to use the second choice of terminators.

Note that with a string terminator, the terminator is *not* included when the function returns. However, the input buffer must be able to hold the input string plus the termination characters. After the terminator is read in, a "\0" byte is written over the first character of the terminator resident in the buffer.

In the buffered version of `Read()`, there is no terminator. In this mode, the routine is just trying to read in an entire buffer of data before the specified time elapses. Like the other routines, the time can be as short as 0 milliseconds or as long as `FOREVER`. When the parameter is set to 0, the routine will just try to read in as many bytes as possible until it either completes or runs out of characters and returns.

When these functions return, they will always give an accurate rendering of the elapsed time in the `ElapsedTime` public data member. The `ByteCount` member will contain the number of bytes being returned to the calling function. This means that the characters read in as part of the terminator will not be counted in the total returned to the calling program.

```
virtual int Write( int c, long milliseconds = 0 )
```

`Write(int, long)` performs the opposite function of `Read( long )` by writing a single byte out to the serial port. Like the other I/O functions, `Write()` has an optional parameter that specifies a minimum number of milliseconds that the function will wait for a successful output. If it isn't specified, the milliseconds parameter defaults to a value of 0. A parameter of 0 means that the function will attempt to perform the output one time only, returning the warning message `RS232_TIMEOUT` if unsuccessful.

`Write()` sets the two public data members used by the other I/O functions. `ByteCount` will be set to either a 1 or a 0, depending on whether the output was successful or not. The `ElapsedTime` data element will contain the count of elapsed milliseconds that the function waited while trying to output the single character.

`Write()` will call the virtual function `IdleFunction()` while it is waiting to perform output. This function is operating-system dependent and can be redefined by a derived class. In addition, the idle function can abort the I/O function by returning an error code when it is called.

```
virtual int Write( void *buffer,
                   unsigned int count = 0,
                   long milliseconds = 0,
                   char *terminator = 0 )
```

The `Write(void *buffer)` routine manages to become even more complicated than `Read(void *buffer)`. It has the same list of parameters, which features the addition of the count and terminator parameters. Unlike the previous function, however, in this case the count parameter has a default value as well.

The reason for the addition of these new parameters and defaults is the same as in `Read()`. This function has a split personality, with the ability to output both raw buffers of data and formatted strings with termination. When the count parameter is set to a positive integer, it means that the function is performing a traditional buffer output. In this case, the count parameter is relied upon for an accurate count of the number of characters to be sent.

If the `count` parameter is set to 0, the function is operating on what is expected to be a string. In this case, the `count` parameter is ignored, and the length of the string is determined by looking for a "\0" string termination character. After the character is found, the function then outputs the bytes in the string.

As in the previous function, the two most commonly used termination strings will be "\r" and "\r\n". Which one of these is appropriate depends on what sort of data the receiving end expects.

This function returns one of the standard error codes based on how well it managed to output the entire buffer. A return of `RS232_SUCCESS` means that the entire buffer as well as the optional termination string made it out. A return of `RS232_TIMEOUT` means that the routine ran out of time before completing its task. This running out of time usually occurs because of a blocked condition due to handshaking.

The `ElapsedTime` and `ByteCount` public data members are set up to work much as you would expect. `ElapsedTime` returns a count of the number of milliseconds that the function spent waiting to send the data. `ByteCount` returns the count of characters actually transmitted, which includes the termination string, when used.

```
int Peek( void )
```

This function is simply a front-end that sends a function call to `Peek( void *)`, with a request for just one byte of data. It is included as a convenience for the programmer. The end of this chapter includes a listing of the actual function in RS232.CPP. Note that this function will return RS232_TIMEOUT if no character is available. It will also return with a valid count in ByteCount.

int ReadSettings(Settings &settings)

This short function provides access to the private data member Settings. As a safeguard, the Settings data member is kept privately, so you need to have this access function to return a copy of the values.

RS232Error ErrorStatus(void)

This is another access function that used to return the value of a private data member, in this case error_status. Because this data member can't be changed by functions outside the class, you require an access function.

int DebugLineCount(void)

Another access function that allows an outside function to determine the number of lines of debug output produced by this class. This is simply a way to read the value of debug_line_count, which is a private data member.

A very short example program

With just a few of the mandatory and nonvirtual functions from the RS232 class, you can easily build a simple terminal program. By simple, I mean a program whose sole purpose is to route serial input to the screen and keyboard input to the serial port. In addition to the mandatory functions shown earlier, you need only a derived class that can open a port on your PC. The listing that follows shows this type of simple program.

```
#include <stdio.h>
#include <conio.h>
#include "rs232.h"

//
// Don't try to compile this program; it is
// strictly hypothetical! It is intended to
// demonstrate the brevity of code needed to
// produce a simple terminal program using
// the member function of class RS232
//

int main()
```

```
{
  int c;
  Comport port( COM1, 9600, 'N', 8, 1 );

  for ( ; ; ) {
    if ( port.RXSpaceUsed() > 0 )
      if ( (c = port.Read()) >= RS232_SUCCESS )
        putc( c, stdout );
    if ( kbhit() ) {
      c = getch();
      if ( c == 27 )
        break;
      port.Write( c );
    }
  }
}
```

As I state earlier in this chapter, you could easily use the C++ driver code developed in this book and still continue programming as if you were working with C. In the preceding example, the only real oddity from a C perspective is the constructor for the (hypothetical) `Comport` object. Other than that, the code is more or less ANSI C. Admittedly, the member function calls (`port.Write()`) look somewhat strange, but they are still legitimate C. Even if your C experience is very limited, you should be able to read this code and modify it without too much difficulty.

The optional functions

There are 16 optional functions defined in the `RS232` class. I have made these optional mainly because the functions aren't supported by nearly as many drivers as the mandatory functions.

Although the optional functions may be somewhat more rare than the mandatory functions, good drivers will still support them, and application programmers should feel free to use them. The code that uses these functions, however, has to be ready to receive an `RS232_NOT_SUPPORTED` message when calling any of them.

`virtual ~RS232( void )`

The destructor for class `RS232` is virtual. Using a virtual destructor provides an advantage over using a nonvirtual destructor. With a virtual destructor, utility code can destroy port objects without knowing anything about their class. Note that in the header file `RS232.H`, an empty function is created to be the destructor for the base class. When destroying a derived class, the destructor for the base class will be called first. It just happens that you don't need to do anything in the base destructor.

The fact that this is an optional function is really not important to anyone but the implementer of a derived class. To the end user, it won't matter.

```
virtual int Break( long milliseconds = 300 )
```

The ability to send a line break is not available in every serial driver, so I have included it here as an optional feature. Remember that a break signal is not an actual character; sending it is an operation that is very different from a normal character. When a UART sends a break, it actually changes the line to a spacing condition and holds it there for a relatively long time. In this way, it will be recognized as a break signal regardless of the baud rate and other settings of the two receivers.

One place where break signals are used to good effect is when a user is first logging in to a UNIX system. When an incoming caller first connects to a UNIX system, the two ends are frequently set to different baud rates. The break signal provides an unambiguous message to the remote end, letting it know the baud rate must be changed.

The default length of the break is 300 milliseconds — long enough to provide a usable break on just about any system. However, the programmer can override this setting if needed. Note that the time spent while waiting for the break to finish is spent in the virtual `IdleFunction()`, doing whatever is recommended for that particular operating environment. Under MS-DOS, this consists of doing nothing at all.

```
virtual int SoftwareOverrunError( int clear = UNCHANGED )
```

This optional function manages a diagnostic function. A software overrun error occurs when an incoming character is received and there is no room for it in the buffer. The interrupt service routine has no choice but to throw the character away. In this situation, many drivers set a flag so that the application program can respond appropriately.

This function simply returns the state of the overrun flag. If the optional argument is set to be true, the flag is also cleared after it has been read. If the parameter is false, or no parameter is given, then the flag remains set.

Note that the overrun flag is not present in the `RS232` class definition, because it is an optional feature. However, as with all optional features, there must be a base class implementation of the function. In this case, the base class implementation just returns the `RS232_NOT_SUPPORTED` error to the calling program.

```
virtual int XonXoffHandshaking( int setting = UNCHANGED )
virtual int RtsCtsHandshaking( int setting = UNCHANGED )
virtual int DtrDsrHandshaking( int setting = UNCHANGED )
```

These three functions do essentially the same thing. Each one has a dual purpose. Each function can be used to just read the current setting of the handshaking for a port, or it can be used to turn handshaking on or off.

When the function is called with no arguments, or with `UNCHANGED` as the argument, all it does is return the current state of the handshaking. If the new setting is something other than `UNCHANGED` (`ENABLE` and `DISABLE` being the recommended alternatives), the current state of that form of handshaking is either enabled or disabled. The function will return the previous state of the handshaking for that mode.

The function returns the state of the handshaking *before* the new control takes place so that a programmer can set the handshaking mode and save the previous mode with one function call. If the function call returned the new setting of the handshake mode, two calls need to be made to store the old value and one to set the new one. Also, it would be redundant to set it and then return the value that was just set.

Certainly, not every driver will support these optional functions. Worse, complications will accompany support of these features. For example, some drivers allow only one handshaking mode to be set at a time, so setting one might clear the others. Other drivers will support one of the modes, but not the others. These peculiarities go with the territory.

The base class versions of these functions can be found in `RS232.CPP`, and they do nothing more than return the warning message `RS232_NOT_SUPPORTED`. If a derived class doesn't support these functions, the base class version will return the error flag to the program.

```
virtual int Dtr( int setting = UNCHANGED )
virtual int Rts( int setting = UNCHANGED )
```

These two functions are used to either read or control the state of the two RS-232 output lines normally supported on a PC. When not being used for handshaking, DTR and RTS have many other uses, according to the needs of the application programmer.

To read the current state of these control lines, the programmer simply calls either of these functions with no parameters or with the single argument set to `UNCHANGED`. If the argument is some other value besides `UNCHANGED`, it will be interpreted as a boolean value and the control line will either be set or cleared, depending on its value. I suggest that you use the constants `SET` and `CLEAR` to make your programs more readable.

When the argument is used and the function sets the output line to a new value, it still returns a value indicating the previous state of the line. This is done so that the programmer can set the line to a new state and store the old state with a single function call.

Most drivers will support these functions. If for some reason a driver doesn't support this function, the default virtual function for the base class will be called. The base class versions of these functions simply return the `RS232_NOT_SUPPORTED` warning error to the programmer.

```
virtual int Peek( void *buffer, unsigned int count )
```

Many times, it is useful to be able to look ahead and see what is coming up in the input buffer without actually extracting any data. Many drivers implement various forms of a so-called peek function, with the majority at least supporting the ability to peek ahead one character into the buffer. This virtual function lets the caller peek ahead an arbitrary number of characters into the input buffer, stuffing the results into the user-supplied data area.

The value returned by this function indicates how many bytes were actually read into the buffer. A count lower than the number requested by the caller doesn't necessarily mean that only that many bytes are in the buffer. Instead, it may well mean that the driver can look ahead only that far into the buffer. As with all the other functions, a value less than zero means that an error occurred.

The base class implementation of this function does nothing more than return the RS232_NOT_SUPPORTED error message.

```
virtual int RXSpaceFree( void )
virtual int TXSpaceUsed( void )
```

These two functions correspond to the two buffer size functions found in the mandatory support area. These functions are not mandatory and are generally not quite as useful as the mandatory ones. For example, you may have a pressing need to know how much space is free in the transmit buffer. If a program has data to go out, it needs to know whether it will be able to send it. The knowledge about how much space is still in use in the transmit buffer is not as pressing, however.

The TXSpaceUsed() function still can be useful. For example, when you're preparing to exit a communications program, it is usually a good idea to wait until the transmit buffer has finished sending all its data. If it was in the middle of sending a screen full of logout data to a user when the program exited, the odds are that the data stream would be cut off.

Likewise, RXSpaceFree() is not as urgently needed as RXSpaceUsed(). The space used function tells the programmer whether it is time to service the input data. The space free function can alert you to an overflow condition, but you usually leave that up to the driver, anyway.

Both of these functions are defined in the base class with the typical return of RS232_NOT_SUPPORTED. If a derived class supports these functions, it needs to supply virtual implementations so that they get called rather than the base version.

```
virtual int FlushTXBuffer( void )
virtual int FlushRXBuffer( void )
```

FlushTXBuffer() and FlushRXBuffer() are another pair of useful functions that aren't supported in every driver. This function throws away all the data queued up for output in the transmit buffer. For example, this function would be useful when a system has dumped out a few screenfuls of data in the process of being transmitted and the user at the other end hits the break key. Rather than the remote end having to wait through the lengthy process of dumping all the data, a simple call to `FlushTXBuffer()` will discard all that data in the output buffer.

Although these functions are not always supported, they should be relatively easy to implement. Most systems use a simple buffering system for storing data pending transmission. To flush the buffer, you would simply move the head pointer back to where the tail pointer is. Usually, interrupts must be disabled, but other than that it isn't particularly difficult.

The base class implementation of this function is a one-line function that just returns the `RS232_NOT_SUPPORTED` error message.

```
virtual char *ErrorName( RS232Error error )
```

The `ErrorName()` function translates an error code from the `RS232Error` enumerated type into a readable ASCII string. This lets the error be presented to the user of the program in a reasonable manner.

Traditionally, errors are implemented via a master list of error codes that could be accessed anywhere in the program. But when you're implementing a traditional error system like this for the `RS232` class, it is fairly difficult to extend the list to include new errors introduced from derived classes. Under C++, you would like to be able to leave your base class definition alone, even when you add a new derived class. However, to add a new error under the traditional system, you would have to edit the header file with the error definitions (`RS232.H` in this program) and then edit the function that translates the error names.

In class `RS232` a new system accomplishes this goal without too much trouble. The implementation of `ErrorName()` in the base class can translate all of the predefined error codes. The error names are assigned sequentially, with the first warning message starting at `RS232_WARNING`, (with a value of -100) and working up to `RS232_NEXT_FREE_WARNING`. The fatal errors start with `RS232_ERROR`, (with a value of -200) and work up to `RS232_NEXT_FREE_ERROR`. The base implementation of `ErrorName()` knows how to translate this predefined list of errors.

A derived class that wants to add its own error codes can start assigning them as its own enumerated type. The first warning defined by the derived class would be assigned a value of `RS232_NEXT_FREE_WARNING`, and the first fatal error would be assigned a value of `RS232_NEXT_FREE_ERROR`. The derived class would then be free to assign as many new error names as it wanted.

To properly translate an error code, the derived class then needs to implement its own virtual function `ErrorName()`. The new derived version of `ErrorName()` checks the error code to see whether it was defined by the base class or the derived class. If the derived class was responsible for the error code, it would return the translated version to the caller. If the error code was one defined by the base class, the base version of `ErrorName()` would be called.

This system of "passing it up the line" allows for essentially never-ending chains of error codes to be defined by nested derived classes. To help you clear up any confusion over this operation, I give you an actual example. A code fragment from the `PC8250` class, which is developed in Chapter 3, follows. This fragment shows how `PC8250` would support the addition of a single new error code called `PC8250_UART_NOT_FOUND`.

First, when developing a new list of errors, you must define the new enumerated type. The new type `PC8250Error` does this, presumably somewhere in a header file. It defines the first error in the fatal error list as being defined by `RS232_NEXT_FREE_ERROR`. If a warning message were being added as well, it would be defined as having the value `RS232_NEXT_FREE_WARNING`.

```
enum PC8250Error {
  PC8250_UART_NOT_FOUND = RS232_NEXT_FREE_ERROR,
  PC8250_NEXT_FREE_ERROR,
  PC8250_NEXT_FREE_WARNING = RS232_NEXT_FREE_WARNING };

char * PC8250::ErrorName( RS232Error error )
{
  if ( error < RS232_NEXT_FREE_ERROR && error >= RS232_ERROR )
    return RS232::ErrorName( error );
  if ( error < RS232_NEXT_FREE_WARNING && error >= RS232_WARNING )
    return RS232::ErrorName( error );
  if ( error >= RS232_SUCCESS )
    return RS232::ErrorName( error );
  switch ( error ) {
    case PC8250_UART_NOT_FOUND : return( "UART not found" );
    default                    : return( "Undefined error" );
  }
}
```

After the error messages have been defined, the definition of the `ErrorName()` function for the derived class is fairly simple. The version of this function for the `PC8250` class demonstrates this clearly. The code first checks to see whether the error message is in the range of predefined fatal errors. If it is, the base class version of `ErrorName()` should be able to do the translation, so the parameters are passed along. The scoping operator "::" lets you pass the function call up the line.

Next, the routine checks to see whether the error message is a predefined warning message from the base class or the predefined success message. If the error message is one of the predefined messages, the call is passed up the line to the base class.

If the routine falls through these tests, it can then translate the error code on its own by checking against the list of errors it knows about. The translation is made and the correct ASCII string is returned to the calling function.

If another function were derived from class `PC8250`, the same sort of linkage could be achieved. The new class would have to start its new list of messages, starting at `PC8250_NEXT_FREE_ERROR` and `PC8250_NEXT_FREE_WARNING`. When the derived version of `ErrorName()` was called, it would check to see whether the error message belonged to the new class. If not, the error number would just be passed up the line to `PC8250::ErrorName()`, where the same process would be repeated until someone performed a translation.

The ability to add to the library without having to modify the existing code strengthens the case for C++. Once again, these features could be developed using ANSI C, but a thorough implementation would involve fairly significant overhead and some rigorous gymnastics.

```
virtual int IdleFunction( void )
```

The idle function is a virtual function that is called while one of the data input or output routines waits for data. Although this is a virtual function, a derived class does not necessarily need to implement it. The function has two important properties. First, it can yield control to other processes so as to be a good citizen in a non-preemptive multitasking environment. Second, it detects an abort condition and passes it back to the input routine.

The base version of `IdleFunction()` for MS-DOS returns only an `RS232_SUCCESS` to the calling function. Under MS-DOS, there generally isn't any penalty for hogging the CPU as long as interrupts are enabled, and this implementation does just that. Later in this book, I develop versions of `IdleFunction()` for other environments. These will tend to be somewhat more sophisticated when cooperating with other processes.

Even though the base version of `IdleFunction()` doesn't check for any abort conditions, a derived class may want to do so. Reasons for aborting an input or output function include loss of carrier or a user-initiated break, among others.

```
virtual int FormatDebugOutput ( char *buffer = 0,
                                int line_number = -1 )
```

This virtual function is similar to `ErrorName()` in that it depends on sharing the work load with classes farther up the hierarchy. The basic concept behind `FormatDebugOutput()` is that for any given class of serial port, there should be a descriptive set of output data to assist in diagnosing any problems with the port, or perhaps just in assessing operations.

When working with a class hierarchy, you can assume that the base class and each derived class have a certain amount of data to print out. How do you then coordinate the output from each of these functions?

The system developed here allows each class to contribute a few lines to the debug output, which all combines for a complete picture of the state of the port. This works if each class can recognize two things about its formatted output. First, the class must know how many lines it will contribute to the formatted debug output and, second, it must know on which line its output begins.

A user function uses `FormatDebugOutput()` in a relatively simple way. The output from this function consists of a number of lines. The actual number is determined by calling the member function `DebugLineCount()`, which just returns the value in the private data member, `debug_line_count`. After this information is known, the user application can just call the formatting routine repeatedly, once for each line, and print out the buffer after it has been formatted. The sample code that follows would do this.

```
char buffer[ 81 ];
int i;

printf( "\n" );
for ( i = 0 ; i < port1.DebugLineCount() ; i++ )
{
    port1.FormatDebugOutput( buffer, i );
    puts( buffer );
}
```

When the virtual function for a derived class such as `PC8250` is called, it will handle some of the lines of debug output itself and pass other ones up the line to the parent classes from which it is derived. A special feature of the `FormatDebugOutput()` function makes this bookkeeping relatively easy. When called with no arguments, rather than return an `RS232_SUCCESS` value, this function returns the number of lines that it will take up. In its present implementation, the base class of `RS232` takes up three lines. Thus, a derived version of `FormatDebugOutput()` would pass the function call up to `RS232::FormatDebugOutput()` when called with a line number of 0, 1, or 2. When the number is greater than that, the derived class will begin printing out its own data.

The line numbers used by the formatting routine in a derived class are determined when a member of the class is constructed. In the class `PC8250`, developed in the next chapter, an additional private data member is initialized in the constructor. This private data member is named `first_debug_output_line`. The constructor calling the formatting function in the base class (with no arguments) is responsible for initializing it. The total number of debug output lines are then stored in the private data member `debug_line_counter`. The code that follows shows a portion of the constructor.

```
PC8250::PC8250( enum RS232PortName port,
                long baud_rate,
                char parity,
                int word_length,
                int stop_bits )
{
    port_name = port;
```

```
first_debug_output_line = RS232::FormatDebugOutput();
debug_line_count = FormatDebugOutput();
error_status = RS232_SUCCESS;
    .
    .
    .
```

The constructor determines the first line of output for the derived class. It does this by calling the base class version of the formatting routine with no arguments: RS232::FormatDebugOutput(). The number returned tells how many lines the base class will be using; therefore, this is the number of the first line to be printed.

The constructor next determines the total number of output lines. It does this by calling the version of FormatDebugOutput() for this class. That function will add the number of lines it needs to print to the number required for the base class and will return the total.

The listing that follows shows how the formatting routine actually manages this data. The process looks a lot like the algorithm used by the ErrorName() function. First, if the buffer parameter is null, the formatting routine was called with no arguments and the caller wants to know how many lines can be produced by this routine. If this is the case, the actual count is returned, which consists of all the lines produced by the base class, plus two additional lines for this class.

```
int xxxx::FormatDebugOutput( char *buffer, int line_number )
{
    if ( buffer == 0 )
        return( first_debug_output_line + 2 );
    if ( line_number < first_debug_output_line )
        return RS232::FormatDebugOutput( buffer, line_number );
    switch( line_number - first_debug_output_line )
    {
        case 0 :
            sprintf( buffer, "Derived class: xxxx Line 0" );
            break;
        case 1 :
            sprintf( buffer, "Line 1" );
            break;
        default :
            return RS232_ILLEGAL_LINE_NUMBER;
    }
    return RS232_SUCCESS;
}
```

If the line number passed to this routine happens to be less than the first line of debug output used by this class, the function call is passed up the line to the base class for processing. Finally, if the line happens to be greater than the first line of output used by the derived class, it is managed locally.

Just as with the `ErrorName()` function, this nesting concept can be extended indefinitely, with each derived class contributing its lines of debug output. Most important, you can achieve this extendibility without modifying the base class.

The Code

The code for the class definitions used in this chapter is found in three files, consisting of one header file and two C++ source files. Following are explanations of the general content of these files.

ON THE CD This code for the class definitions is found on the accompanying CD-ROM.

RS232.H	This file contains the complete definition of the base `RS232` class. Every file that will be developing serial classes for the derived classes in this book must include this header file. The code for this file is in Listing 2-1.
RS232.CPP	The default virtual function definitions are found in this file. These are relatively uninspiring because all they do is return error messages. Two of the exceptions to this are `FormatDebugOutput()` and `ErrorName()`. Both of these virtual functions are explained earlier in this chapter. The `Read()` and `Write()` functions are both in this source file as well. The code for this file is in Listing 2-2.
MSDOS.CPP	This file contains two operating-system-specific functions. `IdleFunction()` was discussed earlier in this section. The other function, `ReadTime()`, is discussed in subsequent chapters. The code for this file is in Listing 2-3.

Listing 2-1: RS232.H

```
// ********************* START OF RS232.H *********************
//
// This header file contains the definitions for the base
// class RS232.
//
```

```
#ifndef _RS232_DOT_H
#define _RS232_DOT_H

#include "portable.h"
#include <conio.h>

enum RS232PortName { COM1 = 0, COM2,  COM3,  COM4,
                     COM5,    COM6,   COM7,  COM8 };

enum RS232Error {    RS232_SUCCESS              = 0,

// Warning errors

                     RS232_WARNING              = -100,
                     RS232_FUNCTION_NOT_SUPPORTED,
                     RS232_TIMEOUT,
                     RS232_ILLEGAL_BAUD_RATE,
                     RS232_ILLEGAL_PARITY_SETTING,
                     RS232_ILLEGAL_WORD_LENGTH,
                     RS232_ILLEGAL_STOP_BITS,
                     RS232_ILLEGAL_LINE_NUMBER,
                     RS232_NO_MODEM_RESPONSE,
                     RS232_NO_TERMINATOR,
                     RS232_DTR_NOT_SUPPORTED,
                     RS232_RTS_NOT_SUPPORTED,
                     RS232_RTS_CTS_NOT_SUPPORTED,
                     RS232_DTR_DSR_NOT_SUPPORTED,
                     RS232_XON_XOFF_NOT_SUPPORTED,
                     RS232_NEXT_FREE_WARNING,

// Fatal Errors

                     RS232_ERROR                = -200,
                     RS232_IRQ_IN_USE,
                     RS232_PORT_NOT_FOUND,
                     RS232_PORT_IN_USE,
                     RS232_ILLEGAL_IRQ,
                     RS232_MEMORY_ALLOCATION_ERROR,
                     RS232_NEXT_FREE_ERROR };

//
// These constants are used as parameters to RS232 member functions.
//

const int UNCHANGED = -1;
const int FOREVER = -1;
```

```cpp
const int DISABLE = 0;
const int CLEAR = 0;
const int ENABLE = 1;
const int SET = 1;
const int RESET = 1;
const int REMOTE_CONTROL = -1;

//
// The Settings class provides a convenient mechanism for saving or
// assigning the state of a port.
//

class Settings
{
    public :
        long BaudRate;
        char Parity;
        int WordLength;
        int StopBits;
        int Dtr;
        int Rts;
        int XonXoff;
        int RtsCts;
        int DtrDsr;
        void Adjust( long baud_rate,
                     int parity,
                     int word_length,
                     int stop_bits,
                     int dtr,
                     int rts,
                     int xon_xoff,
                     int rts_cts,
                     int dtr_dsr );
};

//
// Class RS232 is the abstract base class used for any serial port
// class. RS232 cannot be instantiated. Only fully defined
// classesderived from RS232 can actually be created and used.
//

class RS232
{
    protected :
```

```cpp
        RS232PortName port_name;
        Settings saved_settings;
        Settings settings;
        RS232Error error_status;
        int debug_line_count;

// Mandatory protected functions

        virtual int read_buffer( char *buffer,
                            unsigned int count ) = 0;
        virtual int write_buffer( char *buffer,
                            unsigned int count = -1 ) = 0;
        virtual int read_byte( void ) = 0;
        virtual int write_byte( int c ) = 0;

    public :
        unsigned int ByteCount;
        long ElapsedTime;

//   Mandatory functions. All derived classes must define these.

        virtual RS232Error Set( long baud_rate = UNCHANGED,
                            int parity = UNCHANGED,
                            int word_length = UNCHANGED,
                            int stop_bits = UNCHANGED ) = 0;
        virtual int TXSpaceFree( void ) = 0;
        virtual int RXSpaceUsed( void ) = 0;
        virtual int Cd( void ) = 0;
        virtual int Ri( void ) = 0;
        virtual int Cts( void ) = 0;
        virtual int Dsr( void ) = 0;
        virtual int ParityError( int clear = UNCHANGED ) = 0;
        virtual int BreakDetect( int clear = UNCHANGED ) = 0;
        virtual int FramingError( int clear = UNCHANGED ) = 0;
        virtual int HardwareOverrunError(int clear=UNCHANGED) = 0;

// Optional Functions. Derived class are not required to
// support these.

        virtual ~RS232( void ){ ; }
        virtual int Break( long milliseconds = 300 );
        virtual int SoftwareOverrunError( int clear = UNCHANGED );
        virtual int XonXoffHandshaking( int setting = UNCHANGED );
        virtual int RtsCtsHandshaking( int setting = UNCHANGED );
```

```
                virtual int DtrDsrHandshaking( int setting = UNCHANGED );
                virtual int Dtr( int setting = UNCHANGED );
                virtual int Rts( int setting = UNCHANGED );
                virtual int Peek( void *buffer, unsigned int count );
                virtual int RXSpaceFree( void );
                virtual int TXSpaceUsed( void );
                virtual int FlushRXBuffer( void );
                virtual int FlushTXBuffer( void );
                virtual char *ErrorName( int error );
                virtual int IdleFunction( void );
                virtual int FormatDebugOutput( char *buffer = 0,
                                               int line_number = -1 );

        // Nonvirtual functions. These work the same for all classes.

                int Read( void *buffer,
                        unsigned int count,
                        long milliseconds = 0 );
                int Read( void *buffer,
                        unsigned int count,
                        long milliseconds,
                        char *terminator );
                int Write( void *buffer,
                          unsigned int count = 0,
                          long milliseconds = 0,
                          char *terminator = 0 );
                int Read( long milliseconds = 0 );
                int Write( int c, long milliseconds = 0 );
                int Peek( void );
                int ReadSettings( Settings &copy ) { copy = settings;
                                                    return RS232_SUCCESS; }
                RS232Error ErrorStatus( void ) { return error_status; }
                int DebugLineCount( void ) { return debug_line_count; }
};


// A miscellaneous support function. This may be implemented
// differently by different environments.

long ReadTime( void );

#endif   // #ifndef _RS232_DOT_H

// ********************* END OF RS232.H *********************
```

Listing 2-2: RS232.CPP

```cpp
// ******************** START OF RS232.CPP ********************
//
// This C++ file contains the definitions for all
// functions defined for the base class. Most of these
// are dummy functions that do nothing but return a warning
// message to the calling routine. A well-defined derived class
// will usually define new versions of these virtual functions,
// which means they will never be called.
//

#include "portable.h"
#include <stdio.h>
#include <string.h>
#include <ctype.h>
#include "rs232.h"

// FlushRXBuffer() doesn't have to be defined for every
// derived class. This default function should be able to flush
// the buffer using the mandatory read_buffer() function.
// Classes such as PC8250 that have direct access to their
// receive buffer can implement more efficient versions than this
// if they want.

int RS232::FlushRXBuffer( void )
{
    char buf[ 32 ];

    for ( ; ; ) {
        if ( error_status != RS232_SUCCESS )
            return error_status;
        read_buffer( buf, 32 );
        if ( ByteCount == 0 )
            break;
    }
    return RS232_SUCCESS;
}

// Peek( void ) isn't a virtual function. This is one of the
// few normal member functions in class RS232. It peeks at a
// single byte using the Peek( char *, int ) function.

int RS232::Peek( void )
{
```

```
        char c;
        int status;

        if ( error_status < RS232_SUCCESS )
            return error_status;
        if ( ( status = Peek( &c, 1 ) ) < RS232_SUCCESS )
            return status;
        if ( ByteCount < 1 )
            return RS232_TIMEOUT;
        return (int) c;
}

//
// This member function returns the character translation for one
// of the error codes defined in the base class. It is called by
// the ErrorName() function for a derived class after checking to
// see whether the error code is not a new one defined by the
// derived class.

char * RS232::ErrorName( int error )
{
    switch ( error ) {
        case RS232_SUCCESS                  :
            return( "Success" );

        case RS232_WARNING                  :
            return( "General Warning" );
        case RS232_FUNCTION_NOT_SUPPORTED   :
            return( "Function not supported" );
        case RS232_TIMEOUT                  :
            return( "Timeout" );
        case RS232_ILLEGAL_BAUD_RATE        :
            return( "Illegal baud rate" );
        case RS232_ILLEGAL_PARITY_SETTING   :
            return( "Illegal parity setting" );
        case RS232_ILLEGAL_WORD_LENGTH      :
            return( "Illegal word length" );
        case RS232_ILLEGAL_STOP_BITS        :
            return( "Illegal stop bits" );
        case RS232_ILLEGAL_LINE_NUMBER      :
            return( "Illegal line number" );
        case RS232_NO_TERMINATOR            :
            return( "No terminator" );
```

```
        case RS232_NO_MODEM_RESPONSE       :
            return( "No modem response" );
        case RS232_DTR_NOT_SUPPORTED        :
            return( "DTR control not supported" );
        case RS232_RTS_NOT_SUPPORTED        :
            return( "RTS control not supported" );
        case RS232_RTS_CTS_NOT_SUPPORTED    :
            return( "RTS/CTS handshaking not supported" );
        case RS232_DTR_DSR_NOT_SUPPORTED    :
            return( "DTR/DSR handshaking not supported" );
        case RS232_XON_XOFF_NOT_SUPPORTED   :
            return( "XON/XOFF handshaking not supported" );

        case RS232_ERROR                    :
            return( "General Error" );
        case RS232_IRQ_IN_USE               :
            return( "IRQ line in use" );
        case RS232_PORT_NOT_FOUND           :
            return( "Port not found" );
        case RS232_PORT_IN_USE              :
            return( "Port in use" );
        case RS232_ILLEGAL_IRQ              :
            return( "Illegal IRQ" );
        case RS232_MEMORY_ALLOCATION_ERROR  :
            return( "Memory allocation error" );

        default                             :
            return( "???" );
    }
}

//
// The base class contributes four lines of output to the Debug
// output. Note that it returns the number 4 if called with a
// null buffer, to pass this information on. The four lines of
// output contain everything the base class knows about the port,
// which are its current settings, saved settings, port name, and
// error status. For values of line_number greater than three, the
// derived class provides additional lines of debug output. Note
// that this function is called by the version of
// FormatDebugOutput() defined for the derived class.

int RS232::FormatDebugOutput( char *buffer, int line_number )
{
```

```c
        if ( buffer == 0 )
            return 4;

    switch( line_number ) {
        case 0 :
            sprintf( buffer, "Base class: RS232   "
                             "COM%-2d   "
                             "Status: %-35.35s",
                             port_name + 1,
                             ErrorName( error_status ) );
            return RS232_SUCCESS;
        case 1 :
            sprintf( buffer, "Byte count: %5u   "
                             "Elapsed time: %9ld   "
                             "TX Free: %5u   "
                             "RX Used: %5u",
                             ByteCount,
                             ElapsedTime,
                             TXSpaceFree(),
                             RXSpaceUsed() );
            return RS232_SUCCESS;
        case 2 :
            sprintf( buffer,
                     "Saved port: %6ld,%c,%2d,%2d   "
                     "DTR,RTS: %2d,%2d   "
                     "XON/OFF,RTS/CTS,DTR/DSR: %2d,%2d,%2d",
                     saved_settings.BaudRate,
                     saved_settings.Parity,
                     saved_settings.WordLength,
                     saved_settings.StopBits,
                     saved_settings.Dtr,
                     saved_settings.Rts,
                     saved_settings.XonXoff,
                     saved_settings.RtsCts,
                     saved_settings.DtrDsr );
            return RS232_SUCCESS;

        case 3 :
            sprintf( buffer,
                     "Current port: %6ld,%c,%1d,%1d   "
                     "DTR,RTS: %2d,%2d   "
                     "XON/OFF,RTS/CTS,DTR/DSR: %2d,%2d,%2d",
                     settings.BaudRate,
                     settings.Parity,
```

```
                    settings.WordLength,
                    settings.StopBits,
                    settings.Dtr,
                    settings.Rts,
                    settings.XonXoff,
                    settings.RtsCts,
                    settings.DtrDsr );
            return RS232_SUCCESS;

        default :
            return RS232_ILLEGAL_LINE_NUMBER;
    }
}

// This nonvirtual member function operates by repeatedly
// calling the read_byte() function for the derived class. It
// handles the optional milliseconds parameter, which determines
// how long the function will wait for input before returning a
// timeout. The idle function is called while waiting.

int RS232::Read( long milliseconds )
{
    int c;
    long start_time;
    int idle_status = RS232_SUCCESS;

    ElapsedTime = 0;
    ByteCount = 0;
    if ( error_status < RS232_SUCCESS )
        return error_status;
    start_time = ReadTime();
    for ( ; ; ) {
        c = read_byte();
        if ( c >= 0 )
            break;
        if ( milliseconds != FOREVER &&
            ( ReadTime() - start_time ) >= milliseconds )
            break;
        if ( ( idle_status = IdleFunction() ) < RS232_SUCCESS )
            break;
    }
    ElapsedTime = ReadTime() - start_time;
    if ( idle_status < RS232_SUCCESS )
        return idle_status;
```

```
        if ( c >= 0 ) {
            ByteCount = 1;
            return c;
        }
        return RS232_TIMEOUT;
}

// This nonvirtual member function of class RS232 operates by
// repeatedly calling the virtual function write_byte() for the
// derived class. The milliseconds parameter defines how long
// the function will keep trying before giving up. While
// waiting, the idle function is called.

int RS232::Write( int c, long milliseconds )
{
    int write_status;
    int idle_status = RS232_SUCCESS;
    long start_time;

    ElapsedTime = 0;
    ByteCount = 0;
    if ( error_status < 0 )
        return error_status;
    start_time = ReadTime();
    for ( ; ; ) {
        write_status = write_byte( c );
        if ( write_status != RS232_TIMEOUT )
            break;
        if ( milliseconds != FOREVER &&
             ( ReadTime() - start_time ) >= milliseconds )
            break;
        if ( ( idle_status = IdleFunction() ) < RS232_SUCCESS )
            break;
    }
    ElapsedTime = ReadTime() - start_time;
    if ( idle_status < RS232_SUCCESS )
        return idle_status;
    if ( write_status < RS232_SUCCESS )
        return write_status;
    ByteCount = 1;
    return RS232_SUCCESS;
}

// This nonvirtual member function of class RS232 writes out
```

```c
// a buffer using the virtual write_buffer() routine. It has
// two additional parameters beyond those used by write_buffer(),
// which are a timeout value and a terminator. The terminator
// can be used to automatically append a CR/LF pair to output
// strings.

int RS232::Write( void *buffer,
                  unsigned int count,
                  long milliseconds,
                  char *terminator )
{
    char *b = ( char * ) buffer;
    long start_time;
    unsigned int byte_count;
    int idle_status = RS232_SUCCESS;
    int write_status;

    ElapsedTime = 0;
    ByteCount = 0;
    if ( error_status < 0 )
        return error_status;

    byte_count = 0;
    start_time = ReadTime();
    if ( count == 0 )
        count = strlen( b );
    for ( ; ; ) {
        write_status = write_buffer( b, count );
        byte_count += ByteCount;
        b += ByteCount;
        count -= ByteCount;
        if ( count == 0 && terminator != 0 ) {
            count += strlen( terminator );
            b = terminator;
            terminator = 0;
            continue;
        }
        if ( write_status != RS232_TIMEOUT || count == 0 )
            break;
        if ( milliseconds != FOREVER &&
             ( ReadTime() - start_time ) >= milliseconds )
            break;
        if ( ( idle_status == IdleFunction() ) < RS232_SUCCESS )
            break;
```

```
    }
    ElapsedTime = ReadTime() - start_time;
    ByteCount = byte_count;
    if ( idle_status < RS232_SUCCESS )
        return idle_status;
    if ( write_status < RS232_SUCCESS )
        return write_status;
    else if ( count > 0 )
        return RS232_TIMEOUT;
    else
        return RS232_SUCCESS;
}

// There are two versions of the nonvirtual ReadBuffer()
// function defined for the base class. They differ only in what
// causes their normal termination. This version terminates only
// when it reads in a full buffer of data, or when it times out. The
// next version stops when it sees the terminator string
// specified as a parameter.

int RS232::Read( void *buffer,
                 unsigned int count,
                 long milliseconds )
{
    long start_time;
    unsigned int byte_count;
    char *b = (char *) buffer;
    int read_status;
    int idle_status = RS232_SUCCESS;

    ElapsedTime = 0;
    ByteCount = 0;
    if ( error_status < 0 )
        return error_status;
    start_time = ReadTime();
    byte_count = 0;
    for ( ; ; ) {
        read_status = read_buffer( b, count );
        byte_count += ByteCount;
        count -= ByteCount;
        b += ByteCount;
        if ( read_status != RS232_TIMEOUT || count == 0 )
            break;
        if ( milliseconds != FOREVER &&
```

```
                ( ReadTime() - start_time ) >= milliseconds )
            break;
        if ( ( idle_status = IdleFunction() ) < RS232_SUCCESS )
            break;
    }
    *b = '\0';
    ElapsedTime = ReadTime() - start_time;
    ByteCount = byte_count;
    if ( idle_status < RS232_SUCCESS )
        return idle_status;
    else
        return read_status;
}

// This version of ReadBuffer() looks for a termination string
// in the incoming data stream. Because of this, it has to read
// in characters one at a time instead of in blocks. It looks
// for the terminator by doing a strncmp() after every new
// character is read in, which is probably not the most efficient
// way of doing it.

int RS232::Read( void *buffer,
                 unsigned int count,
                 long milliseconds,
                 char *terminator )
{
    long start_time;
    unsigned int byte_count;
    char *b = (char *) buffer;
    int idle_status = RS232_SUCCESS;
    int c;
    int term_len;

    term_len = strlen( terminator );
    ElapsedTime = 0;
    ByteCount = 0;
    if ( error_status < 0 )
        return error_status;
    start_time = ReadTime();
    byte_count = 0;
    for ( ; ; ) {
        c = read_byte();
        if ( c >= 0 ) {
            byte_count++;
```

```
                count--;
                *b++ = (char) c;
                if ( byte_count >= (unsigned int) term_len ) {
                    if (strncmp(b-term_len,terminator,term_len)==0) {
                        b -= term_len;
                        c = RS232_SUCCESS;
                        byte_count -= term_len;
                        break;
                    }
                }
                if ( count == 0 )
                    break;
            } else {
                if ( c != RS232_TIMEOUT )
                    break;
                if ( milliseconds != FOREVER &&
                    ( ReadTime() - start_time ) >= milliseconds )
                    break;
                if ( (idle_status = IdleFunction()) < RS232_SUCCESS )
                    break;
            }
        }
        *b = '\0';
        ElapsedTime = ReadTime() - start_time;
        ByteCount = byte_count;
        if ( idle_status < RS232_SUCCESS )
            return idle_status;
        else if ( c < RS232_SUCCESS )
            return c;
        else
            return RS232_SUCCESS;
}

// All of the remaining functions defined here are optional
// functions that won't be defined for every class. The default
// versions of these virtual functions just return an error
// message.

int RS232::Break( long duration )
{
    UNUSED( duration );
    return RS232_FUNCTION_NOT_SUPPORTED;
}

int RS232::SoftwareOverrunError( int clear )
```

```
{
    UNUSED( clear );
    return RS232_FUNCTION_NOT_SUPPORTED;
}

int RS232::FlushTXBuffer( void )
{
    return RS232_FUNCTION_NOT_SUPPORTED;
}

int RS232::RXSpaceFree( void )
{
    return RS232_FUNCTION_NOT_SUPPORTED;
}

int RS232::TXSpaceUsed( void )
{
    return RS232_FUNCTION_NOT_SUPPORTED;
}

int RS232::XonXoffHandshaking( int enable )
{
    UNUSED( enable );
    return RS232_FUNCTION_NOT_SUPPORTED;
}

int RS232::RtsCtsHandshaking( int enable )
{
    UNUSED( enable );
    return RS232_FUNCTION_NOT_SUPPORTED;
}

int RS232::DtrDsrHandshaking( int enable )
{
    UNUSED( enable );
    return RS232_FUNCTION_NOT_SUPPORTED;
}

int RS232::Dtr( int setting )
{
    UNUSED( setting );
    return RS232_FUNCTION_NOT_SUPPORTED;
}

int RS232::Rts( int setting )
```

```cpp
{
    UNUSED( setting );
    return RS232_FUNCTION_NOT_SUPPORTED;
}

int RS232::Peek( void *buffer, unsigned int count )
{
    UNUSED( buffer );
    UNUSED( count );
    return RS232_FUNCTION_NOT_SUPPORTED;
}

void Settings::Adjust( long baud_rate,
                       int parity,
                       int word_length,
                       int stop_bits,
                       int dtr,
                       int rts,
                       int xon_xoff,
                       int rts_cts,
                       int dtr_dsr )
{
    if ( baud_rate != UNCHANGED )
          BaudRate = baud_rate;
    if ( parity != UNCHANGED )
        Parity = (char) toupper( parity );
    if ( word_length != UNCHANGED )
        WordLength = word_length;
    if ( stop_bits != UNCHANGED )
        StopBits = stop_bits;
    if ( dtr != UNCHANGED )
        Dtr = dtr;
    if ( rts != UNCHANGED )
        Rts = rts;
    if ( xon_xoff != UNCHANGED )
        XonXoff = xon_xoff;
    if ( rts_cts != UNCHANGED )
        RtsCts = rts_cts;
    if ( dtr_dsr != UNCHANGED )
        DtrDsr = dtr_dsr;
}

// ********************* END OF RS232.CPP *********************
```

Listing 2-3: MSDOS.CPP

```cpp
// ******************** START OF MSDOS.CPP ********************
//
// This module contains O/S-specific routines. These routines are
// all defined for MS-DOS. When the target O/S is OS/2, Windows,
// or UNIX, different versions of these routines must be
// linked in.
//

#include <dos.h>
#include "rs232.h"
#include "_msdos.h"

// The default idle function for MS-DOS does nothing.

int RS232::IdleFunction( void )
{
    return RS232_SUCCESS;
}


//
// ReadTime() returns the current time of day in milliseconds.
//

long ReadTime( void )
{
    union REGS r;
    long milliseconds;

    r.h.ah = 0x2c;
    int86( 0x21, &r, &r );
    milliseconds = (long) r.h.dl * 10;         // dl : hundredths
    milliseconds += (long) r.h.dh * 1000;      // dh : seconds
    milliseconds += (long) r.h.cl * 60000L;    // cl : minutes
    milliseconds += (long) r.h.ch * 3600000L;  // ch : hours
    return( milliseconds );
}
// ******************** END OF MSDOS.CPP ********************
```

Summary

The `RS232` class described in this chapter lays the groundwork for all of the derived classes that will be used in the rest of this book. It implements some code that is platform independent, but leaves much of the work of creating a full implementation to derived classes. If you understand how class `RS232` interfaces with the rest of your program, you can write communications software that works with a wide variety of hardware and operating systems.

Chapter 3

The PC8250 Class

IN THIS CHAPTER

- The 8250 UART
- The standard COM card
- PC8250 driver structure
- Support classes
- A test program

IN THIS CHAPTER I present a fully functional interface to the IBM PC standard communications ports derived from the RS232 class. This driver will support all of the standard and optional virtual functions from this class, meaning that it will be fully compatible with any software written to use the RS232 class. The PC8250 class will work only with 16-bit real-mode programs, which means programs that run either under MS-DOS or in a DOS box under Windows.

The PC8250 class will also play a key role in working with the nonintelligent multiport board drivers described in the next chapter. Object-oriented programming should enable properly written code to be reused for new applications.

Because this is 16-bit code, you will need to compile it using a 16-bit compiler. Microsoft and Borland both have frozen their 16-bit compilers, Microsoft at version 1.52, and Borland at 4.5. You will need one of these to build this code; don't try using current releases of the 32-bit compilers!

> **NOTE:** The 16-bit programs for MS-DOS can read and write directly to hardware components such as the 8250 UARTs in the PC. The 32-bit programming model for Windows NT/9X doesn't support this direct access to hardware. Programs that are 32 bits can access hardware only via device drivers, VxDs, or other operating system interfaces.

The 8250 UART

In Chapter 1, I go over the history of the venerable 8250 UART family as it relates to the IBM PC. Certainly, IBM's choice of the Intel 8088 as the CPU for the PC is one of the most influential hardware decisions in history. Although the choice of the National Semiconductor 8250 as the UART on the PC COM card may seem like a footnote in comparison, it has had a considerable impact as well.

Both the IBM PC BIOS and MS-DOS itself left out any significant driver support for RS-232 interface cards. Accordingly, communications software developers have had to work directly with the hardware. Over the years, thousands of communications programs have been written to access the 8250 registers directly, ranging from top-quality professional software down to inexpensive shareware. The installed base of communications software users who support 8250 family of UARTs has grown so much that it is difficult to support anything else.

Because so much communications code talks directly to the 8250 hardware, PC and peripheral manufacturers have not had too many choices regarding UARTs for the PC ISA. Basically, if a UART is not completely 8250 compatible, it isn't going to sell. Any nonstandard hardware will require custom software to work, and most reasonable people just aren't interested in replacing off-the-shelf software with custom implementations.

This is really more of a problem to the end user than it is to the programmer. The 8250 is not a particularly high-powered chip, so power users are finding that their existing hardware is running out of gas. Programmers can't do much to squeeze more performance out of existing parts, so they continue writing code that works with the standard until something better comes along. The techniques developed in this book will help you ensure that your software is ready for the change when it happens.

The move to 32-bit Windows in the form of Windows NT, 9X, and 2000 will eventually solve the 8250 straitjacket problem. Code that writes directly to the PC hardware such as that in the `PC8250` class will eventually give way to 32-bit protected-mode code that talks to a driver. Until all those legacy machines have been upgraded, the code presented in this chapter will still be relevant and useful.

8250 register set

The 8250 UART and its close family members are controlled by approximately 11 (the exact number depends on how you view things) hardware registers. On the IBM PC standard COM cards, these registers are mapped into a block of eight consecutive I/O ports. In general, hardware designed to work with Intel CPU architectures usually maps to the I/O bus, leaving the higher-speed memory bus to peripherals that have large blocks of shared memory, such as video cards.

The I/O bus on most PCs is a 16-bit bus that operates at a slower speed than the memory bus. Unlike conventional memory, the I/O bus has only a few different machine instructions for accessing hardware. The 8088 instruction set only has four output and four input instructions, with a few more added to later versions of Intel processors. But this RISC-like implementation doesn't seem to cause any particular hardship to systems-level programming. Most of the difficulties implementing communications software are timing and hardware related, and are not related to an anemic instruction set.

The registers found in the 8250 family are shown in Table 3-1.

TABLE 3-1 8250 FAMILY REGISTER DEFINITIONS

Register Name	Offset	Abbreviation	Access Type
Receiver Buffer Register	0	RBR	Read Only
Transmit Holding Register	0	THR	Write Only
Interrupt Enable Register	1	IER	Read/Write
Interrupt Identification Register	2	IIR	Read Only
FIFO Control Register (16550)	2	FCR	Write Only
Line Control Register	3	LCR	Read/Write
Modem Control Register	4	MCR	Read/Write
Line Status Register	5	LSR	Read Only
Modem Status Register	6	MSR	Read Only
Scratch Register (16450/550)	7	SCR	Read/Write
Divisor Latch (16 bits)	0/1	DL	Read/Write

Each of these registers has its own well-defined role to play in the proper operation of an 8250 family UART. The offsets listed in the preceding table refer to the offsets from the base address of the UART on the I/O bus. For example, COM1 on an IBM PC is normally configured to be at address 0x3F8. Because the Scratch Register is defined as having an offset of 7, it will appear at address 0x3FF and can be accessed with an input or output instruction. Note that the addresses on the UART could be mapped differently if necessary; IBM simply mapped the UART the conventional way.

> **NOTE:** Addresses in this book are always given in hexadecimal, or base 16. Because hex numbers are given in C++ programs with a 0x prefix, that convention is used in the text as well.

The next few sections discuss each of the UART's registers in greater detail.

RECEIVE BUFFER REGISTER

The Receive Buffer Register (RBR) is the address from which data that the UART has received from an RS-232 line can be read into the computer. The serial stream of bits coming in from the modem or other RS-232 device get assembled into a byte and stored in the RBR. The CPU actually gets the data from the UART by executing an input instruction at the base address of the UART. This means that on COM1, you can read in a byte from the UART by executing a piece of assembly code that looks like this:

```
INPUT:      MOV     DX,3F8H
            IN      AL,DX
```

C++ programmers can't execute CPU instructions quite as easily, but the Run Time Library has simple routines to do the same thing:

```
int data = inp( 0x3f8 );
```

The 8250 uses a technique for its input and output registers known as *double buffering*. This means that inside the chip are a pair of registers for input and a pair for output. On the input side, the UART uses one register as a temporary holding area for a byte coming down the RS-232 line. As each bit comes in, it is shifted into this holding register. After 7 or 8 bits (depending on the UART settings) have come in, the UART decides that it has assembled a complete data word. At this point, the word is dumped from the receiver holding register to the RBR. The holding register can then begin assembling the next RS-232 byte coming down the line, while the last word rests comfortably in the buffer register.

Thus, the programmer has a minimum of one data word time to read the byte from the RBR before the next word is completely assembled and loaded. As soon as the next word is completely assembled, it is written out into the RBR, obliterating the current contents. So, response time is critical to the accurate reception of the input data.

Not long ago, this amount of time was more than adequate. A 300-baud modem transmits a maximum of only 30 bytes per second, so each data word has a maximum response time of around 33 milliseconds. But today, not too many applications exist for 300-baud modems. The standard interface is probably 57.6 Kbps or

115.2 Kbps. At 57.6 Kbps, characters arrive at the UART as often as six per millisecond. Even on today's fast machines, 175 microseconds is a very brief interval.

UARTs with on-chip buffering such as the 16550 represent the most practical solution to this problem. The 16550 has a 16-byte receiver buffer, allowing for significantly longer durations between servicing the chip. The 16550 UART can be configured to generate an interrupt when the very first character enters the FIFO, which then leaves 15 more data word times before loss of data. This can cause a dramatic increase in performance, even on a very fast machine.

TRANSMIT HOLDING REGISTER

Just like on the receive side of the UART, the transmit side is double buffered. The character actually being shifted out one bit at a time to the RS-232 line is contained in the Transmitter Buffer. The next character to be sent is held in the Transmit Holding Register (THR). When the transmitter completes shifting out the last bit from the current output byte, it immediately moves the byte from the THR into the Transmit Buffer. At that point, the UART lets the CPU know by way of a data bit or an interrupt that it is ready to accept another character. If the processor can write a new data byte to the THR before the next character is done shifting out, a continuous stream of RS-232 characters will be sent.

The transmitter's response time is not nearly as critical as the receiver's. If the CPU is a little slow moving the next character into the transmit buffer, the RS-232 line will suffer some "dead air" when nothing is being transmitted. The computer will be wasting some of its data bandwidth on nothing, but no data will be lost.

Nonetheless, when the 16550 was designed, it incorporated a 16-byte FIFO buffer on the transmitter side as well. When the CPU knows that the transmit buffer is empty, it can immediately load up the TX FIFO with 16 data words ready to be sent. The CPU won't be bothered again for 16 more data word times, allowing for much less overhead when transmitting blocks of data.

INTERRUPT ENABLE REGISTER

The 8250 family of UARTs can generate interrupts based on four classes of events. These events are as follows (see Figure 3-1):

- ◆ Receive Data Available
- ◆ Transmit Holding Register Empty
- ◆ Modem Status Line Change
- ◆ Line Status Event

Depending on the type of interface to the 8250, one or more of these interrupts may be in use at any time. As I've already stated, the BIOS talks to the 8250 without using any of these interrupt types, which renders it nearly useless for any serious work.

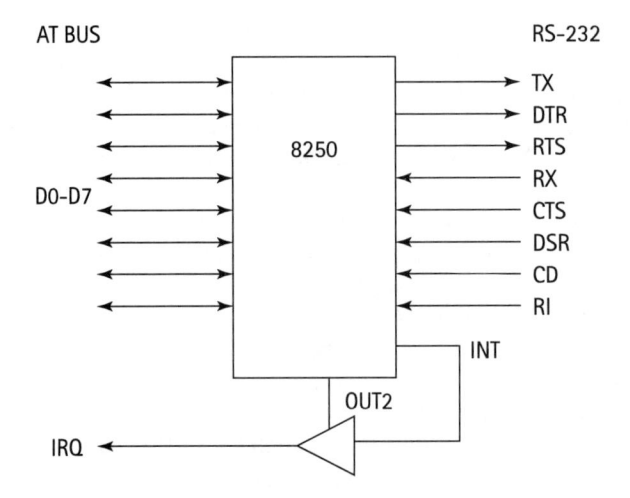

```
         AT BUS                          RS-232
            ←→  ┌─────────┐  →  TX
            ←→  │         │  →  DTR
            ←→  │  8250   │  →  RTS
            ←→  │         │  ←  RX
    D0-D7   ←→  │         │  ←  CTS
            ←→  │         │  ←  DSR
            ←→  │         │  ←  CD
            ←→  │         │  ←  RI
                │         │  →  INT
                │  OUT2   │
    IRQ   ←─────◁─────────┘
```

Figure 3-1: The four types of 8250 Interrupts

The four types of interrupts are enabled via individual bits in the Interrupt Enable Register (IER). Table 3-2 shows the bit map of the IER. Writing a 1 to the bit in the register enables that particular interrupt. Note that the IER is a read/write register, which means that the programmer can read the bits back out of the register at any time. This is convenient when programming the register because you can set or clear an individual bit.

TABLE 3-2 THE INTERRUPT ENABLE REGISTER

7	6	5	4	3	2	1	0
Not Used	Not Used	Not Used	Not Used	Modem Status	Line Status	Transmit Holding Register Empty	Received Data Available

When developing the device driver for the 8250, you must ask which of the four interrupts to enable and when. Clearly the most important interrupt to support in any driver software is the Receive Data Available (RDA) interrupt. With any real world application running on conventional RS-232 hardware, it is simply not possible to poll the UART fast enough to read in all incoming data. The only solution is the RDA interrupt. But then you must ensure that your code can respond to the interrupt rapidly enough to not lose any data.

The Transmit Holding Register Empty (THRE) interrupt is also useful, but it can be safely ignored under certain circumstances. In a single-tasking environment such as MS-DOS, with the right type of application, polled-mode output will prove more than satisfactory to the task at hand. When transmitting data, the CPU simply sits in a polling loop, waiting for the THRE to become empty before sending each character. The CPU wastes an awful lot of time doing nothing but waiting, but often this is still the best approach.

The modem status interrupt is generated any time one of the four incoming modem status lines to the UART changes state. The 8250 family has four incoming modem status lines that are normally connected to CTS, DSR, CD, and RI.

The 8250 driver developed in this chapter will have modem status interrupts enabled at all times. Many applications can get by without enabling these interrupts, but having them on makes it particularly easy to manage hardware flow control. When one of the two modes of hardware flow control is enabled, you want your driver to be able to either start or stop interrupts when an incoming CTS or DSR line changes state.

If the modem status interrupts weren't turned on, there would be a polling problem. When the 8250 driver was in a blocked state while waiting for CTS or DSR to go high, your driver would have to be polling the state of the modem status lines. Otherwise, when the line went high again, you would have no way of knowing it was time to begin transmission again.

There is a downside to enabling modem status interrupts, however. First, as I mentioned in Chapter 1, if a cable leaves some of the modem status lines unconnected, they can pick up noise from adjacent data lines in the cable. This can result in massive floods of modem status interrupts, with an interrupt being generated for literally every bit that is input or output.

Even if the modem status lines are properly connected on the cable, most of the modem status interrupts just waste CPU cycles. If hardware handshaking isn't being used, many applications will work properly by just polling the input lines. But with the 8250 architecture being what it is, you have to accept the necessity of leaving these interrupts turned on.

The final interrupt that can be turned on in the 8250 is the Line Status Interrupt (LSI). There are four line status conditions that can generate an interrupt. Parity errors occur when an incoming character doesn't obey the parity that the UART has been programmed to expect. A Framing Error occurs when an incoming character doesn't appear to have a valid stop bit. A Break Detect occurs when the incoming RS-232 line stays at the logic 0 state for an entire character, time, including start, stop, and data bits. The final line status interrupt condition occurs when the CPU fails to service an 8250 interrupt rapidly enough, resulting in the loss of a character. The 8250 terminology for this condition is an Overrun Error. In this book, I refer to this particular error as a Hardware Overrun Error to clearly differentiate it from a buffer overflow in the interrupt service routine.

The 8250 driver developed in this chapter will run with line status interrupts enabled at all times. However, no real-time action will be taken when a line status interrupt occurs. Instead, the interrupt bit will just be ORed into a cumulative register that keeps track of cumulative line status errors.

For general-purpose software, it isn't always clear how to respond to a line status interrupt. For example, during a terminal emulation session, there usually isn't any way to retry a transmission, so errors cannot be corrected. On the other hand, file transfer protocols will usually detect errors that occur during a reception, so the line status bits become redundant.

If an error-free connection were of paramount importance, I would probably rewrite this driver to respond differently to line-status interrupts. When the interrupt occurs, the application program could be alerted immediately, allowing it to take whatever action the programmer deems necessary.

INTERRUPT ID REGISTER

When an interrupt does occur, the CPU will respond by entering an Interrupt Service Routine (ISR). This is a special piece of code designed to handle the incoming hardware event rapidly and efficiently. After it takes control of the machine, the ISR needs to decide what action to take. For the 8250, this means reading in the Interrupt ID Register (IIR). This 8-bit register has five valid states, shown in Table 3-3.

TABLE 3-3 THE INTERRUPT ID REGISTER VALUES

IIR Contents	Interrupt Type	Priority
0	Modem Status Interrupt	Lowest
2	Transmit Holding Register Empty	Third
4	Received Data Available	Second
6	Line Status	Highest
1	No Interrupt Pending	N/A

When the ISR takes control, a good approach to take is to code a loop that repeatedly reads the contents of the IIR. If the IIR contents indicate that an interrupt needs to be serviced, the appropriate handler routine can be dispatched. If the value 1 is read out of the IIR, no interrupts are pending and the routine can exit, returning control to the main program.

With most variations of the 8250, it's possible for the interrupt service routine to just read in a single value from the IIR, dispatch a handler, and then exit. If any other interrupts need to be serviced, the ISR will be fired up again by the system. However, that approach has a couple of problems. First, if the 8250 is in a very active state, managing a high number of interrupts, it is much more efficient for the CPU to handle as much activity as is possible while in the ISR.

Second, a few variations of the 8250 will fail to correctly interrupt 80x86 processors if only one interrupt at a time is serviced. Later in this chapter, I offer details about this particular problem.

The four interrupt types in the 8250 have specific actions that must be taken to clear the interrupt state. If these actions aren't properly taken after reading the IIR, the UART can get into a hang state, unable to generate further interrupts until the last one is cleared. The four interrupt categories follow.

Line Status Interrupt:	Clearing this interrupt just requires that the CPU read the Line Status Register.
Modem Status Interrupt:	Reading the Modem Status Register clears this interrupt.
Received Data Available:	Reading the data from the Receiver Buffer Register clears this interrupt.
Transmit Holding Register:	When the Transmit Holding Register goes empty, there are two ways to clear the interrupt. Just reading the Interrupt ID Register will clear it, as will sending a byte to the transmitter.

The THRE interrupt is particularly important. If the interrupt service routine fails to reload the transmit register when it is empty, no further interrupts will occur. Thus, the program might be ready to send out data to the transmitter, but it may never receive an interrupt to let it know it can.

LINE CONTROL REGISTER / BAUD RATE DIVISOR

The Line Control Register (LCR) is used to set up the data transmission parameters for the 8250 UART. An additional parameter, the baud rate, is indirectly controlled by this register. The LCR is divided into five different fields, which are controlled with nonintuitive bit field values. Table 3-4 shows how the fields are broken out across the 8-bit register.

TABLE 3-4 THE LINE CONTROL REGISTER BIT SETTINGS

7	6	5	4	3	2	1	0
Divisor Latch Access Bit	Break Control	Parity Control Bits			Number of Stop Bits	Word Length Select	

The two least significant bits in the LCR are used to control the number of bits in a word transmitted by the UART. The 8250 has the capability to transmit words of 5, 6, 7, or 8 bits. Not many applications use words of a length other than 7 or 8, but they can. Table 3-5 details the four possible settings of this bit field.

TABLE 3-5 THE WORD LENGTH BIT FIELD IN THE LCR

Bit Field Value	Resulting Word Length
00	5 bits
01	6 bits
10	7 bits
11	8 bits

The stop bits setting is merely a binary flag. A value of 1 indicates that two stop bits should be used; 0 means that a single stop bit is used. For most applications, the slightly faster throughput afforded by using just a single stop bit is usually the desired setting. However, on a noisy line with continuous data flow, two stop bits may be required to quickly recover synchronization when an error occurs.

Decoding the functions of the three parity bits can be difficult at first. For one thing, there are three bits, which allow for eight different settings. However, the UART actually has only five different parity settings. The reason for this is that the three bits operate somewhat independently so that each one controls a different aspect of the parity settings. The actual binary decoding of the parity bits is shown in Table 3-6.

The least significant bit in the parity select field is the parity enable bit. When this bit is clear, no parity is generated or checked under any conditions. If this bit is set, the next two bits determine what sort of parity is actually generated. The second bit in the field is the even parity select bit. Usually, if this bit is set, even parity is used, and if it is clear, odd parity is used. However, the setting of the third bit, the stick parity control, can overrule this bit. If the stick parity bit is set, an extra bit is appended to the data, but the value of the bit is independent of the actual data contents. If a stick parity of 1 is selected, the extra bit is always 1; if a stick parity of 0 is selected, the extra bit is always a 0. The previous bit, the even parity select bit, controls the setting of the extra bit.

The stick parity setting is rarely used but is still available, and many drivers will at least support it. Using a 0 bit for stick parity is referred to as Space parity, a 1 is referred to as Mark parity.

TABLE 3-6 THE PARITY BIT FIELD IN THE LCR

Stick Parity Bit	Even Parity Bit	Parity Enable Bit	Effect
0	0	0	No parity
0	0	1	Odd Parity
0	1	0	No Parity
0	1	1	Even Parity
1	0	0	No Parity
1	0	1	Mark Parity
1	1	0	No Parity
1	1	1	Space Parity

Calculating exactly what the parity settings do for each bit field can be somewhat confusing. But you can create a switch statement one time for setting the parity and forget about it after that. That is the approach I take in this book.

The break bit in the LCR is used to send a break signal on the outgoing RS-232 line. A break signal is not a properly formatted character like the ones normally sent on the outbound line. Rather, a break signal is created when the UART forces the transmit line to a logic 0 and holds it there for significantly longer than a single character time. Generally a break signal should last at least 250 milliseconds. Using a long time guarantees that a break will be interpreted correctly even at very low baud rates.

The 8250 has no built-in break timer, so sending a break becomes a manual operation. Asserting the break bit in the LCR puts the line into a spacing condition. The line has to be held there while the main program counts off enough CPU ticks to amount to a significant fraction of a second. After that, the bit is cleared and the UART goes back to normal operations.

The final bit in the LCR is the Baud Rate Divisor Latch Access Bit (DLAB). The LCR directly controls all of the RS-232 transmission parameters for the UART, except for the baud rate. The 8250 has a flexible baud rate generator that is configured by loading a 16-bit divisor with a value determined by the program. The 8250 designers at National Semiconductor apparently were unhappy with the idea of having a register map with more than eight entries, so they mapped the two 8-byte components of the baud rate divisor into the same locations as the transmit register and the interrupt enable register (register offsets of 0 and 1). A single bit, the DLAB, determines which set of registers is actually mapped at any given moment.

To write to the baud-rate divisor, the programmer just asserts the DLAB in the LCR and then writes out the two bytes of the divisor to register positions 0 and 1. Register 0 gets the least significant byte, register 1 gets the most significant. After the baud rate is set, the DLAB is cleared and register positions 0 and 1 revert to their normal mode of operation.

Problems can arise if an interrupt occurs while the DLAB is in an unknown state. For example, if the port has data arriving at the same time that you decide to modify the baud rate, you can run into trouble. Imagine that your main program sets the DLAB so that it can access the baud rate divisor values, and just then an incoming character triggers an interrupt. The interrupt service routine will then read what it thinks is valid data from the RDR, but it will actually be reading the LSB of the baud rate divisor. This is not a good thing!

One way to handle this problem is for the ISR to save and restore the state of the DLAB bit at the entry and exit of the ISR. A simpler method, which I use here, is to disable interrupts while changing the baud rate.

On the IBM PC, the transmitter and receiver for standard COM ports derive their clock from a 115.2 KHz fundamental clock that is divided by the baud-rate divisor. This sets the maximum baud rate to 115.2Kbps (except for the undefined case when the divisor is 0). The rate was set to 115.2 KHz because that rate divides down nicely to frequently used rates such as 9600 and 2400 bps.

The design of the IBM COM port hardware also prohibits the use of split baud rates, in which the transmitter and receiver are operating at different speeds. The 8250 could operate in this mode with a different hardware setup. However, few applications require this feature. Applications that must use split baud rates have to use custom hardware.

MODEM CONTROL REGISTER

The Modem Control Register (MCR) sets or clears the four output lines from the 8250 UART. The UART lines are conventionally labeled as DTR, RTS, OUT1, and OUT2. Table 3-7 details the bit settings used in the MCR, and Table 3-8 shows what function the control bits perform on an IBM PC COM card.

OUT1 and OUT2 are undedicated lines that hardware designers can use for whatever purposes they wish. On a standard IBM PC COM card, OUT1 is not connected to anything. On the same type of card, OUT2 enables or disables the interrupt line to the PC bus. When OUT2 is low, the interrupt output from the 8250 UART is electrically disconnected from the bus so that other peripheral cards are free to use the interrupt line. When OUT2 is high, the 8250 interrupt line will be driving the interrupt line either high or low, depending on its current state.

Note that this ability to disconnect the card from the interrupt line is very important for PC COM cards. There are only 16 interrupt lines on the PC ISA bus, and most of those are dedicated to specific purposes. This means that devices often have to share a single line, using it one at a time. When it comes to COM cards, you normally set them up to share a single interrupt line between COM1 and COM3 and another line between COM2 and COM4. In order for this sharing to work, you have to have a way to disconnect a one card from an interrupt line in order for the other to work. You can see more about the implications of this later.

TABLE 3-7 THE BIT SETTINGS IN THE MCR

7	6	5	4	3	2	1	0
Unused				Loopback	OUT2	OUT1	RTS	DTR

The DTR and RTS lines are used just as you would expect them to be. On the IBM COM card, they directly control the RTS and DTR output lines to the RS-232 connector. The 8250 UART doesn't have any automatic modes of operation that can change either of these control lines. Instead, the lines have to be controlled by the driver software. If you want to implement RTS/CTS flow control, for example, the ISR will have to toggle these bits at the correct trigger points based on buffer states.

More advanced UARTs in the same family do have built-in support for RTS/CTS handshaking. The method for enabling that is discussed later in this chapter.

TABLE 3-8 FUNCTIONS OF THE MCR BITS ON THE PC COM CARD

Control Bit	Function
Loopback	Loops back data and control lines
OUT2	Enables interrupts on PC COM card
OUT1	Not connected, does nothing on PC COM card
RTS	Conventional modem control line
DTR	Conventional modem control line

The final bit in the MCR of concern is the Loopback bit. This bit can be used to place the UART into internal Loopback mode for testing. When this bit is set, the output of the transmitter is internally routed to the input of the receiver. This means that if you write out a character to the THR, you should see the same character appear in the RBR after just one character time.

Although Loopback mode sounds like a useful thing to have in the UART, in practice it has one small flaw. As soon as the chip is placed into Loopback mode, the four output bits, OUT1, OUT2, RTS, and DTR, are all disconnected from the

UART output pins and instead are routed back internally to connect to the four modem inputs. The modem control outputs are dropped to logic 0 states for the duration of the output tests. Because of this, the low OUT2 pin on the UART disables any PC interrupts from taking place. If you want to test the UART in Loopback mode, you will need to write code that uses polled-mode input, because the card is not going to be able to generate any interrupts.

The MCR is another read/write register. This is convenient for programmers because they can determine the actual state of the output lines at any time. Additionally, they can easily modify the state of a single output line by reading in the MCR, changing the state of a single bit, and then writing the contents back out.

LINE STATUS REGISTER

The Line Status Register (LSR) is a read-only register that has seven bits of information regarding the state of the RS-232 data transmission. Table 3-9 shows the value of the actual bits in question. Four of the bits in the LSR are used to flag incoming data errors or conditions. The other three bits give the status of the transmit and receive buffers.

TABLE 3-9 THE LINE STATUS REGISTER

7	6	5	4	3	2	1	0
Not Used	Transmitter Empty	Transmitter Transmit Holding Register Empty	Break Detected	Framing Error	Parity Error	Overrun Error	Data Ready

The four error status bits are used to signal events, not conditions. As such, they will be cleared as soon as they are read. This means that if the programmer wants to keep track of these error conditions, it is critical that the four error bits be recorded *every* time the LSR is read in. For example, the LSR may be polled in the interrupt service routine to determine whether the Transmitter is ready to accept a new byte. If the LSR is read in during the polling, the contents of the four error bits will then be cleared. Accordingly, the status of those four bits needs to be updated after the LSR is read.

The definitions and use of the seven bits in the LSR follow:

Data Ready: This bit is used to indicate that a new byte has been read in from the RS-232 line and is ready to be read out of the Receiver Buffer Register. After the character is read in, Data Ready is cleared.

Overrun Error:	A Hardware Overrun Error occurs when a new byte is read in from the RS-232 line before the last one was read out. This bit is set to indicate that at least one character was lost.
Parity Error:	If an incoming character does not have a parity setting that the UART is expecting, this bit is set.
Framing Error:	If an incoming character doesn't have a valid stop bit, the Framing Error bit is set. This condition usually indicates a noisy line, mismatched baud rates between the sender and the receiver, or an incoming break.
Break Detect:	A break consists of an incoming RS-232 line in the logical "0" state for at least one entire character time, including start and stop bits. Most breaks will actually remain in the logic 0 state for much longer, but one character time is the minimum.
Transmit Holding Register Empty:	When the Transmit Holding Register is empty, it means that the UART is ready for the CPU to load another character for transmission. If the Transmit Holding Register is loaded before the Transmitter itself becomes empty, transmission will continue with no gap between the characters except the stop and start bits. This allows for maximum use of the RS-232 bandwidth.
Transmitter Empty:	This bit is used to signal that the transmitter is empty. Probably the most important time this bit is used is when closing a port. If a programmer wants to be sure that every byte that is supposed to be sent has actually gone out on the line, this bit must be polled.

MODEM STATUS REGISTER

The Modem Status Register (MSR) has two matched sets of four bits each. The first set of bits indicates the current *states* of the four incoming modem control lines. The next set of four bits record *events*, namely a change in any one of the four lines. Just like in the Line Status Register, the status bits will always reflect the current state of the incoming line, but the event bits will be cleared after they are read in for the first time. Table 3-10 shows the position of these eight bits in the MSR.

TABLE 3-10 THE MODEM STATUS REGISTER

7	6	5	4	3	2	1	0
Carrier Detect	Ring Indicator	Data Set Ready	Clear to Send	Change in CD	Change in RI	Change in DSR	Change in CTS

In your implementation of the 8250 driver, any time one of the four modem status lines changes state, an interrupt will be generated. In the interrupt service routine, you read in the MSR and check to see which bits have changed by looking at bits 0 through 3. In the PC8250 class, the two bits that matter the most are the DSR and CTS bits. Event flags in either of these bits can trigger either a stop or start of transmitter interrupts, if hardware handshaking is turned on.

8250 lookalikes

Most of the UARTs found in the PCs today are compatible with the 8250 family. However, a couple of exceptions are worth noting, and one will receive some additional support from the device interface developed here.

The most important of the 8250 variants is known as the 16550. The 16550 is downward compatible with the 8250 at the register level. This means that an IBM PC application that writes directly to the 8250 chips will still work properly with the 16550. But the 16550 has additional features that can be enabled via a hidden register. Most important among these is a 16-byte FIFO (first in, first out) buffer on both the transmit and receive sides. The FIFOs are enabled and controlled by way of the FIFO Control Register (FCR). The FCR is a write-only register located at offset 2, which is shared by the read-only IIR.

The 16550 is electrically compatible with the 8250 as well. The 16550 UART can be plugged into an existing 8250 socket, and it will work without code changes. This not only enables end users to replace their 16450 (the faster twin of the 8250) and 8250 UARTs with a better performing one, but also gives manufacturers of PCs and interface boards the capability to upgrade their designs by simply replacing one part.

Microsoft's hardware specifications now require that Windows-compatible PCs use UARTs with at least a 16-byte FIFO on board, so the 16550 is now the standard UART on most new machines. The core logic of the UART is usually embedded in a motherboard chip set, combined with other necessary logic, such as IDE disk controllers, parallel port interfaces, and so on.

Table 3-11 shows the bit settings in the 16550 FIFO Control Register. To use the Transmit and Receive FIFOs, the FIFO Enable bit in position 0 needs to be set. After this bit is set, the input and output buffers on the UART are no longer just double buffered; instead they have a 16-byte buffer.

TABLE 3-11 THE 16550 FIFO CONTROL REGISTER

7	6	5	4	3	2	1	0
RX Interrupt	Unused	Unused	DMA Mode	TX FIFO Reset	RX FIFO Reset	Trigger Level	FIFO Enable

The 16-byte FIFO on the receive side cures a major problem for many PC users. When the serial port is operating at relatively high speeds — say, 38400 bps or greater — users will frequently find that they are getting large numbers of hardware overrun errors. Many activities on a PC can disable interrupts for significant periods of time. Prime suspects for this problem are device drivers that need to have unfettered access to hardware.

For maximum protection against loss of data, the 16-byte RX FIFO can be set up to generate an interrupt when it has only a single character in it. After it has received just one character, the UART can then generate an interrupt and know that it has 15 more character times left before the processor has to respond. This use of the FIFO nearly always cures the problem of hardware overruns.

The interrupt trigger level is set by bits 7 and 6, the RX Trigger Level bits. These two bits have four possible settings, which determine how full the FIFO has to be before generating an interrupt. When a system is having problems with hardware overruns, the earliest possible setting can be used, giving the maximum time allowance for interrupts to be disabled before an error occurs. The four possible settings for these two bits have the effect shown in Table 3-12.

TABLE 3-12 THE TRIGGER LEVEL BITS IN THE 16550 FIFO CONTROL REGISTER

Bit Setting	Trigger Level
0	1 Character in the FIFO
1	4 Characters in the FIFO
2	8 Characters in the FIFO
3	14 Characters in the FIFO

If a system isn't plagued with hardware overruns, the maximum setting can be selected, which will not generate an interrupt until the FIFO is nearly full. This drastically reduces the number of interrupts on a busy system, which results in more efficient operation.

If characters are not streaming in continuously, the 16550 won't wait indefinitely before generating an interrupt. Regardless of the FIFO count, if no new characters come in for three character times, the 16550 will generate an interrupt if any characters are waiting in the FIFO.

The transmit FIFO is a little less complicated. It generates an interrupt only when empty. When the Transmit Holding Register Empty interrupt occurs, the ISR can simply stuff 16 characters into the transmitter, whereas on a normal 8250, it can only send one.

The two reset bits in the FCR are used when initializing. They simply take care of properly resetting the transmit and receive FIFOs.

The DMA bit in the FCR is used to control DMA transfers on the part of the UART. In general, most systems aren't configured to take advantage of this capability.

Detecting the presence of a 16550 is relatively simple. During the initialization phase of the UART, the FIFOs can be enabled by writing the correct control word to the FCR. The 16550 has an additional two bits in the bit positions 6 and 7 of the Interrupt ID Register. If the FIFOs are properly enabled, a read of the IIR will show 1s in those two positions, and the program can begin using both the transmit and receive FIFOs.

If both bits aren't set, a word with all zeros should immediately be written out to the FCR. Two problems can arise if the programmer doesn't do this. First, some early versions of the 16550 had bugs that prevented the FIFOs from working properly. These versions of the part had only one of the two bits set. Because the FIFOs won't work on these parts, they need to be disabled. Second, there is another 8250 lookalike called the Intel 82510. The 82510 uses the FCR for completely different purposes and will be rendered unusable if you don't clear the register at this point. Writing a 0 back to the FCR will reset the 82510 to 8250 compatibility mode.

Extensions to the 8250 design

A few manufacturers have decided that a little more tinkering with the basic 8250 concept would be fun for everyone involved. Two popular results have been the 16650 and the 16750 UARTs. These two chips extend the size of the FIFO to 32 and 64 bytes, respectively. Better yet, these UARTs implement on-chip RTS/CTS handshaking. With the standard 8250 family, RTS/CTS handshaking must be implemented in software, usually as part of the interrupt service routine. Moving this function out of the CPU's arena of responsibility and into that of the UART makes good sense and should provide for a more responsible system.

The 16650 and 16750 are found on some custom multiport boards but generally have not been added to any current motherboard designs. The code presented in this chapter supports basic 8250 and 16550 functions, but does not have the code to support the advanced features in these newer parts. However, you should be able to quickly add these features armed with little more than the data sheet for the part. You can get a 16750 data sheet from the Texas Instruments Web site.

> **NOTE:** Texas Instruments' Web site can be found at http://www.ti.com. Use its search engine to search for UART and you will find the datasheets for its parts.

8250 oddities

Just reading the data sheet for the 8250 parts can give a programmer a false sense of security. Writing programs that conform strictly to the specifications of the part has often led to nonfunctional code. You should know about a few bugs and operational problems with the 8250 family.

INTERRUPT PULSING

One 8250 bug was particularly useful to IBM PC programmers. The designers of the first IBM PC hardware and BIOS elected to operate the 8259 interrupt controller in edge-triggered mode, rather than use the more conventional level triggering. This means that to generate a new interrupt, a device has to actually take the interrupt line from a logic 0 to a logic 1. After an interrupt has been serviced, the device in question has to lower its interrupt line and raise it again to get more service.

In theory, the 8250 should keep its interrupt line asserted as long as interrupts are pending. However, doing so can cause trouble. If a programmer finished servicing interrupts on an 8250 and exited the ISR at the same time another incoming character arrived, the 8259 interrupt controller might not recognize that another interrupt occurred. In practice, however, the initial 8250 design pulsed the interrupt line low after each interrupt condition was cleared. Because of this, the hardware worked properly with an edge-triggered interrupt controller. This bug is now considered a feature and is required for proper operation with most communications software.

JUMP STARTING INTERRUPTS

Another "feature" of the early 8250 family UARTs gave programmers an easy way to jump-start transmit interrupts. As specified, an 8250 should generate a TX interrupt only when the THR goes empty. This register goes empty when a character is moved into the Transmit Register and starts being shifted out to the RS-232 data line.

In practice, however, programmers found that just enabling TX interrupts when the THR was empty was enough to generate a TX interrupt. Programmers could take a convenient shortcut when sending the very first character out the UART. All a programmer had to do was load the character into the buffer used by the ISR and then enable TX interrupts. At that point, an interrupt would automatically be generated, and the ISR could take care of the details of transmitting the character.

Unfortunately, some later versions of the 8250 family fixed this bug so that TX interrupts only occurred when they should. This had the unexpected effect of suddenly causing lots of working application software to break, much to the consternation of the owners of new brand-name computers. Because many of these chips are still in circulation, communications programmers have had to adjust.

The solution to this problem is actually quite simple and should be a standard part of every programmer's communications software. If TX interrupts aren't presently running and a character needs to be transmitted, the programmer needs to manually write the first character out to the THR as if in polled-mode operation, and *then* enable TX interrupts. The first character will "prime the pump" by generating an interrupt when it is shifted to the transmitter. After that, interrupts will run in the traditional manner, with a new one following the transmission of each character.

EXTRA MODEM STATUS INTERRUPTS

One annoying bug found both in original National Semiconductor chips as well as some clone chips is the false modem status interrupt. The IIR can report a modem status interrupt when none has occurred. This can easily lead to trouble with the ISR code.

The best solution to the false modem status interrupt is to always check the "changed" bits in the MSR when servicing this interrupt. By checking these bits, the ISR will take action only on a particular modem status line if a change in state has actually occurred on that line.

MOTHERBOARD TIMING

When IBM first introduced the AT, it published a Technical Reference Manual that included a complete listing of the BIOS for this machine. If you looked at the INT 14H service routines that access the COM ports for the AT, you probably noticed some sequences of 8086 assembly language that looked like this:

```
LOOP:   IN      AL,DX
        JMP     .+$
        JNZ     LOOP
```

The exact purpose of the `JMP .+$` code wasn't spelled out clearly at all in the code listings, so the reader had to dig in the Technical Reference Manual. Eventually, if you looked hard enough, you found a statement from IBM to the effect that the I/O Bus had some timing problems. If the 8086 processor executed back-to-back I/O instructions, bus timing could cause a read or write error. Thus the inserted delays.

The use of the `JMP .+$` instruction had a few further implications. Any one of the jump instructions on this processor would flush the instruction prefetch queue on the processor, resulting in an inordinately long delay. Apparently, IBM did not feel that a simple NOP instruction would use up enough cycles for everything to work properly.

Communications programmers everywhere have taken the hint, and all of our programs are now liberally salted with `JMP .+$` sequences. However, some nagging doubts remain. For example, as future generations of processors run faster, will the current sequences ever become too short? Will future processors find ways of maintaining a valid prefetch queue even through JMP instructions? The answers to these questions appear to be somewhat murky.

THE MISSING DR BIT

The integrated UART used in some 3COM (formerly U.S. Robotics) internal modems have a quirk that can cause trouble for unwary communications programs. This UART is a 16550 type buffered chip, and like all the UARTs in this family, it will generate a received data interrupt before the FIFO is full if it times out waiting for a new character. When this happens, the US Robotics UART generates an RX Data interrupt, but it doesn't turn on the Data Ready bit in the Line Status Register.

This can be confusing to a naïve Interrupt Service Routine. In general, you would expect that the Data Ready bit would *always* be set if there was incoming data to be read. Instead, to accommodate this bug, you need to assume that if an RX Data interrupt occurs, there is at least one valid byte in the input FIFO, regardless of whether the Data Ready bit is set or not.

The Standard COM Card

The standard IBM-compatible communications card has few surprises. The original card developed by IBM was an exercise in minimalism, offering as little supporting functionality as possible in order to let the 8250 do its job. The card supported the standard RS-232 input and output lines, an 8-bit interface between the AT I/O bus and the UART registers, and added support for an interrupt line.

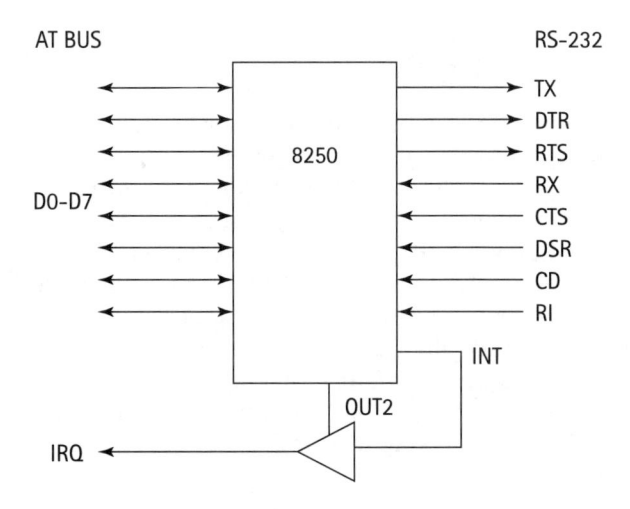

Figure 3-2: The IBM COM card

For various reasons (discussed in Chapter 1), the IBM COM card design has not changed for 10 years or so. The COM card in most systems sold today is electrically identical to the one used in 1982, with a possible UART upgrade to the pin-compatible 16550. The only real improvements have been in reduced manufacturing costs.

Laptop oddities

Makers of notebook and laptop computers have had major difficulties with the standard COM card. For the designers of these machines, the sun rises and sets around power consumption. Because of this, most of the parts used in portable computers are of the CMOS variety, known for very low power consumption. However, early designers of portable computers did not have CMOS versions of 8250-compatible UARTs available. Some portable machine designers, such as those at Data General, were brave enough to use nonstandard UARTs. Needless to say, these machines are no longer being manufactured.

The next best alternative was to include circuitry that kept the COM card in a powered-down state most of the time, only turning on power to the UART when given special commands. Before using communications software users had to invoke special power management commands to power up the UART. This compromise seems to have been effective, and most laptops today have the ability to control power to internal UARTs.

To the COM programmer, this situation presents something of a dilemma. No standard commands exist to universally power up and turn off these laptop COM cards. This means that users have to be savvy enough to encapsulate their COM programs with batch files or other software that manages the power. Unfortunately, for most laptop users this is out of the question. So, COM software often runs into difficulties on laptops.

How interrupts work on the PC

Probably the single greatest fear that keeps people from working with PC communications software is that of interrupts. Writing an Interrupt Service Routine takes a programmer a step deeper than normal applications programming. An ISR has to work directly with hardware in an environment very unforgiving of mistakes.

Despite these obstacles, *every* PC programmer can write and use a simple ISR to service 8250 family UARTs. The ISR developed in the last half of this chapter will be somewhat more complex than the ISR you would write the first time around, but it is still relatively straightforward. And although any programmer can make mistakes, virtually nothing can go wrong in this ISR that can't be fixed by judicious application of the front panel reset switch. As long as you save your source frequently, you have nothing to fear from working with an ISR.

Hardware basics

Like most microprocessors, the Intel 80x86 family has built-in support for interrupts. If you look at the hardware data sheet for the 8088 (the IBM world's first brush with Intel), you will see a pair of pins labeled INTR and INTA. These two pins are more properly referred to as *Interrupt Request* and *Interrupt Acknowledge*. With the proper hardware in place, these two pins allow an external piece of hardware to interrupt the processor and so to save its current state and go off to manage some time-critical task.

Most computers, however, must manage more than a single source of interrupts. The IBM PC family started with support for eight external interrupt sources and expanded that number to 16 with the introduction of the AT. Even before adding any external peripherals, many of these interrupt sources are taken up by standard equipment: the timer tick, keyboard interrupt, floppy and hard disk controller, and so on.

The addition of a part known as the 8259 Programmable Interrupt Controller (PIC) lends support to these various interrupt sources. This chip accepts up to eight external interrupt sources and manages them so that the 80x86 CPU doesn't have to. The 8259 takes care of prioritizing external interrupts and presenting them to the processor in an orderly fashion. The 8259 won't let lower-priority interrupts interfere with higher-priority ones, and it won't let an interrupt interrupt itself.

The 8259 was developed well before the 8088 began its quest to take over the world. It supports several different modes of operation, designed to support different families of CPUs. The original designers of the hardware and BIOS for the IBM PC had to choose from several possible implementations of interrupts on their machines. Unfortunately for all of us, they elected to use edge-triggered interrupts.

Edge-triggered interrupts differ from conventional level-triggered interrupts in precisely the way their names imply. On the IBM PC, the 8259 operates in edge-triggered mode. This means that the PIC will consider an interrupt to be valid only when the interrupt line makes the transition from a logic 0 to a logic 1. Had the PC designers chosen to use level-triggered mode, the 8259 would consider a line to be interrupting any time the interrupt line is asserted.

I find the choice of edge-triggered interrupts less than desirable because it essentially mandates against the use of shared interrupt lines on the standard PC architecture. There is a relatively simple solution for the electrical problem of having multiple cards all driving the same line. Using an *open collector* configuration, any number of cards can drive the same interrupt line. In this configuration, sometimes referred to as a *wired OR,* any card that tries to assert the interrupt line will bring it high. The cards that are not driving the line high will not try to pull the interrupt line low.

In the open collector scheme, the interrupt controller would simply generate an interrupt any time the interrupt line was active. One card might be trying to interrupt the CPU, or five cards might. The BIOS and the interrupt servers must check every device attached to the line for service requirements.

In edge-triggered mode, the wired-OR configuration simply won't work. Figure 3-3 gives a graphical description of the problem. Imagine that two devices were connected to the same IRQ line on the PC bus, using an open collector configuration. If the first device initiated an interrupt, it would raise its interrupt line, and the CPU would initiate the interrupt service routine. So far, things would be working properly.

```
Device 1 IRQ ____|‾‾‾‾‾‾‾‾‾‾‾‾‾‾
Device 1 IRQ _____|‾‾‾‾‾|____
Interrupt Service
   Routine Starts
Interrupt Service
   Routine Ends
```

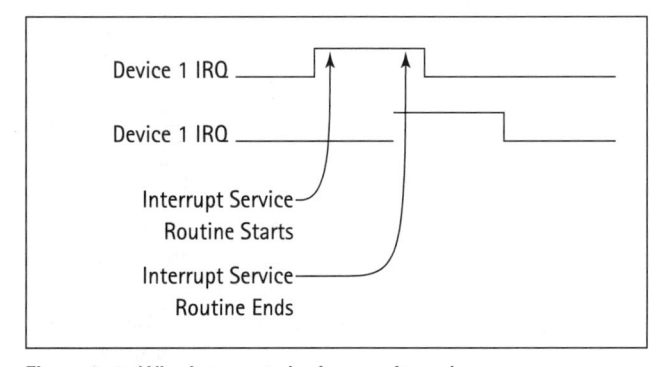

Figure 3-3: Why interrupt sharing won't work

During the course of servicing the first device, the second device might try to initiate another interrupt. Unfortunately, the interrupt line is already high, so when the second device raises the line, it just remains high. Because the 8259 on the PC requires a transition from low to high in order to generate an interrupt, nothing happens.

Of course, on the PC, you never come this close to sharing interrupts anyway. Peripheral cards designed for the PC don't use open collector drivers; they use standard TTL outputs to drive the bus. Because of this, if two devices were trying to use the same line as in Figure 3-3, they would clash, and the voltage levels on the bus would probably be invalid, leading to unpredictable results.

This affects communications programmers when attempting working with COM1 and COM3 or COM2 and COM4 simultaneously. The only way to get this to work on the PC is to operate one of the ports in polled mode. It just can't be done properly with both cards in interrupt mode, despite occasional reports to the contrary.

IBM saw the light when it developed the Micro Channel architecture. MCA machines were able to share interrupts, which meant that IBM could offer eight standard COM ports without adding additional interrupt lines. The demise of the Micro Channel product line illustrates the point that just making good architectural decisions doesn't guarantee market success.

PC8250 Driver Structure

The remainder of this chapter discusses the implementation of the PC8250 class. PC8250 is a class derived from class RS232 and is designed to work with various types of hardware that use this UART. In this chapter, the PC8250 class will interface with standard IBM COM cards. In the next chapter, I use the same class to interface with nonintelligent multiport boards.

The interrupt service routine

A fairly sizable body of code makes up the PC8250 class. It is a fully featured class derived from RS232, so it supports quite a few virtual functions. However, to really understand this class, you must understand the ISR.

As I state earlier in this chapter, the 8250 family of UARTs has four different interrupts. This particular class will be using all four types of interrupts: the Transmit Holding Register Empty interrupt, the Receive Data interrupt, the Modem Status interrupt, and the Line Status Interrupt.

The ISR is essentially four tightly packed subroutines, each handling its own type of interrupt. These routines will need to run and terminate in the shortest possible time, so as not to tie up the system with a lot of interrupt overhead. Most of the work done during the interrupt service routine consists of modifying elements in a data structure that is a subset of the PC8250 class.

Listing 3-1 shows the header file that contains the definitions for the PC8250 class. To understand how this class operates, you must understand the struct isr_data definition. This conventional C structure contains the information used by the interrupt service routine when processing an interrupt for a given port. After you understand how the interrupt service routine manipulates the data in that structure, you will be able to follow the rest of the support code for this particular class.

Listing 3-1: PC8250.H

```
//
//  PC8250.H
//
//  Source code from:
//
//  Serial Communications Developer's Guide, 2nd Edition
//  by Mark Nelson, IDG Books, 1999
//
//  Please see the book for information on usage.
//
//  This header file has all of the definitions and prototypes
//  needed to use the PC8250 class.  This file should be included
```

```cpp
//  by any code that needs to access this class.  For an example,
//  see the PC8250 test program, TEST232.CPP.
//

#ifndef _PC8250_DOT_H
#define _PC8250_DOT_H

#include "rs232.h"
#include "queue.h"
#include "pcirq.h"
#include "_8250.h"

// A few type definitions used with this class.

enum PC8250Error {
        PC8250_UART_NOT_FOUND        = RS232_NEXT_FREE_ERROR,
        PC8250_NEXT_FREE_ERROR,
        PC8250_HANDSHAKE_LINE_IN_USE = RS232_NEXT_FREE_WARNING,
        PC8250_NEXT_FREE_WARNING };

enum UARTType { UART_8250, UART_16550, UART_UNKNOWN };

enum handshaking_bits {  dtr_dsr = 1, rts_cts = 2, xon_xoff = 4 };

class PC8250;

// The ISR data is contained in a conventional C structure instead of
// a class.  The ISR is much easier to work with as a normal C function
// instead of a member function, and as such it wants to work with
// structures instead of classes.

struct isr_data_block {
    int uart;
    UARTType uart_type;
    volatile int overflow;
    volatile int tx_running;
    volatile unsigned int rx_int_count;
    volatile unsigned int tx_int_count;
    volatile unsigned int ms_int_count;
    volatile unsigned int ls_int_count;
    volatile unsigned int line_status;
    unsigned int handshaking;
    volatile unsigned int blocking;
    volatile unsigned int blocked;
```

Chapter 3: The PC8250 Class 131

```cpp
        volatile int send_handshake_char;
        volatile unsigned int modem_status;
        Queue TXQueue;
        Queue RXQueue;
};

// The Handler class is used when multiple ports share an
// interrupt, such as on a multiport board or a Microchannel bus.

class Handler {
    public :
        virtual RS232Error AddPort( RS232PortName port_name,
                                    struct isr_data_block *data ) = 0;
        virtual void DeletePort( RS232PortName port_name ) = 0;
};

class PC8250 : public RS232
{
    private :
        struct isr_data_block *isr_data;
        enum irq_name irq;
        int interrupt_number;
        int first_debug_output_line;
        int fifo_setting;
        Handler *interrupt_handler;

        void check_uart( void );
        void read_settings( void );
        RS232Error write_settings( void );
        void set_uart_address_and_irq( Handler *handler,
                                       int uart_address,
                                       irq_name irq_line );
        virtual int read_buffer( char *buffer,
                                 unsigned int count );
        virtual int write_buffer( char *buffer,
                                  unsigned int count = -1 );
        virtual int read_byte( void );
        virtual int write_byte( int c );
        void check_rx_handshaking( void );

    public :
        PC8250( enum RS232PortName port_name,
                long baud_rate = UNCHANGED,
                char parity = UNCHANGED,
```

```cpp
                    int word_length = UNCHANGED,
                    int stop_bits = UNCHANGED,
                    int dtr = SET,
                    int rts = SET,
                    int xon_xoff = DISABLE,
                    int rts_cts = DISABLE,
                    int dtr_dsr = DISABLE,
                    Handler *handler = 0,
                    int uart_address = 0,
                    irq_name irq_line = ILLEGAL_IRQ );
        virtual ~PC8250( void );
        virtual RS232Error Set( long baud_rate = UNCHANGED,
                                int parity = UNCHANGED,
                                int word_length = UNCHANGED,
                                int stop_bits = UNCHANGED );
        virtual int TXSpaceFree( void );
        virtual int RXSpaceUsed( void );
        virtual int Break( long milliseconds = 300 );
        virtual int Cd( void );
        virtual int Ri( void );
        virtual int Cts( void );
        virtual int Dsr( void );
        virtual int ParityError( int clear = UNCHANGED );
        virtual int BreakDetect( int clear = UNCHANGED );
        virtual int FramingError( int clear = UNCHANGED );
        virtual int HardwareOverrunError( int clear = UNCHANGED );
        virtual int SoftwareOverrunError( int clear = UNCHANGED );
        virtual int XonXoffHandshaking( int setting = UNCHANGED );
        virtual int RtsCtsHandshaking( int setting = UNCHANGED );
        virtual int DtrDsrHandshaking( int setting = UNCHANGED );
        virtual int Dtr( int setting = UNCHANGED );
        virtual int Rts( int setting = UNCHANGED );
        virtual int PeekBuffer( void *buffer, unsigned int count );
        virtual int RXSpaceFree( void );
        virtual int TXSpaceUsed( void );
        virtual int FlushRXBuffer( void );
        virtual int FlushTXBuffer( void );
        virtual char * ErrorName( int error );
        virtual int FormatDebugOutput( char *buffer = 0,
                                       int line_number = -1 );
};

#endif // #ifndef _PC8250_DOT_H

// *********************** END OF PC8250.H ***********************
```

It may seem odd that I have gone to all the trouble of creating a `PC8250` class and then packed all the ISR data into its own structure. However, I have good reasons for doing so. To have access to all of the protected elements of the `PC8250` class, a function needs to be a member function of class `PC8250`, or a member function of a friend class. With our current implementations of C++, it just isn't easy to have an interrupt service routine operate as member function, because it doesn't have access to the `this` pointer. An even more important concern is that of interfacing to assembly language. One of the natural steps in the refinement of an interrupt service routine is rewriting it in assembly language for speed. By keeping all the data the ISR needs to access in a conventional C structure, it becomes much easier to write assembly language code to access it. Typically, compilers make it fairly easy to access members of ordinary C structures.

The isr_data structure

The `isr_data` structure has 16 data members that completely define the state of the UART as far as the ISR is concerned. A list of these member definitions follows:

`uart:`	This is the address of the 8250 family UART. The ISR and other class member functions need this address to access the UART.
`uart_type:`	The UART can either be an 8250 or a member of the 16550 family. The ISR needs to know what type the UART is so that it can try to use the receive FIFO if it is available.
`overflow:`	This flag is set if a software overflow of the RX buffer occurs.
`tx_running:`	This flag is set when a character is loaded into the Transmitter. It lets the ISR know that it can expect a TX interrupt to occur in the future. After the last character has been transmitted, no more TX interrupts will occur and this flag is cleared.
`rx_int_count:`	This counter keeps track of how many RX interrupts have occurred. This is useful for debugging.
`tx_int_count:`	This counter is used to track how many TX interrupts have occurred.
`ms_int_count:`	This is the third of the four interrupt counter; it keeps a count of how many modem status interrupts have occurred.
`ls_int_count:`	The final counter is used to maintain a count of line status interrupts.

line_status:
Every time a line status interrupt occurs, the status bits are ORed into this word. It can be checked at any time for a cumulative look at the line status bits.

handshaking:
This word has three bits that can be set for the three different types of handshaking. The bits are defined in enum handshaking_bits. They are packed into a word like this so that they can be tested as a group to see whether any form of handshaking is in effect.

blocking:
This word uses the same bits as the handshaking data member to indicate when a particular form of handshaking has been invoked to stop transmission from the remote end.

blocked:
This word uses the same bits as the handshaking data member to indicate when a handshake signal has been received from the remote end blocking us from transmitting.

send_handshake_char:
When an XON or XOFF character needs to be sent, the traditional approach is to either wait for the 8250 to be ready to accept another character, or to stuff the XON or XOFF at the head of the queue. Both of these approaches have problems, so the PC8250 class takes a completely different approach. Each PC8250 object has a special flag word used to indicate when an XON or XOFF needs to be sent. The word is set to −1 when no special protocol characters need to be set, and to the protocol character when one is ready to be transmitted. The TX interrupt handler looks at this word first so as to transmit the handshake character ahead of any active data in the TX buffer.

modem_status:
Every time a modem status interrupt occurs, the modem status data is read into this word. When one of the member functions needs to know the state of the modem status word, it can just check this data member.

TXQueue:
This QUEUE object contains all of the characters queued up for transmission.

RXQueue: This QUEUE object contains all of the characters that have been received but not yet read in by the application program.

Note that you do use C++ objects in the ISR to manipulate the TX and RX Queues. Even though the ISR can't easily be a member function, it has no problem manipulating C++ objects, and this is an example of it. Because most of the member functions for the QUEUE class are defined as inline functions, you should see a good improvement in performance by using C++ rather than C for the ISR.

Most of the data in the isr_data is labeled with the C keyword volatile. This lets the compiler know that those values may be modified by another process, so the compiler can be careful not to count on data being constant. This prevents the compiler from performing certain optimizations that could cause this code not to work.

The remainder of the data members of class PC8250 are defined in the PC8250 class and are not accessed by the ISR. None of them is publicly accessible, so they can be manipulated only by members of class PC8250. They are defined here:

isr_data: This is a pointer to the isr_data structure discussed previously. Each PC8250 object has a single isr_data structure allocated for it, and keeps a pointer to the data here.

irq: The IRQ line the port is attached to.

interrupt_number: The actual interrupt number used on the PC by the IRQ line.

first_debug_output_line: The first line of debug output that is output by the member function of class PC8250. All of the lines smaller than this one will be passed up to class RS232 for definition.

fifo_setting: The trigger level used for the UART if it was a 16550. The default is 14, but heavily loaded systems may want to lower the number.

handler: 8250 UARTs that are sharing an interrupt, such as those on a multiport board, will have a command interrupt handler that dispatches the handlers for individual UARTs. This pointer points to the handler this UART belongs to. If it is a standalone UART that isn't sharing interrupts with any other device, this will be NULL.

Listing 3-2 is a listing of the ISR, found in file `ISR_8250.CPP`. The main entry point for the ISR is near the top of the file, at function `isr_8250()`. This function takes a single argument, which is a pointer to the data structure defined in the `PC8250` class header file. Note that the ISR is called by an ISR manager found in file `PCIRQ.CPP`, which is discussed later in this chapter.

By itself, `isr_8250()` is a very simple function. All it does is sit in a loop, reading the Interrupt ID Register from the UART. As long as a valid interrupt ID is read out of the register, it is processed by one of the four handlers. When the loop finally processes all of the interrupts, the 8250 should drop its interrupt request line, which means the PC's 8259 interrupt controller will recognize the next interrupt as a new one.

One comment in the source code that deserves some attention relates to stack overflow checking. Most C compilers have an option that allows the compiler to generate code at the entry of every routine to check for stack overflow. This works well for the most part, and prevents many problems, but it most emphatically won't work for code inside an ISR. The stack being used while in the ISR is different from what the compiler expects, and this will cause the overflow checking code to get confused. If the error checking causes the program to abort while in the middle of an interrupt, the results are usually catastrophic.

Both Borland and Microsoft have command-line options to turn stack checking on or off. To prevent a user of the `PC8250` class from turning on stack checking in the ISR, I've placed the following special code in `RS232.H`:

```
#ifdef _MSC_VER
# pragma check_stack( off )
#endif

#ifdef __BORLANDC__
# pragma option -N-
#endif
```

These two pragmas will override any option you select in your make file or command line. Note that if you are adapting this code to work with some other 16-bit real-mode compiler, you will need to be sure that stack checking is never inadvertently turned on.

The ISR code

Listings 3-2 through 3-5 are the source listings for files `ISR_8250.CPP`, `_PC8250.H`, `_8250.H`, and `ASCII.H`, respectively. The first file contains all the source code used in the interrupt service routine for the `PC8250` class. The second header file, `_PC8250.H`, is a private header file used by both the main body of the `PC8250` class and the ISR. `_8250.H` contains a set of constants that define all of the registers and bit masks used when communicating with an 8250 class UART. These are stored in a separate file because they are used by many of the other classes developed in this book. Finally, `ASCII.H` contains the definitions for many commonly used ASCII characters. The ISR needs these for the definitions of `XON` and `XOFF`, used with software handshaking.

Listing 3-2: ISR_8250.CPP

```
//
//  ISR_8250.CPP
//
//  Source code from:
//
//  Serial Communications Developer's Guide, 2nd Edition
//  by Mark Nelson, IDG Books, 1999
//
//  Please see the book for information on usage.
//
//  All of the code used in the 8250 interrupt service
//  routine is found in this file.  The Queue class inline
//  functions are pulled in from QUEUE.H

#include <dos.h>
#include "pc8250.h"
#include "_pc8250.h"
#include "ascii.h"

// Prototypes for the internal handlers called by the ISR.

void handle_modem_status_interrupt( struct isr_data_block *data );
void handle_tx_interrupt( struct isr_data_block *data );
void handle_rx_interrupt( struct isr_data_block *data );
```

```c
// This is the main body of the 8250 interrupt handler.  It
// sits in a loop, repeatedly reading the Interrupt ID
// Register, and dispatching a handler based on the
// interrupt type.  The line status interrupt is so simple
// that it doesn't merit its own handler.

void isr_8250( struct isr_data_block * data )
{
    _enable();
    for ( ; ; ) {
        switch( inp( data->uart + INTERRUPT_ID_REGISTER ) & 7 ) {
            case IIR_MODEM_STATUS_INTERRUPT :
                handle_modem_status_interrupt( data );
                break;
            case IIR_TX_HOLDING_REGISTER_INTERRUPT :
                handle_tx_interrupt( data );
                break;
            case IIR_RX_DATA_READY_INTERRUPT :
                handle_rx_interrupt( data );
                break;
            case IIR_LINE_STATUS_INTERRUPT :
                data->ls_int_count++;
                data->line_status |= inp( data->uart + LINE_STATUS_REGISTER );
                break;
            default :
                return;
        }
    }
}

// The modem status interrupt handler has to do three
// things.  It has to handle RTS/CTS handshaking.  It has
// to handle DTR/DSR handshaking, and it has to update the
// modem_status member of the isr_data structure.

void handle_modem_status_interrupt( struct isr_data_block *data )
{
    data->ms_int_count++;
        data->modem_status =
            (unsigned int)
                inp( data->uart + MODEM_STATUS_REGISTER );
    if ( data->handshaking & rts_cts )
        if ( data->modem_status & MSR_DELTA_CTS ) // Has CTS changed?
            if ( data->modem_status & MSR_CTS ) {
```

```
                    if ( data->blocked & rts_cts ) {
                        data->blocked &= ~rts_cts;
                        jump_start( data );
                    }
                } else {
                    if ( !( data->blocked & rts_cts ) )
                        data->blocked |= rts_cts;
                }
    if ( data->handshaking & dtr_dsr )
        if ( data->modem_status & MSR_DELTA_DSR )
            if ( data->modem_status & MSR_DSR ) {
                if ( data->blocked & dtr_dsr ) {
                    data->blocked &= ~dtr_dsr;
                    jump_start( data );
                }
            } else {
                if ( !( data->blocked & dtr_dsr ) )
                    data->blocked |= dtr_dsr;
            }
}

// The TX interrupt is fairly simple.  All it has to do is
// transmit the next character, if one is available.  Depending
// on whether or not a character is available, it will set or
// clear the tx_running member.  Note that here and in
// jump_start(), the handshake_char gets first shot at going
// out.  This is normally an XON or XOFF.

void handle_tx_interrupt( struct isr_data_block *data )
{
    int c;

    data->tx_int_count++;
    if ( data->send_handshake_char >= 0 ) {
        outp( data->uart + TRANSMIT_HOLDING_REGISTER,
                data->send_handshake_char );
        data->send_handshake_char = -1;
    } else if ( data->blocked ) {
        data->tx_running = 0;
    } else {
        c = data->TXQueue.Remove();
        if ( c >= 0 )
            outp( data->uart + TRANSMIT_HOLDING_REGISTER, c );
        else
```

```
            data->tx_running = 0;
        }
    }

// The RX interrupt handler is divided into two nearly
// independent sections.  The first section just reads in the
// character that has just been received and stores it in a
// buffer.  If the UART type is a 16550, up to 16 characters
// might be read in.  The next section of code handles the
// possibility that a handshaking trigger has just occurred,
// modifies any control lines or sends an XOFF as needed.

void handle_rx_interrupt( struct isr_data_block *data )
{
    int c;
    int mcr;
    int lsr;

    data->rx_int_count++;
// The receive data section
    for ( ; ; ) {
        c = inp( data->uart + RECEIVE_BUFFER_REGISTER );
        if ( data->handshaking & xon_xoff ) {
            if ( c == XON ) {
                data->blocked &= ~xon_xoff;
                jump_start( data );
                return;
            } else if ( c == XOFF ) {
                data->blocked |= xon_xoff;
                return;
            }
        }
        if ( !data->RXQueue.Insert( (char) c ) )
            data->overflow = 1;
        if ( data->uart_type == UART_8250 )
            break;
        lsr = inp( data->uart + LINE_STATUS_REGISTER );
        data->line_status |= lsr;
        if ( ( lsr & LSR_DATA_READY ) == 0 )
            break;
    }

// The handshaking section
```

```
        if ( data->handshaking ) {
            if ( data->RXQueue.InUseCount() > HighWaterMark ) {
                if ( ( data->handshaking & rts_cts ) &&
                     !( data->blocking & rts_cts ) ) {
                    mcr = inp( data->uart + MODEM_CONTROL_REGISTER );
                    mcr &= ~MCR_RTS;
                    outp( data->uart + MODEM_CONTROL_REGISTER, mcr );
                    data->blocking |= rts_cts;
                }
                if ( ( data->handshaking & dtr_dsr ) &&
                     !( data->blocking & dtr_dsr ) ) {
                    mcr = inp( data->uart + MODEM_CONTROL_REGISTER );
                    mcr &= ~MCR_DTR;
                    outp( data->uart + MODEM_CONTROL_REGISTER, mcr );
                    data->blocking |= dtr_dsr;
                }
                if ( ( data->handshaking & xon_xoff ) &&
                     !( data->blocking & xon_xoff ) ) {
                    data->blocking |= xon_xoff;
                    if ( data->send_handshake_char == XON ) {
                        data->send_handshake_char = -1;
                    } else {
                        data->send_handshake_char = XOFF;
                        jump_start( data );
                    }
                }
            }
        }
    }
}

// Any time transmit interrupts need to be restarted, this
// routine is called to do the job.  It gets the interrupts
// running again by sending a single character out the TX
// register manually.  When that character is done
// transmitting, the next TX interrupt will start.  The
// tx_running member of the class keeps track of when we can
// expect another TX interrupt and when we can't.

void jump_start( struct isr_data_block *data )
{
    int c;

// Both tx_running and blocked can change behind my back in the
// ISR, so I have to disable interrupts if I want to be able to
```

```
    // count on them.

        _disable();
        if ( !data->tx_running ) {
            if ( ( c = data->send_handshake_char ) != -1 )
                data->send_handshake_char = -1;
            else if ( !data->blocked )
                c = data->TXQueue.Remove();
            if ( c >= 0 ) {
                outp( data->uart, c );
                data->tx_running = 1;
            }
        }
        _enable();
}


// *********************** END OF ISR_8250.CPP ***********************
```

Listing 3-3: _PC8250.H

```
//
//  _PC8250.H
//
//  Source code from:
//
//  Serial Communications Developer's Guide, 2nd Edition
//  by Mark Nelson, IDG Books, 1999
//
//  Please see the book for information on usage.
//
//  This header file provides prototypes for functions that are shared
//  between the PC8250 class and the PC8250 ISR routines.  This header
//  file is only for use by the PC8250 class, not the end user of the
//  class.
//

#ifndef __PC8250_DOT_H
#define __PC8250_DOT_H

void jump_start( struct isr_data_block *data );
void isr_8250( struct isr_data_block * data );

#endif // #ifndef __PC8250_DOT_H


// *********************** END OF _PC8250.H ***********************
```

Listing 3-4: _8250.H

```
//
//    _8250.H
//
//    Source code from:
//
//    Serial Communications Developer's Guide, 2nd Edition
//    by Mark Nelson, IDG Books, 1999
//
//    Please see the book for information on usage.
//

#ifndef __8250_DOT_H
#define __8250_DOT_H

//
// These are the definitions for the 8250 and 16550 UART
// registers.  They are used in both the ISR and the main
// class functions.
//

const int TRANSMIT_HOLDING_REGISTER          = 0x00;
const int RECEIVE_BUFFER_REGISTER            = 0x00;
const int INTERRUPT_ENABLE_REGISTER          = 0x01;
const int    IER_RX_DATA_READY               = 0x01;
const int    IER_TX_HOLDING_REGISTER_EMPTY   = 0x02;
const int    IER_LINE_STATUS                 = 0x04;
const int    IER_MODEM_STATUS                = 0x08;
const int INTERRUPT_ID_REGISTER              = 0x02;
const int    IIR_MODEM_STATUS_INTERRUPT      = 0x00;
const int    IIR_TX_HOLDING_REGISTER_INTERRUPT = 0x02;
const int    IIR_RX_DATA_READY_INTERRUPT     = 0x04;
const int    IIR_LINE_STATUS_INTERRUPT       = 0x06;
const int FIFO_CONTROL_REGISTER              = 0x02;
const int    FCR_FIFO_ENABLE                 = 0x01;
const int    FCR_RCVR_FIFO_RESET             = 0x02;
const int    FCR_XMIT_FIFO_RESET             = 0x04;
const int    FCR_RCVR_TRIGGER_LSB            = 0x40;
const int    FCR_RCVR_TRIGGER_MSB            = 0x80;
const int    FCR_TRIGGER_01                  = 0x00;
const int    FCR_TRIGGER_04                  = 0x40;
const int    FCR_TRIGGER_08                  = 0x80;
const int    FCR_TRIGGER_14                  = 0xc0;
const int LINE_CONTROL_REGISTER              = 0x03;
```

```
    const int   LCR_WORD_LENGTH_MASK        = 0x03;
    const int   LCR_WORD_LENGTH_SELECT_0    = 0x01;
    const int   LCR_WORD_LENGTH_SELECT_1    = 0x02;
    const int   LCR_STOP_BITS               = 0x04;
    const int   LCR_PARITY_MASK             = 0x38;
    const int   LCR_PARITY_ENABLE           = 0x08;
    const int   LCR_EVEN_PARITY_SELECT      = 0x10;
    const int   LCR_STICK_PARITY            = 0x20;
    const int   LCR_SET_BREAK               = 0x40;
    const int   LCR_DLAB                    = 0x80;
    const int MODEM_CONTROL_REGISTER        = 0x04;
    const int   MCR_DTR                     = 0x01;
    const int   MCR_RTS                     = 0x02;
    const int   MCR_OUT1                    = 0x04;
    const int   MCR_OUT2                    = 0x08;
    const int   MCR_LOOPBACK                = 0x10;
    const int LINE_STATUS_REGISTER          = 0x05;
    const int   LSR_DATA_READY              = 0x01;
    const int   LSR_OVERRUN_ERROR           = 0x02;
    const int   LSR_PARITY_ERROR            = 0x04;
    const int   LSR_FRAMING_ERROR           = 0x08;
    const int   LSR_BREAK_DETECT            = 0x10;
    const int   LSR_THRE                    = 0x20;
    const int MODEM_STATUS_REGISTER         = 0x06;
    const int   MSR_DELTA_CTS               = 0x01;
    const int   MSR_DELTA_DSR               = 0x02;
    const int   MSR_TERI                    = 0x04;
    const int   MSR_DELTA_CD                = 0x08;
    const int   MSR_CTS                     = 0x10;
    const int   MSR_DSR                     = 0x20;
    const int   MSR_RI                      = 0x40;
    const int   MSR_CD                      = 0x80;
    const int DIVISOR_LATCH_LOW             = 0x00;
    const int DIVISOR_LATCH_HIGH            = 0x01;


#endif // #ifndef _8250_DOT_H

// ********************* END OF _8250.H *********************
```

Listing 3-5: ASCII.H

```
//
//  ASCII.H
//
```

```
//  Source code from:
//
//  Serial Communications Developer's Guide, 2nd Edition
//  by Mark Nelson, IDG Books, 1999
//
//  Please see the book for information on usage.
//

#ifndef _ASCII_DOT_H
#define _ASCII_DOT_H

const int BS   = 8;
const int LF   = 10;
const int CR   = 13;
const int DLE  = 16;
const int XON  = 17;
const int XOFF = 19;
const int CAN  = 24;
const int ESC  = 27;

#endif // #ifndef _ASCII_DOT_H
// ******************* END OF ASCII.H *******************
```

THE MODEM STATUS INTERRUPT HANDLER

The code that is invoked to handle this type of interrupt is found in routine handle_modem_status_interrupt(). The easy work in this routine is done right away. The MSI counter is incremented, and the current value of the MSR is read in and stored in the isr_data structure used throughout the ISR.

With that job done, the routine can work on the more difficult portion of its job: managing handshaking lines. If either DTR/DSR or RTS/CTS handshaking is in effect, a change in state of those control lines means that the transmitter of the UART will either be blocked or unblocked.

The CTS and DSR code handlers are identical, except for the specific bits that they manipulate. Each routine first checks whether a specific control line has changed by looking at the delta bit in the MSR.

If the appropriate delta bit hasn't changed, the ISR skips over the rest of the handshaking code. If the appropriate line has changed, the next step is to look for a change in state.

If the transmitter is already in a blocked state and the status line has just gone high, a change of state has occurred. To go from blocked to unblocked, the ISR must do two things. First, it needs to clear the appropriate bit in the blocked data member. Second, it must call the jump_start() routine. If conditions are right, `jump_start()` restarts transmit interrupts, meaning that no blocking states exist and there is data to be transmitted.

If the transmitter isn't blocked and the status line goes low, the state has changed in the opposite direction. The routine has only set the appropriate bit in the `blocked` data member. The next time a transmit interrupt occurs, the transmit routine takes note of the blocked state and shuts down interrupts.

THE TX INTERRUPT HANDLER

The TX interrupt handler has only a few decisions to make. First, it checks to see whether a handshake character needs to be sent. Any time another routine in either the main class or the ISR needs to send a handshake character, it stuffs the character into the `send_handshake_char` data element. When the TX interrupt handler executes, it checks to see whether `send_handshake_char` contains a character (a value of -1 means no character). If a character is found there, the TX interrupt handler sends it out immediately and the handler exits.

If there is no handshake character to be sent, the transmit handler next checks to see whether it is in a blocked state. If so, transmit interrupts are shut down, signified by the `tx_running` data member being set to 0, and an exit is taken.

If the `blocked` data member is clear, none of the three handshaking modes is in effect and the transmitter is free to send any available characters. The `Remove()` member function of the `TXQueue` object is called to remove any characters that are waiting for transmission. If one is successfully removed from the queue, it is transmitted and the routine exits. If there aren't any characters waiting to be transmitted, the `tx_running` element is cleared to indicate that no more Transmit Interrupts can be expected, and the handler exits.

The important thing to remember about the transmitter interrupt is that although it is always enabled, it becomes quiescent if a TX interrupt occurs and the transmitter is not reloaded with a new character. This state is indicated by the `tx_running` data member being set to 0. After this is set to 0, starting interrupts up again requires a call to `jump_start()` to get things going again (`jump_start()` is very similar in structure to the transmit interrupt handler).

THE RECEIVE INTERRUPT HANDLER

The receive interrupt handler is the longest of the four handlers. It has chores to handle for both directions of handshaking in addition to receiving the data, so it ends up occupying more lines of code than any of the other interrupt routines.

After incrementing its interrupt counter, the receive handler first goes into a loop where it reads in all of the characters pending in the UART. For a normal 8250, this means just reading in a single character. For a 16550, the FIFO could contain as many as 16 characters. If the UART is in the 16550 family, the routine checks the Line Status Register at the end of the loop to see whether the `LSR_DATA_READY` bit is still set. If it is, another character is read in from the Receive Buffer Register.

While in the receive loop, the interrupt handler has to perform a couple of additional chores. If the incoming character is an XON or an XOFF, and XON/XOFF handshaking has been enabled, the handler may have to either block or unblock transmission. In addition, nonhandshaking characters must all be placed into the receive buffer and the overflow flag set if this insertion fails.

After all the available characters have been read in and acted on, the receive interrupt handler then has to manage all three types of handshaking. If handshaking is enabled and if the receive buffer is above the high-water mark, each of the three handshaking methods is checked. For the two hardware handshaking methods (RTS/CTS and DTR/DSR), the routine checks to see whether that type of handshaking is enabled and then whether it is not currently blocking. If not, the appropriate modem control line is lowered. Next, the XON/XOFF status is checked. If an XOFF needs to be sent, the blocking bit is set and the handshake character is set to XOFF. Finally, `jump_start()` needs to be called to get transmit interrupts running again, in case they are presently off, and to send the XOFF character, if it was set.

One thing to note about the `send_handshake_char` data member is that it is at least remotely possible that when your receive routine wants to send an XOFF, there is still an XON waiting to be sent. If so, you assume that the remote end is still blocked from a previous XOFF, and you don't send another one. A similar test is performed by the receive interrupt handler when it is time to send an XON during the process of reading characters out of the receive buffer.

THE LINE STATUS HANDLER

The final one of the four interrupt handlers is so short that it doesn't even need its own routine. When an LSI occurs, the current value in the line status register is read out and ORed in with the `line_status` member of the `isr_data` structure. This means that any line status error that occurs will cause the appropriate to be set, and it will remain set until it is cleared by a call to the appropriate `RS232` member function call.

```
jump_start()
```

One additional important piece of code in the ISR routines is the `jump_start()` routine. Both in the ISR and the `PC8250` member functions call `jump_start()` when they need to restart transmit interrupts. It is safe to call `jump_start()` even with transmit interrupts already running; the routine will simply return without doing anything.

The `jump_start()` routine has only to check if the `tx_running` member is already set to be true. If not, that TX interrupt needs to be restarted. To do so, the next character to be transmitted needs to be pushed into the UART transmitter. If a handshake character needs to go out, `jump_start()` sends it immediately. If no handshake character needs to go out, the routine first checks to be sure that none of the three blocked bits is set, and then it tries to pull a character out of the Transmit buffer. If a character is available, it is stuffed into the transmitter and the `tx_running` member is set.

All this must be done under the cover of disabled interrupts. If a member function were to call `jump_start()` and find that `tx_running` was not set, it would be possible to begin the process of restarting interrupts, only to have an incoming modem status interrupt start up the process for you. This could lead to a character being stuffed out into the transmit buffer when it shouldn't be. Wrapping up all the code inside disabled interrupts prevents this from happening. This routine should be able to execute quickly, so having interrupts disabled won't adversely affect system performance.

PC8250.CPP

The source file `PC8250.CPP` (Listing 3-6) contains all the source code to support the use of `class PC8250`. The only code for this class that doesn't show up in this file is the interrupt service routine code that is found in `ISR_8250.CPP`. This source file is relatively long, but most of the code in it is used to develop the small member functions for this class.

The `PC8250.CPP` source code is on the CD-ROM.

Listing 3-6: PC8250.CPP

```
//
//    PC8250.CPP
//
//    Source code from:
//
//    Serial Communications Developer's Guide, 2nd Edition
//    by Mark Nelson, IDG Books, 1999
//
//    Please see the book for information on usage.
//
//    This file contains most of the code used in the PC8250
//    class.  The remainder of the code can be found in
//    ISR_8250.CPP, which has the ISR and its support code.
//

#include <stdio.h>
#include <dos.h>
#include <ctype.h>
#include <conio.h>
```

```c
#include "rs232.h"
#include "pc8250.h"
#include "_pc8250.h"
#include "ascii.h"

// Data used to initialize UART addresses and IRQ lines.

static int Uarts[]          = { 0x3f8,  0x2f8,  0x3e8,  0x2e8 };
static enum irq_name IRQs[] = { IRQ4,   IRQ3,   IRQ4,   IRQ3 };

// This is the one and only constructor for an object of class
// PC8250.  A quick look at PC8250.H will show you that all of
// the parameters in the list except the port have default
// values, so the list isn't as overwhelming as it might look.

PC8250::PC8250( RS232PortName port,
                long baud_rate,
                char parity,
                int word_length,
                int stop_bits,
                int dtr,
                int rts,
                int xon_xoff,
                int rts_cts,
                int dtr_dsr,
                Handler *handler,
                int uart_address,
                irq_name irq_line )
{
    int mcr;

    interrupt_handler = handler;
    port_name = port;
    error_status = RS232_SUCCESS;

// This section of code initializes most of the items in the
// isr_data structure, which contains all of the items used in
// the ISR.

    isr_data = new isr_data_block;
    if ( isr_data == 0 ) {
        error_status = RS232_MEMORY_ALLOCATION_ERROR;
        return;
```

```
    }
    set_uart_address_and_irq( handler, uart_address, irq_line );
    if ( error_status < RS232_SUCCESS )
        return;
    isr_data->overflow = 0;
    isr_data->tx_running = 0;
    isr_data->tx_int_count = 0;
    isr_data->rx_int_count = 0;
    isr_data->ls_int_count = 0;
    isr_data->ms_int_count = 0;
    isr_data->line_status = 0;
    isr_data->handshaking = 0;
    isr_data->blocking = 0;
    isr_data->blocked = 0;
    isr_data->send_handshake_char = -1;

// PC8250 has to share the debug output with the parent
// class.  To determine where our first line starts, we call the
// FormatDebugOutput() function from our parent class.

    first_debug_output_line = RS232::FormatDebugOutput();
    debug_line_count = FormatDebugOutput();

// Determine whether the UART is there and what type it is.

    check_uart();
    if ( error_status < RS232_SUCCESS )
        return;

//  Save all of the old UART settings, and then set it to the
//  new ones passed to the constructor.

    read_settings();
    saved_settings = settings;
    settings.Adjust( baud_rate,
                     parity,
                     word_length,
                     stop_bits,
                     dtr,
                     rts,
                     xon_xoff,
                     rts_cts,
                     dtr_dsr );
    write_settings();
```

// Here we set up the interrupt handler, then turn on
// interrupts. After this code is done the UART will be
// running.

```
    outp( isr_data->uart + INTERRUPT_ENABLE_REGISTER, 0 );
    mcr = inp( isr_data->uart + MODEM_CONTROL_REGISTER );
    mcr |= MCR_OUT2;
    mcr &= ~MCR_LOOPBACK;
    outp( isr_data->uart + MODEM_CONTROL_REGISTER, mcr );
    if ( interrupt_handler == 0 ) {
        error_status = ConnectToIrq( irq,
                                     isr_data, (void (*)(void *))
                                     isr_8250 );
        if ( error_status < RS232_SUCCESS ) {
            outp( isr_data->uart + MODEM_CONTROL_REGISTER, 0 );
            outp( isr_data->uart + INTERRUPT_ENABLE_REGISTER, 0 );
            return;
        }
    } else {
        error_status = interrupt_handler->AddPort( port_name,
                                                   isr_data );
        if ( error_status < RS232_SUCCESS )
            return;
    }
    inp( isr_data->uart );   // Clear any pending interrupts
    inp( isr_data->uart + INTERRUPT_ID_REGISTER );
    _disable();
    isr_data->modem_status =
        (unsigned int)
            inp( isr_data->uart + MODEM_STATUS_REGISTER );
    outp( isr_data->uart + INTERRUPT_ENABLE_REGISTER,
          IER_RX_DATA_READY + IER_TX_HOLDING_REGISTER_EMPTY +
          IER_MODEM_STATUS + IER_LINE_STATUS );
    outp( 0x20, 0xc0 + IRQ3 - 1 );
    _enable();
```

// Finally, set up the last few parameters and exit.

```
    Dtr( settings.Dtr );
    Rts( settings.Rts );
    XonXoffHandshaking( settings.XonXoff );
    RtsCtsHandshaking( settings.RtsCts );
    DtrDsrHandshaking( settings.DtrDsr );
}
```

```cpp
void PC8250::set_uart_address_and_irq( Handler *handler,
                                       int uart_address,
                                       irq_name irq_line )
{

// If I have a handler or have a defined irq_line, I won't
// use the default IRQs.  If I have a uart_address, I won't
// use the default UART address.

    if ( handler == 0 && irq_line == ILLEGAL_IRQ ) {
        if ( port_name > COM4 )
            error_status = RS232_PORT_NOT_FOUND;
        else
            irq = IRQs[ port_name ];
    } else
        irq = irq_line;

    if ( uart_address == 0 ) {
        if ( port_name > COM4 )
            error_status = RS232_PORT_NOT_FOUND;
        else
            isr_data->uart = Uarts[ port_name ];
    } else
        isr_data->uart = uart_address;
}

// The destructor has a much easier time of it than the
// constructor.  It disables interrupts, then restores the line
// settings of the UART.

PC8250::~PC8250( void )
{
    if ( error_status == RS232_SUCCESS ) {
        outp( isr_data->uart + INTERRUPT_ENABLE_REGISTER, 0 );
        outp( isr_data->uart + MODEM_CONTROL_REGISTER, 0 );
        if ( interrupt_handler == 0 )
            DisconnectFromIRQ( irq );
        else
            interrupt_handler->DeletePort( port_name );
        settings = saved_settings;
        write_settings();
        Dtr( settings.Dtr );
        Rts( settings.Rts );
    }
```

```
    if ( isr_data != 0 )
        delete isr_data;
}

// This routine determines if a UART is present, and if so,
// whether or not it is a 16550.  If it is a 16550, the FIFO is
// enabled with a trigger at 14 bytes.

void PC8250::check_uart( void )
{
    int temp;

    outp( isr_data->uart + FIFO_CONTROL_REGISTER, 0 );
    temp = inp( isr_data->uart + INTERRUPT_ID_REGISTER );
    if ( ( temp & 0xf8 ) != 0 ) {
        isr_data->uart_type = UART_UNKNOWN;
        error_status = RS232_PORT_NOT_FOUND;
        return;
    }
    outp( isr_data->uart + FIFO_CONTROL_REGISTER,
            FCR_FIFO_ENABLE + FCR_TRIGGER_14 );
    temp = inp( isr_data->uart + INTERRUPT_ID_REGISTER );
    if ( ( temp & 0xf8 ) == 0xc0 ) {
        isr_data->uart_type = UART_16550;
        fifo_setting = 14;
    } else {
        isr_data->uart_type = UART_8250;
        fifo_setting = 0;
        outp( isr_data->uart + FIFO_CONTROL_REGISTER, 0 );
    }
}

// After any function that reads data from the ISR buffers,
// this routine is called.  If the read operation dropped us
// below a handshaking trigger point, this routine will figure
// out what action to take.

void PC8250::check_rx_handshaking()
{
    int mcr;

// Take a quick exit if we aren't handshaking, blocking, or if
// the RX Queue is not below the low-water mark.
```

```
        if ( !isr_data->handshaking || !isr_data->blocking )
            return;
        if ( isr_data->RXQueue.InUseCount() > LowWaterMark )
            return;

    // If RTS/CTS handshaking is in effect, I raise RTS.

        if ( ( isr_data->handshaking & rts_cts ) &&
             ( isr_data->blocking & rts_cts ) ) {
            _disable();
            mcr = inp( isr_data->uart + MODEM_CONTROL_REGISTER );
            mcr |= MCR_RTS;
            outp( isr_data->uart + MODEM_CONTROL_REGISTER, mcr );
            isr_data->blocking &= ~rts_cts;
            _enable();
        }

    // If DTR/DSR handshaking is in effect, I raise DTR.

        if ( ( isr_data->handshaking & dtr_dsr ) &&
             ( isr_data->blocking & dtr_dsr ) ) {
            _disable();
            mcr = inp( isr_data->uart + MODEM_CONTROL_REGISTER );
            mcr |= MCR_DTR;
            outp( isr_data->uart + MODEM_CONTROL_REGISTER, mcr );
            isr_data->blocking &= ~dtr_dsr;
            _enable();
        }

    // If XON/XOFF is in effect, I send an XON.  Note that if
    // there is a pending XOFF that never made it out, I cancel it
    // and don't send anything else.

        if ( ( isr_data->handshaking & xon_xoff ) &&
             ( isr_data->blocking & xon_xoff ) ) {
            _disable();
            isr_data->blocking &= ~xon_xoff;
            if ( isr_data->send_handshake_char == XOFF )
                isr_data->send_handshake_char = -1;
            else {
                isr_data->send_handshake_char = XON;
                jump_start( isr_data );
            }
            _enable();
```

```
    }
}

// This routine just pulls out a byte and checks for
// handshaking activity.

int PC8250::read_byte( void )
{
    int c;

    if ( error_status < 0 )
        return error_status;
    c = isr_data->RXQueue.Remove();
    if ( c < 0 )
        return RS232_TIMEOUT;
    check_rx_handshaking();
    return c;
}

// When sending a byte to the output buffer, I have to check
// to see if the TX interrupt system needs to be restarted.

int PC8250::write_byte( int c )
{
    if ( error_status < 0 )
        return error_status;
    if ( !isr_data->TXQueue.Insert( (unsigned char) c ) )
        return RS232_TIMEOUT;
    if ( !isr_data->tx_running && !isr_data->blocked )
        jump_start( isr_data );
    return RS232_SUCCESS;
}

// read_buffer() pulls in only as many bytes as are
// immediately available.  Any high-level functions such as
// timing out or looking for a terminator are handled by one of
// the higher level Read() routines from class RS232.

int PC8250::read_buffer( char *buffer, unsigned int count )
{
    ByteCount = 0;
    if ( error_status < 0 )
        return error_status;
    while ( isr_data->RXQueue.InUseCount() ) {
```

```
            if ( count <= 0 )
                break;
            *buffer++ = (char) isr_data->RXQueue.Remove();
            count--;
            ByteCount++;
        }
        *buffer = '\0';
        if ( ByteCount > 0 )
            check_rx_handshaking();
        if ( count > 0 )
            return RS232_TIMEOUT;
        else
            return RS232_SUCCESS;
    }

// write_buffer() sends as many characters as the buffer can
// immediately manage.  Like read_buffer(), it relies on higher
// level routines from class RS232 to perform the nicer functions
// such as adding termination, timing, etc.

int PC8250::write_buffer( char *buffer, unsigned int count )
{
    ByteCount = 0;
    if ( error_status < 0 )
        return error_status;
    for ( ; ; ) {
        if ( count == 0 )
            break;
        if ( !isr_data->TXQueue.Insert( *buffer ) )
            break;
        buffer++;
        count--;
        ByteCount++;
    }
    if ( !isr_data->tx_running && !isr_data->blocked )
        jump_start( isr_data );
    if ( count > 0 )
        return RS232_TIMEOUT;
    else
        return RS232_SUCCESS;
}

// The Queue functions make it easy to flush the RX queue.
// After emptying it all, we need to be sure that handshaking
```

```c
// gets managed.

int PC8250::FlushRXBuffer( void )
{
    if ( error_status < RS232_SUCCESS )
        return error_status;
    _disable();
    isr_data->RXQueue.Clear();
    _enable();
    check_rx_handshaking();
    return RS232_SUCCESS;

}

// write_settings() is a protected routine called by the
// constructor and the public Set() function.  It is long and
// stringy, mostly because setting up the UART is just a long
// case of setting or clearing bits in control registers.  It
// might be possible to modularize this code, but it wouldn't be
// particularly useful.

RS232Error PC8250::write_settings( void )
{
    int lcr;
    int divisor_high;
    int divisor_low;
    RS232Error status = RS232_SUCCESS;
    long result_baud;

    if ( settings.BaudRate <= 0 || settings.BaudRate > 115200L ) {
        settings.BaudRate = 9600;
        status = RS232_ILLEGAL_BAUD_RATE;
    }
    divisor_low = (int) ( ( 115200L / settings.BaudRate ) & 0xff );
    divisor_high = (int) ( ( 115200L / settings.BaudRate ) > 8 );
    result_baud = 115200L / ( 115200L / settings.BaudRate );
    if ( result_baud != settings.BaudRate ) {
        settings.BaudRate = result_baud;
        status = RS232_ILLEGAL_BAUD_RATE;
    }
    lcr = inp( isr_data->uart + LINE_CONTROL_REGISTER );
    lcr |= LCR_DLAB;
    _disable();
    outp( isr_data->uart + LINE_CONTROL_REGISTER, lcr );
```

```c
            outp( isr_data->uart + DIVISOR_LATCH_LOW, divisor_low );
            outp( isr_data->uart + DIVISOR_LATCH_HIGH, divisor_high );
            lcr &= ~LCR_DLAB;
            outp( isr_data->uart + LINE_CONTROL_REGISTER, lcr );
            _enable();
            lcr &= ~LCR_PARITY_MASK;
            switch ( toupper( settings.Parity ) ) {
                case 'O' :
                    lcr |= LCR_PARITY_ENABLE;
                    break;
                case 'E' :
                    lcr |= LCR_PARITY_ENABLE + LCR_EVEN_PARITY_SELECT;
                    break;
                case 'M' :
                    lcr |= LCR_PARITY_ENABLE + LCR_STICK_PARITY;
                    break;
                case 'S' :
                    lcr |= LCR_PARITY_ENABLE +
                           LCR_EVEN_PARITY_SELECT +
                           LCR_STICK_PARITY;
                    break;
                default :
                    settings.Parity = 'N';
                    status = RS232_ILLEGAL_PARITY_SETTING;
                case 'N' :
                    break;
            }
            lcr &= ~LCR_WORD_LENGTH_MASK;
            switch ( settings.WordLength ) {
                case 5 :
                    break;
                case 6 :
                    lcr |= LCR_WORD_LENGTH_SELECT_0;
                    break;
                case 7 :
                    lcr |= LCR_WORD_LENGTH_SELECT_1;
                    break;
                default :
                    settings.WordLength = 8;
                    status = RS232_ILLEGAL_WORD_LENGTH;
                case 8 :
                    lcr |= LCR_WORD_LENGTH_SELECT_0 +
                           LCR_WORD_LENGTH_SELECT_1;
                    break;
```

```
        }
        lcr &= ~LCR_STOP_BITS;
        switch ( settings.StopBits ) {
            default :
                settings.StopBits = 1;
                status = RS232_ILLEGAL_STOP_BITS;
            case 1 :
                break;
            case 2 :
                lcr |= LCR_STOP_BITS;
                break;
        }
        outp( isr_data->uart + LINE_CONTROL_REGISTER, lcr );
        return status;
}

// read_settings() is the protected inverse of
// write_settings().  This routine just reads in the state of the
// UART into a settings object.  This is done when the routine
// starts up, so that the RS232 class will always have the saved
// settings available for restoration when the RS232 port is
// closed.

void PC8250::read_settings( void )
{
    int lcr;
    int mcr;
    int divisor_low;
    int divisor_high;

    lcr = inp( isr_data->uart + LINE_CONTROL_REGISTER );
    lcr |= LCR_DLAB;
    _disable();
    outp( isr_data->uart + LINE_CONTROL_REGISTER, lcr );
    divisor_low = inp( isr_data->uart + DIVISOR_LATCH_LOW );
    divisor_high = inp( isr_data->uart + DIVISOR_LATCH_HIGH );
    lcr &= ~LCR_DLAB;
    outp( isr_data->uart + LINE_CONTROL_REGISTER, lcr );
    _enable();

    if ( divisor_high | divisor_low )
        settings.BaudRate =
                115200L / ( ( divisor_high << 8 ) + divisor_low );
    else
```

```
            settings.BaudRate = -1;
    switch ( lcr & LCR_PARITY_MASK ) {
        case LCR_PARITY_ENABLE :
            settings.Parity = 'O';
            break;
        case LCR_PARITY_ENABLE + LCR_EVEN_PARITY_SELECT :
            settings.Parity = 'E';
            break;
        case LCR_PARITY_ENABLE + LCR_STICK_PARITY :
            settings.Parity = 'M';
            break;
        case LCR_PARITY_ENABLE +
              LCR_EVEN_PARITY_SELECT +
              LCR_STICK_PARITY :
            settings.Parity = 'S';
            break;
        default :
            settings.Parity = 'N';
            break;
    }
    switch ( lcr & LCR_WORD_LENGTH_MASK ) {
        case 0 :
            settings.WordLength = 5;
            break;
        case LCR_WORD_LENGTH_SELECT_0 :
            settings.WordLength = 6;
            break;
        case LCR_WORD_LENGTH_SELECT_1 :
            settings.WordLength = 7;
            break;
        case LCR_WORD_LENGTH_SELECT_0 + LCR_WORD_LENGTH_SELECT_1 :
            settings.WordLength = 8;
            break;
    }
    switch ( lcr & LCR_STOP_BITS ) {
        case 0 :
            settings.StopBits = 1;
            break;
        default :
            settings.StopBits = 2;
            break;
    }
    mcr = inp( isr_data->uart + MODEM_CONTROL_REGISTER );
    settings.Dtr = ( mcr & MCR_DTR ) != 0;
```

```
        settings.Rts = ( mcr & MCR_RTS ) != 0;
        settings.XonXoff = -1;
        settings.RtsCts = -1;
        settings.DtrDsr = -1;
}

// Set() takes advantage of code used by the constructor to
// set up some of the UART parameters.

RS232Error PC8250::Set( long baud_rate,
                       int parity,
                       int word_length,
                       int stop_bits )
{
    settings.Adjust( baud_rate,
                     parity,
                     word_length,
                     stop_bits,
                     UNCHANGED,
                     UNCHANGED,
                     UNCHANGED,
                     UNCHANGED,
                     UNCHANGED );
    return write_settings();
}

// This virtual routine is easily handled by a Queue member
// function.

int PC8250::TXSpaceFree( void )
{
    if ( error_status < RS232_SUCCESS )
        return error_status;
    return isr_data->TXQueue.FreeCount();
}

// The same thing is true here.

int PC8250::RXSpaceUsed( void )
{
    if ( error_status < RS232_SUCCESS )
        return error_status;
    return isr_data->RXQueue.InUseCount();
}
```

```c
// The 8250 UART doesn't have an intelligent BREAK function,
// so we have to just sit on the line while the BREAK goes out.
// Hopefully the IdleFunction() can do something useful while
// this takes place.

int PC8250::Break( long milliseconds )
{
    int lcr;
    long timer;

    if ( error_status < RS232_SUCCESS )
        return error_status;
    timer = ReadTime() + milliseconds;
    lcr = inp( isr_data->uart + LINE_CONTROL_REGISTER);
    lcr |= LCR_SET_BREAK;
    outp( isr_data->uart + LINE_CONTROL_REGISTER, lcr );
    while ( ReadTime() < timer )
        IdleFunction();
    lcr &= ~LCR_SET_BREAK;
    outp( isr_data->uart + LINE_CONTROL_REGISTER, lcr );
    return RS232_SUCCESS;
}

// The four modem status functions just check the bits that
// were read in the last time a modem status interrupt took
// place, and return them to the calling routine.

int PC8250::Cd( void )
{
    if ( error_status < RS232_SUCCESS )
        return error_status;
    return ( isr_data->modem_status & MSR_CD ) ? 1 : 0;
}

int PC8250::Ri( void )
{
    if ( error_status < RS232_SUCCESS )
        return error_status;
    return ( isr_data->modem_status & MSR_RI ) ? 1 : 0;
}

int PC8250::Cts( void )
{
    if ( error_status < RS232_SUCCESS )
```

```
        return error_status;
    return ( isr_data->modem_status & MSR_CTS ) ? 1 : 0;
}

int PC8250::Dsr( void )
{
    if ( error_status < RS232_SUCCESS )
        return error_status;
    return ( isr_data->modem_status & MSR_DSR ) ? 1 : 0;
}

// The four line status routines are similar to the modem
// status routines in that they just check a bit in a data
// member.  However, they also have an optional parameter that
// can be used to clear the error flag.  This is just a matter of
// clearing the same bit.

int PC8250::ParityError( int reset )
{
    int return_value;

    if ( error_status < RS232_SUCCESS )
        return error_status;
    return_value =
            ( isr_data->line_status & LSR_PARITY_ERROR ) ? 1 : 0;
    if ( reset != UNCHANGED && reset != 0 ) {
        _disable();
        isr_data->line_status &= ~LSR_PARITY_ERROR;
        _enable();
    }
    return return_value;
}

int PC8250::BreakDetect( int reset )
{
    int return_value;

    if ( error_status < RS232_SUCCESS )
        return error_status;
    return_value =
        ( isr_data->line_status & LSR_BREAK_DETECT ) ? 1 : 0;
    if ( reset != UNCHANGED && reset != 0 ) {
        _disable();
        isr_data->line_status &= ~LSR_BREAK_DETECT;
```

```cpp
        _enable();
    }
    return return_value;
}

int PC8250::FramingError( int reset )
{
    int return_value;

    if ( error_status < RS232_SUCCESS )
        return error_status;
    return_value =
        ( isr_data->line_status & LSR_FRAMING_ERROR ) ? 1 : 0;
    if ( reset != UNCHANGED && reset != 0 ) {
        _disable();
        isr_data->line_status &= ~LSR_FRAMING_ERROR;
        _enable();
    }
    return return_value;
}

int PC8250::HardwareOverrunError( int reset )
{
    int return_value;

    if ( error_status < RS232_SUCCESS )
        return error_status;
    return_value =
        ( isr_data->line_status & LSR_OVERRUN_ERROR ) ? 1 : 0;
    if ( reset != UNCHANGED && reset != 0 ) {
        _disable();
        isr_data->line_status &= ~LSR_OVERRUN_ERROR;
        _enable();
    }
    return return_value;
}

// This just reads in the status bit from the isr_data
// structure, and optionally clears it.

int PC8250::SoftwareOverrunError( int clear )
{
    int temp = isr_data->overflow;
    if ( clear ) {
```

```c
            _disable();
            isr_data->overflow = 0;
            _enable();
        }
        return temp;
}


// The three handshaking functions all have approximately the
// same mode of operation.  If the setting parameter is set to
// UNCHANGED, they just return a boolean indicating whether or
// not handshaking is in effect.  If handshaking is being turned
// on or off, things become a little more complicated.  The
// major complication is that after setting the bits needed by
// the ISR to handshake, they also have to take action to make
// sure the control lines and XON/XOFF output are where they need
// to be to accurately get things started.

int PC8250::XonXoffHandshaking( int setting )
{
    if ( setting != UNCHANGED ) {
        if ( setting )
            isr_data->handshaking |= xon_xoff;
        else {
            isr_data->handshaking &= ~xon_xoff;
            isr_data->blocked &= ~xon_xoff;
// If blocking, I need to send an XON
            if ( isr_data->blocking & xon_xoff ) {
                _disable();
                if ( isr_data->send_handshake_char == -1 )
                    isr_data->send_handshake_char = XON;
                else
                    isr_data->send_handshake_char = -1;
                _enable();
            }
          // Restart TX if I was blocked, or have to send and XON
            jump_start( isr_data );
            isr_data->blocking &= ~xon_xoff;
        }
        settings.XonXoff = ( setting != 0 );
    }
    return( ( isr_data->handshaking & xon_xoff ) != 0 );
}

int PC8250::RtsCtsHandshaking( int setting )
```

```c
{
    int old_setting;

    if ( setting != UNCHANGED ) {
        old_setting = isr_data->handshaking & rts_cts;
        isr_data->handshaking &= ~rts_cts;
        isr_data->blocking &= ~rts_cts;
        isr_data->blocked &= ~rts_cts;
        if ( setting ) {
            Rts( 1 );
            _disable();
            if ( ( isr_data->modem_status & MSR_CTS ) == 0 )
                isr_data->blocked |= rts_cts;
            isr_data->handshaking |= rts_cts;
            _enable();
            settings.Rts = REMOTE_CONTROL;
        } else {
            if ( old_setting )
                Rts( 1 );  //If handshaking to go off, set RTS high
            if ( isr_data->blocked == 0 )
                jump_start( isr_data );
        }
        settings.RtsCts = ( setting != 0 );
    }
    return( ( isr_data->handshaking & rts_cts ) != 0 );
}

int PC8250::DtrDsrHandshaking( int setting )
{
    int old_setting;

    if ( setting != UNCHANGED ) {
        old_setting = isr_data->handshaking & dtr_dsr;
        isr_data->handshaking &= ~dtr_dsr;
        isr_data->blocking &= ~dtr_dsr;
        isr_data->blocked &= ~dtr_dsr;
        if ( setting ) {
            Dtr( 1 );
            _disable();
            if ( ( isr_data->modem_status & MSR_DSR ) == 0 )
                isr_data->blocked |= dtr_dsr;
            isr_data->handshaking |= dtr_dsr;
            _enable();
            settings.Dtr = REMOTE_CONTROL;
```

```
            } else {
                if ( old_setting )
                    Dtr( 1 );  //If turning handshaking off, set RTS high
                if ( isr_data->blocked == 0 )
                    jump_start( isr_data );
            }
            settings.DtrDsr = ( setting != 0 );
        }
        return( ( isr_data->handshaking & dtr_dsr ) != 0 );
}

// Just reading the state of the control line is relatively
// easy.  The setting returned is just the stored value in the
// settings element.  However, both of the next two routines have
// to handle setting or clearing the line as well.  This only
// gets complicated if handshaking is turned on.  If it is, these
// routines refuse to play with the control lines.

int PC8250::Dtr( int setting )
{
    int mcr;

    if ( setting != UNCHANGED ) {
        if ( isr_data->handshaking & dtr_dsr )
            return PC8250_HANDSHAKE_LINE_IN_USE;
        else {
            settings.Dtr = setting;
            _disable();
            mcr = inp( isr_data->uart + MODEM_CONTROL_REGISTER );
            if ( setting )
                mcr |= MCR_DTR;
            else
                mcr &= ~MCR_DTR;
            outp( isr_data->uart + MODEM_CONTROL_REGISTER, mcr );
            _enable();
        }
    }
    return settings.Dtr;
}

int PC8250::Rts( int setting )
{
    int mcr;
```

```cpp
        if ( setting != UNCHANGED ) {
            if ( isr_data->handshaking & rts_cts )
                return PC8250_HANDSHAKE_LINE_IN_USE;
            else {
                settings.Rts = setting;
                _disable();
                mcr = inp( isr_data->uart + MODEM_CONTROL_REGISTER );
                if ( setting )
                    mcr |= MCR_RTS;
                else
                    mcr &= ~MCR_RTS;
                outp( isr_data->uart + MODEM_CONTROL_REGISTER, mcr );
                _enable();
            }
        }
        return settings.Rts;
}

// PeekBuffer uses the class Queue function to read as many
// bytes as possible from the RXBuffer.

int PC8250::PeekBuffer( void *buffer, unsigned int count )
{
    if ( error_status < RS232_SUCCESS )
        return error_status;
    ByteCount =
        isr_data->RXQueue.Peek( (unsigned char *) buffer, count );
    ( (char *) buffer )[ ByteCount ] = '\0';
    return RS232_SUCCESS;
}

// The next two functions just return a count using a Queue
// class primitive function.

int PC8250::RXSpaceFree( void )
{
    if ( error_status < RS232_SUCCESS )
        return error_status;
    return isr_data->RXQueue.FreeCount();
}

int PC8250::TXSpaceUsed( void )
{
    if ( error_status < RS232_SUCCESS )
```

```
        return error_status;
    return isr_data->TXQueue.InUseCount();
}

// Flushing the TX buffer is easy when using the Queue class
// primitive.

int PC8250::FlushTXBuffer( void )
{
    if ( error_status < RS232_SUCCESS )
        return error_status;
    _disable();
    isr_data->TXQueue.Clear();
    _enable();
    return RS232_SUCCESS;
}

// The debug output routine has three possible modes.  If the
// buffer passed to it is a null, it means it should just return
// the total number of lines used by the the output, which is 6
// plus the number used by the base class.  If the line number
// requested is less than where we start, the request is passed
// up the line to the base class.  Finally, if it is one of our
// lines, the buffer is formatted and returned to the calling
// routine.

int PC8250::FormatDebugOutput( char *buffer, int line_number )
{
    if ( buffer == 0 )
        return( first_debug_output_line +  6 );
    if ( line_number < first_debug_output_line )
        return RS232::FormatDebugOutput( buffer, line_number );
    switch( line_number - first_debug_output_line ) {
        case 0 :
            sprintf( buffer,
                    "Derived class: PC8250    "
                    "UART: %04x  "
                    "Overflow: %1d  "
                    "TX Running: %1d  "
                    "Line Status: %02x",
                    isr_data->uart,
                    ( isr_data->overflow ) ? 1 : 0,
                    ( isr_data->tx_running ) ? 1 : 0,
                    isr_data->line_status );
```

```
            break;
        case 1 :
            sprintf( buffer,
                    "TX Head, Tail, Count %4d %4d %4d "
                    "RX Head,Tail,Count %4d %4d %4d",
                    isr_data->TXQueue.Head(),
                    isr_data->TXQueue.Tail(),
                    isr_data->TXQueue.InUseCount(),
                    isr_data->RXQueue.Head(),
                    isr_data->RXQueue.Tail(),
                    isr_data->RXQueue.InUseCount() );
            break;
        case 2 :
          sprintf( buffer,
                    "Counts: TX: %5u   RX: %5u   MS: %5u   LS: %5u  "
                    "CTS/DSR/RI/CD: %d%d%d%d",
                    isr_data->tx_int_count,
                    isr_data->rx_int_count,
                    isr_data->ms_int_count,
                    isr_data->ls_int_count,
                    ( isr_data->modem_status & MSR_CTS ) ? 1 : 0,
                    ( isr_data->modem_status & MSR_DSR ) ? 1 : 0,
                    ( isr_data->modem_status & MSR_RI ) ? 1 : 0,
                    ( isr_data->modem_status & MSR_CD ) ? 1 : 0 );
            break;
        case 3 :
            sprintf( buffer,
                    "Handshake DTR/RTS/XON : %d%d%d   "
                    "Blocking: %d%d%d   "
                    "Blocked: %d%d%d   "
                    "Handshake char: %04x",
                    ( isr_data->handshaking & dtr_dsr ) ? 1 : 0,
                    ( isr_data->handshaking & rts_cts ) ? 1 : 0,
                    ( isr_data->handshaking & xon_xoff ) ? 1 : 0,
                    ( isr_data->blocking & dtr_dsr ) ? 1 : 0,
                    ( isr_data->blocking & rts_cts ) ? 1 : 0,
                    ( isr_data->blocking & xon_xoff ) ? 1 : 0,
                    ( isr_data->blocked & dtr_dsr ) ? 1 : 0,
                    ( isr_data->blocked & rts_cts ) ? 1 : 0,
                    ( isr_data->blocked & xon_xoff ) ? 1 : 0,
                    isr_data->send_handshake_char );
            break;
        case 4 :
          sprintf( buffer,
```

```c
                        "Parity Err: %d   "
                        "Break Det: %d   "
                        "Overrun Err: %d  "
                        "Framing Err: %d  "
                        "FIFO Setting: %2d",
                        ( isr_data->line_status & LSR_PARITY_ERROR )
                            ? 1 : 0,
                        ( isr_data->line_status & LSR_BREAK_DETECT )
                            ? 1 : 0,
                        ( isr_data->line_status & LSR_OVERRUN_ERROR )
                            ? 1 : 0,
                        ( isr_data->line_status & LSR_FRAMING_ERROR )
                            ? 1 : 0,
                        fifo_setting );
            break;
        case 5 :
            char *uart_name;
            switch( isr_data->uart_type ) {
                case UART_8250   : uart_name = "8250";    break;
                case UART_16550  : uart_name = "16550";   break;
                default          : uart_name = "Unknown"; break;
            }
            sprintf( buffer,
                     "Uart type: %-7s",
                     uart_name );
            break;
        default :
            return RS232_ILLEGAL_LINE_NUMBER;
    }
    return RS232_SUCCESS;
}

// Just like the debug format routine, ErrorName has to pass
// most requests up the line to the base class, saving only a few
// for it to respond to.

char * PC8250::ErrorName( int error )
{
    if ( error < RS232_NEXT_FREE_ERROR && error >= RS232_ERROR )
        return RS232::ErrorName( error );
    if (error < RS232_NEXT_FREE_WARNING && error >= RS232_WARNING)
        return RS232::ErrorName( error );
    if ( error >= RS232_SUCCESS )
        return RS232::ErrorName( error );
```

```
    switch ( error ) {
       case PC8250_UART_NOT_FOUND        :
             return( "UART not found" );
       case PC8250_HANDSHAKE_LINE_IN_USE :
             return( "Handshake line in use" );
       default                           :
             return( "Undefined error" );
   }
}
```

PC8250::PC8250()

This class has only a single constructor. This constructor has a formidable argument list, but every argument except the port number has a default value, so the function can actually be used fairly easily. The first argument is the port name, which is found in the enumerated set RS232PortName, defined in RS232.H. The next four arguments are used to set up the initial line state for the UART: baud_rate, parity, word_length, and stop_bits. In each case, these arguments default to the UNCHANGED value, meaning that the current setting will not be changed.

The next two arguments determine the initial setting of DTR and RTS. Normally, most programs will want to set these two lines high, so the default setting for these two parameters is SET. If some program has a reason for wanting to open the port with either of these two parameters UNCHANGED or CLEAR, the parameter can be specified as part of the constructor.

The next three arguments allow for the three different handshaking modes to be initialized to a defined setting. The default values for XON/XOFF, RTS/CTS, and DTR/DSR handshaking is for all three values to be disabled initially.

The last three arguments are used to specify nonstandard UARTs. A handler is an object of a class Handler. A handler is used when multiple ports are sharing a single interrupt, such as when a multiport board is in use. If no handler is specified, the parameter defaults to a value of 0 and control is automatically routed to that port whenever an interrupt occurs. The next chapter of this book looks at some handlers used in different situations.

The uart_address and irq_line parameters should be self-explanatory. They are needed only when a port doesn't adhere to the standard addresses and IRQ lines defined for the IBM PC. If your application is using standard COM ports, your calls to the constructor will omit these two arguments.

Most of the body of PC8250::PC8250() is concerned with initialization of all the data members of both PC8250 and the base class RS232. The first section of code allocates the isr_data structure that is used by the ISR. The various members of this structure are all initialized, with a few opportunities for failures coming into play.

The debug output parameters are determined dynamically. The first line of output for the PC8250 class depends on what the last number for the RS232 class will be. This is calculated by calling the base class version of the `FormatDebugOutput()` routine, using the scoping operator to override the virtual function selection. After you know the first line number for this class, you can calculate the total number for the derived class by calling the `FormatDebugOutput()` routine for this class.

The next section of code performs all the initialization of the UART. First you must identify the UART type by calling `check_uart()`. If no UART is detected, an error exit is taken. To store the current UART settings in the `saved_setting` data member, `read_settings()` is called. The new settings are initialized to the same state and then the parameters passed to the constructor help set up new settings. The new settings are then applied to the UART using the `set_uart_state()` protected member function. And the line parameters are set to those requested when the constructor was called, but the handshaking parameters and control lines are still in an unknown state.

The UART is then hooked to an interrupt handler. By default, `isr_8250()` will handle interrupts for the UART. If another handler was specified, it will be used instead. The `PC8250` object gets passed to the `Handler` object via the virtual `AddPort()` member function. It is up to the `Handler()` routine to establish its own interrupt handler at that point.

After that, all four interrupts in the 8250 UART are enabled, the `modem_status` data member is initialized, and the UART is up and running. A single output to the 8259 interrupt controller is made to lower the priority of the keyboard interrupt. (The default for the PC is to have keyboard interrupts set at a higher priority than the communications ports, exactly the opposite of the way it should be.) Finally, before the constructor exits, DTR and RTS are set appropriately and the three handshaking types are set to their initialized values.

Because a constructor doesn't return a value, you depend on the `error_status` data member to convey a fatal error back to the calling program. Various errors can occur during initialization, rendering an `RS232` object unusable. By setting `error_status` to an error code, you not only let the calling program know that the constructor failed but also insure that none of the member functions will try to access an invalid port.

`PC8250::set_uart_address_and_irq()`

This private member function is called to do two things. First, it needs to determine the address of the UART as well as the IRQ line on which the UART will generate interrupts. These two parameters can either be specified (from the constructor) or default values will be chosen.

Second, this routine needs to assign the interrupt to a handler. The default handler will always be used for standard PC comm ports, but special hardware such as multiport boards will need special handlers as well.

`PC8250::~PC8250`

The code for the destructor is considerably more simple than that for the constructor. It first disables interrupts in the UART and then calls the interrupt disconnect routine. If a `Handler` object owns the port, then the `Handler::DeletePort()` routine is called to disconnect the port from the interrupt service routine. Otherwise, the `DisconnectFromIRQ()` routine is called to do the job.

The saved settings are then applied to the UART so that its baud rate, parity, and so on are all set back to their values before the port was opened. Finally, the `isr_data` member is deleted and the destructor can exit.

PC8250::check_uart()

This routine is called by the constructor to determine whether a valid UART is present at the address stored in the `isr_data->uart` data member. The simple check done here just looks at the IIR and verifies that the upper 6 bits are all set to 0. Before doing this, the FIFO Control Register is set to 0 because the two FIFO enabled bits could show up in the Interrupt ID Register.

After the presence of the UART is established, the routine checks whether it is a 16550 family UART. If so, the FIFOs are enabled and the RX trigger level is set to 14 bytes. An interrupt will be generated when the FIFO has 14 bytes, doubling the time available to process the interrupt when compared to that available on a conventional 8250 UART.

If this function doesn't find a UART at the specified address, it sets the `error_status` to a fatal error flag, which shuts down all the other member functions in an attempt to minimize any trouble caused by continued use of the object.

PC8250::check_rx_handshaking()

This routine is called after any member function that reads data from the RX buffer. If the RX buffer has passed below the low-water mark and handshaking is in effect, it may be necessary to either raise a handshaking line or send an XON.

Each of the three possible handshaking conditions is handled individually. The DTR/DSR and RTS/CTS code is essentially identical, except for the actual control lines involved. Each checks to see whether the particular mode of handshaking is in effect and whether blocking is in effect. If so and the RX count has dropped below the low water mark, the appropriate control line is raised and the blocking flag is cleared.

The software handshaking code is nearly identical. The major difference is that instead of raising a control line, this code has to issue an XON, which means setting the `send_handshake_character` data member and then calling `jump_start()` to actually cause the transmission.

Note that all three of these routines have to momentarily disable interrupts in order to do their job properly. Both the interrupt service routine and this function are actively manipulating much of the same handshaking data, so you must block interference while critical changes are made.

PC8250::read_byte()

This protected member function is the fundamental read function that is used whenever bytes need to be read in one at a time instead of in block mode. This is necessary any time the single character version of RS232::Read() is called, as well as the mode of RS232::Read() that scans for a terminator string while reading.

This function takes up only a few lines of code because all the hard work necessary to accomplish the read function has already been done elsewhere. Pulling the data out of the RX buffer is done with the Queue::Remove() function (discussed later in this chapter), with an error return if no characters are available. After the character has been read in, a quick call to PC8250::check_rx_handshaking() will handle any handshaking generated by this call. When that is done, the character that has just been read is returned to the calling program.

This is a protected function and is intended to be available only to functions such as RS232::Read(). It is a little more terse than the public functions available to the programmer. In particular, it doesn't support any of the timing options, and doesn't set the ElapsedTime or ByteCount data members. These high-level niceties are handled by other functions.

PC8250::write_byte()

Like read_byte(), this is a protected function that is not intended for direct access by the application programmer. This virtual function is called by high-level functions in the base class such as RS232::Write(int), which also include some of the niceties such as timing information in ElapsedTime. All this function does is check to see whether it can successfully insert the character into the transmit queue using the inline Queue class member function Queue::Insert(). If successful, the routine then checks to see whether transmit interrupts must be restarted. If interrupts appear to be stopped, jump_start() is called to get them going again.

PC8250::read_buffer()

This is the block-oriented equivalent to read_byte(). This protected member function is not intended for direct use by the applications programmer. Instead, it is for the use of the high-level functions in class RS232 such as Read(void*). The read_buffer() function reads in bytes repeatedly into the user-specified buffer until one of two things happens: either the RX buffer goes empty or the user buffer fills up. In either case, the actual number of characters read in is returned to the calling program in the ByteCount data member. The actual return from the function is either RS232_SUCCESS if all of the bytes requested were found, or RS232_TIMEOUT if only an incomplete read was accomplished.

In keeping with a convention used with the RS232 class, the user buffer is terminated with a '\0' character after the characters have all been read in. This is done as a convenience to the programmer, and it comes in handy for many programs. For example, a terminal emulation program can have a code sequence that looks like this:

```
Port->ReadBuffer( buffer, 81 );
cout << buffer;
```

This is a little more efficient than a polling loop where a single character at a time is read in and then echoed out to some output stream. The major implication this has for the programmer is that any read request for n bytes must always be directed toward a buffer that has room for n + 1 bytes.

After `read_buffer()` has finished reading in bytes, it has to check for RX handshaking conditions. This is all managed by `PC8250::check_rx_handshaking()`, so it can be accomplished with a single function call.

The routine then returns the data to the calling routine. Note that the `ElapsedTime` data member is not set here. It would be somewhat redundant, because this function will never wait for more data after the buffer is empty. The higher-level functions that have a timing parameter are in more urgent need of returning an accurate time value.

PC8250::write_buffer()

This is a virtual protected routine that is used by the high-level block-oriented write routines from `class RS232`. Like the previous three functions, it isn't intended for use directly by an application programmer; instead, it is a support routine for other functions.

This function doesn't have any timing constraints, so it simply stuffs characters from the user buffer into the TX Queue until one of two things happens: either the TX Queue fills up and can't handle any more data, or the entire user buffer is sent.

After the routine is done stuffing characters into the TX Queue, it checks to see whether transmit interrupts are actively running. If not, a quick call to `jump_start()` will get things started again.

After interrupts have been started, one of two values is returned to the calling program. `RS232_SUCCESS` is returned if all of the buffer was successfully transmitted. If only some of the buffer was sent, `RS232_TIMEOUT` is sent instead. The calling routine can then check the byte count in `ByteCount` to see how many characters were sent.

PC8250::FlushRXBuffer()

This is an optional virtual function defined in `class RS232`. It is optional because it is already implemented in the base class. `RS232::FlushRXBuffer()` can empty the RX buffer by simply calling `read_buffer()` repeatedly until a `ByteCount` of 0 is returned. At that point, you can assume that the RX buffer is empty.

The `PC8250` class implements its own version of this function simply for efficiency. Because of the implementation of the `Queue` class, emptying a queue is simply a matter of making a single call to an inline function that sets the head and tail pointers to be equal. This is definitely faster and more efficient than making numerous calls to `read_buffer()`, with all of its associated overhead.

After `FlushRXBuffer()` is done clearing the RX Queue, it naturally has to make a call to `PC8250::check_rx_handshaking()` to update any of the handshaking parameters. For example, if the RX buffer was completely full before the call, the driver may have sent an XOFF character to the remote end, indicating that it couldn't handle any more data. After clearing the buffer, this handshake condition would have to be cleared to allow the remote end to send additional data.

You are pretty much guaranteed that this function will return `RS232_SUCCESS` — that is, unless the port is in a fatal error state.

`PC8250::write_settings()`
`PC8250::read_settings()`

These two functions are grouped together here and in the source code because they are perfectly symmetrical. Both operate on the `settings` member of the class. One function reads in all the line settings from the UART and stores them in the `settings` object; the other reads the data from the `settings` object and stores them in the UART. The code they use is very similar.

Both functions are protected and are used only by other member functions, not by the programmer. The `read_settings()` function is called in the constructor of the `PC8250` object and nowhere else. Its settings object is eventually transferred to the `saved_settings` member of the base `RS232` class. The `write_settings()` function is called in three different places. First, it is called in the constructor to establish the initial settings of the UART. It is also called in the destructor to restore the old settings of the UART to their original state. Finally, it is the engine for the `PC8250::Set()` function, which modifies one or more of the UART's line-setting conditions.

These functions aren't available to the end user, at least in part because of their lack of error detection. All data passed to `write_settings()` is already assumed to be valid. In the definition of the `PC8250` class, this is true, because all settings get passed through `Settings::Adjust()` before being used by `write_settings()`. The `read_settings()` function does not verify that the UART it is being told to read is valid or that it, in fact, exists.

Both of these functions set all the UART parameters in one fell swoop. Although there may be some benefit to breaking these routines into smaller individual modules (such as one for setting the baud rate, one for the parity, and so on), this system works well and confines debugging to a single potential point of failure.

Note that for class `PC8250`, no attempt is made by `read_settings()` to save or restore any of the handshaking states. In a class interfacing to an O/S device driver that supports handshaking, it makes sense it makes sense to try to preserve the state. However, no DOS driver is in use with the PC8250 class, so no default handshaking parameters exist. In fact, when you closed the port, there really wouldn't be any way to restore handshaking options, even if you wanted to.

PC8250::Set()

This function takes advantage of a two support functions that were used by the PC8250 constructor. A single call to Settings::Adjust() parses through all the passed parameters, making sure that they are valid, and then updates their values into the settings object in the base class. Next, a single call to write_settings() writes all these new parameters out to the UART, performing a wholesale conversion of parameters.

This routine can, in fact, return with an error code. If any of the parameters passed to Settings::Adjust() look invalid, Set() passes the appropriate error code back to the calling application program.

PC8250::TXSpaceFree()
PC8250::RXSpaceUsed()
PC8250::TXSpaceUsed()
PC8250::RXSpaceFree()

These four functions are grouped because they operate in nearly identical fashions. Two are mandatory virtual functions, whereas the other two are optional. However, because the space free and space used for both the transmit and received queues are readily available to member functions of class PC8250, all four functions are implemented.

Every function just calls one of two inline functions from class Queue for either the RX Queue or the TX Queue. Queue::FreeCount() returns the space free in a queue, and Queue::InUseCount() returns the space in use.

PC8250::Break()

This function generates a break signal on the line. The 8250 class of UART has only minimal support for hardware breaks. To actually transmit a break, a bit in the LCR has to be set. The LCR is then held in that state for as long as necessary for the given break. When time has expired, the break bit in the LCR is lifted and the UART returns to normal operation.

This mode of operation is clearly problematic in a multitasking operating system. Obviously, you don't want to tie up an entire system while you wait for a break signal to complete. The PC8250 class won't generally have to deal with this problem, because MS-DOS is a single-tasking operating system. However, this class can be used in a cooperative multitasking environment such as Windows 3.1. When this is the case, the IdleFunction() used by the RS232 class can be replaced with a function that yields time to the operating system.

Chapter 3: The PC8250 Class 179

```
PC8250::Cd()
PC8250::Ri()
PC8250::Cts()
PC8250::Dsr()
```

These four functions are nearly identical in implementation. Each function just picks a bit from the `modem_status` data member of the ISR data structure. The `modem_status` data member gets updated each time there is a modem status interrupt, so it always has the most recent status of all incoming control lines.

Following the general convention of this library, these functions return only a 1 or a 0. Although any nonzero value is an acceptable boolean under C and C++, programmers will want to store the state of control lines in bit fields or similar C++ classes. Because they return only a single-bit value, these functions can easily be used in this manner.

Although it wouldn't be possible to implement in every class derived from the `RS232` class, a useful enhancement to these functions would be to keep track not just of modem status *states* but modem status *events* as well. For example, because the 8250 generates an interrupt any time a modem status line changes state, you can set a flag if CD drops low so that a BBS program can avoid the problem of missing a momentary drop in carrier. Even more useful would be the ability to detect ring pulses, which can easily be missed when a program is just polling the line with calls to `Ri()`. This sort of event detection will be performed in the Win32 version of the port driver, with event callbacks being promulgated via user-definable member functions.

```
PC8250::ParityError()
PC8250::BreakDetect()
PC8250::FramingError()
PC8250::HardwareOverrunError()
```

These four functions are similar to the previous four modem status functions. Each of them just checks the state of a bit in the `line_status` word. Whenever a line status interrupt occurs, `line_status` is ORed with the contents of the UART's LSR. This means that the bits in `line_status` contain a cumulative record of all the line status events that have occurred while the system has been running.

Although the stickiness of the line status bits is necessary for catching error events, these functions must also safely clear the flags so that a program can detect the next occurrence of an event. These functions differ from the four modem status functions in that the optional reset parameter for each can clear the line status bit.

Because the ISR can modify the `line_status` word while these routines are in the process of modifying it, the modification has to be made while interrupts are disabled. Because the only thing that happens while interrupts are disabled is the modification of a flag in memory, it isn't likely to have any impact on system performance.

Like the modem status functions, these functions also return only a 1 or a 0 for the state value, although presumably any boolean value would do.

`PC8250::SoftwareOverrunError()`

Like the hardware line status function, this function returns the state of an event, in this case the overflow of the receive buffer. However, this event is strictly a software matter, unlike the UART line status events. When the ISR receives a character and has no room for it in the RX buffer, it sets the `overflow` flag in the `isr_data` structure. This function just returns the value of that flag.

This function also has an optional parameter that can be used to clear the software overrun flag.

`PC8250::XonXoffHandshaking()`

This function also has a dual purpose. When called without any arguments, it just returns a boolean value to indicate whether handshaking is enabled. To do so, it checks the setting of the `xon_xoff` bit in the `isr_data->handshaking` word. If it is set, handshaking is enabled and the function returns a 1. If it is clear, that form of handshaking is disabled and a 0 is returned.

Turning handshaking on is relatively simple: All the routine has to do is set the `xon_xoff` bit in the handshaking status word. This doesn't even have to be done with interrupts disabled, because the ISR doesn't ever modify the handshaking status word. After this bit is set, the next incoming data byte will automatically trigger the ISR to send an XOFF if the receive buffer is past the high-water mark. That way, you don't have to worry about manually putting the port into a blocking state.

However, when turning off handshaking, you have to take some extra things into consideration. Because the port may have previously been in handshaking mode, the transmitter could be in a blocked state, and the port may have at some time issued an XOFF and gone into a blocking state. To manage this, the routine first clears the `xon_xoff` bit in the handshaking status word. After this is done, the blocked and blocking states won't change unless you do so manually. If the port is in the blocked state, it received an XOFF from the remote end at some time and is still waiting for an XON. Clearing the `xon_xoff` bit in the `isr_data->blocked` word will solve half the problem. But clearing the status bit won't start the transmitter up again. You can resume the transmission of interrupts later in the routine. A call to `jump_start()` will begin transmit interrupts again by pulling the next available character out of the `TXQueue` and sending it out the transmitter—if and only if the other blocked bits are clear.

If the `xon_xoff` bit is set in the `isr_data->blocking` word, an XOFF was sent to the remote end to block it from further transmission. Because handshaking is turned off, the remote end won't ever receive an XON to get it started again unless it is sent out now. This routine takes care of that by checking the blocking bit and setting the `send_handshake_char` bit to XON. If the `send_handshake_char` character still has the last XOFF character in it, `send_handshake_char` is canceled and nothing is sent.

After all this work is done and the call to `jump_start()` has been made, the `XonXoff` flag in the settings data member of the base class is set to the appropriate value, and the function returns.

`PC8250::RtsCtsHandshaking()`
`PC8250::DtrDsrHandshaking()`

These two functions do exactly the same thing as the previous function does, which is to report on a handshaking state and, optionally, change it. However, these functions perform their handshaking using the modem control lines, instead of by transmitting XON and XOFF characters, so they have to operate somewhat differently. The code for these two functions is nearly identical, with the only difference being which of the RS-232 control lines they work with.

Like the XON/XOFF function, when called with no arguments these functions just return their current handshaking status. A 1 means that handshaking is enabled and a 0 means that it is disabled. As with the previous function, when the parameter is set to a 1 or a 0, a new handshaking mode is selected and requires a bit more effort to handle.

When either RTS/CTS or DTR/DSR handshaking is being enabled, the appropriate control line (RTS or DTR) is first set to a logic 1 so that the remote end won't initially be blocked. Then, with interrupts disabled, the state of the corresponding input control line is checked via the `modem_status` word. If CTS or DSR is low, the appropriate blocked bit is set. No other characters will be sent because the next TX interrupt will detect the blocked state. Finally, the `rts_cts` bit in the handshaking bit is set, and interrupts are enabled. The remote end isn't blocked, but if the `RXQueue` is past the high-water mark, the next RX interrupt will cause a blocking event and the appropriate modem control line will be lowered.

When handshaking is being enabled, the `Settings.Rts` and/or `Settings.Dtr` bits are also set to the somewhat odd value of `REMOTE_CONTROL`. This special value is used to indicate that the line is being used for handshaking and can be expected to change on a regular basis.

The sequence of events that takes place when hardware handshaking is being disabled is much simpler. If hardware handshaking was previously enabled, the appropriate control line is raised to a level 1 to make sure that any blocking status is cleared. After raising the line and clearing the appropriate bits in the `handshaking`, `blocked`, and `blocking` bits, a call to `jump_start()` is made. If the transmitter was previously in a blocked state, this will get it restarted.

When the routine exits, its final task is to return the current setting of the appropriate type of handshaking, which it does simply by testing the appropriate bit in the handshaking member of the `isr_data` object.

`PC8250::Dtr()`
`PC8250::Rts()`

These two functions also have two purposes. When called without any parameters, they simply return the current setting of the output modem control line. When called with a parameter other than UNCHANGED, they also set the output of the control line either high or low.

The control line might already be in use as a handshaking line. If this is the case, the request to change the output is rejected with a return code of PC8250_HANDSHAKE_LINE_IN_USE. If the line is not in use for handshaking, its setting is modified as its control bit in the 8250 modem control register is modified. Because the interrupt service routine could also modify the MCR, Rts() and Cts() have to write to the control lines with interrupts disabled.

The settings.Rts or settings.Dsr bits in the base class are also modified when the line is changed. The correct way to examine the settings of these control lines is to read back the settings structure, so these values need to be kept up-to-date.

PC8250::PeekBuffer()

Because the interrupt service routine maintains its receive buffer as a data member of the derived class PC8250, it should be easy to peek into that receive buffer. In this case, it was made even easier by the fact that the Queue class has a member function that will perform the equivalent of the peek buffer on request.

Because of these convenient facts, the PeekBuffer() routine takes up only a few lines of code. A single call to the Queue::Peek() function reads in as many bytes as possible from the RX Queue and returns the count to be stored in the ByteCount data member. The only thing to do at this point is to terminate the buffer with a '\0' character and return to the calling program.

PC8250::FlushTXBuffer()

Flushing the transmit buffer is done using this optional virtual function. It is an optional function because not every driver will have the easy access to the output buffer that class PC8250 has. In this class, a single call to a member function of class Queue for the TX Queue object takes care of clearing the buffer out. This member function is an inline function that just has to set the head and tail pointers of the queue to the same value.

The only complication is that interrupts must be disabled during the clearing operation, because the ISR can modify the queue pointers in the middle of the operation, leading to unexpected results.

PC8250::FormatDebugOutput()

As I describe in Chapter 2, the debug output function has to work in cooperation with the same function in the base class. Each class in a hierarchy of derived classes is free to contribute its own lines of debug output, as many or as few as necessary.

By definition, this function returns a count of the number of lines that it can display when it is called with no arguments. In the constructor for the PC8250 object, you call RS232::FormatDebugOutput() to determine how many lines of output the base class will contribute. You then know which line your first line output will appear on.

As presently coded, the PC8250 class contributes six lines to the debug output. When this routine is called with a buffer pointer set to 0, the caller is asking how many lines total can be expected from you. In this case, you return the total contribution of the base class plus six, for a total of eight.

If this routine is called with a valid buffer pointer, you need to format a line of output and return it to the caller. If the line number requested was less than the total contribution of the base class, the function call is passed up the line to the base class for processing. If, instead, the line number is one of the lines designated for class PC8250, this routine formats it with pertinent data and returns it to the calling function.

The following screen shot shows the output from this routine when called for every line possible (a total of 8). This version of the debug output just attempts to show all of the member data so that a programmer or user can attempt to interpret the current state of the port. Although this type of display may not be particularly useful to the end user of an application, it can be invaluable to a programmer during development.

```
Base class: RS232   COM1    Error status: Success
Saved Settings:     2400,N,8,1   DTR,RTS:  0, 0   XON/OFF,RTS/CTS,DTR/DSR: 0,0,0
Current Settings:   2400,N,8,1   DTR,RTS:  1, 1   XON/OFF,RTS/CTS,DTR/DSR: 0,0,0
Derived class: PC8250   UART: 03f8  Overflow: 0  TX Running: 0  Line Status: 00
TX Head, Tail, Count      6     6     0   RX Head,Tail,Count   330   330    0
Counts: TX:     6   RX:    330   MS:     0   LS:    0   CTS/DSR/RI/CD: 1100
Handshake DTR/RTS/XON : 000   Blocking: 000   Blocked: 000   Handshake char: ffff
Parity Err: 0   Break Det: 0   Overrun Err: 0   Framing Err: 0   FIFO Setting: 0
```

One other nice feature about the debug output is that it is easily extensible. It is relatively easy to derive a new class from PC8250 that retained all the same functionality, but added a few new lines of output to the FormatDebugOutput() routine. This feature demonstrates the strength of C++ in making it easy to add on to existing work.

PC8250::ErrorName()

Like the previous function, the ErrorName() function works by extending the same function in the base class. Each derived class is free to create its own error codes. If they do not overlap with the error codes in the base class, they can be properly translated into ASCII.

Here, three ranges of error codes are defined by the base class. They are the fatal errors, warning errors, and success messages. If the error code passed to this function appears to belong to the base class, the code is passed up to `RS232::ErrorName()` for translation. Otherwise, this routine does its best to translate the error code as one of the ones defined for this class.

Support Classes

Two different support packages are needed to implement the `PC8250` class. The first is the `Queue` class, which is used to support the transmit and receive queues. The second package is the interrupt manager, which is a set of general-purpose code that sets up interrupt handlers. Both packages are rather generic, and I use them elsewhere in the book.

The Queue package

The `Queue` package consists of the `Queue` class definition, along with nine member functions, including the constructor. All but one of the functions are defined as inline functions, for two reasons. First, these functions are used when efficiency is important, such as in the ISR. Execution speed is at an absolute premium in such frequently called routines — ideal applications for inline code. Second, the inline functions are generally very short and, in some cases, inline code may not take much more code space than a separately compiled function combined with calling overhead.

Because most of the functions are inline, most of the code is found in the header file `QUEUE.H` shown in Listing 3-7. `QUEUE.CPP` contains only the lone compiled function, `Queue::Peek()`, shown in Listing 3-8.

Listing 3-7: QUEUE.H

```
//
//  QUEUE.H
//
//  Source code from:
//
//  Serial Communications Developer's Guide, 2nd Edition
//  by Mark Nelson, IDG Books, 1999
//
//  Please see the book for information on usage.
//
//  This header file contains the definitions needed to use the
//  Queue class.  This class is used for both the input and
//  output queues used by class PC8250.  Most of the functions
```

```cpp
//  in this class are defined as inline, as speed is essential
//  in the interrupt service routine.  Those that aren't can
//  be found in QUEUE.CPP
//

#ifndef _QUEUE_DOT_H
#define _QUEUE_DOT_H

#ifdef _MSC_VER
# pragma warning( disable : 4505 )
#endif

const unsigned int QueueSize = 1024;
const unsigned int HighWaterMark = ( QueueSize * 3 ) / 4;
const unsigned int LowWaterMark = QueueSize / 4;

class Queue
{
    private :
        volatile unsigned int head_index;
        volatile unsigned int tail_index;
        volatile unsigned char buffer[ QueueSize ];
    public :
        Queue( void );
        int Insert( unsigned char c );
        int Remove( void );
        int Peek( unsigned char *buffer, int count );
        int InUseCount( void );
        int FreeCount( void );
        int Head( void ) { return head_index; }
        int Tail( void ) { return tail_index; }
        void Clear( void );
};

inline Queue::Queue( void )
{
    head_index = 0;
    tail_index = 0;
}

inline int Queue::Insert( unsigned char c )
{
    unsigned int temp_head = head_index;
```

```cpp
        buffer[ temp_head++ ] = c;
        if ( temp_head >= QueueSize )
            temp_head = 0;
        if ( temp_head == tail_index )
            return 0;
        head_index = temp_head;
        return 1;
    }

    inline int Queue::Remove( void )
    {
        unsigned char c;
        if ( head_index == tail_index )
            return( -1 );
        c = buffer[ tail_index++ ];
        if ( tail_index >= QueueSize )
            tail_index = 0;
        return c;
    }

    inline int Queue::InUseCount( void )
    {
        if ( head_index >= tail_index )
            return head_index - tail_index;
        else
            return head_index + QueueSize - tail_index;
    }

    inline int Queue::FreeCount( void )
    {
        return QueueSize - 1 - InUseCount();
    }

    inline void Queue::Clear( void )
    {
        tail_index = head_index;
    }

    #endif   //  #ifndef _QUEUE_DOT_H

    // ******************** END OF QUEUE.H ********************
```

Listing 3-8: QUEUE.CPP

```cpp
//
//   QUEUE.CPP
//
//   Source code from:
//
//   Serial Communications Developer's Guide, 2nd Edition
//   by Mark Nelson, IDG Books, 1999
//
//   Please see the book for information on usage.
//
// Most of the queue class functions are defined in QUEUE.H as
// inline for speed.  This routine probably won't generate
// inline code with most compilers, and it is not used in the
// ISR, so speed is not as critical.  Thus, it gets defined
// normally.

#include "queue.h"

int Queue::Peek( unsigned char *buf, int count )
{
    unsigned int index = tail_index;
    int total = 0;

    while ( total < count && index != head_index ) {
        *buf++ = buffer[ index++ ];
        if ( index >= QueueSize )
            index = 0;
        total++;
    }
    return total;
}
// ******************** END OF QUEUE.CPP ********************
```

The Queue class functions are used in various places throughout the PC8250 class code. The functions are as follows:

Queue::Queue()   The constructor for the queue sets the head and tail indices to 0. The buffer is allocated automatically as a data member of the queue.

Queue::Insert()   The insertion routine tries to stuff a character into the buffer, advancing the head index. If the buffer is full, the function returns a 0, indicating failure. Otherwise, a 1 is returned, indicating success.

Queue::Remove()	This function tries to remove a character from the buffer, advancing the tail index if successful. If a character can't be removed, a −1 is returned; otherwise, the character is removed and returned.
Queue::Peek()	This is the only function in the package that isn't defined as an inline function. It tries to pull as many characters out of the receive buffer as requested, without advancing the tail pointer. The actual count of characters removed is returned.
Queue::InUseCount()	This function returns the number of characters presently stored in the Queue.
Queue::FreeCount()	This function returns the number of spaces available in the Queue.
Queue::Head()	This function returns the current head index for the queue. The only place this is presently used is in the debug display output.
Queue::Tail()	This function returns the current tail index for the queue. Like the Head() function, this is only presently used in the debug output dump.
Queue::Clear()	This function sets the tail index to the same value as the head index, effectively emptying the queue.

The interrupt manager package

This package is a set of functions that connect and disconnect interrupt routines to and from interrupt vectors. This package has two function calls that are used in the PC8250 class. The ConnectToIRQ() function is used to connect a function to an interrupt vector, and the DisconnectFromIrq() function removes that connection. When a function is connected to an interrupt vector, the connect routine also accepts a parameter specifying a pointer to a data item that is passed to the function when the interrupt occurs. For the PC8250 class, the function is always isr_8250(), and the data item is a pointer to the isr_data structure for the given port.

The interrupt manager works by keeping a separate stub routine for each of the usable IRQs on the PC. When an interrupt is connected to a particular IRQ, a DOS function call is made to connect the interrupt vector for that IRQ to the stub function. When control passes to that stub function, it immediately calls the user-specified function with a pointer to the user-specified data area.

Listing 3-9 shows an example of the PCIRQ.H header file that has the prototypes and definitions used with the IRQ manager routines. All the code for the IRQ manager is found in PCIRQ.CPP, shown in Listing 3-10.

Listing 3-9: PCIRQ.H

```
//
//  PCIRQ.H
//
//  Source code from:
//
//  Serial Communications Developer's Guide, 2nd Edition
//  by Mark Nelson, IDG Books, 1999
//
//  Please see the book for information on usage.
//
//  This header file has the prototypes and definitions used with
//  the IRQ manager routines.  The three public functions have
//  their prototypes here.  All the code for the IRQ manager is
//  found in PCIRQ.CPP.

#ifndef _PCIRQ_DOT_H
#define _PCIRQ_DOT_H

#include "rs232.h"

enum irq_name {  IRQ0 = 0, IRQ1,  IRQ2,  IRQ3,  IRQ4,  IRQ5,
                 IRQ6,     IRQ7,  IRQ8,  IRQ9,  IRQ10, IRQ11,
                 IRQ12,    IRQ13, IRQ14, IRQ15,
                 ILLEGAL_IRQ = -1 };

RS232Error
ConnectToIrq( irq_name irq,
              void *isr_data_block,
              void ( *isr_routine )( void *isr_data_block ) );
int DisconnectFromIRQ( enum irq_name irq );

#endif // #ifndef _PCIRQ_DOT_H

// ******************** END OF PCIRQ.H ********************
```

Listing 3-10: PCIRQ.CPP

```
//
//  PCIRQ.CPP
//
//  Source code from:
//
//  Serial Communications Developer's Guide, 2nd Edition
```

```
//  by Mark Nelson, IDG Books, 1999
//
//  Please see the book for information on usage.
//
//  This module contains the interrupt management code.
//  ConnectToIRQ() is called to establish an interrupt handler
//  function, DisconnectFromIRQ() is called to break the
//  connection.

#include <dos.h>
#include "pcirq.h"

typedef void ( __far __interrupt *HANDLER )( void );

// Prototypes for all the handlers defined here

void __far __interrupt isr2( void );
void __far __interrupt isr3( void );
void __far __interrupt isr4( void );
void __far __interrupt isr5( void );
void __far __interrupt isr7( void );
void __far __interrupt isr10( void );
void __far __interrupt isr11( void );
void __far __interrupt isr15( void );
void __far __interrupt int1b( void );
void __far __interrupt int23( void );

// When any IRQs are hooked by one of our routines, the IRQ code
// disables control-break termination by taking over the two
// control-break vectors. The saved control-break state is
// stored in the following three variables.

static HANDLER old_int1b;
static HANDLER old_int23;
static unsigned char old_dos_break_state;

// A count of the number of handlers currently in use.

static int count = 0;

// This structure keeps track of the state of each of the eight
// possible IRQ lines our program can take over. This includes
// the address of the new handler, the old handler, and most
// importantly, the data pointer passed to the new handler when
```

```c
// it is invoked.

struct {
    enum irq_name irq;
    void *isr_data;
    void ( *isr_routine)( void *isr_data );
    HANDLER handler;
    HANDLER old_isr;
    int old_pic_enable_bit;
} irq_data[] = { { IRQ2,  0, 0, isr2,  0, 0 },
                 { IRQ3,  0, 0, isr3,  0, 0 },
                 { IRQ4,  0, 0, isr4,  0, 0 },
                 { IRQ5,  0, 0, isr5,  0, 0 },
                 { IRQ7,  0, 0, isr7,  0, 0 },
                 { IRQ10, 0, 0, isr10, 0, 0 },
                 { IRQ11, 0, 0, isr11, 0, 0 },
                 { IRQ15, 0, 0, isr15, 0, 0 }
               };

// All of the new ISR handlers are called when the interrupt
// occurs.  All they do is call the hooked routine, passing it
// a pointer to the data block it asked for in the
// ConnectToIRQ() routine.  When this is done, they take care
// of issuing the EOI instruction and then exiting.  The
// "return 1" is necessary for Zortech's interrupt handlers.
// If a "return 0" is used, the handler will then chain to the
// old interrupt, which we don't want.

void __far __interrupt isr2( void )
{
    irq_data[ 0 ].isr_routine( irq_data[ 0 ].isr_data );
    _disable();
    outp( 0x20, 0x20 );
}

void __far __interrupt isr3( void )
{
    irq_data[ 1 ].isr_routine( irq_data[ 1 ].isr_data );
    _disable();
    outp( 0x20, 0x20 );
}

void __far __interrupt isr4( void )
{
```

```c
    irq_data[ 2 ].isr_routine( irq_data[ 2 ].isr_data );
    _disable();
    outp( 0x20, 0x20 );
}

void __far __interrupt isr5( void )
{
    irq_data[ 3 ].isr_routine( irq_data[ 3 ].isr_data );
    _disable();
    outp( 0x20, 0x20 );
}

void __far __interrupt isr7( void )
{
    irq_data[ 4 ].isr_routine( irq_data[ 4 ].isr_data );
    _disable();
    outp( 0x20, 0x20 );
}


// These routines have to send an EOI to the second 8250 PIC
// as well as the first.

void __far __interrupt isr10( void )
{
    irq_data[ 5 ].isr_routine( irq_data[ 5 ].isr_data );
    _disable();
    outp( 0xa0, 0x20 );
    outp( 0x20, 0x20 );
}

void __far __interrupt isr11( void )
{
    irq_data[ 6 ].isr_routine( irq_data[ 6 ].isr_data );
    _disable();
    outp( 0xa0, 0x20 );
    outp( 0x20, 0x20 );
}

void __far __interrupt isr15( void )
{
    irq_data[ 7 ].isr_routine( irq_data[ 7 ].isr_data );
    _disable();
    outp( 0xa0, 0x20 );
```

```c
        outp( 0x20, 0x20 );
}

// The two control-break vectors do nothing, so that Control-C
// and Contrl-Break both have no effect on our program.

void __far __interrupt int1b( void )
{
}

void __far __interrupt int23( void )
{
}

// This utility routine is only used internally to these
// routines.  It sets control of the given interrupt number to
// the handler specifified as a parameter.  It returns the
// address of the old handler to the caller, so it can be
// stored for later restoration.  Note that Zortech stores the
// old handler internally, so we just return a 0.

HANDLER HookVector( int interrupt_number, HANDLER new_handler )
{
    union REGS r;
    struct SREGS s = { 0, 0, 0, 0 };
    HANDLER old_handler = 0;

    r.h.al = (unsigned char) interrupt_number;
    r.h.ah = 0x35;
    int86x( 0x21, &r, &r, &s );
    *( (unsigned __far *) old_handler + 1 ) = s.es;
    *( (unsigned __far *) old_handler ) = r.x.bx;
    s.ds = FP_SEG( new_handler );
    r.x.dx = FP_OFF( new_handler );
    r.h.al = (unsigned char) interrupt_number;
    r.h.ah = 0x25;
    int86x( 0x21, &r, &r, &s );
    return old_handler;
}

// When we are done with an IRQ, we restore the old handler
// here.  Note once again that Zortech does this internally, so
// we don't have to.
```

```c
void UnHookVector( int interrupt_number, HANDLER old_handler )
{
    union REGS r;
    struct SREGS s = { 0, 0, 0, 0 };

    s.ds = FP_SEG( old_handler );
    r.x.dx = FP_OFF( old_handler );
    r.h.al = (unsigned char) interrupt_number;
    r.h.ah = 0x25;
    int86x( 0x21, &r, &r, &s );
}

// When we have taken over an interrupt, we don't want keyboard
// breaks to cause us to exit without properly restoring
// vectors.  This routine takes over the DOS and BIOS
// control-break routines, and sets the DOS BREAK flag to 0.
// The old state of all these variables is saved off so it can
// be restored when the last interrupt routine is restored.

void TrapKeyboardBreak( void )
{
    union REGS r;

    old_int1b = HookVector( 0x1b, int1b );
    old_int23 = HookVector( 0x23, int23 );
    r.h.ah = 0x33;
    r.h.al = 0;
    int86( 0x21, &r, &r );
    old_dos_break_state = r.h.dl;
    r.h.ah = 0x33;
    r.h.al = 1;
    r.h.dl = 0;
    int86( 0x21, &r, &r );
}

// When the last interrupt is restored, we can set the
// control-break vectors back where they belong, and restore
// the old setting of the DOS break flag.

void RestoreKeyboardBreak( void )
{
    union REGS r;

    UnHookVector( 0x1b, old_int1b );
```

```
        UnHookVector( 0x23, old_int23 );
        r.h.ah = 0x33;
        r.h.al = 1;
        r.h.dl = old_dos_break_state;
        int86( 0x21, &r, &r );
}

// When connecting to an IRQ, I pass it an irq number, plus a
// pointer to a function that will handle the interrupt.  The
// function gets passed a pointer to a data block of its choice,
// which will vary depending on what type of interrupt is being
// handled.

RS232Error
ConnectToIrq( enum irq_name irq,
              void *isr_data,
              void ( *isr_routine )( void *isr_data ) )
{
    int i;
    int pic_mask;
    int pic_address;
    int interrupt_number;
    int temp;

    for ( i = 0 ; ; i++ ) {
        if ( irq_data[ i ].irq == irq )
            break;
        if ( irq_data[ i ].irq == IRQ15 )
            return RS232_ILLEGAL_IRQ;
    }
    if ( irq_data[ i ].isr_routine != 0 )
        return RS232_IRQ_IN_USE;
    if ( count++ == 0 )
        TrapKeyboardBreak();
    irq_data[ i ].isr_data = isr_data;
    irq_data[ i ].isr_routine = isr_routine;

    pic_mask = 1 << ( irq % 8 );
    if ( irq < IRQ8 ) {
        pic_address = 0x20;
        interrupt_number = irq + 8;
    } else {
        interrupt_number = irq + 104;
        pic_address = 0xa0;
```

```c
    }
    irq_data[ i ].old_isr = HookVector( interrupt_number,
                                        irq_data[ i ].handler );

    temp = inp( pic_address + 1 );
    irq_data[ i ].old_pic_enable_bit = temp & pic_mask;
    outp( pic_address + 1, temp & ~pic_mask );
    return RS232_SUCCESS;
}

// This routine restores an old interrupt vector.

int DisconnectFromIRQ( enum irq_name irq )
{
    int i;
    int pic_mask;
    int pic_address;
    int interrupt_number;
    int temp;

    for ( i = 0 ; ; i++ ) {
        if ( irq_data[ i ].irq == irq )
            break;
        if ( irq_data[ i ].irq == IRQ15 )
            return 0;
    }
    if ( irq_data[ i ].isr_routine == 0 )
        return 0;

    irq_data[ i ].isr_data = 0;
    irq_data[ i ].isr_routine = 0;

    pic_mask = 1 << ( irq % 8 );
    if ( irq < IRQ8 ) {
        pic_address = 0x20;
        interrupt_number = irq + 8;
    } else {
        interrupt_number = irq + 104;
        pic_address = 0xa0;
    }

    temp = inp( pic_address + 1 );
    temp &= ~pic_mask;
    temp |= irq_data[ i ].old_pic_enable_bit;
    outp( pic_address + 1, temp );
```

```
        UnHookVector( interrupt_number, irq_data[ i ].old_isr );

    if ( --count == 0 )
        RestoreKeyboardBreak();
    return 1;
}
// ******************* END OF PCIRQ.CPP *******************
```

ConnectToIrq()

This function takes three arguments: an IRQ number, a function name, and a data pointer. It attempts to set up the interrupt vectors so that when the interrupt defined for that IRQ takes place, a call is made to the C function specified as an argument with a pointer to the data item.

When the connect routine is called, it also saves off the present status of the 8259 PIC controller for that particular line. When the function is finally disconnected from the interrupt vector, the 8259 state is restored.

When the first port is connected to an interrupt vector, the IRQ manager package also does its best to disable the ability of the user to break out of the program from the keyboard with either Ctrl+C or Ctrl+Break. It does this by taking over INT 23H and INT 1BH, both of which can be invoked when one of these events occur. When the last IRQ is restored to its original state (in `DisconnectFromIRQ()`), the break vectors are restored to their original settings, which will allow the user to break.

`int DisconnectFromIRQ()`

This function takes a single argument, which is an IRQ number. The disconnect function attempts to restore both the old interrupt vector and the enable/disable bit for that IRQ in the 8259 PIC. In the event that there isn't a stored vector for this IRQ, an error value of 0 is returned.

A Test Program

On the CD that accompanies this book, you will find the complete source code for `CHAPT03.CPP`. This is a general-purpose program that lets you test most of the functionality of any of the classes that will be developed in this and following chapters. The customized version of the program used in this chapter is called `CHAP03.CPP`. Following is a screen shot of CHAPT03.EXE with the help screen; this screen is from the program as configured for this chapter while testing a modem connection to a remote system. The top half of the screen shows an interactive session between the keyboard and the `PC8250` port. In this case, the port has been attached to a Practical Peripherals modem and is engaged in an online session. The bottom half of the screen has a description of the function keys that can be pressed for quick testing of many of the features of the class. Plenty of room is left for further customization of the function keys.

```
#                                                                       #
#                  Data General AViiON DG/UX System                     #
#                                                                       #
#=======================================================================#


UniVerse Command Language 9.3
(c) Copyright 1996 Vmark Software Inc. - All Rights Reserved
ACC.DI logged on: Wed Dec 30 21:51:21 1998


DEC vt100 terminal (vt100)


Terminal type is currently VT100.

      Terminal Type          Terminal Description
      -------------------    ---------------------------------------------
        1 ANSI                ANSI emulation
        2 PKH                 PK Harmony (in "Regent 60" emulation)
        3 PROCOMM             ProComm (in "ADDS VP" emulation)
        4 VIEWPOINT           VIEWPOINT, PRISM II, PRISM IV
        5 VT100               vt100 emulation
        6 WYSE                wyse 50 ADDSVP enhanced emulation
        7 WYSE50              Wyse WY-50
        8 WYSE0               Wyse WY-50 (in "ADDSVP" mode) (Original)
Enter terminal type or number:
```

```
F1 Help Toggle        ALT F1 Toggle XON/XOFF
F2 Next port          ALT F2 Toggle RTS/CTS
F3 Spew Toggle        ALT F3 Toggle DTR/DSR
F4 Reading Toggle     ALT F4 Toggle RTS
F5 Set baud rate      ALT F5 Toggle DTR
F6 Set parity         ALT F6 Flush RX Buffer
F7 Set word length    ALT F7 Flush TX Buffer
F8 Set stop bits      ALT F8 Peek at 1 byte
F9 Send break         ALT F9 Read a byte
F10 Exit              ALT F10 Send 1K block
```

The next screen, from CHAPT03.EXE, shows the same program with the help screen turned off. In this mode, the bottom half of the screen shows a port dump, with all the available information that the debug output functions supply. Watching this information while the program runs and function keys are pressed can give you an excellent feel for how the class operates.

```
#                                                                       #
#                  Data General AviiON DG/UX System                     #
#                                                                       #
#=======================================================================#


UniVerse Command Language 9.3
(c) Copyright 1996 Vmark Software Inc. - All Rights Reserved
ACC.DI logged on: Wed Dec 30 21:51:21 1998


DEC vt100 terminal (vt100)

Terminal type is currently VT100.


    Terminal Type         Terminal Description
    -----------------     -----------------------------------------------

    1 ANSI                ANSI emulation
    2 PKH                 PK Harmony (in "Regent 60" emulation)
    3 PROCOMM             ProComm (in "ADDS VP" emulation)
    4 VIEWPOINT           VIEWPOINT, PRISM II, PRISM IV
    5 VT100               vt100 emulation
    6 WYSE                wyse 50 ADDSVP enhanced emulation
    7 WYSE50              Wyse WY-50
    8 WYSE0               Wyse WY-50 (in "ADDSVP" mode) (Original)
Enter terminal type or number:
```

```
Base class: RS232   COM1    Status: Success
Byte count:     0   Elapsed time:      0   TX Free:  1023  RX Used:     0
Saved port:   2400,N, 8, 1  DTR,RTS:  0, 0  XON/OFF,RTS/CTS,DTR/DSR: -1,-1,-1
Current port: 38400,N,8,1   DTR,RTS:  1, 1  XON/OFF,RTS/CTS,DTR/DSR:  0, 0, 0

Derived class: PC8250   UART: 03f8  Overflow: 0  TX Running: 0  Line Status: 6b
TX Head, Tail, Count    48   48     0  RX Head,Tail,Count  748  748     0
Counts: TX:     49  RX:    748  MS:     1  LS:     1  CTS/DSR/RI/CD: 1101
Handshake DTR/RTS/XON : 000  Blocking: 000  Blocked: 000  Handshake char: ffff
Parity Err: 0  Break Det: 0  Overrun Err: 1  Framing Err: 1  FIFO Setting:  0
Uart type: 8250
```

The actual process of building a custom program requires small modifications to two files. First, the actual source file for the test program, TEST232.CPP, has to be changed. Then you make a copy of the program to CHAPT03.CPP. This will be your working copy. (This file as modified here is supplied on your source CD.) When testing different classes, you will have to make very minor adjustments to the main program.

Next, you have to include the header file needed to define the PC8250 class. You just append this to the normal list of header files at the top of the program, so that it looks like this:

```
#include <stdio.h>
#include <stdlib.h>
#include <string.h>
#include <conio.h>
#include <ctype.h>
#include "rs232.h"
#include "textwind.h"
#include "pc8250.h"
```

The standard test program can be configured to test multiple ports simultaneously. As shipped, TEST232.CPP can be configured to test one or two ports by modifying the internal PORT_COUNT definition. If you want to test two ports simultaneously, locate the line of code that looks like this:

```
#define PORT_COUNT 1
```

Simply change it to:

```
#define PORT_COUNT 2
```

Finally, you modify the loop that opens the ports and windows so that it will open a PC8250 port:

```
for ( i = 0 ; i < 1 ; i++ ) {
    switch ( i ) {
        default :
        Ports[ i ] = new PC8250( port_names[ i ],
                                57600L, 'N', 8, 1 );
    }
}
```

ON THE CD — The make file that builds the test program also needs to be slightly modified because each class will require different files to be linked in. These implementation dependent files are defined in a single line in the `makefile` with the symbol `FILES`. The line looks like this:

FILES = pc8250.obj pcirq.obj isr_8250.obj queue.obj

An appropriately modified version of the make file is included on your CD.

Summary

The `PC8250` class is one of the most fully featured classes that I use in this book. Although the code to digest in this chapter is fairly long, it provides an excellent reference that you can use time and time again when developing other classes.

Chapter 4

Shared Interrupt Devices

IN THIS CHAPTER

- ◆ Multiport boards
- ◆ The handler class
- ◆ The Digi Classic board interrupt handler
- ◆ CHAPT04.CPP
- ◆ Multitasking under MS-DOS

IN THIS CHAPTER, I give this book's first demonstration of actual code reuse. The basic PC8250 class developed in the previous chapter works with standard IBM-compatible Comm ports. When you develop some new derivatives of the Handler class, all the code in class PC8250 will work properly with shared interrupt ports of several different varieties. A straightforward implementation of this class will be developed to work with an unintelligent multiport board from Digi International. The Multiport class developed for use with the standard multiport boards from Digi is easily adapted or modified to work with boards from nearly any manufacturer.

> Digi International is a major supplier of multiport board hardware, including hardware that is compatible with the boards used in this chapter and Chapter 5 of this book. You can find it at www.dgii.com.

Multiport Boards

MS-DOS and the original IBM PC BIOS were originally developed to support just two or perhaps four RS-232 ports. The design of the interrupt system also means that only two of the ports can be in use simultaneously.

Users immediately saw the need for applications using 4, 8, or even 16 ports. Third-party manufacturers quickly responded to the demand and began producing nonintelligent multiport boards.

These nonintelligent multiport boards typically contain an array of 8250 family UARTs that can be configured to reside in various slots on the I/O memory bus.

Each of the UARTs appears to the CPU to be more or less identical to a standard RS-232 port, with one important exception. Rather than have each UART directly control an interrupt line, all of the UARTS on the board share a single interrupt line. The board itself supplies hardware logic that manages and performs arbitration between all of these UARTs vying for use of a single interrupt line.

Figure 4-1 shows a typical multiport board. This board is manufactured by Digi International, Minnetonka, Minnesota. The Classic board can be configured with either four or eight 16550 class UARTS. The two large chips on the top of the board are ASICs, each of which emulate four 16550 UARTs. The board can be configured with either one or two of these chips. Most multiport board makers use these combo UARTs to reduce overall board cost.

Figure 4-1: The Digi International Classic board

Unfortunately, there are no standard ways to bring out the RS-232 connections from the card edge, and every manufacturer improvises when it designs a new board. Digi International has a standard extender cable that connects to the card edge via a large D connector, and has four or eight RS-232 cables extending from it. Each of the cables supports the standard signals used on PC RS-232 ports.

Interrupt line sharing – the status register

Multiport boards work by combining the various interrupt lines on the board into a single interrupt that can be effectively presented to the ISA bus. Boards such as the Classic board perform a logical OR of the eight UART lines to create a single interrupt signal. If any of the ports are requesting an interrupt, the interrupt line on the bus will be high.

The problem with this interrupt scheme is obvious. When the interrupt service routine that is attached to the board sees an incoming interrupt, how does it know which port to service?

One obvious way to do this would be to scan through all the UARTs on the board, checking the interrupt pending register in the 8250 class UART. If an interrupt is pending, the UART can be serviced. If not, the UART is left alone.

This is a reasonable system but it tends to be inefficient. A better system is employed by Digi in the Classic board. It has a simple status register that can be read at the start of the ISR. The status register contains a number indicating which of the four or eight UARTs needs servicing. The ISR can then invoke the correct handler for the given UART.

On the Classic board, the act of reading the status register also pulses the IRQ line low so that any other UARTs with pending interrupts will generate another interrupt on the same IRQ line.

Selecting IRQ lines and addresses

Because multiport boards aren't standard PC hardware sanctioned by IBM or Microsoft, the address of the status register can differ depending on both the manufacturer and your installation. Most boards are heavily configurable so that a board can be positioned at any open slot available in the I/O map, and, ideally, can use any open IRQ line.

In the old days, multiport boards were covered with arrays of dip switches and jumpers so that you could select the addresses and IRQs needed by your application. Fortunately, new boards have moved beyond that. In order to achieve Plug and Play compatibility, the Classic board can be set up entirely via software, meaning that all you need is the configuration program supplied by Digi International.

For the example board supplied with this program, I used the configuration program to set the Classic board to use IRQ3, and put the status address at 0x140. Table 4-1 shows the base address of each of the eight UARTS. (Note that I used only the first four of the UARTs for the example.)

TABLE 4-1 CLASSIC BOARD ADDRESSES

Port	Address
COM5	0x100
COM6	0x108
COM7	0x110
COM8	0x118
COM9	0x120
COM10	0x128
COM11	0x130
COM12	0x138

> **NOTE:** When configuring the Classic board for use under MS-DOS, you should turn Plug and Play off. When using the Classic board with Windows 95/98, you should allow the operating system to select the ports by enabling Plug and Play. If you are going to use the board under Windows 95/98, you don't need to use the programming techniques from this chapter, because the board has a standard Windows serial device driver.

Digi International makes things easy on the programmer by having the status register contain the actual number of the port that is requesting interrupt servicing. Other boards often use a bitmap approach, in which each bit in the register signifies an interrupt request, as shown in Figure 4-2.

Status Register

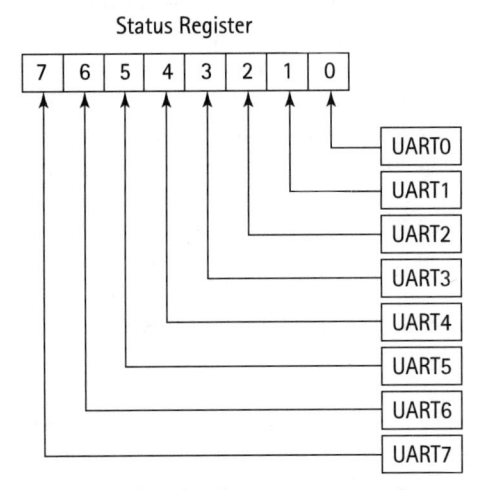

| 7 | 6 | 5 | 4 | 3 | 2 | 1 | 0 |

- Bit 0 → UART0
- Bit 1 → UART1
- Bit 2 → UART2
- Bit 3 → UART3
- Bit 4 → UART4
- Bit 5 → UART5
- Bit 6 → UART6
- Bit 7 → UART7

Figure 4-2: Another frequent status register approach

The Handler Class

As you may recall from Chapter 3, the `PC8250` class had an additional class referenced in its header file named `Handler`. This class was listed as an optional parameter that could be specified in the `PC8250` constructor. Although I don't use it in Chapter 3, the handler class is specified if and when a handler needs to be used to support multiple UARTs per interrupt service routine. Because multiport boards have such a wide variety of architectures, it makes sense to not try to integrate support for all of the various systems into the standard interrupt handler. This means that you develop a base `Handler` class that defines the interface for class `PC8250`, and then derive specific classes for each board type that you intend to support.

Chapter 4: Shared Interrupt Devices

> **NOTE:** The first edition of this book included a `Handler` class developed for shared interrupt ports on the MicroChannel bus. Because this bus is no longer being used, that class isn't documented in this version of the book. That particular class did not make use of a status register; it simply polled all of the UARTs attached to the handler object and invoked the handler for any of them that had an interrupt request flag set.

The `Handler` class is an abstract base class that is defined as having nothing more than a pair of virtual functions. The first of these two functions is used to connect a `PC8250` port to the handler when opening the port; the second virtual function is called to detach it from the handler when closing the port. It is the handler's job to intercept the interrupt, determine which ports need servicing, and invoke the appropriate hardware servicing routines. Because every type of hardware is going to have different ways of handling this task, the base class makes no assumptions whatsoever about data members or other member functions.

A handler is attached to a port during the execution of the `PC8250` constructor. The constructor takes a single argument of a pointer to type `Handler`, which defaults to a value of 0. When a normal `PC8250` port is opened, the handler argument is set to 0 and the constructor calls `ConnectToIrq()` to attach the port to the default interrupt service routine, `isr_8250()`. If a handler is specified, the virtual function `AddPort()` is called instead. `AddPort()` is a member function of the handler, which is an instance of a class derived from the `Handler` class.

In principle, the `Handler` class you write for a board can be implemented any way you want. It has only a few responsibilities. Obviously, you need to be able to construct and destroy it. In addition, the handler must implement its own versions of `AddPort()` and `DeletePort()`. And finally, it needs to take over the management of an interrupt line. This means that it needs to connect to the IRQ when constructed and disconnect from it when destroyed. During its lifetime, it needs to respond to all incoming interrupts and dispatch them to the appropriate ports.

In practice, most multiport boards are relatively similar. Most of the nonintelligent boards on the market today can be controlled via a handler very similar to the one presented later in this chapter. The major factors that will vary from board to board are the following:

- The number of UARTs that are sharing a single interrupt.

- The format of the status register: bit mask or a number. The polarity of the bit mask may also vary.

- Whether just one or multiple ports can be serviced in a single interrupt.

Fortunately, modifying these things is a relatively simple thing, so you should be able to create new handler classes quickly and expect good results.

The Digi Classic Board Interrupt Handler

Opening and using ports on the Classic board is nearly identical to the process of opening standard `PC8250` ports. The only difference is that before any Classic port can be opened, an object of class `Handler` needs to be created to handle interrupts generated by those ports. Because the handler has to be tailored to the specific type of shared interrupt hardware, you need to create a new handler class, in this case `ClassicHandler`.

The constructor

The Classic board is highly configurable, with IRQ support for most of the 16 ISA IRQ lines and a wide variety of possibilities for the UARTs and status register. The `ClassicHandler` object doesn't need to know the address of the UARTs, but it does need to know which IRQ line it is expected to control. It also needs to know the address of the board's status register.

> **ON THE CD** The class definition and constructor prototype in Listing 4-1 show that the constructor takes as parameters the value of the IRQ line used by the board, and the address of the board's status register.

Listing 4-1: The class definitions in CLASSIC.H

```
// ****************** START OF CLASSIC.H ********************
//
// Copyright (c) 1998 Mark R. Nelson. All Rights Reserved.
//
// This header file has all of the definitions and prototypes
// needed to use the ClassicHandler class.


#ifndef _CLASSIC_DOT_H
#define _CLASSIC_DOT_H

#include "rs232.h"
#include "pc8250.h"

struct classic_data {
    int status_register;
    struct isr_data_block *data_pointers[ 8 ];
```

```
};

class ClassicHandler : public Handler {
    private :
        struct classic_data isr_info;
        irq_name irq;
        RS232Error connected;
    public :
        ClassicHandler( irq_name irq_line,
                        int status_register_address );
        ~ClassicHandler( void );
        virtual RS232Error AddPort( RS232PortName port_name,
                                    struct isr_data_block *data );
        virtual void DeletePort( RS232PortName port_name );
};

#endif // #ifndef _CLASSIC_DOT_H

// ******************** END OF CLASSIC.H ********************
```

The `ClassicHandler` constructor clearly has to know the IRQ line for the board. When the handler is created, one of the few things that it actually has to do besides initialize its data members is to connect an ISR to the IRQ line. The location of the status register could conceivably not be defined until one of the ports was added to the handler, but doing it in the handler constructor probably helps clarify the code. A programmer not familiar with the Classic board could look at this code and understand what has happened more quickly than if the status register definition was not shown until its implicit use in the ISR.

Listing 4-2 shows all of the `ClassicHandler` specific class code, which is where you see what the constructor actually does. It takes care of storing the IRQ line and status register addresses, and then initializes the data pointers to the eight ports that can be attached to the handler. Finally, the handler attaches the `classic_isr()` routine to the specified interrupt handler.

Listing 4-2: The class functions in CLASSIC.CPP

```
// ******************** START OF CLASSIC.CPP ********************
//
//

#include <dos.h>
#include "rs232.h"
#include "pc8250.h"
#include "_pc8250.h"
#include "pcirq.h"
```

```c
#include "classic.h"

void classic_isr( struct classic_data *isr_info )
{
    _enable();
    int port = inp( isr_info->status_register );
    port &= 7;
    if ( isr_info->data_pointers[ port ] )
        isr_8250( isr_info->data_pointers[ port ] );
}

ClassicHandler::ClassicHandler( irq_name irq_line,
                                int status_register_address )
{
    int i;

    isr_info.status_register = status_register_address;
    for ( i = 0 ; i < 8 ; i++ )
        isr_info.data_pointers[ i ] = 0;
    irq = irq_line;
    connected = ConnectToIrq( irq,
                              &isr_info,
                              (void (*)( void *)) classic_isr );
}

ClassicHandler::~ClassicHandler( void )
{
    if ( connected == RS232_SUCCESS )
        DisconnectFromIRQ( irq );
}

RS232Error ClassicHandler::AddPort( RS232PortName port_name,
                                    struct isr_data_block *data )
{
    if ( connected != RS232_SUCCESS )
        return connected;
    if ( isr_info.data_pointers[ port_name - COM5 ] )
        return RS232_PORT_IN_USE;
    isr_info.data_pointers[ port_name - COM5 ] = data;
    return RS232_SUCCESS;
}

void ClassicHandler::DeletePort( RS232PortName port_name )
{
```

```
        isr_info.data_pointers[ port_name - COM5 ] = 0;
}

// ******************* END OF CLASSIC.CPP *******************
```

Because the ISR is called from deep inside the hardware, it is not specified as a member function. In addition, all the data manipulated by the ISR is packed into a classic C structure, not a class. Although this isn't absolutely necessary, it is the convention used in this book. The primary reason for this is that if any routines are rewritten in assembly language, it is usually easier to determine member offsets in conventional C structures than in C++ classes.

The C structure used by `ClassicHandler` is defined in CLASSIC.H as `struct classic_data`. This structure has pointers to the `isr_data_block` structures for every port that gets added to the handler, as well as the status register address for the given board.

There is an interesting error-handling mechanism in the Classic board handler. The one place where there is potential for a failed constructor is in the `ConnectToIRQ()` call. If some other port has already taken over that IRQ, an error return will come back to this routine. As usual, because a constructor has no return value, you need to improvise to come up with a method of returning an error.

You store the result of the `ConnectToIRQ()` statement in a member of type `RS232Error` called `connected`. Later, when one of the ports attempts to connect to the handler, the value of connected is checked and, if an error occurred, the add operation is aborted and the error code in `connected` is returned.

The destructor

The destructor for `ClassicHandler` has only to disconnect the `classic_isr()` from the interrupt specified in the constructor. This is done only if the `connected` member indicates that the connection took place properly. You should note that if any of the UARTs connected to the Classic board handler are still generating interrupts, the system will become unstable. The programmer must be sure that all the ports have been properly closed before destroying the handler. Just as in the constructor, however, it is difficult to handle errors in the destructor, so I leave this issue to the discretion of the application programmer.

AddPort()

The two virtual functions that have to be supported by an object derived from `class Handler` are the `AddPort()` and `DeletePort()` functions. These virtual functions are called in the `PC8250` constructor if a handler argument is specified. (This means that you won't ever call them from applications; you just need to be aware that they are used internally.)

The `AddPort()` function has to set up all the information needed by the `classic_isr()` routine to properly handle interrupts for the given port. Two items are important here. First, like all the other interrupt handlers, `classic_isr()` will need a pointer to the `isr_data_block` for the port. All the data needed to process the interrupt by `isr_8250()` is contained in that data block.

Second, `classic_isr()` needs to know what port number this is on the Classic board. The `AddPort()` function has the port name as one of its parameters, so this does get passed to the handler. By convention, I've defined the Classic board ports as COM5 through COM12. So, when constructing the first port on a Classic board, you will use a port number of COM5. Remember that this is just a convention; the important thing is not the port number you use but rather the position of the port on the board. It would be just as easy to label them COM1 through COM8, but using the same names as conventional DOS COM ports COM1 through COM4 would cause unnecessary confusion.

The reason `classic_isr()` needs to know the port number is that in the interrupt service routine, the status report returns a number from 0 to 7 indicating which port needs servicing. Without the `port_name` parameter passed in `AddPort()`, the Classic board handler would have no way of knowing which port corresponds to which value read from the status register. The `isr_data_block` pointer is stored away in an array of pointers for use by the ISR, with the index into the array determined by the `port_name` parameter.

`DeletePort()`

This routine doesn't do anything except to zero out the appropriate element in the array of pointers to `isr_data_block` elements. That way, a new port can be added later with a function call to `AddPort()`. The PC8250 constructor calls this routine after it has shut down interrupts for the specified port, so there should be no possibility of an inadvertent interrupt occurring after the call to `DeletePort()`.

`classic_isr()`

All the work done in the other routines comes to fruition in the ISR for this handler. This routine will be invoked when an interrupt occurs on the IRQ line specified by the constructor to `ClassicHandler`. This routine keeps an array of pointers to the data block needed by `isr_8250()` to process each port. It determines which of the ports to service by reading the contents of the status register. After that value is read in, the routine simply invokes the PC8250 interrupt handler for the given port.

> **NOTE** Many other nonintelligent boards use a status register that has a single bit representing the status of each port. The handler routine for a board of this type can continuously read the contents of the status register and execute the interrupt handler for each port needing servicing. This can result in many ports being serviced during each interrupt.

CHAPT04.CPP

The test program from Chapter 3 needs only a few modifications to test the Classic board. Although `CHAPT03.CPP` could test one or two ports, `CHAPT04.CPP` has been modified to test 5 ports. The configuration shipping with the book is set up to test four ports on the Classic board along with the standard MS-DOS COM1.

Because `CHAPT04.CPP` is so similar to last chapter's program, I don't include the full listing in this chapter. Instead, I just review the differences here. All the differences are confined to roughly the first 75 lines of code, up to the initialization code in `main()`.

Header file inclusion

First, because you will be using the `ClassicHandler` class to act as dispatcher for the board's interrupt, you need to include the appropriate header file:

```
#include "textwind.h"
#include "classic.h"
#include "pc8250.h"
```

Variables and constants

The test program has a count of ports being tested, and that needs to be increased to 5 for this program. To add flexibility, I also keep the names of Classic board ports in an array so that they can be easily changed. In `CHAPT03.CPP`, that array is called `port_names`; in this program, it changes to `classic_port_names`:

```
#define PORT_COUNT 5

RS232PortName classic_port_names[4] = {COM5, COM6, COM7, COM8};
```

In `CHAPT03.CPP`, I test either one or two ports; in this program, I'm testing five simultaneously. So, the code that defines the window layout is modified to produce a new layout during initialization:

```
int window_parms[ PORT_COUNT ][ 4 ] = {
                       {  1,  1, 38, 10 },
                       {  1, 41, 38, 10 },
                       { 13,  1, 38, 10 },
                       { 13, 41, 38, 10 },
                       { 25,  1, 78, 10 }
                     };
```

Adding the Classic handler

Those changes account for all of the variable and initialization changes needed to update the program. The only remaining changes need to be made in the code that opens ports in `main()`. The most important piece of code creates a handler for the Classic board, initializing it with the IRQ and status port address. The new line of code is shown in bold

```
int main()
{
    int i;
    int c;
    char buffer[ 81 ];
    ClassicHandler handler( IRQ3, 0x140 ); // new line
```

The two parameters for the Classic board are ones that you selected during your board configuration. The system I used to test the Classic board had a built in COM1 but no COM2, so I configured it to use IRQ3. I also configured the board to use I/O ports 0x100 through 0x13f for the eight UARTs, and 0x140 for the status port.

Opening ports and windows

Because CHAPT04.CPP is testing five ports rather than two, I have to modify the position of a couple of the windows used for help and status messages:

```
    UserWindow = new TextWindow( 36, 0, 80, 12 );
    StatusLine = new TextWindow( 48, 0, 80, 1 );
```

The final and most important change to the test program is the code that actually opens the ports. Instead of opening two standard MS-DOS ports, I'm opening four Classic board ports and a single COM port:

```
for ( i = 0 ; i < PORT_COUNT ; i++ ) {
    //
    // This switch allows you to mix and match different
    // port types. In this program the first four ports
    // are Digiboard ports, and the last is a standard
    // PC COM1.
    //
    switch ( i ) {
        case 0 :
        case 1 :
        case 2 :
        case 3 :
            Ports[ i ] = new PC8250( classic_port_names[ i ],
```

```
                        57600L, 'N', 8, 1,
                        1, 1,
                        UNCHANGED,
                        UNCHANGED,
                        UNCHANGED,
                        &handler,
                        0x100 + i * 8 );
            break;
        case 4 :
            Ports[ i ] = new PC8250( COM1,
                        57600L,'N',8,1,1,1);
            break;
    }
}
```

This code opens Classic board ports for the first four test windows and a standard MS-DOS com port for the last window.

The Classic board ports have to specify a handler that knows how to dispatch interrupts to the appropriate UART handler. This is the `ClassicHandler` that was declared earlier in the program. In addition, you have to specify the base address of the UART for the given port. The board setup used here has a UART base address of 0x100, 0x108, 0x110, and on up to 0x138.

The parameters that specify the handler and the UART address are not normally used when declaring standard ports, in which case they are set to their default values. In this case, you have five new parameters that aren't normally seen: `xon_xoff`, `rts_cts`, `dtr_dsr`, `handler`, and `uart_address`. You leave the three handshaking parameters unchanged but specify a handler and uart address.

Building and running the program

After making these changes, the program is ready to build and run. You build it using the `CHAPT04.MAK` file after editing it to use either Borland C++ 4.5 or Microsoft Visual C++ 1.5. These are the last 16-bit versions of the two compilers and the last versions that support real mode MS-DOS programming.

Under MS-DOS, I used the Classic configuration program to set up my test board. I told it to not use PNP mode and to use a single shared interrupt line, IRQ3. The status register was set to 0x140 and the UARTs were set to the eight consecutive eight-byte slots starting at I/O address 0x100.

To subject this handler to a really active test, I connected a modem to the first Classic board port and a loopback connector to the second, and I interconnected the third and fourth with a null modem connector. The last port is connected to MS-DOS COM1, which has a second modem connected.

After doing some typing and turning on the spew feature for the last two Classic ports, the resulting screen looks something like that shown in the in the example that follows. Turning on spewing for a port results in the port continually sending out messages that look something like this:

```
Spewing Packet XXX from port XX              This port is in loopback, I can
OK                                           type data and see it return. The
at&v                                         two windows below me are connected
ACTIVE PROFILE:                              with a null modem cable and are
B1 E1 L2 M1 N1 Q0 T V1 W1 X4 Y0 %C3 %        spewing data to one another.
S00:000 S01:000 S02:043 S03:013 S04:06
S10:014 S11:095 S12:050 S18:000 S23:05
S40:104 S41:195 S44:195 S46:138 S48:0

OK
```

```
Spewing packet 2466 from port 3    Spewing packet 2720 from port 2
Spewing packet 2467 from port 3    Spewing packet 2721 from port 2
Spewing packet 2468 from port 3    Spewing packet 2722 from port 2
Spewing packet 2469 from port 3    Spewing packet 2723 from port 2
Spewing packet 2470 from port 3    Spewing packet 2724 from port 2
Spewing packet 2471 from port 3    Spewing packet 2725 from port 2
Spewing packet 2472 from port 3    Spewing packet 2726 from port 2
Spewing packet 2473 from port 3    Spewing packet 2727 from port 2
Spewing packet 2474 from port 3    Spewing packet 2728 from port 2
```

```
STORED PROFILE 1:
B16 B1 E1 L2 M1 N1 P Q0 V1 W0 X4 Y0 &A0 &B1 &C1 &D2 &G0 &K3 &Q5 &R0 &S0 &U0
S00:000 S02:043 S06:002 S07:050 S08:002 S09:006 S10:014 S11:095 S12:050 25:05
S26:001 S30:000 S36:007 S37:000 S38:020 S46:002 S48:007 S63:009 S82:128 95:00
S108:001 S109:4095 S110:006
TELEPHONE NUMBERS:
&Z0=                                         &Z1=
&Z2=                                         &Z3=
OK
```

```
F1 Help Toggle        ALT F1 Toggle XON/XOFF
F2 Next port          ALT F2 Toggle RTS/CTS
F3 Spew Toggle        ALT F3 Toggle DTR/DSR
F4 Reading Toggle     ALT F4 Toggle RTS
F5 Set baud rate      ALT F5 Toggle DTR
F6 Set parity         ALT F6 Flush RX Buffer
F7 Set word length    ALT F7 Flush TX Buffer
F8 Set stop bits      ALT F8 Peek at 1 byte
F9 Send break         ALT F9 Read a byte
F10 Exit              ALT F10 Send 1K block
```

Multitasking under MS-DOS

Earlier in this book I discuss the fact that people frequently want to use multiport boards under MS-DOS in a multitasking configuration. After seeing how the code in this chapter works, I hope you have an idea of why this is difficult to accomplish. It isn't easy to have the interrupt handler reside in one task and have the `PC8250` objects reside in various other tasks running on the same system.

The biggest problem with this is that multitasking is an afterthought on MS-DOS systems. During the DOS heyday, products such as DESQView and DoubleDos were created as add-ons to Microsoft's MS-DOS, but those products are no longer readily available. However, there are still-third party solutions that may allow you to multitask in your particular hardware setup.

> **NOTE:** Caldera, Inc., is still actively selling and supporting DR-DOS, an MS-DOS clone with a fairly substantial heritage. DR-DOS provides an excellent environment for embedded or dedicated systems, and will run on inexpensive hardware the other operating systems can't touch. DR-DOS has a multitasking API that you may be able to use with your communications applications.

Probably the best way to accomplish multitasking with this setup is to create a device driver or a task that functions as one. The ISR and all the open port objects would reside in a single task. Other tasks would then ask the driver for blocks of data and would send it data via some OS-dependent communications mechanism. Under pure MS-DOS, the most general way to do this would be by using 80×86 interrupts. Other environments will usually have specific function calls in their API to accomplish this.

Summary

This chapter presents a representative multiport class that works with Digi multiport boards. Adding support for this new type of hardware only required a minimal amount of code, thanks to the fact that it is able to reuse most of the code in classes `PC8250` and `RS232`.

Chapter 5

Intelligent Multiport Boards

IN THIS CHAPTER

- ◆ The hardware
- ◆ The software interface
- ◆ The Digi International API
- ◆ Summary of INT14 driver functions
- ◆ Configuring your intelligent board
- ◆ Configuring the ports
- ◆ Implementing the DigiBoard class
- ◆ The code
- ◆ CHAPT05.EXE

THE INTELLIGENT multiport board brings with it a host of new advantages and disadvantages. For comparatively large data transfers via RS-232 lines, it is vastly superior to its unintelligent cousin (discussed in Chapter 4.) Despite the extra power they can bring to bear on an RS-232 problem, intelligent boards were frequently overlooked by programmers. Programmers who had written applications using conventional RS-232 ports would have to completely rewrite their applications to convert to this type of board.

Fortunately, object-oriented programming techniques minimize the amount of rewriting for conversion to one of these boards. By developing drivers that are derived from a carefully constructed base class, such as the `RS232` class, applications can switch between different types of hardware with a minimum of trouble. This chapter develops a derived class named `DigiBoard` to illustrate how you can develop an intelligent board interface.

> **Note:** Digi International is a major supplier of multiport board hardware, including hardware that is compatible with the boards used in Chapter 4 and in this chapter of this book. You can reach Digi International at www.dgii.com.

The Hardware

Dozens of different intelligent multiport boards are available for the PC-compatible bus, but most follow the same basic design. Figure 5-1 shows a block diagram of the major components of the board and its interface with the PC.

Most C++ programmers are probably more familiar with the left side of Figure 5-1 — the PC motherboard. The CPU, whether it is an 8088, 80386, or Pentium, has direct connections to various components on the motherboard, such as RAM and BIOS chips. The CPU connects to plug-in cards and other devices via the ISA or PCI bus, which provides a standard interface.

The bus provides several mechanisms for communicating with the processor, including the I/O bus, memory bus, and interrupt lines. For transferring large amounts of data at relatively high speeds, the optimal solution is to use the memory bus. Multiport boards do this using standard RAM chips with special control circuitry that are collectively referred to as *dual port RAM*.

Dual port RAM is simply RAM that has special control circuitry, allowing it to be accessed by two processors (or other devices) simultaneously. Most PCs already have dual port RAM in their video frame buffer. The video data can be read or written to by the PC BIOS, while at the same time a CRT controller is reading the data and forming dots on a raster line.

The dual port RAM on the multiport board provides the connection between the ISA bus and the rest of the multiport board. The dual port RAM is read and written to by the controller CPU on the card. This CPU is the heart of the multiport card. It has direct access to the UARTs on the card, as well as local RAM and ROM.

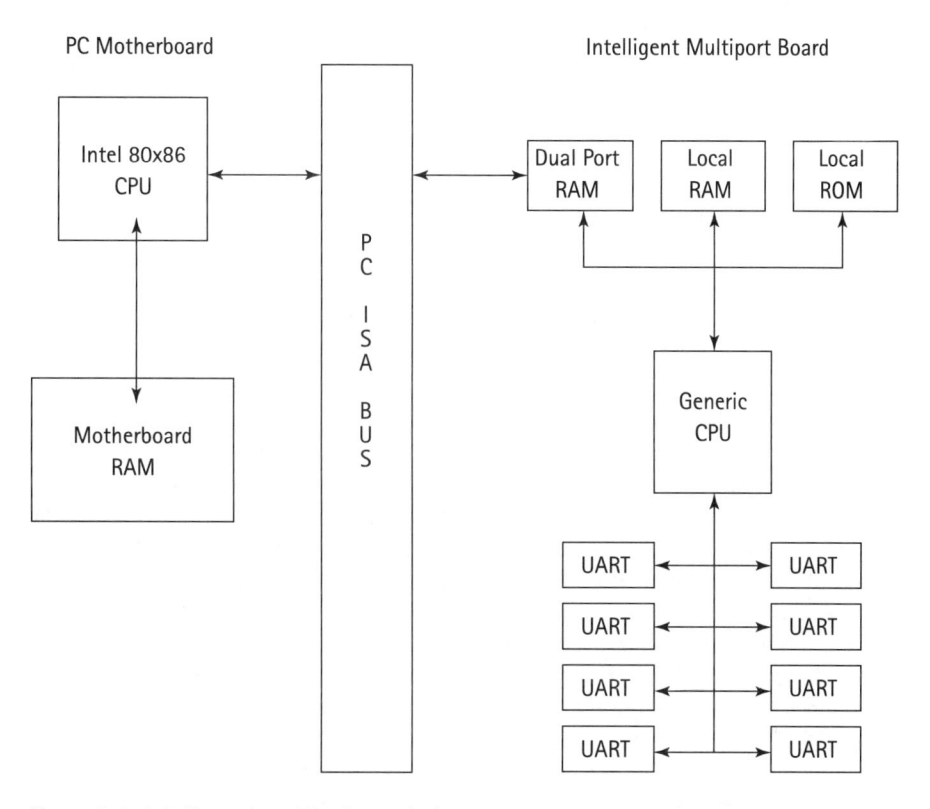

Figure 5-1: Intelligent board hardware design

Design freedom

From a hardware designer's perspective, a multiport board provides a level of freedom uncharacteristic of PC communications equipment. Because the UARTs and CPU are physically separated from the PC, communications is performed using a high-level API, not via direct hardware control. Thus the 8250 compatibility restrictions that dog hardware and software designers alike can be thrown out; they can create a completely new system. More important, the board's CPU does not have to maintain 8088 binary compatibility, meaning that a processor can be selected strictly for its functionality.

Multiport boards, then, have a broad selection of CPUs ranging from lowly 8051 microcontrollers, through conventional 80186 CPUs, to custom RISC machines. UARTs include 16450 chips, Z80 DUARTs, and various other chips rarely seen elsewhere. Typically, the hardware on the board isn't a factor in programming considerations.

Control programs

Clearly, the CPU on the multiport card has to execute a program of its own. The question is, who writes that program? What operating system is the card using? What control do you have over it?

In nearly every case, an application programmer or end user doesn't have to know anything about the program running on the multiport board. The hardware developer creates the software and provides a way for us to load it on to the card. Although end users can customize their hardware, most programmers do not feel it is worth customizing their software to support such a small segment of the market.

Most boards have loader software and perhaps an O/S kernel on EPROM or ROM on the multiport card. Software provided by the manufacturer usually downloads the control program when the PC boots. Although some vendors are courageous enough to put the entire control program on EPROM, most like to retain the flexibility implied by downloading the code into RAM.

After the control program is downloaded and running, it takes control of the UARTs and begins managing their traffic. This traffic includes initialization, interrupt handling, and communications with the PC CPU. Because the card doesn't worry about issues such as the keyboard, MS-DOS interrupts, and video modes, it can concentrate on communications. Using a real-time kernel or O/S instead of MS-DOS helps considerably as well.

The Software Interface

After the control program has been downloaded and is running, you need to establish an interface for sending data and control information back and forth between the PC and the multiport card. No standard has been established for communications protocols; each vendor has gone its own direction.

Two computers communicate via a shared block of memory using procedures that are relatively easy to work out. For most of these boards, communications is established through the use of control blocks. A control block is simply a block of data that one CPU writes out to a memory area. It then uses a semaphore byte to signify that the block is ready for the other CPU. The second CPU signals that it has read in the control block via another semaphore byte. With a carefully controlled protocol, both sides can communicate without memory conflicts.

Listing 5-1 shows sample routines that the PC and the multiport board might use to exchange a control block using shared memory. (Don't try to compile this; it is hypothetical code!) In this case, there is a single semaphore byte. The PC uses the semaphore to set a `BLOCK_FULL` flag when it has written a new block out. The multiport board uses the same semaphore to write a `BLOCK_EMPTY` flag after the block has been successfully transferred.

Listing 5-1: Reading and writing control blocks with shared memory

```
PC::WriteControlBlock( block *data )
{
    while ( semaphore == BLOCK_FULL )
        ;
    *control_block =  *data;
    semaphore = BLOCK_FULL;
}

MultiPortBoard::ReadControlBlock( block *data )
{
    while ( semaphore == BLOCK_EMPTY )
        ;
    *data = *control_block;
    semaphore = BLOCK_EMPTY;
}
```

An algorithm like the one shown here must carefully avoid conflicts between the CPUs. Normally, only a single CPU should have write access to any given block of memory at a time. If both CPUs could write to a single byte simultaneously, neither one could ever be sure of having its data actually being used before being obliterated.

Fortunately, most programmers don't have to deal with multiprocessing issues like these. Most board makers supply driver software that provides a more convenient interface to their boards.

For users of Windows 95/98, the manufacturer's drivers make the ports look as if they were regular serial ports. Application programs that work with standard COM1 and COM2 under Windows 9x will often work with intelligent multiport boards with no changes whatsoever. If you are lucky enough to be in this situation, you can skip ahead to Chapter 10; you don't have to worry a bit about low-level control of your board.

Many projects can't afford the overhead of Windows, and in these cases, you might be forced to use a custom driver written for MS-DOS. Digi International supplies an interface that is loaded as a DOS device driver. The driver will usually provide at least one of two standard interfaces: a DOS device interface and the INT 14H BIOS interface. Some boards provide both, and a few go it alone with a completely nonstandard interface.

The class developed in this chapter uses the Digi International intelligent board driver, so I present the API for its device driver. Because there isn't enough space in this chapter (or this book) to discuss the interfaces for all boards, I concentrate on today's market leader. If you learn how to work with the interface to one board's device driver, working with a different interface will be that much easier.

The Digi International API

Digi International makes quite a few intelligent boards. Figure 5-2 shows a typical example. Over the course of time, Digi managed to unify its intelligent board drivers, providing a uniform interface that works with all of its boards. The universal device driver, CXDOS5.SYS, has an API based on the INT 14H BIOS interface to PC Comm ports. The device driver is loaded upon system bootup and communicates with the intelligent board via a block of shared memory. Programmers can then communicate with the device driver using the same INT 14H API for all boards in the product line.

Figure 5-2: An intelligent multiport board from Digi International

As discussed earlier in the book, the ROM BIOS INT 14H function set is somewhat anemic and isn't really practical for "real world" communications applications. However, a few applications, such as programs that support serial printers, use INT 14H for all their serial port work. Such programs work with unmodified boards from Digi.

Programs such as ones that you will be developing need more features than are available with the standard BIOS set, and Digi has provided them. The extensions to the BIOS found in the CXDOS5.SYS driver set make implementing most of the virtual features found in the RS232 class possible.

All the functions in the Digi API are accessed using the int86() and int86x() function calls in all MS-DOS C and C++ compilers. These functions take register structures as arguments and let you set up the 80x86 registers with any values you choose. The following API listing details the usage of the registers.

One confusing point is the port number that is passed in register DX for every API function call. Under MS-DOS, DX can have a value between 0 and 3 on ISA machines for COM1-COM4. The Digi device driver customarily sets up the ports on the intelligent board as starting at COM5 on ISA. However, these port numbers are entirely arbitrary and can be changed at any time by running the `CXDOSCFG.EXE` program. The programs in this book assume that the board is set up starting at COM5, but it could easily be set at other values.

Function 0: initialize port (BIOS compatible)

This is the standard INT 14H function used to set up a port's parameters. If a baud rate or parity setting isn't available here, the driver has other initialization functions that can be used.

Input registers:

AH :   Set to 0, the function value

AL :   Broken down into four bit fields, shown in the table that follows

DX :   The port number, where COM5 is 4

Return values:

AH :   Set to 0xff if an error occurred; otherwise, set to the line status value

AL :   Set to the reflect the modem status value

The bit settings for the input values of AL are in the following table:

AL BIT FIELD DEFINITIONS

7	6	5	4	3	2	1	0
Baud Rate			Parity		Stop Bits	Word Length	

> **NOTE:** The Digi driver can be set up to emulate either the standard BIOS or the Extended BIOS (EBIOS) introduced with IBM's PS/2 machines. The EBIOS supports a baud rate of 19,200 bps; the standard BIOS does not.

Baud Rate Values :	000	110 (BIOS), 19200 (EBIOS)
	001	150
	010	300
	011	600
	100	1200
	101	2400
	110	4800
	111	9600
Parity values:	00	None
01		Odd
	10	None
	11	Even
Stop bits:	0	1 Stop bit
	1	2 Stop bits
Word length:	00	5 bits
	01	6 bits
	02	7 bits
	03	8 bits

Function 1: output a single character (BIOS compatible)

A single character is placed in the output buffer.

Input registers:

AH :   Set to 1, the function value

AL :   The character to be output

DX :   The port number, where COM5 has a value of 4

Return values:

AH :   Set to the line status value

AL :   Set to the reflect the modem status value

Function 2: input a single character (BIOS compatible)

A single character is read in from the input buffer. Like the BIOS, this function will wait indefinitely for a character to become available.

Input registers:

AH :   Set to 2, the function value

DX :   The port number, where COM5 has a value of 4

Return values:

AH :   Set to the line status value

AL :   The character read in

Note that this function will wait indefinitely for a character before returning.

Function 3: read line and modem status (BIOS compatible)

This function reads in the line and modem status settings for the UART. It is compatible with the BIOS function that does the same thing.

Input registers:

AH :   Set to 3, the function value

DX :   The port number, where COM5 has a value of 4

Return values:

AH :   The port line status

AL :   The port modem status

Function 4: extended port initialization (EBIOS compatible)

The EBIOS was first made available with IBM's PC Convertible and PS/2 lines. It provides for more initialization options for the function 0, particularly in the area of extended baud rates.

Input registers:

AH :	Set to 4, the function value		
AL :	Break flag, 1 for break on, 0 for break off		
BH :	Parity setting:	0	No parity
		1	Odd parity
		2	Even parity
BL :	Stop bits:	0	1 stop bit
		1	2 stop bits
CH :	Word length:	0	5 bits
		1	6 bits
		2	7 bits
		3	8 bits
CL :	Baud rate:	0	110 baud
		1	150 baud
		2	300 baud
		3	600 baud
		4	1200 baud
		5	2400 baud
		6	4800 baud
		7	9600 baud
		8	19200 baud
		9	38400 baud
		10	57600 baud
		11	76800 baud
		12	115200 baud
		13	50 baud
		14	75 baud
		15	134 baud
		16	200 baud
		17	1800 baud

Chapter 5: Intelligent Multiport Boards

DX :   The port number, where COM5 has a value of 4

Return values:

AH :   0xff on error, otherwise the port line status

AL :   The port modem status

Function 5: extended port control (EBIOS compatible)

The EBIOS added a feature sorely missing from the BIOS: the ability to set and clear DTR and RTS.

Input registers:

AH :   Set to 5, the function value

AL :   A value of 0 is used to read the modem control lines

  A value of 1 is used to write the modem control lines

BL :   If writing modem control, bit 0 sets DTR and bit 1 sets RTS

DX :   The port number, where COM5 has a value of 4

Return values:

AH :   The port line status

AL :   The port modem status

BL :   If reading modem control, bit 0 returns DTR; bit 1 returns RTS

Function 6, Subfunction 0: get port name

This function serves two useful purposes. First, it tells you whether the Digi device driver is actually in place and supports a particular port. Second, it lets you know whether the Digi driver has DOS support turned on. *DOS support* means that a device with a name like COM5 has been installed, allowing you to access the port with standard DOS function calls.

Input registers:

AH :   Set to 6, the function value

AL :   Set to 0, the subfunction value

DX :   The port number, where COM5 has a value of 4

Return values:

AH :   Set to 0xff on error

AL :   If no error, set to the highest INT 14H function supported

ES:BX :   A pointer to an eight byte string, containing the port's DOS name (in the format "COMx"); if the driver does not have DOS support, the string "NoDriver" is returned.

Function 6, Subfunction 1: get driver information

This function won't be used in the smart board class developed this chapter, but it can provide useful information. For example, it can be used as a "sanity check" at the beginning of a program to determine whether the Digi driver is in place and, if so, what capabilities it has.

Input registers:

AH :   Set to 6, the function value

AL :   Set to 1, the subfunction value

DX :   The port number, where COM5 has a value of 4

Return values:

AH :   Set to 0xff on error

AL :   If no error, set to the total number of channels supported

BX :   The driver version

CX :   Total number of boards controlled by this driver

DX :   The first port number supported by the driver

Function 6, Subfunction 2: get board information

Like the previous subfunction, this function isn't be used the class developed in this chapter, but can be useful in a configuration or test program.

Input registers:

AH :   Set to 6, the function value

AL :   Set to 2, the subfunction value

BX :   The board number, with 0 being the first board

DX :   Any valid DigiBoard port number

Return values:

AH :	Set to 0xff on error; otherwise, set to the IRQ number		
AL :	Board type :	1	COM/Xi
		2	MC/Xi
		3	PC/Xe
		4	PC/Xi
		5	PC/Xm
		6	CX
		7	PC8K
		8	MC2e
		9	XEM
BX :	The memory segment of the board's dual ported RAM		
CX :	Number of channels on the board		
DX :	The board's I/O port address		
SI :	Port number for the first channel on the board		

Function 6, Subfunction 0xff: get driver name

This function can be used to make sure that the Digi INT 14H support in place is coming from the Universal Digi driver, and not an earlier, incompatible driver.

Input registers:

AH :	Set to 6, the function value
AL :	Set to 0xff, the subfunction value
DX :	Any valid DigiBoard port number

Return values:

AX :	Driver version number
CX :	Number of channels supported
ES:BX :	Pointer to the driver's name, an eight-byte unterminated string; this should normally be "DIGIFEP5"

Function 7: send break

The driver will use this function to send a break signal. This function is a major improvement over the break functions used in many other drivers in this book because it doesn't require that the driver sit in a hot idle loop waiting for the break time to expire.

Input registers:

AH :	Set to 7, the function value
AL :	A value of 0 indicates that the default break time should be used
	A value of 1 indicates that BX contains the break time
BX :	If AL is 1, BX contains the break time in 10 millisecond ticks
DX :	The port number, where COM5 has a value of 4

Return values:

AH :	0xff indicates an error; 0 indicates success

Function 8: alternate status check

This function performs a peek at the next available character in the port's input buffer and returns the current line status.

Input registers:

AH :	Set to 8, the function value
DX :	The port number, where COM5 has a value of 4

Return values:

AH :	0xff is used to indicate that no character was ready to be read
	If AH is not 0xff, it contains the port's line status
AL :	Next input character, if AH is not 0xff

Function 9: clear a port's buffers

This function performs a reset of the port by flushing both the input and output buffers. It is used when the port is initialized.

Input registers:

AH : Set to 9, the function value

DX : The port number, where COM5 has a value of 4

Return values:

AH : 0xff if an error occurred; otherwise 0

Function 0x0A: input buffer count

This function returns a count of the characters presently in the input buffer. It is used as one of the virtual functions inherited from the `RS232` class.

Input registers:

AH : Set to 0x0A, the function value

DX : The port number, where COM5 has a value of 4

Return values:

DH : Set to 0xff if an error occurred

AX : Number of characters in input buffer if DH is not set to 0xff

Function 0x0B: drop a port's handshake lines

This function drops DTR and RTS, even if handshaking is enabled. Usually, the Digi driver ignores requests to change the modem status lines if handshaking is being used on a particular line. With this function, a blocking action could be forced, even if the input buffers haven't passed the high-water mark.

Input registers:

AH : Set to 0x0B, the function value

DX : The port number, where COM5 has a value of 4

Return values:

AH : Set to 0xff if an error occurred; otherwise, set to 0

Function 0x0C: get a port's parameters

This function reads back the current operating parameters of a given port, including the baud rate, parity, word length, and handshaking settings.

Input registers:

AH :   Set to 0x0C, the function value

DX :   The port number, where COM5 has a value of 4

Return values:

AH :   Set to 0xff if an error occurred; otherwise, set to 0

AH :   If not 0xff, software flow control flags

    bit 0 :   XON/XOFF TX flow control

    bit 1 :   XON/XOFF RX flow control

AL :   Hardware flow control flags

    bit 0 :   DTR RX flow control

    bit 1 :   RTS RX flow control

    bit 4 :   CTS TX flow control

    bit 5 :   DSR TX flow control

    bit 7 :   CD TX flow control

BH :   Parity setting

    0 :   No parity

    1 :   Odd parity

    2 :   Even parity

BL :   Stop bits

    0 :   1 stop bit

    1 :   2 stop bits

CH :   Word length

    0 :   5 bits

    1 :   6 bits

    2 :   7 bits

    3 :   8 bits

CL :	Baud rate :	
	0 :	110 baud
	1 :	150 baud
	2 :	300 baud
	3 :	600 baud
	4 :	1200 baud
	5 :	2400 baud
	6 :	4800 baud
	7 :	9600 baud
	8 :	19200 baud
	9 :	38400 baud
	10 :	57400 baud
	11 :	75600 baud
	12 :	115200 baud
	13 :	50 baud
	14 :	75 baud
	15 :	134 baud
	16 :	200 baud
	17 :	1800 baud

Function 0x0D: get pointer to character ready flag

The Digi driver has a character ready flag that can be used to test whether any characters are ready to be read in. The `DigiBoard` class in this chapter uses this function.

Input registers:

AH :	Set to 0x0D, the function value
DX :	The port number, where COM5 has a value of 4

Return values:

ES:BX :	A far pointer to the character ready flag; the flag will contain a 0 if the input buffer for the port is empty, a 0xff if any characters are available

Function 0x0E: write a buffer

This function is used to implement the `write_buffer()` private function for class `DigiBoard`. It simply writes out a buffer full of characters to the intelligent board.

Input registers:

AH :	Set to 0x0E, the function value
CX :	The number of characters in the buffer
DX :	The port number, where COM5 has a value of 4
ES:BX :	A far pointer to the buffer

Return values:

DH :	If an error occurred, set to 0xff
AX :	The actual number of characters transmitted to the intelligent board

Function 0x0F: read a buffer

This function is used to implement the `read_buffer()` private function for class `DigiBoard`. It simply writes out a buffer full of characters to the intelligent board.

Input registers:

AH :	Set to 0x0F, the function value
CX :	The number of characters in the buffer
DX :	The port number, where COM5 has a value of 4
ES:BX :	A far pointer to the buffer

Return values:

AX :	The actual number of characters read from the intelligent board
DH :	If an error occurred, is set to 0xff

Function 0x10: clear RX buffer

This function is used to clear the RX buffer for a particular port. Any and all characters that were pending in the buffer are discarded.

Input registers:

AH :   Set to 0x10, the function value

DX :   The port number, where COM5 has a value of 4

Return values:

AH :   Set to 0xff if an error occurred; otherwise 0

Function 0x11: clear TX buffer

This function is used to clear the TX buffer for a particular port. Any and all characters that were pending in the buffer are discarded.

Input registers:

AH :   Set to 0x11, the function value

DX :   The port number, where COM5 has a value of 4

Return values:

AH :   Set to 0xff if an error occurred; otherwise 0

Function 0x12: get free space in the TX buffer

This function tells how many bytes are available in the TX buffer. This is used to implement one of the virtual functions derived from the RS232 class.

Input registers:

AH :   Set to 0x12, the function value

DX :   The port number, where COM5 has a value of 4

Return values:

AX :   Number of free bytes

Function 0x13: raise a port's handshake lines

This function raises DTR and RTS, even if handshaking is enabled. Normally, the Digi driver ignores requests to change the modem status lines if handshaking is being used on a particular line. With this function, a blocking action could be cleared, even if the input buffers haven't passed below the low-water mark.

Input registers:

AH :   Set to 0x13, the function value

DX :   The port number, where COM5 has a value of 4

Return values:

AH :   Set of 0xff if an error occurred; otherwise set to 0

Function 0x14: peek at character

The Digi driver lets you peek only a single character ahead. This function is used to perform the actual peeking.

Input registers:

AH :   Set to 0x14, the function value

DX :   The port number, where COM5 has a value of 4

Return values:

AH :   If AH is not 0xff, it contains the port's line status

AL :   Next input character, if AH is not 0xff

Function 0x15: get space used in the RX buffer

This function tells how many bytes are present in the RX buffer. This is used to implement one of the virtual functions derived from the RS232 class.

Input registers:

AH :   Set to 0x15, the function value

DX :   The port number, where COM5 has a value of 4

Return values:

AX :   Number of bytes in use

Function 0x1B: get buffer sizes and water marks

This function retrieves the levels of the two water marks and the size of the two buffers.

Input registers:

AH : Set to 0x1B, the function value

AL : The subcommand, indicating which value is to be returned:

　　　0 : Get the TX low-water mark

　　　1 : Get the RX low-water mark

　　　2 : Get the RX high-water mark

DX : The port number, where COM5 has a value of 4

Return values:

AX : The requested water mark

BX : TX buffer size if AL was set to 0; otherwise, the RX buffer size

DH: Set to 0xff on error

Function 0x1C: set handshaking water marks

This function is used to set the high- and low-water marks used by the receiver when performing handshaking.

Input registers:

AH : Set to 0x1C, the function value

AL : The subcommand, indicating which water mark is to be set:

　　　0 : Set the TX low water mark

　　　1 : Set the RX low water mark

　　　2 : Set the RX high water mark

BX : The water mark value

DX : The port number, where COM5 has a value of 4

Return values:

AH : 0xff on error, 0 on success

Function 0x1E: set handshaking

This function is used to establish the form of handshaking used for the given port.

Input registers:

AH :	Set to 0x1E, the function value		
BH :	Software flow control flags		
	Bit 0 :	XON/XOFF TX flow control	
	Bit 1 :	XON/XOFF RX flow control	
	Bit 2 :	Flow control characters are in CX	
BL :	Hardware flow control flags		
	Bit 0 :	DTR RX flow control	
	Bit 1 :	RTS RX flow control	
	Bit 4 :	CTS TX flow control	
	Bit 5 :	DSR TX flow control	
	Bit 7 :	DC TX flow control	
CH :	New XOFF character, if specified in BH		
CL :	New XON character, if specified in BH		
DX :	The port number, where COM5 has a value of 4		

Return values:

AH :   0xff on error, 0 on success

Function 0x20: enable/disable BIOS pacing

In order to emulate the BIOS, the Digi intelligent board can emulate the BIOS pacing on the read and write functions. When trying to write, the BIOS checks for both CTS and DSR to be asserted and will wait for up to 500 milliseconds before returning. You don't want to have to handle this with the current driver, so these functions are disabled.

Input registers:

AH :   Set to 0x20, the function value

AL :   Set to 1 to enable BIOS pacing, 0 to clear the pacing function

DX :   The port number, where COM5 has a value of 4

Return values:

AH :   0xff on error, 0 on success

Function 0xFD: get buffer counts

This function is used to retrieve the number of characters in the transmit or receive buffers. Note that for this function to be enabled, the Digi driver must be installed with EBIOS support.

Input registers:

AH :   Set to 0xfd, the function value

AL :   Set to 1 to get the TX buffer count, 2 to get the RX buffer count

DX :   The port number, where COM5 has a value of 4

Return values:

CX :   The buffer count

Summary of INT14 Driver Functions

Table 5-1 shows a quick reference chart of the functions provided by the Digi driver. You might want to refer to this chart when looking at the code that implements class `DigiBoard`.

TABLE 5-1 THE DIGI DRIVER INT 14H INTERFACE

Function	Description
0	BIOS compatible port parameter initialization
1	BIOS compatible single character output
2	BIOS compatible single character input
3	BIOS compatible read line status and modem status registers
4	EBIOS compatible extended port initialization

Continued

TABLE 5-1 THE DIGI DRIVER INT 14H INTERFACE *(Continued)*

Function	Description
5	EBIOS compatible modem line control
6	Get driver information
7	Send break
8	Check line status and peek at character buffer
9	Clear buffers
0x0A	Input buffer count
0x0B	Drop handshaking lines
0x0C	Read operating port parameters
0x0D	Get pointer to the character ready flag
0x0E	Write a buffer to a port
0x0F	Read a buffer from a port
0x10	Clear the RX buffer
0x11	Clear the TX buffer
0x12	Get the TX buffer free space count
0x13	Raise a port's handshake lines
0x14	Peek at the next input character
0x15	Get the count of space used in the RX buffer
0x1B	Get buffer sizes and handshaking water marks
0x1C	Set the handshaking water marks
0x1E	Set the type of handshaking
0x20	Enable/Disable BIOS pacing
0xFD	Get buffer counts

Configuring Your Intelligent Board

Writing a class to interact with one of the Digi International boards is a fairly straightforward assignment. Getting an intelligent multiport board installed and operating on your system isn't. Unfortunately, this book isn't long enough to accommodate a chapter on board installation, although you might wish it were.

The MS-DOS device driver that interfaces with class `DigiBoard` is named `XEMDOS5.SYS`. This file is normally shipped with the Intelligent Board, along with printed documentation on how to configure the board. You may want to download the latest copy of the driver from Digi's Web site at `http://www.dgii.com`.

> **NOTE:** You can also use the INT14 interface when you install Digi's Windows 3.1 device driver. Digi's Windows 3.1 driver also supports the standard Windows Comm port API, so it probably makes more sense to have your application write to the standard interface.

A configuration program named `XEMCFG.EXE` accompanies the device driver. This program lets you set up the board and port parameters that the intelligent board will be set to when the system boots. You will need to run `XEMCFG.EXE` at least once to set up the board to work with this class.

The following output is from the opening screen of the `XEMCFG.EXE` program. When you first run the configuration program, it asks you for the pertinent information that defines the interface with the board. You need to be fairly comfortable with PC hardware to make it past this stage unscathed. The ISA architecture boards require you to specify the shared RAM memory address, I/O port address, number of ports, and so on. Digi provides some documentation and tools to help with this phase. In particular, you may find Digi's utility program `DIGIMMAP.EXE` helpful in locating a section of unused memory suitable for the shared RAM interface with the board.

```
DigiCHANNEL CONFIGURATION PARAMETERS

    Adapter   Type Window  Memory      I/O    IRQ    # of    Start    Driver
    #         Size Window  Port        #      Chnls  Chnl#   Support
    ------------------------------------------------------------------------
    1         Xr   32k     D0000h      0324   0      8       4        DOS/EBIOS
    +----------------------------------------------------------------------+
```

```
Memory Window Starting Addresses :

8)   80000h  9)   90000h  A)   A0000h  B)   B0000h  C) C0000h  D) D0000h  E) E0000h
     F) 88000h  G) 98000h  H) A8000h  I) B8000h  J) C8000h  K) D8000h  L) E8000h

Enter Selection :
```

The Board Type, Memory Window, and I/O Port parameters are all just reflections of the way you have set up your board. You need to enter values in these fields that show how you have configured the board. The memory address and I/O port are both defined by jumpers or DIP switches on the board. The biggest difficulty with these is making sure that the values you choose don't conflict with existing hardware. The memory map setting has to coexist with 32-bit memory managers, hardware RAM caching, video and network boards, and 8/16-bit addressing conflicts.

The board used in this chapter has an IRQ that can generate interrupts on certain events that take place on the board. The `DigiBoard` driver will not take advantage of those events, so the IRQ should be disabled by setting it to a value of 0.

The number of channels on the board should match your actual hardware. Digi sells most of its boards in various port sizes, with 4-, 8-, and 16-port configurations available.

The starting channel parameter is somewhat arbitrary. By default, the port numbers start at COM5 on ISA machines. However, the actual value really only matters in the applications that talk to the ports. The value used in `XEMCFG.EXE` is the same value that will be loaded into the DX register before making an INT 14H function call. Remember that the value for COM5 is 4 because IBM defined COM1 as being 0 to the INT 14H BIOS.

The final parameter listed for the board definition is "Driver Support." This parameter simply defines which function calls the driver will accept. If DOS support is requested, an MS-DOS device called COMx will be defined for each port. This means that a program could conceivably open up COM15 and send output via the Digi board without having any special knowledge of how the board works. EBIOS support means that the driver will accept the standard EBIOS function calls as well as the BIOS calls. For the `DigiBoard` class used here, EBIOS support is required. DOS support can be included, but the `DigiBoard` class won't use it directly. It sometimes comes in handy when testing your configuration, as shown in the next section.

Configuring the Ports

Ports are configured using `XEMCFG.EXE` as well. Fortunately, the port configuration is not particularly critical to the successful operation of the board. The parameters entered here define the settings of the individual ports at system startup, but any parameter can be overridden when the constructor for a `DigiBoard` object is first called.

The following output is from the port configuration screen that you will see when you first start up `XEMCFG.EXE`. When you first enter the port configuration screen, you see a list of all the ports available on the board, along their current settings.

```
Adapter 1 PARAMETERS
     CHANL    BAUD    MODE     RX FLOW        TX FLOW      NAME
     ---------------------------------------------------------------
       4      38400   8,N,1      NONE         DSR/CTS      COM5
       5       9600   8,N,1      NONE         DSR/CTS      COM6
       6       9600   8,N,1      NONE         DSR/CTS      COM7
       7       9600   8,N,1      NONE         DSR/CTS      COM8
       8       9600   8,N,1      NONE         DSR/CTS      COM9
       9       9600   8,N,1      NONE         DSR/CTS      COM10
      10       9600   8,N,1      NONE         DSR/CTS      COM11
      11       9600   8,N,1      NONE         DSR/CTS      COM12

          A)    50  B)    75  C)   110  D) 134.5  E)   150  F)   200
          G)   300  H)   600  I)  1200  J)  1800  K)  2400  L)  4800
          M)  9600  N) 19200  O) 38400  P) 57600  Q) 76800  R)115200
             S) 14400    T) 28800   U)230400
Select Baud Rate :
```

The handshaking parameters may be the only thing in the configuration menu that ends up being important. Although most programs will initialize the handshaking values when the port is opened, they are not required to do so. By leaving the handshaking parameters out of the constructor, the port will be opened with handshaking set to UNCHANGED. In this case, a port could be opened in a blocking state owing to a low or missing handshake line.

To avoid this problem, I set all my ports to boot up with no handshaking. Then they can transmit immediately, even if I neglect to set up handshaking.

Additionally, if handshaking is not enabled immediately, during the debug phase, I can dump data out of the COM ports with the simple MS-DOS command line:

```
C> ECHO This is a test > COM5
```

If I have another device hooked up to monitor the connection, or even just a breakout box, I can see some activity on the TX lines, which lets me know that things are at least partly working. Note that this test will work only if you configured the driver to include DOS support.

Implementing the DigiBoard Class

Although getting the Digi hardware to work properly can be difficult, interfacing with the XEMDOS5.SYS device driver is fairly simple. This driver doesn't have to worry about interrupt handling. Any interrupts that occur as a result of incoming or outgoing data are handled directly on the DigiBoard by a dedicated processor.

Unlike the classes I developed previously to work with the PC8250 class UARTs, this class doesn't do too much low-level work. For example, when you want to read a buffer full of data in the PC8250 class, the read_byte() routine has to check the input queue for data, extract as much as it can, and then manage the incoming handshaking lines. In the DigiBoard class, you just have to ask the XEMDOS5.SYS driver for the data and it does all the work.

The Code

Listings 5-2 and 5-3 contain the listings for DIGI.H and DIGI.CPP, the two files that together implement class DigiBoard. One of the first things to note in DIGI.H is that it has a full implementation of the virtual functions defined in the base class RS232. Digi designed an API flexible and complete enough to do the job.

> **ON THE CD** Listings 5-2 and 5-3 are on the companion CD-ROM.

DIGI.H extends the range of errors defined in RS232.H by only a single new error, which is DIGIBOARD_DRIVER_NOT_FOUND. This fatal error is returned when an attempt is made to open a port that isn't controlled by the Digi device driver. Other than that, the header file for class `DigiBoard` is pretty much directly derived from class `RS232`.

Listing 5-2: The class definition in DIGI.H

```
//
// DIGI.H
//
// Source code from:
//
//   Serial Communications Developer's Guide, 2nd Edition
//   by Mark Nelson, IDG Books, 1999
//
//   Please see the book for information on usage.
//
// This header file has the definitions and prototypes needed
// to use the DigiBoard classes.

#ifndef _DIGI_DOT_H
#define _DIGI_DOT_H

#include <dos.h>
#include "rs232.h"

// A few type definitions used with this class.

enum DigiBoardError {
    DIGIBOARD_DRIVER_NOT_FOUND      = RS232_NEXT_FREE_ERROR,
    DIGIBOARD_NEXT_FREE_ERROR,
    DIGIBOARD_NEXT_FREE_WARNING     = RS232_NEXT_FREE_WARNING };

class DigiBoard : public RS232
{
    private :
        int line_status;
        int first_debug_output_line;
        void read_settings( void );
        RS232Error write_settings( void );
        int valid_port( void );
        virtual int read_buffer( char *buffer,
                                 unsigned int count );
        virtual int write_buffer( char *buffer,
                                  unsigned int count = -1 );
        virtual int read_byte( void );
        virtual int write_byte( int c );
```

```cpp
        public :
            DigiBoard( enum RS232PortName port_name,
                       long baud_rate = UNCHANGED,
                       char parity = UNCHANGED,
                       int word_length = UNCHANGED,
                       int stop_bits = UNCHANGED,
                       int dtr = SET,
                       int rts = SET,
                       int xon_xoff = DISABLE,
                       int rts_cts = DISABLE,
                       int dtr_dsr = DISABLE );
            virtual ~DigiBoard( void );
            virtual RS232Error Set( long baud_rate = UNCHANGED,
                                    int parity = UNCHANGED,
                                    int word_length = UNCHANGED,
                                    int stop_bits = UNCHANGED );
            virtual int TXSpaceFree( void );
            virtual int RXSpaceUsed( void );
            virtual int Break( long milliseconds = 300 );
            virtual int Cd( void );
            virtual int Ri( void );
            virtual int Cts( void );
            virtual int Dsr( void );
            virtual int ParityError( int clear = UNCHANGED );
            virtual int BreakDetect( int clear = UNCHANGED );
            virtual int FramingError( int clear = UNCHANGED );
            virtual int HardwareOverrunError( int clear = UNCHANGED );
            virtual int XonXoffHandshaking( int setting = UNCHANGED );
            virtual int RtsCtsHandshaking( int setting = UNCHANGED );
            virtual int DtrDsrHandshaking( int setting = UNCHANGED );
            virtual int Dtr( int setting = UNCHANGED );
            virtual int Rts( int setting = UNCHANGED );
            virtual int PeekBuffer(void *buffer, unsigned int count);
            virtual int RXSpaceFree( void );
            virtual int TXSpaceUsed( void );
            virtual int FlushRXBuffer( void );
            virtual int FlushTXBuffer( void );
            virtual char * ErrorName( int error );
            virtual int FormatDebugOutput( char *buffer = 0,
                                           int line_number = -1 );
};

#endif // #ifndef _DIGI_DOT_H

// *********************** END OF DIGI.H ***********************
```

Chapter 5: Intelligent Multiport Boards

Most of the code in `DIGI.CPP` should be fairly simple to follow given the documentation on the `XEMDOS5.SYS` API earlier in this chapter. The majority of the functions just make one or two calls via the INT 14H interface and return to the calling routine. Note that the `line_status` private member of class `DigiBoard` is updated after most of the function calls. This allows you to keep track of any line status events on a cumulative basis.

Listing 5-3: The DigiBoard class implementation in DIGI.CPP

```
//
//   DIGI.CPP
//
//   Source code from:
//
//   Serial Communications Developer's Guide, 2nd Edition
//   by Mark Nelson, IDG Books, 1999
//
//   Please see the book for information on usage.
//
// This file contains all of the code used by the DigiBoard class.
// All access of the DigiBoard is done via the INT 14H interface
// described in the DOC file available from DigiBoard.
//

#include <stdio.h>
#include <ctype.h>
#include "pc8250.h"
#include "rs232.h"
#include "digi.h"

// The DigiBoard constructor is nice and simple. It has to read
// in the old settings to save them, then set new ones according
// to the parameters passed in the constructor. The only private
// member exclusive to the derived class is the line-status flag,
// which is initialized to 0. The call to function 0x20 is used
// to disable BIOS timing emulation.

DigiBoard::DigiBoard( RS232PortName port,
                      long baud_rate,
                      char parity,
                      int word_length,
                      int stop_bits,
                      int dtr,
                      int rts,
                      int xon_xoff,
                      int rts_cts,
```

```
                     int dtr_dsr )
{
    union REGS r;

    port_name = port;
    error_status = RS232_SUCCESS;

    first_debug_output_line = RS232::FormatDebugOutput();
    debug_line_count = FormatDebugOutput();
    if ( !valid_port() ) {
        error_status = (RS232Error) DIGIBOARD_DRIVER_NOT_FOUND;
        return;
    }
    read_settings();
    saved_settings = settings;
    settings.Adjust( baud_rate,
                     parity,
                     word_length,
                     stop_bits,
                     dtr,
                     rts,
                     xon_xoff,
                     rts_cts,
                     dtr_dsr );
    write_settings();
    r.h.ah = 0x20;
    r.h.al = 0;
    r.x.dx = port_name;
    int86( 0x14, &r, &r );
    line_status = 0;
}

// The destructor just restores the old state, nothing more.

DigiBoard::~DigiBoard( void )
{
    settings = saved_settings;
    write_settings();
}

//
// A call to function 0x0c and 0x05 are needed to read all the
// parameters found in the Settings class. All that is
// needed after that is a bunch of switch statements to convert
// the enumerated results that come back from the driver to
```

```
// settings usable by programmers.
//

void DigiBoard::read_settings( void )
{
    union REGS r;

    settings.BaudRate = -1L;
    settings.Parity = '?';
    settings.WordLength = -1;
    settings.StopBits = -1;
    settings.Dtr = -1;
    settings.Rts = -1;
    settings.XonXoff = -1;
    settings.RtsCts = -1;
    settings.DtrDsr = -1;
    r.h.ah = 0xc;
    r.x.dx = port_name;
    int86( 0x14, &r, &r );
    if ( r.h.ah == 0xff )
        return;
    switch ( r.h.cl ) {
        case 0x00 : settings.BaudRate = 110L;    break;
        case 0x01 : settings.BaudRate = 150L;    break;
        case 0x02 : settings.BaudRate = 300L;    break;
        case 0x03 : settings.BaudRate = 600L;    break;
        case 0x04 : settings.BaudRate = 1200L;   break;
        case 0x05 : settings.BaudRate = 2400L;   break;
        case 0x06 : settings.BaudRate = 4800L;   break;
        case 0x07 : settings.BaudRate = 9600L;   break;
        case 0x08 : settings.BaudRate = 19200L;  break;
        case 0x09 : settings.BaudRate = 38400L;  break;
        case 0x0a : settings.BaudRate = 57600L;  break;
        case 0x0b : settings.BaudRate = 75600L;  break;
        case 0x0c : settings.BaudRate = 115200L; break;
        case 0x0d : settings.BaudRate = 50L;     break;
        case 0x0e : settings.BaudRate = 75L;     break;
        case 0x0f : settings.BaudRate = 134L;    break;
        case 0x10 : settings.BaudRate = 200L;    break;
        case 0x11 : settings.BaudRate = 1800L;   break;
    }
    switch ( r.h.bh ) {
        case 0 : settings.Parity = 'N'; break;
        case 1 : settings.Parity = 'O'; break;
        case 2 : settings.Parity = 'E'; break;
```

```
        }
        switch ( r.h.ch ) {
            case 0 : settings.WordLength = 5; break;
            case 1 : settings.WordLength = 6; break;
            case 2 : settings.WordLength = 7; break;
            case 3 : settings.WordLength = 8; break;
        }
        switch ( r.h.bl ) {
            case 0 : settings.StopBits = 1; break;
            case 1 : settings.StopBits = 2; break;
        }
        settings.XonXoff = ( r.h.ah & 3 ) ? 1: 0;
        settings.DtrDsr = ( r.h.al & 0x21 ) ? 1 : 0;
        settings.RtsCts = ( r.h.al & 0x12 ) ? 1 : 0;
        r.x.dx = port_name;
        r.h.ah = 5;
        r.h.al = 0;
        int86( 0x14, &r, &r );
        settings.Dtr = ( r.h.bl & MCR_DTR ) ? 1 : 0;
        settings.Rts = ( r.h.bl & MCR_RTS ) ? 1 : 0;
}

// Setting the DigiBoard up with all the parameters found in the
// Settings class requires three INT 14H calls. Function 4
// sets the standard communications parameters, Function 5 sets
// the modem control lines, and function 0x1e sets up handshaking.
//

RS232Error DigiBoard::write_settings( void )
{
    union REGS r;
    RS232Error status = RS232_SUCCESS;

    r.x.dx = port_name;
    r.h.ah = 4;
    r.h.al = 0;
    switch ( toupper( settings.Parity ) ) {
        case 'E' : r.h.bh = 1; break;
        case 'O' : r.h.bh = 2; break;
        default  : settings.Parity = 'N';
                   status = RS232_ILLEGAL_PARITY_SETTING;
        case 'N' : r.h.bh = 0; break;
    }
    switch ( settings.StopBits ) {
        default : settings.StopBits = 1;
```

Chapter 5: Intelligent Multiport Boards 253

```c
                  status = RS232_ILLEGAL_STOP_BITS;
       case 1   : r.h.bl = 0; break;
       case 2   : r.h.bl = 1; break;
   }
   switch ( settings.WordLength ) {
       case 5   : r.h.ch = 0; break;
       case 6   : r.h.ch = 1; break;
       case 7   : r.h.ch = 2; break;
       default  : settings.WordLength = 8;
                  status = RS232_ILLEGAL_WORD_LENGTH;
       case 8   : r.h.ch = 3; break;
   }
   switch ( settings.BaudRate ) {
       case 110L    : r.h.cl = 0x00; break;
       case 150L    : r.h.cl = 0x01; break;
       case 300L    : r.h.cl = 0x02; break;
       case 600L    : r.h.cl = 0x03; break;
       case 1200L   : r.h.cl = 0x04; break;
       case 2400L   : r.h.cl = 0x05; break;
       case 4800L   : r.h.cl = 0x06; break;
       default      : settings.BaudRate = 9600L;
                      status = RS232_ILLEGAL_BAUD_RATE;
       case 9600L   : r.h.cl = 0x07; break;
       case 19200L  : r.h.cl = 0x08; break;
       case 38400L  : r.h.cl = 0x09; break;
       case 57600L  : r.h.cl = 0x0a; break;
       case 76800L  : r.h.cl = 0x0b; break;
       case 115200L : r.h.cl = 0x0c; break;
       case 50L     : r.h.cl = 0x0d; break;
       case 75L     : r.h.cl = 0x0e; break;
       case 134L    : r.h.cl = 0x0f; break;
       case 200L    : r.h.cl = 0x10; break;
       case 1800L   : r.h.cl = 0x11; break;
   }
   int86( 0x14, &r, &r );
   r.x.dx = port_name;
   r.h.ah = 0x1e;
   r.h.bh = (unsigned char) ( ( settings.XonXoff ) ? 3: 0 );
   r.h.bl = (unsigned char) ( ( settings.RtsCts ) ? 0x12 : 0 );
   r.h.bl |= ( settings.DtrDsr ) ? 0x21 : 0;
   int86( 0x14, &r, &r );
   r.x.dx = port_name;
   r.h.ah = 5;
   r.h.al = 1;
   r.h.bl = (unsigned char) ( ( settings.Dtr ) ? 1 : 0 );
```

```c
        r.h.bl |= ( settings.Rts ) ? 2 : 0;
        int86( 0x14, &r, &r );
        return status;
}

// Function 6 is called to return the name of the port, but
// it also functions effectively as a check to see whether the
// DigiBoard considers the port to be a valid one.

int DigiBoard::valid_port( void )
{
    union REGS r;

    r.x.dx = port_name;
    r.h.ah = 6;
    r.h.al = 0;
    int86( 0x14, &r, &r );
    return ( r.h.ah != 0xff );
}

// Reading a byte uses the two BIOS emulation functions, one to
// read in the modem status, and the other to read the character.
// This function, like many of the other ones, updates the
// line status flags with the result read back from the board.

int DigiBoard::read_byte( void )
{
    union REGS r;

    if ( error_status < 0 )
        return error_status;
    r.h.ah = 3;
    r.x.dx = port_name;
    int86( 0x14, &r, &r );
    line_status |= r.h.ah;
    if ( r.h.ah & LSR_DATA_READY ) {
        r.h.ah = 2;
        r.x.dx = port_name;
        int86( 0x14, &r, &r );
        line_status |= r.h.ah;
        return( r.h.al );
    }
    return( RS232_TIMEOUT );
}
```

```c
// This function also uses a standard BIOS function call.

int DigiBoard::write_byte( int c )
{
    union REGS r;

    if ( error_status < 0 )
        return error_status;
    r.x.dx = port_name;
    r.h.ah = 0x01;
    r.h.al = (char) c;
    int86( 0x14, &r, &r );
    line_status |= r.h.ah;
    if ( r.h.ah & 0x80 )
        return RS232_TIMEOUT;
    return RS232_SUCCESS;
}

// DigiBoard has two private functions, 14 and 15, which are
// used to read or write blocks of data. They both transfer
// as much data as possible, then return a count.

int DigiBoard::read_buffer( char *buffer, unsigned int count )
{
    union REGS r;
    struct SREGS s;

    if ( error_status < 0 )
        return error_status;
    r.x.dx = port_name;
    r.x.cx = count;
    r.h.ah = 0x0f;
    s.es = (unsigned int) ( (long) (void __far *) buffer > 16 );
    r.x.bx = (unsigned int) (long) (void __far *) buffer;
    int86x( 0x14, &r, &r, &s );
    ByteCount = r.x.ax;
    buffer[ ByteCount ] = '\0';
    if ( ByteCount != count )
        return RS232_TIMEOUT;
    return( RS232_SUCCESS );
}

int DigiBoard::write_buffer( char *buffer, unsigned int count )
{
    union REGS r;
```

```c
    struct SREGS s;

    if ( error_status < RS232_SUCCESS )
        return error_status;

    r.x.dx = port_name;
    r.x.cx = count;
    r.h.ah = 0x0e;
    s.es = (unsigned int) ( (long) (void __far *) buffer > 16 );
    r.x.bx = (unsigned int) (long) (void __far *) buffer;
    int86x( 0x14, &r, &r, &s );
    ByteCount = r.x.ax;
    if ( ByteCount != count )
        return RS232_TIMEOUT;
    return RS232_SUCCESS;
}

// This function does no work on its own. Instead, it uses
// the adjust function to change the settings member, then
// calls the write_settings() function to do the job.

RS232Error DigiBoard::Set( long baud_rate,
                           int parity,
                           int word_length,
                           int stop_bits )
{
    settings.Adjust( baud_rate,
                     parity,
                     word_length,
                     stop_bits,
                     UNCHANGED,
                     UNCHANGED,
                     UNCHANGED,
                     UNCHANGED,
                     UNCHANGED );
    return write_settings();
}

// DigiBoard function 7 sets a break of a variable time in 10
// millisecond ticks.

int DigiBoard::Break( long milliseconds )
{
    union REGS r;
```

```c
        if ( error_status < RS232_SUCCESS )
            return error_status;
    r.x.dx = port_name;
    r.h.ah = 7;
    r.h.al = 1;
    r.x.bx = (int) ( milliseconds / 10 );
    int86( 0x14, &r, &r );
    return RS232_SUCCESS;
}

// All four of the modem status functions just use BIOS function
// 3 to read in the MSR of the UART. They then just mask off
// the appropriate bit from the MSR and return a boolean value
// to the calling program.

int DigiBoard::Cd( void )
{
    union REGS r;

    if ( error_status < RS232_SUCCESS )
        return error_status;
    r.x.dx = port_name;
    r.h.ah = 3;
    int86( 0x14, &r, &r );
    line_status |= r.h.ah;
    return ( r.h.al & MSR_CD ) != 0;
}

int DigiBoard::Ri( void )
{
    union REGS r;

    if ( error_status < RS232_SUCCESS )
        return error_status;
    r.x.dx = port_name;
    r.h.ah = 3;
    int86( 0x14, &r, &r );
    line_status |= r.h.ah;
    return ( r.h.al & MSR_RI ) != 0;
}

int DigiBoard::Cts( void )
{
    union REGS r;
```

258   Serial Communications Developer's Guide, Second Edition

```
        if ( error_status < RS232_SUCCESS )
            return error_status;
    r.x.dx = port_name;
    r.h.ah = 3;
    int86( 0x14, &r, &r );
    line_status |= r.h.ah;
    return ( r.h.al & MSR_CTS ) != 0;
}

int DigiBoard::Dsr( void )
{
    union REGS r;

    if ( error_status < RS232_SUCCESS )
        return error_status;
    r.x.dx = port_name;
    r.h.ah = 3;
    int86( 0x14, &r, &r );
    line_status |= r.h.ah;
    return ( r.h.al & MSR_DSR ) != 0;
}

// Like the modem status functions, the four line status functions
// use BIOS function 3 to read the LSR from the UART, then mask
// off the appropriate bits and return a logical true or false to
// the calling program.

int DigiBoard::ParityError( int reset )
{
    union REGS r;
    int status;

    if ( error_status < RS232_SUCCESS )
        return error_status;
    r.x.dx = port_name;
    r.h.ah = 3;
    int86( 0x14, &r, &r );
    line_status |= r.h.ah;
    status = ( line_status & LSR_PARITY_ERROR ) != 0;
    if ( reset != UNCHANGED && reset != 0 )
        line_status &= ~LSR_PARITY_ERROR;
    return status;
}

int DigiBoard::BreakDetect( int reset )
```

```
{
    union REGS r;
    int status;

    if ( error_status < RS232_SUCCESS )
        return error_status;
    r.x.dx = port_name;
    r.h.ah = 3;
    int86( 0x14, &r, &r );
    line_status |= r.h.ah;
    status = ( line_status & LSR_BREAK_DETECT ) != 0;
    if ( reset != UNCHANGED && reset != 0 )
        line_status &= ~LSR_BREAK_DETECT;
    return status;
}

int DigiBoard::FramingError( int reset )
{
    union REGS r;
    int status;

    if ( error_status < RS232_SUCCESS )
        return error_status;
    r.x.dx = port_name;
    r.h.ah = 3;
    int86( 0x14, &r, &r );
    line_status |= r.h.ah;
    status = ( line_status & LSR_FRAMING_ERROR ) != 0;
    if ( reset != UNCHANGED && reset != 0 )
        line_status &= ~LSR_FRAMING_ERROR;
    return status;
}

int DigiBoard::HardwareOverrunError( int reset )
{
    union REGS r;
    int status;

    if ( error_status < RS232_SUCCESS )
        return error_status;
    r.x.dx = port_name;
    r.h.ah = 3;
    int86( 0x14, &r, &r );
    line_status |= r.h.ah;
    status = ( line_status & LSR_OVERRUN_ERROR ) != 0;
```

```
        if ( reset != UNCHANGED && reset != 0 )
            line_status &= ~LSR_OVERRUN_ERROR;
        return status;
    }

    // The five handshaking and modem control functions are all
    // basically lazy. They modify the appropriate value in
    // the settings member, then call write_settings() to do the
    // real work.

    int DigiBoard::XonXoffHandshaking( int setting )
    {
        if ( setting != UNCHANGED ) {
            settings.XonXoff = ( setting != 0 );
            write_settings();
        }
        return settings.XonXoff;
    }

    int DigiBoard::RtsCtsHandshaking( int setting )
    {
        if ( setting != UNCHANGED ) {
            settings.RtsCts = ( setting != 0 );
            write_settings();
        }
        return settings.RtsCts;
    }

    int DigiBoard::DtrDsrHandshaking( int setting )
    {
        if ( setting != UNCHANGED ) {
            settings.DtrDsr = ( setting != 0 );
            write_settings();
        }
        return settings.DtrDsr;
    }

    int DigiBoard::Dtr( int setting )
    {
        if ( setting != UNCHANGED ) {
            settings.Dtr = ( setting != 0 );
            write_settings();
        }
        return ( settings.Dtr != 0 );
    }
```

```
int DigiBoard::Rts( int setting )
{
    if ( setting != UNCHANGED ) {
        settings.Rts = ( setting != 0 );
        write_settings();
    }
    return ( settings.Rts != 0 );
}

// DigiBoard lets us peek ahead by only one byte into the
// input buffer. If there is a character there, this function
// reads it in and stores it in the appropriate place.

int DigiBoard::PeekBuffer( void *buffer, unsigned int count )
{
    union REGS r;

    if ( count ) {
        r.h.ah = 3;
        r.x.dx = port_name;
        int86( 0x14, &r, &r );
        line_status |= r.h.ah;
        if ( r.h.ah & 0x80 )
            return RS232_ERROR;
        if ( r.h.ah & 1 ) {
            r.h.ah = 0x14;
            r.x.dx = port_name;
            int86( 0x14, &r, &r );
            line_status |= r.h.ah;
            *( (char *) buffer ) = r.h.al;
            ByteCount = 1;
        } else
            ByteCount = 0;
    }
    return RS232_SUCCESS;
}

// These functions all use private digiboard INT 14 calls to
// return buffer counts. The only complication is that there
// is no direct way to determine the RX space free. It has to
// be calculated indirectly as the RX buffer size - the buffer
// space used.

int DigiBoard::TXSpaceUsed( void )
{
```

```c
    union REGS r;

    if ( error_status < RS232_SUCCESS )
        return error_status;
    r.x.dx = port_name;
    r.h.ah = 0xfd;
    r.h.al = 1;
    int86( 0x14, &r, &r );
    return( r.x.cx );
}

int DigiBoard::TXSpaceFree( void )
{
    union REGS r;

    if ( error_status < RS232_SUCCESS )
        return error_status;
    r.x.dx = port_name;
    r.h.ah = 0x12;
    int86( 0x14, &r, &r );
    return r.x.ax;
}

int DigiBoard::RXSpaceUsed( void )
{
    union REGS r;

    if ( error_status < RS232_SUCCESS )
        return error_status;
    r.x.dx = port_name;
    r.h.ah = 0x0a;
    int86( 0x14, &r, &r );
    return r.x.ax;
}

int DigiBoard::RXSpaceFree( void )
{
    union REGS r;
    int buffer_size;

    if ( error_status < RS232_SUCCESS )
        return error_status;

    r.x.dx = port_name;
    r.h.ah = 0x1b;
```

```c
    r.h.al = 1;
    int86( 0x14, &r, &r );
    buffer_size = r.x.bx;
    r.h.ah = 10;
    r.x.dx = port_name;
    int86( 0x14, &r, &r );
    return( buffer_size - r.x.ax );
}

// DigiBoard provides two private INT 14 calls to handle flushing
// the TX and RX buffers.

int DigiBoard::FlushRXBuffer( void )
{
    union REGS r;

    if ( error_status < RS232_SUCCESS )
        return error_status;
    r.x.dx = port_name;
    r.h.ah = 0x10;
    int86( 0x14, &r, &r );
    return RS232_SUCCESS;
}

int DigiBoard::FlushTXBuffer( void )
{
    union REGS r;

    if ( error_status < RS232_SUCCESS )
        return error_status;
    r.x.dx = port_name;
    r.h.ah = 0x11;
    int86( 0x14, &r, &r );
    return RS232_SUCCESS;
}

int DigiBoard::FormatDebugOutput( char *buffer, int line_number )
{
    union REGS r;

    if ( buffer == 0 )
        return( first_debug_output_line +  4 );
    if ( line_number < first_debug_output_line )
        return RS232::FormatDebugOutput( buffer, line_number );
    switch( line_number - first_debug_output_line ) {
```

```c
            case 0 :
                r.x.dx = port_name;
                r.h.ah = 6;
                r.h.al = 1;
                int86( 0x14, &r, &r );
                sprintf( buffer,
                         "Derived class: DigiBoard   "
                         "Boards/Channels: %2d/%2d   "
                         "Ver: %2x.%02x   1st Port: COM%-2d",
                         r.x.cx,
                         r.x.ax,
                         r.h.bh, r.h.bl,
                         r.x.dx + 1 );
                break;
            case 1 :
                ParityError( UNCHANGED );
                sprintf( buffer,
                         "Parity Err: %d   "
                         "Break Det: %d   "
                         "Overrun Err: %d   "
                         "Framing Err: %d   ",
                         ( line_status & LSR_PARITY_ERROR ) ? 1 : 0,
                         ( line_status & LSR_BREAK_DETECT ) ? 1 : 0,
                         ( line_status & LSR_OVERRUN_ERROR ) ? 1 : 0,
                         ( line_status & LSR_FRAMING_ERROR ) ? 1 : 0
                       );
                break;
            case 2 :
                sprintf( buffer,
                         "Buffer Counts: RX Used/Free: %5u/%5u   "
                         "TX Used/Free: %5u/%5u",
                         RXSpaceUsed(),
                         RXSpaceFree(),
                         TXSpaceUsed(),
                         TXSpaceFree() );
                break;
            case 3 :
                sprintf( buffer,
                         "RI: %2d   CD: %2d   CTS: %2d   DSR: %2d",
                         Ri(), Cd(), Cts(), Dsr() );
                break;
            default :
                return RS232_ILLEGAL_LINE_NUMBER;
        }
        return RS232_SUCCESS;
```

```
}

char * DigiBoard::ErrorName( int error )
{
    if ( error < RS232_NEXT_FREE_ERROR && error >= RS232_ERROR )
        return RS232::ErrorName( error );
    if (error < RS232_NEXT_FREE_WARNING && error >= RS232_WARNING)
        return RS232::ErrorName( error );
    if ( error >= RS232_SUCCESS )
        return RS232::ErrorName( error );
    switch ( error ) {
        case DIGIBOARD_DRIVER_NOT_FOUND    :
            return( "Driver not found" );
        default                            :
            return( "Undefined error" );
    }
}
```

CHAPT05.EXE

Modifying CHAPT03.EXE to work properly with the DigiBoard class is fairly simple. The easiest way to proceed is to use the version of the program created for Chapter 4. First, I modified the list of include files to pull in DIGI.H instead of CLASSIC.H. DIGI.H contains the definition of class DigiBoard.

```
#include <stdio.h>
#include <stdlib.h>
#include <string.h>
#include <conio.h>
#include <ctype.h>
#include "rs232.h"
#include "textwind.h"
#include "digi.h"
#include "pc8250.h"
```

In CHAPT04.CPP, I created an object of type ClassicHandler at the start of main(). This line of code can be deleted, as it is not needed by the intelligent board class. Finally, I just changed the line of code that used to open the classic board ports so that it reads like this:

```
Ports[ i ] = new DigiBoard( classic_port_names[ i ],
                            57600L, 'N', 8, 1 );
```

To build this program, you need to change the definition of the FILES in CHAPT04.MAK to include the DIGI.OBJ instead of CLASSIC.OBJ. You can then proceed with building the program as defined in previous chapters.

After you make CHAPT05.EXE, you should then be able to talk to an intelligent Digi board. Assuming that you are successful in installing the hardware on your system, you should see a screen shot such as the following.

```
This port has a loopback connector      STORED PROFILE 1:
attached, so it copies whatever I       B16 B1 E1 L2 M1 N1 P Q0 V1 W0 X4 Y0 &0
type in.                                S00:000 S02:043 S06:002 S07:050 S08:05
                                        S26:001 S30:000 S36:007 S37:000 S38:00
                                        S108:001 S109:4095 S110:006
                                        TELEPHONE NUMBERS:
                                        &Z0=                                  =
                                        &Z2=                                  =
                                        OK
```

```
The third and fourth ports are              Spewing packet 14108 from port 2
connected with a null modem cable, so    Spewing packet 14109 from port 2
the spew being sent from this port       Spewing packet 14110 from port 2
is being received and displayed in       Spewing packet 14111 from port 2
the fourth port...                       Spewing packet 14112 from port 2
                                         Spewing packet 14113 from port 2
                                         Spewing packet 14114 from port 2
                                         Spewing packet 14115 from port 2
                                         Spewing packet 14116 from port 2
```

```
Base class: RS232   COM8    Status: Success
Byte count:    23  Elapsed time:       0  TX Free:  4095  RX Used:     0
Saved port:   9600,N, 8, 1  DTR,RTS:  1, 1  XON/OFF,RTS/CTS,DTR/DSR:  0, 1, 1
Current port: 57600,N,8,1   DTR,RTS:  1, 1  XON/OFF,RTS/CTS,DTR/DSR:  0, 0, 0
Derived class: DigiBoard    Boards/Channels:  1/ 8  Ver:  4.03  1st Port: COM5
Parity Err: 0  Break Det: 0  Overrun Err: 0  Framing Err: 0
Buffer Counts: RX Used/Free:     32/ 8159  TX Used/Free:      0/ 4095
RI:  0  CD:  1  CTS:  1  DSR:  1
```

Owing to the fact that the Digi board offloads much of the processing requirements from the PC to the card, you can easily put all ports in Spew mode with CHAPT05.EXE and keep up with the load at high baud rates. This just wouldn't be possible with a nonintelligent multiport card.

Summary

It's not too difficult to implement the class to support intelligent Digi boards. Unfortunately, this experience is only a warmup for other boards. Each intelligent board manufacturer has a proprietary interface with its own peculiarities, pluses, and minuses. Most are based on the INT 14H BIOS calls, but their similarities all end there.

Fortunately, the last strongholds of these proprietary drivers are MS-DOS and Windows 3.1. As you move into the standardized 32-bit Windows platforms, it becomes much easier to interface to drivers that conform to an existing API defined by the operating system.

Chapter 6

The BIOS and EBIOS Classes

IN THIS CHAPTER

- ◆ BIOS Details
- ◆ Problems
- ◆ The Code
- ◆ Inheritance
- ◆ BIOSPort/EBIOSPort class test

ACCORDING TO ITS original design, the IBM PC was supposed to allow developers to write hardware-independent code. All system hardware was supposed to be accessed via a standardized BIOS interface. For some services, such as access to the hard disk, this method has been fairly successful. When developers want to read to or write from the hard disk on a PC, they either use the BIOS indirectly by making MS-DOS function calls, or they use it directly via the INT 13H interface. However, the BIOS designers did not provide interrupt-driven support for the COM ports, which forced programmers to bypass the BIOS and write programs that directly accessed the hardware.

When writing code for standard comm ports on the IBM PC, the developer will usually use code such as that shown in Chapter 3 that implements the `PC8250` class, for reasons of efficiency. However, there are good reasons for supporting the BIOS and EBIOS classes as well:

- ◆ To interface with hardware that is not 8250 compatible. Over the years, some computers have used nonstandard hardware and provided support by replacing the standard BIOS routines with custom implementations.

- ◆ The INT 14H API is used as an interface for several different network access protocols. Many competing systems exist for accessing modems across a network, such as Novell's NASI. Most of these systems support INT 14H access, with proprietary extensions.

- ◆ Some BBS *Door Programs* need to talk to serial ports on a PC via a FOSSIL driver, which is an extension of the IBM PC BIOS. The FOSSIL driver is discussed later in this chapter.

♦ Intelligent boards, such as those from Digi International, support a BIOS or EBIOS interface. The `BIOSPort` class I present in this chapter will work well with intelligent boards from Digi.

BIOS Details

The BIOS designers provided a set of services for access to the serial ports on the PC, collectively accessed via 80x86 interrupt 14H. The original IBM PC BIOS provided four functions, which gave very limited support for polled mode I/O via the two system COM ports. The PS/2 introduced two additional function calls as part of the *Extended BIOS*, or what I sometimes refer to as EBIOS. Although you might have a hard time finding a PS/2 today, many systems support the Extended BIOS. Descriptions of the six functions follow.

Function 0: initialize port (BIOS)

This function is used to initialize the transmission parameters for the port. Some software that uses the INT 14H API interprets function 0 as the equivalent of opening a port. However, no equivalent function that closes a port is defined for the BIOS.

Input registers:

AH: Set to 0, the function value

AL: Broken down into four bit fields, shown in the table that follows.

DX : The port number, starting at 0 for COM1

Return values:

AH: The current line status

AL: Set to reflect the modem status value.

The bit settings for the input values of AL areas are in the following table:

AL BIT FIELD DEFINITIONS

7	6	5	4	3	2	1	0
Baud Rate			Parity		Stop Bits	Word Length	

Baud Rate Values:	000	110
	001	150
	010	300
	011	600
	100	1200
	101	2400
	110	4800
	111	9600
Parity values:	00	None
	01	Odd
	10	None
	11	Even
Stop bits:	0	1 Stop bit
	1	2 Stop bits
Word length:	02	7 bits
	03	8 bits

Function 1: output a single character (BIOS)

This function sends a single character out the port. When you're using the actual BIOS, this function obeys IBM's version of half-duplex transmission. DTR and RTS are asserted before the character is sent. The BIOS routine then waits for CTS and DSR to be asserted before sending the character. In the event that the control lines don't ever go high, a timeout error is returned after a nominal wait, usually on the order of a second.

Input registers:

AH :   Set to 1, the function value

AL :   The character to be output

DX :   The port number, starting at 0 for COM1

Return values:

AH :   Timeout error if bit 7 is set, else the current line status

Function 2: input a single character (BIOS)

This function also obeys IBM's version of RS-232 half-duplex signaling. When the function is called, DTR is first asserted, and then the routine waits for DSR to be asserted. If the input DSR signal remains at a low level after the nominal timeout of one to two seconds, an error is returned. If DSR signal does come high, the routine waits again for a character to be ready in the RX buffer. A timeout error is returned if no character arrives; otherwise, the character is returned.

Input registers:

AH :   Set to 2, the function value

DX :   The port number, starting at 0 for COM1

Return values:

AH :   Timeout error if bit 7 is set, else the current line status

AL :   The character read in

Function 3: read line and modem status (BIOS)

This routine is nice and simple. It just reads in the two status register values and returns them in AH and AL. Although the IBM documentation indicates that this return could return a timeout bit in position 7 of AH, the BIOS cannot actually generate a timeout error for this function.

Input registers:

AH: Set to 3, the function value

DX: The port number, starting at 0 for COM1

Return values:

AH: The port line status

AL: The port modem status

Function 4: extended port initialization (extended BIOS)

This function was added with the PS/2 line in order to support a few more line settings.

Input registers:

AH:	Set to 4, the function value		
AL:	Break flag, 1 for break on, 0 for break off		
BH:	Parity setting:	0	No parity
		1	Odd parity
		2	Even parity
		3	Mark parity
		4	Space parity
BL:	Stop bits:	0	1 stop bit
		1	2 stop bits
CH:	Word length:	0	5 bits
		1	6 bits
		2	7 bits
		3	8 bits
CL:	Baud rate:	0	110 baud
		1	150 baud
		2	300 baud
		3	600 baud
		4	1200 baud
		5	2400 baud
		6	4800 baud
		7	9600 baud
		8	19200 baud
DX:	The port number, starting at 0 for COM1		

Return values:

AH:	The port line status
AL:	The port modem status

Function 5, Subfunction 0: read modem control register (extended BIOS)

Function 5 added the ability to read in the current settings for DTR and RTS and to set them to any desired values.

Input registers:

AH: Set to 5, the function value

AL: Set to 0, the subfunction value

DX: The port number, starting at 0 for COM1

Return values:

AH: The port line status

AL: The port modem status

BL: The modem control register contents

Function 5, Subfunction 1: write modem control register (extended BIOS)

This function adds the ability to write to the Modem Control Register, providing a way to directly control DTR and RTS via the BIOS.

Input registers:

AH: Set to 5, the function value

AL: Set to 1, the subfunction value

BL: Bit 0 controls DTR, bit 1 controls RTS

DX: The port number, starting at 0 for COM1

Return values:

AH: The port line status

AL: The port modem status

Problems

Looking over the BIOS and EBIOS functions, you can spot a number of problem areas. Although you can implement a BIOS class, quite a few pieces are missing. The INT 14H API does not support advanced features, such as handshaking. In addition, the following points will cause various degrees of trouble:

- No error codes are returned from the BIOS calls. This is a major problem if you are trying to open the port, because no way exists to determine whether a port even exists.

- BIOS ports require the use of IBM's version of RS-232 control. If an attempt is made to read or write when the appropriate input control lines are low, the BIOS will delay for many hundreds of milliseconds before returning. But if the routines returned immediately, your code could manage the delay. It would be even better if the control line management could be disabled.

- No BIOS function to close a port exists. This missing feature in the BIOS API causes trouble for software that attempts to emulate the INT 14H functions, such as modem access software that works on networks.

- The selection of available baud rates is very limited. There is no practical reason for this restriction; it's really just a result of laziness on the part of the BIOS designers.

- There is no handshaking of any kind. This would be tough to implement properly in a polled environment, but it would have been useful as a BIOS extension.

- No function is provided to read in the current settings of the UART. The Extended BIOS offers a minor improvement here by letting you read in the state of the Modem Control Register, giving you the settings of DTR and RTS.

Because of these problems, the BIOS interface should be used only when absolutely necessary. Probably the best use of class `BIOSPort` is as a base for a derived class with a better level of functionality.

The Code

The two files that define the `BIOSPort` and `EBIOSPort` classes are `BIOSPORT.H` and `BIOSPORT.CPP`. Both files are listed in their entirety in Listings 6-1 and 6-2. The code for the two classes defined here is fairly easy to follow with the help of the BIOS function definitions given previously.

The most important thing to know when using these classes is which specific functions are *not* supported by the BIOS. Unfortunately, the list is fairly long.

Functions not supported by either class:

- `SoftwareOverrunError()`
- `XonXoffHandshaking()`
- `RtsCtsHandshaking()`
- `DtrDsrHandshaking()`
- `Peek()`
- `FlushRXBuffer()`
- `FlushTXBuffer()`
- `RXSpaceFree()`
- `TXSpaceUsed()`

Functions supported only by class EBIOS:

- `Dtr()`
- `Rts()`
- `Break()`

These two classes make good use of an often-mentioned C++ feature: inheritance. Because the input, output, and status functions are identical for the BIOSPort and `EBIOSPort` classes, it makes sense to derive `EBIOSPort` directly from `BIOSPort`. `EBIOSPort` then has to have its own private implementations of a few new functions, and of the `write_settings()` and `read_settings()` functions, but it shares several other functions with its parent class.

Inheritance

One of the interesting things to note in this class is the use of inheritance. Although all the classes in this book were derived from the `RS232` class, they did not inherit any usable code. `RS232` is an abstract class that doesn't actually do anything on its own.

In this case, class `EBIOSPort` inherits all the methods and data from the `BIOSPort` class. One of the interesting problems to overcome here lies in the area of initialization. Because the `EBIOSPort` supports different baud rates and parities, it needs its own version of `write_settings()`, which has to be called in the constructor. It also has the ability to read the current state of DTR and RTS, so it has a `read_settings()` function, whereas `BIOSPort` doesn't.

When constructing an object of a derived class, the C++ compiler generates code to first construct an instance of the parent class. This means that when the EBIOSPort constructor is called, an instance of BIOSPort will have already been created. You don't want to execute the constructor code because it works completely differently in each of the two classes.

To get around this problem, I created a protected version of the default constructor, BIOSPort::BIOSPort(void). This is the constructor that the compiler will call by default when creating an instance of BIOSPort. This constructor doesn't attempt to initialize any of the settings, which means that the port will still be uninitialized when the EBIOSPort constructor gets called.

The void BIOSPort constructor is set as protected simply for safety reasons. Calling this constructor will create a BIOSPort object that is in a dangerous state. Because the port has not actually been initialized, there is no telling what would happen if it were inadvertently used. By making it protected, you ensure that it can be used only by a derived class, which will presumably know that it is dealing with a dangerously uninitialized object. Listing 6-1 shows the header file (BIOSPORT.H) for the two BIOS classes and Listing 6-2 shows BIOSPORT.CPP, the code for the two BIOS classes

Listing 6-1: BIOSPORT.H: the header file for the two BIOS classes

```
// ****************** START OF BIOSPORT.H *******************
//
//    Source code from:
//
//    Serial Communications Developer's Guide, 2nd Edition
//    by Mark Nelson, IDG Books, 1999
//
//    Please see the book for information on usage.
//
//
//    This header file has all of the definitions and prototypes
//    needed to use the BIOSPort and EBIOSPort classes. This file
//    should be included by any module that needs to access either
//    of the classes.

#ifndef _BIOSPORT_DOT_H
#define _BIOSPORT_DOT_H

#include <dos.h>
#include "rs232.h"

class BIOSPort : public RS232
{
    protected :
        int line_status;
```

```cpp
            int first_debug_output_line;
            RS232Error write_settings( void );
            virtual int read_buffer( char *buffer,
                                     unsigned int count );
            virtual int write_buffer( char *buffer,
                                      unsigned int count = -1 );
            virtual int read_byte( void );
            virtual int write_byte( int c );
            BIOSPort( void );

        public :
            BIOSPort( enum RS232PortName port_name,
                      long baud_rate = UNCHANGED,
                      char parity = UNCHANGED,
                      int word_length = UNCHANGED,
                      int stop_bits = UNCHANGED,
                      int dtr = SET,
                      int rts = SET,
                      int xon_xoff = DISABLE,
                      int rts_cts = DISABLE,
                      int dtr_dsr = DISABLE );
            virtual ~BIOSPort( void );
            virtual RS232Error Set( long baud_rate = UNCHANGED,
                                    int parity = UNCHANGED,
                                    int word_length = UNCHANGED,
                                    int stop_bits = UNCHANGED );
            virtual int TXSpaceFree( void );
            virtual int RXSpaceUsed( void );
            virtual int Cd( void );
            virtual int Ri( void );
            virtual int Cts( void );
            virtual int Dsr( void );
            virtual int ParityError( int clear = UNCHANGED );
            virtual int BreakDetect( int clear = UNCHANGED );
            virtual int FramingError( int clear = UNCHANGED );
            virtual int HardwareOverrunError( int clear = UNCHANGED );
            virtual int FormatDebugOutput( char *buffer = 0,
                                           int line_number = -1 );
};

class EBIOSPort : public BIOSPort
{
    protected :
        RS232Error write_settings( void );
        void read_settings( void );
```

```
                int first_debug_output_line;
                int break_on;

        public :
                EBIOSPort( enum RS232PortName port_name,
                           long baud_rate = UNCHANGED,
                           char parity = UNCHANGED,
                           int word_length = UNCHANGED,
                           int stop_bits = UNCHANGED,
                           int dtr = SET,
                           int rts = SET,
                           int xon_xoff = DISABLE,
                           int rts_cts = DISABLE,
                           int dtr_dsr = DISABLE );
                ~EBIOSPort( void );
                virtual RS232Error Set( long baud_rate = UNCHANGED,
                                       int parity = UNCHANGED,
                                       int word_length = UNCHANGED,
                                       int stop_bits = UNCHANGED );
                virtual int Break( long milliseconds = 300 );
                virtual int Dtr( int setting = UNCHANGED );
                virtual int Rts( int setting = UNCHANGED );
                virtual int FormatDebugOutput( char *buffer = 0,
                                               int line_number = -1 );
};

#endif // #ifndef _BIOSPORT_DOT_H

// ******************** END OF BIOSPORT.H ********************
```

Listing 6-2: BIOSPORT.CPP: the code for the two BIOS classes

```
// ******************** START OF BIOSPORT.CPP ********************
//
// This file contains all of the code used by the BIOSPort and
// EBIOSPort classes.
//

#include <stdio.h>
#include <ctype.h>
#include "rs232.h"
#include "biosport.h"
#include "_8250.h"

// The BIOSPort constructor doesn't have very much work to do. It
// sets all the saved settings to invalid values because none of
```

```
// them can be accessed. It has to set up the debug output, then
// set all the port settings, and then return. Note that
// there is no way to detect an error when attempting to access
// a BIOS port, so the constructor always succeeds.

BIOSPort::BIOSPort( RS232PortName port,
                    long baud_rate,
                    char parity,
                    int word_length,
                    int stop_bits,
                    int dtr,
                    int rts,
                    int xon_xoff,
                    int rts_cts,
                    int dtr_dsr )
{
    port_name = port;
    error_status = RS232_SUCCESS;

    first_debug_output_line = RS232::FormatDebugOutput();
    debug_line_count = FormatDebugOutput();
    saved_settings.BaudRate = -1L;
    saved_settings.Parity = '?';
    saved_settings.WordLength = -1;
    saved_settings.StopBits = -1;
    saved_settings.Dtr = -1;
    saved_settings.Rts = -1;
    saved_settings.XonXoff = -1;
    saved_settings.RtsCts = -1;
    saved_settings.DtrDsr = -1;
    settings.Adjust( baud_rate,
                     parity,
                     word_length,
                     stop_bits,
                     dtr,
                     rts,
                     xon_xoff,
                     rts_cts,
                     dtr_dsr );
    write_settings();
    line_status = 0;
}

// The void constructor is called by the inherited class EBIOSPort
// when it is being constructed. Because EBIOSPort will initialize
```

```
// all the settings, this constructor just initializes the debug
// output. Note that this constructor is protected, because it
// doesn't create a properly initialized port that could be used
// as an object by itself.

BIOSPort::BIOSPort( void )
{
    first_debug_output_line = RS232::FormatDebugOutput();
    debug_line_count = FormatDebugOutput();
}

// There is no BIOS function to close a port, so the destructor
// doesn't have to do anything.

BIOSPort::~BIOSPort( void )
{
}

// The write_settings function is fairly limited when it comes to
// options. There are lots of opportunities for errors here.
// Note that if the constructor attempts an invalid settings, the
// error code never gets returned to the calling program, because
// the constructor doesn't return a value.

RS232Error BIOSPort::write_settings( void )
{
    union REGS r;
    RS232Error status = RS232_SUCCESS;
    r.x.dx = port_name;
    r.h.ah = 0;
    r.h.al = 0;
    switch ( toupper( settings.Parity ) ) {
        case 'E' : r.h.al |= 0x18; break;
        case 'O' : r.h.al |= 0x08; break;
        default  : settings.Parity = 'N';
                   status = RS232_ILLEGAL_PARITY_SETTING;
        case 'N' : r.h.al |= 0x00; break;
    }
    switch ( settings.StopBits ) {
        case 1   : r.h.al |= 0; break;
        default  : settings.StopBits = 2;
                   status = RS232_ILLEGAL_STOP_BITS;
        case 2   : r.h.al |= 4; break;
    }
    switch ( settings.WordLength ) {
```

```c
            case 5    : r.h.al |= 0; break;
            case 6    : r.h.al |= 1; break;
            case 7    : r.h.al |= 2; break;
            default   : settings.WordLength = 8;
                        status = RS232_ILLEGAL_WORD_LENGTH;
            case 8    : r.h.al |= 3; break;
        }
        switch ( settings.BaudRate ) {
            case 110L   : r.h.al |= 0x00; break;
            case 150L   : r.h.al |= 0x20; break;
            case 300L   : r.h.al |= 0x40; break;
            case 600L   : r.h.al |= 0x60; break;
            case 1200L  : r.h.al |= 0x80; break;
            case 2400L  : r.h.al |= 0xa0; break;
            case 4800L  : r.h.al |= 0xc0; break;
            default     : settings.BaudRate = 9600L;
                          status = RS232_ILLEGAL_BAUD_RATE;
            case 9600L  : r.h.al |= 0xe0; break;
        }
        int86( 0x14, &r, &r );
        if ( settings.Dtr != -1 ) {
            settings.Dtr = -1;
            status = RS232_DTR_NOT_SUPPORTED;
        }
        if ( settings.Rts != -1 ) {
            settings.Rts = -1;
            status = RS232_RTS_NOT_SUPPORTED;
        }
        if ( settings.RtsCts != -1 ) {
            settings.RtsCts = -1;
            status = RS232_RTS_CTS_NOT_SUPPORTED;
        }
        if ( settings.DtrDsr != -1 ) {
            settings.DtrDsr = -1;
            status = RS232_DTR_DSR_NOT_SUPPORTED;
        }
        if ( settings.XonXoff != -1 ) {
            settings.XonXoff = -1;
            status = RS232_XON_XOFF_NOT_SUPPORTED;
        }
        return status;
    }

    // If the data ready bit is set in the UART LSR, this routine
    // calls the BIOS function to read the character. Otherwise,
```

Chapter 6: The BIOS and EBIOS Classes 283

```c
// it returns a timeout. Even if the data ready bit is set, this
// routine is still vulnerable to hanging up in a several-second
// delay if the incoming DSR line is not set.

int BIOSPort::read_byte( void )
{
    union REGS r;

    if ( error_status < 0 )
        return error_status;
    r.h.ah = 3;
    r.x.dx = port_name;
    int86( 0x14, &r, &r );
    line_status |= r.h.ah;
    if ( r.h.ah & LSR_DATA_READY ) {
        r.h.ah = 2;
        r.x.dx = port_name;
        int86( 0x14, &r, &r );
        line_status |= r.h.ah;
        if ( ( r.h.ah & 0x80 ) == 0 )
            return( r.h.al );
    }
    return( RS232_TIMEOUT );
}

// This function also uses a standard BIOS function call. It is
// also vulnerable to a delay in the event that DSR or CTS is not
// set.

int BIOSPort::write_byte( int c )
{
    union REGS r;

    if ( error_status < 0 )
        return error_status;
    r.x.dx = port_name;
    r.h.ah = 0x01;
    r.h.al = (char) c;
    int86( 0x14, &r, &r );
    line_status |= r.h.ah;
    if ( r.h.ah & 0x80 )
        return RS232_TIMEOUT;
    return RS232_SUCCESS;
}
```

```cpp
RS232Error BIOSPort::Set( long baud_rate,
                          int parity,
                          int word_length,
                          int stop_bits )
{
    settings.Adjust( baud_rate,
                     parity,
                     word_length,
                     stop_bits,
                     UNCHANGED,
                     UNCHANGED,
                     UNCHANGED,
                     UNCHANGED,
                     UNCHANGED );
    return write_settings();
}

// The next four routines all execute the BIOS call that reads
// in the MSR. The appropriate bit is then masked out, and the
// result is returned to the calling routine.

int BIOSPort::Cd( void )
{
    union REGS r;

    if ( error_status < RS232_SUCCESS )
        return error_status;
    r.x.dx = port_name;
    r.h.ah = 3;
    int86( 0x14, &r, &r );
    line_status |= r.h.ah;
    return ( r.h.al & MSR_CD ) != 0;
}

int BIOSPort::Ri( void )
{
    union REGS r;

    if ( error_status < RS232_SUCCESS )
        return error_status;
    r.x.dx = port_name;
    r.h.ah = 3;
    int86( 0x14, &r, &r );
    line_status |= r.h.ah;
    return ( r.h.al & MSR_RI ) != 0;
```

```
}

int BIOSPort::Cts( void )
{
    union REGS r;

    if ( error_status < RS232_SUCCESS )
        return error_status;
    r.x.dx = port_name;
    r.h.ah = 3;
    int86( 0x14, &r, &r );
    line_status |= r.h.ah;
    return ( r.h.al & MSR_CTS ) != 0;
}

int BIOSPort::Dsr( void )
{
    union REGS r;

    if ( error_status < RS232_SUCCESS )
        return error_status;
    r.x.dx = port_name;
    r.h.ah = 3;
    int86( 0x14, &r, &r );
    line_status |= r.h.ah;
    return ( r.h.al & MSR_DSR ) != 0;
}

// The four routines that check line status bits operate almost
// identically to the modem status routines. The only difference
// is that the line status bits are accumulated in a private data
// member, so instead of just checking the bit in the LSR, these
// routines have to check the current state ORed with the
// cumulative state. In addition, each of the routines has the
// option of either leaving the bit set or clearing it after
// reading it.

int BIOSPort::ParityError( int reset )
{
    union REGS r;
    int status;

    if ( error_status < RS232_SUCCESS )
        return error_status;
    r.x.dx = port_name;
```

```c
    r.h.ah = 3;
    int86( 0x14, &r, &r );
    line_status |= r.h.ah;
    status = ( line_status & LSR_PARITY_ERROR ) != 0;
    if ( reset != UNCHANGED && reset != 0 )
        line_status &= ~LSR_PARITY_ERROR;
    return status;
}

int BIOSPort::BreakDetect( int reset )
{
    union REGS r;
    int status;

    if ( error_status < RS232_SUCCESS )
        return error_status;
    r.x.dx = port_name;
    r.h.ah = 3;
    int86( 0x14, &r, &r );
    line_status |= r.h.ah;
    status = ( line_status & LSR_BREAK_DETECT ) != 0;
    if ( reset != UNCHANGED && reset != 0 )
        line_status &= ~LSR_BREAK_DETECT;
    return status;
}

int BIOSPort::FramingError( int reset )
{
    union REGS r;
    int status;

    if ( error_status < RS232_SUCCESS )
        return error_status;
    r.x.dx = port_name;
    r.h.ah = 3;
    int86( 0x14, &r, &r );
    line_status |= r.h.ah;
    status = ( line_status & LSR_FRAMING_ERROR ) != 0;
    if ( reset != UNCHANGED && reset != 0 )
        line_status &= ~LSR_FRAMING_ERROR;
    return status;
}

int BIOSPort::HardwareOverrunError( int reset )
{
```

```c
    union REGS r;
    int status;

    if ( error_status < RS232_SUCCESS )
        return error_status;
    r.x.dx = port_name;
    r.h.ah = 3;
    int86( 0x14, &r, &r );
    line_status |= r.h.ah;
    status = ( line_status & LSR_OVERRUN_ERROR ) != 0;
    if ( reset != UNCHANGED && reset != 0 )
        line_status &= ~LSR_OVERRUN_ERROR;
    return status;
}

// The formatted debug output for BIOSPort is sparse. It prints
// out two lines of information that dump the states of the MSR
// and LSR.

int BIOSPort::FormatDebugOutput( char *buffer, int line_number )
{
    if ( buffer == 0 )
        return( first_debug_output_line +  2 );
    if ( line_number < first_debug_output_line )
        return RS232::FormatDebugOutput( buffer, line_number );
    switch( line_number - first_debug_output_line ) {
        case 0 :
            sprintf( buffer,
                     "Derived class: BIOSPort  "
                     "RI: %2d  CD: %2d  CTS: %2d  DSR: %2d",
                     Ri(), Cd(), Cts(), Dsr() );
            break;
        case 1 :
            Ri();
            sprintf( buffer,
                     "Parity Err: %d  "
                     "Break Det: %d  "
                     "Overrun Err: %d  "
                     "Framing Err: %d",
                     ( line_status & LSR_PARITY_ERROR ) ? 1 : 0,
                     ( line_status & LSR_BREAK_DETECT ) ? 1 : 0,
                     ( line_status & LSR_OVERRUN_ERROR ) ? 1 : 0,
                     ( line_status & LSR_FRAMING_ERROR ) ? 1 : 0
                   );
            break;
```

```
            default :
                return RS232_ILLEGAL_LINE_NUMBER;
        }
        return RS232_SUCCESS;
}

// The read_buffer routine is set up to continue reading in data
// as long as the data ready bit is set in the LSR. With a true
// BIOS, this means that it will generally read in only a single
// byte before returning to the Read() routine. It is up to the
// calling program to make sure a time value is set up so that
// multiple bytes can be read in. Note that a BIOS emulation
// system will usually be able to feed in an entire buffer with a
// call.

int BIOSPort::read_buffer( char *buffer, unsigned int count )
{
    union REGS rin;
    union REGS rout;

    ByteCount = 0;
    if ( error_status < 0 )
        return error_status;
    rin.x.dx = port_name;
    while ( count > 0 ) {
        rin.h.ah = 3;
        int86( 0x14, &rin, &rout );
        line_status |= rout.h.ah;
        if ( ( rout.h.ah & LSR_DATA_READY ) == 0 )
            break;
        rin.h.ah = 2;
        int86( 0x14, &rin, &rout );
        line_status |= rout.h.ah;
        if ( rout.h.ah & 0x80 )
            break;
        *buffer++ = rout.h.al;
        count--;
        ByteCount++;
    }
    *buffer = '\0';
    if ( count > 0 )
        return RS232_TIMEOUT;
    else
        return RS232_SUCCESS;
}
```

```c
// Like read_buffer(), the write_buffer routine will usually
// be able to write only a single byte when using a true BIOS
// implementation. It is up to the caller to invoke Write() with
// a long enough time delay to be able to send the entire buffer.
// A BIOS emulation system will usually be able to take in the
// entire buffer with one call to write_buffer().

int BIOSPort::write_buffer( char *buffer, unsigned int count )
{
    union REGS rin;
    union REGS rout;

    rin.x.dx = port_name;
    ByteCount = 0;
    if ( error_status < 0 )
        return error_status;
    while ( count > 0 ) {
        rin.h.ah = 3;
        int86( 0x14, &rin, &rout );
        line_status |= rout.h.ah;
        if ( ( rout.h.ah & LSR_THRE ) == 0 )
            break;
        rin.h.ah = 1;
        rin.h.al = (char) *buffer++;
        int86( 0x14, &rin, &rout );
        if ( rout.h.ah & 0x80 )
            break;
        line_status |= rout.h.ah;
        buffer++;
        count--;
        ByteCount++;
    }
    if ( count > 0 )
        return RS232_TIMEOUT;
    else
        return RS232_SUCCESS;
}

// If the THRE bit is set, there is room for one byte; if clear,
// there is room for 0 bytes.

int BIOSPort::TXSpaceFree( void )
{
    union REGS r;
```

```c
        if ( error_status < RS232_SUCCESS )
            return error_status;
    r.x.dx = port_name;
    r.h.ah = 3;
    int86( 0x14, &r, &r );
    line_status |= r.h.ah;
    if ( r.h.ah & LSR_THRE )
        return 1;
    else
        return 0;
}

// If the data ready bit is set, there is one byte present in the
// buffer, else 0.

int BIOSPort::RXSpaceUsed( void )
{
    union REGS r;

    if ( error_status < RS232_SUCCESS )
        return error_status;
    r.x.dx = port_name;
    r.h.ah = 3;
    int86( 0x14, &r, &r );
    line_status |= r.h.ah;
    if ( r.h.ah & LSR_DATA_READY )
        return 1;
    else
        return 0;
}

// EBIOSPort has a few extra functions above and beyond BIOSPort.
// It has the ability to read in the old state of DTR and RTS,
// and can send a break signal. It also has a few extra baud
// rates and other line settings.

EBIOSPort::EBIOSPort( RS232PortName port,
                      long baud_rate,
                      char parity,
                      int word_length,
                      int stop_bits,
                      int dtr,
                      int rts,
                      int xon_xoff,
                      int rts_cts,
```

```
                            int dtr_dsr )
{
    port_name = port;
    error_status = RS232_SUCCESS;

    first_debug_output_line = BIOSPort::FormatDebugOutput();
    debug_line_count = FormatDebugOutput();
    read_settings();
    saved_settings = settings;
    settings.Adjust( baud_rate,
                     parity,
                     word_length,
                     stop_bits,
                     dtr,
                     rts,
                     xon_xoff,
                     rts_cts,
                     dtr_dsr );
    break_on = 0;
    write_settings();
    line_status = 0;
}

EBIOSPort::~EBIOSPort( void )
{
}

// The only additional information that I have to offer with this
// output routine is the setting of the break flag, which will
// usually be clear.

int EBIOSPort::FormatDebugOutput( char *buffer, int line_number )
{
    if ( buffer == 0 )
        return( first_debug_output_line + 1 );
    if ( line_number < first_debug_output_line )
        return BIOSPort::FormatDebugOutput( buffer, line_number );
    switch( line_number - first_debug_output_line ) {
        case 0 :
            sprintf( buffer,
                     "Derived class: EBIOSPort   "
                     "Break flag: %2d",
                     break_on );
            break;
        default :
```

```
            return RS232_ILLEGAL_LINE_NUMBER;
    }
    return RS232_SUCCESS;
}

// There are exactly two settings that I can read here: the state
// of Dtr and Rts. It isn't much, but I read them both in and
// set the rest of the values to be invalid.

void EBIOSPort::read_settings( void )
{
    union REGS r;

    r.x.dx = port_name;
    r.h.ah = 5;
    r.h.al = 0;
    int86( 0x14, &r, &r );
    settings.Dtr = ( ( r.h.bl & 0x1 ) != 0 );
    settings.Rts = ( ( r.h.bl & 0x2 ) != 0 );
    settings.BaudRate = -1L;
    settings.Parity = '?';
    settings.WordLength = -1;
    settings.StopBits = -1;
    settings.XonXoff = -1;
    settings.RtsCts = -1;
    settings.DtrDsr = -1;
}

// write_settings() uses a different function for the EBIOS, so it
// has a few extra settings to support.

RS232Error EBIOSPort::write_settings( void )
{
    union REGS r;
    RS232Error status = RS232_SUCCESS;

    r.x.dx = port_name;
    r.h.ah = 4;
    if ( break_on )
        r.h.al = 1;
    else
        r.h.al = 0;
    switch ( toupper( settings.Parity ) ) {
        case 'E' : r.h.bh = 1; break;
        case 'O' : r.h.bh = 2; break;
```

```
            default  : settings.Parity = 'N';
                       status = RS232_ILLEGAL_PARITY_SETTING;
            case 'N' : r.h.bh = 0; break;
        }
        switch ( settings.StopBits ) {
            case 1   : r.h.bl = 0; break;
            default  : settings.StopBits = 2;
                       status = RS232_ILLEGAL_STOP_BITS;
            case 2   : r.h.bl = 1; break;
        }
        switch ( settings.WordLength ) {
            case 5   : r.h.ch = 0; break;
            case 6   : r.h.ch = 1; break;
            case 7   : r.h.ch = 2; break;
            default  : settings.WordLength = 8;
                       status = RS232_ILLEGAL_WORD_LENGTH;
            case 8   : r.h.ch = 3; break;
        }
        switch ( settings.BaudRate ) {
            case 110L   : r.h.cl = 0x00; break;
            case 150L   : r.h.cl = 0x01; break;
            case 300L   : r.h.cl = 0x02; break;
            case 600L   : r.h.cl = 0x03; break;
            case 1200L  : r.h.cl = 0x04; break;
            case 2400L  : r.h.cl = 0x05; break;
            case 4800L  : r.h.cl = 0x06; break;
            default     : settings.BaudRate = 9600L;
                          status = RS232_ILLEGAL_BAUD_RATE;
            case 9600L  : r.h.cl = 0x07; break;
            case 19200L : r.h.cl = 0x08; break;
        }
        int86( 0x14, &r, &r );
        r.x.dx = port_name;
        r.h.ah = 5;
        r.h.al = 1;
        r.h.bl = (unsigned char) ( ( settings.Dtr ) ? 1 : 0 );
        r.h.bl |= ( settings.Rts ) ? 2 : 0;
        int86( 0x14, &r, &r );
        if ( settings.RtsCts != -1 ) {
            settings.RtsCts = -1;
            status = RS232_RTS_CTS_NOT_SUPPORTED;
        }
        if ( settings.DtrDsr != -1 ) {
            settings.DtrDsr = -1;
            status = RS232_DTR_DSR_NOT_SUPPORTED;
```

```cpp
        }
        if ( settings.XonXoff != -1 ) {
            settings.XonXoff = -1;
            status = RS232_XON_XOFF_NOT_SUPPORTED;
        }
        return status;
}

// EBIOSPort can set Dtr and Rts, BIOSPort can't.

int EBIOSPort::Dtr( int setting )
{
    if ( setting != UNCHANGED ) {
        settings.Dtr = ( setting != 0 );
        write_settings();
    }
    return ( settings.Dtr != 0 );
}

int EBIOSPort::Rts( int setting )
{
    if ( setting != UNCHANGED ) {
        settings.Rts = ( setting != 0 );
        write_settings();
    }
    return ( settings.Rts != 0 );
}

int EBIOSPort::Break( long milliseconds )
{
    long timer;

    if ( error_status < RS232_SUCCESS )
        return error_status;
    timer = ReadTime() + milliseconds;
    break_on = 1;
    write_settings();
    while ( ReadTime() < timer )
        IdleFunction();
    break_on = 0;
    write_settings();
    return RS232_SUCCESS;
}
```

```
RS232Error EBIOSPort::Set( long baud_rate,
                           int parity,
                           int word_length,
                           int stop_bits )
{
    settings.Adjust( baud_rate,
                     parity,
                     word_length,
                     stop_bits,
                     UNCHANGED,
                     UNCHANGED,
                     UNCHANGED,
                     UNCHANGED,
                     UNCHANGED );
    return write_settings();
}
```

Testing the BIOS Classes

Building a version of CHAPT03 to test these two classes requires the usual steps. Naturally, the version created here will be called CHAPT06, and its makefile will be called CHAPT06.MAK. First, copy CHAPT03.MAK to CHAPT06.MAK, then modify the definition of FILES to look like this:

```
FILES = biosport.obj pcirq.obj\
        rs232.obj textwind.obj msdos.obj
```

This will cause the make system to compile and link the code for this class in with the rest of the code needed for CHAPT06.CPP, without any of the code needed for unused classes.

The second step is to copy CHAPT03.CPP to CHAPT06.CPP, then perform the usual modifications. For my particular version of the test program, I first modify the port count to be set to 2, as I am testing with COM2 and COM3. Immediately below that line I define the port name array with the ports that I plan to use:

```
#define PORT_COUNT 2
RS232PortName port_names[ 4 ] = { COM2, COM3 };
```

Finally, I modify the switch statement that creates the new *BIOSPort* objects to look like this:

```
for ( i = 0 ; i < PORT_COUNT ; i++ ) {
    Ports[ i ] = new BIOSPort( port_names[ i ],
                               9600L, 'N', 8, 1, 1, 1 );
```

On my system, COM2 is connected to a loopback connector, and COM3 is an internal modem. The following output illustrates the program running in this configuration.

```
This port has a loopback connector,   OK
and thus copies everything I type     at&v
directly back to the input port.      ACTIVE PROFILE:
                                      B1 E1 L1 M1 N1 Q0 T V1 W0 X4 Y0 &C1 &0
The second port is connected to a     S00:000 S01:000 S02:043 S03:013 S04:06
modem.                                S10:014 S11:095 S12:050 S18:000 S25:00
                                      S46:138 S48:007 S95:000

                                      STORED PROFILE 0:
                                      B1 E1 L1 M1 N1 Q0 T V1 W0 X4 Y0 &C1 &
                                      S00:000 S02:043 S06:002 S07:050 S08:00
                                      S36:007 S37:000 S40:104 S41:195 S46:1

                                      STORED PROFILE 1:
                                      B1 E1 L1 M1 N1 Q0 T V1 W0 X4 Y0 &C1 &
                                      S00:000 S02:043 S06:002 S07:050 S08:00
                                      S36:007 S37:000 S40:104 S41:195 S46:1

Base class: RS232  COM3   Status: Success
Byte count:      0  Elapsed time:      0  TX Free:    1  RX Used:     0
Saved port:     -1,?,-1,-1  DTR,RTS: -1,-1  XON/OFF,RTS/CTS,DTR/DSR: -1,-1,-1
Current port:   9600,N,8,1  DTR,RTS: -1,-1  XON/OFF,RTS/CTS,DTR/DSR: -1,-1,-1
Derived class: BIOSPort  RI: 0  CD: 0  CTS: 1  DSR: 1
Parity Err: 0  Break Det: 0  Overrun Err: 0  Framing Err: 0
```

The only other modification needed to CHAPT06.CPP is to add the appropriate include line to bring BIOSPORT.H and all its definitions into the file. The list of header files should look like this:

```
#include "portable.h"
#include <stdio.h>
#include <stdlib.h>
#include <string.h>
#include <conio.h>
#include <ctype.h>
#include "rs232.h"
#include "textwind.h"
#include "biosport.h"
```

There are several inherent problems with the BIOS drivers. Perhaps the foremost is that the BIOS doesn't have an error return for a missing port, so the `BIOSPort` constructor executes successfully regardless of the existence of the port.

In addition, there is no good way to determine whether a given configuration supports EBIOS. So a port opened with the `EBIOSPort` constructor may operate incorrectly when in fact a port exists.

Finally, if you are truly using the PC BIOS and not emulation software, you will face truly horrendous obstacles when it comes to reading data. Without interrupt support, you will likely miss enormous masses of input data due to slow polling. In fact, if I attempt to use the test program's spew mode on my `BIOSPort` object, I basically am stuck with a complete failure.

This leaves us with a fairly dangerous set of `RS232` objects. Although they may be our only choice for access of COM ports under many configurations, we are going to be extremely dependent on proper configuration of the software by end users. In the event that the end user doesn't understand his or her setup, these objects will work poorly or not at all.

Summary

The IBM PC BIOS provides a standard interface to serial ports. Not only does it work with standard PC serial ports, but many manufacturers of custom communications hardware use the same interface to communicate with their hardware. The `BiosPort` and `EBiosPort` classes described in this chapter insure that you have code in your toolkit that works with these interfaces.

Chapter 7

The FOSSIL Interface

IN THIS CHAPTER

- ◆ A history review
- ◆ The FOSSIL specification
- ◆ Sources of more information
- ◆ The source code for class Fossil
- ◆ The program CHAPT07.EXE
- ◆ The test program results

THE FOSSIL DRIVER IS a good idea that should have taken over the PC world. But just being a good idea wasn't enough, and FOSSIL drivers have been relegated to niche applications. This chapter documents the FOSSIL interface and develops a class derived from `RS232` that utilizes the FOSSIL interface for communications.

Note that the FOSSIL interface was very much a part of the BBS world, which today has largely vanished. You may still find that you need to use software or hardware that supports this interface, so regardless of the status of BBS-ing in general, it seems like a good idea to keep a `Fossil` class handy.

History

FOSSIL is an acronym for *Fido-Opus-Seadog Standard Interface Layer*. The development of the first FOSSIL was an attempt to define a level of standardization missing from the IBM PC. As I've already mentioned, the IBM PC BIOS support for serial ports is simply not up to the task of serious serial communications. Early pioneers in the IBM PC BBS world had to implement custom versions of serial interface code that interfaced directly with the PC hardware.

Although most BBS authors successfully implemented their own serial interfaces, this approach still created numerous problems. First, the BBS authors wanted to concentrate on interesting problems such as providing good user interfaces or developing nationwide mail networks. Instead, they often found themselves debugging system hardware problems for the vast array of machines that BBS sysops were attempting to bring up.

An even more serious problem was related to door programs and external protocols. A *door program* is an external program that can be executed by a user logged in on a BBS. By giving a BBS the ability to call external programs, the BBS author opens the doors to a wide variety of support programs written by enterprising programmers. Popular BBS programs of old, such as PCBoard, had literally hundreds of door programs available, performing tasks ranging from mail delivery to games to callback verifiers.

External protocols were another feature useful for BBS authors. When a new file transfer protocol such as ZMODEM became popular, an external protocol driver allowed a BBS to add support for that protocol without modification to the BBS code. Without external protocol programs, every time BBS authors or users wanted to add a new file transfer protocol, they would be required to alter the BBS source code. External door programs such as Chuck Forsberg's DSZ.COM made new protocols available much more quickly than would have been possible if every BBS system had to be modified.

In the early 1980s, door programs and external protocols were not easy to implement. Once again, even for the simplest external program, the programmer had to sit down and write an entire library of serial interface code.

The solution

The early BBS implementers decided to do what IBM or Microsoft should have done, which was to define a set of system services for the PC serial port. The FOSSIL specification was the result. A FOSSIL driver can be implemented as a device driver, a TSR, or even part of the system BIOS. It is simply a piece of software that provides access to the serial ports on a PC using a set of extensions to the BIOS INT 14H services.

By placing the interrupt-driven serial support in a standalone driver, the BBS writer no longer had to devote substantial amounts of code to supporting serial hardware. Even better, external door programs and protocol drivers could now take advantage of the same driver, making their lives much simpler. After the BBS program opened a port and configured it, the door program didn't even have to worry about setting the baud rate or handshaking options!

The early definition of FOSSIL envisioned a future in which BBS programs could run on virtually any hardware and O/S built on Intel 80x86 platform. By simply building a FOSSIL driver for a particular computer, all existing BBS software would work without changes.

In practice, this idea was somewhat successful. Several good FOSSIL drivers are available for standard PCs. In addition, noncompatible computers such as the DEC Rainbow were able to run BBS software after an appropriate FOSSIL driver was developed. FOSSIL drivers for standard PCs have been quick to take advantage of features such as 16550 FIFO buffering. Waiting for every door and BBS program to take advantage of the same thing might have taken years.

Better yet, the FOSSIL interface provided hardware manufacturers with an instant market for their products. A multiport board manufacturer could write a FOSSIL driver for their board and instantly be useful to dozens of different BBS programs. For example, even today, Comtrol provides a FOSSIL driver for its RocketPort line of boards.

The FOSSIL Specification

The FOSSIL specification defines the complete interface between the application program and the serial interface hardware. The FOSSIL specification is up to release 5, and is not likely to ever be updated. You can find the document describing the entire interface on the source CD for this book.

The FOSSIL interface defines a very complete set of functions for talking to serial hardware. The only major functions that you can't implement in the `RS232` class are direct control of the RTS line and DTR/DSR handshaking. This is a considerable improvement over the simple interface provided by the IBM PC BIOS! Some of the FOSSIL functions are essentially duplicates of the BIOS functions and are noted as such here.

In addition to the serial port interface, the FOSSIL definition includes support for a few other basic system services, such as keyboard input, screen output, and timer tick support. For the purposes of class `Fossil` as defined here, these are not relevant. Curious readers can look up the specification.

Function 0: initialize port (BIOS)

This function is identical to IBM BIOS function 0, with one exception. The FOSSIL spec supports 19200 and 38400 BPS initialization. To do so, they replaced the port settings for 110 and 150 baud with those two values. See Chapter 6 on the BIOS driver for a complete definition of the bit settings.

Input registers:

AH :	Set to 0, the function value
AL :	Broken down into four bit fields. See Chapter 6 for details.
DX :	The port number, starting at 0 for COM1

Return values:

AH :	The current line status
AL :	Set to the reflect the modem status value.

Function 1: transmit a single byte (BIOS)

This function is identical to the INT 14H BIOS function to transmit a byte. The primary difference here is that the character does not get immediately transmitted. Instead, it is placed into the queue of characters waiting to be transmitted as TX interrupts occur.

Input registers:

AH :	Set to 1, the function value
AL :	The character to be transmitted
DX :	The port number, starting at 0 for COM1

Return values:

AH :	The current line status
AL :	Set to the reflect the modem status value.

Function 2: get a received character (BIOS)

This function is used to read in an input character from the received character buffer. It is designed to be compatible with INT 14H BIOS function 2, which tries to read a character in from the UART receiver buffer. Because this routine waits for a character rather than returns immediately on an empty buffer, class Fossil uses an alternate function for reading data with a return upon failure.

Input registers:

AH :	Set to 2, the function value
DX :	The port number, starting at 0 for COM1

Return values:

AH :	Timeout error if bit 7 is set, else the current line status
AL :	The character read in

Function 3: read status registers (BIOS)

This function is compatible with INT 14H BIOS function 3. It simply reads in the current status of the modem status register and the line status register, and returns the results.

Input registers:

AH :	Set to 3, the function value
DX :	The port number, starting at 0 for COM1

Return values:

AH :	The port line status
AL :	The port modem status

Function 4: open serial port

This function addresses a major oversight in the original PC BIOS. It is called to open a serial port before any other services are required. This lets the FOSSIL device driver know that the port is about to be used, which allows it to allocate system resources, such as memory buffers. It also lets the FOSSIL lock out other processes from using the port in a multitasking environment. The other useful feature provided by this function is the ability to cause the open request to fail. If the FOSSIL device driver is installed and the appropriate COM port is available, the success code is returned. If the driver isn't installed or the port isn't present, the application program is informed of the failure. This prevents application programs from attempting to work with hardware that is nonexistent or is engaged with another program.

Input registers:

AH :	Set to 4, the function value
DX :	The port number, starting at 0 for COM1

Return values:

AX :	Set to 0x1954 if successful
BL :	Maximum function number supported by this FOSSIL driver
BH :	FOSSIL revision supported

Function 5: close port

This function is every bit as useful as function 4. It allows the system to reallocate resources and disable the serial hardware after an application is no longer using the port. This function is sorely missing from the IBM PC BIOS. Although the BIOS itself may not need this function, many systems that perform BIOS emulation would benefit greatly from this function. For example, a program implementing modem access across a network doesn't have any way to let the modem server know that it is done with a modem when the program exits. FOSSIL function 5 gives the application that capability.

Input registers:

AH :   Set to 5, the function value

DX :   The port number, starting at 0 for COM1

Return values:

None

Function 6: control DTR

This function gives the application the ability to raise or lower DTR. IBM added this capability to the Extended BIOS, which became available after the FOSSIL was already implemented. Because of this, the function number and parameters are not compatible with the Extended BIOS.

In addition, it is important to note that the FOSSIL spec does not offer a function to control RTS. It is automatically asserted when the port is opened and will change only if RTS/CTS handshaking is on.

Input registers:

AH :   Set to 6, the function value

AL: Set to 1 to raise DTR, 0 to lower DTR'

DX :   The port number, starting at 0 for COM1

Return values:

None

Function 8: flush the TX buffer

This function doesn't return until all the characters in the TX buffer have been transmitted. The function isn't used in class `Fossil` because it takes away one's ability to do other processing in the idle function. It also offers the possibility of long delays should the transmitter be blocked due to a handshaking event.

Input registers:

AH :   Set to 8, the function value

DX :   The port number, starting at 0 for COM1

Return values:

Nothing

Function 9: purge the input buffer

This function lets the application program throw out all the characters presently pending in the RX buffer. Because the BIOS doesn't have an input buffer, it doesn't have an analogous function.

Input registers:

AH :   Set to 9, the function value

DX :   The port number, starting at 0 for COM1

Return values:

Nothing

Function 0x0A: purge the output buffer

This function lets the application program throw out all the characters presently pending in the TX buffer. Once again, because the BIOS doesn't have an output buffer, it doesn't have an analogous function. Note that this function differs from function 8 in that none of the characters presently residing in the TX buffer will be transmitted when this function is called.

Input registers:

AH :   Set to 0x0A, the function value

DX :   The port number, starting at 0 for COM1

Return values:

Nothing

Function 0x0B: transmit with no wait

This function adds a single character to the output buffer. Unlike function 1, it will not wait indefinitely if the TX buffer is presently full. Instead, it returns immediately with an error flag, so the application program can continue processing. The Fossil class uses this function rather than function 1 because it offers additional flexibility.

Input registers:

AH :	Set to 0x0B, the function value
AL :	The character to be added to the transmit buffer
DX :	The port number, starting at 0 for COM1

Return values:

AX :	Set to 1 if the character was added to the buffer, 0 if it wasn't

Function 0x0C: single character peek

This function is called to peek one character ahead in the RX buffer. Although being able to peek ahead an arbitrary number of bytes would be nice, as is possible in class *PC8250*, this is a big improvement over the BIOS, which offers no peek function.

Input registers:

AH :	Set to 0x0C, the function value
DX :	The port number, starting at 0 for COM1

Return values:

AH :	Set to 0 if a character was read, 0xff if not
AL :	The next character in the buffer if AH is set to 0

Function 0x0F: select flow control

This function allows the application program to select which handshaking options to use. The FOSSIL driver supports RTS/CTS flow control, as well as independent XON/XOFF flow control for the transmitter and receiver. Class *RS232* does not support split handshaking, so only bidirectional flow control is used by class Fossil.

Input registers:

AH :	Set to 0x0F, the function value
AL :	Flow control bits
	Bit 0: Enable XON/XOFF reception to stop the transmitter
	Bit 1: Enable RTS/CTS flow control
	Bit 2: Must be set to 0
	Bit 3: Enable XON/XOFF transmission when the RX buffer passes the high-water mark
DX :	The port number, starting at 0 for COM1

Return values:

None

Function 0x18: read a buffer

This is a function that is sorely missing from the BIOS interface. It allows a block of data to be read in from the port all at one time. This is generally much more efficient than reading in a single byte at a time, as the BIOS forces you to do. Once again, this function might not be useful to the BIOS itself, but software that emulates the BIOS interface would have benefited greatly from a function like this. Note that this function reads in as many characters as possible, then returns immediately.

Input registers:

AH :	Set to 0x18, the function value
CX :	The number of characters requested
DX :	The port number, starting at 0 for COM1
ES :	Segment of the buffer that is to receive the data
DI :	Offset of the buffer

Return values:

AX :	The count of characters actually transferred.

Function 0x19: write a buffer

This function is the converse of function 0x18. It allows a block of data to be transferred to the TX buffer with a single call. This is usually much more efficient than sending the characters one at a time. This function will attempt to place as many characters as possible in the TX buffer, then return immediately.

Input registers:

AH :	Set to 0x19, the function value
CX :	The number of characters to be sent
DX :	The port number, starting at 0 for COM1
ES :	Segment of the buffer that contains the data to be sent
DI :	Offset of the buffer

Return values:

AX :	The count of characters actually transferred.

Function 0x1A: break control

This function is used to either set or clear a breaking condition on a port. This is another function that was added to the Extended BIOS after the FOSSIL definition, which is why the FOSSIL driver function call is not compatible with the EBIOS.

Input registers:

AH :	Set to 0x1A the function value
AL :	Set to 1 to start breaking, 0 to stop
DX :	The port number, starting at 0 for COM1

Return values:

None

Function 0x1B: get FOSSIL driver information

This is a general-purpose function that returns information about the presently installed FOSSIL driver. The block of data returned from the driver has the following structure:

```
struct fossil_struct {
    short int structure_size;
    short int revision;
    char FAR *fossil_name;
    short int input_buffer_size;
    short int input_bytes_available;
    short int output_buffer_size;
    short int output_bytes_available;
    char screen_width;
    char screen_height;
    char baud_rate_id;
}
```

These fields should be fairly self-explanatory. Not all of them are used by class `Fossil`, but many of them are. Some, such as the `fossil_name` element, are helpful in a general sense and are printed with the debug output.

Input registers:

AH :	Set to 0x1B the function value
CX :	Size in bytes of the buffer that will receive the data
DX :	The port number, starting at 0 for COM1
ES :	Segment of the buffer that is to receive the data
DI :	Offset of the buffer

Return values:

AX :	The count of bytes actually sent to the user buffer

Sources

Given the well-crafted FOSSIL specification, the next logical question is: Where are all these wonderful FOSSIL device drivers? One good place would be the Simtel file repository, found at `http://www.simtel.net`. Searching the MS-DOS archives with the keyword FOSSIL yields a respectable page or two of files, with a few FOSSIL drivers and quite a few programs that use FOSSIL drivers.

Probably the best-known FOSSIL driver for IBM PCs under MS-DOS is X00.SYS, by Ray Gwinn. Another popular driver is BNU, by David Nugent. Both are available on Simtel. Both drivers are fully featured and can be loaded as device drivers from your CONFIG.SYS file or as TSRs from the command line. Both have some excellent debugging features that can help during the development process.

The Source Code

The source code shown here implements class `Fossil`. This class implements nearly every virtual function included in the base class, `RS232`. The only missing functions are the following:

- `DtrDsrHandshaking()`
- `Cts()`
- `SoftwareOverrunError()`

There just aren't any hooks in the FOSSIL specification to let you implement these missing functions. However, the functionality you get from the FOSSIL driver is an order of magnitude ahead of the `BIOSPort` class.

The `Fossil` class is derived from the `BIOSPort` class. It can take advantage of nine functions in the `BIOSPort` class. The four-line status and the four-modem status functions are identical, as is the `read_byte()` function. The rest of the functionality for this class had to be built from scratch. It makes sense to take advantage of the previously written functions, as well as the two lines of debug output available from the `BIOSPort` class. If the code has already been written, you might as well take advantage of it!

ON THE CD

Listings 7-1 and 7-2 provide the definition and implementation of class `Fossil` in source files `FOSSIL.H` and `FOSSIL.CPP`. These two files will be used in the example program `CHAPT07.CPP`, which is found on the CD-ROM. This demo program for class `Fossil` can be built with the 16 bit versions of Microsoft's and Borland's C++ compilers.

All of the code in this book can be found on the CD-ROM, along with sample make files.

Listing 7-1: FOSSIL.H: the header file for class Fossil

```
// ********************** START OF FOSSIL.H **********************
//
//
// This header file has all the definitions and prototypes needed
// to use the Fossil class. This file should be included by any
// module using that specific class.

#ifndef _FOSSIL_DOT_H
#define _FOSSIL_DOT_H
```

Chapter 7: The FOSSIL Interface 311

```cpp
#include <dos.h>
#include "rs232.h"
#include "biosport.h"

// Note that the Fossil class is derived from BIOSPort. BIOSPort
// provides nine virtual functions that work properly with a FOSSIL
// driver. This is a good example of code reuse.

class Fossil : public BIOSPort
{
    protected :
        int first_debug_output_line;
        RS232Error write_settings( void );
        virtual int read_buffer( char *buffer,
                                 unsigned int count );
        virtual int write_buffer( char *buffer,
                                  unsigned int count = -1 );
        virtual int write_byte( int c );
        Fossil( void );

    public :
        Fossil( enum RS232PortName port_name,
                long baud_rate = UNCHANGED,
                char parity = UNCHANGED,
                int word_length = UNCHANGED,
                int stop_bits = UNCHANGED,
                int dtr = SET,
                int rts = SET,
                int xon_xoff = DISABLE,
                int rts_cts = DISABLE,
                int dtr_dsr = DISABLE );
        virtual ~Fossil( void );
        virtual RS232Error Set( long baud_rate = UNCHANGED,
                                int parity = UNCHANGED,
                                int word_length = UNCHANGED,
                                int stop_bits = UNCHANGED );
        virtual int TXSpaceFree( void );
        virtual int RXSpaceUsed( void );
        virtual int FormatDebugOutput( char *buffer = 0,
                                       int line_number = -1 );
        virtual int RXSpaceFree( void );
        virtual int TXSpaceUsed( void );
        virtual int Break( long milliseconds = 300 );
```

```cpp
            virtual int XonXoffHandshaking( int setting = UNCHANGED );
            virtual int RtsCtsHandshaking( int settings = UNCHANGED );
            virtual int Dtr( int settings = UNCHANGED );
            virtual int Peek( void *buffer, unsigned int count );
            virtual int FlushRXBuffer( void );
            virtual int FlushTXBuffer( void );
};

#endif // #ifndef _FOSSIL_DOT_H

// ******************** END OF FOSSIL.H ********************
```

Listing 7-2: FOSSIL.CPP: the implementation file for class Fossil

```cpp
// ******************** START OF FOSSIL.CPP ********************
//
//
//
// This file contains all of the code used by the Fossil class.
//

#include <stdio.h>
#include <string.h>
#include <ctype.h>
#include "rs232.h"
#include "fossil.h"
#include "_8250.h"

// The following two structures and the constructor code are here to
// support the fossil_info class. The single constructor for this
// class executes FOSSIL function 0x1B, which loads the fossil
// information block into the fossil_struct structure. The
// contents of struct fossil_struct are stored in their own
// separate structure to guarantee proper offsets and packing
// of all data members.

struct fossil_struct {
    short int structure_size;
    short int revision;
    char __far *ident;
    short int input_buffer_size;
    short int input_bytes_available;
    short int output_buffer_size;
    short int output_bytes_available;
};
```

```
class fossil_info : public fossil_struct {
    public :
         fossil_info( int port_number );
};

fossil_info::fossil_info( int port_number )
{
    union REGS r;
    struct SREGS s;

    r.x.dx = port_number;
    r.x.cx = sizeof( fossil_struct );
    s.es = (unsigned)((long)(void __far *) &structure_size > 16);
    r.x.di = (unsigned int) (long) (void __far *) &structure_size;
    r.h.ah = 0x1b;
    int86x( 0x14, &r, &r, &s );
}

// The Fossil constructor looks very similar to the BIOSPort
// constructor. It differs in just a couple respects. First, the
// port open function provided by the FOSSIL driver lets you detect
// when the port isn't present or the driver isn't loaded. This
// gives this constructor an error exit. Second, one of the data
// members in the saved_settings is initialized to 1, which is
// where it always is when the FOSSIL driver is installed.

Fossil::Fossil( RS232PortName port,
                long baud_rate,
                char parity,
                int word_length,
                int stop_bits,
                int dtr,
                int rts,
                int xon_xoff,
                int rts_cts,
                int dtr_dsr )
{
    union REGS r;

    port_name = port;
    error_status = RS232_SUCCESS;

    first_debug_output_line = BIOSPort::FormatDebugOutput();
```

```
        debug_line_count = FormatDebugOutput();
        r.h.ah = 4;
        r.x.dx = port_name;
        r.x.bx = 0;
        int86( 0x14, &r, &r );
        if ( r.x.ax != 0x1954 ) {
            error_status = RS232_PORT_NOT_FOUND;
            return;
        }
        saved_settings.BaudRate = -1L;
        saved_settings.Parity = '?';
        saved_settings.WordLength = -1;
        saved_settings.StopBits = -1;
        saved_settings.Dtr = -1;
        saved_settings.Rts = -1;
        saved_settings.XonXoff = -1;
        saved_settings.RtsCts = -1;
        saved_settings.DtrDsr = -1;
        settings = saved_settings;
        settings.Dtr = 1;
        settings.XonXoff = 0;
        settings.RtsCts = 0;
        settings.Adjust( baud_rate,
                        parity,
                        word_length,
                        stop_bits,
                        dtr,
                        rts,
                        xon_xoff,
                        rts_cts,
                        dtr_dsr );
        write_settings();
        line_status = 0;
    }

    // Unlike the BIOSPort destructor, the FOSSIL driver actually has
    // a function call that lets the FOSSIL driver know that the port
    // is no longer in use.

    Fossil::~Fossil( void )
    {
        union REGS r;

        if ( error_status == RS232_SUCCESS ) {
```

Chapter 7: The FOSSIL Interface 315

```c
        r.x.dx = port_name;
        r.h.ah = 5;
        int86( 0x14, &r, &r );
    }
}

// The Fossil version of write_settings is nearly the same as the
// BIOSPort version. It has additional code to set DTR and the
// two handshaking options.

RS232Error Fossil::write_settings( void )
{
    union REGS r;
    RS232Error status = RS232_SUCCESS;

    r.x.dx = port_name;
    r.h.ah = 0;
    r.h.al = 0;
    switch ( toupper( settings.Parity ) ) {
        case 'E' : r.h.al |= 0x18; break;
        case 'O' : r.h.al |= 0x08; break;
        default  : settings.Parity = 'N';
                   status = RS232_ILLEGAL_PARITY_SETTING;
        case 'N' : r.h.al |= 0x00; break;
    }
    switch ( settings.StopBits ) {
        case 1 : r.h.al |= 0; break;
        default : settings.StopBits = 2;
                  status = RS232_ILLEGAL_STOP_BITS;
        case 2 : r.h.al |= 4; break;
    }
    switch ( settings.WordLength ) {
        case 5    : r.h.al |= 0; break;
        case 6    : r.h.al |= 1; break;
        case 7    : r.h.al |= 2; break;
        default   : settings.WordLength = 8;
                    status = RS232_ILLEGAL_WORD_LENGTH;
        case 8    : r.h.al |= 3; break;
    }
    switch ( settings.BaudRate ) {
        case 19200L : r.h.al |= 0x00; break;
        case 38400L : r.h.al |= 0x20; break;
        case 300L   : r.h.al |= 0x40; break;
        case 600L   : r.h.al |= 0x60; break;
```

```cpp
                case 1200L   : r.h.al |= 0x80; break;
                case 2400L   : r.h.al |= 0xa0; break;
                case 4800L   : r.h.al |= 0xc0; break;
                default      : settings.BaudRate = 9600L;
                               status = RS232_ILLEGAL_BAUD_RATE;
                case 9600L   : r.h.al |= 0xe0; break;
        }
        int86( 0x14, &r, &r );
// Set up DTR
        r.x.dx = port_name;
        r.h.ah = 6;
        r.h.al = (unsigned char) settings.Dtr;
        int86( 0x14, &r, &r );
// Set up handshaking
        r.x.dx = port_name;
        r.h.ah = 0x0f;
        r.h.al = 0;
        if ( settings.RtsCts )
            r.h.al |= 2;
        if ( settings.XonXoff )
            r.h.al |= 9;
        int86( 0x14, &r, &r );

        if ( settings.Rts != -1 ) {
            settings.Rts = -1;
            status = RS232_RTS_NOT_SUPPORTED;
        }

        if ( settings.DtrDsr != -1 ) {
            settings.DtrDsr = -1;
            status = RS232_DTR_DSR_NOT_SUPPORTED;
        }
        return status;
}

// The Fossil debug output adds the fossil ID from the
// fossil_info data structure, and a couple of buffer
// counts not found in the BIOSPort class.

int Fossil::FormatDebugOutput( char *buffer, int line_number )
{
    if ( buffer == 0 )
        return( first_debug_output_line + 2 );
```

```cpp
        if ( line_number < first_debug_output_line )
            return BIOSPort::FormatDebugOutput( buffer, line_number );
        fossil_info port_data( port_name );
        switch( line_number - first_debug_output_line ) {
            case 0 :
                sprintf( buffer,
                         "Derived class: Fossil   "
                         "TX Used: %5u   RX Free: %5u",
                         TXSpaceUsed(),
                         RXSpaceFree() );
                break;
            case 1 :
                strcpy( buffer, "FOSSIL Id: " );
                {
                    for ( int i = 0 ; i < 60 ; i++ )
                        buffer[ i+ 11 ] = port_data.ident[ i ];
                    buffer[ i + 11 ] = '\0';
                }
                break;
            default :
                return RS232_ILLEGAL_LINE_NUMBER;
        }
        return RS232_SUCCESS;
    }

    RS232Error Fossil::Set( long baud_rate,
                            int parity,
                            int word_length,
                            int stop_bits )
    {
        settings.Adjust( baud_rate,
                         parity,
                         word_length,
                         stop_bits,
                         UNCHANGED,
                         UNCHANGED,
                         UNCHANGED,
                         UNCHANGED,
                         UNCHANGED );
        return write_settings();
    }

    // This function uses the FOSSIL version of the single character
    // output function, because it returns immediately, unlike the BIOS
```

```cpp
// function.


int Fossil::write_byte( int c )
{
    union REGS r;

    if ( error_status < 0 )
        return error_status;
    r.x.dx = port_name;
    r.h.ah = 0x0b;
    r.h.al = (char) c;
    int86( 0x14, &r, &r );
    if ( r.x.ax )
        return RS232_SUCCESS;
    return RS232_TIMEOUT;
}

// The read_buffer and write_buffer functions take advantage of
// the dedicated FOSSIL functions that transfer blocks of data
// with a single function call.

int Fossil::read_buffer( char *buffer, unsigned int count )
{
    union REGS r;
    struct SREGS s;

    ByteCount = 0;
    if ( error_status < 0 )
        return error_status;

    r.x.dx = port_name;
    r.h.ah = 0x18;
    r.x.cx = count;
    s.es = (unsigned int) ( (long) (void __far *) buffer > 16 );
    r.x.di = (unsigned int) (long) (void __far *) buffer;
    int86x( 0x14, &r, &r, &s );
    ByteCount = r.x.ax;
    buffer[ ByteCount ] = '\0';
    if ( ByteCount != count )
        return RS232_TIMEOUT;
    return( RS232_SUCCESS );
}
```

```
int Fossil::write_buffer( char *buffer, unsigned int count )
{
    union REGS r;
    struct SREGS s;

    if ( error_status < RS232_SUCCESS )
        return error_status;

    r.x.dx = port_name;
    r.x.cx = count;
    r.h.ah = 0x19;
    s.es = (unsigned int) ( (long) (void __far *) buffer > 16 );
    r.x.di = (unsigned int) (long) (void __far *) buffer;
    int86x( 0x14, &r, &r, &s );
    ByteCount = r.x.ax;
    if ( ByteCount != count )
        return RS232_TIMEOUT;
    return RS232_SUCCESS;
}


// The following four functions all get their data from the
// fossil_info data structure. The data is loaded automatically
// by the fossil_info constructor.

int Fossil::TXSpaceFree( void )
{
    if ( error_status < RS232_SUCCESS )
        return error_status;

    fossil_info port_data( port_name );

    return( port_data.output_bytes_available );
}

// Ray Gwinn's driver, X00.SYS, doesn't return exactly the numbers
// expected here, so I adjust them if the FOSSIL driver turns out
// to be his.

int Fossil::TXSpaceUsed( void )
{
    if ( error_status < RS232_SUCCESS )
        return error_status;
```

```c
    fossil_info port_data( port_name );
    if ( port_data.ident[ 0 ] == 'R' &&
         port_data.ident[ 1 ] == 'a' &&
         port_data.ident[ 2 ] == 'y' )
        return( port_data.output_buffer_size -
                port_data.output_bytes_available - 1 );

    return( port_data.output_buffer_size -
            port_data.output_bytes_available );
}

int Fossil::RXSpaceUsed( void )
{
    if ( error_status < RS232_SUCCESS )
        return error_status;

    fossil_info port_data( port_name );

    return( port_data.input_buffer_size -
            port_data.input_bytes_available );
}

int Fossil::RXSpaceFree( void )
{
    if ( error_status < RS232_SUCCESS )
        return error_status;

    fossil_info port_data( port_name );

    return( port_data.input_bytes_available );
}


// The FOSSIL driver adds a dedicated Break function, which is
// missing from the BIOS specification.

int Fossil::Break( long milliseconds )
{
    long timer;
    union REGS r;

    if ( error_status < RS232_SUCCESS )
        return error_status;
    timer = ReadTime() + milliseconds;
```

```
        r.h.ah = 0x1a;
        r.h.al = 1;
        r.x.dx = port_name;
        int86( 0x14, &r, &r );
        while ( ReadTime() < timer )
            IdleFunction();
        r.h.ah = 0x1a;
        r.h.al = 0;
        r.x.dx = port_name;
        int86( 0x14, &r, &r );
        return RS232_SUCCESS;
}

// The two handshaking commands don't really do any work, they
// just modify the data structure and then let write_settings()
// perform FOSSIL function calls necessary to make the actual
// changes.

int Fossil::XonXoffHandshaking( int setting )
{
    if ( error_status < RS232_SUCCESS )
        return error_status;
    if ( setting != UNCHANGED ) {
        settings.XonXoff = ( setting != 0 );
        write_settings();
    }
    return settings.XonXoff;
}

int Fossil::RtsCtsHandshaking( int setting )
{
    if ( error_status < RS232_SUCCESS )
        return error_status;
    if ( setting != UNCHANGED ) {
        settings.RtsCts = ( setting != 0 );
        write_settings();
    }
    return settings.RtsCts;
}

// The FOSSIL driver has a unique function for setting DTR.
// Unfortunately, it doesn't offer a similar function for RTS.

int Fossil::Dtr( int setting )
```

```
{
    if ( error_status < RS232_SUCCESS )
        return error_status;
    if ( setting != UNCHANGED ) {
        settings.Dtr = ( setting != 0 );
        write_settings();
    }
    return settings.Dtr;
}


// The FOSSIL driver can only peek ahead a single byte, and I use
// that function here.

int Fossil::Peek( void *buffer, unsigned int count )
{
    union REGS r;

    if ( error_status < RS232_SUCCESS )
        return error_status;
    ByteCount = 0;
    if ( count ) {
        r.h.ah = 0x0c;
        r.x.dx = port_name;
        int86( 0x14, &r, &r );
        if ( r.h.ah == 0 ) {
            *(char *)buffer = r.h.al;
            ByteCount = 1;
        }
    }
    return RS232_SUCCESS;
}


// The two flush functions have special FOSSIL commands to get the
// job done.

int Fossil::FlushRXBuffer( void )
{
    union REGS r;

    if ( error_status < RS232_SUCCESS )
        return error_status;
    r.h.ah = 10;
    r.x.dx = port_name;
    int86( 0x14, &r, &r );
```

```
        return RS232_SUCCESS;
}

int Fossil::FlushTXBuffer( void )
{
    union REGS r;

    if ( error_status < RS232_SUCCESS )
        return error_status;
    r.h.ah = 9;
    r.x.dx = port_name;
    int86( 0x14, &r, &r );
    return RS232_SUCCESS;
}

// ******************** END OF FOSSIL.CPP ********************
```

Building CHAPT07.EXE

Creating the test program for this chapter just requires a couple of minor changes to the basic test program, CHAPT03.CPP. First, add a single include file to the list of includes so that the header file FOSSIL.H is used. The resulting list should look like this:

```
#include "portable.h"
#include <stdio.h>
#include <stdlib.h>
#include <string.h>
#include <conio.h>
#include <ctype.h>
#include "rs232.h"
#include "textwind.h"
#include "fossil.h"
```

Note that BIOSPORT.H is included by FOSSIL.H, so it doesn't need to appear in this list.

The second modification I made to TEST232.CPP instructed it to open every port as a FOSSIL port. The resulting code at the start of main( ) looked like this:

```
switch ( i ) {
    default :
        Ports[ i ] = new FOSSIL( port_names[ i ],
                                 9600, 'N', 8, 1 );
}
```

When this code executes, it will attempt to open any test ports as FOSSIL ports. If the FOSSIL constructor returns an error, the port won't be opened. Note that in this test program, I defined only a single port. Not all FOSSIL drivers can open more than one port at a time, so this seemed to be a prudent approach.

The final step necessary to create a `CHAPT07.EXE` is to create the makefile, `CHAPT03.MAK`. The FILES definition line should be modified to look like this:

```
FILES = BIOSPORT.OBJ FOSSIL.OBJ
```

A Test Run

`CHAPT07.EXE` produced the following output. This program is being run in conjunction with a version of X00.SYS, a popular MS-DOS FOSSIL driver. The exact version of the FOSSIL driver can be determined by noting the bottom line of the debug output.

The actual performance of a FOSSIL driver is dependent on the driver itself. I have noticed tremendous variations in the speed of drivers, the memory space they occupy, and even whether they correctly implement all FOSSIL features. You will have to experiment a bit to determine which ones will work best for you.

```
+------------------------------------+
|OK                                  |
|atdt 250-3778                       |
|CARRIER 9600                        |
|                                    |
|PROTOCOL: LAP-M                     |
|                                    |
|COMPRESSION: V.42BIS                |
|                                    |
|CONNECT 9600                        |
|                                    |
+------------------------------------+
Base class: RS232  COM1   Status: Success
Byte count:     0 Elapsed time:       0 TX Free:    511 RX Used:    0
Saved port:     -1,?,-1,-1  DTR,RTS: -1,-1  XON/OFF,RTS/CTS,DTR/DSR: -1,-1,-1
Current port:   9600,N,8,1  DTR,RTS:  1,-1  XON/OFF,RTS/CTS,DTR/DSR:  0, 0,-1
Derived class: BIOSPort  RI:  0  CD:  1  CTS:  1  DSR:  1
Parity Err: 0  Break Det: 0  Overrun Err: 0  Framing Err: 0
Derived class: FOSSIL  TX Used:     0  RX Free:    512
FOSSIL Id: Ray Gwinn's double aught buckshot driver, X00 V1.24




Toggle XON/XOFF handshaking returns: 0
```

Summary

The FOSSIL interface was a good idea that arose from the BBS community that flourished in the late 1980s and early 1990s. The FOSSIL specification, built on the standard BIOS interface, added enough additional functionality to create a versatile and useful programming tool. The `Fossil` class developed in this chapter takes full advantage of the interface, and can prove useful to you in your MS-DOS projects.

Chapter 8

Terminal Emulation

IN THIS CHAPTER

- Reasons for emulating a terminal
- Escape sequences
- ANSI.SYS
- A terminal class
- A test program
- The AnsiTerminal class
- Terminal emulation code debugging
- The BaseWindow class
- The TextWindow class

How to Create the Test Program

This chapter presents a working framework for performing terminal emulation. Terminal emulation software lets your PC act as though it is a smart terminal communication with another computer via an RS-232 link. This is particularly useful when you are supporting legacy applications that once ran on dedicated terminals.

Why Emulate a Terminal?

One of the first questions that beginning communications programmers often ask is, "How do I clear the screen of a PC attached to my Point of Sale System?" This typical new programmer will usually have learned how to create nice-looking screens for his or her programs using runtime library functions such as clrscr(), gotoxy(), and textcolor(). The same programmer then finds out, much to her dismay, that these functions don't work properly when used for the interface code in a communications program.

The reason for this is fairly simple, but grasping it does require a little understanding of the hardware involved. Most display devices, ranging from DEC

VT-100 terminals to IBM PC VGA monitors, save the contents of the display in a specialized piece of hardware referred to as a *frame buffer*. In text modes on the PC, the frame buffer is just a block of memory that has two bytes for each character on the screen. One byte per character contains the actual display value of the character, in 8-bit IBM ASCII. The second byte for each character contains the display attribute.

On the PC, all I have to do to clear the screen is step through display memory, setting each character to an ASCII blank, and each attribute to simple white on black. Thus, a 16-bit version of `clrscr()` could be written to look like this:

```
void clrscr( void )
{
    char __far *screen = (char __far *) 0xb8000000L;

    for ( int row = 0 ; row < 25 ; row++ )
        for ( int col = 0 ; col < 80 ; col++ ) {
            *screen++ = ' ';
            *screen++ = 0x07;
        }
}
```

This routine just writes out blanks with a normal display attribute to every position on the screen. It is extremely fast and is easy to implement, which is why most 16-bit MS-DOS C and C++ compilers come with a routine that accomplishes the same thing.

Getting this same thing to happen across an RS-232 communications link is considerably more difficult, however. If I want to clear the screen on a PC hooked up to my data entry system via a modem, I can't just create a far pointer that lets me directly access the frame buffer on the remote system. Instead, I have to rely on traditional protocols to let me accomplish something similar.

Escape Sequences

In the days before desktop computers, most interactive computing was done via remote terminals attached to timeshared computers. These remote terminals had the same problem as our communications programmer: the main computer didn't have any way to directly address memory on the terminal, thus had no way to write to different areas all over the screen quickly and easily.

Hardware and firmware designers quickly developed protocols to overcome this difficulty. When designing the RS-232 interface between the computer and the terminal, designers added a protocol that let programmers step outside the traditional ASCII display characters to send terminal control sequences. A *terminal control sequence* is just a special set of input that sends a display or formatting command to the terminal.

For example, one early display terminal was the DEC VT-52. A programmer who wanted to clear an area on the screen of a VT-52 could send the two-character sequence ESC J. This command told the VT-52 to clear everything from the cursor to the end of the screen. Another sequence could be used to position the cursor at the home position immediately before this command, resulting in a completely clear screen with just a few characters transmitted.

In order to distinguish these commands from normal display data, screen control commands were frequently prefaced with the ASCII ESC (Escape) character, 0x1b. The Escape code would not show up as part of a normal display sequence, so it provided an unambiguous way to distinguish special command sequences. Because so many terminal manufacturers used control sequences that started with the Escape character, these sequences came to be known generically as *escape sequences*.

Terminal intelligence

Early terminals that responded to control sequences were dubbed *smart terminals*, to distinguish them from *dumb terminals*, which could only display text. A dumb terminal acted as nothing much more than a fully electronic teletype, able to print at the bottom line of the screen and scroll text upward as it progressed.

Today, every terminal sold is a smart terminal, so this usage is not as meaningful as it was at one time.

Tower of babel

Over the past 25 years or so, every manufacturer of display terminals has deemed it appropriate to create a unique and proprietary set of Escape sequences to control its particular terminals. One can see an example of the confusion that this causes by looking at the termcap file shipped with most UNIX systems. The termcap file futilely attempts to define all the possible sequences for any terminal that could conceivably be connected to a UNIX system. The result is a file containing several 100 kilobytes of cryptic runes that works often, but not always.

In a perhaps futile attempt to cut down on this confusion, the American National Standards Institute (ANSI) has created a specification known as ANSI X3.64, "Additional Controls for Use with American National Standard Code for Information Interchange." This specification defines a set of Escape Sequences that can be used to handle most of the commands needed by ASCII display terminals.

> ANSI X3.64 was withdrawn and replaced by the international standard ISO 6429 in 1992. You can order ISO 6429 from ANSI online at http://web-store.ansi.org/AnsiCatalog/AnsiCat.asp.

ANSI X3.64 includes commands such as:

- Cursor movement
- Setting horizontal and vertical tabs
- Delete character/line
- Insert character/line
- Define protected areas

ANSI X3.64 really can't claim much success in the world of ASCII display terminals. Some manufacturers have adopted ANSI-like command sets for the terminals; others offer it as a secondary command set. But for the most part, developers still have to contend with the same Tower of Babel as that which existed 15 years ago. The only difference today is that there are more dialects to master.

ANSI.SYS

IBM and Microsoft created a device driver called *ANSI.SYS* that supports a very limited subset of the ANSI X3.64 command set. This driver would allow software that was written to work with display terminals to run on the IBM PC with no fundamental changes. In practice, it has been used mostly as an accessory to .BAT files, allowing batch file programmers to create flashy screens in what are otherwise simple programs.

Although ANSI.SYS may not have been particularly useful for communications programmers, it did have one unintended side effect. By defining a standard for terminal Escape sequences used on the PC, it gave the same communications programmers a standard to program to. Because the actual set of commands is so short and simple, it began finding its way into both shareware programs such as Procomm and Telix, as well as commercial programs such as Crosstalk. (As this is being written, Procomm and Telix have matured into commercial programs, but Crosstalk has disappeared.)

The official definition of the command set used by ANSI.SYS can be found in the *IBM DOS Technical Reference Manual*. For the most part, the commands conform to those in the ANSI/ISO standard, although there is some variation. It is important to recognize that this is a very limited subset of the official specification. Software written for terminals that conform more closely to the specifications, such as DEC's VT-220, will often have trouble with the more limited IBM version.

ANSI.SYS escape sequences

The official specification for ANSI X3.64 gives a common format that all ANSI command sequences should follow. Each command starts with an ASCII *ESC* code,

0x1b, which serves notice that an Escape sequence has started. An '[' character immediately follows most of the commands, although not all. Immediately following that is a set of 0 or more numeric parameters, separated by semicolons. (Just to keep things interesting, a very few ANSI commands have a punctuation character such as '=' pr '?' as a parameter.) Finally, a one- or two-character command character terminates the command. Table 8-1 summarizes these components.

TABLE 8-1 THE COMPONENTS OF AN ANSI COMMAND SEQUENCE

Components	Description
ESC	All commands start with the Escape code
'['	Used with most, but not all, commands
Parameter	A number composed of ASCII digits '0' through '9'
';'	The separator used between parameters
Command prefix	An optional prefix between ' ' and '/' (0x20 and 0x2f) can precede the command character.
Command	Normally the command character lies in the range between ASCII '@' and '~' (0x40 and 0x7e).

The IBM version of ANSI.SYS modifies this sequence somewhat. First, normal ANSI parameters are always ASCII representations of decimal numbers. For example, a typical cursor positioning command might look like this:

```
ESC[23;1H
```

Simple C code to issue this command might look like this:

```
printf( "\x1b[%d;%dH", row, column );
```

IBM and Microsoft extended the parameter definition to allow for the use of character strings as parameters. This means that in addition to normal numeric parameters, an ANSI input parser also has to be able to accommodate quoted strings, which might look like this:

```
ESC[0;68;"dir";13p
```

This sequence, which is quoted directly from the IBM manual, redefines function key F10 to issue the DIR command followed by a carriage return.

The following sequences are supported by ANSI.SYS as shipped with MS-DOS and IBM-DOS:

Cursor Position: `ESC[#;#H` -or- `ESC[#;#f`

This command moves the cursor to the row and column specified in the first two parameters. The default for each of the two parameters is 1, so one or both can be omitted. The row and column numbers used by ANSI.SYS are 1 based, which means the upper-left corner of the screen is row 1, column 1.

Cursor Up: `ESC[#A`

This command moves the cursor up by the number of rows specified by the numeric parameter. If the parameter is not given, it defaults to 1. The cursor won't try to move past the first row on the screen.

Cursor Down: `ESC[#B`

This command moves the cursor down by the number of rows specified by the numeric parameter. If the parameter is not given, it defaults to 1. The cursor won't try to move down past the last row on the screen.

Cursor Right: `ESC[#C`

This command moves the cursor right by the number of columns specified by the numeric parameter. If the parameter is not given, it defaults to 1. The cursor won't try to move past the last column on the screen.

Cursor Left: `ESC[#D`

This command moves the cursor left by the number of columns specified by the numeric parameter. If the parameter is not given, it defaults to 1. The cursor won't try to move past the first column on the screen.

Device Status Request: `ESC[6n`

This command causes ANSI.SYS to issue a cursor position report, which has the format:

```
ESC[#;#R
```

The two numeric parameters in the cursor position report give the current row and column of the cursor. This command is frequently used as a way to determine whether a PC is performing ANSI emulation.

Save Cursor Position: `ESC[s`

This command saves the current row and column of the cursor. The cursor can be restored to the saved position with the next command, `Restore Cursor Position`.

Restore Cursor Position: `ESC[u`

This command restores the cursor row and column to the position saved previously with the `Save Cursor Position` command.

Erase Screen: `ESC[2J`

This command is used to erase the entire display. The cursor is returned to position 1,1 after the screen is erased.

Erase to End of Line: `ESC[K`

This command erases all positions from the cursor to the end of the current row. The cursor position isn't modified.

Set Colors: ESC[#;...;#m

This command is used to set custom display colors on the screen. Any number of color commands can be combined into a single escape sequence. The numeric parameters defined for this command are as follows:

0	Reset color to white on black
1	Set foreground color to high intensity
4	Turn on underline (meaningful only on a monochrome display)
5	Set the blinking attribute
7	Reverse video
8	Invisible attribute
30	Set the foreground color to black
31	Set the foreground color to red
32	Set the foreground color to green
33	Set the foreground color to yellow
34	Set the foreground color to blue
35	Set the foreground color to purple
36	Set the foreground color to cyan
37	Set the foreground color to white
40	Set the background color to black
41	Set the background color to red
42	Set the background color to green
43	Set the background color to yellow
44	Set the background color to blue
45	Set the background color to purple
46	Set the background color to cyan
47	Set the background color to white

Set Mode: ESC[=#h -or-
ESC[?7h

This command sets the video to one of the seven predefined BIOS video modes, or optionally turns on character wrapping at the end of the line. The mode commands are defined as follows:

0   Set mode to 40 x 25 black and white

1   Set mode to 40 x 25 color

2   Set mode to 80 x 25 black and white

3   Set mode to 80 x 25 color

4   Set mode to 320 x 200 color

5   Set mode to 320 x 200 black and white

6   Set mode to 640 x 200 black and white

7   Enable wrap at the end of line

Note that this command, and Reset Mode, which follows, are among the few that use a punctuation character as a parameter instead of a number. This requires some special code in any ANSI parsing routine.. The default value of the numeric parameter is 0.

Reset Mode: ESC[=#l -or-
                                 ESC[?7l

This command behaves identically to Set Mode except that it will disable wrap at the end of the line if the numeric parameter is 7.

Keyboard Key Reassignment: ESC[#;#;...#p

ANSI.SYS has the ability to redefine keyboard output for any key. This is the function that required the extension of the ANSI specification to allow for quoted strings. The syntax of this command is straightforward. The key to be redefined is specified using either the first or the first two parameters. Standard ASCII keys are defined using a single numeric parameter; extended function keys are defined using a 0 in the first parameter followed by a scan code in the second. The remaining parameters in the list are concatenated to form a single string, which is the new definition.

For example, an escape sequence to redefine function key F1 to sound a beep (by issuing an MS-DOS command when F1 is pressed) would look like this:

```
ESC[0;59;"echo ";7;13p
```

Redefining the Z key on the keyboard to perform the same function would take a command like this:

```
ESC[90;"echo ";7;13p
```

ANSI.SYS keyboard sequences

ANSI.SYS doesn't have anything to say about what sort of characters should be issued when a given key is pressed. It concerns itself only with sequences sent *to* a terminal, not those issued *by* the terminal. However, the `AnsiTerminal` class developed here does perform translation of keystrokes, compatible with existing ANSI X3.64 terminals (see Table 8-2).

TABLE 8-2 ANSITERMINAL KEYBOARD TRANSLATIONS

Characters	Keystrokes
Left Arrow	ESC[D
Home	ESC[H
Right Arrow	ESC[C
End	ESC[F
Up Arrow	ESC[A
PgUp	ESC[I
Down Arrow	ESC[B
PgDn	ESC[G
Insert	ESC[L
F1	ESC[M
Shift F1	ESC[Y
Ctrl F1	ESC[k
Alt F1	ESC[w
F2	ESC[N
Shift F2	ESC[Z
Ctrl F2	ESC[l
Alt F2	ESC[x
F3	ESC[O
Shift F3	ESC[a

Continued

TABLE 8-2 ANSITERMINAL KEYBOARD TRANSLATIONS *(Continued)*

Characters	Keystrokes
Ctrl F3	ESC[m
Alt F3	ESC[y
F4	ESC[P
Shift F4	ESC[b
Ctrl F4	ESC[n
Alt F4	ESC[z
F5	ESC[Q
Shift F5	ESC[c
Ctrl F5	ESC[o
Alt F5	ESC[@
F6	ESC[R
Shift F6	ESC[d
Ctrl F6	ESC[p
Alt F6	ESC[[
F7	ESC[S
Shift F7	ESC[e
Ctrl F7	ESC[q
Alt F7	ESC[\
F8	ESC[T
Shift F8	ESC[f
Ctrl F8	ESC[r
Alt F8	ESC[]
F9	ESC[U
Shift F9	ESC[g
Ctrl F9	ESC[s
Alt F9	ESC[^
F10	ESC[V

Characters	Keystrokes
Shift F10	ESC[h
Ctrl F10	ESC[t
Alt F10	ESC[_

A Terminal Class

The terminal class needs to perform a simple task. It needs to filter data going in both directions, to and from the RS-232 port. Keystrokes being sent to the RS-232 port need to be translated to escape (or other) sequences. RS-232 input needs to have Escape sequences filtered out and translated into screen activity.

Listing 8-1 shows the definition of the Terminal base class. With this virtual base class, it is extremely simple to write a short program that performs terminal emulation. The example program for this chapter, TESTERM.CPP, uses a derived class, AnsiTerminal, to actually perform terminal emulation.

Listing 8-1: TERMINAL.H

```
// ******************* START OF TERMINAL.H *******************
//
// This header file contains the definitions for the base class
// Terminal. It is a virtual base class, so you can't create an
// instance of it directly; you must derive a class from it and
// implement the pure virtual functions. One example of such a
// class is AnsiTerminal, defined in Chapter 13 of the book.
//

#ifndef _TERMINAL_DOT_H
#define _TERMINAL_DOT_H

#include "rs232.h"
#include "BaseWind.h"

class Terminal {
protected :
    RS232 *port;
    BaseWindow *window;
public :
    Terminal( RS232 &p, BaseWindow &w )
```

```
    {
        port = &p;
        window = &w;
    }
    virtual int ReadPort( void ) = 0;
    virtual void Display( int c ) = 0;
    virtual void WriteKey( int c ) = 0;
    virtual ~Terminal( void ){ ; }
};

#endif // #ifndef _TERMINAL_DOT_H
```

The three functions that the `Terminal` class needs to perform take care of all the basic terminal emulation functions. Although more sophisticated classes might need additional public features, you don't have to add anything to get a fully functioning program. The public functions defined by the base class are defined in the following section.

`Terminal( RS232 &p, BaseWindow &w )`

This is the constructor for the base class. Although the base class cannot be instantiated by itself, any derived class should call this constructor before entering its constructor. All this constructor does is set up the internal protected pointers to an `RS232` port object and a `BaseWindow` object.

Although the `RS232` object should be fairly familiar to you by this point, the `BaseWindow` object is a member of a class that hasn't been discussed before in this book. `BaseWindow` is just a very simple abstract class. `BaseWindow` defines a simple interface that provides the screen I/O functions needed by a terminal emulator. As it happens, I've already been using a class derived from `BaseWindow` to perform much of the screen I/O used in test programs in this book. `TextWindow` uses the PC BIOS to create windows, put data on the screen, insert and delete lines, and so on. It is presented later in this chapter with little or no discussion. `TextWindow` could easily be replaced by a more sophisticated class, as long as it implements the pure virtual functions of `BaseWindow`, such as `Clear()`, `Goto()`, `SetPosition()`, and so on.

`int ReadPort( void )`

A very simple terminal program that doesn't perform any sort of emulation would probably read characters in directly from the RS-232 port using a call to `RS232::Read()`. When performing terminal emulation, this strategy begins to have problems. The normal display data coming in from the port will be interspersed with escape sequences, and the terminal program would have to filter those out and act on them.

The virtual function `ReadPort()` relieves the emulation program of having to worry about this. Instead of directly calling the `Read()` function, the terminal program calls `Terminal::ReadPort()`. This function reads data in from the RS-232 port and actively filters out terminal escape sequences. The escape sequences are translated into function calls that operate on the screen, whereas normal display characters are passed back to the calling program.

The nice part about `ReadPort()` is that the base class describes virtually nothing about the internal workings of this function. This leaves the derived class free to implement its filtering function however works best for it, while maintaining a nice, simple interface to the calling program.

`int Display( int c )`

For the `AnsiTerminal` class, this function is a simple inline piece of code that writes a character directly out to the screen. However, other Terminal classes may need to perform different processing here, which can be accomplished by developing a more sophisticated virtual function. A good example of this might be the VT-52 terminal. This terminal can be set into graphics mode, in which normal ASCII characters are translated into a different character set used for drawing lines, boxes, and so on. This could be accomplished easily with a simple version of `Display()`.

`void WriteKey( int c )`

Most `Terminal` classes will want to translate IBM PC extended keys into different sequences, such as the ANSI escape sequences documented here. The `WriteKey()` function is responsible for taking a standard key code as input, and writing out whatever sequence is necessary to the RS-232 port.

Some terminals have more complicated keyboard mapping systems than that found in the `AnsiTerminal` class, allowing for different key mappings to be selected by terminal escape sequences. In addition, allowing for user-controlled remapping of the keyboard using this function would be relatively simple.

A Test Program

`TESTTERM.CPP`, shown in Listing 8-2, is the listing for the program that is used to test the `AnsiTerminal` class. A couple of interesting things are notable about this program. One striking feature is the relative simplicity of a program that has to deal with three complex classes. Another is that the program operates on base classes only, which means that replacing either the port type or the terminal emulation is simply a matter of changing the constructor.

Listing 8-2: TESTTERM.CPP

```cpp
// ***************** START OF TESTTERM.CPP ****************
//
// This test program implements a simple IBM ANSI terminal
// emulator. With a properly designed class, a terminal emulator
// amounts to just a few lines of code, because all the work
// here is being done by the AnsiTerminal object. Note that
// the Terminal and RS232 objects are both pointers to the
// base class, not the derived class. This shows how terminal
// emulation can be performed without the programmer knowing
// anything about the emulation code or the display class.
//

#include "rs232.h"
#include "pc8250.h"
#include "ascii.h"
#include "ansiterm.h"
#include "textwind.h"

main()
{
    TextWindow window( 0, 0, 80, 25 );
    RS232 *port = new PC8250( COM1, 19200, 'N', 8, 1 );
    Terminal *terminal = new AnsiTerminal( *port, window );
    int c;

    window << "Press F10 to exit...\n";
    port->RtsCtsHandshaking( 1 );
    for ( ; ; ) {
        c = terminal->ReadPort();
        if ( c < 0 && c != RS232_TIMEOUT )
            break;
        if ( c >= 0 )
            terminal->Display( c );
        c = window.ReadKey();
        if ( c == F10 )
            break;
        if ( c != 0 )
            terminal->WriteKey( c );
    }
    delete terminal;
    delete port;
    return 0;
}
```

```
// ****************** END OF TESTTERM.CPP *******************
```

In TESTTERM.CPP, all interpretation of escape sequences is being done in the class member function ReadPort(). Any escape sequences in the input stream are pulled out by this function and acted on immediately. Normal characters are passed through to TESTTERM.CPP, which then immediately displays them.

Class AnsiTerminal

Implementation of the AnsiTerminal class is fairly painless. The most difficult piece of code in the entire class is the parser, which breaks incoming escape sequences down into a list of parameters. After the incoming escape sequence has been broken down, the individual routines that execute each of the ANSI command sequences are very simple.

Listing 8-3 shows ANSITERM.H, the header file with the class definition for the AnsiTerminal class. In addition to the four virtual functions defined by the base Terminal class, AnsiTerminal has a constructor and a fairly lengthy list of private data and function members. These members are described immediately following the listing.

Listing 8-3: ANSITERM.H

```
// ****************** START OF ANSITERM.H *******************
//
// This is the public definition for the AnsiTerminal class.
// It has just three public functions, as well as a constructor
// and a destructor.
//

#ifndef _ANSITERM_DOT_H
#define _ANSITERM_DOT_H

#include "terminal.h"

class AnsiTerminal : public Terminal {
private :
    void parse( void );
    int parse_ansi_string( void );
    void position_cursor( void );
    void cursor_move( int row_dir, int col_dir );
    void cursor_position_report( void );
    void erase_in_display( void );
    void erase_in_line( void );
```

```
        void save_position( void );
        void restore_position( void );
        void set_color( void );
        void set_mode( void );
        char *ansi_parms[ 16 ];
        int parm_count;
        int saved_row;
        int saved_col;
        char **keys;
        char **extended_keys;
public :
        AnsiTerminal( RS232 &p, BaseWindow &w );
        virtual ~AnsiTerminal( void );
        virtual int ReadPort( void );
        virtual void Display( int c ){ *window << (char) c; }
        virtual void WriteKey( int c );
};

#endif   // #ifdef _ANSITERM_DOT_H

// ******************* END OF ANSITERM.H *********************
```

```
char *ansi_parms[ 16 ]
int parm_count
```

These two data members are used when parsing the input escape sequence. The constructor allocates a set of character arrays and places pointers to them in the `ansi_parms[]` pointer array. During parsing, each incoming parameter is stored in an element of the array, starting at position 0. The `parm_count` index always points to the element of the array currently being accessed. When the parser returns, the last parameter should be the ANSI command character, which can be accessed in `ansi_parms[parm_count]`.

```
int saved_row
int saved_col
```

These two members support the ANSI commands to save and restore the current cursor position. When the command to save the position is received, the cursor position is written into these two data members. When the command to restore the cursor position is received, it is read out of the two data members and used to update the screen.

```
char **keys
char **extended_keys
```

These two 256-element arrays contain the list of keyboard translations. Standard key sequences representing "normal" IBM ASCII keystrokes are stored in the `keys[]` array. Extended keys, which are referenced by a scan code, are stored in the `extended_keys[]` array. Most of the keys have a null pointer in their key translation array, in which case just the normal ASCII code is sent.

The `AnsiTerminal` class doesn't support the key redefinition command, but having these two arrays in place makes it a fairly simple matter to add support for this function.

```
virtual int ReadPort( void )
```

This public virtual function normally just reads in the current value from the `RS232` port and returns whatever it read to the calling program. The exception occurs when the incoming character is an ASCII ESC code. If this is the case, it marks the beginning of an incoming Escape sequence. The incoming sequence is handled by the `parse()` function, and the command is acted on. Finally, the value `RS232_TIMEOUT` is returned to the calling program, indicating that no character was received.

```
void parse( void )
```

This member function is called when an incoming ESC is detected. Its job is to read in the rest of the Escape sequence, parse it, and execute the command requested by the remote end.

In reality, this routine doesn't do too much work on its own. As soon as it is called, it invokes `parse_ansi_string()` to break the incoming sequence down into a list of usable parameters. After that routine returns, the rest of `parse()` executes the appropriate member function based on a big switch statement. The real work is all done elsewhere.

```
int parse_ansi_string( void )
```

This routine has the hardest job of any function in the `AnsiTerminal` class. It has to take that incoming string of characters and break it down into a list of parameters stored in the `ansi_parms[]` array so that they can be successfully processed by other routines.

This routine operates as a simple state machine, which is always in one of four states:

READY_TO_READ: The state machine starts here, when it is ready to read in the first character of an upcoming parameter. It returns to this state every time it reads in the ';' character used to separate parameters. Reading a non-numeric character other than the double quote (""") in this position signals the end of an ANSI Escape sequence.

READING_DIGITS: After the first digit in a numeric parameter has been read in, the parser moves to this state. It stays in this state until it reads the ';' character, indicating that another parameter is coming, or some other non-numeric character, which should be the command parameter.

READING_STRING: After the initial '"' character is read in, indicating the start of a quoted string, the parser moves to this state and stays there until the trailing '"' character is found.

DONE_WITH_STRING: The trailing quote character puts the parser in this state, where it then waits for either the ';' character, indicating that another parameter is coming, or a non-numeric command character.

`void position_cursor( void )`

Escape sequences 'H' and 'f' invoke this member function. It converts the two parameters in `ansi_parms[]` to row and column coordinates, then uses the `BaseWindow::SetPosition()` function to position the cursor. If either of the row or column parameters is missing, the value of 1 is used as the default. Note that the row and column address parameters passed by the Escape sequence are 1 based rather than 0 based as the `BaseWindow` class expects, so some additional conversion is done.

`void cursor_move( int row_dir, int col_dir )`

This member function is used to support the four cursor movement commands generated by Escape sequences 'A', 'B', 'C', and 'D'. The two direction parameters should be set to 1, 0, or -1 to indicate the direction of movement for the row and column.

This function checks the `ansi_parms[]` array to see whether a value was passed, in which case it is used as the distance to travel measured in rows or columns. If no value was passed, the distance defaults to 1. It relies on the `SetPosition()` command to avoid trying to move outside the current bounds of the window.

`void cursor_position_report( void )`

When the "ESC[6n" command is received, IBM's version of ANSI.SYS sends a cursor position report, which is in the form "ESC[#;#R", where the two numeric parameters are the row and column. This function takes care of sending the cursor position report, getting the current row and column using the `BaseWindow::GetPosition()` command, and then formatting the string and sending it out to the RS232 port.

```
void erase_in_display( void )
```

The ANSI command to erase some or all of the display actually has three different modes, depending on the parameter that is sent in the "ESC[#J" command. IBM ANSI.SYS recognizes only a parameter value of 2, which is used to clear the entire screen. `AnsiTerminal` accomplishes this by calling `BaseWindow::Clear()`, followed by `BaseWindow::SetPosition()` to home the cursor.

```
void erase_in_line( void )
```

Like the previous command, the ANSI specification gives several possible parameters that can be passed with the "ESC[#K" command. The version supported by IBM ANSI.SYS is called when the parameter is either not present or is set to 0. This command erases the current line from (and including) the cursor position to the end of the line. Because the `BaseWindow` class doesn't have a member function to do this, it is accomplished by first reading the cursor position with `BaseWindow::GetPosition()`, and then by getting the width of the line with `BaseWindow::GetDimensions()`. The line is filled with blanks using the insertion operator, '<<', then the cursor position is restored with `BaseWindow::SetPosition()`.

```
void save_position( void )
```

The "ESC[s" command is an extension of the ANSI specification that is unique to ANSI.SYS. All this command does is read the current cursor position by calling `BaseWindow::GetPosition()` and storing it in the member data elements `saved_row` and `saved_col`.

```
void restore_position( void )
```

Like the previous command, the "ESC[u" command is unique to ANSI.SYS. This command restores the settings stored previously in `saved_row` and `saved_col` by calling `BaseWindow::SetPosition()`.

```
void set_color( void )
```

The code to execute this command is somewhat more complicated than any of the previous commands. First, rather than have a single parameter, this command can have any number of numeric parameters strung together. Second, there are 21 possible parameters, each of which modifies the screen's current display attribute.

`set_color()` accomplishes this by executing a loop that starts with the first parameter and works through the list in `ansi_parms[]`. The loop terminates when it reaches the value of `parm_count`, which is the index for the ANSI command value and is one past the last parameter.

Each parameter in the list is processed by first retrieving the current display attribute with a call to `BaseWindow::GetAttribute()`. The attribute is then modified, either by changing the foreground color or the background color, or by replacing it with an entirely new attribute. All this is accomplished by a large switch statement that does the job in a very straightforward manner. Finally, the new attribute is set using the `BaseWindow::SetAttribute()` command.

```
void set_mode( void )
```

The "ESC[=#h" and "ESC[=#l" commands are used to set new video modes. ANSI.SYS will change the display into various video modes, such as 40 by 25 text mode and 320 by 200 graphics mode. In addition, a parameter value of 7 is used to set and reset end of line wrap mode.

The implementation of the two mode commands in `AnsiTerminal` doesn't support any of the mode values except 7, which controls wrap mode. This accomplishes its task by calling the `BaseWindow::SetWrap()` function.

```
AnsiTerminal( RS232 &p, TextWindow &w )
```

The constructor for an object of type `AnsiTerminal` first calls the base class constructor, which takes care of assigning the `BaseWindow` and `RS232` pointers that are used by the class. Next, it takes care of setting up the output screen by calling the `Clear()`, `Goto()`, and `SetWrap()` members of class `BaseWindow`.

After the output screen has been set up, the next thing the constructor does is allocate the memory used in the `ansi_parms[]` array, as well as the two key code translation arrays. Finally, the two key code translation arrays are initialized with their default values.

```
virtual ~AnsiTerminal( void )
```

The `AnsiTerminal` destructor frees the memory allocated for the three arrays used during the emulation and then exits.

```
virtual void Display( int c )
```

The `Display()` routine is used to display normal characters that make it through the escape sequence filtering. For ANSI emulation, this is nice and simple. The characters are just output to the `BaseWindow` using the insertion operator.

```
virtual void WriteKey( int c )
```

This function checks to see whether the key is one of the extended key codes or a standard ASCII code. Depending on which it is, a translation is looked up from one of the two key code translation tables. If a translation exists, it is sent. If no translation exists and the key is a standard ASCII key, the key value is sent. Extended keys aren't sent if no translation exists.

The implementation for class `AnsiTerminal` is shown in Listing 8-4. It accompanies the declarations for the class given in `ANSITERM.H` in Listing 8-3.

Listing 8-4: ANSITERM.CPP

```
// **************** START OF ANSITERM.CPP ****************
//
//
// This file contains all the code to support the AnsiTerm
// class, which is a terminal emulation class that supports
// the IBM PC ANSI.SYS control sequences.

#include <stdio.h>
#include <stdlib.h>
#include <string.h>
#include "terminal.h"
#include "ansiterm.h"

// These two defines can be used to help debug the terminal
// emulation class. DEBUG is used to split the screen and
// provide a bottom window that displays escape sequences as
// they are parsed. KEYBOARD_FAKE lets you input escape
// sequences from the keyboard.

//#define KEYBOARD_FAKE
#define DEBUG

//
// The debug macro in this file is meant to be used
// when only debugging in MS-DOS. A bit of additional code would
// need to be written under Windows to create a debug window.
// So, you turn off the debug macro if you are building a
// Windows program.
//
#if defined( _WINDOWS ) && defined( DEBUG )
#undef DEBUG
#endif

#if defined( DEBUG )
#include "textwind.h"
BaseWindow *debug_window;
#endif
```

```c
// This is a list of keyboard mappings that are defined when the
// emulator first starts. These key mappings can be remapped
// dynamically, although this class does not support the feature.
// These values are loaded into the mapping arrays when the
// constructor executes.

struct key_strings {
    int key_value;
    char *translation;
} initial_key_translations[] = { { LEFT,        "\x1b[D"  },
                                 { RIGHT,       "\x1b[C"  },
                                 { UP,          "\x1b[A"  },
                                 { DOWN,        "\x1b[B"  },
                                 { HOME,        "\x1b[H"  },
                                 { END,         "\x1b[F"  },
                                 { PGUP,        "\x1b[I"  },
                                 { PGDN,        "\x1b[G"  },
                                 { INSERT,      "\x1b[L"  },
                                 { F1,          "\x1b[M"  },
                                 { F2,          "\x1b[N"  },
                                 { F3,          "\x1b[O"  },
                                 { F4,          "\x1b[P"  },
                                 { F5,          "\x1b[Q"  },
                                 { F6,          "\x1b[R"  },
                                 { F7,          "\x1b[S"  },
                                 { F8,          "\x1b[T"  },
                                 { F9,          "\x1b[U"  },
                                 { F10,         "\x1b[V"  },
                                 { SHIFT_F1,    "\x1b[Y"  },
                                 { SHIFT_F2,    "\x1b[Z"  },
                                 { SHIFT_F3,    "\x1b[a"  },
                                 { SHIFT_F4,    "\x1b[b"  },
                                 { SHIFT_F5,    "\x1b[c"  },
                                 { SHIFT_F6,    "\x1b[d"  },
                                 { SHIFT_F7,    "\x1b[e"  },
                                 { SHIFT_F8,    "\x1b[f"  },
                                 { SHIFT_F9,    "\x1b[g"  },
                                 { SHIFT_F10,   "\x1b[h"  },
                                 { CONTROL_F1,  "\x1b[k"  },
                                 { CONTROL_F2,  "\x1b[l"  },
                                 { CONTROL_F3,  "\x1b[m"  },
                                 { CONTROL_F4,  "\x1b[n"  },
                                 { CONTROL_F5,  "\x1b[o"  },
                                 { CONTROL_F6,  "\x1b[p"  },
```

```
                        { CONTROL_F7,   "\x1b[q"  },
                        { CONTROL_F8,   "\x1b[r"  },
                        { CONTROL_F9,   "\x1b[s"  },
                        { CONTROL_F10,  "\x1b[t"  },
                        { ALT_F1,       "\x1b[w"  },
                        { ALT_F2,       "\x1b[x"  },
                        { ALT_F3,       "\x1b[y"  },
                        { ALT_F4,       "\x1b[z"  },
                        { ALT_F5,       "\x1b[@"  },
                        { ALT_F6,       "\x1b[["  },
                        { ALT_F7,       "\x1b[\\" },
                        { ALT_F8,       "\x1b[]"  },
                        { ALT_F9,       "\x1b[^"  },
                        { ALT_F10,      "\x1b[_"  },
                        { 0,            0         }
                   };

//
// The constructor sets up the pointers to the port and the
// TextWindow objects. It puts the window in a predefined
// state, allocates the memory for the ANSI string parsing
// storage, and then initializes the key maps. If the DEBUG macro
// is turned on, the screen is split and a second debug text
// window is opened.
//

AnsiTerminal::AnsiTerminal( RS232 &p, BaseWindow &w )
    : Terminal( p, w )
{
    int key;
    char *translation;

    window->Clear();
    window->Goto();
    window->SetWrap( 1 );
    saved_row = 0;
    saved_col = 0;
    for ( int i = 0 ; i < 15 ; i++ )
        ansi_parms[ i ] = new char[ 81 ];
    ansi_parms[ 15 ] = 0;
    keys = new char *[ 256 ];
    extended_keys = new char *[ 256 ];
    for ( i = 0 ; i < 256 ; i++ ) {
        if ( keys )
```

```
                    keys[ i ] = 0;
            if ( extended_keys )
                extended_keys[ i ] = 0;
        }
        for ( i = 0;
              initial_key_translations[ i ].translation != 0;
              i++ )
        {
            key = initial_key_translations[ i ].key_value;
            translation = initial_key_translations[ i ].translation;
            if ( extended_keys && key > 256 )
                extended_keys[ ( key > 8 ) & 0xff ] = translation;
            else if ( keys )
                keys[ key ] = translation;
        }
#if defined( DEBUG )
    Set43LineMode( 1 );
    debug_window = new TextWindow( 25, 0, 80, 18 );
    debug_window->SetWrap( 1 );
#endif
}


//
// ReadPort filters port input for the end application. If
// it sees the first character of an escape sequence, it gets
// parsed and the application never sees it. Normal characters
// get passed straight back to the application. Note that if
// the KEYBOARD_FAKE macro is defined, input comes from the
// keyboard instead of the port.
//
int AnsiTerminal::ReadPort( void )
{
    int c;

#ifdef KEYBOARD_FAKE
    while ( ( c = window->ReadKey() ) == 0 )
        ;
    if ( c == F10 )
        return RS232_ERROR;
#else
    c = port->Read();
#endif
    if ( c == ESC ) {
        parse();
```

```
            return RS232_TIMEOUT;
        }
        return c;
}

//
// The destructor for an AnsiTerminal objects just has to free
// up the memory allocated for the ANSI parser. If DEBUG is
// turned on, the screen is restored to 25-line mode.

AnsiTerminal::~AnsiTerminal( void )
{
    for ( int i = 0 ; i < 15 ; i++ )
        delete[] ansi_parms[ i ];
    delete[] keys;
    delete[] extended_keys;
#if defined( DEBUG ) && !defined( _WINDOWS )
    Set43LineMode( 0 );
#endif
}

// This is the actual parser that reads in ANSI strings. It
// is just a fairly simple state machine that sits in a loop
// reading in characters until it detects the end of an ANSI
// sequence. When it is done, the ansi_parms[] array holds a
// list of numeric and quoted strings, and parm_count is the
// index to the last valid string. Error handling is
// nonexistent; if anything odd happens, the routine just returns
// with a failure.

int AnsiTerminal::parse_ansi_string( void )
{
    int index;
    enum { READY_TO_READ,
           READING_DIGITS,
           READING_STRING,
           DONE_WITH_STRING } scan_state;
    int c;

    parm_count = 0;
    index = 0;

    for ( int i = 0 ; i < 15 ; i++ )
        if ( ansi_parms[ i ] != 0 )
```

```c
            memset( ansi_parms[ i ], 0, 81 );
#ifdef KEYBOARD_FAKE
    while ( ( c = window->ReadKey() ) == 0 )
        ;
#else
    c = port->Read( 200 );
#endif
    if ( c != '[' )
        return 0;

    scan_state = READY_TO_READ;
    for ( ; ; ) {
        if ( index >= 80 || ansi_parms[ parm_count ] == 0 )
            return 0;
#ifdef KEYBOARD_FAKE
        while ( ( c = window->ReadKey() ) == 0 )
            ;
#else
        c = port->Read( 1000 );
#endif
        if ( c < 0 )
            return 0;
        switch ( scan_state ) {
          case READY_TO_READ:
            if ( parm_count == 0 && ( c == '=' || c == '?' ) )
              ansi_parms[ parm_count++ ][ 0 ] = (char) c;
            else if ( c == '"' ) {
              scan_state = READING_STRING;
              ansi_parms[ parm_count ][ index++ ] = (char) c;
            } else if ( c >= '0' && c <= '9' ) {
              ansi_parms[ parm_count ][ index++ ] = (char) c;
              scan_state = READING_DIGITS;
            } else if ( c == ';' ) {
              parm_count++;
              index = 0;
            } else {
              ansi_parms[ parm_count ][ index ] = (char) c;
              return 1;
            }
            break;
          case READING_DIGITS :
            if ( c == ';' ) {
              parm_count++;
              index = 0;
```

```
              scan_state = READY_TO_READ;
            } else if ( c >= '0' && c <='9' )
              ansi_parms[ parm_count ][ index++ ] = (char) c;
            else {
              ansi_parms[ ++parm_count ][ 0 ] = (char) c;
              return 1;
            }
            break;
          case READING_STRING :
            if ( c == '"' )
              scan_state = DONE_WITH_STRING;
            ansi_parms[ parm_count ][ index++ ] = (char) c;
            break;
          case DONE_WITH_STRING :
            if ( c == ';' ) {
              parm_count++;
              index = 0;
              scan_state = READY_TO_READ;
            } else {
              ansi_parms[ ++parm_count ][ 0 ] = (char) c;
              return 1;
            }
            break;
        }
    }
}

// This routine is the high-level controller for the terminal
// emulation class. It calls parse_ansi_string() to break the
// escape sequence down into usable components, then dispatches
// the appropriate member function to do the work. If DEBUG is
// switched on, the escape sequence is dumped out to the debug
// window.

void AnsiTerminal::parse( void )
{
    if ( parse_ansi_string() ) {
#if defined( DEBUG )
        debug_window->Goto();
        DisplayAttribute att = debug_window->GetAttribute();
        debug_window->SetAttribute( att ^ 0x77 );
        *debug_window << "ESC [ ";
        for ( int i = 0 ; i <= parm_count; i++ )
            *debug_window << "<" << ansi_parms[ i ] << ">";
```

```
            *debug_window << "  ";
            window->Goto();
#endif
        switch( ansi_parms[ parm_count ][ 0 ] ) {
            case 'A' : cursor_move( -1, 0 ); break;
            case 'B' : cursor_move( 1, 0 ); break;
            case 'C' : cursor_move( 0, 1 ); break;
            case 'D' : cursor_move( 0, -1 ); break;
            case 'H' : position_cursor(); break;
            case 'J' : erase_in_display(); break;
            case 'K' : erase_in_line(); break;
            case 'f' : position_cursor(); break;
            case 'l' : set_mode(); break;
            case 'h' : set_mode(); break;
            case 'm' : set_color(); break;
            case 'n' : cursor_position_report(); break;
            case 's' : save_position(); break;
            case 'u' : restore_position(); break;
        }
    }
}

// ESC[#;#f and ESC[#;#H
//
// These two commands have the same effect: to position
// the cursor at a location specified by the two numbers, which
// are a row and column sequence. One or both parameters can be
// omitted, in which case the default value of 1 is used. Note
// that row and column numbers in ANSI are 1 based, whereas the
// BaseWindow class numbers are 0 based.

void AnsiTerminal::position_cursor()
{
    int row;
    int col;

    if ( parm_count > 0 )
        row = atoi( ansi_parms[ 0 ] );
    else
        row = 1;
    if ( parm_count > 1 )
        col = atoi( ansi_parms[ 1 ] );
    else
        col = 1;
```

```
        window->SetPosition( row - 1, col  - 1 );
}

// ESC[#A   Cursor up
// ESC[#B   Cursor down
// ESC[#C   Cursor right
// ESC[#D   Cursor left
//
// These four commands are all handled with this member function.
// The single numeric parameter defaults to 1 if it is omitted.
// Any movement outside the screen bounds is ignored by the
// BaseWindow functions, so this routine doesn't have to worry
// about it.

void AnsiTerminal::cursor_move( int row_dir, int col_dir )
{
    int offset;
    int row;
    int col;

    if ( parm_count > 0 )
        offset = atoi( ansi_parms[ 0 ] );
    else
        offset = 1;
    window->GetPosition( row, col );
    row += offset * row_dir;
    col += offset * col_dir;
    window->SetPosition( row, col );
}

// ESC[6n   Device Status Report
//
// This command is handled by issuing a Cursor Position Report
// sequence, ESC[#;#R, with the two numeric parameters being the
// row and column number. Note that handling the command this way
// is somewhat idiosyncratic to the PC.

void AnsiTerminal::cursor_position_report( void )
{
    int row;
    int col;
    char temp[ 40 ];

    if ( parm_count != 1 )
```

```
        return;
    if ( strcmp( ansi_parms[ 0 ], "6" ) != 0 )
        return;
    window->GetPosition( row, col );
    sprintf( temp, "%c[%d;%dR", ESC, row + 1, col + 1 );
    port->Write( temp );
}

// ESC[2J   Erase in display
//
// The official ANSI version of this command will erase some or
// all of the display, depending on the value of the numeric
// parameters. The IBM PC version supports only parameter 2, which
// erases the entire display. The cursor is homed as part of this
// command.

void AnsiTerminal::erase_in_display( void )
{
    if ( parm_count != 1 )
        return;
    if ( strcmp( ansi_parms[ 0 ], "2" ) != 0 )
        return;
    window->Clear();
    window->SetPosition( 0, 0 );
}

// ESC[K   Erase in line
//
// This is another ANSI command that is only partially supported
// by IBM ANSI. When no numeric parameter is given, the line is
// erased from the cursor position to the end of the line.

void AnsiTerminal::erase_in_line( void )
{
    int row;
    int col;
    int width;
    int height;
    int i;

    if ( parm_count != 0 )
        return;
    window->GetPosition( row, col );
    window->GetDimensions( width, height );
```

```
        for ( i = col ; i < width; i++ )
            *window << ' ';
        window->SetPosition( row, col );
}

// ESC[s   Save Cursor Position
//
// This command saves off the current cursor position for later
// restoration. This is an IBM extension to the ANSI standard.

void AnsiTerminal::save_position( void )
{
    if ( parm_count != 0 )
        return;
    window->GetPosition( saved_row, saved_col );
}

// ESC[u   Restore Cursor Position
//
// Another IBM extension to the ANSI standard. This command
// restores the previously saved cursor position.
//

void AnsiTerminal::restore_position( void )
{
    if ( parm_count != 0 )
        return;
    window->SetPosition( saved_row, saved_col );
}

// ESC[#;#;...;#m   Set Graphics Rendition
//
// This command sets the current display attributes to various
// attributes. Multiple command parameters can be strung
// together in unlimited combinations. This implementation is
// limited to 14 parameters.

void AnsiTerminal::set_color( void )
{
    int command;
    int att;

    for ( int i = 0 ; i < parm_count ; i++ ) {
        command = atoi( ansi_parms[ i ] );
```

```
            att = window->GetAttribute();
            switch( command ) {
               case 0  : att = NORMAL_ATTRIBUTE;        break;
               case 1  : att = att | 8;                 break;
               case 5  : att = att | 0x80;              break;
               case 7  : att = REVERSE_ATTRIBUTE;       break;
               case 8  : att = INVISIBLE_ATTRIBUTE;     break;
               case 30 : att = ( att & 0xf0 ) | 0x00; break;
               case 31 : att = ( att & 0xf0 ) | 0x04; break;
               case 32 : att = ( att & 0xf0 ) | 0x02; break;
               case 33 : att = ( att & 0xf0 ) | 0x0e; break;
               case 34 : att = ( att & 0xf0 ) | 0x01; break;
               case 35 : att = ( att & 0xf0 ) | 0x05; break;
               case 36 : att = ( att & 0xf0 ) | 0x03; break;
               case 37 : att = ( att & 0xf0 ) | 0x07; break;
               case 40 : att = ( att & 0x0f ) | 0x00; break;
               case 41 : att = ( att & 0x0f ) | 0x40; break;
               case 42 : att = ( att & 0x0f ) | 0x20; break;
               case 43 : att = ( att & 0x0f ) | 0x60; break;
               case 44 : att = ( att & 0x0f ) | 0x10; break;
               case 45 : att = ( att & 0x0f ) | 0x50; break;
               case 46 : att = ( att & 0x0f ) | 0x30; break;
               case 47 : att = ( att & 0x0f ) | 0x70; break;
            }
            window->SetAttribute( att );
         }
      }

      // ESC[=#h   ESC[=#l   Set/Reset Mode
      // ESC[=h    ESC[=l
      // ESC[=0h   ESC[=0l
      // ESC[?7h   ESC[?7l
      //
      // This command is used to change the current video mode. The
      // TextWindow class used here doesn't support changing modes, so
      // most versions of this command aren't supported. The single
      // exception is the last version, which turns line wrap on or off.
```

```
void AnsiTerminal::set_mode( void )
{
    if ( parm_count != 2 )
        return;
    if ( strcmp( ansi_parms[ 0 ], "?" ) != 0 &&
         strcmp( ansi_parms[ 0 ], "=" ) != 0 )
        return;
    if ( strcmp( ansi_parms[ 1 ], "7" ) != 0 )
        return;
    switch( ansi_parms[ 2 ][ 0 ] ) {
        case 'h' : window->SetWrap( 1 ); break;
        case 'l' : window->SetWrap( 0 ); break;
    }
}

// Writing a key to the serial port is done by checking to see
// whether a translation is defined. If not, the key itself is
// sent out. Otherwise, the translation is sent.

void AnsiTerminal::WriteKey( int key )
{
    char *translation;

    if ( extended_keys && key > 256 ) {
        translation = extended_keys[ ( key > 8 ) & 0xff ];
        if ( translation != 0 )
            port->Write( translation );
    } else {
        if ( keys )
            translation = keys[ key & 0xff ];
        else
            translation = 0;
        if ( translation != 0 )
            port->Write( translation );
        else
            port->Write( key );
    }
}

// ****************** END OF ANSITERM.CPP ******************
```

Debugging Hooks

Debugging terminal emulation code can be difficult. Doing so involves two problems in particular. First, as the escape codes are transmitted from the remote terminal, they are deliberately filtered out of the input stream, so they aren't visible to the programmer during debugging. Because of this, it is difficult to tell whether or not the emulation code is responding properly to escape sequences-- you can't see what sequences are being received.

Second, it isn't always easy to convince a remote system to send the exact sequences that you want to test. For example, you may never be able to get the Linux system you are using to send the "ESC[s" sequence needed to save the cursor row and position.

These two problems are handled by providing special debugging code inside the `AnsiTerminal` class. Two special macros enable the debugging code when they are defined.

The first macro is called `DEBUG`. When `DEBUG` is defined, which is done by virtue of a preprocessor #define statement in `ANSITERM.CPP`, some extra code is enabled. This code has the effect of opening up a debug window that displays ANSI Escape sequences as they are parsed.

The `DEBUG` code accomplishes this by putting the screen into 43-line mode when the `AnsiTerminal` constructor is called, and by creating a second text window that occupies the bottom half of the screen. (Note that the DEBUG macro is enabled only during debugging of MS-DOS Text mode programs.) The top 25 lines are still used for normal terminal emulation. During the parsing of input data, the Escape sequences are displayed in the debug window.

The debug output follows. . During the course of a BBS session, scores of escape sequences are shown in the debug window. Although this may seem somewhat overwhelming, it is usually fairly easy to spot simple problems with a complete output dump such as this. Working on more complicated problems may require modification of the code that displays the escape sequences. For example, the following sample screen (with `DEBUG` turned off,) could be modified to show only certain sequences, or perhaps to filter other sequences out.

The second macro used to help during the debugging process is called `KEYBOARD_FAKE`. The name of the macro describes exactly what it does: allows you to fake escape sequences using keyboard input. When the `KEYBOARD_FAKE` macro is turned on, input that normally comes from the RS232 port is instead read in from the keyboard. In this way, you can input whatever escape sequences you want to test without struggling to convince a remote system to send them to you over an RS-232 link.

```
             +-----------------------------------------+
         +-++-+                     +-++-+
     _ __ _  +--+ - ---+       _ __ _ ---+ ---+ + +        _
      _ ++ _ _ --_ __  _        _ ++ __ --  _ __ _         _
       _ -   - + + - -   -       - - ---+ - - +--+         _
_____+-----------------------------------------+_____
                      WILDCAT! Version 3
_____+-----------------------------------------+_____

___+------------------+_+-------------+_+-------------+_+------------------+___
___  M essage Menu     ___ H elp Level ___ U ser List  ___ Q uestionnaires   ___
___  C omments         ___ N ewsletter ___ F iles Menu ___ T alk to Nodes    ___
___  J oin Conference  ___ G oodbye    ___ P age Sysop ___ I nitial Welcome  ___
  _  Y our Settings    _ _ W hos Online_ _ V erify User_ _ 1 Sysop Menu       _
  _  S ystem Stats     _ _ B ulletins   _ _ D oors      _ _ ? Command Help    _
   +------------------+ +-------------+ +-------------+ +------------------+
    Conference: CommLib Conference    Time On: 0   Time Remaining: 100

   Command > ?


><33><40><m>  ESC [ <0><1><37><40><m>  ESC [ <0><1><32><40><m>  ESC [ <0><1><37>
<40><m>  ESC [ <0><1><33><40><m>  ESC [ <0><1><37><40><m>  ESC [ <0><32><40><m>
  ESC [ <0><1><33><40><m>  ESC [ <0><1><37><40><m>  ESC [ <0><1><33><40><m>  ESC
 [ <0><1><37><40><m>  ESC [ <0><1><33><40><m>  ESC [ <0><1><37><40><m>  ESC [ <0>
<1><33><40><m>  ESC [ <0><1><37><40><m>  ESC [ <0><1><33><40><m>  ESC [ <0><1><3
7><40><m>  ESC [ <0><1><33><40><m>  ESC [ <0><1><37><40><m>  ESC [ <0><1><33><40
><m>  ESC [ <0><1><37><40><m>  ESC [ <0><1><33><40><m>  ESC [ <0><1><37><40><m>
  ESC [ <0><37><40><m>  ESC [ <0><1><37><40><m>  ESC [ <0><1><33><40><m>  ESC [ <
0><1><37><40><m>  ESC [ <0><1><33><40><m>  ESC [ <0><1><37><40><m>  ESC [ <0><1>
<33><40><m>  ESC [ <0><1><37><40><m>  ESC [ <0><1><33><40><m>  ESC [ <0><1><37><
40><m>  ESC [ <0><1><37><40><m>  ESC [ <0><1><33><40><m>  ESC [ <0><1><37><40><m
>  ESC [ <0><1><33><40><m>  ESC [ <0><1><37><40><m>  ESC [ <0><1><33><40><m>  ES
C [ <0><1><37><40><m>  ESC [ <0><1><33><40><m>  ESC [ <0><1><37><40><m>  ESC [ <
0><1><37><40><m>  ESC [ <0><1><37><40><m>  ESC [ <0><1><33><40><m>  ESC [ <0><1>
<37><40><m>  ESC [ <0><1><33><40><m>  ESC [ <0><1><37><40><m>  ESC [ <0><1><33><
40><m>  ESC [ <0><1><37><40><m>  ESC [ <0><1><37><40><m>
```

The BaseWindow Class

Terminal emulators need to perform output to display devices, but you don't want to tie your terminal emulation classes to any specific hardware or software. In C++, when you want to define an abstract interface, you usually create a class with pure virtual functions. For your terminal emulators, this interface is defined in class BaseWindow.

BaseWindow is mostly just thin air containing eight pure virtual functions that have to be defined by derived classes. However, it does have two actual data members, wrap and attribute, plus a couple of functions that manipulate them. However, using those two members for useful purposes is still left up to the derived classes.

BaseWindow is entirely defined in a single file, BASEWIND.H, with no cpp file needed. The functions actually implemented by this base class are so short that it makes sense to define them as inline and include them in the header file shown in Listing 8-5.

Listing 8-5: BASEWIND.H

```
// ********************* BaseWind.h *********************
//
// This header file contains the entire definition and
// implementation of class BaseWindow. BaseWindow is an abstract
// base class that is used to define an interface between
// terminal emulation code and a concrete display device. The
// class that implements the display code on some target device
// will be derived from this class and will have to implement
// the pure virtual functions declared in this class.
//

#ifndef _BASE_WINDOW_DOT_H
#define _BASE_WINDOW_DOT_H

#include "rs232.h"
#include "ascii.h"

enum DisplayAttribute { NORMAL_ATTRIBUTE = 0x07,
                        REVERSE_ATTRIBUTE = 0x70,
                        INVISIBLE_ATTRIBUTE = 0 };

class BaseWindow {
public :
   BaseWindow()
   {
```

```
        wrap = 0;
        attribute = NORMAL_ATTRIBUTE;
    }
    virtual ~BaseWindow( void ){ ; }
    void SetWrap( int setting ){ wrap = setting; }
    DisplayAttribute GetAttribute( void ) { return attribute; }
    virtual BaseWindow &operator<<( char c ) = 0;
    virtual BaseWindow &operator<<( char *pStr ) = 0;
    virtual void Clear( void ) = 0;
    virtual void Goto( void ) = 0;
    virtual void SetAttribute( int a ) = 0;
    virtual int SetPosition( int row, int col ) = 0;
    virtual void GetPosition( int &rol, int &col ) = 0;
    virtual void GetDimensions( int &width, int &height ) = 0;
protected :
    int wrap;
    DisplayAttribute attribute;
};


//
// Keyboard definitions for codes returned from ReadKey().
// These are BIOS codes from MS-DOS, but I'll keep using
// them under Windows for consistency.
//

const int F1          = 0x3b00;
const int F2          = 0x3c00;
const int F3          = 0x3d00;
const int F4          = 0x3e00;
const int F5          = 0x3f00;
const int F6          = 0x4000;
const int F7          = 0x4100;
const int F8          = 0x4200;
const int F9          = 0x4300;
const int F10         = 0x4400;
const int ALT_F1      = 0x6800;
const int ALT_F2      = 0x6900;
const int ALT_F3      = 0x6a00;
const int ALT_F4      = 0x6b00;
const int ALT_F5      = 0x6c00;
const int ALT_F6      = 0x6d00;
const int ALT_F7      = 0x6e00;
const int ALT_F8      = 0x6f00;
```

```
const int ALT_F9       = 0x7000;
const int ALT_F10      = 0x7100;
const int CONTROL_F1   = 0x5e00;
const int CONTROL_F2   = 0x5f00;
const int CONTROL_F3   = 0x6000;
const int CONTROL_F4   = 0x6100;
const int CONTROL_F5   = 0x6200;
const int CONTROL_F6   = 0x6300;
const int CONTROL_F7   = 0x6400;
const int CONTROL_F8   = 0x6500;
const int CONTROL_F9   = 0x6600;
const int CONTROL_F10  = 0x6700;
const int SHIFT_F1     = 0x5400;
const int SHIFT_F2     = 0x5500;
const int SHIFT_F3     = 0x5600;
const int SHIFT_F4     = 0x5700;
const int SHIFT_F5     = 0x5800;
const int SHIFT_F6     = 0x5900;
const int SHIFT_F7     = 0x5a00;
const int SHIFT_F8     = 0x5b00;
const int SHIFT_F9     = 0x5c00;
const int SHIFT_F10    = 0x5d00;
const int UP           = 0x4800;
const int DOWN         = 0x5000;
const int LEFT         = 0x4b00;
const int RIGHT        = 0x4d00;
const int HOME         = 0x4700;
const int END          = 0x4f00;
const int PGUP         = 0x4900;
const int PGDN         = 0x5100;
const int INSERT       = 0x5200;
const int DELETE_KEY   = 0x5300;

const int ALT_A = 0x1e00;
const int ALT_B = 0x3000;
const int ALT_C = 0x2e00;
const int ALT_D = 0x2000;
const int ALT_E = 0x1200;
const int ALT_F = 0x2100;
const int ALT_G = 0x2200;
const int ALT_H = 0x2300;
const int ALT_I = 0x1700;
const int ALT_J = 0x2400;
const int ALT_K = 0x2500;
```

```
const int ALT_L = 0x2600;
const int ALT_M = 0x3200;
const int ALT_N = 0x3100;
const int ALT_O = 0x1800;
const int ALT_P = 0x1900;
const int ALT_Q = 0x1000;
const int ALT_R = 0x1300;
const int ALT_S = 0x1f00;
const int ALT_T = 0x1400;
const int ALT_U = 0x1600;
const int ALT_V = 0x2f00;
const int ALT_W = 0x1100;
const int ALT_X = 0x2d00;
const int ALT_Y = 0x1500;
const int ALT_Z = 0x2c00;

#endif // #ifndef _BASE_WINDOW_DOT_H

// ******************* End of BaseWind.h *******************
```

The functions defined in class `BaseWindow` represent the sum total of everything needed in a display device by your terminal emulation code. Any derived class that wants to work with the terminal emulation classes need only implement these functions properly and it can be a terminal emulation target. The functions defined in this class are described in the following paragraphs.

`BaseWindow()`

The constructor for the `BaseWindow` class turns off the `wrap` member and sets the `attribute` member to the `NORMAL_ATTRIBUTE` setting.

`~BaseWindow()`

The destructor for `BaseWindow` does nothing at all.

`void SetWrap( int setting )`

This function sets the logical member `wrap` to the value passed in the parameter. If `wrap` is set to be true, derived clases are expected to wrap at the end of the line. This means that if the emulator tries to write text past the last column of the display, the derived class should issue a carriage-return linefeed pair and continue writing at the start of a new line.

`DisplayAttribute GetAttribute()`

This member function returns the current display attribute for the display device. Display attributes in this class are simply one-byte tokens. Derived classes have flexibility over how to use the tokens, but class `AnsiTerm` will set the attributes as if the device is a PC screen accessed by the BIOS. This means that the lower four bits of the attribute will be the foreground color for the display, and the upper four bits will be the background color.

```
BaseWindow &operator<<( char c ) (pure virtual)
```

The insertion operator is used to output a single character to the display. The character is written using the current display attribute, and the position of the cursor is updated. This is a pure virtual function and must be implemented by derived classes.

```
BaseWindow &operator<<( char *pStr ) (pure virtual)
```

This insertion operator performs the same basic insertion function, except that it performs it on a null-delimited string of characters instead of a single character. This is a pure virtual function and must be implemented by derived classes.

```
void Clear()(pure virtual)
```

This pure virtual function is called to clear the screen. Clearing means that ASCII spaces are written to every possible display position using the current display attribute. The position of the cursor doesn't change through the clear operation.

```
void Goto( void ) (pure virtual)
```

This function is called to set the focus to the window in question. (The window with the focus will be the window that receives all keyboard input.) In the event that the program is managing multiple text or GUI windows, this function can be used to force control to go to a specific window. This function is used by the terminal emulation functions when the emulator output focus is switching between the main window and the debug window. This is a pure virtual function, and must be implemented by derived classes.

```
void SetAttribute( int a ) (pure virtual)
```

This pure virtual function is defined to set the current display attribute to a new byte. Until the attribute is changed, all characters will be displayed using this attribute. Remember that the lower four bits of this attribute pick one of the sixteen colors for the foreground color and the upper four bits select the background color.

```
int SetPosition( int row, int col ) (pure virtual)
```

This function sets the cursor position to the row and column passed in as arguments. The row and column are 0 base. If the command is successful in setting the new row and column, it returns a true value; if it fails, a false value. This is a pure virtual function and must be implemented by derived classes.

```
void GetPosition( int &rol, int &col ) (pure virtual)
```

This pure virtual function retrieves the current row and column of the cursor.

```
void GetDimensions( int &width, int &height ) (pure virtual)
```

This function returns the height and width of the display device in character cells.

The TextWindow Class

The workhorse class used throughout this book for screen output in 16-bit MS-DOS mode is `TextWindow`. As it happens, `TextWindow` is derived from `BaseWindow`, so you can use it as the target for terminal emulation. You do this by passing a pointer to a newly created `TextWindow` object to the constructor of the terminal emulator. Because a `TextWindow` is also a `BaseWindow`, the pointer is accepted and used properly.

The functions that `AnsiTerminal` needs to use in order to perform terminal emulation are all defined in `BaseWindow`. However, the specific implementations of these functions can be found in `TextWindow.cpp` and might be worth a quick look just to help you increase your understanding of the class.

The one function not defined as part of `AnsiTerminal` that is actually used by the terminal emulator in this chapter is given here.

```
int ReadKey( void )
```

This function reads in a key from the keyboard. If no key is present in the keyboard buffer, it returns a 0. Extended keys are returned with a 0 in the low byte and the extended IBM keyboard scan code in the upper byte.

The source code for the `TextWindow` class appears in Listings 8-6 and 8-7. These source files are also used in several other 16-bit test programs in various chapters of this book.

Listing 8-6: TEXTWIND.H

```
// ******************* START OF TEXTWIND.H *********************
//
//
// Text windows are used by utility and test programs to provide
```

```cpp
// a convenient set of display functions under MS-DOS.

#ifndef _TEXTWIN_DOT_H
#define _TEXTWIN_DOT_H

#include <dos.h>
#include <conio.h>
#include "BaseWind.h"
#ifdef _MSC_VER
# pragma warning( disable : 4505 )
#endif


// The TextWindow class is a very limited display class that
// uses the BIOS for all of its input and output. It supports
// just a few basic operations, but these are enough for test
// and demonstration programs.

class TextWindow : public BaseWindow {
    protected:
        static int count;
        unsigned char start_row;
        unsigned char start_col;
        unsigned char width;
        unsigned char height;
        int border;
        unsigned char row;
        unsigned char col;
        unsigned int *save_buffer;
        void write_char( unsigned char c );
        void write_repeated_chars( unsigned char c, int count );
        void position( int r, int c );
        void save_window();
        void save_border();
        void restore_window();
        void restore_border();
    public :
        TextWindow( int r, int c, int w, int h );
        ~TextWindow();
        BaseWindow& operator<<( char c );
        BaseWindow& operator<<( int c );
        BaseWindow& operator<<( char *s );
        virtual void Clear( void );
        void AddBorder( void );
```

```
        void DisplayTitle( char *title );
        void Scroll( unsigned char line_count );
        int SetPosition( int row, int col );
        void GetPosition( int &rol, int &col );
        virtual void GetDimensions( int &width, int &height );
        virtual void SetAttribute( int a )
        {
            attribute = (DisplayAttribute) a;
        }
        virtual void Goto( void );
        int ReadKey( void );
};

// A couple of simple access routines that are short enough
// to define as inline.

inline void TextWindow::GetPosition( int &r, int &c )
{
    r = row;
    c = col;
}

inline void TextWindow::GetDimensions( int &w, int &h )
{
    w = width;
    h = height;
}

// This class provides a very handy way to save a cursor position
// and restore it later.

class SaveCursor {
    protected :
        unsigned char row;
        unsigned char col;
    public :
        SaveCursor();
        ~SaveCursor();
};

inline SaveCursor::SaveCursor( void )
{
    union REGS r;
```

```
        r.h.ah = 3;
        r.h.bh = 0;
        int86( 0x10, &r, &r );
        row = r.h.dh;
        col = r.h.dl;
    }

    inline SaveCursor::~SaveCursor( void )
    {
        union REGS r;

        r.h.ah = 2;
        r.h.dh = row;
        r.h.dl = col;
        r.h.bh = 0;
        int86( 0x10, &r, &r );
    }

    // PopupWindow is a class derived from TextWindow. It is almost
    // identical to TextWindow except for the fact that it saves the
    // underlying text when created and restores it when destroyed.

    class PopupWindow : public TextWindow {
        protected :
            SaveCursor saved_cursor;
        public :
            PopupWindow( int r, int c, int w, int h );
    };

    // A couple of handy support routines

    int Menu( char *menu[] );
    int ReadLine( char *prompt, char *buffer, int length );
    void Set43LineMode( int control );


#endif   //  #ifdef _TEXTWIN_DOT_H

// ******************* END OF TEXTWIN.H *******************
```

Listing 8-7: TEXTWIND.CPP

```
// ***************** START OF TEXTWIND.CPP *****************
//
//
```

```
//
// This file contains all the code needed to support the
// Text Windows used for example programs in this book. These
// are "quick and dirty" text windows, using the BIOS for most of
// the work.

#include <stdlib.h>
#include <string.h>
#include <dos.h>
#include <conio.h>
#include <ctype.h>
#include <bios.h>
#include "textwind.h"

// This static data member keeps track of how many windows are
// open. When the count drops to zero, cleanup work can be done.

int TextWindow::count = 0;

// write_char uses the BIOS function to write the current
// character using the window attribute. This function is a
// protected member function and is used by the << operator.

inline void TextWindow::write_char( unsigned char c )
{
    union REGS r;

    r.h.ah = 9;
    r.h.al = c;
    r.h.bl = attribute;
    r.h.bh = 0;
    r.x.cx = 1;
    int86( 0x10, &r, &r );
}

// This protected function uses the BIOS parameter to write a
// single character repeatedly. This is much faster than writing
// individual characters in a loop. It is used for writing the
// border and clearing the screen.

inline void TextWindow::write_repeated_chars( unsigned char c,
                                              int count )
{
    union REGS r;
```

```c
    r.h.ah = 9;
    r.h.al =  c;
    r.h.bl =  attribute;
    r.x.cx = count;
    r.h.bh = 0;
    int86( 0x10, &r, &r );
}

// This protected member function positions the cursor at the
// desired position relative to the text window. The protected
// function doesn't check for validity of the row and column
// values. It also doesn't set the row and column data
// members.

inline void TextWindow::position( int r, int c )
{
    union REGS rin;

    r += start_row;
    c += start_col;
    rin.h.ah = 2;
    rin.h.dh = (unsigned char) r;
    rin.h.dl = (unsigned char) c;
    rin.h.bh = 0;
    int86( 0x10, &rin, &rin );
}

// This public member function positions the cursor in a
// window. It also stores the new position in the row and column
// data members.

int TextWindow::SetPosition( int r, int c )
{
    union REGS rin;

    if ( r < 0 || c < 0 )
        return 0;
    if ( r >= (int) height || c >= (int) width )
        return 0;
    row = (unsigned char) r;
    col = (unsigned char) c;
    r += start_row;
    c += start_col;
    rin.h.ah = 2;
```

```c
        rin.h.dh = (unsigned char) r;
        rin.h.dl = (unsigned char) c;
        rin.h.bh = 0;
        int86( 0x10, &rin, &rin );
        return 1;
}

// This public member function positions the cursor in the current
// location of the window defined by *this.

void TextWindow::Goto( void )
{
    union REGS rin;

    rin.h.ah = 2;
    rin.h.dh = (unsigned char) ( row + start_row );
    rin.h.dl = (unsigned char) ( col + start_col );
    rin.h.bh = 0;
    int86( 0x10, &rin, &rin );
}

// This public function uses the BIOS to scroll a text window.

inline void TextWindow::Scroll( unsigned char line_count )
{
    union REGS r;

    r.h.ah = 6;
    r.h.al = line_count;
    r.h.ch = start_row;
    r.h.cl = start_col;
    r.h.dh = (unsigned char) ( start_row + height - 1 );
    r.h.dl = (unsigned char) ( start_col + width - 1 );
    r.h.bh = attribute;
    int86( 0x10, &r, &r );
}

// This routine writes a formatted character to the output
// window. Special processing is performed for the CR, LF, and
// BS keys.

BaseWindow& TextWindow::operator<<( char c )
{
    switch ( c ) {
```

```
            case '\r' :
                col = 0;
                break;
            case '\n' :
                col = 0;
        row += 1;
                break;

            case '\b' :
                if ( col > 0 )
                    col--;
                break;
            default :
                position( row, col );
                write_char( c );
                col++;
                if ( col >= width ) {
                    if ( wrap ) {
                        col = 0;
                        row++;
                    } else
                        col--;
                }
        }
        if ( row >= height ) {
            row = (unsigned char) ( height - 1 );
            Scroll( 1 );
        }
        position( row, col );
        return *this;
}

// This routine writes a formatted string to the output
// window. Special processing is performed for the CR, LF, and
// BS keys.

BaseWindow& TextWindow::operator<<( char *s )
{
    unsigned char c;

    while ( ( c = *s++ ) != '\0' ) {
        switch ( c ) {
            case '\r' :
                col = 0;
```

```
                    break;
                case '\n' :
                    col = 0;
                    row += 1;
                    break;
                case '\b' :
                    if ( col > 0 )
                        col--;
                    break;
                default :
                    position( row, col );
                    write_char( c );
                    col++;
                    if ( col >= width ) {
                        if ( wrap ) {
                            col = 0;
                            row += 1;
                        } else
                            col--;
                    }
                    break;
            }
            if ( row >= height ) {
                row = (unsigned char) ( height - 1 );
                Scroll( 1 );
            }
            position( row, col );
        }
        return *this;
}

BaseWindow& TextWindow::operator<<( int c )
{
    return operator<<( (char) c );
}

// The only constructor for a text window just defines the
// starting row and column, and the width and height.
// Constructing a window doesn't actually draw anything on the
// screen.

TextWindow::TextWindow( int r, int c, int w, int h )
{
    count++;
```

```
        start_row = (unsigned char ) r;
        start_col = (unsigned char ) c;
        width = (unsigned char) w;
        height = (unsigned char) h;
        border = 0;
        save_buffer = 0;
        row = 0;
        col = 0;
}

// The destructor for a text window restores any saved data
// that was under the window. It also repositions the cursor if
// the last window was just closed.

TextWindow::~TextWindow( void )
{
    if ( save_buffer ) {
        restore_window();
        if ( border )
            restore_border();
        delete save_buffer;
    }
    count--;
    if ( count == 0 ) {
        start_row = 0;
        start_col = 0;
        position( 23, 0 );
    }
}

// Clearing the window is easy.

void TextWindow::Clear( void )
{
    Scroll( 0 );
}

// This function writes the border out around the window. If
// a save buffer has been established, the data under the border
// is saved.

void TextWindow::AddBorder( void )
{
    unsigned char r;
```

```
    SaveCursor a;

    if ( save_buffer && border == 0 )
        save_border();
    border = 1;
    position( -1, -1 );
    write_char( 218 );
    position( -1, width );
    write_char( 191 );
    position( height, -1 );
    write_char( 192 );
    position( height, width );
    write_char( 217 );
    for ( r = 0 ; r < height ; r++ ) {
        position( r, -1 );
        write_char( 179 );
        position( r, width );
        write_char( 179 );
    }
    position( -1, 0 );
    write_repeated_chars( 196, width );
    position( height, 0 );
    write_repeated_chars( 196, width );
}

// The title just gets displayed on top of the border.

void TextWindow::DisplayTitle( char *s )
{
    int col = 0;

    if ( ( strlen( s ) + 2 ) > width )
        return;
    if ( !border )
        AddBorder();
    SaveCursor save_it;
    position( -1, col++ );
    write_char( 180 );
    while ( *s ) {
        position( -1, col++ );
        write_char( *s++ );
    }
    position( -1, col );
    write_char( 195 );
```

```cpp
    }

    // Popup windows save the area under the window. This
    // function saves the main window; another one saves the border
    // area.

    void TextWindow::save_window( void )
    {
        union REGS rpos;
        union REGS rread;
        union REGS rout;
        int i;
        SaveCursor save_it;

    // Allocate enough space for the window plus the border. To
    // simplify the storage issues, I treat the save buffer as the
    // screen array followed by a border array. The border array
    // will have weird indexing, but the screen array won't.

        if ( save_buffer == 0 )
            save_buffer = new unsigned int[(width+2)*(height+2)];
        if ( save_buffer ) {
            i = 0;
            rpos.h.ah = 2;
            rpos.h.bh = 0;
            rread.h.ah = 8;
            rread.h.bh = 0;
            for ( rpos.h.dh = start_row ;
                    rpos.h.dh < (unsigned char) (start_row+height);
                    rpos.h.dh++ )
                for ( rpos.h.dl = start_col ;
                        rpos.h.dl < (unsigned char) (start_col+width);
                        rpos.h.dl++ ) {
                    int86( 0x10, &rpos, &rout );
                    int86( 0x10, &rread, &rout );
                    save_buffer[ i++ ] = rout.x.ax;
                }
        }
    }

    // When a popup window is destroyed, the area under it is
    // restored. This function restores the text under the window,
    // but doesn't do anything about the border.
```

```
void TextWindow::restore_window( void )
{
    union REGS rpos;
    union REGS rwrite;
    union REGS rout;
    int i;
    SaveCursor save_it;

    if ( !save_buffer )
        return;
    i = 0;
    rpos.h.ah = 2;
    rpos.h.bh = 0;
    rwrite.h.ah = 9;
    rwrite.h.bh = 0;
    rwrite.x.cx = 1;
    for ( rpos.h.dh = start_row ;
          rpos.h.dh < (unsigned char) ( start_row + height );
          rpos.h.dh++ )
        for ( rpos.h.dl = start_col ;
              rpos.h.dl < (unsigned char) ( start_col + width );
              rpos.h.dl++ ) {
            int86( 0x10, &rpos, &rout );
            rwrite.h.al = (unsigned char) save_buffer[ i ];
            rwrite.h.bl = (unsigned char)(save_buffer[i++]>8);
            int86( 0x10, &rwrite, &rout );
        }
}

// When a popup window is saved, the border has to be saved as
// well. The main window is saved in a standard row-by-column
// order in the save buffer. The border area is stored somewhat
// more haphazardly, right here.

void TextWindow::save_border( void )
{
    union REGS rpos;
    union REGS rread;
    union REGS rout;
    int i;
    SaveCursor save_it;

    if ( save_buffer == 0 )
        return;
```

```c
        i = width * height;
        rpos.h.ah = 2;
        rpos.h.bh = 0;
        rread.h.ah = 8;
        rread.h.bh = 0;
        for ( rpos.h.dl = (unsigned char) ( start_col - 1 );
              rpos.h.dl < (unsigned char) ( start_col + width + 1 ) ;
              rpos.h.dl++ ) {
            rpos.h.dh = (unsigned char) ( start_row - 1 );
            int86( 0x10, &rpos, &rout );
            int86( 0x10, &rread, &rout );
            save_buffer[ i++ ] = rout.x.ax;
            rpos.h.dh = (unsigned char) ( start_row + height );
            int86( 0x10, &rpos, &rout );
            int86( 0x10, &rread, &rout );
            save_buffer[ i++ ] = rout.x.ax;
        }
        for ( rpos.h.dh = start_row ;
              rpos.h.dh < (unsigned char) ( start_row + height ) ;
              rpos.h.dh++ ) {
            rpos.h.dl = (unsigned char) ( start_col - 1 );
            int86( 0x10, &rpos, &rout );
            int86( 0x10, &rread, &rout );
            save_buffer[ i++ ] = rout.x.ax;
            rpos.h.dl = start_col;
            rpos.h.dl = (unsigned char)( rpos.h.dl + width );
            int86( 0x10, &rpos, &rout );
            int86( 0x10, &rread, &rout );
            save_buffer[ i++ ] = rout.x.ax;
        }
}

// This protected function restores the border in the same odd
// order that it was saved.

void TextWindow::restore_border( void )
{
    union REGS rpos;
    union REGS rwrite;
    union REGS rout;
    int i;
    SaveCursor save_it;

    if ( save_buffer == 0 )
```

```
            return;
    i = width * height;
    rpos.h.ah = 2;
    rpos.h.bh = 0;
    rwrite.h.ah = 9;
    rwrite.h.bh = 0;
    rwrite.x.cx = 1;
    for ( rpos.h.dl = (unsigned char) ( start_col - 1 );
          rpos.h.dl < (unsigned char)( start_col + width + 1 );
          rpos.h.dl++ ) {
        rpos.h.dh = (unsigned char) ( start_row - 1 );
        int86( 0x10, &rpos, &rout );
        rwrite.h.al = (unsigned char) save_buffer[ i ];
        rwrite.h.bl = (unsigned char)( save_buffer[ i++ ] > 8 );
        int86( 0x10, &rwrite, &rout );
        rpos.h.dh = (unsigned char) ( start_row + height );
        int86( 0x10, &rpos, &rout );
        rwrite.h.al = (unsigned char) save_buffer[ i ];
        rwrite.h.bl = (unsigned char)( save_buffer[ i++ ] > 8 );
        int86( 0x10, &rwrite, &rout );
    }
    for ( rpos.h.dh = start_row;
          rpos.h.dh < (unsigned char) ( start_row + height ) ;
          rpos.h.dh++ ) {
        rpos.h.dl = (unsigned char) ( start_col - 1 );
        int86( 0x10, &rpos, &rout );
        rwrite.h.al = (unsigned char) save_buffer[ i ];
        rwrite.h.bl = (unsigned char) ( save_buffer[ i++ ] > 8 );
        int86( 0x10, &rwrite, &rout );
        rpos.h.dl = (unsigned char) ( start_col + width );
        int86( 0x10, &rpos, &rout );
        rwrite.h.al = (unsigned char) save_buffer[ i ];
        rwrite.h.bl = (unsigned char) ( save_buffer[ i++ ] > 8 );
        int86( 0x10, &rwrite, &rout );
    }
}

// A popup window is just like a text window except that it
// has an automatic save buffer and save cursor. The constructor
// doesn't do anything except make a text window and then save
// it.

PopupWindow::PopupWindow( int r, int c, int w, int h )
         : TextWindow( r, c, w, h )
```

```c
{
    save_window();
}

// This internal utility routine hides the cursor by moving it
// off the screen. It is used in the menu code.

inline void hide_cursor( void )
{
    union REGS r;
    r.h.ah = 2;
    r.h.dh = 25;
    r.h.dl = 0;
    r.h.bh = 0;
    int86( 0x10, &r, &r );
}

int Menu( char *menu[] )
{
    int items;
    int maxlen;
    int length;
    int i;
    int c;
    int selection;

    items = 0;
    maxlen = 0;
    while ( ( length = strlen( menu[ items ] ) ) != 0 ) {
        items++;
        if ( length > maxlen )
            maxlen = length;
    }
    if ( items == 0 )
        return -1;
    PopupWindow w( 5, 25, maxlen + 2, items );
    w.Clear();
    w.AddBorder();
    for ( i = 0 ; i < items ; i++ ) {
        w.SetPosition( i, 1 );
        w << menu[ i ];
    }
    selection = 0;
    for ( ; ; ) {
```

```
            w.SetAttribute( REVERSE_ATTRIBUTE );
            w.SetPosition( selection, 1 );
            w << menu[ selection ];
            hide_cursor();
            while ( ( c = w.ReadKey() ) == 0 )
                ;
            w.SetAttribute( NORMAL_ATTRIBUTE );
            w.SetPosition( selection, 1 );
            w << menu[ selection ];
            switch ( c ) {
                case 27 : //Escape
                    return( -1 );
                case 13 : // CR
                    return( selection );
                case HOME :
                    selection = 0;
                    break;
                case END :
                    selection = items - 1;
                    break;
                case DOWN :
                    if ( selection < ( items - 1 ) )
                        selection++;
                    break;
                case UP :
                    if ( selection > 0 )
                        selection--;
                    break;
                default :
                    for ( i = ( selection + 1 ) % items ;
                          i != selection ;
                          i = ( i + 1 ) % items ) {
                        if (toupper(c)==toupper(menu[i][0]))
                        {
                            selection = i;
                            break;
                        }
                    }
                    break;
            }
        }
#ifdef _MSC_VER
    return -1;// To pass /W4 under Microsoft, not really needed
#endif
```

```
}

int ReadLine( char *prompt, char *buffer, int length )
{
    int c;
    int count;

    PopupWindow w( 5, 10, 60, 1 );
    w.Clear();
    w.AddBorder();
    w << prompt << ' ';
    count = 0;

    for ( ; ; ) {
        while ( ( c = w.ReadKey() ) == 0 )
            ;
        switch ( c ) {
            case ESC :
                return 0;
            case CR :
                buffer[ count ] = '\0';
                return 1;
            case BS :
                if ( count > 0 ) {
                    count--;
                    w << BS;
                    w << ' ';
                    w << BS;
                }
                break;
            default :
                if ( c >= ' ' && c <= 0x7f ) {
                    if ( count < length ) {
                        buffer[ count++ ] = (char) c;
                        w << c;
                    }
                }
        }
    }
#ifdef _MSC_VER
    return -1; // To pass /W4 under Microsoft, not really needed
#endif
}
```

```c
// ReadKey returns a 0 if no key is ready. The _bios_keybrd()
// routine under Borland C++ has trouble if a Ctrl-Break has been
// pressed, so I replace it with the equivalent int86() function
// call for that compiler only.

int TextWindow::ReadKey( void )
{
#ifdef __TURBOC__
    union REGS r;
    r.h.ah = 1;
    int86( 0x16, &r, &r );
    if ( r.x.flags & 0x40 )   // Test for the zero flag
        return 0;
    r.h.ah = 0;
    int86( 0x16, &r, &r );
    if ( r.h.al != 0 )
        return r.h.al;
    else
        return r.x.ax;
#else   // #ifdef __TURBOC__
    int c;

// Under Borland C, this function will never return true if
// CTRL-BREAK has been pressed, effectively closing the keyboard.

    if ( _bios_keybrd( _KEYBRD_READY ) == 0 )
        return 0;
    c = _bios_keybrd( _KEYBRD_READ );
    if ( ( c & 0xff ) == 0 )   // A normal ASCII key
        return c;
    else
        return c & 0xff;       // A function or other extended key
#endif // #ifdef __TURBOC__ ... #else
}

// This is an unsophisticated way to change to 43-line mode, or
// to 50-line mode on a VGA. Note that it doesn't disable EGA
// cursor emulation, so if you try to change the cursor size,
// strange things might happen. All this routine does to change
// modes is select the appropriate size font, 8x8 for 43 line
// mode, else 8x14 or 8x16.

void Set43LineMode( int control )
{
```

```
        union REGS r;

        if ( control ) {
            r.h.ah = 0x11;
            r.h.al = 0x12;
            r.h.bl = 0;
            int86( 0x10, &r, &r );
        } else {
            r.h.ah = 0x14;   // Change to 11 for EGA
            r.h.al = 0x12;
            r.h.bl = 0;
            int86( 0x10, &r, &r );
            r.h.ah = 0;
            r.h.al = 3;  // Change to 2 for BW80
            int86( 0x10, &r, &r );
        }
}

// ************* END OF TEXTWIND.CPP **************
```

Making the Test Program

The test program for this chapter, TESTTERM.CPP, can be created using the make file shown in Listing 8-8. Just like the make files used in the previous chapters, you just need to remove the comment prefix from the line containing the commands for your particular compiler.

Listing 8-8: TESTTERM.MAK: the make file for the test program

```
# ****************** START OF TESTTERM.MAK ******************
#
#
# This is the make file for the terminal emulation test program.
# Just remove the leading comment line from your compiler, then
# execute:
#
#           Borland and Zortech:  make -ftestterm.mak
#
#           Microsoft:            nmake -ftestterm.mak
#

#CC = tcc -w
#CC = bcc -w
#CC = ztc -b
CC = cl /W4 /AL
```

```
FILES = pc8250.obj isr_8250.obj queue.obj ansiterm.obj pcirq.obj

.cpp.obj:
  $(CC) -c $<

testterm.exe : testterm.obj rs232.obj textwind.obj msdos.obj
$(FILES)
                $(CC) testterm.obj rs232.obj textwind.obj msdos.obj
$(FILES)

# ****************** END OF TESTTERM.MAK *******************
```

Summary

In this chapter, you have learned the basics of terminal emulation. To do a good job with terminal emulation, you must be able to monitor data that arrives on the serial port as well as keystrokes that are entered by the user. Both of these functions are encapsulated in a `Terminal` class. You derive specific versions of the `Terminal` class for any given type of terminal. The derived class created in this chapter emulates terminals that implement the ANSI standard embraced by MS-DOS.

All of this is tied together in a 16-bit MS-DOS demo program. The `Ansi Terminal` class needs help from a display class in order to talk to the hardware. For the demo program in this chapter, the `TextWindow` class provides this function. In Chapter 13, a 32-bit terminal emulation is shown under Windows for which a GUI-based display class is used.

Chapter 9

The Win16 Driver

IN THIS CHAPTER

- ◆ How Windows programming differs from MS-DOS
- ◆ The Windows device driver
- ◆ The communications API
- ◆ Designing a class that uses the Win16 API
- ◆ A Win16 test program
- ◆ Building Test232.EXE

WITH THE RELEASE OF version 3.0, Microsoft Windows became the desktop GUI of choice in the IBM compatible world. While most users seemed to be enamored with the easy-to-use interface, C programmers had to deal with the difficulties in learning a complex API and a new set of programming tools. For RS-232 programmers, working with Win16 meant working with a device driver instead of writing directly to the hardware. It also meant adopting a new event-driven programming paradigm. Although rarely fatal, experienced programmers often found this new way of thinking to be quite painful.

Because of the flexibility of C++, communications programmers don't have to get completely wrapped up in the never-ending arguments over whether Windows is a gift from the gods or an abomination. To us communications programmers, , it is just another platform to support with another class. Since the O/S dependent portions of the communications code was virtualized, adding support for Windows is just another chapter in this book, instead of the religious conversion some zealots would like it to be.

Windows Programming

Programmers who are accustomed to writing code for MS-DOS applications have to make some major adjustments to start developing applications for Microsoft Windows. If you are trained to write conventional text-based programs, you must clear two conceptual hurdles that are fairly difficult.

The first difficulty new Windows programmers encounter is shifting their point of view to an event-driven programming system. Most of you learned to write programs that go out and seek events such as user input and using functions such as `getc()`. Under MS-Windows, the events seek you out, forcing themselves on your programs whether you are ready for them or not.

The second difficulty for new Windows programmers is adjusting to the graphical user interface. Simple C I/O statements such as `printf()` no longer work under MS-Windows. Instead, you have to learn the intricacies of menus and dialog boxes, and learn how to write to the screen using bit mapped proportional fonts.

In this chapter, I am not going to write too much about these difficulties; rather, I concentrate mostly on the communications aspects of Windows programming. Fortunately, control of the communications ports under MS-Windows is fairly straightforward. Windows has a set of new functions that you have to learn, but applying them doesn't take a major paradigm shift.

The Microsoft Windows 16-Bit Device Driver

The 16-bit versions of Windows are often put down as not being real operating systems. Although there may be some truth in those assusations, Win16 does perform one O/S function for communications programmers: shielding applications developers from harder. As a result, the techniques used in Chapter 3 to talk to the UART directly in the `PC8250` class just won't work under Windows. Communicating directly with the hardware is always discouraged, and frequently impossible. Instead, Windows requires users to talk to the RS-232 ports via a device driver.

Using a device driver has some disadvantages. Developers are constrained by the limitations of both the driver API and the driver implementation. However, the benefits of a well-designed driver should outweigh the disadvantages. The most important benefit of the well-designed driver is that it provides a standard interface that you can use to communicate with all sorts of different hardware. The `Win16Port` class developed in this chapter can talk just as easily to an intelligent DigiBoard as a standard PC COM1. All that you need in each case is a vendor-provided device driver.

The Communications API

The Win16 communications API consists of a set of 17 function calls. Although these functions are designed to also support a few basic operations on printer ports, for the most part they are oriented strictly towards RS-232 operations. In addition to these function calls, the communications API is heavily dependent on a pair of structures — the `DCB` and `COMSTAT` structures. The following is a list of the Windows comm API functions:

`BuildCommDCB()`

`ClearCommBreak()`

`CloseComm()`

`EnableCommNotification()`

`EscapeCommFunction()`

`FlushComm()`

`GetCommError()`

`GetCommEventMask()`

`GetCommState()`

`OpenComm()`

`ReadComm()`

`SetCommBreak()`

`SetCommEventMask()`

`SetCommState()`

`TransmitCommChar()`

`UngetCommChar()`

`WriteComm()`

`DCB` structure

`COMSTAT` structure

Note that nearly all the functions in the communications group of the Windows API take an integer argument named `idComDev` as their first argument. This is the port identifier returned by Windows when the port is first opened with the `OpenComm()` call.

```
int BuildCommDCB( LPCSTR lpszDef, DCB FAR *lpdcb )
```

This function is used to build a `DCB`, or Device Control Block. The DCB (explained in detail later in this chapter) contains all the user controllable settings for the port, which includes the standard parity, baud rate, and so on. This function takes an input string of the form `COM1:9600,N,8,1`, and fills in the DCB settings with the appropriate values. The port can then be set to those values by calling the `SetCommState()` command.

This function may be of some use to programmers who are setting up the port based on keyboard input. You won't use it in the `Win16Port` class, as you may want to have more comprehensive control over the port.

This function returns a 0 if successful, or a -1 if an error occurs.

`int ClearCommBreak( int idComDev )`

The Windows API supports break signaling in a fairly rudimentary fashion. `SetCommBreak()` puts the port into a breaking condition, and this function clears the breaking condition. The single parameter is the port ID returned from the `OpenComm()` function. This function returns a 0 if successful, -1 if there is an error. The `Win16Port` class calls this function in the virtual Break function.

`int CloseComm( int idComDev )`

The `CloseComm()` function closes the port and makes it available for other programs running under Windows. The single argument is the port ID returned from the `OpenComm()` function. The function returns a 0 if successful and a -1 on error.

The `Win16Port` class calls this function as part of its destructor.

```
BOOL EnableCommNotification( int idComDev,
                             HWND hwnd,
                             int cbWriteNotify,
                             int cbOutQueue )
```

This function was introduced as part of the API in Windows 3.1. It sets up the port identified by the `idComDev` parameter to generate `WM_COMMNOTIFY` events to be sent to the window identified by `hwnd`. Three types of events can be generated. `CN_RECEIVE` and `CN_TRANSMIT` events are generated when a specified amount of activity occurs on the input or output buffers. `CN_EVENT` events are used to track events such as incoming parity errors, breaks, or modem status line changes.

Using events to notify a program that activity is occurring in the communications driver is a very natural way to do things under Windows. Unfortunately, the notification functions in Win16 seem to be plagued by serious operation restrictions and bugs, and are probably not suitable for use in a general-purpose class. Because of this, the `Win16Port` class doesn't take advantage of these events.

`EnableCommNotification` returns a zero on failure, a non-zero when successful.

`LONG EscapeCommFunction( int idComDev, int nFunction )`

This function is used to handle a few miscellaneous things that aren't covered elsewhere in the Windows API. The `nFunction` argument determines what function is actually performed on the specified port. The argument values used in the `Win16Port` class are:

```
CLRDTR  : Drops DTR on the specified port.
CLRRTS  : Drops RTS on the specified port.
SETDTR  : Sets DTR on the specified port.
SETRTS  : Sets RTS on the specified port.
```

These functions all return a zero if the function is successful, and a value less than zero on failure.

```
int FlushComm( int idComDev, int fnQueue )
```

This function is used to flush either the input or output buffers for the port specified by the `idComDev` parameter. If the `fnQueue` argument is zero, the transmit buffer is flushed. If non-zero, the receiver buffer is flushed. This function is used to implement the `FlushRXQueue()` and `FlushTXQueue()` virtual functions in the `Win16Port` class.

A return value of zero indicates success. A return value that is less than zero indicates an invalid device was specified. A return greater than zero indicates an error on the specified device.

```
int GetCommError( int idComDev, COMSTAT FAR *lpStat )
```

This function returns the current status of the given port. The return value is a mask consisting of various bit settings, defining things such as line status flags, software buffer overruns, and transmit timeouts.

The `COMSTAT` structure returned by this function returns an additional status byte with more information about handshaking, plus a count indicating how many characters are present in both the transmit and receive buffer.

`GetCommError()` is called by the `Win16Port` class member functions whenever an error occurs, or an error status check is requested. Most of the flags returned directly by this function are ORed into a cumulative line status word, which can be cleared when the status function is called.

The error codes relevant to the `Win16Port` class are:

CE_BREAK	An incoming break was detected.
CE_CTSTO	A CTS timeout occurred while transmitting a character. This error will occur only when CTS pacing is enabled in the DCB structure.
CE_DSRTO	A DSR timeout occurred while transmitting a character. This error will occur only when DSR pacing is enabled in the DCB structure.
CE_FRAME	An incoming framing error was detected.

CE_MODE	This error is returned when either the port handle is invalid, or an invalid mode is requested.
CE_OVERRUN	A hardware overrun error was detected.
CE_RLSDTO	A CD timeout occurred while transmitting a character. This error will occur only when CD pacing is enabled in the DCB structure.
CE_RXOVER	This bit is set when a software receive buffer overrun error occurs.
CE_RXPARITY	An incoming parity error was detected.
CE_TXFULL	The TX buffer was full when a character transmission was attempted.

```
UINT GetCommEventMask( int idComDev, int fnEvtClear )
```

The Comm Event Mask is a word that is maintained by the Windows device driver. It is used to keep track of line status events, such as an incoming break signal, changes in the modem status lines, and so on. The events that are to be monitored by this word are selected by the setup function `SetCommEventMask()`.

During the function call, any of the bits can be cleared after it is read. The bits to be cleared are selected in the `fnEvtClear` bit mask.

This function isn't used by the `Win16Port` class. All of the events that could be detected using this function are detected in other ways.

```
int GetCommState( int idComDev, DCB FAR *lpdcb )
```

`GetCommState()` is called to request that the device drive load the current state of the requested port into a DCB structure. The DCB data contains all of the user definable items, including things such as the baud rate, parity, and other line settings. The exact details of the DCB contents will be detailed later in this section.

The `WindowsPort` class calls this function in the `read_settings()` member function. This is called in the constructor to initialize the DCB.

This function returns a zero when successful, less than zero on failure.

```
int OpenComm( LCSTR lpszDevControl,
              UINT cbInQueue,
              UINT cbOutQueue )
```

This is the function used under Win16 to open a communications port (or a printer port). The first parameter contains a string with the port name, such as COM1. The next two parameters are used to specify the size of the input and output buffers.

When successful, this function returns an integer ID greater than or equal to zero. In the event of an error, one of several possible error returns less than zero is given.

This function is used in the constructor to open the port. In the event that the function returns an error code, the Windows error code is translated to an RS232 class error code and is stored in the `error_status` member, which flags the object as unusable to the rest of the member functions.

The error returns that can come back from this function are:

IE_BADID	A bad or invalid device was selected.
IE_BAUDRATE	A bad or invalid baud rate was selected.
IE_BYTESIZE	A bad or invalid word length was selected.
IE_DEFAULT	The default parameters are invalid.
IE_HARDWARE	The hardware is in use by another program, and can't be opened.
IE_MEMORY	A memory allocation error occurred when trying to reserve buffer space for the device.
IE_NOPEN	The device is not open.
IE_OPEN	The device has already been opened.

```
int ReadComm( int idComDev, void FAR *lpvBuf, int cbRead )
```

ReadComm() is used in the `Win16Port` class to read both single bytes and blocks of data. You can expect the following three parameters: a port ID, a buffer pointer, and a count of bytes requested.

The return code from this function is a little complicated. The function always returns the count of bytes read in. In the event that an error occurs, the count of bytes is negated and a negative number is returned. In turn, the actual error code for the read function can be retrieved using the `GetCommError()` function. Because it isn't possible to distinguish an error when a count of zero is returned, the programmer should *always* call `GetCommError()` when that value is encountered.

```
int SetCommBreak( int idComDev )
```

SetCommBreak() is used in tandem with `ClearCommBreak()` to issue break signals from the given port. This function is called to put the port into a breaking condition. The program then has to idle wait for a for specific period of time and clear the breaking condition. After that, the port is ready to resume its normal function.

A successful break initiation causes a zero to be returned. An error condition causes a return of less than zero.

```
UINT FAR* SetCommEventMask( int idComDev, UINT fuEvtMask )
```

This function is called to cause Windows to record certain error and status events in a word in the driver. The events that the program wants to monitor are specified in the bit mask parameter. Typical events include changes in modem status lines and incoming line status errors.

The `Win16Port` class calls this function, but it has a slightly backhanded reason for doing so. All of the events that can be accessed with the event mask are also returned by the `GetCommError()` function, which means that the information recorded in the event mask is redundant. However, the event mask also gives you an undocumented way to get some other information that is not available using the Windows API.

Looking through the Windows API for communications functions, you will find that most of the virtual functions defined in class `RS232` are fairly easy to implement. The one serious omission is the absence of functions to read the current state of the incoming modem status lines. Although the event mask lets you see when the status lines *change* state, you don't have a way to directly read them.

Some early pioneers of communications programming under Windows dug around a little bit and found that the communications driver stored a copy of the 8250 Modem Status Register at a fixed location 35 bytes after the event mask word. Word spread, and enough programmers began using this feature that it has become an unacknowledged feature of the API. Until new functions are added to directly support reading these lines, it is likely that Microsoft and other device driver developers will be forced into continuing to support this feature.

The `Win16Port` constructor reads in the event mask, and then forms a far pointer to the modem status register, which is used anytime one of the lines is read in.

The communications port bits that can be set or cleared as part of the event mask are:

EV_BREAK	This flag is used to detect incoming breaks.
EV_CTS	An event will be generated when CTS changes state.
EV_CTSS	When the event occurs, this bit will either be set or cleared to indicate the state of CTS during the last modem status event.
EV_DSR	An event will occur when DSR changes state.
EV_ERR	This bit is used to enable events on line status errors.
EV_RING	This bit is either set or cleared to indicate the state of the incoming RI bit during the last modem status event.

EV_RLSD   This bit is used to enable events caused by the CD line changing state.

EV_RLSDS   This bit is either set or cleared to indicate the state of the incoming RI bit during the last modem status event.

EV_RXCHAR   This bit is used to generate an event anytime a new incoming character is detected.

EV_RXFLAG   This bit is set to generate an event anytime the special event character is received. The event character can be specified in the DCB structure.

EV_TXEMPTY   This bit is used to generate an event whenever the transmitter goes empty.

`int SetCommState( const DCB FAR * lpdcb )`

The `SetCommState()` function is used to set the port's parameters to the values specified in the DCB. This basically sets all of the port parameters that are under the user's control. This function is called in the `write_settings()` virtual function to configure the port.

This function returns a zero when it is successful, or a negative number on failure.

`int TransmitCommChar( int idComDev, char chTransmit )`

This function is used to transmit a single character out of the specified port. It returns a zero when successful, or a negative number on failure. The `Win16Port` class uses the more versatile `WriteComm()` function to support output in both the `write_byte()` and `write_buffer()` functions.

`int UngetCommChar( int idComDev, char chUnget )`

This function is used to stuff a character back into the receive buffer after it has been read. Note that the buffer only has the ability to absorb a single character, so this function cannot be called more than once consecutively. The `Win16Port` class does not use this function.

`UngetCommChar()` returns a zero on success, a value less than zero on failure.

```
int WriteComm( int idComDev,
               const void FAR *lpvBuf,
               int cbWrite )
```

`WriteComm()` is the function used by both `write_byte()` and `write_buffer()` to send data out to the port. The three arguments to this function define the port, a pointer to the data to be sent, and a count of bytes to be written.

Like the `ReadComm()` function, `WriteComm()` returns a count of bytes whether or not an error occurs. If an error occurred during writing, the byte count is negated. A negative or zero byte count means the caller needs to check for an actual error code with `GetCommError()`.

`WriteComm()` has an unusual way of handling requests for more data than it can presently handle. If the TX buffer doesn't have enough room for the entire block of data to be transmitted, `WriteComm()` will blithely write over existing data in the buffer until the output is complete. Because of this, it is important to only request an output count less than or equal to the current space available in the output buffer.

struct DCB

The DCB structure is used by the `SetCommState()` and `GetCommState()` functions to read and write the current settings of the comm port. This is done via the long list of data elements in this structure, which are defined below:

BYTE Id	This contains the integer ID returned from the `OpenComm()` function. This value is used throughout the Comm API functions to identify the port.
UINT BaudRate	This is the current baud rate for the port. Some values that are too large to fit in an unsigned integer have special constants that have an upper byte of 0xff.
BYTE ByteSize	The current word length setting for the UART.
BYTE Parity	The current parity setting for the UART. Unfortunately, instead of using easy-to-remember characters, as are used in class `RS232`, this value must be set to one of several defined constants.
BYTE StopBits	The number of stop bits to be used by the UART.
UINT RlsTimeout	This setting specifies the maximum amount of time that the driver will wait for the CD signal to become true during transmission. The value is expressed in milliseconds. This setting, along with the next two settings, is always left at zero by the `WindowsPort` class.
UINT CtsTimeout	The maximum amount of time the driver will wait for the CTS signal to be asserted.
UINT DsrTimeout	The maximum amount of time the driver will wait for the DSR signal to be asserted.

Chapter 9: The Win16 Driver   399

UINT fBinary	This flag bit determines whether the port is in binary (raw) mode. When in non-binary mode, the port will register an End of File when the EOF character is received. The `Win16Port` class always operates in binary mode.
UINT fRtsDisable	If this bit is set, the RTS signal is disabled and will remain low. This setting is not used by the `Win16Port` class to control RTS. Instead, the escape function is invoked with the set/clear RTS function.
UINT fParity	If this bit is set, parity checking is enabled. When this bit is set, parity errors will be detected and reported.
UINT fOutxCtsFlow	If this flag is set, CTS will be used to control the port's transmission. The `Win16Port` class uses this flag to implement RTS/CTS flow control.
UINT fOutxDsrFlow	This bit is used to implement the transmit half of DTR/DSR flow control.
UINT fDtrDisable	This bit is used to disable DTR for the duration of the setting. The `Win16Port` class uses an escape function to control DTR, so this bit will always be clear.
UINT fOutX	This bit is used to enable XON/XOFF control of the transmitter.
UINT fInX	This bit is used to enable XON/XOFF control in the `Win16Port` receiver. This causes the port to issue an XOFF character when the receiver passes the high water mark.
UINT fPeChar	It is possible to cause the windows driver to replace characters that were received with bad parity with a special flag character. This bit controls that feature. This bit is always clear in the `Win16Port` class.
UINT fNull	This flag specifies that null ('\0') characters are to be discarded.
UINT fChEvt	This flag is used to enable events upon reception of a special event character. The `Win16Port` class does not use this feature.
UINT fDtrflow	This flag is used to cause the receiver to use DTR to control the flow of data coming into the receiver buffer.
UINT fRtsflow	This flag is used to cause the receiver to use RTS to control the flow of data coming into the receiver buffer.

`char XonChar`	This byte contains the XON character used by both the receiver and transmitter for flow control.
`char XoffChar`	This byte contains the XOFF character used by both the receiver and transmitter for flow control.
`UINT XonLim`	This specifies the minimum number of characters allowed in the receiver before an XON is issued.
`UINT XoffLim`	This byte specifies the high water mark in the RX buffer. When there is only room for this number of characters remaining, an XOFF will be issued to stop input.
`char PeChar`	If the `fPeChar` flag is set, this character will be substituted for any incoming characters that were received with a parity error.
`char EofChar`	If the port is not in Binary mode, this character will be treated as an EOF character.
`char EvtChar`	If the `fChEvt` flag is set, the receipt of this incoming character will generate an event flag.

struct COMSTAT

The `COMSTAT` structure is filled in by the `GetCommError()` function. It contains three data members:

`BYTE status`	The status byte has a set of flags that keep track of a few things related to the transmitter. The seven flags used in this byte are:

`CSTF_CTSHOLD`	If this flag is set, it indicates that the transmitter is waiting for the CTS line to go high before transmitting a character.
`CSTF_DSRHOLD`	This flag is used to indicate that the transmitter is waiting for DSR to go high before transmitting a character.
`CSTF_RLSDHOLD`	This flag indicates that the transmitter is waiting for CD to go high before transmitting a character.
`CSTF_XOFFHOLD`	This flag indicates that the transmitter is holding while waiting to receive an XON.

	CSTF_XOFFSENT	This flag indicates that an XOFF character was sent to the remote end. Under certain configurations, the Windows device driver has the ability to halt transmission immediately after sending an XOFF character. This is because there are some systems that will treat *any* character following an XOFF as if it were an XON. This is an unusual configuration, and isn't supported directly by the `Win16Port` class.
	CSTF_EOF	This flag indicates that the EOF character was received.
	CSTF_TXIM	When this flag is set, it means there is still a character waiting to be transmitted.
UINT cbInQue		This structure element indicates how many characters are currently in the receiver buffer.
UINT cbOutQue		This structure element indicates how many characters are currently in the transmit buffer.

Putting It Together

The Windows communications API matches up very well with the member functions in the `RS232` class. The only function that can't be implemented using straightforward API calls is the `RS232::Peek()` virtual function, which looks into the input buffer. In theory, this could be hacked together using the `UngetCommChar()` function (which doesn't work properly with Windows 3.1). In practice this has enough difficulties to make it not worth attempting.

Listing 9-1 shows the header file that defines the `Win16Port` class. A quick look at the header file shows that this is a very generic class definition. The only place it deviates too much from the norm is in the addition of a few private data members:

```
int line_status;
char FAR * modem_status_register;
DCB saved_dcb;
DCB dcb;
```

The two `DCB` structures are used in conjunction with the `settings` and `saved_settings` members defined as part of the base class. In many of the other classes that were used so far, the settings argument was enough to keep track of all the information needed to define the port. The Windows communications port has quite a few other attributes that are stored in the DCB, so a copy of the current DCB is kept. In addition, the original settings of the port are stored in a DCB so that it can be restored with its original settings when the port closes.

The `modem_status_register` is a pointer to the undocumented copy of the UART's MSR in the driver's data area. This pointer is used anytime the modem status functions, such as `Cts()`, are called.

The `line_status` structure element is used to accumulate the status bits returned from the `GetCommError()` function. Whenever the error function is called, the resulting bits are ORed into the `line_status` word so that they can be checked by one of the line status functions such as `HardwareOverrunError()`. The line status bits are optionally cleared when the status functions are invoked.

Note that the `line_status` structure element also accumulates the software buffer overflow error bit, which isn't strictly a line status error.

Listing 9-1: WIN16.H

```
// ******************* START OF WIN16.H *******************
//
//
// This file contains the definitions and declarations
// necessary to use the Win16Port class.

#ifndef _WIN16_DOT_H
#define _WIN16_DOT_H

#include "rs232.h"
#include "_8250.h"

// New error codes defined for the Win16Port class.

enum Win16PortError {
        WINDOWS_PORT_DEFAULT_PARAMETERS = RS232_NEXT_FREE_ERROR,
        WINDOWS_PORT_NOT_OPEN,
        WINDOWS_PORT_ALREADY_OPEN,
        WINDOWS_PORT_HANDSHAKE_LINE_IN_USE,
        WINDOWS_PORT_NEXT_FREE_ERROR,
        WINDOWS_PORT_NEXT_FREE_WARNING = RS232_NEXT_FREE_WARNING };

// The Win16Port class declaration looks similar to most of the
// other classes. It has nearly complete support for all of the
// virtual functions in the RS232 class.
```

```cpp
class Win16Port : public RS232
{
    private :
        int first_debug_output_line;
        int handle;
        int line_status;
        char FAR * modem_status_register;
        DCB saved_dcb;
        DCB dcb;
        void read_settings( void );
        RS232Error write_settings( void );
        RS232Error translate_windows_error( int error );
        virtual int read_buffer( char *buffer,
                                 unsigned int count );
        virtual int write_buffer( char *buffer,
                                  unsigned int count = -1 );
        virtual int read_byte( void );
        virtual int write_byte( int c );

    public :
        Win16Port( enum RS232PortName port_name,
                   long baud_rate = UNCHANGED,
                   char parity = UNCHANGED,
                   int word_length = UNCHANGED,
                   int stop_bits = UNCHANGED,
                   int dtr = SET,
                   int rts = SET,
                   int xon_xoff = DISABLE,
                   int rts_cts = DISABLE,
                   int dtr_dsr = DISABLE );
        virtual ~Win16Port( void );
        virtual RS232Error Set( long baud_rate = UNCHANGED,
                                int parity = UNCHANGED,
                                int word_length = UNCHANGED,
                                int stop_bits = UNCHANGED );
        virtual int TXSpaceFree( void );
        virtual int RXSpaceUsed( void );
        virtual int Break( long milliseconds = 300 );
        virtual int SoftwareOverrunError( int clear = UNCHANGED );
        virtual int Cd( void );
        virtual int Ri( void );
        virtual int Cts( void );
        virtual int Dsr( void );
```

```
                virtual int ParityError( int clear = UNCHANGED );
                virtual int BreakDetect( int clear = UNCHANGED );
                virtual int FramingError( int clear = UNCHANGED );
                virtual int HardwareOverrunError( int clear = UNCHANGED );
                virtual int XonXoffHandshaking( int setting = UNCHANGED );
                virtual int RtsCtsHandshaking( int setting = UNCHANGED );
                virtual int DtrDsrHandshaking( int setting = UNCHANGED );
                virtual int Dtr( int setting = UNCHANGED );
                virtual int Rts( int setting = UNCHANGED );
                virtual int RXSpaceFree( void );
                virtual int TXSpaceUsed( void );
                virtual int FlushRXBuffer( void );
                virtual int FlushTXBuffer( void );
                virtual char * ErrorName( int error );
                virtual int FormatDebugOutput( char *buffer = 0,
                                               int line_number = -1 );
};

#endif // #ifndef _WIN16_DOT_H

// ******************* END OF WIN16.H *******************
```

> The code that implements the Win16Port class is shown in Listing 9-2. The virtual functions are all constructed using very straightforward calls to the Windows API.

Listing 9-2: WIN16.CPP

```
// ******************* START OF WIN16.CPP *******************
//
//
// This file contains the source code that implements the
// Win16Port class. This class uses the Windows 3.1 comm
// driver.

#include <windows.h>
#include <ctype.h>
#include "win16.h"

#define INPUT_BUFFER_SIZE 1024
#define OUTPUT_BUFFER_SIZE 1024
```

```cpp
// The Win16Port constructor opens the port using the MS-Windows
// function call OpenComm(). It then does the standard reading of
// the existing settings, saving them, and then writing the new
// settings. Note that you acquire a pointer to the internal
// driver byte that has the Modem Status Lines.

Win16Port::Win16Port( RS232PortName port,
                      long baud_rate,
                      char parity,
                      int word_length,
                      int stop_bits,
                      int dtr,
                      int rts,
                      int xon_xoff,
                      int rts_cts,
                      int dtr_dsr )
{
    char name[ 15 ];

    port_name = port;
    error_status = RS232_SUCCESS;
    line_status = 0;

    first_debug_output_line = RS232::FormatDebugOutput();
    debug_line_count = FormatDebugOutput();

    wsprintf( name, "COM%d", port_name + 1 );
    handle = OpenComm( name,
                       INPUT_BUFFER_SIZE,
                       OUTPUT_BUFFER_SIZE );
    if ( handle < 0 ) {
        error_status = translate_windows_error( handle );
        return;
    }
    modem_status_register =
        (char FAR *) SetCommEventMask( handle, 0 );
    modem_status_register += 35;
    read_settings();
    saved_settings = settings;
    saved_dcb = dcb;
    settings.Adjust( baud_rate,
                     parity,
                     word_length,
                     stop_bits,
```

```
                        dtr,
                        rts,
                        xon_xoff,
                        rts_cts,
                        dtr_dsr );
    write_settings();
}

// The destructor restores the previous settings, then closes the
// port using the Windows call.

Win16Port::~Win16Port( void )
{
    if ( error_status == RS232_SUCCESS ) {
        settings = saved_settings;
        dcb = saved_dcb;
        write_settings();
        CloseComm( handle );
    }
}

// The set function looks much like the Set function for all the
// other RS232 derivatives seen in the book. It just adjusts the
// current port settings, then calls write_settings() to do the
// dirty work.

RS232Error Win16Port::Set( long baud_rate,
                           int parity,
                           int word_length,
                           int stop_bits )
{
    settings.Adjust( baud_rate,
                     parity,
                     word_length,
                     stop_bits,
                     UNCHANGED,
                     UNCHANGED,
                     UNCHANGED,
                     UNCHANGED,
                     UNCHANGED );
    return write_settings();
}

// read_settings() does most of its work on the DCB associated
```

```cpp
// with the current port. All of the settings that it can figure
// out are found in the DCB. The current settings of RTS and DTR
// can't be found, so they are set to -1, indicating that they are
// unknown.

void Win16Port::read_settings( void )
{
    int status;
    RS232Error error;

    status = GetCommState( handle, &dcb );
    if ( status < 0 ) {
        error = translate_windows_error( status );
        if ( error >= RS232_ERROR )
            error_status = error;
        return;
    }
    if ( ( dcb.BaudRate & 0xff00 ) == 0xff00 )
        switch( dcb.BaudRate ) {
            case CBR_110     : settings.BaudRate = 110;       break;
            case CBR_300     : settings.BaudRate = 300;       break;
            case CBR_600     : settings.BaudRate = 600;       break;
            case CBR_1200    : settings.BaudRate = 1200;      break;
            case CBR_2400    : settings.BaudRate = 2400;      break;
            case CBR_4800    : settings.BaudRate = 4800;      break;
            case CBR_9600    : settings.BaudRate = 9600;      break;
            case CBR_14400   : settings.BaudRate = 14400;     break;
            case CBR_19200   : settings.BaudRate = 19200;     break;
            case CBR_38400   : settings.BaudRate = 38400L;    break;
            case CBR_56000   : settings.BaudRate = 56000L;    break;
            case CBR_128000  : settings.BaudRate = 128000L;   break;
            case CBR_256000  : settings.BaudRate = 256000L;   break;
            default          : settings.BaudRate = -1;        break;
        } else
            settings.BaudRate = dcb.BaudRate;
    switch ( dcb.Parity ) {
        case NOPARITY    : settings.Parity = 'N'; break;
        case ODDPARITY   : settings.Parity = 'O'; break;
        case EVENPARITY  : settings.Parity = 'E'; break;
        case MARKPARITY  : settings.Parity = 'M'; break;
        case SPACEPARITY : settings.Parity = 'S'; break;
        default          : settings.Parity = '?'; break;
    }
    settings.WordLength = dcb.ByteSize;
```

```
        switch ( dcb.StopBits ) {
            case ONESTOPBIT   : settings.StopBits = 1; break;
            case ONE5STOPBITS :
            case TWOSTOPBITS  : settings.StopBits = 2; break;
            default           : settings.StopBits = -1; break;
        }
        settings.Rts = -1;
        settings.Dtr = -1;
        settings.XonXoff = dcb.fOutX;
        settings.RtsCts = dcb.fRtsflow;
        settings.DtrDsr = dcb.fDtrflow;
}

// write_settings() does almost everything it needs to do by
// modifying the DCB and then calling SetCommState(). Setting
// RTS and DTR is done by sending an escape function to the
// driver.

RS232Error Win16Port::write_settings( void )
{
    int set_status;
    RS232Error status = RS232_SUCCESS;

    if ( settings.BaudRate <= 19200L )
        dcb.BaudRate = (int) settings.BaudRate;
    else if ( settings.BaudRate == 38400L )
        dcb.BaudRate = CBR_38400;
    else
       status = RS232_ILLEGAL_BAUD_RATE;
    switch ( toupper( settings.Parity ) ) {
        case 'N' : dcb.Parity = NOPARITY; break;
        case 'E' : dcb.Parity = EVENPARITY; break;
        case 'O' : dcb.Parity = ODDPARITY; break;
        case 'M' : dcb.Parity = MARKPARITY; break;
        case 'S' : dcb.Parity = SPACEPARITY; break;
        default : status = RS232_ILLEGAL_PARITY_SETTING; break;
    }
    switch ( settings.WordLength ) {
        case 8 : dcb.ByteSize = 8; break;
        case 7 : dcb.ByteSize = 7; break;
        case 6 : dcb.ByteSize = 6; break;
        case 5 : dcb.ByteSize = 5; break;
        default : status = RS232_ILLEGAL_PARITY_SETTING; break;
    }
```

```
    switch ( settings.StopBits ) {
        case ONESTOPBIT   : dcb.StopBits = 1; break;
        case ONE5STOPBITS :
        case TWOSTOPBITS  : dcb.StopBits = 2; break;
        default : status = RS232_ILLEGAL_STOP_BITS; break;
    }
    if ( settings.Rts == 0 )
        EscapeCommFunction( handle, CLRRTS );
    else if ( settings.Rts == 1 )
        EscapeCommFunction( handle, SETRTS );
    if ( settings.Dtr == 0 )
        EscapeCommFunction( handle, CLRDTR );
    else if ( settings.Dtr == 1 )
        EscapeCommFunction( handle, SETDTR );
    dcb.fOutX = dcb.fInX = ( settings.XonXoff != 0 );
    dcb.fOutxCtsFlow = dcb.fRtsflow = ( settings.RtsCts != 0 );
    dcb.fOutxDsrFlow = dcb.fDtrflow = ( settings.DtrDsr != 0 );
    set_status = SetCommState( &dcb );
    if ( set_status == 0 )
        return status;
    return translate_windows_error( set_status );
}

// The Windows port driver sends back its own error codes in
// certain stituations. This function translates them to their
// class RS232 equivalents.

RS232Error Win16Port::translate_windows_error( int error )
{
    switch ( error ) {
        case IE_BADID     :
            return RS232_PORT_NOT_FOUND;
        case IE_BAUDRATE  :
            return RS232_ILLEGAL_BAUD_RATE;
        case IE_BYTESIZE  :
            return RS232_ILLEGAL_WORD_LENGTH;
        case IE_DEFAULT   :
            return (RS232Error) WINDOWS_PORT_DEFAULT_PARAMETERS;
        case IE_HARDWARE  :
            return RS232_PORT_IN_USE;
        case IE_MEMORY    :
            return RS232_MEMORY_ALLOCATION_ERROR;
        case IE_NOPEN     :
            return (RS232Error) WINDOWS_PORT_NOT_OPEN;
```

```
            case IE_OPEN      :
                return (RS232Error) WINDOWS_PORT_ALREADY_OPEN;
            default           :
                return RS232_ERROR;
    }
}

// ReadComm() does all the work necessary to implement this
// function.

int Win16Port::read_byte( void )
{
    int result;
    unsigned char c;
    COMSTAT comstat;

    if ( error_status < 0 )
        return error_status;
    result = ReadComm( handle, &c, 1 );
    if ( result > 0 )
        return (int) c;
    line_status |= GetCommError( handle, &comstat );
    return RS232_TIMEOUT;
}

// Before calling WriteComm(), I check to be sure there is room
// for a new character in the output queue. When that is
// determined, WriteComm() does the rest of the work.

int Win16Port::write_byte( int c )
{
    int result;
    COMSTAT comstat;

    if ( error_status < 0 )
        return error_status;
    line_status |= GetCommError( handle, &comstat );
    if ( comstat.cbOutQue == OUTPUT_BUFFER_SIZE )
        return RS232_TIMEOUT;
    result = WriteComm( handle, &c, 1 );
    if ( result > 0 )
        return RS232_SUCCESS;
    line_status |= GetCommError( handle, &comstat );
    return RS232_TIMEOUT;
```

```
}

// The read_buffer() routine is slightly more complicated than
// read_byte(), but it still calls ReadComm() to do most of the
// work. It just has to take into account the possibility that
// an incomplete read may take place.

int Win16Port::read_buffer( char *buffer, unsigned int count )
{
    int result;
    COMSTAT comstat;

    ByteCount = 0;
    if ( error_status < 0 )
        return error_status;
    result = ReadComm( handle, buffer, (int) count );
    if ( result > 0 )
        ByteCount = result;
    else {
        ByteCount = -result;
        line_status |= GetCommError( handle, &comstat );
    }
    if ( ByteCount < count )
        return RS232_TIMEOUT;
    else
        return RS232_SUCCESS;
}

// Like read_buffer(), this routine is basically just an extension
// of its single byte sibling. However, it has to take into
// account the possibility that a partial buffer write may occur.

int Win16Port::write_buffer( char *buffer, unsigned int count )
{
    int result;
    COMSTAT comstat;
    unsigned int buffer_space;

    ByteCount = 0;
    if ( error_status < 0 )
        return error_status;
    line_status |= GetCommError( handle, &comstat );
    buffer_space = OUTPUT_BUFFER_SIZE - comstat.cbOutQue;
    if ( buffer_space > count )
```

```
        result = WriteComm( handle, buffer, count );
    else
        result = WriteComm( handle, buffer, buffer_space );
    if ( result > 0 )
        ByteCount = result;
    else {
        ByteCount = -result;
        line_status |= GetCommError( handle, &comstat );
    }
    if ( ByteCount < count )
        return RS232_TIMEOUT;
    return RS232_SUCCESS;
}

// This function has a dedicated Windows API call to do its work.

int Win16Port::FlushRXBuffer( void )
{
    int status;

    if ( error_status < RS232_SUCCESS )
        return error_status;
    status = FlushComm( handle, 1 );
    if ( status != 0 )
        return translate_windows_error( status );
    return RS232_SUCCESS;
}

// The COMSTAT structure returned from GetCommError contains
// the information you need to determine how the space in both
// the TX and RX buffers is presently being used.

int Win16Port::TXSpaceFree( void )
{
    COMSTAT comstat;

    if ( error_status < RS232_SUCCESS )
        return error_status;
    line_status |= GetCommError( handle, &comstat );
    return OUTPUT_BUFFER_SIZE - comstat.cbOutQue;
}

int Win16Port::RXSpaceUsed( void )
{
```

```
        COMSTAT comstat;

    if ( error_status < RS232_SUCCESS )
        return error_status;
    line_status |= GetCommError( handle, &comstat );
    return comstat.cbInQue;
}

// The Windows API function takes care of sending the break.

int Win16Port::Break( long milliseconds )
{
    long timer;

    if ( error_status < RS232_SUCCESS )
        return error_status;
    SetCommBreak( handle );
    timer = ReadTime() + milliseconds;
    while ( ReadTime() < timer )
        IdleFunction();
    ClearCommBreak( handle );
    return RS232_SUCCESS;
}

// The four Modem Status routines all take advantage of directly
// peeking at the MSR byte inside the driver. They just mask off
// the bit they are interested in, and return a logical result to
// the calling routine.

int Win16Port::Cd( void )
{
    if ( error_status < RS232_SUCCESS )
        return error_status;
    return ( *modem_status_register & MSR_CD ) != 0;
}

int Win16Port::Ri( void )
{
    if ( error_status < RS232_SUCCESS )
        return error_status;
    return ( *modem_status_register & MSR_RI ) != 0;
}

int Win16Port::Cts( void )
```

```
{
    if ( error_status < RS232_SUCCESS )
        return error_status;
    return ( *modem_status_register & MSR_CTS ) != 0;
}

int Win16Port::Dsr( void )
{
    if ( error_status < RS232_SUCCESS )
        return error_status;
    return ( *modem_status_register & MSR_DSR ) != 0;
}

// The four line status routines and the software overrrun error
// detect routine all get their information from the
// Windows API function GetCommError(). It returns all the line
// status bits, rearranged by Windows just for fun.

int Win16Port::SoftwareOverrunError( int clear )
{
    COMSTAT comstat;
    int return_value;

    if ( error_status < RS232_SUCCESS )
        return error_status;
    line_status |= GetCommError( handle, &comstat );
    return_value = ( ( line_status & CE_RXOVER ) != 0 );
    if ( clear != UNCHANGED && clear != 0 )
        line_status &= ~CE_RXOVER;
    return return_value;
}

int Win16Port::ParityError( int reset )
{
    COMSTAT comstat;
    int return_value;

    if ( error_status < RS232_SUCCESS )
        return error_status;
    line_status |= GetCommError( handle, &comstat );
    return_value = ( ( line_status & CE_RXPARITY ) != 0 );
    if ( reset != UNCHANGED && reset != 0 )
        line_status &= ~CE_RXPARITY;
    return return_value;
```

```cpp
}

int Win16Port::BreakDetect( int reset )
{
    COMSTAT comstat;
    int return_value;

    if ( error_status < RS232_SUCCESS )
        return error_status;
    line_status |= GetCommError( handle, &comstat );
    return_value = ( ( line_status & CE_BREAK ) != 0 );
    if ( reset != UNCHANGED && reset != 0 )
        line_status &= ~CE_BREAK;
    return return_value;
}

int Win16Port::FramingError( int reset )
{
    COMSTAT comstat;
    int return_value;

    if ( error_status < RS232_SUCCESS )
        return error_status;
    line_status |= GetCommError( handle, &comstat );
    return_value = ( ( line_status & CE_FRAME ) != 0 );
    if ( reset != UNCHANGED && reset != 0 )
        line_status &= ~CE_FRAME;
    return return_value;
}

int Win16Port::HardwareOverrunError( int reset )
{
    COMSTAT comstat;
    int return_value;

    if ( error_status < RS232_SUCCESS )
        return error_status;
    line_status |= GetCommError( handle, &comstat );
    return_value = ( ( line_status & CE_OVERRUN ) != 0 );
    if ( reset != UNCHANGED && reset != 0 )
        line_status &= ~CE_OVERRUN;
    return return_value;
}
```

```cpp
// All of the handshaking functions rely on write_settings() to do
// the dirty work of actually changing the settings. They then
// return the current setting to the caller.

int Win16Port::XonXoffHandshaking( int setting )
{
    if ( error_status < RS232_SUCCESS )
        return error_status;
    if ( setting != UNCHANGED ) {
        settings.XonXoff = ( setting != 0 );
        write_settings();
    }
    return( settings.XonXoff );
}

int Win16Port::RtsCtsHandshaking( int setting )
{
    if ( error_status < RS232_SUCCESS )
        return error_status;
    if ( setting != UNCHANGED ) {
        settings.RtsCts = ( setting != 0 );
        write_settings();
    }
    return( settings.RtsCts );
}

int Win16Port::DtrDsrHandshaking( int setting )
{
    if ( error_status < RS232_SUCCESS )
        return error_status;
    if ( setting != UNCHANGED ) {
        settings.DtrDsr = ( setting != 0 );
        write_settings();
    }
    return( settings.DtrDsr );
}

// Setting DTR and RTS is done with a Windows API Escape code.
// The escape sequence is undocumented but widely known, and
// used by so much software it is unlikely to ever change.

int Win16Port::Dtr( int setting )
{
    if ( error_status < RS232_SUCCESS )
```

```cpp
            return error_status;
    if ( setting != UNCHANGED ) {
        if ( settings.DtrDsr == 1 )
            return WINDOWS_PORT_HANDSHAKE_LINE_IN_USE;
        else {
            if ( ( settings.Dtr = setting ) == 1 )
                EscapeCommFunction( handle, SETDTR );
            else
                EscapeCommFunction( handle, CLRDTR );
        }
    }
    return settings.Dtr;
}

int Win16Port::Rts( int setting )
{
    if ( error_status < RS232_SUCCESS )
        return error_status;
    if ( setting != UNCHANGED ) {
        if ( settings.RtsCts == 1 )
            return WINDOWS_PORT_HANDSHAKE_LINE_IN_USE;
        else {
            if ( ( settings.Rts = setting ) == 1 )
                EscapeCommFunction( handle, SETRTS );
            else
                EscapeCommFunction( handle, CLRRTS );
        }
    }
    return settings.Rts;
}

// All the information needed to perform the following functions
// is found in the COMSTAT function returned by GetCommError().


int Win16Port::RXSpaceFree( void )
{
    COMSTAT comstat;

    if ( error_status < RS232_SUCCESS )
        return error_status;
    line_status |= GetCommError( handle, &comstat );
    return INPUT_BUFFER_SIZE - comstat.cbInQue;
}
```

```
int Win16Port::TXSpaceUsed( void )
{
    COMSTAT comstat;

    if ( error_status < RS232_SUCCESS )
        return error_status;
    line_status |= GetCommError( handle, &comstat );
    return comstat.cbOutQue;
}

// The Windows API provides a dedicated function to perform this
// task.

int Win16Port::FlushTXBuffer( void )
{
    int status;

    if ( error_status < RS232_SUCCESS )
        return error_status;
    status = FlushComm( handle, 0 );
    if ( status != 0 )
        return translate_windows_error( status );
    return RS232_SUCCESS;
}

// The debug output includes a complete dump of the current DCB
// structure for the port, which describes virtually everything
// windows knows about the port. The only thing left out here
// which could be interesting in the COMSTAT structure.

int Win16Port::FormatDebugOutput( char *buffer, int line_number )
{
    if ( buffer == 0 )
        return( first_debug_output_line +  7 );
    if ( line_number < first_debug_output_line )
        return RS232::FormatDebugOutput( buffer, line_number );
    switch( line_number - first_debug_output_line ) {
        case 0 :
            wsprintf( buffer,
                    (LPSTR) "Derived class: Win16Port    "
                    "Ri: %2d  Cts: %2d  Cd: %2d  Dsr: %2d  "
                    "RX Overrun: %d",
                    Ri(), Cts(), Cd(), Dsr(),
                    SoftwareOverrunError() );
```

```
            break;
    case 1 :
        wsprintf( buffer,
                    "TX Used: %5d   RX Free: %5d  "
                    "Parity Err: %d  Break: %d   "
                    "Overrun: %d  Framing Err: %d",
                    TXSpaceUsed(), RXSpaceFree(),
                    ParityError(),
                    BreakDetect(),
                    HardwareOverrunError(),
                    FramingError() );
            break;
    case 2 :
        wsprintf( buffer,
                    "DCB: RlsTimeout: %04x   CtsTimeout: %04x  "
                    "DsrTimeout: %04x   fBinary: %1d",
                    dcb.RlsTimeout,
                    dcb.CtsTimeout,
                    dcb.DsrTimeout,
                    dcb.fBinary );
            break;
    case 3 :
        wsprintf( buffer,
                    "DCB: fRtsDisable: %1d   fParity: %1d   "
                    "fOutxCtsFlow: %1d   fOutxDsrFlow: %1d",
                    dcb.fRtsDisable,
                    dcb.fParity,
                    dcb.fOutxCtsFlow,
                    dcb.fOutxDsrFlow );
            break;
    case 4 :
        wsprintf( buffer,
                    "DCB: fDtrDisable: %1d   fOutX: %1d  "
                    "fInx: %1d   fPeChar: %1d  "
                    "fNull: %1d   fChEvt: %1d",
                    dcb.fDtrDisable,
                    dcb.fOutX,
                    dcb.fInX,
                    dcb.fPeChar,
                    dcb.fNull,
                    dcb.fChEvt );
            break;
    case 5 :
        wsprintf( buffer,
                    "DCB: fDtrflow: %1d   fRtsflow: %1d  "
```

```
                            "XonChar: %02x   XoffChar: %02x  "
                            "XonLim: %04x   XoffLim: %04x",
                            dcb.fDtrflow,
                            dcb.fRtsflow,
                            dcb.XonChar,
                            dcb.XoffChar,
                            dcb.XonLim,
                            dcb.XoffLim );
                break;
            case 6 :
                wsprintf( buffer,
                            "DCB: PeChar: %02x   EofChar: %02x  "
                            "EvtChar: %02x   TxDelay: %04x",
                            dcb.PeChar,
                            dcb.EofChar,
                            dcb.EvtChar,
                            dcb.TxDelay );
                break;
            default :
                return RS232_ILLEGAL_LINE_NUMBER;
        }
        return RS232_SUCCESS;
}


char * Win16Port::ErrorName( int error )
{
    if ( error < RS232_NEXT_FREE_ERROR && error >= RS232_ERROR )
        return RS232::ErrorName( error );
    if (error < RS232_NEXT_FREE_WARNING && error >= RS232_WARNING)
        return RS232::ErrorName( error );
    if ( error >= RS232_SUCCESS )
        return RS232::ErrorName( error );
    switch ( error ) {
        case WINDOWS_PORT_DEFAULT_PARAMETERS :
            return "Default parameters in error";
        case WINDOWS_PORT_NOT_OPEN :
            return "Port not open";
        case WINDOWS_PORT_ALREADY_OPEN :
            return "Port already open";
        case WINDOWS_PORT_HANDSHAKE_LINE_IN_USE :
            return "Handshake line in use";
        default :
            return( "Undefined error" );
```

```
        }
}

// For Win16, you need a pair of OS specific routines to handle a
// couple of timing issues properly. In a program that really uses
// the idle function you might want to replace this function with
// one that performs a PeekMessage() call

int RS232::IdleFunction( void )
{
    return RS232_SUCCESS;
}

//
// ReadTime() returns the current time of day in milliseconds. It
// uses the Windows specific tick count function, instead of
// polling MS-DOS or the BIOS.
//

long ReadTime( void )
{
    return GetTickCount();
}

// ******************** END OF WIN16.CPP ********************
```

In the previous chapters, the two O/S dependent functions were contained in a file called MSDOS.CPP. The O/S specific functions for 16-bit Windows are now contained in WIN16.CPP. The first is the idle function, which is called whenever one of the functions is waiting for input. Under MS-DOS, there really isn't anything to do in the idle function. Of course, the programmer could use the idle function for other activity, but it isn't essential.

Under MS-Windows, the idle function needs to be redefined. Because MS-Windows is a cooperative multitasking system, you need to give time back to the O/S. This is usually done with a loop that calls the Windows PeekMessage() function as shown in the following example. Unfortunately, the exact format of this loop is going to vary slightly depending on how the Windows application is implemented. Because of this uncertainty, the generic function is still a "do-nothing" function in WIN16.CPP:

```
    while ( PeekMessage ( &msg, 0, 0, 0, PM_REMOVE ) ) {
        TranslateMessage ( &msg );
        DispatchMessage ( &msg );
    }
```

The `ReadTime()` function makes a direct call to a Windows API function, which providentially returns the time in the exact format that you need it.

> **Note:** Because the `PeekMessage()` function returns time to the O/S, you can safely use it to wait for input from the RS-232 port. However, this sort of programming isn't really in the spirit of event-driven Windows programming.
>
> To avoid extended waits for characters while keeping your programs responsive, I recommend using a timer to periodically read the entire contents of the input buffer. A terminal emulation program can process all incoming data every 100 milliseconds or so and can be a good program and a good Win16 citizen.

A Win16 Test Program

The standard test program used in the previous chapters is not going to help you under the Windows programming environment. `CHAPT03.CPP` is a useful program, but it makes heavy use of video BIOS services, which just won't work under Windows.

Many beginning Windows programmers are dismayed to find that writing even the simplest "Hello, world!" program can take hundreds of lines of boilerplate code. The amount of code needed to create the Windows equivalent of `CHAPT03.CPP` would run unfortunately into at least 1,000 lines of C code, which is probably more than most readers want to try to digest.

The reason a terminal program under Win16 is so complicated is simply one of displaying a text window of constantly changing data. Windows doesn't provide a convenient class with cursor addressing and an easy-to-modify text display. However, for this test program, I take a shortcut that lets you do almost everything you want without too much trouble. (Note that I bite the bullet and actually produce a true Win32 terminal emulation program later in this book.)

> **On the CD:** For this test program, `TERMW16.CPP` (see Listing 9-3), I'm using a basic Win16 multiline edit control. Any Windows user is familiar with the use of this control, as it is used for input in nearly any program that requires user input. However, to make it truly useful, you need to override some of the control's behavior using a common Windows programming technique called *subclassing*.

In this case, the only behavior that you override for the edit control is its action when receiving a character from the keyboard. Because you are using the edit control as a terminal control, you capture the incoming characters and send it to the serial port instead. When the device connected on the other end sends characters back to you over the serial port, those characters are sent to the edit control for displays as if they were actual typed characters.

Note that this program doesn't sit in an eternal polling loop waiting for characters to come in from the keyboard and serial port. The keyboard characters are sent as Windows events, and are handled as they arrive. The serial port is polled for data every 100 ms, and all incoming data is displayed. The resulting program acts and feels like a well-behaved Win16 program with quick response and no degradation to the rest of the system.

Listing 9-3: TERMW16.CPP

```
// ******************* START OF TERMW16.CPP *******************
//
// This is a simple demo program that exercises the Win16Port
// class under Windows 3.1. This program uses a subclassed
// edit control for display of incoming data. Any keystrokes
// sent to the subclassed control from the keyboard are
// intercepted and sent out the open comm port. Data that
// is read in from the comm port is sent to the edit control
// as if it were actual keyboard data, which then displays it.
//
// This is okay for a demo/test program, but it isn't robust
// enough for a real application. In particular, it will
// eventually run out of memory, as none of the input data is
// ever flushed from the edit control's buffer. Also, special
// characters sent to the control, such as arrow keys, will
// have  results that cause the app to misbehave.
//
#include <windows.h>
#include "win16.h"

//
// Even though this is a C++ program, it operates
// under Win16, which is basically a C framework.
// So you end up with a few global variables, which
// would be frowned upon in some quarters.
//

FARPROC pDefaultEditProc = 0;  // Pointer to the normal WinProc
                               // for the edit control.
HWND hEdit = 0;                // Handle of the embedded edit
```

```
                                    // control.
    Win16Port *pCommPort = 0;       // Pointer to the comm port
                                    // opened in WinMain and kept open.


//
// This is the subclassed edit control procedure. It only
// overrides one piece of behavior, which is the WM_CHAR
// message. When the user types a character from the keyboard,
// you don't want it to go into the edit control, you actually
// want to send it out the comm port. This guy takes care
// of it.
//
// The really important thing this control does is take care
// of displaying the data that is read in from the comm port.
// You send those to the edit control from the polling loop
// with a special value of lParam that indicates you need to
// deal with them.
//

long FAR PASCAL _export EditProc( HWND hwnd,
                                  UINT message,
                                  UINT wParam,
                                  LONG lParam )
{
    switch ( message ) {
        case WM_CHAR :
            if ( lParam == 0xffffffffl )
                lParam = 0x1e0001L;  /* A normal lParam */
            else {
                pCommPort->Write( (char) wParam );
                return 1;
            }
            break;
    }
    //
    // Here you use the default procedure to handle any message
    // besides WM_CHAR. You also handle the special WM_CHAR sent
    // in from the polling loop. The polling loop sends data to
    // be displayed with a special lParam value of 0xffffffffl,
    // which you then discard and replace with a value that
    // gets sent with a 'normal' keystroke
    //
    return CallWindowProc( pDefaultEditProc,
                           hwnd,
```

```
                        message,
                        wParam,
                        lParam );
}

//
// The windows procedure for my frame window. This is
// a really simple window procedure, because you rely
// on the child edit control to do all the work. All
// you do of any significance in here is to create the edit
// child when you are created, set up a timer to let you
// poll the serial port periodically, and resize the
// child control if you are resized.
//
long FAR PASCAL _export WndProc( HWND hwnd,
                                 UINT message,
                                 UINT wParam,
                                 LONG lParam )
{
  switch ( message ) {
  //
  // I want a unique frame without resizing handles, and
  // I set it up here. I could have done it by calling
  // CreateWindowEx() in Win Main, but this requires
  // less typing.
  //
  case WM_NCCREATE:
  {
    LONG exstyle = GetWindowLong( hwnd, GWL_EXSTYLE );
    exstyle |= WS_EX_DLGMODALFRAME;
    SetWindowLong( hwnd, GWL_EXSTYLE, exstyle );
    return 1 ;
  }
  //
  // When the frame window is ready, I create the embedded
  // child edit control, hook its procedure, and start up
  // a 100 millisecond timer.
  //
  case WM_CREATE:
  {
    HANDLE hInstance = ( (LPCREATESTRUCT) lParam)->hInstance;
    hEdit = CreateWindow( "edit",
                          NULL,
                          WS_CHILD       | WS_VISIBLE       |
```

```
                            WS_HSCROLL   | WS_VSCROLL        |
                            WS_BORDER    | ES_LEFT           |
                            ES_MULTILINE | ES_AUTOHSCROLL    |
                            ES_AUTOVSCROLL,
                            0, 0, 0, 0,
                            hwnd, 1,
                            hInstance,
                            NULL ) ;
    FARPROC pEditProc =
              MakeProcInstance( (FARPROC) EditProc, hInstance );
    pDefaultEditProc = (FARPROC)GetWindowLong(hEdit, GWL_WNDPROC);
    SetWindowLong( hEdit, GWL_WNDPROC, (LONG) pEditProc );
    SetTimer( hwnd, 1000, 100, 0 );
    return 0 ;
}
//
// Every timer tick I read in all the characters I can handle
// from the serial port, and send them to the edit control which
// is tricked into thinking they are regular keystrokes. One
// thing I have to do as a bit of preprocessing is to through
// out CR characters and just process LFs. If don't do this
// every input line gets an extra LF.
//
case WM_TIMER :
{
  char buf[ 256 ];
  pCommPort->Read( buf, 255, 0 );
  int count = pCommPort->ByteCount;
  if ( count > 0 )
    for ( int i = 0 ; i < count ; i++ )
      if ( buf[ i ] != '\r' )
        SendMessage( hEdit, WM_CHAR, buf[ i ], 0xffffffffL );
  break;
}
//
// If the frame window gets the focus for some reason, you
// immediately delegate it to the child edit control.
//
case WM_SETFOCUS:
  SetFocus( hEdit );
  return 0;
//
// I only get resized on creation, but even so I have to deal
// with it by resizing the child edit control so that it fills
```

```
    // the frame.
    //
    case WM_SIZE:
          MoveWindow( hEdit,
                      0, 0,
                      LOWORD( lParam ), HIWORD( lParam ),
                      TRUE );
          return 0 ;
    case WM_DESTROY :
      PostQuitMessage (0) ;
      return 0 ;
    }
    return DefWindowProc( hwnd, message, wParam, lParam );
}

//
// WinMain is the same everywhere.
//
int PASCAL WinMain( HANDLE hInstance,
                    HANDLE hPrevInstance,
                    LPSTR /* lpszCmdLine */,
                    int nCmdShow )
{
    pCommPort = new Win16Port( COM2, 19200L, 'N', 8, 1 );
    if ( pCommPort == 0 || pCommPort->ErrorStatus() < 0 ) {
        MessageBox( 0,
                    "Error opening port!",
                    "TERMW16 Error",
                    MB_OK );
        return 0;
    }
    if ( !hPrevInstance ) {
        WNDCLASS wndclass ;
        wndclass.style         = CS_HREDRAW | CS_VREDRAW ;
        wndclass.lpfnWndProc   = WndProc ;
        wndclass.cbClsExtra    = 0 ;
        wndclass.cbWndExtra    = 0 ;
        wndclass.hInstance     = hInstance ;
        wndclass.hIcon         = LoadIcon(NULL, IDI_APPLICATION);
        wndclass.hCursor       = LoadCursor ( NULL, IDC_ARROW );
        wndclass.hbrBackground = GetStockObject(WHITE_BRUSH);
        wndclass.lpszMenuName  = NULL ;
        wndclass.lpszClassName = "TermClass";
        RegisterClass (&wndclass) ;
```

```
    }

    HWND hwnd = CreateWindow( "TermClass",
                              "Term31",
                              WS_CAPTION      |
                              WS_SYSMENU      |
                              WS_MINIMIZEBOX,
                              CW_USEDEFAULT,
                              CW_USEDEFAULT,
                              600, 350,
                              NULL,
                              NULL,
                              hInstance,
                              NULL );

    ShowWindow( hwnd, nCmdShow );
    UpdateWindow( hwnd );

    MSG msg;
    while ( GetMessage ( &msg, NULL, 0, 0 ) ) {
        TranslateMessage( &msg );
        DispatchMessage( &msg );
    }
    delete pCommPort;
    return msg.wParam;
}
```

The resulting program works very well for testing and shows that the serial port works as expected. However, if you decide to use the edit control in a true Win16 program, you still have a bit more work to do. For simplicity, cursor control is completely ignored by TESTW16, which causes trouble if a user presses arrow keys while typing text.

An even more serious problem will arise if the Edit control runs out of memory. It stores incoming data in a 32K buffer, which will continue filling as TESTW16 runs. When that memory fills up, the control won't accept any more data, and thus will appear dead. The best approach to this is probably to monitor the amount of memory in use in the control, and release large amounts when the control appears to be filling up.

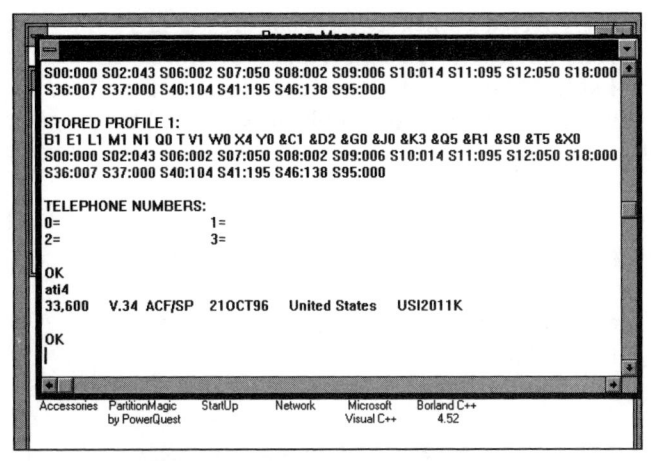

Figure 9-1: TERMW16 in action

Building TEST232W.EXE

Most Win16 programs have an RC file that holds dialog templates, icons, strings, and so on. TESTW16 manages without any of that stuff, so you don't have to worry about that file. However, the project does have the required DEF file that passes information to the linker. The DEF file is shown in its entirety in Listing 9-4.

This file is on the CD-ROM that accompanies this book.

Listing 9-4: TERMW16.DEF

```
NAME       TERMW16
EXETYPE    WINDOWS
CODE       PRELOAD MOVEABLE DISCARDABLE
DATA       PRELOAD MOVEABLE MULTIPLE
HEAPSIZE   1024
STACKSIZE  8192

EXPORTS
```

All the MS-DOS programs covered earlier in the book had a single file that worked with both Borland's and Microsoft's 16-bit compilers. However, that proved to be a bit awkward with TERMW16, so I created two separate make files. They are shown in Listings 9-5 and 9-6. Instructions that describe how to build the program with the make file is embedded in the file.

Listing 9-5: TERMW16B.MAK

```
# ****************** START OF TERMW16B.MAK ******************
#
# This is one of two make files for the Win16 test program.
# This version builds the project using Borland C++. Build
# the file with the following command:
#
#         Borland :              make -f termw16b.mak
#
# To build using Microsoft Visual C++, use termw16m.mak
#

CC = bcc -ml -WS -c

termw16.exe : rs232.obj termw16.obj win16.obj
  tlink    @&&|
 /v -Twe -c -C -x +
c0wl.obj+
rs232.obj+
termw16.obj+
win16.obj
termw16
termw16
import.lib+
crtldll.lib
termw16.def
|


# ****************** END OF TERMW16B.MAK ******************
```

Listing 9-6: TERMW16M.MAK

```
# ****************** START OF TERMW16M.MAK ******************
#
# This is one of two make files for the Win16 test program.
# This version builds the project using Microsoft C++. Build
# the file with the following command:
#
```

```
#            Microsoft : nmake -f termw16m.mak
#
# To build using Borland C++, use TERMW16B.MAK
#

CC = cl /W3 /AM /GA

.cpp.obj:
    $(CC) -c /W3 /AM /GA $<

termw16.exe : rs232.obj termw16.obj win16.obj
        echo >NUL @<<termw16.CRF
termw16 +
win16 +
rs232
termw16
termw16
oldnames libw commdlg shell olecli olesvr mlibcew
termw16.def;
<<
        link /NOLOGO /ONERROR:NOEXE /NOD /PACKC:61440 /ALIGN:16 @termw16.CRF
        $(RC) $(RESFLAGS) $@

# ****************** END OF TERMW16M.MAK ******************
```

Summary

Although it is certainly true that writing Windows applications can require a lot of education and work, Microsoft did a good job of supplying all the tools needed for our communications needs. The Windows API fit neatly into the RS232 class, doing better than any other interface except for the completely customized PC8250 class.

Writing a great Windows communications application is still going to require a lot of work. But at least you can expect to find yourself on familiar ground when using the Win16Port class.

Chapter 10

The Win32 Comm API

IN THIS CHAPTER

- Win32 programming differences
- The Win32 device driver
- The Communications API

WHEN I WAS WRITING the first edition of this book back in 1991 and 1992, Windows 3.*x* was still in its rapid ascent to total domination of the desktop. MS-DOS was still a very important platform as well. Windows NT was still in beta, and its 32-bit API was still not even visible on industry radar. Because of this, the Win32 serial API didn't even get a mention, much less a class of its own.

Eight years later, we find ourselves in entirely different waters. The 32-bit serial API used in Windows NT, Windows 95, and Windows 98 is unquestionably the most important one to developers, at least in terms of numbers.

This current state of affairs in the desktop programming world means that the Win32 class presented in this chapter may well be the most important serial communications tool you have in your toolbox. You get all the details on the Win32 comm API in this chapter, and then see it integrated with class `RS232` in the next two chapters.

Win32 Programming Differences

At first glance, you might look at the Win32 serial interface and suppose that it was nearly identical to the Win16 driver. However, although the driver retains some of the functions and structures used under 16 bit Windows, it differs in several fundamental ways.

Comm ports as file objects

Although much of the code used to set up and control the serial port looks the same, the API has undergone a complete transformation in a couple of areas. Win16 had a dedicated function called `OpenComm` that returned a special handle. That special handle was then used with dedicated functions `ReadComm()` and `WriteComm()` to read and write data.

Under Win32, comm ports are treated in many ways as if they were devices that could be accessed by the file system. Ports are opened using the standard `CreateFile()` function, and data is read using `ReadFile()` and `WriteFile()`, as if the port were just another file object. This philosophy is a bit of a throwback to the way devices are accessed under UNIX.

As you will see in this chapter, making ports look like files doesn't really buy you anything. Because of the unique requirements that serial ports impose on your programs, you almost never get to reuse any existing code written to access other devices or file systems.

Threading a must

The original Win16 API for serial ports was designed to work with event-driven programs. In theory, as incoming data was received or outgoing buffers emptied, messages would be sent to the program that owned the port. Likewise, changes in modem status lines generate events of their own.

The Win32 approach to serial I/O takes a completely different tack. Instead of responding to events, the Win32 serial API expects you to spawn threads that wait on input and status events. These threads will block while waiting for interesting events to happen, which means that they won't be using any valuable CPU time while idle.

The mechanism behind this approach is Win32 overlapped I/O. When the port is opened with the `CreateFile()` function call, using the flag `FILE_FLAG_OVERLAPPED` tells the O/S that the file is going to be used in overlapped mode. This means that calls to `ReadFile()` and `WriteFile()` will typically return immediately, without waiting for their operations to complete.

After making calls to `ReadFile()` and `WriteFile()`, the thread then waits for the completion event. While it waits for that event, it can also respond properly if the port is closed, and an I/O error takes place or a timeout occurs.

Writing safe code that works with multiple threads is tricky. Mistakes are easy to make but often difficult to detect. But the designers of the Win32 serial API have virtually mandated that threads be used for input and output. Attempting to read or write from your main thread can cause your program to lock up for indefinite periods of time.

> You can easily see the perils of attempting to perform serial I/O from your main thread under Windows 95/98. Just set up a Hyperterm session that talks directly to a comm port with either hardware or software handshaking. Block Hyperterm's output by either sending it an XOFF or dropping CTS from a second PC or terminal. If you type a single character in Hyperterm's window from this blocked state, the program will lock up and remain completely unresponsive to anything until the blocking condition is removed.

The Win32 Device Driver

The rest of this chapter covers the basics of the Win32 comm API. The functions and data structures described here are used in the next chapter to implement the `Win32Port` class.

Data structures

The data structures described here are used as arguments to various functions in the Comm API. Unfortunately, these are simple C structures with no supporting member functions, so all access is done with direct member access.

DCB

The `DCB` is the structure used to set most of the operating parameters of the port via the `SetCommState()` function. The `DCB` has a huge list of members that are all important when setting up the port. In Chapter 11, the `Win32Port` class uses a simple `DCB` wrapper class to simplify manipulation of some of these members. Table 10-1 defines the members are defined.

TABLE 10-1 THE DCB STRUCTURE MEMBERS

Member type and name	Description
DWORD DCBlength	This member holds the size of the `DCB` structure. This is normally initialized before calling any API function that uses the `DCB`. The appropriate value is `sizeof(DCB)`.
DWORD BaudRate	The port's baud rate. Under Win16, the `DCB` was a 16-bit value, so it couldn't hold values as high as 115200 or greater. To work around this, the Win16 API had special constant values that could be used for certain rates. Although these special values are still supported by the Win32 API, they are no longer necessary and won't be used by the `Win32Port` class.
DWORD fBinary	This flag is set when the port is operating in binary mode. Microsoft's documentation states that this bitfield value should always be set to `TRUE`.
DWORD fParity	This flag enables parity checking on input data. The *Parity* member of the `DCB` determines what sort of parity is expected, this member determines whether the UART will actually check the parity of the incoming data.

Continued

TABLE 10-1 THE DCB STRUCTURE MEMBERS *(Continued)*

Member type and name	Description
DWORD fOutxCtsFlow	This flag member determines whether the incoming CTS line provides flow control for the output stream. The DCB allows CTS and RTS flow control to be turned on and off independently of one another.
DWORD fOutxDsrFlow	This flag member determines whether the incoming DSR line provides flow control for the output stream. As with the previous flag, the DCB allows DTR and DSR flow control to be turned on and off independently of one another.
DWORD fDtrControl	This member provides control over the DTR output line. It can be set to one of three values. DTR_CONTROL_HANDSHAKE uses DTR as a flow control line that restrains incoming data. If that value is not selected, DTR_CONTROL_ENABLE or DTR_CONTROL_DISABLE will raise or drop the line.
DWORD fDsrSensitivity	This line is used to enable the use of DSR as a data validation signal. When this asserted, the driver will ignore any incoming data seen while DSR is low. The Win32Port class doesn't take advantage of this feature, but it would be easy to enable in a customized version of the class.
DWORD fOutX	This binary flag determines whether XON/XOFF flow control is applied to the transmitter. If it is set, the transmitter stops when an incoming XOFF character is seen, and doesn't restart until and XON is seen. Note that the Win32 API allows you to control the transmit and receive versions of all types of flow control independently, but the Win32Port class, will always set the two to the same state.
DWORD fInX	Specifies whether XON and XOFF are used to control incoming data.
DWORD fErrorChar	When this flag is set, the Win32 serial driver will replace any incoming data that has a parity error with a special error character. The error character used will be determined by the ErrorChar member. This feature is not supported by the Win32Port class, but you may find it useful in your own design.

Member type and name	Description
DWORD fNull	If this flag is set, incoming NULL characters are discarded. This is another one of the Win32 API features that aren't used in the *Win32Port* class, but might prove useful in specific applications.
DWORD fRtsControl	If this member is set to RTS_CONTROL_HANDSHAKE, the RTS line is used to throttle incoming data when the input buffer is 75% full. The RTS line is dropped when the input buffer drops below 25% full. To simply raise or drop the RTS line, settings of RTS_CONTROL_DISABLE and RTS_CONTROL_ENABLE are used. And finally, the Win32API provides the RTS_CONTROL_TOGGLE setting. This final setting asserts RTS while there is data present in the transmitter and drops RTS when the TX buffer is empty.
DWORD fAbortOnError	If this flag is set, read and write operations are aborted when an error is detected. The transmitter and receiver will remain shut down until the ClearCommError() function is called.
WORD XonLim	When XON/XOFF handshaking is enabled, this value dictates the point when an XON is sent to re-enable the remote transmitter after an XOFF has been sent. Typically, this value will be set to a value approximately 25% of the size of the receive buffer.
WORD XoffLim	When XON/XOFF handshaking is enabled, this value dictates the point at which an XOFF is sent, disabling transmission from the remote transmitter. The value here defines the number of bytes free in the receive buffer when the trigger is reached. Typically, this value will be set to approximately 25% of the size of the receive buffer. So, for example, a 1,000-byte buffer will often have both this member and XonLim set to 256.
BYTE ByteSize	This value determines the number of bits per byte in the words sent and received by the UART. Although values from five to eight can be used, most PC applications will set this member to seven or eight.
BYTE Parity	This word determines the parity scheme to be used by the transmitter and receiver. Supported values are NO_PARITY, EVEN_PARITY, ODD_PARITY, MARK_PARITY, and SPACE_PARITY.

Continued

TABLE 10-1 THE DCB STRUCTURE MEMBERS *(Continued)*

Member type and name	Description
BYTE StopBits	The number of stop bits used in the current UART setting. This can be set to ONESTOPBIT, TWOSTOPBITS, or ONE5STOPBITS. The final setting supports the 1.5 stop bits setting, which, in the 8250 family UARTs, is used only with the offbeat word size of five bits.
char XonChar	The character sent to re-enable transmission when XON/XOFF handshaking is being used. This is normally XON, which is 0x11, or Ctrl+Q.
char XoffChar	The character sent to disable transmission from the remote end when XON/XOFF handshaking is enabled. This is normally XOFF, which is 0x13 or Ctrtl+S.
char ErrorChar	The character sent when a parity error is received. If the fErrorChar member is set, an incoming character with a parity error is replaced with this special character.
char EofChar	Under Windows 3.1, in theory you could convince the comm driver to recognize a special EOF character on incoming data by putting the EOF char in this member and setting the fBinary member to FALSE. Under Win32, Microsoft specifically says that only binary mode is supported; therefore, this member would seem to have no purpose.
char EvtChar	The Serial event mechanism can be configured to generate an event every time a specific character arrives. If the event mechanism is configured to do this, the character is defined in this member.

COMMTIMEOUTS

This structure is used to set up the timeout values used when reading and writing data to and from the serial port. The structure is used in calls to SetCommTimeouts() and GetCommTimeouts(), which are discussed later in this section. The member type and names are described in the following table.

Member type and name	Description
DWORD ReadIntervalTimeout	This is the idle line timeout in milliseconds. A call to `ReadFile()` for a given report will return before completion after this amount of time passes without any incoming characters. A value of 0 here means that timeouts aren't used. A value of `MAXDWORD` in this word combined with a value of 0 in the next two words means that all read operations will return immediately with whatever characters are presently available.
DWORD ReadTotalTimeoutMultiplier DWORD ReadTotalTimeoutConstant	The previous word in the structure is used to set an inter-character timeout. These two words are combined to create an overall timeout for a given read operation. The total timeout is determined by adding the `ReadTotalTimeoutConstant` to the product of `ReadTotalTimeout Multiplier` and the number of bytes requested. So, if the first value is 1 millisecond and the second is 500 milliseconds, a read operation requesting 1,000 characters would time out unconditionally after 1.5 seconds. A value of 0 for both of these values means that no overall read timeout will be used.
DWORD WriteTotalTimeoutMultiplier DWORD WriteTotalTimeoutConstant	These timeout values work just like the previous two read timeout values. Calculating the overall timeout for a write operation is done by multiplying the `WriteTotalTimeoutMultiplier` by the number of bytes being written, and then adding the `WriteTotalTimeoutConstant`.

COMMCONFIG

This structure is used to describe arguments to the `CommConfigDialog()` function, which provides an easy way to set and modify port parameters. The member type and names are described in the following table.

Member type and name	Description
DWORD dwSize	The size of the structure. Like many of the structures used in Win32, you should initialize this member with sizeof(COMMCONFIG) before using the structure with any Win32 API function calls. This size element is needed because different device types may extend this structure with provider-specific data.
WORD wVersion	Set to 1.
DCB dcb	A copy of the current DCB for the device. The members of this structure are modified by the call to CommConfigDialog() call.
DWORD dwProviderSubType	The type of port, which varies according to device configuration. For generic use of this structure, a reasonable value to use here is PST_RS232. The actual values for this data, as well as the remaining provider specific data, can be found by making a call to the GetCommProperties() function.
DWORD dwProviderOffset	The offset in bytes to the provider specific data in this structure. A value of 0 indicates that there isn't any provider specific data.
DWORD dwProviderSize	The size of the provider-specific data.
WCHAR wcProviderData[1]	The starting point of the provider specific data. Obviously, if there is any data, the size of this element may very well be greater than 1. However, C doesn't provide for strict definition of variable length structures, so this syntax is necessary.

COMMPROP

This structure is used by GetCommProperties() to return information about a comm port driver. Most of the information in this structure describes capabilities of the comm driver, which might be used later when attempting to configure the port. The member type and names are described in the following table.

Chapter 10: The Win32 Comm API 441

Member type and name	Description
WORD wPacketLength	Like many of the structures used in the Win32API, COMMPROP is a variable-length object. Depending on the type of device for which you are making a query, an indeterminate number of bytes may be appended to the end of the structure. To deal with this in a safe manner, you often have to put the actual length of the structure in its first member. wPacketLength simply holds the size of the structure. (Why it is confusingly referred to as a packet is unclear.)
WORD wPacketVersion	A call to GetCommProperties() will return some information about the version of the Windows API that is returning the information in this member.
DWORD dwServiceMask	A bitmask defining which services are implemented by the driver. It appears that the only value possible in this member is SP_SERIALCOMM.
DWORD dwMaxTxQueue	The maximum TX buffer size. (Be sure to note that this is the maximum size for the internal buffer used by the driver. In the Win32Port class implemented in the next chapter, an external buffer is maintained that is used to feed data to the driver.) A value of 0 means that the driver doesn't impose a maximum size.
DWORD dwMaxRxQueue	The maximum RX buffer size. (See the comment for the previous member regarding internal vs. external buffers.) Like the previous member, a value of 0 here means that the buffer doesn't impose a maximum.
DWORD dwMaxBaud	The maximum baud rate. Traditional 8250 devices will usually return 115.2 Kbps as the maximum baud rate. Unfortunately, the value stored in this member is not a plain numeric value; it is one of about 20 bit masks ranging from BAUD_075 up to BAUD_128K. Refer to the SDK documentation or header files for values ranging from BAUD_075 to BAUD_128K. BAUD_USER indicates that nonstandard baud rates can be programmed.
DWORD dwProvSubType	This word contains the provider type. Most of the devices this book is concerned with will have values of PST_RS232 or PST_MODEM.

Continued

(Continued)

Member type and name	Description
`DWORD dwProvCapabilities`	Another bit mask. The possible values that can be masked into this word are shown here: `PCF_16BITMODE`: The serial device supports a special 16-bit mode. I have never encountered a device that actually uses this capability. `PCF_DTRDSR`: The driver supports DTR/DSR handshaking. `PCF_INTTIMEOUTS`: Interval timeouts are supported. `PCF_PARITY_CHECK`: Parity checking is supported. `PCF_RLSD`: Monitoring the incoming RLSD (Carrier Detect) line is supported. `PCF_RTSCTS`: RTS/CTS handshaking is supported. `PCF_SETXCHAR`: The driver supports programmable setting of the XON and XOFF characters used in handshaking. `PCF_SPECIALCHARS`: Special characters are supported. `PCF_TOTALTIMEOTS`: Total timeouts are supported. `PCF_XONXOFF`: XON/XOFF handshaking are supported.
`DWORD dwSettableParams`	This bit mask shows which parameters can be adjusted. The bits defined for the mask areas follows: `SP_BAUD`: The baud rate is adjustable. `SP_DATABIT`: The word size is adjustable. `SP_HANDSHAKING`: Hardware and software handshaking can be enabled and disabled. `SP_PARITY`: Parity generation can be turned on and off. `SP_PARITY_CHECK`: Incoming parity detection is programmable. `SP_RLSD`: Incoming RLSD (Carrier Detect) detection can be enabled or disabled. `SP_STOPBITS`: The number of stop bits can be programmed.

Member type and name	Description
DWORD dwSettableBaud	The baud rates that can be selected. The same bit masks are used for this word as in the dwMaxBaud member.
WORD wSettableData	A mask specifying the available choices for word size for the given port. The values are defined as DATABITS_X, where X can take values of 5, 6, 7, 8, 16, and 16X. 16X is defined by Microsoft as a special wide path through serial hardware lines.
WORD wSettableStopParity	The API designers at Microsoft decided to combine two types of parameters in one bit mask. This word supports masks of two varieties: STOPBITS_XX and PARITY_YY. XX can take on values of 10, 15, and 20 for the normal stop bit settings of 1, 1.5, and 2. The YY values for the parity are NONE, ODD, EVEN, MARK, and SPACE.
DWORD dwCurrentTxQueue	The current size of the driver's internal output buffer. A return value of 0 indicates that the driver doesn't care to share this information.
DWORD dwCurrentRxQueue	The size of the internal driver's receive buffer. Like the previous member, a value of 0 returned in this member indicates that the driver doesn't want to share this information.
DWORD dwProvSpec1	
DWORD dwProvSpec2	Microsoft indicates that these words are reserved for device specific information, and should not be used unless you are aware of the requirements for the driver you are using.
WCHAR wcProvChar[]	This member marks the start of device specific data of a variable length. Different drivers will append data of different lengths to this structure. The actual value can be determined by checking the wPacketLength mamber. If the device is a modem, this member should be the start of a MODEMDEVCAPS structure.

OVERLAPPED

This structure is used by `ReadFile()` and `WriteFile()` to manage overlapped I/O. The structure is passed to the function and then left alone until the asynchronous I/O is complete. The same structure is then passed to `GetOverlappedResult()` to get the final data on the I/O operation. The member type and names are described in the following table.

Member type and name	Description
`DWORD Internal` `DWORD InternalHigh`	During the progress of the I/O operation, these two words are used by the Win32 I/O functions to maintain the state of the call. You leave these members alone.
`DWORD Offset`	This member specifies the position at which the I/O operation is to start. Because serial I/O ports aren't random access devices, you always set this value to 0 before calling the function.
`DWORD OffsetHigh`	The high word of the offset. (This allows for the possibility of files with 64-bit offset values.) You don't use this word, either.
`HANDLE hEvent`	Handle of an event that is used to signal the calling process when the I/O operation completes. The `Win32Port` class uses this handle to wait for completion. The event must be created by the calling process and should be reset before calling the I/O operation.

The communications API

Microsoft identifies more than 20 functions as being part of the communications API. I add four more functions that aren't necessarily just for communications but are essential nonetheless. The resulting list is a bit overwhelming:

```
BuildCommDCB
BuildCommDCBAndTimeouts
ClearCommBreak
ClearCommError
CloseHandle
CreateFile
CommConfigDialog
EscapeCommFunction
GetCommConfig
```

```
GetCommMask
GetCommModemStatus
GetCommProperties
GetCommState
GetCommTimeouts
GetDefaultCommConfig
GetOverlappedResult
PurgeComm
ReadFile
SetCommBreak
SetCommConfig
SetCommMask
SetCommState
SetCommTimeouts
SetDefaultCommConfig
SetupComm
TransmitCommChar
WaitCommEvent
WriteFile
```

Despite the overwhelming size of the list, things aren't all that bad. First, the Win32Port class doesn't use all of these functions; some of them are only needed for special functions. Second, the Win32Port class does an effective job of hiding the Win32 API behind the general purpose class interface.

The descriptions of the functions follow. Note that all these functions are documented by Microsoft as part of the Win32 API, which should be your resource for complete documentation.

```
BOOL BuildCommDCB( LPCTSTR lpDef, LPDCB lpDCB )
```

lpDef   Pointer to an ASCII string that is in the same format as the command line MODE command used to configure serial ports.

LpDCB   Pointer to a DCB that will be filled in completely by this command.

returns   The function returns TRUE if it succeeds and FALSE if it fails. Like most Win32 functions, the cause of the error can be determined using the GetLastError() function.

This is a utility function that can be used to fill in all the values in the DCB structure. (The DCB structure is used to configure ports and is described in the previous section.) This is strictly a convenience function and isn't used in the Win32Port class. The lpDef command is simply a formatting command that uses the same format as the command line MODE command. Traditional MS-DOS versions of the MODE command would typically look like this:

```
mode com2:9600,e,7,2
```

The Win98 version of the same command might look like this:

```
mode com2 baud=9600 parity=E data=7 stop=2
```

After the DBC structure is filled out by this command, it can be applied to a port with the `SetCommState()`.

```
BOOL BuildCommDCBAndTimeouts( LPCTSTR lpDef,
                              LPDCB lpDCB,
                              LPCOMMTIMEOUTS lpCommTimeouts )
```

`lpDef`	Pointer to an ASCII string that is in the same format as the command line `MODE` command used to configure serial ports.
`lpDCB`	Pointer to a `DCB` that will be filled in completely by this command.
`lpCommTimeouts`	Pointer to a timeout structure that will be filled in by this function.
`returns`	The function returns `TRUE` if it succeeds and `FALSE` if it fails. Like most Win32 functions, the cause of the error can be determined using the `GetLastError()` function.

This function fills in the `DCB` argument just like the previous one, but also fills in the timeout structure. After being initialized, the timeout structure can be passed as an argument to the `SetCommTimeouts()` function. The values placed in the timeout structure depend on the presence or absence of a `TO=xx` argument in the ASCI string. If xx is `ON`, the timeout structure is set up to have an arbitrary timeout. If xx is `OFF`, the timeout structure is set up to have no timeout. If the `TO=xx` tokens are not in the ASCII setup string, the timeout structure is unchanged.

This function, like the previous one, is simply a convenience function to help avoid the hassle of filling in the fields of the `DCB` and `COMMTIMEOUT` structure manually. The motivations behind this are good, but the `Win32Port` class doesn't use either of these functions, preferring to do things the hard way.

BOOL CLEARCOMMBREAK(HANDLE HFILE)

`hFile`	The handle referring to the open comm port.
`returns`	The function returns `TRUE` if it succeeds and `FALSE` if it fails. Like most Win32 functions, the cause of the error can be determined using the `GetLastError()` function.

Chapter 10: The Win32 Comm API 447

This function is called to take the port out of the breaking state and restore it to normal output. The port is put into the breaking state by the `SetCommBreak()` function, which causes the transmission line to send a continuous stream of 0 bits with no intervening stop bits. (This is also referred to as *continuous spacing*.)

This function is used in the Win32Port class to bring the port out of the break state.

```
BOOL CloseHandle( HANDLE hObject )
```

hObject   The handle referring to the open comm port.

returns   The function returns TRUE if it succeeds and FALSE if it fails. Like most Win32 functions, the cause of the error can be determined using the GetLastError() function.

This function closes an open comm port and stops all input and output. This function is used in the Win32Port class to close a port in the object's destructor.

```
HANDLE CreateFile( LPCTSTR lpFileName,
                   DWORD dwDesiredAccess,
                   DWORD dwSharedMode,
                   LPSECURITY_ATTRIBUTES lpSecurity,
                   DWORD dwCreationDisposition,
                   DWORD dwFlagsAndAttributes,
                   HANDLE hTemplateFile )
```

lpFileName   The name of the port to be opened. Normally, this will be COMxx. Under Win16, there is a limit of eight ports, which has been lifted under Win32. However, ports with a number greater than COM9 should be opened by using the name "\\.\COMxx". For C/C++ programmers, the backslashes must be doubled up, leading to the hideous-looking port name of "\\\\.\\COMxx". Because this syntax also works for ports lower than COM10, it's usually easiest to use it for all calls to CreateFile().

dwDesiredAccess   This can be any combination of GENERIC_READ and GENERIC_WRITE. When opening communications port, it really only makes sense to use both, which is what is done in the Win32Port class.

dwSharedMode   The Win32 API provides for several file-sharing options in this argument, but none of them really make sense for serial ports. The Win32Port class always passes a 0 for this argument.

lpSecurity | Like the previous argument, the various possibilities for security don't really make sense for serial ports, so the `Win32Port` always passes a 0 in this argument.

dwCreationDisposition | You don't really have any choice about creating new serial ports, so this argument will always be passed as `OPEN_EXISTING` when working with communications devices.

dwFlagsAndAttributes | When opening serial ports, there are two flags used here. The first, `FILE_ATTRIBUTE_NORMAL` is used by convention, and may not even be strictly necessary. The second, `FILE_FLAG_OVERLAPPED`, is used to indicate that the file will be used to perform overlapped I/O. You don't need to use this to open a communications port, but as I discuss earlier in this chapter, you really have to use multithreaded overlapped I/O to get effective, safe use of your ports under Win32.

hTemplateFile | This argument is used when creating files, but it doesn't make any sense with serial ports, so you pass a value of 0 always.

returns | This function returns `INVALID_HANDLE_VALUE` if it fails, in which case `GetLastError()` must be used to determine the reason for the failure. Otherwise, the return value is the handle that will be used for all functions that access the port.

Although it's kind of neat to think of every device on the system as if it were some sort of file, it's not always a very good fit. You use the `CreateFile()` function to open a port, and it returns a handle as if it were a file, but most of the possible arguments that this function uses are meaningless in this context. However, it is the only way to open a port under Win32, so that's what you use in the `Win32Port` class.

```
BOOL CommConfigDialog( LPTSTR lpszName,
                       HWND hWNd,
                       LPCOMMCONFIG lpCC )
```

lpFileName | The name of the port to be configured. This will normally be a simple string of the format `"COMx"`.

hWnd   The handle to the window that will own the dialog box. You normally pass the handle of the main window in your application here; that ensures that the configuration will be modal with respect to your app.

lpCC   Pointer to a COMMCONFIG function. At a minimum, you need to initialize the dwSize member of this structure before calling the function. The contents of this structure should include the DCB for your port, which will be modified by this routine.

This function provides a handy way to provide a port configuration function in your program. The configuration dialog box that this function invokes may have custom features provided by a hardware vendor, which relieves you of the burden of developing custom dialogs for every type of hardware out there.

To use this routine for standard port requires only a minimal amount of code. Just these two lines of code are enough to invoke the dialog box:

```
COMMCONFIG cfg = { sizeof( COMMCONFIG ), 0 };
CommConfigDialog( "COM2", m_hWnd, &cfg );
```

That code in an MFC app brings up the dialog box shown in Figure 10-1.

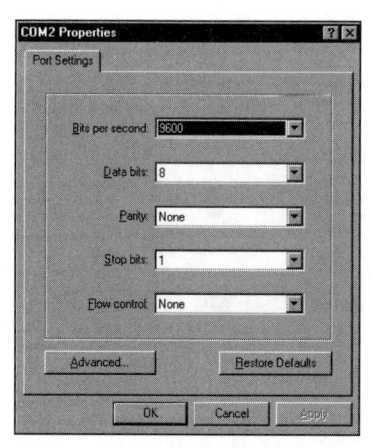

Figure 10-1: CommConfigDialog() for a standard serial port

The standard serial port setup is nice, but getting a free version of this simple dialog box isn't a huge time saver. The odds are good that you'll want your own version of this dialog box, anyway. However, when it comes to configuring modems, the amount of labor to be saved is considerably more. In particular, every modem potentially has its own specialized setup information, which might take days of work to add to a dialog.

The following code fragment shows how you might go about using the `CommConfigDialog` to configure a modem:

```
DWORD size = sizeof( COMMCONFIG ) + sizeof( MODEMSETTINGS );
COMMCONFIG *pCfg = (COMMCONFIG *) calloc( size, 1 );
char *name = "Boca 33.6 Kbps Internal FD34FSVD";
if ( GetDefaultCommConfig( name, pCfg, &size ) )
  CommConfigDialog( name, m_hWnd, pCfg );
```

Note that the COMMCONFIG structure has a private data area for modem devices, which you have to account for by allocating extra space. You also use the `GetDefaultCommConfig()` function to fill in the structure with valid data. This function call produces the dialog box shown in Figure 10-2.

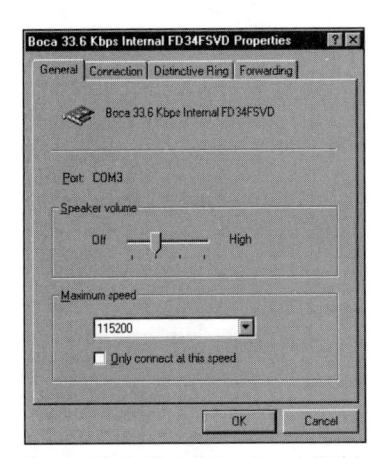

Figure 10-2: The dialog box called by GetDefaultCommConfig()

This dialog box has quite a bit of modem information that you get to configure without any extra work.

```
BOOL EscapeCommFunction( HANDLE hFile, DWORD dwFunc )
```

hFile   The handle of the port to be used. This is the handle that was returned by the `CreateFile()` function call that opens the port.

dwFunc   The function to be performed on the port. The values that can be used for this function are listed in the following table below.

returns   `TRUE` if the function succeeded, `FALSE` if it didn't.

Chapter 10: The Win32 Comm API

This function is a grab bag of miscellaneous functions (which are described in the following table). All but two of the functions that can be invoked from `EscapeCommFunction()` are duplicated elsewhere in the comm API. Because of this, the function isn't used in the Win32Port class.

Function Name	Action
CLRDTR	Clears the DTR line on the port. Management of DTR can also be done via the DCB structure, which is what the Win32Port class uses.
CLRRTS	Clears the RTS output line on the port. Like DTR, the RTS line can also be controlled via the DCB structure, which is what the Win32Port class uses.
SETDTR	Assert the DTR line on the port.
SETRTS	Assert the RTS line on the port.
SETXOFF	This function causes the port to behave as though an XOFF had been received. This is one of two functions that can be performed only using EscapeCommFunction. Although this function might be useful for testing, it wasn't included in the class in Chapter 11.
SETXON	Causes the port to behave as though an XON had just been received. This has no equivalent in the rest of the Win32 comm API.
SETBREAK	Stops sending characters and puts the line into the breaking state. The Win32Port class uses the SetCommBreak() API function when a break output is needed.
CLRBREAK	Takes the line out of the breaking state and begins sending characters again.

```
BOOL GetCommConfig( HANDLE hFile,
                    LPCOMMCONFIG lpCC,
                    LPDWORD lpdwSize )
```

hFile The handle of the port to be used. This is the handle that is returned by the `CreateFile()` function used to open the port.

lpCC A pointer to a `COMMCONFIG` structure. As you saw in the preceding example code for `CommConfigDialog`, this structure may have additional space appended to it for device specific data.

lpdwSize   A pointer to a DWORD containing the size of the COMMCONFIG structure. Because the size of the structure varies depending on the device type, this value needs to be passed to the function. Upon a successful return, this value will contain the number of bytes in the returned structure. If the function fails, this word should show the number of bytes that are needed by the function.

returns   Returns TRUE upon success, FALSE upon failure.

If you just wanted to get the contents of the DCB for a port, you would just call the GetCommState() function. It fills in a DCB structure with the current values for a given port. Calling GetCommConfig() fills in all the values of the DCB, plus a block of data that varies among different device types.

This is useful for a couple of different reasons. First, if you know what the device-specific data type is, you can then examine the current configuration. For example, if the attached device is a modem, you know that the wcProviderData values in the COMMCONFIG structure are a MODEMSETTINGS structure.

Second, and perhaps even more useful, you can use the COMMCONFIG structure read out of this call as input to the CommConfigDialog() function, which lets you set up the various features of the device. After the user modifies settings in the dialog, you can call SetCommConfig(), which will update the device-specific features without your even needing to know about it.

Unfortunately, using GetCommConfig() to retrieve modem parameters requires that you pass a modem handle to the function, not a comm port handle. Calling this function with a handle returned from CreateFile() will always invoke the standard comm port dialog box, not the modem config dialog box. The procedures for getting a modem handle are discussed in the TAPI chapter.

BOOL GetCommMask(HANDLE hFile, LPDWORD lpEvtMask)

hFile   The handle of the port to be used. This is the handle that is returned when you open the port using CreateFile().

lpEvtMask   A pointer to a DWORD that will receive the returned event mask.

Returns   TRUE if the function succeeds; FALSE if it fails.

An open comm port can be set up to report certain asynchronous events as they occur via a call to WaitCommEvent. The events that will be reported from this function are defined in a single DWORD mask, with the bits relevant to serial ports described in the following table.

Chapter 10: The Win32 Comm API

Mask Bit	Function
EV_BREAK	An incoming break was detected.
EV_CTS	The incoming CTS modem signal line changed state.
EV_DSR	The incoming DSR modem signal line changed state.
EV_ERR	A line status error occurred. This can be a framing error, parity error, or overrun error.
EV_RING	The incoming ring signal changed state. Microsoft has acknowledged that this signal is not properly handled under Win 95/98 (although it is under NT,) which means that incoming rings are not properly reported as comm events. I have had success using EV_RINGTE in addition to EV_RING; see the next entry in this table.
EV_RINGTE	This event mask was dropped from the comm API during the switch from Windows 3.1 to Win32, which means it isn't even included in the SDK header files. (I simply define it as 0x2000, its internally defined value.) However, adding it to the comm event mask causes the Win32 API to properly generate an event on the trailing edge of each incoming ring event, allowing you to detect incoming ring properly.
EV_RLSD	The RLSD (Carrier Detect) line changed state.
EV_RX80FULL	The RX buffer has reached the 80% full mark.
EV_RXCHAR	A character was received by the UART and handed off to the driver for internal buffering.
EV_RXFLAG	The special flag character defined in the DCB was received.
EV_TXEMPTY	The last character in the device driver's buffer has been sent to the UART.

The comm events used in the Win32Port driver are EV_BREAK, EV_CTS, EV_DSR, EV_RING, EV_RINGTE, and EV_RLSD.

BOOL GetCommModemStatus(HANDLE hFile, LPDWORD lpModemStat)

hFile	The handle of the port to be used. This is the handle that is returned by the CreateFile() function used to open the port.
lpModemStat	Pointer to a DWORD that will receive the modem status bits.

returns   TRUE on success, FALSE on failure. Like most of the functions in the Win32 comm API, a call to GetLastError() should be made to determine the exact cause of any failure.

This function allows you to directly interrogate the serial driver to determine the current status of the four modem input signals. The masks used to define the bits for the four input lines are as follows:

MS_CTS_ON

MS_DSR_ON

MS_RING_ON

MS_RLSD_ON

This function is used by the Win32Port class to implement the four functions that return the current state of these modem lines.

BOOL GetCommProperties(HANDLE hFile, LPCOMMPROP lpCommProp)

hFile   The handle of the port to be used. This is the handle that is returned by the CreateFile() function used to open the port.

lpModemStat   Pointer to a COMMPROP structure that will receive the data regarding the port. The wPacketLength member should be initialized with the size of the structure before the function is called.

returns   TRUE on success; FALSE on failure. Like most of the functions in the Win32 comm API, a call to GetLastError() should be made to determine the exact cause of any failure.

This function returns a structure that gives a lot of information regarding which settable parameters are supported by this device. It's easy to generalize everything you know about standard 8250 family UARTs to all other devices, but in many cases, this is bad thinking. Some devices will support features above and beyond the normal 8250 feature set; others will support fewer. This isn't necessarily all a bad deal. After all, how often do you need to program your UART for 75 baud, 5 bits, 1.5 stop bits, and Mark parity?

BOOL GetCommState(HANDLE hFile, LPDCB lpDCB)

hFile   The handle of the port to be used. This is the handle that is returned by the CreateFile() function used to open the port.

Chapter 10: The Win32 Comm API 455

lpDCB   Pointer to a DCB structure that will receive the data regarding the port. The DCBLength member should be initialized to give the size of the structure.

returns   TRUE on success; FALSE on failure. Like most of the functions in the Win32 comm API, a call to GetLastError() should be made to determine the exact cause of any failure.

This function fills in all the members in the DCB, yielding a wealth of information regarding the state of the port. Nearly all the configurable parameters used by the Win32Port class are controlled by settings in the DCB structure.

```
BOOL GetCommTimeouts( HANDLE hFile,
                      LPCOMMTIMEOUTS lpCommTimeouts )
```

hFile   The handle of the port to be used. This is the handle that is returned by the CreateFile() function used to open the port.

lpCommTimeouts   Pointer to a COMMTIMEOUTS structure that will receive the timeout data for the port. Unlike most of the other Get...() functions, this one does not require that the first member of the COMMTIMEOUTS structure be initialized with the size of the structure.

returns   TRUE on success, FALSE on failure. Like most of the functions in the Win32 comm API, a call to GetLastError() should be made to determine the exact cause of any failure.

This function reads in the current timeout settings for the port. Input operations have two timeout values: an interval timeout that applies to each input character, and a total timeout that applies to the input of an entire buffer. Output operations just have a total timeout value. Details on the contents and meaning of this structure are documented in the previous section's discussion of the COMMTIMEOUT structure.

The Win32Port class developed in Chapter 11 doesn't do much with this structure. Because you are using overlapped I/O for reads and writes, you want read and write operations to return immediately whether they are complete or not. Therefore, your timeout values are always set to the minimal settings.

```
BOOL GetDefaultCommConfig( LPCSTR lpszName,
                           LPCOMMCONFIG lpCC,
                           LPDWORD lpdwSize )
```

lpszName	The name of the port in question. Note that nearly all other comm functions expect the handle to an open port, whereas this function wants just a name. That means that you can get the default configuration for a port without opening it.
lpCC	Pointer to a COMMCONFIG structure that will receive the configuration data for the port. As is so often the case, this structure can be different sizes depending on the amount of device-specific data appended to its tail. Unlike many of the other functions, you don't communicate this by preloading the first member in the structure with the size. Instead, you use the next parameter.
lpdwSize	Pointer to a DWORD containing the size of the lpCC parameter. If the function call succeeds, it passes back the actual count of bytes used in this parameter. If the function call fails, this value is returned with the number of bytes needed.
returns	TRUE on success, FALSE on failure. Like most of the functions in the Win32 comm API, a call to GetLastError() should be made to determine the exact cause of any failure.

This function is used to determine the default configuration for a given port. The COMMCONFIG structure used to communicate this information contains a complete copy of the default DCB, which gives you most of the information needed. See the description of CommConfigDialog() for a snippet of code that shows how this function can be used to set port parameters.

```
BOOL GetOverlappedResult( HANDLE     hFile,
                          LPOVERLAPPED lpOverlapped,
                          LPDWORD    lpNumberOfBytes,
                          BOOL       bWait )
```

hFile   The handle of the port that was used to perform the read or write. This is the handle that is returned by the CreateFile() function used to open the port. (Or file, in other contexts.)

lpOverlapped	A pointer to the OVERLAPPED structure that was passed to the ReadFile() or WriteFile() function call that initiated the I/O process.
lpNumberOfBytes	A pointer to a DWORD that will receive the actual count of bytes that were transferred by the read or write operation. Despite the fact that this is an overlapped I/O operation, owing to timeouts, it still may not return the number of bytes requested.
bWait	If this flag is TRUE, this function call won't return until the I/O operation is complete. In the Win32Port class, you never call GetOverlappedResult() until the I/O operation is complete, so you don't use this parameter.

BOOL PurgeComm(HANDLE hFile, DWORD dwFlags)

hFile	The handle of the port to be affected. This is the handle that is returned by the CreateFile() function used to open the port.
dwFlags	Pointer to a DWORD that contains a bit mask detailing what operations this function is supposed to accomplish. The possible bits that can be set in this mask are detailed in the following table.
returns	TRUE on success, FALSE on failure. Like most of the functions in the Win32 comm API, a call to GetLastError() should be made to determine the exact cause of any failure.

This function is used to abort input or output operations currently in progress on an open port. The exact operation performed by this function call is determined by the bits set in the dwFlags command mask. Any combination of command is legal. The following bits can be set in the mask word:

Mask	Action
PURGE_TXABORT	All character output in progress is terminated. Any pending overlapped operation is completed, which will generate an event indicating that the write operation is done.
PURGE_RXABORT	All character input operations in progress are terminated. An overlapped I/O operation in progress is completed, with the appropriate event being set.

Continued

(Continued)

Mask	Action
PURGE_TXCLEAR	This command directs the device driver to clear the output buffer. The output buffer could conceivably have thousands of characters waiting for output, so this command mask is frequently used in conjunction with the PURGE_TXABORT command flag.
PURGE_RXCLEAR	This command clears the device driver's input buffer. This is also frequently used in conjunction with the PURGE_RXABORT command flag.

```
BOOL ReadFile( HANDLE hFile,
               LPVOID lpBuffer,
               DWORD nNumberOfBytesToRead,
               LPDWORD lpNumberOfBytesRead,
               LPOVERLAPPED lpOverlapped )
```

hFile	The handle of the port being used for the read. This is the handle that is returned by the `CreateFile()` function used to open the port. Note that `ReadFile()` is also used to read data from files; this description is intended to cover only its use for input and output via the serial port.
lpBuffer	A pointer to a buffer that will receive the input data.
nNumberOfBytesToRead	The number of bytes requested. The `lpBuffer` parameter should be able to hold at least this many characters.
lpNumberOfBytesRead	Pointer to a DWORD that will receive the number of bytes read during the function call. Note that when the function returns, this number will contain the number of characters written so far, and won't change as the background read operation proceeds. When the asynchronous read completes, the actual number of characters transferred needs to be determined by a call to `GetOverlappedResult()`.
lpOverlapped	Pointer to an OVERLAPPED structure. This is the structure that will be updated as an asynchronous read progresses.

returns   Returns TRUE if the function succeeds, which will happen only if the requested number of characters were present in the device's input buffer. The function returns FALSE if it fails to read all the characters. However, if GetLastError() returns a value of ERROR_IO_PENDING, it means that an overlapped read is in progress.

This is the only function in the Win32 API that can be used to read data from the serial port. Under Win32, I/O operations can be either synchronous or asynchronous, but for serial ports, it is almost impossible to manage a full-duplex connection without using asynchronous I/O, so that is how the Win32Port class does all of its I/O.

Performing asynchronous input calls on a port requires that the port shall have been opened with the FILE_FLAG_OVERLAPPED flag. All calls to ReadFile() subsequent to that must pass in a pointer to an OVERLAPPED structure. If all goes well, one of two possible things will then happen.

If the serial port had enough data to fill the requested buffer, the function returns immediately with a TRUE return value, and the data is immediately available.

If the serial port wasn't able to fill the request, an asynchronous read begins. This means that the calling process has to leave the input buffer and the OVERLAPPED object alone until the O/S signals that the read is complete. This is done by setting the event that was passed to the ReadFile() call in the OVERLAPPED structure.

After that event is set, a call to GetOverlappedResult() is done to see how many bytes were transferred, at which point the port is ready to perform more input.

```
BOOL  SetCommBreak( HANDLE hFile )
```

hFile   The handle of the target port. This is the handle that is returned by the CreateFile() function used to open the port.

returns   TRUE if the function succeeds; FALSE if it fails. Like most of the functions discussed in this chapter, you will have to call GetLastError() to determine the specific cause of failure.

This function is used to begin the transmission of a break on a specific comm port. Note that transmission of characters is suspended during this time. Unfortunately, Win32 denies any responsibility for timing the duration of the break. This means that after calling this function to begin the break, the calling program will have to wait for a specific amount of time before calling ClearCommBreak() to restore normal communications.

```
BOOL SetCommConfig( HANDLE hCommDev,
                    LPCOMMCONFIG lpCC,
                    DWORD dwSize )
```

hFile   The handle of a comm device. Most of the functions in this chapter require a handle to a serial port, but this function can also take a modem handle. The procedures needed to get a modem handle are discussed in Chapter 15.

lpCC   Pointer to a COMMCONFIG structure. This structure needs to be properly filled out for this function to work.

dwSize The size of the COMMCONFIG structure. Because the structure has a variable amount of data appended to it, the actual length needs to be specified. Of course, the first member of the structure, dwSize, contains this information as well, so this is somewhat redundant.

This function can be used to configure a comm device or modem. Because the COMMCONFIG structure contains a complete DCB, this function is a superset of SetCommState(), the configuration function used in the Win32Port class.

The reason you would use this function rather than SetCommState() is to configure additional properties above and beyond those found in the DCB. For example, a modem device will have a MODEMSETTINGS structure appended to the COMMCONFIG structure. The elements of that additional data could be loaded with a call to GetCommConfig(), modified with a call to CommConfigDialog(), and then updated with this function call.

BOOL SetCommMask(HANDLE hFile, DWORD dwEvtMask)

hFile   The handle of the port to be used. This is the handle that is returned when you open the port using CreateFile.

lpEvtMask   A pointer to a DWORD that contains the event mask that is going to be used for the port.

Returns   TRUE if the function succeeds, FALSE if it fails.

An open comm port can be set up to report certain asynchronous events as they occur via a call to WaitCommEvent. The events that will be reported from this function are defined in a single DWORD mask, with the bits relevant to serial ports shown in the following table.

Mask Bit	Function
EV_BREAK	An incoming break was detected.
EV_CTS	The incoming CTS modem signal line changed state.
EV_DSR	The incoming DSR modem signal line changed state.
EV_ERR	A line status error occurred. This can be a framing error, parity error, or overrun error.
EV_RING	The incoming ring signal changed state. Microsoft has acknowledged that this signal is not properly handled under Win 95/98 (although it is under NT,) which means that incoming rings are not properly reported as comm events. I have had success using EV_RINGTE in addition to EV_RING; see the next entry in this table.
EV_RINGTE	This event mask was dropped from the comm API during the switch from Windows 3.1 to Win32, which means that it isn't even included in the SDK header files. (I simply define it as 0x2000, its internally defined value.) However, adding it to the comm event mask causes the Win32 API to properly generate an event on the trailing edge of each incoming ring event, allowing you to detect incoming ring properly.
EV_RLSD	The RLSD (Carrier Detect) line changed state.
EV_RX80FULL	The RX buffer has reached the 80% full mark.
EV_RXCHAR	A character was received by the UART and handed off to the driver for internal buffering.
EV_RXFLAG	The special flag character defined in the DCB was received..
EV_TXEMPTY	The last character in the device driver's buffer has been sent to the UART.

The comm events used in the Win32Port driver are EV_BREAK, EV_CTS, EV_DSR, EV_RING, EV_RINGTE, and EV_RLSD. They are set up with a call to this function at the start of the input thread and are unchanged for the entire time that the port is open.

```
BOOL SetCommState( HANDLE hFile, LPDCB lpDCB )
```

462   Serial Communications Developer's Guide, Second Edition

    hFile   The handle of the port to be set up. This is the handle that is returned by the CreateFile() function used to open the port.

    lpDCB   Pointer to a DCB structure that will be used to set the new configuration of the port. This structure needs to be properly filled out of the function to work. Probably the safest way to do this is to initially fill out the DCB with a call to GetCommState(), the modifying the members that you need to change.

    returns   TRUE on success, FALSE on failure. Like most of the functions in the Win32 comm API, a call to GetLastError() should be made to determine the exact cause of any failure.

SetCommState() is used to set nearly all of the configurable parameters for a serial port. This includes settings for baud rate, parity, word size, stop bits, and handshaking. See the description of the DCB structure earlier in this chapter for a complete description of the members that affect the serial port.

```
BOOL SetCommTimeouts( HANDLE hFile,
                      LPCOMMTIMEOUTS lpCommTimeouts  )
```

    hFile   The handle of the port to be used. This is the handle that is returned by the CreateFile() function used to open the port.

    lpCommTimeouts   Pointer to a COMMTIMEOUTS structure that contains the new the timeout data for the port. A description of the members of this structure is given earlier in the chapter.

    returns   TRUE on success, FALSE on failure. Like most of the functions in the Win32 comm API, a call to GetLastError() should be made to determine the exact cause of any failure.

This function is used to set the read and write timeouts for the port. Under the Win32 regime, you don't have much use for these timeouts, because your asynchronous I/O calls have to be set up to time out immediately, which allows the functions to continue in overlapped I/O mode.

If you want to use the port in nonoverlapped mode, this function will let you set reasonable timeouts so that your I/O calls don't hang your app or thread while waiting for completion.

```
BOOL SetDefaultCommConfig( LPCSTR lpszName,
                           LPCOMMCONFIG lpCC,
                           LPDWORD lpdwSize )
```

lpszName	The name of the port in question. Note that nearly all other comm functions define their first argument to be a handle to an open port, whereas this function wants just a name. That means that you can set the default configuration for a port without opening it.
lpCC	Pointer to a COMMCONFIG structure that contains the configuration data for the port. As is so often the case, this structure can be different sizes depending on the amount of device-specific data appended to its tail. For example, if the device is a modem, a MODEMSETTINGS structure is appended to the end of the COMMCONFIG structure.
lpdwSize	Pointer to a DWORD containing the size of the lpCC parameter.
returns	TRUE on success, FALSE on failure. Like most of the functions in the Win32 comm API, a call to GetLastError() should be made to determine the exact cause of any failure.

This function is used to set the default configuration of a device; that is, the configuration that will be present when the port is first opened. Probably the best way to use this function is to first fill in the COMMCONFIG structure with a call to GetDefaultCommConfig(), and then modify the members of the DCB to match your preferences. After you have things the way you like them, call this function to establish the default configuration.

```
BOOL SetupComm( HANDLE hFile,
                DWORD dwInQueue,
                DWORD dwOutQueue )
```

hFile	The handle of the port to be modified. This is the handle that is returned by the CreateFile() function used to open the port.
dwInQueue	The requested size of the port's input buffer. The actual capabilities of the port might not allow for the buffer size you request. To be sure that the device can support the size you request, you could call GetCommProperties() and examine the dwMaxTxQueue member in the COMMPROP structure it returns.
dwOutQueue	The requested size of the port's output buffer. Once again, you could query the maximum size the driver allows before attempting to set this value.
returns	TRUE on success, FALSE on failure. Like most of the functions in the Win32 comm API, a call to GetLastError() should be made to determine the exact cause of any failure.

With just a quick glance at this function's name, you might think it was responsible for the complete setup of the Win32 serial port. Nothing could be further from the truth; all it does is set up the sizes of the driver's input and output buffers. A much better name would be `SetupCommBufferSizes()`.

In the `Win32Port` class presented in the next chapter, I arbitrarily set up the buffer sizes to be 1K bytes each. However, operating as I am in asynchronous mode, the actual size of the driver's buffers isn't as important as it might be in other situations. The size of the internal buffers that you use to store feed data to and from the driver is much more important.

```
BOOL TransmitCommChar( HANDLE hFile, char cChar )
```

hFile   The handle of the port that is being asked to transmit a character. This is the handle that is returned by the `CreateFile()` function used to open the port.

cChar   The character to be immediately transmitted out of the port.

returns   `TRUE` on success, `FALSE` on failure. Like most of the functions in the Win32 comm API, a call to `GetLastError()` should be made to determine the exact cause of any failure.

This function is used to stuff a character out of the transmit side of a serial port ahead of everything else in the output buffers. This type of function can be indispensable when you are trying to implement your own protocols. For example, you might use this function to send an acknowledgment of a packet immediately, instead of waiting for the current output buffer to drain.

```
BOOL WaitCommEvent( HANDLE hFile,
                    LPDWORD lpEvtMask,
                    LPOVERLAPPED lpOverlapped )
```

hFile   The handle of the port being monitored. This is the handle that is returned by the `CreateFile()` function used to open the port.

lpEvtMask   A pointer to a `DWORD` that will receive the value of the event that caused the wait to complete. The list of possible values is shown in the following table

lpOverlapped If the serial port was opened with the `FILE_FLAG_OVERLAPPED` flag, you must supply an `OVERLAPPED` structure to this call.

This function is used to wait for incoming events from a serial port. Like both the read and write functions, it works in asynchronous mode if the port was opened in overlapped mode. This means that you can call this function and then do other things while you wait for the event to be signaled. In the `Win32Port` class, the input thread calls this function and the `ReadFile()` function, andthen waits for either one to generate a signal, while also waiting for a possible event killing the thread.

If the function returns immediately, you can check the event mask that was returned to see which event caused the return. If you have to wait for the function to complete asynchronously, you have to first call `GetOverlappedResult()` and then examine the contents of the event mask.

The event mask can return one of the following values:

EvtMask Value	Meaning
EV_BREAK	An incoming break was detected.
EV_CTS	The incoming CTS modem signal line changed state.
EV_DSR	The incoming DSR modem signal line changed state.
EV_ERR	A line status error occurred. This can be a framing error, parity error, or overrun error.
EV_RING	The incoming ring signal changed state. Microsoft has acknowledged that this signal is not properly handled under Win 95/98 (although it is under NT,) which means that incoming rings are not properly reported as comm events. I have had success using EV_RINGTE in addition to EV_RING; see the next entry in this table.
EV_RINGTE	This event mask was dropped from the comm API during the switch from Windows 3.1 to Win32, which means that it isn't even included in the SDK header files. (I simply define it as 0x2000, its internally defined value.) However, adding it to the comm event mask causes the Win32 API to properly generate an event on the trailing edge of each incoming ring event, allowing you to detect incoming ring properly.
EV_RLSD	The RLSD (Carrier Detect) line changed state.
EV_RXCHAR	A character was received by the UART and handed off to the driver for internal buffering.
EV_RXFLAG	The special flag character defined in the DCB was received.
EV_TXEMPTY	The last character in the device driver's buffer has been sent to the UART.

```
BOOL WriteFile( HANDLE hFile,
                LPVOID lpBuffer,
                DWORD nNumberOfBytesToWrite,
                LPDWORD lpNumberOfBytesWritten,
                LPOVERLAPPED lpOverlapped )
```

hFile	The handle of the port being used for the write. This is the handle that is returned by the `CreateFile()` function used to open the port. Note that `WriteFile()` is also used to write data to files; this description is intended only to cover its use for input and output via the serial port.
lpBuffer	A pointer to a buffer containing the output data.
nNumberOfBytesToWrite	The number of bytes to be sent from the buffer out the serial port. The `lpBuffer` parameter should contain all of the characters at the time of the function call.
lpNumberOfBytesWritten	Pointer to a `DWORD` that will receive the number of bytes written during the function call. Note that when the function returns, this number will contain the number of characters written so far, and won't change as the background write operation proceeds. When the asynchronous read completes, the actual number of characters written needs to be determined by a call to `GetOverlappedResult()`.
lpOverlapped	Pointer to an `OVERLAPPED` structure. This is the structure that will be updated as an asynchronous read progresses.
returns	Returns `TRUE` if the function succeeds, which will happen only if all of the characters could be transferred to the output buffer immediately. The function returns `FALSE` if it fails to write all of the characters. However, if `GetLastError()` returns a value of `ERROR_IO_PENDING`, it means that an overlapped write is in progress.

This is the only function in the Win32 API that is normally used to write data to the serial port. (`TransmitCommChar()` also sends characters, but only under unique conditions.) Under Win32, I/O operations can be either synchronous or asynchronous, but for serial ports, it is almost impossible to manage a full duplex connection without using asynchronous I/O, so that is how the `Win32Port` class does all of its I/O.

Performing asynchronous output on a port requires that the port have been opened with the FILE_FLAG_OVERLAPPED flag. All calls to WriteFile() subsequent to that must pass in a pointer to an OVERLAPPED structure. If all goes well, one of two possible things will then happen:

- If the serial port had enough room to accommodate the requested buffer, the function returns immediately with a TRUE return value.

- If the serial port doesn't have the space to fill the request, an asynchronous write begins. This means the calling process has to leave the output buffer and the OVERLAPPED object alone until the O/S signals that the write is complete. This is done by setting the event that was passed to the WriteFile() call in the OVERLAPPED structure.

After that event is set, a call to GetOverlappedResult() is done to see how many bytes were transferred, at which point the port is ready to perform more output.

Summary

As you can see, Win32 offers a very comprehensive API for communications programmers. However, like most APIs from Redmond, it isn't particularly programmer friendly. Writing even the most elementary Windows communications program is a fairly sizable exercise. In Chapter 11, I present a class that wraps up the API, making it somewhat more palatable. In Chapter 12, you can see the resulting Win32Port class used in a demo program that gets a lot of work out of not too much code.

Chapter 11

The Win32Port Class

IN THIS CHAPTER

- ◆ The Win32Port Class
- ◆ Microsoft's working sample, MTTTY.C, and how Win32Port class works
- ◆ The IdleFunction under Win32

IN CHAPTER 10, you saw that the Win32 API for serial communications is big and awkward. It has a long list of functions, plus a few overstuffed data structures and no clear road map on how to make it all work together.

In this chapter, you will see how to put these functions together into a working class. The `Win32Port` class is derived from the base class `RS232` and has a complete implementation of the functions provided in that class. Furthermore, the class is a well-behaved Win32 citizen and fits in nicely with the Windows event-driver programming model.

The Win32Port Class

Although class `Win32Port` doesn't exploit every possible feature of the Win32 serial API, it does provide the basic functionality needed by a majority of comm programs. Adding in some of the bells and whistles provided by the driver team in Redmond should be achievable without too much trouble when the need arises.

MTTTY.C – documentation by example

You could make a convincing argument that Microsoft doesn't provide a comprehensive source of documentation on the Win32 serial API. In typical fashion, the components of the API are described in simple functional terms, but a thorough roadmap to use of the API is sorely lacking.

Fortunately, Microsoft did provide a lone sample program that gives a good demonstration of how it intended Win32 serial port access to work. This program, `MTTTY.C`, can be found on Microsoft's Web site and on the MSDN CDs.

`MTTTY.C` is the short name for they `MultiThreaded TTY Program`, a set of source code and documentation by Allen Denver. MTTTY is a simple terminal program that lets you open a port, read and write data, view incoming modem status lines, and capture incoming data (shown in Figure 11-1).

The real value to MTTTY is that it provides a functioning framework for exploring how to perform simple input and output using independent threads. As you are probably tired of reading, attempting to do serial I/O from your program's main thread is a recipe for disaster.

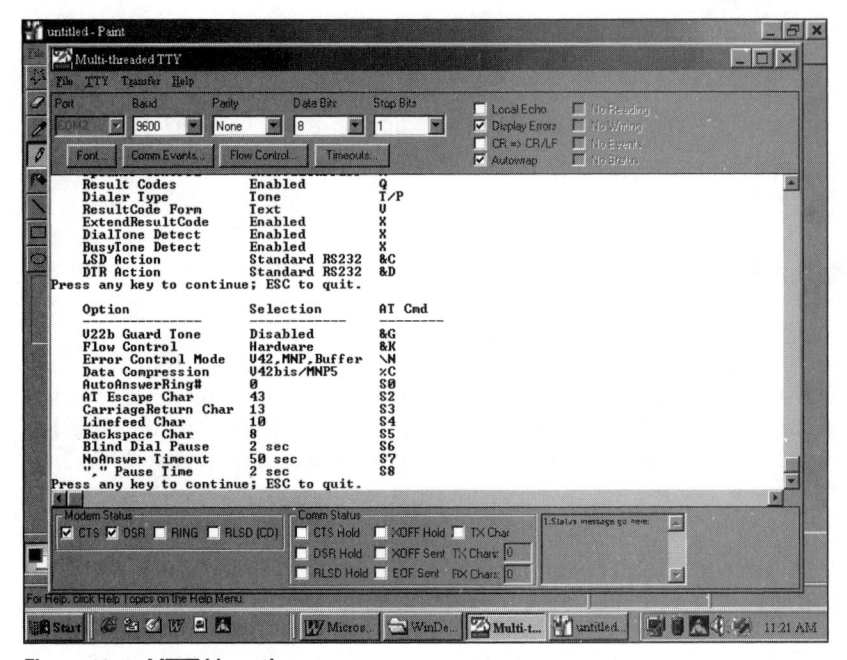

Figure 11-1: MTTTY in action

It would be great if either the Win32 API or MTTTY encapsulated the serial API in a usable C++ class definition. Unfortunately, you aren't that lucky. Both the API and MTTTY use old-fashioned C, with little attempt at encapsulation. MTTTY provides a good example of useful, working code, but it wasn't written with an eye toward reusability.

In addition to providing a working example that uses the Win32 API, MTTTY also is an excellent test program. Allen Denver's sample program provides a nearly complete interface to the elements of the DCB and allows you to see all incoming status information. It is an invaluable tool for experimenting with serial hardware and the API.

Threading architecture and conventions

If you are able to understand how the Win32 API works from the descriptions in Chapter 10, you shouldn't have too much trouble understanding how the

Win32Port class works. Being able to follow the API doesn't mean that you can write a new Win32 wrapper class in a day, but you should be able to see how this one works.

The one really difficult part of both creating and understanding this class is dealing with the fact that it must use separate threads for reading and writing data, as well as receiving status messages. With the advent of the Win32 API, Microsoft began trying to convince programmers that having multiple threads in a program was a really great thing. In my opinion, nothing could be further from the truth. Having multiple threads that access the same data is notoriously dangerous and frequently is done without serious consideration of whether any benefit will accrue from the decision.

> **Note:** Microsoft has a history of pushing questionable programming practices. Through the early 90s, Microsoft was an ardent advocate of using DLLs wherever possible to package code, even when there was clearly no good reason to do so. Today, users of Windows frequently find themselves descending into "DLL Hell" when improper versioning and installation procedures give them mismatched sets of programs and corresponding DLLs. Unfortunately, Microsoft has painted all of us into the corner it already owns, so you are forced to deal with the situation using various hacks and quick fixes. No systemic solutions appear anywhere on the horizon.

Like it or not, a Win32 app is going to have to use threads, and the Win32Port class is no exception. There are a few places where you want to exercise extreme caution with your threads:

- **Startup.** When a thread is first initialized, you have little or no control over how soon the thread begins execution. It may start immediately and begin working before you're ready for it. Or you may mistakenly believe that the thread is up and running when it has yet to execute a single cycle.

- **Shutdown.** When it comes time to terminate a thread, you want to be able to stop it in a reasonable amount of time. It has to be responsive to your request to stop, and as it exits, it should free up all resources that it has allocated.

- **Shared objects.** It is critical that any object that can be accessed by multiple threads be protected if necessary.

When the Win32Port object is created, it attempts to open the port with a call to CreateFile(). If the port is successfully opened, the constructor starts two threads: one for output of data and one for input of data and status. (This is based on the design of MTTTY.C. A more refined solution would probably split the data input and status thread into two separate threads.)

These two threads don't depend on any global data objects. All the data items they use are either automatic variables created when the thread starts, or members of the `Win32Port` object to which they belong. The ones you have to worry about sharing are the members of the class.

One data member that the main thread and the two worker threads share is the port handle, `m_hPort`. By the design, the operating system expects this to be used from multiple threads, so, fortunately, you don't have to manage it at all. The only things you need to be concerned with are having the handle properly created before the two worker threads start, and ensuring that the two worker threads exit before the handle is closed.

Two data objects you really worry about are the input and output queues that store data as it is being sent or received. These objects will be accessed frequently by the main thread and worker threads as things happen on the port. For efficiency, the data is stored in a standard C++ library `deque<char>` object, which is designed to efficiently add and remove data from either end. To avoid corruption, this object is wrapped up in a class that protects all access to the underlying object with a critical section. The resulting class, `MTQueue`, is documented in this section.

Both of these worker threads operate in basically the same fashion. They run in an infinite loop, which has three sections. The first section sets up requests for various actions, including input, output, and status notification. All these actions should take place very quickly. The second section of the loop consists of a wait for multiple events. The resulting events can be either responses from the requests set up in the first part of the loop, or messages from the main thread of the program. (One of the most important messages is the kill thread message, which tells the thread to exit.) Finally, the end of the loop consists of managing the response to whichever event was detected. After that is done, the loop repeats.

The Win32 threading API has no real knowledge of the structure of C++ programs and expects threads to be independent C++ routines. To accommodate this restriction while still making use of C++, each of the two threads are defined as static member functions of class `Win32Port`. The threads receive a copy of the `this` pointer for their controlling object when they are initialized, and therefore have access to all members of the class.

The next sections go over the details of operation of the two threads. Understanding these threads is really all that you need to understand the `Win32Port` class.

The output thread

The output thread does only one job, making it a bit simpler than the input thread. It is presently broken up into two subroutines, which are both structured in the same three-section infinite loop described earlier.

When the output thread first starts, it has to set up an array of handles that will signal it that some action needs to be taken. The code that does that is shown here:

```
void Win32Port::OutputThread(void * arglist)
{
   Win32Port *port = (Win32Port *) arglist;
   HANDLE handles[ 3 ] = { port->m_hKillOutputThreadEvent,
                           port->m_hWriteRequestEvent,
                           port->m_hBreakRequestEvent };
```

> **NOTE:** The fully documented source for this code is included in the listing of Win32Port.cpp in Chapter 12. Please refer to that listing to see the input and output threads in their entirety.

Note that all three event handles are members of the Win32Port object. These event handles will all be set by routines in the main thread and will be cleared automatically by the Win32 API when they are responded to in the output thread.

The three event members used here have the following definitions:

m_hKillOutputThreadEvent

This event is set by the main thread when the port is being closed. The output thread must respond to this by exiting as quickly as possible. Delay can be troublesome because the main thread must wait until the output thread exits before it can continue with whatever it needs to do.

m_hWriteRequestEvent

This event is set to indicate that the main program has placed some data in the transmit buffer and wants it to be transmitted. When the output thread detects that this event is set, it calls the output_worker() routine, which tries to send all of the data in the transmit queue.

m_hBreakRequestEvent

This event is set when the Break() member of the main thread is called by the application. This indicates that the user wants to send a break, which is handled immediately.

Before starting the main loop, one additional function call is made:

```
port->TxNotify();
```

This is the notification routine that lets the owner of the port know that the TX buffer is empty. The notification routine gets called every time the output worker routine manages to empty the buffer, plus once in the startup code.

After this array of handles is set up and the initial notification message is sent, the main loop is entered. The loop runs until boolean variable `done` is set, which happens when the `m_hKillOutputThreadEvent` is set by the main program. The first thing that happens in the main loop is that you wait for one of the three events to be setand then take the appropriate action. The entire loop is shown here:

```
for ( bool done = false ; !done ; ) {
  switch ( WaitForMultipleObjects( 3, handles, FALSE, FALSE ) )
  {
    case 0 : // m_hKillOutputThreadEvent
      done = true;
      break;
    case 1 : // m_hWriteRequestEvent
      done = port->output_worker();
      break;
    case 2 : // m_hBreakRequestEvent
      SetCommBreak( port->m_hPort );
      SleepEx( port->m_iBreakDuration, FALSE );
      ClearCommBreak( port->m_hPort );
      break;
    default :
      assert( false );
  }
}
```

This code is nice and simple (and will look really simple in comparison to the input thread), but you can see that you defer a little bit of the hard work to a second worker routine. Class member function `output_worker()` is called whenever the main thread notifies you that it has placed more data in the TX queue. It has a structure that is nearly identical to that shown here.

When `output_worker()` starts up, it also has to set up an array of event handles that it will wait for in its loop. However, there is one important difference between `output_worker()` and the main output thread. `output_worker()` has to create one of the event handles that it will use. This is the event handle used by the overlapped I/O part of the Win32 file system. When a call is made to `WriteFile()` with an `OVERLAPPED` structure that contains the event handle, you can count on the file system to set the event when the I/O operation is complete.

The resulting code that sets up the handles looks like this:

```
bool Win32Port::output_worker()
{
```

```
OVERLAPPED AsyncWriteInfo = { 0 };
AsyncWriteInfo.hEvent = CreateEvent( NULL, TRUE, FALSE, NULL );
assert( AsyncWriteInfo.hEvent );
HANDLE handles[ 2 ] = { m_hKillOutputThreadEvent,
                        AsyncWriteInfo.hEvent };
bool killed = false;
```

You can see by the choice of handles that while you are waiting for output to complete, you are also waiting for the kill thread event. If you didn't wait for it as well, a port close operation could hang for a long period of time waiting for an output operation to complete. The output worker returns a value of TRUE to the output thread after it completes if it has seen the kill thread flag, FALSE if it exited normally. This lets the output thread exit quickly if the kill command has come down. An internal flag called killed is used to return that status information to the calling output thread.

After setting up the handle array, the output_worker() is ready to begin transmitting characters. It operates in a loop just like the output thread, setting up an output and then waiting for an event before doing anything else. The first step is to get a batch of characters and attempt to start the I/O operation with a call to WriteFile():

```
for ( bool done = false ; ; !done ) {
  char data[ 500 ];
  int count = m_TxQueue.Extract( data, 500 );
  if ( count == 0 ) {
    TxNotify();
    break;
  }
```

The first thing you do in the loop is to extract as many as 500 characters from the transmit queue. If no characters are available in the buffer, it means that the buffer is empty and this routine can return. If that's the case, it also calls the TxNotify() member function to let the main thread of the program know that there is room for a new batch of characters in the TX queue. Otherwise, the loop continues.

With a buffer full of characters ready to transmit, all you have to do is call WriteFile(), which will send the characters to the Win32 driver. Three things can happen when you call WriteFile() at this point. If something is wrong with the port, the function call might return an immediate error. If the port is working and you have given it a manageable request, it might accept all the characters immediately. If the port is relatively busy, it will go into overlapped mode, letting you know that you are going to have to wait a bit before the I/O operation is complete.

The code that calls the write function and handles the three possible results is shown here. Note that WriteFile() returns TRUE if the write operation is completed successfully, and FALSE if not. If FALSE is returned, you have to do additional testing to see whether an error occurred or you are simply in overlapped mode.

```
DWORD result_count;
  if ( !WriteFile( m_hPort,
                   data,
                   count,
                   &result_count,
                   &AsyncWriteInfo ) ) {
    if ( GetLastError() == ERROR_IO_PENDING ) {
      switch ( WaitForMultipleObjects( 2,
                                       handles,
                                       FALSE,
                                       INFINITE ) )
      {
        case 0 : //m_hKillOutputThreadEvent
          done = true;
          killed = true;
          PurgeComm( m_hPort, PURGE_TXABORT );
          break;

        case 1 : //AsyncWriteInfo.hEvent
          if ( !GetOverlappedResult( m_hPort,
                                     &AsyncWriteInfo,
                                     &result_count,
                                     FALSE ) ||
               result_count != count )
          {
            if ( GetLastError() == ERROR_IO_PENDING )
              clear_error();
            else
              translate_last_error();
            done = true;
          }
          break;

        default :
          assert( false );
          done = true;
      }
    } else {
      translate_last_error();
      done = true;
    }
```

```
  } else {
  if ( result_count != count ) {
    translate_last_error();
    done = true;
  }
}
```

Note that if `WriteFile()` returns `FALSE`, you check `GetLastError()` to see whether things are working normally. If the current error code is `ERROR_IO_PENDING`, it means an overlapped I/O operation has started and you can now wait for an event to signal that you are done. If some other error code was returned, you call `translate_error()` and return. Member function `translate_error()` is used to convert Win32 error codes to the codes defined in the `RS232` class.

If the file went into overlapped mode, the wait for multiple objects waits for an event to signal that the I/O operation is complete. When that happens, you call Win32 API function `GetOverlappedResult()` to check on the status of the write and the number of characters transferred.

If the write operation succeeded, either immediately or after a delay, you go back to the top of the loop and try to get another batch of data. This iteration through the loop continues until the TX buffer goes empty.

If a failure occurs, the `error_status` member of the object will be set to the appropriate value, putting the port into an error state. Generally, the calling thread will have to do something drastic to repair the error at this point, including closing the port and reopening it.

The input thread

The input thread is a lot more complicated, for several reasons. First, it has to be reading all the time, not just on demand. The output thread can call a worker routine from time to time when there's output to send, and then return to the main body of the thread when done. Because you don't know when incoming data will arrive, the input thread has to be reading all the time.

Second, the input thread has to deal with two different kinds of input. It sets up an overlapped call to receive data with `ReadFile()`, and it also sets up overlapped input of errors and modem status changes with a call to `WaitCommEvent()`. Therefore, there is more code in the first part of the main loop when you have to set up the I/O. Likewise, there is more code immediately after you return from the wait for event call, because there are more things that can happen. Each of them has to be handled, so there is just more code to wade through.

Some of the setup code at the start of the input thread is similar to that of the output thread. The start of `InputThread()` shown here looks similar to the start of the output thread:

```
void Win32Port::InputThread( void * arglist )
{
```

```
Win32Port *port = (Win32Port *) arglist;
OVERLAPPED AsyncReadInfo = { 0 };
OVERLAPPED AsyncStatusInfo = { 0 };
AsyncReadInfo.hEvent = CreateEvent( NULL, TRUE, FALSE, NULL );
AsyncStatusInfo.hEvent = CreateEvent( NULL, TRUE, FALSE, NULL );
```

Just like at the start of the output thread, you first have to acquire a pointer to the object that controls the port by casting the initial argument passed by the Win32 API. You also have to create OVERLAPPED objects that will be used to read data and wait for comm events. Both of these overlapped structures need an event that will be used to signal the thread, so the two events are created before the main loop starts.

Like the output thread, the main loop starts up by initiating a ReadFile() and a WaitForCommEvent(). In addition, the main loop watches for two other events: a kill thread event and an event notifying it that space has opened up in the RX buffer. All together, the four events that will be waited on in the loop are aggregated into an array:

```
HANDLE handles[ 4 ] = { port->m_hKillInputThreadEvent,
                        AsyncReadInfo.hEvent,
                        AsyncStatusInfo.hEvent,
                        port->m_hReadRequestEvent };
```

This is the array that will be used in the call to WaitForMultipleObjects() in the middle of the main loop.

INPUT DATA

The input thread will always have a read operation in progress as long as space is available in the input buffer, m_RxQueue. Read operations are set up with a call to ReadFile(), with a request for up to 500 characters. The actual number of characters is limited to the amount of space available in m_RxQueue, with a maximum of 500. If there is no space at all, the call to ReadFile() is skipped. When there is space, the call is made like this:

```
if ( !ReadFile( port->m_hPort,
                read_buffer,
                bytes_to_read,
                &dwBytesRead,
                &AsyncReadInfo ) )
```

Like the call to WriteFile() seen earlier, the call to ReadFile() can return with success immediately, or fail. On failure, an error code of ERROR_IO_PENDING means that an overlapped read is now in progress and everything is okay. If the call to ReadFile() returns with success, it means it has returned some data for use to process immediately. Any other type of failure means that something bad has happened.

When the `ReadFile()` function returns with an immediate success code, you examine the contents of `dwBytesRead`, which will show how many bytes were read. When that happens, you stuff the received characters into the RX queue and execute a call to the notification routine:

```
if ( dwBytesRead ) {
  port->m_RxQueue.Insert( read_buffer, dwBytesRead );
  port->RxNotify( dwBytesRead );
}
```

If an overlapped read is in effect, you don't process any data until the appropriate event flag is set. When that event flag is detected after a `WaitForMultipleObjects()` call, you have to check the status of the read with a call to `GetOverlappedResult()`:

```
if ( !GetOverlappedResult( port->m_hPort,
                           &AsyncReadInfo,
                           &dwBytesRead,
                           FALSE ) )
{
  assert( GetLastError() == ERROR_OPERATION_ABORTED );
} else {
  if ( dwBytesRead ) {
    port->m_RxQueue.Insert( read_buffer, dwBytesRead );
    port->RxNotify( dwBytesRead );
  }
}
```

Note that this code also takes into account the possibility that the input operation might have been aborted. This can happen when the `FlushRXBuffer()` member function is called.

There are times in the input thread when you won't have a read in progress. This occurs when the RX queue object is full. When that is the case, you simply don't execute the call to `ReadFile()`. You can tell whether the read is in progress by examining the value of a member called `m_bInputThreadReading`, which is set or cleared in the input thread.

When the RX buffer is full, the input thread may find itself stuck in a `WaitForMultipleObjects()` call with nothing happening. When the main thread of the program reads some data out of the `m_RxQueue` object, it needs to tell the input thread that it can wake up and get back to work. This is accomplished by checking the value of `m_bInputThreadReading` whenever the main thread of the program calls member function `Read()`. If some data is read out of the Rx queue, and it appears that the input thread isn't reading, event handle `m_hReadRequest Event` is set. This wakes up the input thread, which will run through its main loop and, ideally, start a read. The code in private member `read_buffer()` (called by public function `Read()`) that makes this happen looks like this:

```
ByteCount = m_RxQueue.Extract( buffer, count );
buffer[ ByteCount ] = '\0';
if ( !m_bInputThreadReading )
    SetEvent( m_hReadRequestEvent );
```

MODEM STATUS AND LINE ERRORS

At the same time that the main loop of the input thread is waiting for data input, it is also waiting for incoming events. The Win32 API has a list of events that it can respond to:

- `EV_BREAK`: An incoming break is detected on the input line.
- `EV_CTS`: The incoming CTS modem status line changed polarity.
- `EV_DSR`: The incoming DSR modem status line changed polarity.
- `EV_ERR`: An incoming line status error was detected. Line status errors can be parity errors, hardware overrun errors, or framing errors.
- `EV_RING`: An incoming ring signal was detected on the RI line.
- `EV_RLSD`: The incoming RLSD/CD modem status line changed parity.
- `EV_RXCHAR`: One or more characters were received and stored in the input buffer.
- `EV_RXFLAG`: The special event character was detected. This is the special character that can be defined in the DCB. You don't use this capability in the `Win32Port` driver.
- `EV_TXEMPTY`: The last character in the driver's buffer has been sent.

You select the events you want to watch for through a call to `SetCommMask()`. Because you want to wait for most of the events listed here, you call `SetCommMask()` once before entering the main loop of the input thread:

```
SetCommMask( port->m_hPort,
             EV_BREAK  | EV_CTS   | EV_DSR   | EV_RXCHAR |
             EV_ERR    | EV_RING  | EV_RLSD  | EV_RINGTE );
```

Note that you also add the undocumented `EV_RINGTE` to the list of events you're watching for. This constant is defined in `Win32Port.h`, so don't look for it in your

Windows header files. Under Windows 95 and 98, the `EV_RINGTE` event is fired on the trailing edge of the incoming RI modem status line, which allows you to properly detect incoming ring. The `EV_RING` event doesn't work properly and shouldn't be relied on.

After the mask is properly set up, you initiate your wait for comm events with a call to `WaitCommEvent()`. This function operates just like `ReadFile()` in that it can return immediately with success if there are pending events. If there are no pending events, it should return with a failure indication and an error code of `ERROR_IO_PENDING`. If the function fails with a different error code, it means something bad has happened. The normal invocation looks like this:

```
if ( !WaitCommEvent( port->m_hPort,
                     &dwCommEvent,
                     &AsyncStatusInfo ) ) {
  assert( GetLastError() == ERROR_IO_PENDING );
  waiting_on_status = true;
} else {
  port->check_modem_status( false, dwCommEvent );
  port->clear_error();
}
```

In the preceding code, the call to `WaitCommEvent()` can return an error of `ERROR_IO_PENDING`, in which case you just set a flag indicating that you are going to wait for a status message. If the function returns a success indication, it means that you some events are pending immediately. You deal with incoming events in the two member functions `check_modem_status()` and `clear_error()`, which are discussed in the next section.

If the function doesn't return its result immediately, you move into the main loop where you wait for one of the events to be set. When the event flag is set, you have to check the result with a call to `GetOverlappedResult()`. Just like when you call the function after a call to `ReadFile()` completes, you have to take into account the possibility of an error. If you don't see one, it means you can process the status events with a calls to `check_modem_status()` and `clear_error()`:

```
DWORD dwOverlappedResult;
if ( !GetOverlappedResult( port->m_hPort,
                           &AsyncStatusInfo,
                           &dwOverlappedResult,
                           FALSE ) ) {
  assert( GetLastError() == ERROR_OPERATION_ABORTED );
} else {
  port->check_modem_status( false, dwCommEvent );
  port->clear_error();
}
```

Two functions are called when a status event is detected: `check_modem_status()` and `clear_error()`. The first function monitors the state of the modem status lines and keeps track of them for the other members of the class. The second function keeps track of line status errors for the other members of the class, plus it clears the errors so that communications can continue.

The public member functions of class `Win32Port` that actually check the state of the line status errors and modem lines don't call the Win32 API functions that check those values. Instead, they just check the internal data stored by calls to `check_modem_status()` and `clear_error()`. For example, every time that an event is detected, `check_modem_status()` reads the current modem line states into a member called `m_dwModemStatus`:

```
GetCommModemStatus( m_hPort, &m_dwModemStatus );
```

Because this notification routine will be called every time a modem status line changes, you can be confident that `m_dwModemStatus` contains the current state of those lines. Thus, a function that returns one of the modem status bits to the caller doesn't have to call the windows API:

```
int Win32Port::Cts()
{
    return ( MS_CTS_ON & m_dwModemStatus ) != 0;
}
```

The line status members are maintained in a similar fashion. However, the internal state for the line status bits are maintained in a cumulative fashion. Every time you read in a new set of line status bits, the new values are ORed with the current cumulative value:

```
DWORD errors;
ClearCommError( m_hPort, &errors, comstat );
m_dwErrors |= errors;
```

The routines that read the line status bits have the option of clearing the bit in addition to just reading it. Those routines typically look like this:

```
return_value = m_dwErrors & CE_BREAK;
if ( clear != UNCHANGED && clear != 0 )
    m_dwErrors &= ~CE_BREAK;
return return_value;
```

Notification

The input and output threads do more than just collect data for the main thread to analyze. They also perform notification of key events as they occur. These notification messages allow the program using class Win32Port to be event driven, which is a nice way to write Windows programs.

The eleven notification routines in class Win32Port are all virtual functions that do absolutely nothing. This means that, by default, your program won't receive any notification messages. To enable notification, you must create a new class that is derived directly from Win32Port. You can then write your own virtual notification routines that will be called by the input and output threads as things happen.

The demo program for the Win32Port class does just that, creating a new class called MyWin32Port, with just a constructor, eleven virtual functions, and a member that contains the handle of a notification window. The notification functions are extremely short, doing nothing more than sending a Windows message to the main window of the program.

It's important to minimize the amount of work you do in the notification routines. Because they are being called from a different thread of execution, you run the risk of running into serious problems if you attempt to access any data structures that are in use by your main thread. My technique of sending a Windows message and then returning is an easy way to send a signal to the main thread of your program in a thread-safe fashion. When you receive the message in your main thread, you are free to act on it without restrictions.

Five of the notification functions are sent from clear_error(). This function is called with an error mask that you can check. You examine each of the bits found in the error word returned from ClearCommError() and call the appropriate routines:

```
if ( errors & CE_BREAK )
  BreakDetectNotify();
if ( errors & CE_FRAME )
  FramingErrorNotify();
if ( errors & CE_OVERRUN )
  HardwareOverrunErrorNotify();
if ( errors & CE_RXPARITY )
  ParityErrorNotify();
if ( errors & CE_RXOVER )
  SoftwareOverrunErrorNotify();
```

Four of the notification routines are called from the check_modem_status() routine. Three of the routines (notification routines for CD/RLSD, CTS, and DSR) pass in the current state of the input control line so that the program knows whether the line is high or low. The fourth notification routine, OnRiNotify(), is always called with a parameter of 0. Normally, the 8250 family of UARTs doesn't generate an event when RI goes high, only when it goes low. The implementation of OnRiNotify() here reflects this.

The final two routines are RxNotify() and TxNotify(). The first is called anytime new data is read from the driver and put in the Win32Port object's m_RxQueue.

The second is called when a write operation leaves `m_TxQueue` completely empty. (Note that there may still be as many as 500 bytes in the driver's buffer.) Using these two routines to trigger I/O can give you a very efficient program.

To help programs start up properly, `TxNotify()` is called when the port is first opened. The four modem status routines are also called with the current state of their respective lines when the program starts. This gives your program the ability to maintain information about the state of the modem lines without ever reading the values directly. That's the way the demo program operates.

Class member overview

You've seen class `RS232` implemented in quite a few different fashions throughout the book; `Win32Port` is yet another example. Class `Win32Port` is derived directly from class `RS232` and implements its required functions in a very standard way. The two striking differences between this class and other implementations of class `RS232` from this book are the following:

1. The actual interface with the serial ports is done in separate threads of execution. Outside of configuration calls, the main thread in your program won't call any functions that talk directly to the serial API.

2. The class provides a set of events that let you do your programming in nonsequential fashion. Windows programs, or at least their GUI components, work by responding to events from the user and the O/S. With class `Win32Port`, you have the opportunity to write your comm program to do nearly all its work in response to various events, such as the transmit buffer going empty.

Now that you've had a chance to see how the worker threads work, you should be able to follow the routines that make up the rest of the class. I look first at the public member functions defined in this class, and then at the private functions that do much of the real work.

If you encounter some rough spots trying to understand what various members do, review the operations of the two worker threads; then examine the commented source attached to the end of Chapter 12.

WIN32PORT PUBLIC MEMBER FUNCTIONS

These are the functions that you will call directly in order to use the `Win32Port` class. This section of the chapter describes the functions and their arguments.

```
Win32Port( const string &port_name,
           long baud_rate = UNCHANGED,
           char parity = UNCHANGED,
           int word_length = UNCHANGED,
           int stop_bits = UNCHANGED,
```

```
int dtr = SET,
int rts = SET,
int xon_xoff = DISABLE,
int rts_cts = DISABLE,
int dtr_dsr = DISABLE )
```

This is the constructor for class `Win32Port`. It attempts to open and initialized the given comm port. If the initialization succeeds, the various port parameters are written into the device, and the input and output threads are started. If the initialization fails, the port is left in an unopened state. You can tell the difference between the two states by simply examining the `error_status` member of the class immediately after constructing the port. An `error_status` value less than 0 means the port is nonfunctioning:

```
RS232 *port = new Win32Port( "COM2", 19200 );
if ( port->ErrorStatus() < RS232_SUCCESS ) {
    delete port;
    AfxMessageBox( "Port failed to open!" );
    return;
}
```

Note that this constructor differs slightly from the constructors that you have used in other device types seen elsewhere in the book. Rather than pass an integer value ranging from COM1 through COM8 for the port name, you actually pass a string. There are two reasons for this. First, a serial port under Win32 can have a name that doesn't fit into the COMx naming structure, such as MODEM34. Second, ports with a number greater than 9 have to be opened with a name like \\.\COM10, which means that you need a little bit more flexibility than you have with simple integers.

Most of the default parameters can be left off the constructor when opening a port. In fact, most applications will work properly if just the port name and baud rate are passed in, with everything else left as a default parameter.

> **NOTE** This class also has a default constructor that does nothing but initialize the input and output queues. It is used by derived classes that want to perform their own startup. The TAPI class described in a later chapter uses this constructor. See `Win32Port.h` for details.

```
~Win32Port()
```

The destructor for this class has to perform quite a few important cleanup items in order to free up all the resources that were allocated when the port is opened. The first and most important thing that needs to happen is the killing of the input and output threads. You do this by setting the two events that direct the threads to terminate, and then waiting for the system to signal that this has happened.

After that completes, the only remaining task is to close the port and then destroy all the events that have been created to support the class.

```
RS232Error Set( long baud_rate = UNCHANGED,
                int parity = UNCHANGED,
                int word_length = UNCHANGED,
                int stop_bits = UNCHANGED )
```

This function is defined in the base class and is overridden here. Because of various support functions, the implementation of the routine is very simple. Function `Settings::Adjust()` is called to update all the appropriate members of the `settings` member of the base class. The updated members are then written out to the driver by calling private member functions `write_settings()`. The new values should take effect immediately.

```
int Dtr( int setting = UNCHANGED )
int Rts( int setting = UNCHANGED )
```

These two functions do the same thing, which is to change the current setting of an output modem control line. Both functions do their work by first adjusting the appropriate member of the `settings` member of the class and then calling `write_settings()` to let the driver know that things should change. The return value of the function will be 0 or 1 if the current setting is okay. A value of `WIN32_HANDSHAKE_LINE_IN_USE` will be returned if an attempt was made to modify the state of the line while it is being used for handshaking.

Both of these functions can be called with no argument at all, in which case the default argument value of `UNCHANGED` is passed in. When this is the case, the `settings` member is not modified and `write_settings()` isn't called. The current setting of the modem control line is returned, which is all the caller normally wants when the function is called with no arguments.

```
int TXSpaceFree()
int TXSpaceUsed()
int RXSpaceUsed()
int RXSpaceFree()
```

All four of these functions call member functions of either m_RxQueue or m_TxQueue to return the appropriate number. One important thing to note about these functions is that you don't take into account any data that is present in the Win32 driver's buffers, which makes these figures slightly misleading. Because you use relatively small buffers in the driver (500 bytes), this oversight is probably not too significant. The class could be modified to use the driver's buffer size as well, but this is probably not a critical piece of information.

```
int DtrDsrHandshaking( int setting = UNCHANGED )
int RtsCtsHandshaking( int setting = UNCHANGED )
int XonXoffHandshaking( int setting = UNCHANGED )
```

These three functions are used to set and/or read the three different types of handshaking that can be used on a Win32Port object. If the function is called with no arguments, it simply returns the current setting. If it is called with a specific value, the setting is updated.

The three versions of this function all operate in exactly the same way. This code fragment that modifies DTR/DSR handshaking is nearly identical to the same code for the other two types of handshaking.

```
if ( setting != UNCHANGED ) {
   settings.DtrDsr = setting != 0;
   RS232Error error = write_settings();
   if ( error < RS232_SUCCESS )
       return error;
}
return settings.DtrDsr;
```

As you can see, all you have to do is modify the current value of the given member in the settings structure (which is a member of the base class, RS232.) After that, the member function write_settings() takes care of doing the hard work, which is to update the state of the driver.

You'll see this same type of operation for all the other attributes that are controlled by values in the settings structure: an easy modification of a member of the structure, followed by a call to write_settings().

```
int FormatDebugOutput( char *buffer = 0, int line_number = -1 )
```

This function is used to create lines of debug output for help in debugging. An example of how you might use it in a program looks like this:

```
char buffer[ 82 ];
DWORD written = 0;
for ( int i = 0 ; i < m_pPort->DebugLineCount() ; i++ ) {
```

```
            m_pPort->FormatDebugOutput( buffer, i );
            strcat( buffer, "\n" );
            WriteConsole( m_hConsoleOutput,
                          buffer,
      strlen( buffer ),
      &written,
      0 );
            }
}
```

The preceding code is lifted directly from the test program developed for class Win32Port. The output is shown in Figure 11-2.

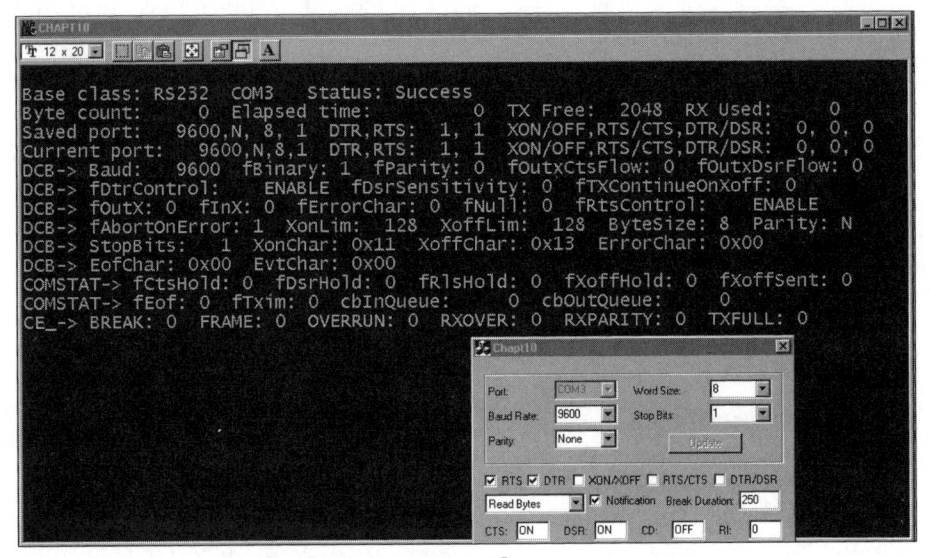

Figure 11-2: The output from FormatDebugOutput()

FormatDebugOutput() is an interesting function because it doesn't work exactly the way you expect most virtual functions to work. Instead of completely taking over the role of the base class, the RS232 version of FormatDebugOutput() expects to work in cooperation with the version of the base class.

In the preceding example, the first four lines of debug output are actually generated by the base class. That is possible because the Win32Port version of this function passes the responsibility up to the base class using this code:

```
if ( line_number < first_debug_output_line )
      return RS232::FormatDebugOutput( buffer, line_number );
```

Chapter 11: The Win32Port Class

The value of `first_debug_output_line` is set up in the constructor of the port by calling the base class version of `FormatDebugOutput()` with a buffer argument of 0.

The version of this function that does the next nine lines of output is just a fairly pedestrian dump of internal data. Six of the lines are needed just to dump the contents of the DCB. The next two lines are called to dump the current contents of the `COMSTAT` structure returned by a call to `ClearCommError()`. This data includes the current state of the driver's handshaking, as well as the amount of space in use in the input and output driver buffers.

The final line of debug output is used to display the current setting of all the error bits in `m_dwErrors`, the cumulative error word. This is the word that is ORed with the any new errors read in during the call to `ClearCommError()`.

Adding additional lines of output to this class is fairly simple. If you derive a new class from `Win32Port`, you can use the version of `Win32Port::FormatDebugOutput()` as a model. Simply defer all possible calls to the `Win32Port` version of the function, and don't start printing your own version out until all of the two base class lines have been formatted. This also implies that you will have your own private copy of the `first_debug_output_line` member.

In your private class constructor, you would include a line like this that determines how many lines of output the two base classes would use:

```
MyClass::MyClass()
{
    .
    .
    .
    first_debug_output_line = Win32Port::FormatDebugOutput();
```

Then you would write your own function that started like this:

```
int MyClass::FormatDebugOutput( char *buffer, int line_number )
{
  if ( buffer == 0 )
    return( first_debug_output_line + XXX );
  if ( line_number < first_debug_output_line )
    return Win32Port::FormatDebugOutput( buffer, line_number );
  switch ( line_number - first_debug_output_line ) {
  case 0 :
    sprintf( buffer,
             "My formated data: %x",
```

In this code fragment, XXX is the count of lines that your formatted output will add to the output stream.

```
int ParityError( int clear = UNCHANGED )
int BreakDetect( int clear = UNCHANGED )
int FramingError( int clear = UNCHANGED )
int HardwareOverrunError( int clear = UNCHANGED )
int SoftwareOverrunError( int clear = UNCHANGED )
```

These five functions are all designed to report and optionally clear errors that are detected through calls to `ClearCommError()`. Each of the errors sets a different bit in an error word that is ORed in with `m_dwErrors` each time `ClearCommError()` is called. All five routines have basically the same code, which looks similar to this core code from `ParityError()`:

```
return_value = ( m_dwErrors & CE_RXPARITY ) != 0;
if ( clear != UNCHANGED && clear != 0 )
    m_dwErrors &= ~CE_RXPARITY;
return return_value;
```

The return value is derived from a simple test to see whether the given bit is set in `m_dwErrors`. The bit can optionally be cleared after its state is read in.

```
int Break( long milliseconds = 300 )
```

Under many of our other drivers, a command to send a break was handled by simply stopping whatever you were doing, setting the break output on a UART, and then waiting in a hard spin loop for a time delay to complete.

This strategy doesn't work under Win32 for a couple of reasons. First, the output to the UART is actually controlled by the output thread, and that will be a different thread from the one that actually calls the `Break()` function. Second, tight loops that wait for a fixed delay are viewed poorly by Windows programmers, for good reasons.

So your job in this function is to set an event that wakes up the output thread and asks it to send a break. You also need to pass the time desired for the break, which you do in a slightly convoluted method. Instead of attempting to pass the actual number to the output thread, you just set the `m_iBreakDuration` member of the class and let the output thread get the value there.

The code that does this also limits the duration of the break to 1000 ms. This might seem a bit rigid to you, but you need to keep in mind that the output thread is locked up tight for the duration of the break. If you inadvertently sent a break duration of 10 years, you might have trouble destroying your `Win32Port` object when the time comes.

Chapter 11: The Win32Port Class

This is the core code from the `Break()` function:

```
if ( milliseconds > 1000 )
    m_iBreakDuration = 1000;
else
    m_iBreakDuration = milliseconds;
SetEvent( m_hBreakRequestEvent );
```

```
int Cd( void )
int Ri( void )
int Cts( void )
int Dsr( void )
```

These four functions all read modem status bits. The `Win32Port` driver doesn't allow the main thread to talk directly to the Win32 driver to read these items. Instead, it insists that it examine the state of the modem lines stored in member `m_dwModemStatus`. This is the `DWORD` that is updated with the current status every time a status event is reported by the call to `WaitCommEvent()` function call.

The core code for all four routines looks something like this:

```
return ( MS_RLSD_ON & m_dwModemStatus ) != 0;
```

This is just a test of the appropriate bit in `m_dwModemStatus`. You're obviously depending on the fact that the input thread will see a status event every time a modem status line changes.

```
int Peek( void *buffer, unsigned int count )
```

The `Peek()` function is designed to read as many bytes as requested from the input buffer without actually removing them from the buffer. The `Win32Port` interpretation of this member function looks for bytes only in the `m_RxQueue` member. Although some bytes may be in the driver buffer that don't have visibility to the `Peek()` member, this architecture insures that those bytes will move out of the driver's buffer an into the `Win32Port::m_RxQueue` member quickly.

The actual mechanism by which this movement takes place is the `MTdeque::Peek()` function. This function uses the `MTdeque`'s critical section to protect the object during the process of transferring the bytes to the buffer passed to the `Peek()` function.

```
int FlushRXBuffer( void )
```

The goal of this function is to completely flush all incoming RX data that has been read by the UART. In the configuration used by `Win32Port`, there are two different buffers that could each contain some data: the `m_RxQueue` member of the class and the driver's internal buffer. The first can be cleared using the `MTdeque::Clear()` member function, and the second can be cleared with the Win32 API function `PurgeComm()`.

After performing both of these functions, you are now left with a possible complication. If the input thread was not reading data because of a full buffer, you need to give it a wake-up call so that it will start reading again. You do so by setting the same event that is used to wake up the Input thread when some data is read. The final core code of this function looks like this:

```
m_RxQueue.Clear();
PurgeComm( m_hPort, PURGE_RXCLEAR );
if ( !m_bInputThreadReading )
    SetEvent( m_hReadRequestEvent );
```

The last line of code in the above fragment will wake up the input thread if it was idling because of a full buffer.

`int FlushTXBuffer( void )`

This function has the same basic problem as the previous one. It has to delete all the data from two different output buffers: the `m_TxQueue` member of class `Win32Port`, and the internal driver's buffer. It takes care of this by first clearing the `m_TxQueue` buffer owned by the `Win32Port` object and then calling the Win32 API function `PurgeComm()` with the `PURGE_TXCLEAR` argument to clear the driver's buffer.

`char *ErrorName( int error )`

This function is similar to `FormatDebugOutput()` in that it doesn't follow the traditional role of a virtual function in a derived class. Instead of completely superseding the functionality of `RS232::ErrorName()`, this function merely adds a bit to it. It does so by calling `RS232::ErrorName()` to translate the error names that were defined in the base class, and performing translation only on the functions defined in `Win32Port.h`.

WIN32PORT PROTECTED MEMBER FUNCTIONS

These functions are protected and, as such, will not be called directly by users of the `Win32Port` class. A few of these functions are virtual functions defined in the base class as utility functions; the remainders are utility functions used internally by other members of the class.

`int read_buffer( char *buffer, unsigned int count )`

This function is defined as pure virtual in the base class RS232. Its job is to supply bytes from the input port to function RS232::Read(void *). The Read() function in the base class is the one called by users of the class; it takes care of managing timeouts and a few other items. All read_buffer() has to do is get as many characters as it can out of the buffer as soon as possible.

In class Win32Port, that is a fairly easy task. All read_buffer() has to do is call MTdeque::Extract() and ask for count characters. The resulting count is returned and stored in member ByteCount, which is used by RS232::Read().

read_buffer() has to take into account the possibility that the input thread has stopped reading data for lack of room. If it reads some characters in from m_RxQueue and afterward sees that the m_bInputThreadReading member is still false, it sets event m_hReadRequestEvent so that the input thread will wake up and attempt to call ReadFile() again.

```
int write_buffer( char *buffer, unsigned int count = -1 )
```

This function is also defined as pure virtual in the base class RS232. The Write(void *) function in class RS232 depends on write_buffer() to do the actual work of writing bytes to the device. This function in turn must be defined by the derived class and must implement an interface to the device in question.

For class Win32Port, the write_buffer() function has just two things to do. First, it has to insert as many characters as possible into the m_TxQueue member, keeping track of the exact number that were transferred in ByteCount. Second, it has to set the m_hWriteRequestEvent event to let the output thread know that some data has been added to the queue. If the output thread was in an idle state, this action will wake it up and put it to work.

The key lines of code in this routine are as follows:

```
ByteCount = m_TxQueue.Insert( buffer, count );
::SetEvent( m_hWriteRequestEvent );
```

If the output thread is idle when write_buffer() is called, setting the event will ensure that it wakes up and starts processing the output buffer.

```
int read_byte( void )
```

Like read_buffer(), read_byte() is declared as pure virtual in the base class RS232. It is used by the Read() function that reads a single character. It does the same work as read_buffer(), just one byte at a time.

```
Int write_byte( int c )
```

This function is the single character counterpart to write_buffer(). It, too, is declared as pure virtual in the base class, meaning that it must be defined in a derived class. It is used by `RS232::Write( int c )` to perform the actual transfer of characters to the Win32 device driver. Internally, it is nearly identical to `write_buffer()`, with a buffer size of 1 byte.

`RS232Error write_settings()`

This function is called in the constructor and in any other function that modifies any of the `settings` member of the class. It takes care of setup for the standard port parameters common to all devices derived from class `RS232`:

- Baud Rate
- Parity
- Word Length
- Stop Bits
- DTR
- RTS
- DTR/DSR Handshaking
- RTS/CTS Handshaking
- XON/XOFF Handshaking

The functions (including the constructor) that modify these values in the `settings` member of the class then call `write_settings()`. `write_settings()` takes its current values and modifies the settings of the DCB to correspond to them. It then calls the Win32 API function `SetCommState()`, which takes the contents of the `DCB` and updates the physical device.

`void read_settings()`

This function is called in the `Win32Port` constructor. It calls the Win32 API function `GetCommState()`, which reads the current state of the comm port into a temporary `DCB`. The values in that temporary `DCB` are then parsed and stored in the `settings` structure.

The constructor calls this function so that it can read the settings of the port and store them in the base class member `saved_settings`. You go along with this theory in class `Win32Port` by reading the port settings right after you open it, and storing them off. However, you don't go along with the basic philosophy of class `RS232`, which holds that you should restore a port to the condition you found it in when you are done with it.

There really isn't any point in restoring the port to the condition you found it in under Win32. Before you open the port, Windows arbitrarily sets it to a specific default configuration, which means that the concept of any previous state is bogus. Even more important, under Win32, you can't borrow a port from another application, use it for a while, and then give it back in the same state you found it in. After you close a port, anything you did to it while it was open is quickly forgotten by the O/S. The next person to open it will see it once again in the default condition dictated by the O/S.

```
void check_modem_status( bool first_time, DWORD event_mask )
```

This is an extremely important protected member of class `Win32Port`. It is used only internally by the class and in fact is called only from the input thread. The input thread calls this function two different times. Normally, it calls it whenever it receives an event from the `WaitCommEvent()` call it makes. This can happen immediately after the function is called, or after an overlapped wait.

The function is also called when the input thread first starts up. When that happens, it is called with the `first_time` argument set to `TRUE`. For both functions, argument `event_mask` is passed in with a mask showing which modem status lines have changed.

When the function is first called, before doing anything else, it reads in the current settings of the modem status lines via a call to `GetModemStatus()`:

```
GetCommModemStatus( m_hPort, &m_dwModemStatus );
```

Note that the results of the read go into the class member `m_dwModemStatus`. If the main thread calls any of the functions that query the settings of the modem status lines, they will actually get their results from this member.

After reading in the modem status, the function then has to perform notification. This consists of making calls to the virtual notification routines:

- ◆ `CtsNotify()`
- ◆ `DsrNotify()`
- ◆ `CdNotify()`
- ◆ `RiNotify()`

The purpose of these notification calls is to let an application that is using notification always have the current settings of the modem status lines. Each of the notification lines is called for one of two reasons. First, if the `first_time` argument is true, notification is always called. This action ensures that the user's application will be properly initialized with the current modem settings. Second, if the `event_mask` parameter has the appropriate mask bit set (masks used here are `EV_CTS`, `EV_DSR`, `EV_RLSD`, `EV_RING`, and `EV_RINGTE`), the corresponding notification event is called. Checking for the presence of the event mask keeps you from calling the notification function when nothing has changed.

One final note about modem status line notification. The 8250 UART is designed to generate an interrupt when the state of modem input lines CTS, DSR, and CD change state, either from low to high or high to low. This isn't the case with the RI line. The UART is programmed to generate an interrupt only on the trailing edge of the RI line. This restriction allows users of the UART to count rings by simply counting notification events.

The designers of the Win32 serial API were somewhat confused about this mode of operation. Even though the 8250 family UARTs don't make it possible, the Win32 driver team supports an EV_RING comm event, which appears to be designed to fire when RI goes from low to high or high to low. This event doesn't work properly under Win95 and Win98. It fires from time to time, but apparently only when RI is high at the time that one of the other three input lines changes state.

The undocumented event EV_RINGTE actually works the way the 8250 designers expected their part to be used. It fires an event every time the RI line goes from high to low. This is good, but it presents a bit of a problem for the notification function user. It means that every time RiNotify() is called, it will be passed a state value of 0. Therefore, your application should consider an invocation of RiNotify() to mean that a single incoming ring has occurred, regardless of whether the state passed in is one or zero.

```
void clear_error( COMSTAT *comstat = 0 )
```

This function is analogous to check_modem_status(). It is called whenever the input thread sees an incoming event from a call to WaitCommEvent(). Its job is to call ClearCommError(), which tells it whether any line status or other software buffer overflow errors have occurred. If they have, the appropriate bits are ORed into the m_dwErrors class member and the relevant notification routines are called.

The code that checks the error and then updates the status word in the class looks something like this:

```
DWORD errors;
ClearCommError( m_hPort, &errors, comstat );
m_dwErrors |= errors;
```

This function cares only about the four standard UART line status errors, plus the software buffer overflow error that is generated. There may be other errors generated by the Win32 device driver, but they are ignored by this routine. (Of course, they are still cleared, allowing the port to continue operation.)

The five member functions that allow a caller in the main thread to check the status of these errors just tests the m_dwErrors member for the presence of the specific bit in question. The result of that test is returned to the calling thread.

Unlike check_modem_status(), this function is called from a couple of other places in the class. It is called from FormatDebugString() because that routine needs to fill in the contents of a COMSTAT object by calling ClearCommErrror().

(It needs the `COMSTAT` object in order to check on the number of bytes in use in the driver's buffer.) Because a line status error can be flagged on any call to `Clear CommError()`, it makes sense to call it in only one routine. That way, no error detection or notification will be missed by a coding oversight.

`RS232Error translate_last_error()`

This function is called when a fatal error on the port occurs. Its job is to translate the Win32 error code returned from the Win32 API call `GetLastError()` into an internal error code. At this time, the function translates only two Windows errors into errors supported by the class:

```
switch ( m_dwWindowsError = GetLastError() )
{
    case ERROR_ACCESS_DENIED  :
        return error_status = RS232_PORT_IN_USE;
    case ERROR_FILE_NOT_FOUND :
        return error_status = RS232_PORT_NOT_FOUND;
}
return error_status = (RS232Error) WIN32_CHECK_WINDOWS_ERROR;
```

If the Windows error doesn't match up with either of these predefined error codes, the catch-all error code of `WIN32_CHECK_WINDOWS_ERROR` is returned. This directs the end user's program to look at the value stored in `m_dwWindowsError` to see what caused the failure.

```
bool output_worker();
void OutputThread( void * arglist );
void InputThread( void *arglist );
```

These three functions do most of the work for the input and output thread. They are discussed earlier in this chapter.

WIN32PORT NOTIFICATION MEMBER FUNCTIONS

The functions in this section are called by other routines in class `Win32Port` to notify your application that some event has occurred. You will normally use a class derived from `Win32Port` that overrides these functions, customizing them to notify your program in the manner that works best for you.

`void RxNotify( int byte_count )`

This routine is called by the input thread every time any data is actually read in from the serial port. The single argument is passed to the caller to give an exact count of bytes that have been read in for this particular call.

This notification routine is used to do all the I/O for the demo program, in a manner which works well for a terminal emulator. The demo program defines a derived class, `MyWin32Port`, that has an implementation of this function. The derived version of the function simply sends a Windows message to the main window of the program.

That main window of the program handles the message in a routine called `OnRxNotify`: This routine then merely has to read in all the data that is ready in the queue and display it on the screen. The inner part of the routine looks like this:

```
for ( ; ; ) {
  char buffer[ 128 ];
  int result = m_pPort->Read( buffer, 127 ) ;
  if ( m_pPort->ByteCount == 0 )
    break;
  DWORD written = 0;
  WriteConsole( m_hConsoleOutput,
                &buffer,
                m_pPort->ByteCount,
                &written, 0 );
}
```

The beauty of using this method is that main program doesn't have to spend any time polling the port; it simply waits to be told that there is some incoming data ready to process.

`void TxNotify()`

This notification routine is called when the output thread has just emptied the `m_TxQueue` buffer. This is a good time to send more data, because there should still be plenty of characters making their way through the device driver buffer and out to the UART. If the 500-byte internal driver buffer is completely filled by the output thread, there is more than enough time to call the `Write()` member function and ensure that the pipeline stays full.

Sometimes you may want your RS-232 driver to let you know when all the internal buffers are actually emptied. Although class `Win32Port` doesn't perform this particular type of notification, you could modify the class to do this, because the serial API provides a message letting you know when the internal TX buffers are empty.

The sample program uses the TX notification in two different ways. First, it keeps a count of TX notification events (as long as the Notification check box is selected) and updates the count so that you can see it in action. Second, the sample program uses the TX notification event when it is in spew mode.

Spew mode in the sample is enabled by clicking the Spew button. When this mode is turned on, the app automatically sends a new line of text every time a TX notification message arrives. This creates a steady stream of output data without putting too much of a burden on the application.

```
void ParityErrorNotify()
void FramingErrorNotify()
void HardwareOverrunErrorNotify()
void SoftwareOverrunErrorNotify()
void BreakDetectNotify()
```

These five functions all get called from the `clear_error()` function, and only from that function. `clear_error()` is normally called only from the input thread when status events are returned from the call to `WaitCommEvent()`, but it can also be called from the `FormatDebugOutput()` routine.

The demo program doesn't take any interesting action when it sees these errors; it simply updates an error counter for each of the possible error types and prints it out to an edit control associated with the particular error.

```
void CtsNotify( bool status )
void DsrNotify( bool status )
void CdNotify( bool status )
void RiNotify( bool status )
```

These functions get called only from `check_modem_status()`, which is called only from the input thread. All the member functions are called when the thread first starts up, guaranteeing that the calling program will have an accurate report on the state of all modem lines, even if they never change.

Every time the call to `WaitCommEvent()` returns with new input, you check the state of all modem lines and call the appropriate notification lines for any changed data. As is mentioned many times in this chapter, you will not normally see a notification message when the RI line goes from low to high, but only when it drops from high to low. This fact means that you should get only a single notification message on each incoming ring.

WIN32PORT CONSTANTS

The Win32Port class has a couple of constants defined for use within the class. You won't need to use them in your application code.

```
MAX_INPUT_BUFFER_SIZE
MAX_OUTPUT_BUFFER_SIZE
```

These two values are defined as enumerated types in class `Win32Port`, which is really just a sneaky way of defining constant values. They determine the size of the `MTQueue` objects that hold the input and output buffers. They are presently defined as 2048 bytes each but are obviously quite easy to change.

The size of the internal buffers used by the Win32 drivers is currently hardcoded as 500 for both input and output. This might be a good value to convert into a constant, but it would need to be done with care because the size of the device driver's buffer might affect other code in a few places.

EV_RINGTE = 0x2000

This is the undocumented event type that you use for tracking incoming ring events. Under Windows 95/98, EV_RINGTE detects incoming rings the way you want it to; EV_RING doesn't.

WIN32PORT DATA MEMBERS

Most of the data members in this class are protected, so you won't use them in your program. They are documented here to help you understand the class listings in Chapter 12.

HANDLE m_hPort

This is the HANDLE value that is returned from the call to CreateFile() made in the constructor. More or less every function call to the Win32 API related to the serial port expects to see this member as a parameter. Note that although this is usually a valid port handle, it might be set to INVALID_HANDLE_VALUE or 0 if the port didn't open. When this is the case, the error_status member of the base class should reflect that the port is not in a good state.

int m_iBreakDuration

This member sets the duration of a break in milliseconds. When the main thread of your application calls the Break() function, the duration argument it passes to the call is stored in this member. When the output thread gets around to actually performing the break, it looks in this member to see how long it should keep the break active.

int first_debug_output_line

This member holds the value of the first debug output line that you print in this class, instead of deferring to the base class. When the object is first constructed, a call is made to RS232::FormatDebugOutput() to see how many lines of output it reserves to itself. When Win32Port::FormatDebugOutput() is called, it checks this value to see whether it should attempt to format the line itself or whether it should pass it up to the base class.

bool m_bInputThreadReading

Chapter 11: The Win32Port Class

The section of this chapter discussing the input and output thread shows that the input thread will always have a read in progress as long as there is room in the m_RxQueue member of the class. As long as that is the case, this member is set to true. When m_RxQueue is full, no more reads can be scheduled and this member is set to false.

One of the more useful things you do with this member is use it to check to see whether input is stalled after you read some data from m_RxQueue. If input is disabled after you have removed some bytes from the queue, you can restart it by setting the appropriate event.

DWORD m_dwWindowsError

Any of the Win32 API calls that can generate an error will read in the error and store it in this member. If the error_status member of the object is set to WIN32_CHECK_WINDOWS_ERROR, the caller needs to examine this DWORD value to see what Windows didn't like.

long m_hOutputThread
long m_hInputThread

These two handles refer to the input and output threads. Those threads should be active the whole time the port is open. When it comes time to destroy the object, the destructor waits for an event to be signaled on each of these handles before exiting. A signal on the thread handle means that the thread has exited.

MTdeque m_TxQueue
MTdeque m_RxQueue

These two objects hold the queues that contain all the input or output data for the port. They are supplemented somewhat by the internal buffers of the Win32 drivers, which are generally somewhat smaller. But these buffers are the ones you have control over, and they are where you do all of your writes and reads.

Dcb m_Dcb

This member contains the current DCB for the port. Nearly all the port's operating parameters are controlled by the DCB. Normally, changing something like the baud rate is done by first modifying the value in this member and then calling SetCommState() with the port handler and a pointer to this member.

DWORD m_dwErrors

Whenever an error event is detected by a return value from the call to WaitCommEvent(), the resulting error bits are ORed in with this value. That makes m_dwErrors a cumulative repository for the five error bits that are detected this way. The calls to see whether the errors are set check this DWORD to see whether the corresponding bit is set. When those same calls are called with an attempt to clear the given errors, the bit is cleared in this word.

DWORD m_dwModemStatus

This DWORD contains all the modem status bits that are read in after every event detected by a return from WaitCommEvent(). The main thread never gets to check the modem status bits directly by polling the driver; it always has to check this DWORD to see what the current settings are.

HANDLE m_hKillOutputThreadEvent
HANDLE m_hKillInputThreadEvent

These two events are used to kill the input and output threads. They are set only when the destructor decides that it is time to shut those threads down. Every time the two threads call WaitForMultipleEvents() in their main loop, one of the things they are waiting for is one of these two events.

HANDLE m_hWriteRequestEvent

When the m_TxQueue member of the class has been drained of all its data, the output thread stops transmitting and just idles. When the main thread of your program loads some more data into m_TxQueue for transmission, it calls this routine to notify the output thread that there is some more data to transmit. The output thread is always waiting on this flag in its call to WaitForMultipleEvnets(), so it will always wake up when this event is set.

HANDLE m_hReadRequestEvent

When the m_RxQueue buffer gets full, the input thread has to stop reading and just kill time waiting for another thread to use some of the data and make more space in the buffer. When that happens, the thread that freed up space in the buffer sets this event. That wakes up the input thread so that it can fire off another call to ReadFile(), attempting to fill the space that was just opened up in the m_RxQueue buffer.

HANDLE m_hBreakRequestEvent

When the main thread of your program wants to send a break, it doesn't call the SetCommBreak() function of the Win32 API directly. Instead, it sets this event, which eventually wakes up the output thread. The output thread then takes care of generating the break.

Helper class — MTDeque

Data objects that are accessed from multiple threads live in great peril. Anytime two threads start trying to modify a data structure at the same time, there is potential for serious trouble. Things get even worse when you have a multiprocessor computer on which two threads can truly be running at the exact same time.

Programmers usually rely on the O/S to provide us with semaphores, mutexes, critical sections, and various other tools to protect these data objects. If you use them correctly, you can successfully use multiple threads without shooting yourself in the virtual foot.

The data objects in the greatest peril in this class are the input and output buffers. Class members m_RxQueue and m_TxQueue are used to transfer blocks of data back and forth between your program's main thread and the input and output threads owned by Win32Port. These rather complex data structures are not even thread safe as they ship from Microsoft. Should two threads be attempting to work on this simultaneously, scrambled data would surely result.

Class MTdeque is designed to deal with this problem. This class has a protected member, m_Queue, that is just a deque<char> from the standard C++ library. This is a good data structure for use as a buffer because it is optimized for quick removal or insertion from either end. Just what you need for a buffer used to manage transfer of data between two threads.

By embedding the deque<char> object as a protected member, you have complete control over any access to the object. The following member functions constitute the complete API for this object:

Clear()	Erases all the data from m_Queue. After this call returns, the object is empty.
Extract()	Extracts a single byte from m_Queue.
Extract(char *, int)	Extracts a block of bytes from m_Queue, up to a maximum count.
Insert(char)	Inserts a single character into m_Queue.
Insert(char *, int)	Inserts a block of characters into m_Queue.
Peek(char *, int)	Peeks at a block of data in m_Queue, up to a maximum count.
SpaceFree()	Returns the amount of space free in m_Queue. The number of bytes that the container may hold is limited to the count specified in m_iMaxSize, which is set in the constructor.
SpaceUsed()	Returns the number of bytes currently in m_Queue.

Each of these member functions has to be able to guarantee that it will be the only thread manipulating m_Queue at any one time. This is accomplished through the use of a Win32 CRITICAL_SECTION object, m_Lock. This object is created in the constructor with a call to InitializeCriticalSection() and is not destroyed until the destructor is called. All access to m_Queue is wrapped up between calls to EnterCriticalSection() and LeaveCriticalSection(). A typical use of the critical section is shown here:

```
int Insert( char c )
{
    int return_value;
    ::EnterCriticalSection( &m_Lock );
    if ( m_Queue.size() < m_iMaxSize ) {
        m_Queue.push_back( c );
        return_value = c & 0xff;
    } else
        return_value = -1;
    ::LeaveCriticalSection( &m_Lock );
    return return_value;
}
```

All the members of MTdeque are defined as inline functions in the header file. With luck, the compiler will then be able to generate very efficient implementations.

Helper class — Dcb

Class Dcb is a simple class that is derived directly from the DCB structure. (Deriving from a C structure might seem unusual, but it works.) Win32Port member m_Dcb is an object of this new class. Because class Dcb derives directly from the DCB structure, you can pass a pointer to member m_Dcb to any of the Win32 API functions that expect a pointer to a DCB. Public derivation also means that you can access any of the DCB members directly if needed.

The main reason this class exists is simply to tidy up some of the routines used to modify the standard port parameters. Class Dcb has short access routines for all the properties in the Settings class, which are the properties that can be modified by members of class RS232. Those member functions are as follows:

- SetBaudRate()
- SetParity()
- SetWordLength()
- SetStopBits()
- SetDtr()

- SetRts()
- SetXonXoff()
- SetDtrDsr()
- SetRtsCts()

A typical implementation of one of those routines is shown here:

```
void Dcb::SetParity( int parity, RS232Error &error )
{
  switch ( toupper( parity ) ) {
    case 'N'       : fParity = FALSE; Parity = NOPARITY;    break;
    case 'E'       : fParity = TRUE;  Parity = EVENPARITY;  break;
    case 'O'       : fParity = TRUE;  Parity = ODDPARITY;   break;
    case 'M'       : fParity = TRUE;  Parity = MARKPARITY;  break;
    case 'S'       : fParity = TRUE;  Parity = SPACEPARITY; break;
    case UNCHANGED : break;
    default        : error = RS232_ILLEGAL_PARITY_SETTING;
  }
};
```

The preceding function takes care of setting the two different members of the DCB structure affected by parity settings, in addition to checking for legal values. This makes the code in class Win32Port a little less cluttered.

The one additional element that the Dcb class provides is a constructor that puts all the members of the DCB structure in a known state. Once again, this just helps to cut down on the clutter in class Win32Port.

The IdleFunction Under Win32

In this chapter, I don't discuss much about the timed versions of class RS232 member functions Read() and Write(). When attempting to read or write a buffer full of data, you can pass these functions a timeout value, which tells them to keep trying to do the job for a specific amount of time.

These timed versions basically sit and poll the driver, idling in a loop while waiting for space to free up or characters to come in. Tying up the CPU is a bad thing in many environments, and class RS232 deals with this problem by calling virtual function IdleFunction() each pass through the loop.

Ideally, you could write your Win32 communications programs to be completely event driven, in which case you wouldn't even worry about these timed functions. But making your programs to be event driven is not always convenient or even practical. So the important thing is to write a version of `IdleFunction()` that lets your program integrate properly with Windows.

If you are doing your serial communications work in a background thread, you can write an idle function that kills time in a very cooperative manner. You can either modify the base class, `Win32Port`, or create a new version of the function in your derived class. A function that works well in a background thread might look like this:

```
int MyDerivedClass::IdleFunction( void )
{
    SleepEx( 100, FALSE );
    return RS232_SUCCESS;
}
```

This idle function simply sleeps for 100 milliseconds, which should place only a very light burden on the system. You can tweak the time to larger or smaller values depending on the type of data flow you are expecting. Ideally, any time you wait too long, your input data buffers should start filling up, which means that you won't have to call the idle routine again for some time.

If you are reading data from your program's main thread, things are a little different. Under Windows, you have to keep servicing messages regardless of what you are doing. A program that sleeps or sits in a tight loop for a long period of time will seem locked up to its user, making everyone unhappy.

The way around this is to service the message loop while you are waiting:

```
int MyDerivedClass::IdleFunction( void )
{
    MSG msg;
    while ( PeekMessage( &msg, NULL, 0, 0, PM_REMOVE ) )
    {
        TranslateMessage( &msg );
        DispatchMessage(&msg);
    }
    return RS232_SUCCESS;
}
```

This idle function keeps your user interface active while you are waiting. You need to be careful with this approach, though. Your program logic has to be aware of the fact that a read or write to the serial port is in progress. If you let the user push a button that starts another I/O operation while the first one is still in progress, you are going to have problems!

Summary

Class `Win32Port` is far and away the most complicated class you've seen so far in this book. It makes use of multiple threads of execution, has a flexible notification system, and fully implements the member functions of base class `RS232`. This chapter provides a complete description of the class. Chapter 12 shows how to use these classes in a sample program and gives the listings for class `Win32Port` and all its supporting classes.

Chapter 12

The Win32Test Program

IN THIS CHAPTER

- A console-based test program
- The Source Code

THIS CHAPTER INCLUDES a Win32Test program with the charismatic name of CHAPT12. The test program is functionally similar to test programs used for the 16-bit MS-DOS programs. Through use of the dialog box control panel, you should be able to use the test program to exercise all the member functions of class Win32Port.

CHAPT12.EXE – A Console-Based Test Program

This short test program lets you test and exercise the Win32Port class opens a text-based console window where the results of input and output are displayed, and has a control panel dialog box that lets you call functions and perform diagnostics on the port. The dialog box is set to be always topmost so that you don't have to search for it every time you want to perform an operation.

The console-based window is admittedly a bit cheesy to see in a Windows application, but it lets you concentrate on the meat of this chapter: the Win32Port class. If the test program also had to create and maintain a terminal window, there would be a huge body of source code that distracted us from the main topic of the chapter.

The creation and maintenance of a terminal window is a topic unto itself and is developed thoroughly in the next chapter.

The test program, CHAPT12.EXE, is an MFC program written to work with Visual C++ 5.x and later. The program uses MFC strictly for message passing and not much else. Although tying a demo program to one specific development environment is not necessarily a good thing, keep in mind that the Win32Port class works fine with any compiler or environment. Additionally, CHAPT12.EXE does not make extensive use of MFC features, so porting it to a different environment should be a straightforward task.

The dialog-based control panel

When CHAPT12.EXE first starts up, you are presented with a dialog box that has most of its buttons disabled, as shown in Figure 12-1.

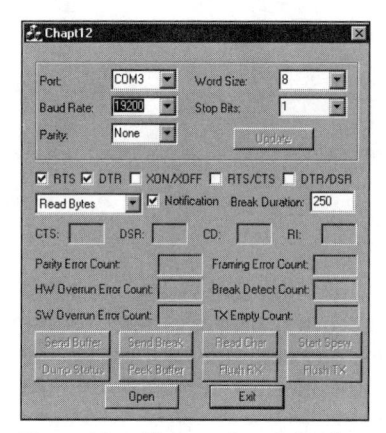

Figure 12-1: The opening dialog box of CHAPT12.EXE

In the initial state, you can set most of the port parameters to their desired values, but all of the action buttons are in the disabled state. After you have settings in the state for the port you will be using, you press the Open button, which opens the port, creates the console window, and enables most of the controls on the dialog box.

In this state, the console window acts much like a standard terminal emulator. Characters typed to the screen will be sent out the port, and data coming in the port will be echoed to the screen. The setup should look something like Figure 12-2.

CHAPT12.EXE is thoroughly documented and at heart is a very simple program. The source code is fairly large, but only because it handles many different commands. Because the source is available for study, I don't discuss it in any detail in this chapter. However, I do go over the various controls on the control panel and talk about what they do or what they indicate.

Port combo box
This control is enabled only when the port is closed. It lets you select the port that you are going to open. It comes preloaded with the names COM1 through COM4, but you are free to enter any text you like.

After the port is opened, this control is disabled. You can't change the port number on an open port; to change ports; you must first close the existing port, and then change the port name, and then open the new port.

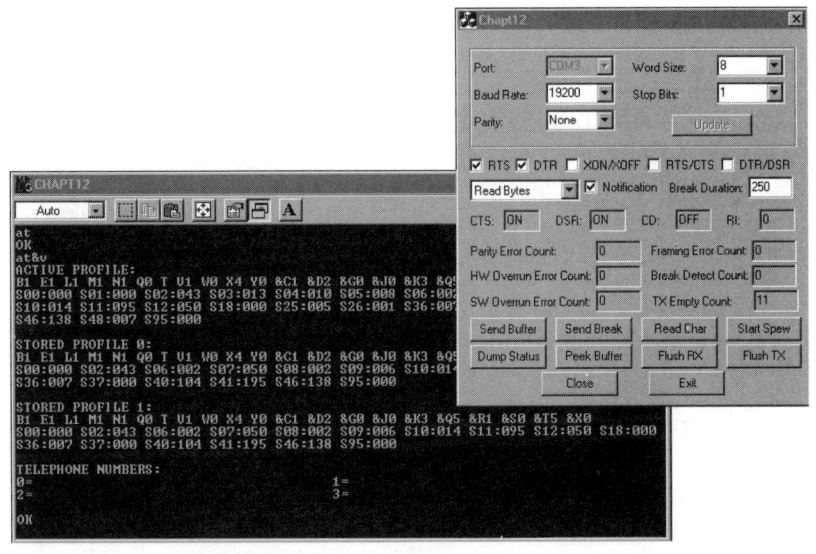

Figure 12-2: CHAPT12.EXE with an open port

Baud Rate combo box

Parity combo box

Word Size combo box

Stop Bits combo box
These four combo boxes control the most common of the port settings. The settings can be modified at will while the port is closed. When the Open button is pressed to open the port, the current values in the combo boxes are used to attempt to open the port.

After the port is open, you can still change the values of these settings freely. However, the settings won't be modified until you press the Update button.

Update button
When the port is closed, the Update button is disabled. After the port is opened, the button is enabled and can be used at any time. The Update button only applies the Baud Rate, Parity, Word Size, and Stop Bits settings to the port. You can make modifications to these settings at will without having them affect the port; it takes a press of the Update button for them to be applied. Note that all the other settings on this control panel take effect immediately upon modification.

RTS check box

DTR check box
These two check boxes directly modify the state of RTS and DTR in the port. If the port is open, the new values are applied immediately. If the port is closed, the settings will be used when the port is opened.

Note that clicking these boxes when the corresponding type of handshaking is selected is ineffective; the handshaking setting overrides any attempt to modify the control line directly.

XON/XOFF check box

RTS/CTS check box

DTR/DSR check box
These three check boxes directly modify the state of the three types of handshaking available on a `Win32` port. If the port is open, the handshaking setting is changed immediately after the box is checked or unchecked. If the port is closed, the new value will be used when the port is opened.

Read Bytes drop-down list
This drop-down list has three choices, which affect the way input bytes are read for display on the console screen. When the main window of this application receives an `RxNotify()` event message, it selects from one of three possible actions:

Read Bytes	When this setting is selected, input bytes will be read one at a time until the input buffer is exhausted.
Read Buffer	Under this setting, input data will be read into an input buffer, up to 128 bytes at a time, until the input is exhausted.
Suppress Reads	With this setting, `RxNotify()` messages are ignored, with the handler doing nothing. This setting allows you see what sort of behavior the `Win32Port` class exhibits as its buffers fill up.

Notification check box
If this check box is disabled, all incoming notification messages are ignored. For this particular application, that means that not much happens.

Break Duration edit control
The contents of this edit box are used when the `Send Break` button is depressed. The value entered here is passed as the parameter to `SendBreak()`. The default value of 250 milliseconds is probably good for most applications.

CTS edit control

DSR edit control

CD edit control
These three edit controls are all permanently set to the read-only state, which means that you can't enter new values. Changes are made only by the program. The three controls will always say either `ON` or `OFF`, reflecting the current state of the incoming RS-232 status line.

RI edit control
This edit control operates a little differently than the other three. Because of the way notification works on the RI line, it isn't likely that you would ever see this box in an `ON` state. RI notification will usually occur only on the trailing edge of the RI signal, which means that it will almost always be in the `OFF` state when the notification event occurs.

So instead, you display a count of RI notifications in this edit box. Every time a new incoming ring burst completes, you should see the RI counter increment.

Parity Error Count edit control

HW Overrun Error Count edit control

SW Overrun Error Count edit control

Framing Error Count edit control

Framing Error Count edit control

TX Empty Count edit control
All these edit controls are always in the read-only state, meaning that you can't change them with the keyboard; only the program can change them. All the controls simply keep a count of the six different types of notification. A properly operating port should never see any of these notifications occur except for the `TX Empty Count` event, which will fire every time the output buffer is emptied.

Send Buffer button
This button is disabled until the port is opened. At that point, it can be used to send a short buffer out the port. If you set the baud rate of the port to a very low value,

say 300 baud, you can press this button fast enough to saturate the driver system, which can help test the performance of both the driver and the class under difficult conditions.

Send Break button
When the port is open, this button can be pressed to send a break on the output line of the port. The duration of the break is determined by the number contained in the `Break Duration` edit control

Read Char button
Pressing this button when the port is open generates a call to `Read()`, which attempts to read a character out of the buffer immediately. If you have set the read mode to `Suppress Reads`, you can read in the data from the input port one byte at a time. The display of these bytes will give you an output screen something like that shown in Figure 12-3.

Figure 12-3: A succession of Read Char button depressions

Start Spew/Stop Spew button
This button is used to take the open port in and out of spew mode. When the port is in spew mode, every time the main window receives a `TxNotify()` message, it sends another spew packet out the port. This has the effect of keeping a continuous stream of data running out the port, as shown in Figure 12-4. The legend on the button changes to reflect the fact that it toggles back and forth from spew mode.

Dump Status button
Pressing this button while the port is open causes a complete status dump to be displayed in the console window. A complete dump consists of calling `Win32 Port::FormatDebugOutput()` for all defined lines. A display of the output from this command was shown earlier in the chapter, in the definition of `FormatDebug Output()`.

Chapter 12: The Win32Test Program 515

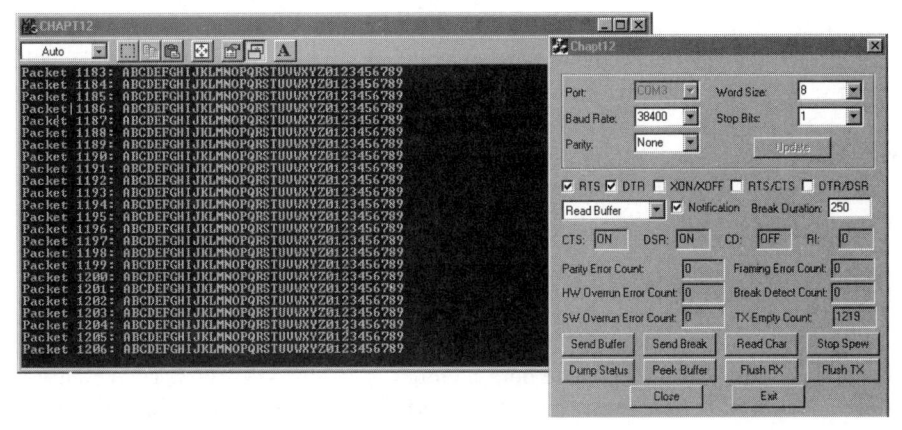

Figure 12-4: Spew in progress

Peek Buffer button
When the port is open, this button can be depressed to peek into the input buffer. This is usually effective only when the read mode is set to suppress reads of incoming data. The Peek() function call executed by the handler attempts to peek at 3000 bytes, but it displays only the first 40, as shown in Figure 12-5.

Figure 12-5: Output of the Peek Buffer operation

Flush RX button

Flush TX button
Pressing either of these buttons when the port is open does exactly what it says: It flushes the appropriate buffer. Although this doesn't do anything visible, you can see the effects by pressing the Dump Status button before and after the flush operation. Note that the flush operation should clear both the class buffers and the buffers used internally by the driver.

Open/Close button

This button changes state depending on the current state of the port. It does exactly what it says, either opening or closing the port.

Exit

If the port is open, the Exit button closes it. After that potential bit of cleanup, the program exits.

The customized derived class

In order to support notification, `Chapt10` uses a derived class called `MyWin32Port`. This derived class has exactly one data member: `m_hNotifyWindow`. The constructor for `MyWin32Port` initializes this member with the value of the main window for `Chapt10`.

The derived class has 11 virtual notification functions defined, and every one of them looks very similar to this:

```
void RiNotify( bool status )
{
    ::PostMessage( m_hNotifyWindow, WM_RI_NOTIFY, status, 0 );
}
```

As you can see, this function just posts a message to the target window. A set of 11 private messages is defined for the use of this class, as follows:

```
const int WM_SERIAL_RX_NOTIFY               = WM_USER + 0x1000;
const int WM_PARITY_ERROR_NOTIFY            = WM_USER + 0x1001;
const int WM_BREAK_DETECT_NOTIFY            = WM_USER + 0x1002;
const int WM_FRAMING_ERROR_NOTIFY           = WM_USER + 0x1003;
const int WM_HARDWARE_OVERRUN_ERROR_NOTIFY  = WM_USER + 0x1004;
const int WM_SOFTWARE_OVERRUN_ERROR_NOTIFY  = WM_USER + 0x1005;
const int WM_CTS_NOTIFY                     = WM_USER + 0x1006;
const int WM_DSR_NOTIFY                     = WM_USER + 0x1007;
const int WM_CD_NOTIFY                      = WM_USER + 0x1008;
const int WM_RI_NOTIFY                      = WM_USER + 0x1009;
const int WM_TX_NOTIFY                      = WM_USER + 0x100a;
```

Remember from the discussion earlier in the chapter that these notification functions are called from a different thread of execution than your main thread, so it is important that they are short and simple. Posting a Windows message and then returning is about as simple as you can get, and it defers all the serious work to whoever receives the message.

> **ON THE CD**
>
> The project files for this chapter are included in the source section of the CD that accompanies the book. If you copy the entire directory tree to your hard drive, you should be able to simply open and build the project. Note that the project file was created to be compatible with the current version of Microsoft's compiler which was, at the time this book was written, Visual C++ 5.0. Later versions of Visual C++ should be able to read in and convert the project to the appropriate level.

The Source Code

The rest of this chapter contains all the source code (Listings 12-1 through 12-5) used to implement Win32Port. The source to the sample program is not listed; you will need to refer to the CD for listings.

Listing 12-1: Win32Port.h

```
//
//  WIN32PORT.H
//
//  Source code from:
//
//  Serial Communications Developer's Guide, 2nd Edition
//  by Mark Nelson, IDG Books, 1999
//
//  Please see the book for information on usage.
//
// This file contains the class definition for Win32Port. This
// class implements a version of class RS232 that works with the
// Win32 serial API. The implementation of this class is in file
// Win32Port.cpp. Although the sample programs in this book use
// MFC, this class should work independently of any application
// framework.
//

#ifndef WIN32PORT_H
#define WIN32PORT_H

#include <deque>
#include <string>
using namespace std;
```

```cpp
#include "rs232.h"
#include "Dcb.h"
#include "MTDeque.h"

//
// These are the enumerated error values added to the class
// specifically to support the Win32Port class. One of these items
// requires a bit of explanation. If an error type of
// WIN32_CHECK_WINDOWS_ERROR is returned, the caller will have to
// examine m_dwWindowsError to see what Windows thinks the error
// is. Because there is a nearly limitless number of possible
// error returns from calls the Windows API, it isn't possible to
// account for every single error return, so this is the kitchen
// sink value.
//
enum Win32PortError {
    WIN32_CHECK_WINDOWS_ERROR = RS232_NEXT_FREE_ERROR,
    WIN32_SETTINGS_FAILURE,
    WIN32_HANDSHAKE_LINE_IN_USE
};


class Win32Port : public RS232
{
//
// Constructors and destructors
//
public :
    Win32Port( const string &port_name,
               long baud_rate = UNCHANGED,
               char parity = UNCHANGED,
               int word_length = UNCHANGED,
               int stop_bits = UNCHANGED,
               int dtr = SET,
               int rts = SET,
               int xon_xoff = DISABLE,
               int rts_cts = DISABLE,
               int dtr_dsr = DISABLE );
    virtual ~Win32Port();

protected :
    Win32Port() : m_TxQueue( MAX_OUTPUT_BUFFER_SIZE ),
                  M_RxQueue( MAX_INPUT_BUFFER_SIZE ){}
//
```

Chapter 12: The Win32Test Program 519

```
// These enumerated values are used internally by the Win32Port
// class. Note that the two buffer size values can be modified
// if your application has different requirements.
//
    enum { MAX_INPUT_BUFFER_SIZE = 2048 };
    enum { MAX_OUTPUT_BUFFER_SIZE = 2048 };
    enum { EV_RINGTE = 0x2000 };
//
// These members are all used internally, and aren't needed
// by any code outside the Win32Port class.
//
    HANDLE m_hPort;           // Handle of the port, used everywhere
    int m_iBreakDuration;
    int first_debug_output_line;
    bool m_bInputThreadReading;
    DWORD m_dwWindowsError;
    long m_hOutputThread;
    long m_hInputThread;
    MTdeque m_TxQueue;        //Outbound data queue
    MTdeque m_RxQueue;        //Incoming data queue
    Dcb m_Dcb;                //Current DCB settings
    DWORD m_dwErrors;         //Cumulative line status error bits
    DWORD m_dwModemStatus;    //Current modem status bits
    //
    // These five Win32 events are all used to communicate
    // requests to the input and output threads.
    //
    HANDLE m_hKillOutputThreadEvent;
    HANDLE m_hKillInputThreadEvent;
    HANDLE m_hWriteRequestEvent;
    HANDLE m_hReadRequestEvent;
    HANDLE m_hBreakRequestEvent;
//
// Private member functions not available to code outside the
// class
//
    RS232Error write_settings();
    void read_settings();
    void check_modem_status( bool first_time, DWORD event_mask );
    void clear_error( COMSTAT *comstat = 0  );
    RS232Error translate_last_error();
    bool output_worker();
    static void OutputThread( void * arglist );
    static void InputThread( void *arglist );
```

```cpp
    //
    // The following are the declarations for the RS232 class
    // members that are implemented by Win32Port. Most of these
    // functions have only stubbed versions in the base class, but
    // have actual useful implementations in Win32Port.
    //
public :
    RS232Error Set( long baud_rate = UNCHANGED,
                    int parity = UNCHANGED,
                    int word_length = UNCHANGED,
                    int stop_bits = UNCHANGED );
    int Dtr( int setting = UNCHANGED );
    int Rts( int setting = UNCHANGED );
    int TXSpaceFree( void ){ return m_TxQueue.SpaceFree(); }
    int TXSpaceUsed( void ){ return m_TxQueue.SpaceUsed(); }
    int RXSpaceUsed( void ){ return m_RxQueue.SpaceUsed(); }
    int RXSpaceFree( void ){ return m_RxQueue.SpaceFree(); }
    int DtrDsrHandshaking( int setting = UNCHANGED );
    int RtsCtsHandshaking( int setting = UNCHANGED );
    int XonXoffHandshaking( int setting = UNCHANGED );
    int FormatDebugOutput(char *buffer = 0,int line_number = -1);
    int ParityError( int clear = UNCHANGED );
    int BreakDetect( int clear = UNCHANGED );
    int FramingError( int clear = UNCHANGED );
    int HardwareOverrunError( int clear = UNCHANGED );
    int SoftwareOverrunError( int clear = UNCHANGED );
    int Break( long milliseconds = 300 );
    int Cd( void );
    int Ri( void );
    int Cts( void );
    int Dsr( void );
    int Peek( void *buffer, unsigned int count );
    int FlushRXBuffer( void );
    int FlushTXBuffer( void );
    char *ErrorName( int error );
//
// Virtual functions that this library must implement in order to
// support public library routines in Win32Port
//
protected :
    int read_buffer( char *buffer, unsigned int count );
    int write_buffer( char *buffer, unsigned int count = -1 );
    int read_byte( void );
    int write_byte( int c );
```

```
//
// The following notification functions all have null
// implemementations that do nothing in Win32Port. You implement
// notification in your program by creating a new class derived
// from Win32Port, and create your own versions of these virtual
// functions. The sample program from Chapter 10 shows a simple
// way to accomplish this.
//
    virtual void RxNotify( int byte_count ){};
    virtual void TxNotify(){};
    virtual void ParityErrorNotify(){};
    virtual void FramingErrorNotify(){};
    virtual void HardwareOverrunErrorNotify(){};
    virtual void SoftwareOverrunErrorNotify(){};
    virtual void BreakDetectNotify(){};
    virtual void CtsNotify( bool status ){};
    virtual void DsrNotify( bool status ){};
    virtual void CdNotify( bool status ){};
    virtual void RiNotify( bool status ) {};
};

#endif // #infdef WIN32PORT_H

// EOF Win32Port.h
```

Listing 12-2: Win32Port.cpp

```
//
//   WIN32PORT.CPP
//
//   Source code from:
//
//   Serial Communications Developer's Guide, 2nd Edition
//   by Mark Nelson, IDG Books, 1999
//
//   Please see the book for information on usage.
//
// This file contains the class implementation for Win32Port.
// Win32Port implements a version of class RS232 that works with
// the Win32 serial API. The implementation of this class is in
// file Win32Port. Although the sample programs in this book use
// MFC, this class should work independently of any application
// framework.
//
//
```

```cpp
#include "stdafx.h"
#include <process.h>
#include <cassert>
#include <sstream>
#include <iomanip>
using namespace std;

#include "Chapt10.h"
#include "Win32Port.h"


//
// Under MFC, some heap use tracking is done in debug mode, in an
// attempt to track down memory leaks. This code enables that
// tracking Feel free to delete the five lines that enable this
// feature; they are not necessary for proper operation of the
// Win32Port class.
//
#ifdef _DEBUG
#undef THIS_FILE
static char THIS_FILE[]=__FILE__;
#define new DEBUG_NEW
#endif

//
// The arguments to the Win32Port constructor are the same as the
// arguments passed to the constructurs for all the other
// RS232 derived classes, with one noticeable difference. Instead
// of passing a numeric value such as COM1 or COM2, this guy
// expects a string, for example, "COM2". This is necessary to
// accomodate two special cases. First, comm ports greater than 9
// must be opened with a special string that looks like this:
// "\\.\COM10". Second, some drivers could be using a completely
// different name, such as "USB Port 1".
//
//
// The constructor has a member initialization list that creates
// the input and output queues at the size chosen by the
// enumerated value in the class definition. The MTQueue class
// limits insertions into the internal deque<char> member to the
// value specified in the constructor.
//
Win32Port::Win32Port( const string &port,
```

```
                        long baud_rate      /* = UNCHANGED */,
                        char parity         /* = UNCHANGED */,
                        int  word_length    /* = UNCHANGED */,
                        int  stop_bits      /* = UNCHANGED */,
                        int  dtr            /* = SET       */,
                        int  rts            /* = SET       */,
                        int  xon_xoff       /* = DISABLE   */,
                        int  rts_cts        /* = DISABLE   */,
                        int  dtr_dsr        /* = DISABLE   */ )
    : m_TxQueue( MAX_OUTPUT_BUFFER_SIZE ),
      m_RxQueue( MAX_INPUT_BUFFER_SIZE )
{
//
// Win32Port has to share the debug output with the parent class.
// To determine where the first line starts, you call the
// FormatDebugOutput() function from the parent class.
//
    first_debug_output_line = RS232::FormatDebugOutput();
    debug_line_count = FormatDebugOutput();
    string temp = port;
//
// One of the base class members holds the port_name, which for
// most other class implementations is a value ranging from COM1
// to COM9. Although not every port passed to this class conforms
// to that naming structure, most of them do. You try to extract
// that port name from the one passed in wherever possible. If no
// possible match is made, the value -1 is inserted into the
// port_name member. The only important place where the port_name
// member is used is in the dump status output routine of the
// base class. Initializing it here ensures that the value
// displayed in the debug output will usually match up with the
// value the calling program passed as a port name.
//
    if ( temp.substr( 0, 4 ) == "\\\\.\\" )
        temp = temp.substr( 4, string::npos );
    if ( toupper( temp[ 0 ] ) == 'C' &&
         toupper( temp[ 1 ] ) == 'O' &&
         toupper( temp[ 2 ] ) == 'M' ) {
        temp = temp.substr( 3, string::npos );
        port_name = (RS232PortName) ( atoi( temp.c_str() ) - 1 );
    } else
        port_name = (RS232PortName) -1;
//
// Here is where the real work starts. You open the port using
```

```cpp
// the flags appropriate to a serial port. Using
// FILE_FLAG_OVERLAPPED is critical, because the input and
// output threads depend on the asynchronous capabilities of
// Win32.
//
m_hPort = CreateFile( port.c_str(),
                      GENERIC_READ | GENERIC_WRITE,
                      0,
                      0,
                      OPEN_EXISTING,
                      FILE_ATTRIBUTE_NORMAL |
                        FILE_FLAG_OVERLAPPED,
                      0 );
//
// If you get a valid handle, it means that the port could at
// least be opened. You then try to set a bunch of
// miscellaneous things that the port needs to run properly.
// If everything goes according to plan, when that is all
// done, you start the input and output threads and the port
// is then really running.
//
if ( m_hPort != INVALID_HANDLE_VALUE ) {
    m_dwErrors = 0;       //Clear cumulative line status errors
    m_iBreakDuration = 0;//No break in progress, init to 0
    SetLastError( 0 );    //Clear any Win error in this thread
    read_settings();      //Read and save current port settings
                          //Only needed because base class dumps
                          //the saved settings in debug output
    saved_settings = settings;
    //Init timeous to ensure our overlapped reads work
    COMMTIMEOUTS timeouts = { 0x01, 0, 0, 0, 0 };
    SetCommTimeouts( m_hPort, &timeouts );
    SetupComm( m_hPort, 500, 500 ); //set buffer sizes
    error_status = RS232_SUCCESS;  //clear current class error
    settings.Dtr = 1;       //Set these five values to their
    settings.Rts = 1;       //default values, the Adjust()
    settings.XonXoff = 0;   //function will modify them if
    settings.RtsCts = 0;    //new vals were passed in the args
    settings.DtrDsr = 0;    //to the constructor
    settings.Adjust( baud_rate,
                     parity,
                     word_length,
                     stop_bits,
                     dtr,
```

```
                        rts,
                        xon_xoff,
                        rts_cts,
                        dtr_dsr );
//
// Now write the new settings to the port. If this or any
// other operation has failed, you abort here. The user
// will be able to see that the port is not working due to
// having an error set immediately upon opening.
//
error_status = write_settings();
if ( error_status != RS232_SUCCESS ) {
    CloseHandle( m_hPort );
    m_hPort = 0;
} else {
    //
    // Because the port opened properly, you're ready to
    // start the input and output threads. Before they
    // start, you create the five Win32 events that will
    // be used to pass requests to the threads. Note that
    // the only argument passed to the thread
    // initialization is a pointer to this. The thread
    // needs that pointer to find all of the data in the
    // Win32Port object that it will be manipulating.
    //
    m_hKillInputThreadEvent = CreateEvent( NULL,
                                           FALSE,
                                           FALSE,
                                           NULL );
    m_hKillOutputThreadEvent = CreateEvent( NULL,
                                            FALSE,
                                            FALSE,
                                            NULL );
    m_hWriteRequestEvent = CreateEvent( NULL,
                                        FALSE,
                                        FALSE,
                                        NULL );
    m_hReadRequestEvent = CreateEvent( NULL,
                                       FALSE,
                                       FALSE,
                                       NULL );
    m_hBreakRequestEvent = CreateEvent( NULL,
                                        FALSE,
                                        FALSE,
```

```
                                            NULL );
        m_hInputThread = _beginthread( InputThread,
                                       0,
                                       (void *) this );
        m_hOutputThread = _beginthread( OutputThread,
                                        0,
                                        (void *) this );
    }
}
//
// If the CreateFile() function didn't succeed, you're really
// in a bad state. Just translate any error into something
// intelligible and exit. The user will have to figure out
// that the open failed due to the bad error_status member.
//
else
    translate_last_error();
}

//
// The destructor has only a couple of important things to do. If
// the port was up and running, the handle that was created as a
// result of the call to CreateFile() has to be closed with a
// call to CloseHandle(). The two worker threads created when the
// port was opened both have to be killed, which is done by
// setting an Event that those threads will be continually
// waiting on.When the threads are destroyed, the five events
// created in the constructor can be destroyed as well.
//
// Note that because of the way this destructor works, you are
// vulnerable to getting hung up if one of the two worker threads
// doesn't exit properly. This is a strong incentive toward
// keeping the code in the threads nice and simple.
//
Win32Port::~Win32Port()
{
    TRACE( "Entering Win32Port dtor\n" );
    if ( m_hPort != INVALID_HANDLE_VALUE ) {
        SetEvent( m_hKillOutputThreadEvent );
        SetEvent( m_hKillInputThreadEvent );
        long handles[ 2 ] = { m_hInputThread, m_hOutputThread };
        WaitForMultipleObjects( 2,
                                (HANDLE *) handles,
                                TRUE,
```

```
                              INFINITE );
        CloseHandle( m_hPort );
        m_hPort = INVALID_HANDLE_VALUE;
        CloseHandle( m_hKillInputThreadEvent );
        CloseHandle( m_hKillOutputThreadEvent );
        CloseHandle( m_hWriteRequestEvent );
        CloseHandle( m_hReadRequestEvent );
        CloseHandle( m_hBreakRequestEvent );
    }
}


//
// The structure of the RS232 class called for a single global
// function that was called when the library was sitting in a
// loop waiting for input data to show up. Under Win32, there are
// a couple of different approaches you might want to take when
// implementing this routine. If you are calling the routine from
// your main thread, you want to make sure that your GUI is
// getting some CPU cycles, so you probably want to replace this
// function with a version that operates your message pump. The
// routine might also check for a cancel flag that a user can set
// from inside your application.
//
// If you are calling this routine from a background thread, you
// could conceivably have it sleep for 5 or 10 milliseconds each
// time it is called. If you are actually idle and truly waiting
// for data to either arrive or be sent, it shouldn't cause any
// degradation of your application's throughput, and it will free
// up time for other processes and threads.
//
// Because this is a virtual function, you can override it in your
// derived class and use some object-specific data to determine
// how it behaves.
//
int RS232::IdleFunction( void )
{
    return RS232_SUCCESS;
}


//
// The RS232 base class expects a global ReadTime() function that
// returns the current time in milliseconds. This matches up well
// with the GetTickCount() in the Windows API.
//
```

```
long ReadTime( void )
{
    return GetTickCount();
}


//
// This is the class-specific implementation of the RS232 virtual
// function called Set(). It is called to set the four principal
// attributes of the serial port: baud rate, parity, word size,
// and number of stop bits. It relies on two internal functions
// to actually do all the work. Member function Adjust() is
// called to accept the new settings and store them in the
// internal settings member. write_settings() is then called to
// take those values, make any modifications needed to the DCB,
// and then call the Win32 API functions needed to update the
// physical values in the port. Illegal values can result in the
// error_status member being set to a bad value, which will
// prevent the port from working at all.
//
RS232Error Win32Port::Set( long baud_rate   /* = UNCHANGED */,
                           int parity       /* = UNCHANGED */,
                           int word_length  /* = UNCHANGED */,
                           int stop_bits    /* = UNCHANGED */ )
{
    settings.Adjust( baud_rate,
                     parity,
                     word_length,
                     stop_bits,
                     UNCHANGED,
                     UNCHANGED,
                     UNCHANGED,
                     UNCHANGED,
                     UNCHANGED );
    return write_settings();

}


//
// This is an implementation of the virtual Dtr() function from
// the base class RS232. It doesn't have to do too much work; it
// merely updates the settings member and then calls the
// write_settings() member function to do all the work. It does
// check to see whether DTR/DSR handshaking is in place, and if it
// is,it the nonfatal warning is returned to the calling routine.
```

```
// If handshaking is not enabled, the functionupdates the Dtr
// member in the settings object and calls write_settings() to
// update the physical port. Note that it returns the current
// setting of the Dtr member. If this function is called with no
// arguments by the end user, it doesn't do anything except return
// that value.
//
int Win32Port::Dtr( int setting /* = UNCHANGED */ )
{
    if ( error_status < RS232_SUCCESS )
        return error_status;
    if ( setting != UNCHANGED ) {
        if ( settings.DtrDsr == 1 )
            return WIN32_HANDSHAKE_LINE_IN_USE;
        settings.Dtr = setting != 0;
        RS232Error error = write_settings();
        if ( error < RS232_SUCCESS )
            return error;
    }
    return settings.Dtr;
}

//
// This is an implementation of the virtual Rts() function from
// the base class RS232. It doesn't have to do too much work; it
// merely updates the settings member and then calls the
// write_settings() member function to do all the work. It does
// check to see whether RTS/CTS handshaking is in place, and if
// it is, it returns a nonfatal warning to the calling routine. If
// handshaking is not enabled, the function updates the Rts member
// in the settings object and calls write_settings() to update the
// physical port.
//
// Note that it returns the current setting of the Rts member. If
// this function is called with no arguments by the end user, it
// doesn't do anything except return that value.
//
int Win32Port::Rts( int setting /* = UNCHANGED */ )
{
    if ( error_status < RS232_SUCCESS )
        return error_status;
    if ( setting != UNCHANGED ) {
        if ( settings.RtsCts == 1 )
            return WIN32_HANDSHAKE_LINE_IN_USE;
```

```
            settings.Rts = setting != 0;
            RS232Error error = write_settings();
            if ( error < RS232_SUCCESS )
                return error;
        }
        return settings.Rts;
    }

//
// This is the local implementation of the RS232 member function
// DtrDsrHandshaking. All it has to do is set the member in the
// settings function, then rely on the write_settings() member to
// do all the work. Note that setting this handshaking type to be
// true means that you no longer have direct control over the DTR
// output line. Any attempt to modify DTR will be futile until
// this handshaking value is turned back off.
//
// After finishing its work, this function returns the setting of
// DTR/DSR handshaking for the port. Note that if the user calls
// it with no arguments, it will skip all the setting work and
// just return the value of the current setting.
//
int Win32Port::DtrDsrHandshaking( int setting /* = UNCHANGED */ )
{
    if ( error_status < RS232_SUCCESS )
        return error_status;
    if ( setting != UNCHANGED ) {
        settings.DtrDsr = setting != 0;
        RS232Error error = write_settings();
        if ( error < RS232_SUCCESS )
            return error;
    }
    return settings.DtrDsr;
}

//
// This is the local implementation of the RS232 member function
// RtsCtsHandshaking. All it has to do is set the member in the
// settings function, and then rely on the write_settings() member
// to do all the work. Note that setting this handshaking type to
// be true means that you no longer have direct control over the
// RTS output line. Any attempt to modify RTS will be futile until
// this handshaking value is turned back off.
//
```

```cpp
// After finishing its work, this function returns the setting of
// RTS/CTS handshaking for the port. Note that if the user calls
// it with no arguments, it will skip all the setting work and
// just return the value of the current setting.
//

int Win32Port::RtsCtsHandshaking( int setting )
{
    if ( error_status < RS232_SUCCESS )
        return error_status;
    if ( setting != UNCHANGED ) {
        settings.RtsCts = setting != 0;
        RS232Error error = write_settings();
        if ( error < RS232_SUCCESS )
            return error;
    }
    return settings.RtsCts;
}


//
// This member function is called to either check or modify the
// current software handshaking state of the port. It doesn't have
// to do any of the hard work; that is all taken care of by the
// write_settings() member of the class. The function returns
// the current state of software handshaking in the port. Note
// that if it is called with no argument, it will skip over all
// the code that modifies the value and simply return the current
// state.
//
int Win32Port::XonXoffHandshaking( int setting /* = UNCHANGED */ )
{
    if ( error_status < RS232_SUCCESS )
        return error_status;
    if ( setting != UNCHANGED ) {
        settings.XonXoff = setting != 0;
        RS232Error error = write_settings();
        if ( error < RS232_SUCCESS )
            return error;
    }
    return settings.XonXoff;
}

//
// The following four functions implement the RS232 class
```

```
// member functions that return the values of the modem
// status lines. In this case, all four functions are so similar
// that there is no point in documenting them individually.
//
// All these functions simply look at a specific bit in the
// m_dwModemStatus word to see whether their individual status
// line is set. The modem status word is read in every time a
// change in the status lines is seen by the status thread. You
// have set up WaitCommEvent so that it signals an event every
// time one of the status lines changes.
//
// Note that you can set up a derived class so that your
// application is notified every time one of the lines change.
// This is particularly valuable for monitoring the RI line,
// because it may be  difficult to catch an incoming ring in
// progress.
//

int Win32Port::Cd()
{
    return ( MS_RLSD_ON & m_dwModemStatus ) != 0;
}

int Win32Port::Cts()
{
    return ( MS_CTS_ON & m_dwModemStatus ) != 0;
}

int Win32Port::Dsr()
{
    return ( MS_DSR_ON & m_dwModemStatus ) != 0;
}

int Win32Port::Ri()
{
    return ( MS_RING_ON & m_dwModemStatus ) != 0;
}

//
// Just like the four modem status routines, the four line status
// error routines all take the same form. Each of them checks the
// m_dwErrors for their specific error bit, returning true if the
// bit is set and false if it is not. If the caller invoked the
// function with the clearing option, the bit in the cumulative
```

```
// line status error word will be cleared.
//
int Win32Port::ParityError( int clear /* = UNCHANGED */ )
{
    int return_value;

    if ( error_status < RS232_SUCCESS )
        return error_status;
    return_value = ( m_dwErrors & CE_RXPARITY ) != 0;
    if ( clear != UNCHANGED && clear != 0 )
        m_dwErrors &= ~CE_RXPARITY;
    return return_value;
}

int Win32Port::FramingError( int clear /* = UNCHANGED */ )
{
    int return_value;

    if ( error_status < RS232_SUCCESS )
        return error_status;
    return_value = ( m_dwErrors & CE_FRAME ) != 0;
    if ( clear != UNCHANGED && clear != 0 )
        m_dwErrors &= ~CE_FRAME;
    return return_value;
}

int Win32Port::HardwareOverrunError( int clear /* = UNCHANGED */ )
{
    int return_value;

    if ( error_status < RS232_SUCCESS )
        return error_status;
    return_value = ( m_dwErrors & CE_OVERRUN ) != 0;
    if ( clear != UNCHANGED && clear != 0 )
        m_dwErrors &= ~CE_OVERRUN;
    return return_value;
}

int Win32Port::BreakDetect( int clear /* = UNCHANGED */ )
{
    int return_value;

    if ( error_status < RS232_SUCCESS )
        return error_status;
```

```
        return_value = ( m_dwErrors & CE_BREAK ) != 0;
        if ( clear != UNCHANGED && clear != 0 )
            m_dwErrors &= ~CE_BREAK;
        return return_value;
    }

    //
    // This routine acts just like the previous four. The only
    // difference is the type of error being handled. The software
    // overrun error is set when the driver receives a character
    // but doesn't have room to store it. Unfortunately, there isn't
    // an EV_XXXX routine to force this error to generate an event
    // when it happens, so the status thread ends up checking the comm
    // status after every input buffer.
    //
    int Win32Port::SoftwareOverrunError( int clear /* = UNCHANGED */ )
    {
        int return_value;

        if ( error_status < RS232_SUCCESS )
            return error_status;
        return_value = ( m_dwErrors & CE_RXOVER ) != 0;
        if ( clear != UNCHANGED && clear != 0 )
            m_dwErrors &= ~CE_RXOVER;
        return return_value;
    }

    //
    // This function is called to provoke the output thread into
    // sending a break of a specified duration. You haven't set up any
    // path by which to set the duration of the break; instead, you
    // just store the desired duration in the object and count on the
    // output thread checking there to see what it should be. The
    // output thread is continually checking for the
    // m_hBreakRequestEvent, and when it sees it, it faithfully sends
    // the break.
    //
    int Win32Port::Break( long milliseconds )
    {
        if ( milliseconds > 1000 )
            m_iBreakDuration = 1000;
        else
            m_iBreakDuration = milliseconds;
        SetEvent( m_hBreakRequestEvent );
```

Chapter 12: The Win32Test Program 535

```
        return RS232_SUCCESS;
}

//
// The Peek() function is fairly close to read_buffer(). It takes
// whatever it can get out the input buffer, and returns a count
// of bytes read in ByteCount.
//
int Win32Port::Peek( void *buffer, unsigned int count )
{
    if ( error_status < RS232_SUCCESS )
        return error_status;
    ByteCount = m_RxQueue.Peek( (char *) buffer, count );
    ( (char *) buffer )[ ByteCount ] = '\0';
    return RS232_SUCCESS;
}


//
// The two FlushXxBuffer routines do the same things. Both calls
// have to take care to clear both the internal buffers used by
// the driver, plus the external buffers you kept in the class.
// One is done by a simple member of class MTQueue, the other by
// using a Win32 API call.
//
int Win32Port::FlushRXBuffer()
{
    if ( error_status < RS232_SUCCESS )
        return error_status;
    m_RxQueue.Clear();
    PurgeComm( m_hPort, PURGE_RXCLEAR );
    if ( !m_bInputThreadReading )
        SetEvent( m_hReadRequestEvent );
    return RS232_SUCCESS;
}

int Win32Port::FlushTXBuffer()
{
    if ( error_status < RS232_SUCCESS )
        return error_status;
    m_TxQueue.Clear();
    PurgeComm( m_hPort, PURGE_TXCLEAR );
    return RS232_SUCCESS;
}
```

```cpp
//
// Because you a few error codes are unique to the
// Win32Port class, it makes sense to translate them yourself
// when requested. That's what this function does. Note that most
// of the time, it passes the job up to the base class.
//
char *Win32Port::ErrorName( int error )
{
    if ( error < RS232_NEXT_FREE_ERROR && error >= RS232_ERROR )
        return RS232::ErrorName( error );
    if (error < RS232_NEXT_FREE_WARNING && error >= RS232_WARNING)
        return RS232::ErrorName( error );
    if ( error >= RS232_SUCCESS )
        return RS232::ErrorName( error );
    switch ( error ) {
        case WIN32_CHECK_WINDOWS_ERROR :
            return "Check Windows error code in m_dwWindowsError";
        case WIN32_SETTINGS_FAILURE :
            return "Failure to set port parameters";
        case WIN32_HANDSHAKE_LINE_IN_USE :
            return "Handshake line is already in use";
        default :
            return( "Undefined error" );
    }
}

//
// The last of the locally implemented versions of base class
// functions is FormatDebugOutput(). It should be fairly easy
// to figure out; it simply creates a line of output upon request.
// Note that it has a helper function that is used to format
// single characters for display in a nice, usable format.
//

static string DisplayChar( int val ) {
    char temp[ 2 ] = { val, 0 };
    if ( val >= ' ' && val <= 0x73 )
        return string( temp );
    ostringstream s;
    s << "0x" << setw( 2 ) << setfill( '0' ) << hex << val;
    return s.str();
}
```

Chapter 12: The Win32Test Program   537

```c
int Win32Port::FormatDebugOutput( char *buffer, int line_number )
{
    char *StopBits[ 4 ] = {
        "1",
        "1.5",
        "2",
        "???"
    };
    char *DtrControl[ 4 ] = {
        "DISABLE",
        "ENABLE",
        "HANDSHAKE",
        "???"
    };
    char *RtsControl[ 4 ] = {
        "DISABLE",
        "ENABLE",
        "HANDSHAKE",
        "TOGGLE"
    };
    if ( buffer == 0 )
        return( first_debug_output_line +  9 );
    if ( line_number < first_debug_output_line )
        return RS232::FormatDebugOutput( buffer, line_number );
    switch ( line_number - first_debug_output_line ) {
    case 0 :
        sprintf( buffer,
                "DCB-> Baud: %6d "
                "fBinary: %1d "
                "fParity: %1d "
                "fOutxCtsFlow: %1d "
                "fOutxDsrFlow: %1d",
                m_Dcb.BaudRate,
                m_Dcb.fBinary,
                m_Dcb.fParity,
                m_Dcb.fOutxCtsFlow,
                m_Dcb.fOutxDsrFlow );
        break;
    case 1 :
        sprintf( buffer,
                "DCB-> fDtrControl: %9s "
                "fDsrSensitivity: %1d "
                "fTXContinueOnXoff: %1d ",
                DtrControl[ m_Dcb.fDtrControl ],
```

```
                    m_Dcb.fDsrSensitivity,
                    m_Dcb.fTXContinueOnXoff );
        break;
    case 2 :
        sprintf( buffer,
                    "DCB-> fOutX: %1d     "
                    "fInX: %1d     "
                    "fErrorChar: %1d     "
                    "fNull: %1d     "
                    "fRtsControl: %9s",
                    m_Dcb.fOutX,
                    m_Dcb.fInX,
                    m_Dcb.fErrorChar,
                    m_Dcb.fNull,
                    RtsControl[ m_Dcb.fRtsControl ] );
        break;
    case 3 :
        sprintf( buffer,
                    "DCB-> fAbortOnError: %1d     "
                    "XonLim: %4d     "
                    "XoffLim: %4d     "
                    "ByteSize: %1d     "
                    "Parity: %1c ",
                    m_Dcb.fAbortOnError,
                    m_Dcb.XonLim,
                    m_Dcb.XoffLim,
                    m_Dcb.ByteSize,
                    "NOEMS"[ m_Dcb.Parity] );
        break;
    case 4 :
        sprintf( buffer,
                    "DCB-> StopBits: %3s     "
                    "XonChar: %s     "
                    "XoffChar: %s     "
                    "ErrorChar: %s     ",
                    StopBits[ m_Dcb.StopBits & 3 ],
                    DisplayChar( m_Dcb.XonChar ).c_str(),
                    DisplayChar( m_Dcb.XoffChar ).c_str(),
                    DisplayChar( m_Dcb.ErrorChar ).c_str() );
        break;
    case 5 :
        sprintf( buffer,
                    "DCB-> EofChar: %s     "
                    "EvtChar: %s     ",
```

```
                    DisplayChar( m_Dcb.EofChar ).c_str(),
                    DisplayChar( m_Dcb.EvtChar ).c_str() );
        break;
    case 6 :
    {
        COMSTAT comstat;
        clear_error( &comstat );
        sprintf( buffer,
                 "COMSTAT-> fCtsHold: %1d  "
                 "fDsrHold: %1d  "
                 "fRlsHold: %1d  "
                 "fXoffHold: %1d  "
                 "fXoffSent: %1d",
                 comstat.fCtsHold,
                 comstat.fDsrHold,
                 comstat.fRlsdHold,
                 comstat.fXoffHold,
                 comstat.fXoffSent );
        break;
    }
    case 7 :
    {
        COMSTAT comstat;
        clear_error( &comstat );
        sprintf( buffer,
                 "COMSTAT-> fEof: %1d  "
                 "fTxim: %1d  "
                 "cbInQueue: %5d  "
                 "cbOutQueue: %5d",
                 comstat.fEof,
                 comstat.fTxim,
                 comstat.cbInQue,
                 comstat.cbOutQue );
        break;
    }
    case 8 :
        sprintf( buffer,
                 "CE_-> BREAK: %1d  "
                 "FRAME: %1d  "
                 "OVERRUN: %1d  "
                 "RXOVER: %1d  "
                 "RXPARITY: %1d  "
                 "TXFULL: %1d",
                 ( m_dwErrors & CE_BREAK ) ? 1 : 0,
```

```
                    ( m_dwErrors & CE_FRAME ) ? 1 : 0,
                    ( m_dwErrors & CE_OVERRUN ) ? 1 : 0,
                    ( m_dwErrors & CE_RXOVER ) ? 1 : 0,
                    ( m_dwErrors & CE_RXPARITY ) ? 1 : 0,
                    ( m_dwErrors & CE_TXFULL ) ? 1 : 0 );
            break;
        default :
            return RS232_ILLEGAL_LINE_NUMBER;
    }
    return RS232_SUCCESS;
}

//
// write_byte() is a virtual function declared by class RS232 as a
// pure virtual function. Classes derived from RS232 must
// implement this function to work with their particular hardware
// setup. In your case, that simply means checking to see whether
// there is room in the output queue, and if there is, adding a
// byte to it. You set the event flag that kick starts the output
// thread just in case it was idle, and then return your status.
// Note that if the port is already in an error condition, this
// routine refuses to do anything except return the same error. If
// the buffer is full, you return the nonfatal warning error
// RS232_TIMEOUT.
//

int Win32Port::write_byte( int c )
{
    if ( error_status < 0 )
        return error_status;
    if ( m_TxQueue.SpaceFree() < 0 )
        return RS232_TIMEOUT;
    m_TxQueue.Insert( c );
    ::SetEvent( m_hWriteRequestEvent );
    return RS232_SUCCESS;
}

//
// write_buffer() is another one of the virtual routines that is
// declared by RS232, the base class, as pure virtual. That means
// it is your responsibility to implement it as best you can in
// this derived class. Writing data to your device is easy; you
// just have to load it into the output queue and set the event
// that wakes up the output thread. The actual number of bytes
```

Chapter 12: The Win32Test Program 541

```
// transferred to the output thread is passed back in member
// ByteCount. If not all bytes could fit in the output buffer, the
// nonfatal warning message RS232_TIMEOUT is passed back to the
// caller.
//

int Win32Port::write_buffer( char *buffer, unsigned int count )
{
    ByteCount = 0;
    if ( error_status < 0 )
        return error_status;
    ByteCount = m_TxQueue.Insert( buffer, count );
    ::SetEvent( m_hWriteRequestEvent );
    if ( ByteCount == count )
        return RS232_SUCCESS;
    else
        return RS232_TIMEOUT;
}


//
// read_byte() is one of the functions that is declared as pure
// virtual in base class RS232. You have to implement a specific
// version for your class that knows how to talk to your hardware.
// In this case, you don't have to talk to the hardware or even
// the driver. If any data has arrived, it has been stuffed into
// the input queue. You get a byte if you can, which will be
// returned to the caller. If no byte is available, the caller
// receives the nonfatal warning message RS232_TIMEOUT.
//
// One slightly tricky bit in this code occurs where you test to
// see whether the input thread is currently reading. If the input
// thread runs out of space in its input buffer, it has to stop
// reading. When you read a new character, you just might free up
// some space so that it can start reading again. You aren't going
// to make that decision for the input port, but you do set the
// event to let the input thread know that some space might have
// freed up.
//
int Win32Port::read_byte( void )
{
    if ( error_status < 0 )
        return error_status;
    int ret_val = m_RxQueue.Extract();
    if ( !m_bInputThreadReading )
```

```
        SetEvent( m_hReadRequestEvent );
    if ( ret_val < 0 )
        return RS232_TIMEOUT;
    else
        return ret_val;
}

//
// read_buffer is one of the support routines declared as pure
// virtual in the base class. This means that as a derived class,
// you are responsible for implementing a version that talks to
// your specific hardware or driver. The implementation here
// doesn't talk directly to the driver; you leave that to the
// input thread. You simply try to take all the characters you can
// from the input buffer, returning the actual count that you got
// in the ByteCount member. If you got every character you asked
// for, you return RS232_SUCCESS. If you didn't get everything you
// asked for, you return the nonfatal warning message
// RS232_TIMEOUT.
//
// One slightly tricky bit in this code occurs where you test to
// see whether the input thread is currently reading. If the input
// thread runs out of space in its input buffer, it has to stop
// reading. When you read a new character, you just might free up
// some space so it can start reading again. You aren't going to
// make that decision for the input port, but you do set his event
// to let him know that some space might have freed up.
//
int Win32Port::read_buffer( char *buffer, unsigned int count )
{
    ByteCount = 0;
    if ( error_status < 0 )
        return error_status;
    ByteCount = m_RxQueue.Extract( buffer, count );
    buffer[ ByteCount ] = '\0';
    if ( !m_bInputThreadReading )
        SetEvent( m_hReadRequestEvent );
    if ( ByteCount < count )
        return RS232_TIMEOUT;
    else
        return RS232_SUCCESS;
}

//
```

```
// clear_error() is an internal support routine that is called in
// response to the reception of an asynchronous error event. It
// first clears the comm error flag so that normal operation of
// the port can resume. It ORs the newly received error flags with
// the ones you have already seen in m_dwErrors. Finally, it calls
// a notification function for any incoming errors that have just
// occurred.
//
// One potential trouble spot in this function call is that it is
// called from both the FormatDebugOutput() routine as well as
// inside the receive thread. This opens the window for at least
// the  possibility of missing an incoming error if
// FormatDebugOutput() is called while an incoming error is seen.
// This could be guarded against by adding a critical section, but
// since FormatDebugOutput() is usually only called during testing
// and diagnostics, I didn't add it to this routine.
//

void Win32Port::clear_error( COMSTAT *comstat /* = 0 */ )
{
    COMSTAT c;
    if ( comstat == 0 )
        comstat = &c;
    DWORD errors;
    ClearCommError( m_hPort, &errors, comstat );
    m_dwErrors |= errors;
    if ( errors & CE_BREAK )
        BreakDetectNotify();
    if ( errors & CE_FRAME )
        FramingErrorNotify();
    if ( errors & CE_OVERRUN )
        HardwareOverrunErrorNotify();
    if ( errors & CE_RXPARITY )
        ParityErrorNotify();
    if ( errors & CE_RXOVER )
        SoftwareOverrunErrorNotify();
}

//
// write_settings() is an internal support routine that is only
// used in Win32Port(). Its job is to write the data in the
// settings member to the DCB being used for this port. The
// settings member has the four commonly used settings: baud rate,
// word size, parity, and number of stop bits. It also has current
```

```
// settings for the three different types of handshaking, plus the
// settings for the desired output of DTR and RTS. Once all of
// these things are punched into the DCB, a call to SetCommState()
// will take care of updating the physical device.
//
// There are a lot of things that can go wrong when attempting to
// set the port. You don't consider any of these things to be fatal
// errors, you simply pass the error back to the calling routine.
// However, the calling routine might decide to treat it as a
// fatal error. The constructor does this, treating an error at
// this point as fatal.
//
// Note also that this routine relies heavily on the DCB support
// class. It takes care of writing the correct values to its
// members by means of a bunch of accessor functions.
//

RS232Error Win32Port::write_settings()
{
    RS232Error error = RS232_SUCCESS;
    m_Dcb.SetBaudRate( settings.BaudRate );
    m_Dcb.SetParity( settings.Parity, error );
    m_Dcb.SetWordLength( settings.WordLength, error );
    m_Dcb.SetStopBits( settings.StopBits, error );
    //
    // Even though you think that you're setting up DTR and RTS,
    // you might not actually be pulling it off. If one of the
    // two hardware handshaking protocols is enabled, it will
    // wipe out the DCB setting for the corresponding control
    // line and change it to use handshaking instead.
    //
    m_Dcb.SetDtr( settings.Dtr );
    m_Dcb.SetRts( settings.Rts );
    m_Dcb.SetXonXoff( settings.XonXoff );
    m_Dcb.SetRtsCts( settings.RtsCts );
    m_Dcb.SetDtrDsr( settings.DtrDsr );
    SetCommState( m_hPort, &m_Dcb );
    if ( GetLastError() != 0 ) {
        if ( GetLastError() == ERROR_INVALID_HANDLE )
            return (RS232Error) WIN32_SETTINGS_FAILURE;
        else {
            m_dwWindowsError = GetLastError();
            return (RS232Error) WIN32_CHECK_WINDOWS_ERROR;
        }
```

```
    }
    return error;
}

//
// read_settings() is an internal support routine only used by
// member functions of Win32Port. It is actually only used in one
// place: the constructor. It is responsible for reading the
// settings from the  port as soon as you open it, giving you a
// baseline to start with. If necessary, this means that you can
// open the port in the default state that the system wants it to
// be opened in.
//
// Note that I didn't add accessor functions to the DCB to pull
// these settings out, you just look directly at the DCB members
// to get them. It would have probably been better to add
// translation routines, but it is not really an important issue.
//
void Win32Port::read_settings()
{
    DCB dcb;
    GetCommState( m_hPort, &dcb );
    settings.BaudRate = dcb.BaudRate;
    if ( !dcb.fParity )
        settings.Parity = 'N';
    else
        switch ( dcb.Parity ) {
        case EVENPARITY   : settings.Parity = 'E'; break;
        case ODDPARITY    : settings.Parity = 'O'; break;
        case MARKPARITY   : settings.Parity = 'M'; break;
        case SPACEPARITY  : settings.Parity = 'S'; break;
        default           : settings.Parity = 'N'; break;
        }
    settings.WordLength = dcb.ByteSize;
    if ( dcb.StopBits == ONESTOPBIT )
        settings.StopBits = 1;
    else
        settings.StopBits = 2;
    if ( dcb.fDtrControl == DTR_CONTROL_DISABLE )
        settings.Dtr = 0;
    else
        settings.Dtr = 1;
    if ( dcb.fRtsControl == RTS_CONTROL_DISABLE )
        settings.Rts = 0;
```

```
        else
            settings.Rts = 1;
        if ( dcb.fOutX || dcb.fInX )
            settings.XonXoff = 1;
        else
            settings.XonXoff = 0;
        if ( dcb.fOutxCtsFlow ||
             dcb.fRtsControl == RTS_CONTROL_HANDSHAKE )
            settings.RtsCts = 1;
        else
            settings.RtsCts = 0;
        if ( dcb.fOutxDsrFlow ||
              dcb.fDtrControl == DTR_CONTROL_HANDSHAKE )
            settings.DtrDsr = 1;
        else
            settings.DtrDsr = 0;
}

//
// translate_last_error() is called any time an error occurs when
// a Win32 API function is called. You know how to translate a
// couple of Win32 errors to native versions, but for the most
// part, you just pass the responsibility for interpretation on to
// the caller of the Win32Port function. The value you see is
// stored in the m_dwWindowsError member so that it can be checked
// even in the presence of other intervening problems.
//

RS232Error Win32Port::translate_last_error()
{
    switch ( m_dwWindowsError = GetLastError() )
    {
    case ERROR_ACCESS_DENIED   :
        return error_status = RS232_PORT_IN_USE;
    case ERROR_FILE_NOT_FOUND :
        return error_status = RS232_PORT_NOT_FOUND;
    }
    return error_status = (RS232Error) WIN32_CHECK_WINDOWS_ERROR;
}

//
// InputThread is the function that runs as a separate thread that
// is responsible for reading all input data and status
// information. It is a fairly complex thread, which makes it a
```

```
// bit harder to read than it should be. Outside of setup and
// teardown, the routine sits in  a giant loop that basically
// performs two functions. First, it makes sure that it is
// properly set up to be notified when either incoming data or
// status messages arrive. Status messages consist of line status
// errors and modem status changes. (Note that you don't try to d
// if there is no room for data in the input buffer.) Once that is
// set up, you simply wait for one of four potential events to be
// signaled. The events are 1) a kill message fromt the main
// thread, which comes when the port is being closed, 2) incoming
// data that has been read in from the serial port, 3) a line
// status error or modem status change on the serial port, and 4)
// a read request message, which indicates that some room may have
// been opened up in the input buffer.
//
// The rest of the work in the routine is devoted to figuring out
// what to do in response to those incoming events.
//

void Win32Port::InputThread( void * arglist )
{
    //
    // The thread is passed a pointer to the Win32Port object when
    // it is started up. You have to cast that back to a Win32Port
    // pointer, because of the way Win32 starts a thread function.
    // Since this is a static member function of the class, that
    // gives you carte blanche to access all the protected members
    // of the class. It also means you don't have to mess with
    // creation or management of thread-specific data, as
    // anything you need will be in the object itself.
    //
    Win32Port *port = (Win32Port *) arglist;
    //
    // You call these two functions once when you start up so that
    // all of the initial settings in the modem status and line
    // status words are initialized properly. This also guarantees
    // that the notification functions for the modem status will
    // be called once with the initial values, which will often be
    // a useful thing for the calling program.
    //
    port->check_modem_status( true, 0 );
    port->clear_error();
    //
    // You need OVERLAPPED structures for both of your overlapped
```

```
// functions in this thread: the data read called with
// ReadFile(), and the status read called with WaitCommEvent.
// You could have included these in the Win32Port object, but
// since they aren't used anywhere else, it seemed better to
// confine them to being automatic objects. Each of these
// objects gets an event that you create here as well, they
// are the events used to signal you when you are waiting in
// the big loop.
//
OVERLAPPED AsyncReadInfo = { 0 };
OVERLAPPED AsyncStatusInfo = { 0 };
AsyncReadInfo.hEvent = CreateEvent( NULL, TRUE, FALSE, NULL );
AsyncStatusInfo.hEvent = CreateEvent(NULL, TRUE, FALSE, NULL);
assert( AsyncReadInfo.hEvent );
assert( AsyncStatusInfo.hEvent );
//
// This word is used as an argument to WaitForCommEvent()
//
DWORD dwCommEvent;
//
//   Some initialization
//
bool waiting_on_status = false;
port->m_bInputThreadReading = false;
//
// This array holds the four event handles that are used to
// signal this thread. On each pass through the main loop we
// will be waiting for one of the four to go to the signal
// state, at which time you take action on it.
//
HANDLE handles[ 4 ] = { port->m_hKillInputThreadEvent,
                        AsyncReadInfo.hEvent,
                        AsyncStatusInfo.hEvent,
                        port->m_hReadRequestEvent };

//
// You set all of the conditions that you will be waiting for.
// Note the inclusion of EV_RINGTE, which is an undocumented
// flag that you define in Win32Port.h.
//
SetCommMask( port->m_hPort,
             EV_BREAK | EV_CTS  | EV_DSR  | EV_RXCHAR |
             EV_ERR   | EV_RING | EV_RLSD | EV_RINGTE );
//
```

```cpp
// This is the main loop. It executes until the done flag is
// set, which won't happen until the kill thread message is
// sent. The first part of the loop sets up the read actions,
// the second part waits for something to happen, and the
// final part of the loop deals with whatever happened.
//
for ( bool done = false ; !done ; ) {
    //
    // Under normal conditions this loop should have a read
    // action in progress at all times. The only time this
    // won't be true is when there is no room in the RX queue.
    // You have a member in class Win32Port that defines
    // whether or not a read is presently active. This section
    // of code just makes sure that if no read is currently in
    // progress, you do your best to get one started.
    //
    int bytes_to_read = 0;
    char read_buffer[ 256 ];
    DWORD dwBytesRead;
    if ( !port->m_bInputThreadReading ) {
        bytes_to_read = port->m_RxQueue.SpaceFree();
        if ( bytes_to_read > 256 )
            bytes_to_read = 256;
        //
        // If there is room to add new bytes to the RX queue,
        // and you currently aren't reading anything, you kick
        // off the read right here with a call to ReadFile().
        // There are two possible things that can then happen.
        // If there isn't any data in the buffer, ReadFile()
        // can return immediately with the actual input in
        // progress but not complete. If there was enough data
        // in the input stream already to fulfill the read, it
        // might return with data present.
        //
        if ( bytes_to_read > 0 ) {
            if ( !ReadFile( port->m_hPort,
                            read_buffer,
                            bytes_to_read,
                            &dwBytesRead,
                            &AsyncReadInfo ) )
            {
                // The only acceptable error condition is the
                // I/O pending error, which isn't really an
                // error, it just means the read has been
```

```
                    // deferred and will be performed using
                    // overlapped I/O.
                    //
                    port->m_bInputThreadReading = true;
                } else {
                    // If you reach this point, ReadFile() returned
                    // immediately, presumably because it was able
                    // to fill the I/O request. I put all of the
                    // bytes just read into the RX queue, then
                    // call the notification routine that should
                    // alert the caller to the fact that some data
                    // has arrive.
                    //
                     if ( dwBytesRead ) {
                         port->m_RxQueue.Insert( read_buffer,
                                                 dwBytesRead );
                         port->RxNotify( dwBytesRead );
                     }
                }
            } else {
                // If you reach this point, it means there is no
                // room in the RX queue. you reset the read event
                // (just in case) and go on to the rest of the
                // code in this loop.
                ResetEvent( AsyncReadInfo.hEvent );
            }
        }
        //
        // Unlike the read event, you will unconditionally always
        // have a status even read in progress. The flag
        // waiting_on_status shows you whether or not you are
        // currently waiting. If not, you have to make a call to
        // WaitCommEvent() so that one gets kicked off.
        //
        if ( !waiting_on_status  ) {
            if ( !WaitCommEvent( port->m_hPort,
                                 &dwCommEvent,
                                 &AsyncStatusInfo ) ) {
                // WaitCommEvent() can return immediately if there
                // are status events queued up and waiting for you
                // to read. But normally it should return with an
                // error code of ERROR_IO_PENDING, which means
                // that no events are currently queued, and you
                // will have to wait for something noteworthy to
```

```
            // happen.
            waiting_on_status = true;
        } else {
            // If you reach this point it means that
            // WaitCommEvent() returned immediately, so either
            // a line status error or a modem line state
            // change has occurred. These two routines are
            // called to deal with all those possibilities.
            //
            // The event bits are in dwCommEvent, which was
            // passed to WaitCommEvent() when you called it.
            // The first of these two functions handles all
            // changes in modem status lines, the second deals
            // with line status errors.
            //
            port->check_modem_status( false, dwCommEvent );
            port->clear_error();
        }
    }
    //
    // We've completed the preliminary part of the loop and
    // you are now ready to wait for something to happen. Note
    // that it is possible that either the call to ReadFile()
    // or WaitCommEvent() returned immediately, in which case
    // you aren't actively waiting for data of that event
    // type. If that's true, you have to go back through the
    // loop and try to set up the ReadFile() or
    // WaitCommEvent() again. That's what this first
    // conditional statement is checking for. It would be a
    // simpler statement, but you have to take into account
    // the possibility that you aren't reading because there
    // is no room in the RX queue, in which case you can wait
    // right away.
    //
    if ( waiting_on_status &&
         (port->m_bInputThreadReading || bytes_to_read == 0) ) {
        DWORD result = WaitForMultipleObjects( 4,
                                               handles,
                                               FALSE,
                                               INFINITE );
        //
        // You can return from the wait call with one of four
        // possible results. 0-3 mean that one of the event
        // handles in the array defined above was set by some
```

```
// process. The other is a timeout. If you are nervous
// about waiting forever, you can put a 10- or 20-
// second timeout on this wait, and print a TRACE
// message every time the wait times out. This gives
// you a little bit of a warm feeling that lets you
// know things are really working.
//
switch ( result ) {
// If the first event handle in the array was set, it
// means that the main thread of the program wants to
// close the port. It sets the kill event, and you in
// turn set the done flag. You will then exit from
// the bottom of the loop.
//
case 0 : // kill thread event
    done = true;
    break;
// This case is selected if an overlapped read of data
// has signalled that it is complete. If the
// ReadFile() call completed because it passed in some
// data, you stuff that data into the RX queue and
// call the notification function to alert the user's
// process.
case 1 :
    if ( GetOverlappedResult( port->m_hPort,
                              &AsyncReadInfo,
                              &dwBytesRead,
                              FALSE ) )
    {
     if ( dwBytesRead ) {
      port->m_RxQueue.Insert(read_buffer,dwBytesRead);
      port->RxNotify( dwBytesRead );
     }
    }
    // Since the last ReadFile() operation completed,
    // you are no longer reading data. You set this
    // flag to false so  that you can kick off a new
    // read at the top of the loop.
    port->m_bInputThreadReading = false;
    break;
// When you reach case 2, it means that the
// WaitCommEvent() call completed, which means that
// one of the line status or modem status events has
// been triggered. You don't know which one it is, so
```

```
                // you call the handler for both possibilities,
                // allowing the handler to decide whether something
                // has happened and who to notify about it.
                case 2 : { /* Status event */
                    DWORD dwOverlappedResult;
                    if ( GetOverlappedResult( port->m_hPort,
                                              &AsyncStatusInfo,
                                              &dwOverlappedResult,
                                              FALSE ) ) {
                      port->check_modem_status( false, dwCommEvent );
                      port->clear_error();
                    }
                    // Clear this flag so that a new call to
                    // WaitCommEvent()can be made at the top of the
                    // loop.
                    waiting_on_status = false;
                    break;
                }
                // When you reach case 3, it means that another thread
                // read some data from the RX queue, opening up some
                // room, and noticed that you weren't actively reading
                // data. When this happens, you need to wake up and
                // start a new call to ReadFile() so that you can fill
                // up all that empty  space in the RX queue.
                case 3 :
                    TRACE( "Input thread wakeup event\n" );
                    break;
                default :
                    assert( false );
            }
        }
    }
    //
    // When the input thread has decided to exit, it first kills
    // the two events it created and then exits via a return
    // statement.
    CloseHandle( AsyncReadInfo.hEvent );
    CloseHandle( AsyncStatusInfo.hEvent );
}

//
// The output thread is very similar in structure to the input
// thread, with a few notable differences. Instead of including
// the wait for output data as part of its main loop, the output
```

```cpp
// thread calls a subroutine to actually perform the data output.
// And that output function runs to completion, so you will never
// wait for output to be complete in the main body of the thread
// shown here. It would probably be a useful modification of this
// thread to change it so that pending output is waited for in the
// main thread.
//
void Win32Port::OutputThread(void * arglist)
{
    //
    // As was the case for the input thread, you get a pointer to
    // the Win32Port object passed to you from the calling routine.
    // You just have to cast the pointer, and then you have full
    // access to all members of the port's structure.
    //
    //
    Win32Port *port = (Win32Port *) arglist;
    ..
    // The array of handles you wait for in the main loop has one
    // fewer element than the same array in the input thread.
    // You're waiting for only three things here: a request to
    // send more data via WriteFile(), a request to kill the
    // thread, or a request to send a break.
    HANDLE handles[ 3 ] = { port->m_hKillOutputThreadEvent,
                            port->m_hWriteRequestEvent,
                            port->m_hBreakRequestEvent };
    port->TxNotify();
    for ( bool done = false ; !done ; ) {
        switch ( WaitForMultipleObjects( 3,
                                          handles,
                                          FALSE,
                                          INFINITE ) ) {
        //
        // There are three possible returns from the call that
        // waits for something to happens: the three events and a
        // timeout. The first case means that a thread has
        // attempted to close the port, which results in the kill
        // thread event being set. When that's the case, you
        // modify the control flag for the loop so that control
        // passes out of the the loop when you reach the bottom.
        //
        case 0 : //m_hKillOutputThreadEvent
            done = true;
            break;
```

```
            //
            // Much of the time this loop will be sitting here doing
            // nothing. When an output request comes through, the
            // appropriate event is set and you end up here. You then
            // call the output worker routine to actually dump the
            // output through the serial port.
            //
            case 1 : //m_hWriteRequestEvent
                done = port->output_worker();
                break;
            //
            // If the break event is set, it means you are being
            // requested to send a break out through the given port.
            // The duration of the break has already been set in a
            // member of the object, so all you have to do here is
            // make it happen. Because this is a background thread
            // with no GUI, it's safe to just sit in a sleep call for
            // the duration of the break.
            //
            case 2 : //m_hBreakRequestEvent
                SetCommBreak( port->m_hPort );
                SleepEx( port->m_iBreakDuration, FALSE );
                ClearCommBreak( port->m_hPort );
                break;
            //
            // This can only be bad!
            //
            default :
                assert( false );
                break;
        }
    }
}

//
// When a request comes in to transmit some data, this routine is
// called. It starts things up by calling WriteFile() and then
// waits for the asynchronous I/O to complete. Note that while it
// is waiting for WriteFile() to complete, it can also be notified
// of a kill thread event, in which case it returns immediately.
//

bool Win32Port::output_worker()
{
```

```cpp
            OVERLAPPED AsyncWriteInfo = { 0 };
            AsyncWriteInfo.hEvent = CreateEvent(NULL, TRUE, FALSE, NULL);
            assert( AsyncWriteInfo.hEvent );
            HANDLE handles[ 2 ] = { m_hKillOutputThreadEvent,
                                    AsyncWriteInfo.hEvent };
            bool killed = false;
            for ( bool done = false ; ; !done ) {
                //
                // First get as much data from the output buffer as you
                // can.
                //
                char data[ 500 ];
                int count = m_TxQueue.Extract( data, 500 );
                if ( count == 0 ) {
                    TxNotify();
                    break;
                }
                //
                // Now you enter the transmit loop, where the data will
                // actually be sent out the serial port.
                //
                DWORD result_count;
                if ( !WriteFile( m_hPort,
                                 data,
                                 count,
                                 &result_count,
                                 &AsyncWriteInfo ) ) {
                    //
                    // WriteFile() returned an error. If the error tells
                    // you that the I/O operation didn't complete, that's
                    // okay.
                    //
                    if ( GetLastError() == ERROR_IO_PENDING ) {
                        switch ( WaitForMultipleObjects( 2,
                                                         handles,
                                                         FALSE,
                                                         INFINITE ) ) {
                            //
                            // Case 0 is the thread kill event; you need to
                            // give this up. Because the event is cleared when
                            // you detect it, you have to reset it
                            //
                            case 0 : //m_hKillOutputThreadEvent
                                done = true;
```

```cpp
                killed = true;
                PurgeComm( m_hPort, PURGE_TXABORT );
                break;
            //
            // Case 1 means the WriteFile routine signaled
            // completion. You're not out of the woods
            // completely; there are a few errors you have to
            // check.
            //
            case 1 : //AsyncWriteInfo.hEvent
                // The overlapped result can show that the
                // write event completed, or it stopped for
                // some other reason. If it is some other
                // reason, you exit the loop immediately.
                // Otherwise, you will pass through the loop
                // and kick off another write. Note that
                // a TXFlush() call creates an error here,
                // which you ignore.
                if ( !GetOverlappedResult( m_hPort,
                                           &AsyncWriteInfo,
                                           &result_count,
                                           FALSE ) ||
                     result_count != count ) {
                    if ( GetLastError() == ERROR_IO_PENDING )
                        clear_error();
                    else
                        translate_last_error();
                    done = true;
                }
                break;
            //
            // You had better not ever land here!
            //
            default :
                assert( false );
            }
        } else {
          translate_last_error();
          done = true;
        }
    } else {
        //
        // If you fall through to this point, it means that
        // WriteFile() returned immediately. If it did, it
```

```
                    // means that you were able to send all the
                    // characters requested in the call. If you get here
                    // and all the characters weren't sent, something bad
                    // happened.
                    //
                    if ( result_count != count ) {
                        translate_last_error();
                        done = true;
                    }
                }
            }
        }
        //
        // On the way out, close the event handle
        //
        CloseHandle( AsyncWriteInfo.hEvent );
        return killed;
    }

    //
    // When an asynchronous event is processed from the call to
    // WaitCommEvent(), you have to call this guy to determine what
    // happened. You check each of the modem status lines to see who
    // changed, and then call the notification functions to let the
    // calling process know what happened.
    //
    void Win32Port::check_modem_status(bool first_time,
                                       DWORD event_mask )
    {
        //
        // There shouldn't be anything to prevent you from reading
        // the input lines. If an error occurs, it is bad.
        ///
        if ( !GetCommModemStatus( m_hPort, &m_dwModemStatus ) )
            assert( false );
        //
        // The first_time flag is set one time when this guy is
        // called to force the notification functions to be called.
        // Forcing this to happen means that an application can be
        // sure that it can use the notification functions to
        // determine status.
        //
        if ( first_time ) //report everything
        {
```

```
            CtsNotify( ( MS_CTS_ON & m_dwModemStatus ) != 0 );
            DsrNotify( ( MS_DSR_ON & m_dwModemStatus ) != 0 );
            CdNotify( ( MS_RLSD_ON & m_dwModemStatus ) != 0 );
            RiNotify( 0 );
        } else { //Only report events
            //
            // If it isn't the first time, you send notification
            // only for events that actually occured in the event that
            // caused this function to be invoked
            //
            if ( event_mask & EV_CTS )
                CtsNotify( ( MS_CTS_ON & m_dwModemStatus ) != 0 );
            if ( event_mask & EV_DSR )
                DsrNotify( ( MS_DSR_ON & m_dwModemStatus ) != 0 );
            if ( event_mask & EV_RLSD )
                CdNotify( ( MS_RLSD_ON & m_dwModemStatus ) != 0 );
            //
            // Win95/98 *always* reports an RI event if RI is high
            // when any other line changes. This is not really a good
            // thing. All you're interested in is seeing EV_RINGTE, so
            // you report an event only if RI is low
            //
            if ( event_mask & ( EV_RING | EV_RINGTE ) )
                if ( ( MS_RING_ON & m_dwModemStatus ) == 0 )
                    RiNotify( 0 );
        }
}

// EOF Win32Port.cpp
```

Listing 12-3: DCB.H

```
//
//   DCB.H
//
//   Source code from:
//
//   Serial Communications Developer's Guide, 2nd Edition
//   by Mark Nelson, IDG Books, 1999
//
//   Please see the book for information on usage.
//
// This file contains the class definition for my private DCB
// class. This guy is used internally by the Win32Port class to
```

```
// hold the current DCB. It exists only because I can put in a
// few convenience functions that are used to initialize
// members of the DCB. They make code elsewhere in the program
// a lot less cluttered.
//

#ifndef _DCB_H
#define _DCB_H

struct Dcb : public DCB
{
    Dcb();
    void SetBaudRate( int rate );
    void SetParity( int parity, RS232Error &error );
    void SetWordLength( int word_length, RS232Error &error );
    void SetStopBits( int stop_bits, RS232Error &error );
    void SetDtr( int value );
    void SetRts( int value );
    void SetXonXoff( int value );
    void SetDtrDsr( int value );
    void SetRtsCts( int value );
};

#endif // #ifndef _DCB_H
```

Listing 12-4: Dcb.cpp

```
//
//   DCB.CPP
//
//   Source code from:
//
//   Serial Communications Developer's Guide, 2nd Edition
//   by Mark Nelson, IDG Books, 1999
//
// The m_Dcb member of the Win32Port class is used to hold most
// of the information regarding the current state of the port.
// The only reason that the DCB was encapsulated into this
// class was simply to make the Win32Port code more readable.
// The Win32Port code becomes more readable because a lot of
// the initialization code for the various members is offloaded
// to the Dcb class. Note that this class is derived from the
// DCB structure defined in the WIN32 header files, so any
// function that takes a pointer to a DCB can take a pointer to
```

```
// one of these structures as well.
//

#include "stdafx.h"
#include <cctype>

#include "Chapt10.h"
#include "rs232.h"
#include "Dcb.h"

//
// The Dcb constructor initializes every member of the base
// class DCB so that you get to skip all the initialization
// code you would normally have in a class that has a member of
// this type. In particular, the Win32Port constructor gets to
// take advantage of this by passively allowing the Dcb
// constructor to be invoked.
//

Dcb::Dcb()
{
    DCBlength = sizeof( DCB );//Windows API expects this
    BaudRate = 38400;         //Default baud rate
    fBinary = TRUE;           //In Win32 this is alwaystrue
    fParity = FALSE;          //Our default is no parity
    fOutxCtsFlow = FALSE;     //Default is no RTS/CTS flow control
    fOutxDsrFlow = FALSE;     //Default is no DTR/DSR flow control
    fDtrControl = DTR_CONTROL_ENABLE; //Assert DTR by default
    fDsrSensitivity = FALSE;  //Ignore incoming DSR by default
    fTXContinueOnXoff = FALSE;  //No special action on Xoff
    fOutX = FALSE;            /No outbound XON/XOFF handshaking
    fInX = FALSE;             //No incoming XON/XOFF handshaking
    fErrorChar = FALSE;       //No special char on line errors
    fNull = FALSE;            //No null detection
    fRtsControl = RTS_CONTROL_ENABLE; //Assert RTS by default
    fAbortOnError = TRUE;     //Always respond to errors
    fDummy2 = 0;
    wReserved = 0;
    XonLim = 128;             //Send XON when 128 characters left
    XoffLim = 128;            //Send XOFF when space left = 128
    ByteSize = 8;             //Default word size
    Parity = NOPARITY;        //Default is no parity
    StopBits = ONESTOPBIT;    //Default is one stop bit
    XonChar = 0x11;           //Default XON is ^Q
```

```
        XoffChar = 0x13;              //Default XOFF is ^S
        ErrorChar = 0;                //Not using error char, don't care
        EofChar = 0;                  //Not using EOF char, don't care
        EvtChar = 0;                  //Not using event char, don't care
    };

    //
    // Setting the baud rate is as simple as stuffing it verbatim
    // into the DCB. There are some intricacies regarding baud rate
    // management in the Win32 API, but I don't get into them
    // here.
    //
    void Dcb::SetBaudRate( int rate )
    {
        if ( rate != UNCHANGED )
            BaudRate = rate;
    }


    //
    // Setting parity is done by passing a single character that is
    // the first character in the name of the parity being
    // selected. The actual setting of the parity affects two
    // members of the DCB. The fParity member tells the driver
    // whether to pay any attention to parity. The Parity
    // member tells it which parity to use if fParity is set.

    void Dcb::SetParity( int parity, RS232Error &error )
    {
        switch ( toupper( parity ) ) {
        case 'N'        : fParity = FALSE; Parity = NOPARITY;    break;
        case 'E'        : fParity = TRUE;  Parity = EVENPARITY;  break;
        case 'O'        : fParity = TRUE;  Parity = ODDPARITY;   break;
        case 'M'        : fParity = TRUE;  Parity = MARKPARITY;  break;
        case 'S'        : fParity = TRUE;  Parity = SPACEPARITY; break;
        case UNCHANGED  :                                        break;
        default         : error = RS232_ILLEGAL_PARITY_SETTING;
        }
    };

    //
    // The word length setting is trivial.
    //
    void Dcb::SetWordLength( int word_length, RS232Error &error )
    {
```

```
    switch ( word_length ) {
    case 5          : ByteSize = 5; break;
    case 6          : ByteSize = 6; break;
    case 7          : ByteSize = 7; break;
    case 8          : ByteSize = 8; break;
    case UNCHANGED  : break;
    default         : error = RS232_ILLEGAL_WORD_LENGTH;
    }
}

//
// Setting the number of stop bits is nice and simple. I don't
// take into account the possibility of 1.5 stop bits in this
// function because it serves no practical purpose.
//
void Dcb::SetStopBits( int stop_bits, RS232Error &error )
{
    switch ( stop_bits ) {
    case 1              : StopBits = ONESTOPBIT;  break;
    case 2              : StopBits = TWOSTOPBITS; break;
    case UNCHANGED      :                         break;
    default             : error = RS232_ILLEGAL_STOP_BITS; break;
    }
}

//
// Setting DTR is fairly simple. Note that this has an
// unintended side effect. If DTR/DSR handshaking was enabled
// before this call, it won't be any more. So, you should either
// call this function before you set up handshaking or skip
// the call if handshaking is enabled.
//
void Dcb::SetDtr( int value )
{
    if ( value == UNCHANGED )
        return;
    else if ( value )
        fDtrControl = DTR_CONTROL_ENABLE;
    else
        fDtrControl = DTR_CONTROL_DISABLE;
}

//
// Setting RTS is fairly simple. Note that this has an
```

```cpp
// unintended side effect. If RTS/CTS handshaking was enabled
// before this call, it won't be any more. So, you should either
// call this function before you set up handshaking or skip
// the call if handshaking is enabled.
//
void Dcb::SetRts( int value )
{
    if ( value == UNCHANGED )
        return;
    else if ( value )
        fRtsControl = RTS_CONTROL_ENABLE;
    else
        fRtsControl = RTS_CONTROL_DISABLE;
}

//
// This function either turns XON/XOFF handshking on or off. It
// assumes that the high- and low-water marks have already been
// set to where you would like them and that the definitons of
// the XON and XOFF characters have already been made. Because
// these are set up in the Dcb constructor, the odds are that
// they still have good values.
//
void Dcb::SetXonXoff( int value )
{
    if ( value != UNCHANGED ) {
        if ( value ) {
            fOutX = TRUE;
            fInX = TRUE;
        } else {
            fOutX = FALSE;
            fInX = FALSE;
        }
    }
}

//
// If DTR/DSR handshaking is to be enabled, this function sets
// the control bits for both input and output handshaking. If
// handshaking is not to be enabled, the inbound sensitivity
// bit is turned off. However, you don't do anything about the
// outbound control of DTR if handshaking is to be turned off.
// You assume that the caller will have already set DTR to the
// desired setting.
```

```
//
void Dcb::SetDtrDsr( int value )
{
    if ( value != UNCHANGED ) {
        if ( value ) {
            fDtrControl = DTR_CONTROL_HANDSHAKE;
            fOutxDsrFlow = TRUE;
        } else
            fOutxDsrFlow = FALSE;
    }
}

//
// If RTS/CTS handshaking is to be enabled, this function sets
// the control bits for both input and output handshaking. If
// handshaking is not to be enabled, the inbound sensitivity
// bit is turned off. However, you don't do anything about the
// outbound control of RTS if handshaking is to be turned off.
// You assume that the caller will have already set RTS to the
// desired setting.
//
void Dcb::SetRtsCts( int value )
{
    if ( value != UNCHANGED ) {
        if ( value ) {
            fRtsControl = RTS_CONTROL_HANDSHAKE;
            fOutxCtsFlow = TRUE;
        } else
            fOutxCtsFlow = FALSE;
    }
}

//EOF Dcb.cpp
```

Listing 12-5: MTDeque.h

(Note that there is no `MTDeque.cpp`, all functions are defined inline.)

```
//
//   MTDEQUE.H
//
//   Source code from:
//
```

```cpp
//  Serial Communications Developer's Guide, 2nd Edition
//  by Mark Nelson, IDG Books, 1999
//
//  Please see the book for information on usage.
//
// This file contains the definition for class MTDeque, a
// double-ended queue of type char that is multithread safe.
// This class is used to implemnet the I/O buffers for class
// Win32Port.
//

#ifndef MTDEQUE_H
#define MTDEQUE_H

//
// Class MTdeque is a class used in this program to provide an
// implementation of the standard container deque<T> that is
// safe in a multithread program. This is done by creating a
// semaphore that wraps any member functions that access the
// object. This class is used in the input and output buffers
// for the Win32Port class. deque<T> is a double-ended queue
// and provides fairly fast access to elements in the queue
// from both ends. Although this may not be as fast as a custom
// container designed specifically for this application, using
// standard library classes should give you a nice, safe feeling.
//

class MTdeque
{
//
// All three data members of this class are protectd; anything
// the end user wants to know needs to come from a member
// function. The deque<char> member is where the data is
// actually stored. m_iMaxSize is the suggested maximum size.
// The CRITICAL_SECTION member protects access to the queue
// against the danger of simultaneous calls from multiple
// threads
//
protected :
    const m_iMaxSize;
    deque<char> m_Queue;
    CRITICAL_SECTION m_Lock;

    //
    // Because the m_iMaxSize is a const member, you need to
```

```
        // assign it a value in a member initialization list.
        // You can accept the default constructor for the
        // deque<char> member because it just creates an empty
        // container. And the critical section needs to be
        // initialized using a call to the Win32 API.
        //
public :
    MTdeque( int max_size ) : m_iMaxSize( max_size )
    {
        ::InitializeCriticalSection( &m_Lock );
    }
    //
    // The destructor for the m_Queue member will take care
    // of properly cleaning up all its data. You have to
    // make sure that you use the API call to properly free up
    // the CRITICAL_SECTION object. And that's all!
    //
    ~MTdeque()
    {
        ::DeleteCriticalSection( &m_Lock );
    }
    //
    // This is a multithread safe version of the function
    // that tells you how much free space is in the queue.
    // There is a belt and suspenders check to make sure that you
    // don't return a negative number if the user has
    // somehow exceeded the maximum size of the queue. This
    // shouldn't happen, but if it does for some reason, you
    // are protected against confusion.
    //
    int SpaceFree()
    {
        ::EnterCriticalSection( &m_Lock );
        int size = m_iMaxSize - m_Queue.size();
        ::LeaveCriticalSection( &m_Lock );
        return ( size < 0 ) ? 0 : size;
    }
    //
    // This returns the amount of space used in the queue.
    // Like the previous member, it uses a private
    // critical section object to protect against the
    // possible ravages that may occur if you use this
    // function while a different thread is accessing the
    // queue.
    //
```

```cpp
int SpaceUsed()
{
    ::EnterCriticalSection( &m_Lock );
    int size = m_Queue.size();
    ::LeaveCriticalSection( &m_Lock );
    return size;
}
//
// This is a thread safe version of a function that
// inserts a single character into the queue. It
// protects against exceeding the desired size of the
// queue, and like some of the old stdio C functions,
// it returns the character inserted on success and a
// negative number upon failure. This function is used
// in Win32Port by the write_byte() member function.
//
int Insert( char c )
{
    int return_value;
    ::EnterCriticalSection( &m_Lock );
    if ( m_Queue.size() < m_iMaxSize ) {
        m_Queue.push_back( c );
        return_value = c & 0xff;
    } else
        return_value = -1;
    ::LeaveCriticalSection( &m_Lock );
    return return_value;
}
//
// This overloaded version of Insert() is used to
// insert an entire buffer of characters into the
// deque<char> member of the class. It uses the
// critical section created in the constructor to
// protect you from multithread conflicts during the
// operation. It returns the actual count of characters
// inserted to the caller. If the caller doesn't
// attempt to exceed the maximum character size, the
// function will always succeed.
//
int Insert( char *data, int count )
{
    ::EnterCriticalSection( &m_Lock );
    int actual = m_iMaxSize - m_Queue.size() ;
    if ( actual < 0 )
        actual = 0;
```

```
        if ( count < actual )
            actual = count;
        for ( int i = 0 ; i < actual ; i++ )
            m_Queue.push_back( *data++ );
        ::LeaveCriticalSection( &m_Lock );
        return actual;
    }
    //
    // This function is used to extract a buffer full of
    // characters from the deque<char> member of this
    // class. The user passes a pointer to a buffer and a
    // maximum count of characters desired. In turn, this
    // function extracts as many characters as possible
    // from the the deque<char> and inserts them into the
    // user buffer. It then returns the count of characters
    // to the caller. This function is used by the
    // read_bytes() member of Win32Port.
    //
    int Extract( char *data, int max )
    {
        int i = 0;
        ::EnterCriticalSection( &m_Lock );
        while ( i < max && m_Queue.size() ) {
            data[ i++ ] = m_Queue.front();
            m_Queue.pop_front();
        }
        ::LeaveCriticalSection( &m_Lock );
        return i;
    }
    //
    // Peek is used to look into the buffer without
    // actually removing the characters. Naturally it looks
    // an awful lot like Extract().
    //
    int Peek( char *data, int max )
    {
        ::EnterCriticalSection( &m_Lock );
        if ( max > m_Queue.size() )
            max = m_Queue.size();
        for ( int i = 0 ; i < max ; i++ )
            data[ i ] = m_Queue.begin()[ i ];
        ::LeaveCriticalSection( &m_Lock );
        return i;
    }
    //
```

```
        // This overloaded version of Extract() is used by the
        // read_byte() member of Win32Port to read a single
        // character at a time from the deque<char> member of
        // this class. If a character is available, it is
        // returned directly to the caller in the lower eight
        // bits of the int return value. This function is
        // called by the read_byte() member function of the
        // Win32Port class.
        //
        int Extract()
        {
            int ret_val = -1;
            ::EnterCriticalSection( &m_Lock );
            if ( m_Queue.size() ) {
                ret_val = m_Queue.front() & 0xff;
                m_Queue.pop_front();
            }
            ::LeaveCriticalSection( &m_Lock );
            return ret_val;
        }
        //
        // This member just empties the queue.
        //
        void Clear()
        {
            ::EnterCriticalSection( &m_Lock );
            m_Queue.clear();
            ::LeaveCriticalSection( &m_Lock );
        }
};

#endif

// EOF MTDeque.h
```

Summary

This chapter wrapped up the discussion of the Win32 API. In Chapters 10 and 11, you learned about the underlying Win32 comm API, and saw how it was integrated into class `Win32Port`. This chapter presented the source for that class plus showed you how to test it using the `CHAPT12.EXE` test program. The `Win32Port` class is far and away the most complex RS232 class developed in this book, so the source and internal documentation are large enough to have merited them a chapter of their own.

As you have learned in this chapter, the test program uses a console window for character input and output, and a GUI-based dialog box for various test and control functions. It provides you with a convenient platform for testing all the features of the class in an interactive way and working samples that show you how to use the `Win32Port` class.

Chapter 13

Win32 Terminal Emulation

IN THIS CHAPTER

- ◆ A terminal window class
- ◆ Class Win32 definitions
- ◆ Integration of Win32Term with AnsiTerm
- ◆ The Chapter 13 demo program
- ◆ Suggested improvements

THIS CHAPTER PRESENTS A simple class that you can use to develop terminal emulation software under Win32. The class developed here uses the Win32 API and doesn't use MFC for command routing, so it should be very portable. It does use some components of standard C++ that aren't available under older compilers, so it can't be used with Win16 as is. However, the changes needed to use the class under 16-bit versions of Windows won't be too difficult, should you need to.

The first part of this chapter looks at the code that actually creates a usable screen on the window. This isn't as simple as you might expect, so there is a sizable piece of code to wallow through. You'll then see how that class integrates with the existing terminal emulation class first presented in Chapter 8. Finally, I show you how to put the whole thing together into a simple Windows-based terminal program.

A Terminal Window Class

This section of the chapter presents a class that creates a simple terminal-like window under Win32. A window that acts like a traditional video terminal or DOS console seems like something that should have been included in the standard repertoire of Windows classes, but unfortunately it wasn't.

I've always believed that Microsoft had an ulterior motive for not including a terminal class of windows under Windows. Including a class of this sort would have made it easy to port existing MS-DOS programs to Windows without truly taking advantage of the new GUI. Programs ported this way would still look very similar to their character-based predecessors and might not have the sexy image that our friends in Redmond were looking for.

Please note that in this chapter when I talk about a Terminal Window *class*, I'm talking about a C++ class. The concept of a Window class is also part of the Windows API, and our C++ class will have to use this concept, but for the most part it will be a quiet part of the Windows infrastructure.

Requirements

To do the basic terminal emulation needed to support typical RS-232 based applications, you need a text window that has the following characteristics:

- A virtual window with a fixed number of rows and columns
- A visible cursor that shows at the current insertion point of the window
- Support for fixed-width fonts
- The ability to change the background and foreground colors for each character cell
- The ability to move the cursor and the insertion point

The class presented in this chapter has a few more features that make it easier to use and work with:

- The ability to dynamically change fonts
- Support for window resizing
- Support for OEM fonts so that MS-DOS line-drawing characters can be used
- Horizontal and Vertical scroll bars that appear when the physical size of the window won't permit complete display of the virtual screen

Your first thought for implementing a class of this sort might be to subclass a standard Windows edit control, or perhaps the newer rich text control. Unfortunately, these standard Windows controls come up short when you try to coerce them into terminal emulation. Their design is optimized to user text entry, not interactive displays of large blocks of text.

C++ versus Windows

Before going into detail on a discussion of the member functions of this class, you need an understanding of some important infrastructure required by this class. In this section I'll explain how you are able to merge the Windows API with modern C++ programming techniques, eliminating holdovers of ANSI C such as global variables or mandatory variable names.

Windows was not written with C++ in mind, even if Microsoft has been known to refer to it as being "object oriented." However, the Windows API is flexible enough that you can easily achieve co-existence between it and a language like C++.

In C++, you are used to calling a member function any time you want to interact with an object. This presents a problem when you try to create a C++ object that you want to represent a window. Windows wants to interact with objects via an object called an HWND, or window handle. Windows sends messages to the HWND callbacks to a Window procedure, which usually looks something like this:

```
LRESULT CALLBACK WinProc( HWND hWnd,
                          UINT message,
                          WPARAM wParam,
                          LPARAM lParam )
{
    switch ( message )
    {
        case WM_CREATE:
            PickColors();
            SetFocus( hWnd );
            break;
        case WM_DESTROY:
            CloseDatabase();
```

In the windows callback function, the window is represented by the HWND parameter, and the message is described by the other three parameters. So if your window is also represented by a C++ object, you need to find a way to reference it.

The easiest way would be to use a global pointer that the WinProc could access:

```
MyWindow *pWindow;

int WINAPI WinMain( HINSTANCE hInstance,
                    HINSTANCE /* hPrevInstance */,
                    LPSTR     /* lpCmdLine */,
                    int       nShowCmd )
{
    pWindow = new MyWindow( "My C++ Window" );
    ...

LRESULT CALLBACK WinProc( HWND hWnd,
                          UINT message,
                          WPARAM wParam,
                          LPARAM lParam )
{
```

```
switch ( message )
{
    case WM_SIZE :
        pWindow->HandleSize();
```

This will obviously work, but the idea of using a global variable to access a C++ object is a little unpleasant. It also makes your class much less flexible. The WinProc() that services the class will always require the presence of a global variable, regardless of how you want to set up your code. Plus, you are limited to a single instance of the particular type of window.

A much better way to do this (and the way you do it in the Win32Term class) is to store a pointer to the C++ object in the Window's storage space. When registering a new Window class with the Win API, you have the opportunity to declare the need for extra storage to be associated with a window handle. You do this by putting the number of bytes needed in the cbWndExtra member of the WNDCLASS structure. For example, the registration code in the Win32Term constructor looks like this:

```
if ( !m_bClassRegistered ) {
  WNDCLASS wc = { 0 };
  wc.lpfnWndProc    = WindowProc;
  wc.hInstance      = GetModuleHandle( NULL );
  wc.hCursor        = LoadCursor( NULL, IDC_IBEAM );
  wc.hbrBackground  = ::CreateSolidBrush( RGB( 255, 255, 255 ) );
  wc.lpszClassName  = "Win32TermClass";
  wc.lpszMenuName   = NULL;
  wc.hIcon          = NULL;
  wc.cbWndExtra     = sizeof( Win32Term * );
  RegisterClass( &wc );
  m_bClassRegistered = true;
}
```

The registration shown previously declares the need for enough space to hold one pointer, in this case a pointer to our C++ object that defines the window.

Now that you have convinced Windows to allocate some extra space associated with the HWND, you can access that storage using two Windows API calls: GetWindowLong() and SetWindowLong(). You use the first function at the very start of the Windows procedure to ensure that you have a pointer to the C++ object available for all the message handlers:

```
LRESULT CALLBACK Win32Term::WindowProc( HWND hWnd,
                                        UINT uMsg,
                                        WPARAM wParam,
                                        LPARAM lParam )
```

```
{
    Win32Term *p = (Win32Term *) ::GetWindowLong( hWnd, 0 );
```

For this to work, at some point after the creation of the C++ object you must have stored a pointer to it using a call to SetWindowLong(). There are several different ways that this can be accomplished; Win32Term manages it by passing additional data with the CreateWindow() function.

The Win32Term constructor calls the Windows API function CreateWindow() to actually create the terminal window. The final argument to the CreateWindow() function is a void pointer called lpParam. Most Windows programs pass a NULL value in this position, but in this case you are going pass a pointer to an object of type CreateData, a class that was defined as a nested class of Win32Term. You put a pointer to this in the CreateData structure and pass it in the final argument:

```
    CreateData data = { sizeof( Win32Term * ), this };
    CreateWindow( "Win32TermClass",
                  window_name,
                  WS_CHILD | WS_VISIBLE | WS_VSCROLL | WS_HSCROLL,
                  0,0,
                  0,0,
                  m_hParent,
                  0,
                  GetModuleHandle( NULL ),
                  &data );
}
```

That special data pointer is then passed in to the WinProc when it receives a WM_CREATE message from Windows. By simply casting the lParam value passed into WinProc to a CreateData pointer, you can get the pointer to this, and store it in the reserved storage area associated with that HWND. For example:

```
if ( uMsg == WM_CREATE )
{
  CreateData *pData;
  pData   = ((CreateData UNALIGNED *) lParam)->lpCreateParams;
  SetWindowLong( hWnd, 0, (LONG) pData->pTerm );
}
```

That's a lot of work and a lot to remember, but when it is done, you will be able to get the pointer to the correct object at the start of WinProc, so every function called there can be a member function. And better yet, this system accomplished this goal without the use of any global variables and achieved it with maximum flexibility for the routine that creates and uses the Win32Term window.

Class Win32Term — basic internals

After determining that subclassing wasn't the answer to creating a Terminal Window class, I went straight into development of class Win32Term. This class supports all the mandatory and optional features listed previously, and provides an interface that makes it very easy to use in your Windows programs. The class is completely independent of all the other modules created for this book, making it easy to use with all sorts of programs.

Most Windows programs use proportionally spaced fonts and frequently use multiple fonts in a single window. The code that manages the windows in programs such as Microsoft Word can end up being quite complicated.

A Terminal window, on the other hand, uses fixed space fonts and normally uses only a single font for the entire window. This lets you make some assumptions that help make the code that manages the contents of the window much simpler.

At the core of class Win32Term is a private class definition and a pair of two-dimensional arrays:

```
class Win32Term
{
public :
    struct TextColor
    {
        TextColor( COLORREF f = 0, COLORREF b = 0 )
            :   m_Foreground( f ),
                m_Background( b ) {}
        bool operator!=( const TextColor &that )
        {
            if ( m_Foreground != that.m_Foreground )
                return true;
            return m_Background != that.m_Background;
        }
        COLORREF m_Foreground;
        COLORREF m_Background;
    };
    .
    .  //Skip much of the class definition
    .
    vector< vector<char> >       m_ScreenText;
    vector< vector<TextColor> >  m_ScreenColor;
```

Both of the two-dimensional arrays are sized in the constructor to have the same number of rows and columns as the virtual screen. Thus, any character on the screen is found at m_ScreenText[row][col], and its current color is found at m_ScreenColor[row][col]. (The vector<T> template class might not look familiar to you. `vector<T>` was added to the C++ language when the Standard Template Library was incorporated. It simply provides a convenient way to manipulate arrays in a safe manner.)

With just the definition of these elements, you can already picture what the code to paint the screen looks like. A simplified approach would look something like this:

```
for ( row = 0 ; row < ROWS ; row++ )
    for ( col = 0 ; col < COLS ; col++ ) {
        int x = col * CHAR_WIDTH;
        int y = row * ROW_HEIGHT;
        set_color( m_ScreenColor[row][col] );
        draw_char( x, y, m_ScreenText[row][col] );
    }
```

This is nice and simple, and it isn't as far from the real code as you might think. There are a few complications to deal with, and after those are handled, you have a complete `WM_PAINT` handler:

- If the window being painted is smaller than the virtual window, you might have scroll bars, and thus have to deal with the fact that all the characters in the window are offset from their normal position.

- You don't want to draw every character on the screen, only the ones in the update region.

- Instead of drawing individual characters, you want to pass strings of characters to the `ExtTextOut()` Windows API function, in the interest of efficiency.

Take those factors into consideration and you should be able to follow the logic of the Paint routine for this class. And when you understand the paint routine, there isn't much more to this class.

The screen shot shown in Figure 13-1 shows class `Win32Term` in action. The display is a result of building class `Win32Term` with a special test routine that fills the display with some default data. This can sometimes prove useful for testing the correctness of the display routines.

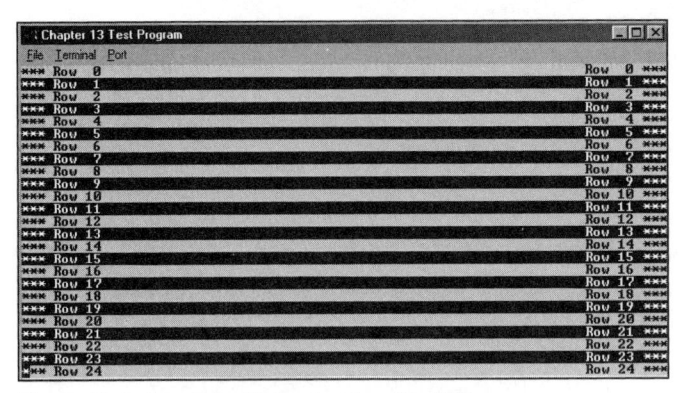

Figure 13-1: A sample display for class `Win32Term`

Class Win32 – Definitions

The remainder of this chapter describes the individual data and code members of class `Win32Term`. These descriptions will be supplemented by the code listings found at the end of the chapter.

Private classes

Three private classes are defined inside class `Win32Term`: `TextColor`, `Pair`, and `CreateData`. `TextColor` and `Pair` are just there for convenience and clarity, whereas `CreateData` is needed to work with the Windows API.

class TextColor

This class is just a container for two `COLORREF` values: `m_Foreground` and `m_Background`. As should be fairly obvious, one object of this type can hold the foreground and background colors for a given cell of text. Class `Win32Term` holds a two-dimensional array that holds an object of this type for every character position on the virtual screen.

You can take advantage of the compiler's built-in definitions for copy constructors, assignments, and destructors, and thus have to write only a couple of member functions for this class. First, you have a constructor that can be used to assign the initial values to the two members of the class. Second, there is a comparison operator, which is used in the `Paint()` member function of class `Win32Term`.

In some ways, `TextColor` is a bit wasteful. Most terminal emulators are going to be limited to a handful of colors, maybe as many as 16 or so. With the current structure of class `TextColor`, you give each cell 32 bits for the foreground and background colors, allowing for any possible 24-bit RGB color. But considering that I am talking about a total allocation of only 16K for a 25×80 screen, perhaps it isn't worth worrying about improving efficiency.

class Pair

class `Pair` is an even sparser implementation of a C++ class than `TextColor`. It has a constructor, and two integer members, x and y. This class exists because there are so many pairs of values in class `Win32Term`. Items such as the scrolling offset, cursor position, character size, and so on all are defined as x, y pairs, with x referring to the horizontal measurement and y referring to the vertical number.

class CreateData

This class is used during the creation of the Win32 window. Under the Windows API, a call to `::CreateWindow()` can include a block of data that gets passed to the Windows procedure responding to the `WM_CREATE` message. The block of data needs to be packaged up in an object identical to `CreateData`.

When the constructor of class `Win32Term` calls `::CreateWindow()` to create its own Win32 window, it passes a pointer to itself in this structure. That allows code inside the Window procedure to access member functions of the `Win32Term` object. This will be discussed in more detail in the documentation on the `Win32Term` constructor.

Data members

If you understand what each of the data members does in the class, you will have no problem with `Win32Term`. Each data member has a simple function that is relatively easy to follow. Any uncertainty about the use of a member can be cleared up quickly with a scan of the source code.

One particularly nice thing about the data members of `Win32Term` is that with one exception, they all have `private` access, which means that the entire range of their operations is confined to the member functions of the class. Not only are the data members not recommended for use by client classes, their access is forbidden by definition of the language.

HWND m_hWnd

`m_hWnd` is the Win32 API handle for the window currently opened by the `Win32Term` object. This window is opened in the constructor for the object and is left open for the lifetime of the C++ object.

Note that this member is the one exception to the rule that all members in the class are protected. Because the `Win32Term` window is generally not a top-level window, you expect it to always have a parent, even if it is only a dialog box or a frame window. The parent of the `Win32Term` object needs to have a copy of the

Win32 handle to perform various operations on the child window such as resizing, moving, and closing.

In the example program seen at the end of the chapter, this handle is accessed for several reasons. First, it can be used after the `Win32Term` constructor is called to verify that a Win32 window was actually created. Second, it is needed to force a repaint of the window under some circumstances. And third, it is used to resize the `Win32Term` window whenever the user resizes the frame window.

It is true that you could pull all of these functions into the `Win32Term` class definition, allowing them to be performed by calling a member function instead of the Win32 API. However, following this path can lead to a class with a thousand shell functions used to call Windows API functions via the class instead of directly. This excess is easily avoided by simply making the one data member public, so that is the way I do it.

HWND m_hParent

The handle of the parent window is `m_hParent`. This handle is passed in to the constructor of the class by the parent and unchanged for the lifetime of the object. You need the value of the parent handle in a few places. For example, in the constructor, when you create the `Win32Term` Win32 window using a call to `::CreateWindow()`, you have to pass the handle of a parent window. You also use this in a call to member function `SetFont()` to get a Device Context during font selection.

TextColor m_CurrentColor

This data member contains color that newly inserted text will have. As you saw earlier in the chapter, `TextColor` contains a `COLORREF` value of both the foreground and background colors. Both colors can be set independently by calling member functions `SetForegroundColor()` and `SetBackgroundColor()`.

The constructor for `Win32Term` sets the foreground color to black and the background color to white.

vector< vector<char> > m_ScreenText

This is a two-dimensional array that contains the screen text. The dimensions of the array are identical to the number of rows and columns passed to the `Win32Term` constructor. Individual characters on the screen can be addressed in this array using standard array notation. For example, in member function `Output( char c )` the character is stored in the array as follows:

```
m_ScreenText[ m_Position.y ][ m_Position.x ] = c;
```

Using a `vector<T>` object instead of a dynamically created `char **` object has several advantages. Creating the array using conventional dynamically created C++ arrays would take several lines of code. In our constructor, setting `m_ScreenText` to the correct dimensions takes just one line:

```
m_ScreenText.resize( rows, vector<char>( cols ) );
```

Other operations are much simpler. For example, when a line feed is being processed and you need to scroll all of the text in the screen up by a line, the `vector<T>` template lets you move a row at a time using code like this:

```
m_ScreenText[ row ] = m_ScreenText[ row + 1 ]
```

And best of all, cleanup of the memory allocated by `m_ScreenText` is done automatically in the destructor without any extra effort!

vector< vector<TextColor> > m_ScreenColor

This two dimensional array contains the foreground and background colors for each cell in the virtual screen. It should have the same dimensions as `m_ScreenText`, the text array.

When you are moving blocks of text, such as when scrolling the screen, the contents of `m_ScreenColor` will always be manipulated in an identical manner as those of `m_ScreenText`.

bool m_bWrap

This Boolean flag controls the way that the terminal behaves when it reaches the final column in the virtual screen. If `m_bWrap` is set to be `true`, the cursor will wrap when it reaches the end of a row. In other words, after a new character is written to the final column on the screen, a carriage return/line feed pair will be simulated.

If `m_bWrap` is `false`, the cursor will remain stuck in the final column of the screen after it reaches that point, and will stay there regardless of how many characters are sent, until it receives a carriage return or line feed character.

bool m_bShowingCursor

Video terminals traditionally have a cursor at the current text entry point, and the `Win32Term` class is not about to be the exception to that rule. You create a visible solid cursor using the Win32 API functions: `ShowCaret()`, `SetCaretPos()`, and `DestroyCaret()`.

Under the Win32 caret regime, you are allowed to show the caret only when the `Win32Term` window has the focus. When the focus goes elsewhere, you are duty bound to destroy the caret. The boolean member variable m_bShowingCursor keeps track of whether you are actually showing the caret at this exact moment or not.

Why should you care whether or not you are showing the caret? Remember that you can have text coming into the window whether it has the focus or not. Every time you add new characters to the Win32Term window, you have to move the cursor position. And when you move the cursor position, you have to decide whether to update the caret position as well. You do that by looking at the m_bShowingCursor member. If it is true, you update the caret position. If it is false, you don't make any attempt to modify the caret position.

HFONT m_hFont

Member m_hFont contains the handle of the font you are currently displaying text in. The Win32Term object must have an active font for its entire lifetime; otherwise it can't display incoming text. You create the font in the constructor and store its handle in member m_hFont. The font will be destroyed in the object's destructor.

The only other time you modify the m_hFont object is when member function SetFont() is called. At that point, you destroy the current font handle in m_hFont and then create a new font and update the handle value.

The m_hFont member is used in the Paint() member function. It is selected into the device context before all the calls to ExtTextOut() that actually paint the text on the screen.

LOGFONT m_lfFont

Under Windows, a LOGFONT structure is used to create a font by calling CreateFontIndirect. Member m_lfFont maintains a copy of the LOGFONT object used to create the current font stored in m_hFont.

When the Win32Term constructor is called, m_lfFont is initialized to select a fixed pitch font using the OEM character set. The lfHeight member of m_lfFont is set to 12, and the face name is set to FixedSys. If you are lucky, this results in the selection of the system-fixed width font, which should be suitable for use as a terminal emulation font.

When the owner of the Win32Term object decides to change to a different font by calling member function SetFont(), a new LOGFONT structure is passed as an argument. This value is then copied into m_lfFont for reference.

In the example program that uses class Win32Term, a copy of m_lfFont is retrieved by making a call to GetLogFont(). That LOGFONT structure is then used to properly initialize the dialog box values in a call to the Win32 system call ChooseFont(). This lets the user see what font is currently selected before choosing a new one.

Pair m_VisibleSize

The x and y values of this member give the current number of pixels that can be used for text in the `Win32Term` window. These values are updated every time the window is resized, and also when a new font is selected.

The actual values in the x and y members of `m_VisibleSize` are not necessarily identical to the size of the window. The `Win32Term` member function that is called upon a `WM_SIZE` message has to determine whether or not vertical and horizontal scroll bars are needed in the current display size. If they are needed, the visible size is reduced by the width and/or height of the scroll bars.

The values in `m_VisibleSize` are used when handling scroll bar messages and when setting up the scroll bars after resizing. When a user clicks on one of the two possible scroll bars while viewing the `Win32Term` window, member functions `VerticalScroll()` and `HorizontalScroll()` are called to scroll the text in the window by a given amount.

```
const Pair m_VirtualSize
```

This data member is initialized in the constructor to the number of rows and columns in the virtual screen. It is a constant value because you don't allow for modifying the layout of the virtual screen during the lifetime of the `Win32Term` object.

The number of rows and columns are used throughout the class, including routines concerned with handling `WM_PAINT` messages, outputting characters or strings, and handling `WM_SIZE` messages.

```
Pair m_ScrollRange
```

This member is meaningful only when scroll bars are present in the output window. The scroll bars are present when the amount of text in the Virtual window won't fit in the visible window. When this is the case, a scroll bar is displayed in the vertical and/or horizontal positions.

When a scroll bar is present on the screen, the Win32 API call `SetScrollRange()` is called to assign a numeric value to the scroll bar's range. This determines what sort of number will be reported to the window procedure when the thumb on the scroll bar is moved.

In the `Win32Term` class, the range of numbers that can be reported by a scroll bar are in the values `m_ScrollRange`. The value in the `m_ScrollRange` x and y members will always be the difference between the number of pixels needed by the virtual screen and the number of pixels actually available for use in the visible window.

```
Pair m_Offset;
```

When the visible screen is smaller than the virtual terminal window, scroll bars are added to the screen and the portion of the visible screen that is presented is controlled by the position of the thumbs on the scroll bars.

At any given time, the first pixel visible in the x and y directions will be stored in `m_Offset`. If the vertical scroll bar is pushed all the way to the top, and the horizontal scroll bar is pushed all the way to the left, the x and y values will be set to 0. If both scroll bars are moved all the way to the opposite ends of their respective ranges, the values in `m_Offset` will be identical to those in `m_ScrollRange`.

The values in `m_Offset` are used whenever virtual screen positions need to be translated into actual locations on the visible window. Naturally this includes the `Paint()` routine, the cursor positioning routines, and even the output routines.

```
Pair m_Position
```

This data member contains the current insertion point in the window. If the window has the focus, it will also contain the position of the cursor. This member is used in the cursor control routines and the `Output()` routines that actually insert new text into the window.

```
Pair m_CharSize
```

This contains the height and width of a character in the currently selected font. You obviously need this information for a couple of important purposes. First, you need it to determine where individual characters are going to be displayed when painting the screen. And second, you need it to determine the desired size of the virtual window.

```
int m_iCharDescent
```

Under Windows, characters are allowed to have descenders that drop below their baselines. For example, lowercase characters such as "g" and "j" will drop below the bottom of the display line. You need take this into account when calculating the amount of space needed to display a given font. This value is set when the font is created in `SetFont()` and is used when calculating screen sizes in the `WM_SIZE` handler.

```
COLORREF m_BorderColor
```

If the visible window is larger than the amount of space needed to display the virtual window, some space is left over on the bottom and right-hand side of the window that won't be used to display text. This border space can be assigned a color using member function `SetBorderColor()`.

Figure 13-2 shows an example of how your screen might look if the visible border color is different than that of the text portion of the window.

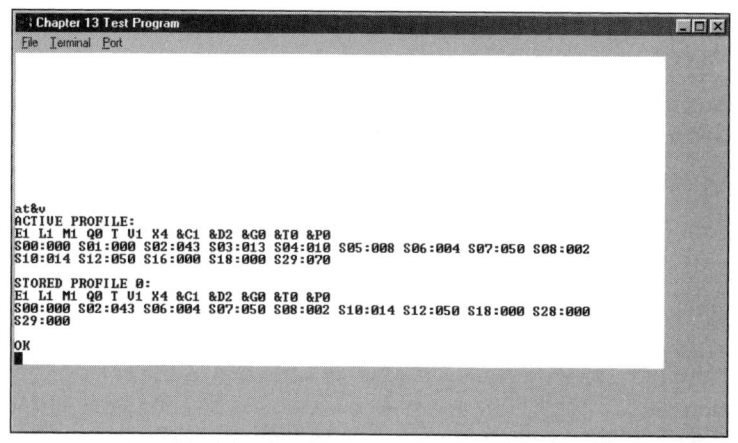

Figure 13-2: A different border color

`static bool m_bClassRegistered`

One of the confusing bits of nomenclature for C++ programmers is the name "Window Class." Windows expects every window created for use in the system to have a Window Class. For our purposes, that class is really not much more than a way to define what procedure will handle messages for the given window.

In our case, the class name is `Win32TermClass` and the window procedure for all windows in that class is `Win32Term::WindowProc()`, a static member function. You have to register this class before you can create any windows that use the window procedure, and you normally do so in the constructor for `Win32Term`. You need to register the class only once, not once per window, so after it is registered the first time, you set this member to be true. From then on, when you check to see whether the class has been registered, you can duck out of doing it again.

Public code members

After reviewing the function of all the data members in the `Win32Term` class, none of the code in this class should present any particular mysteries. Please refer to the listings at the end of this chapter for the definitive word on how things work.

```
Win32Term( HWND hParent,
           const char *window_name,
           int rows,
           int cols )
```

The constructor for class `Win32Term` has a lot to do. In order, it performs the following tasks:

1. Allocate the correct amount of storage for the arrays that hold the screen text and colors.
2. Initialize internal data members to their default settings, including cursor position, wrap flag, and the cursor visible flag.
3. Create the default font and attach it to the object.
4. Set the default colors for the foreground and background, then clear the screen.
5. Create the Window using the Win API call `CreateWindow()`.

Although the call to `CreateWindow()` is the last line of code in the constructor, a bit more work needs to be done. If you look at the class registration code in the constructor, you'll see that the WinProc for this is `Win32Term::WindowProc`:

```
if ( !m_bClassRegistered ) {
  WNDCLASS wc = { 0 };
  wc.lpfnWndProc     = WindowProc;
  wc.hInstance       = GetModuleHandle( NULL );
  wc.hCursor         = LoadCursor( NULL, IDC_IBEAM );
  wc.hbrBackground   = ::CreateSolidBrush( RGB( 255, 255, 255 ) );
  wc.lpszClassName   = "Win32TermClass";
  wc.lpszMenuName    = NULL;
  wc.hIcon           = NULL;
  wc.cbWndExtra      = sizeof( Win32Term * );
  RegisterClass( &wc );
  m_bClassRegistered = true;
}
```

`WindowProc` is a static member function of this class, and it is responsible for dispatching the appropriate handlers for a given `Win32Term` object. The very first time that `WindowProc` is called for a given window should be when the window is created, causing a `WM_CREATE` message to be sent to `WindowProc`. `WindowProc()` does three things that finish the constructor. It sets the `m_hWnd` to the newly created window HWND value, and sets `m_hParent` to the HWND value of the window's parent. It then stores a pointer to `this` in the storage associated with the window.

After the constructor returns, the caller can check the value of `m_hWnd`. If it is non-zero, it means the window was successfully created, has a message loop running, and should be ready to use.

`virtual ~Win32Term()`

When destroying a `Win32Term` window, there are actually two things that have to happen. First, the actual HWND has to be destroyed by Windows. Second, the C++ object has to be destroyed, freeing up all the resources it has. The destructor for class `Win32Term` doesn't attempt to destroy the window associated with it; it simply frees up any resources and then leaves the window to be destroyed by Windows in the normal course of events.

In the sample program presented later in this chapter, the `Win32Term` window is a child of the frame window and is automatically destroyed when the frame window is destroyed. The destructor for the `Win32Term` object is called from the `WM_DESTROY` handler for the frame window, which should mean the destructor is called after the Window proper is already gone.

Most of the objects contained in the `Win32Term` object are destroyed automatically. For example, the `m_ScreenText` array is an automatic variable, so it doesn't need to be destroyed explicitly.

The one item that does need to be destroyed explicitly by the destructor is the `m_hFont` handle. The font created for use by `Win32Term` is freed up by a call to the Win32 API call `DeleteObject()`.

The only other action taken in the destructor is a call to clear the `Win32Term` pointer stored in the data area associated with the Window. This ensures that if any other messages are sent to the Window before it is gone, you won't attempt to invoke a member function on an object that has already been destroyed.

```
void SetForegroundColor( COLORREF color )
```

This member just sets the `m_Foreground` member of the `m_CurrentColor` member to the color passed in by the caller. That color will then be the foreground color used for any text inserted into the window via calls to `Output()`.

```
void SetBackgroundColor( COLORREF color )
```

This member just sets the `m_Background` member of the `m_CurrentColor` member to the color passed in by the caller. That color will then be the background color used for any text inserted into the window via calls to `Output()`. In addition, any space on the screen window cleared as a result of scrolling or a call to `Clear()` will be painted with this color.

```
void SetBorderColor( COLORREF color )
```

If the `Win32Term` window is larger in either dimension than it needs to be to display all the rows or columns of text, the extra portion will be painted in the border color. By default the border color is white, which is the same as the background color of the screen. With that setup it isn't obvious where the normal text screen ends and the border begins. If you want the line of demarcation to be obvious, change the border color so that it no longer matches the background text color.

This function call also forces the window to be repainted, so the change in border color is immediately seen.

```
COLORREF GetForegroundColor()
```

`GetForegroundColor()` returns a copy of the `m_Foreground` member of `m_CurrentColor`.

```
COLORREF GetBackgroundColor()
```

`GetBackgroundColor()` returns a copy of the `m_Background` member of `m_CurrentColor`.

```
COLORREF GetBorderColor()
```

This member returns a copy of the current border color.

```
LOGFONT GetLogFont()
```

The `Win32Term` object keeps an internal copy of the LOGFONT structure used to create the current font being used. This function returns a copy of that LOGFONT structure. It's often useful to be able to retrieve a copy of the LOGFONT structure to use when calling `ChooseFont()` to select a new display font.

```
void Clear()
```

This function sets all the character cells in `m_ScreenText` to blanks and sets the color of all cells to the current foreground and background color. It then invalidates the entire window so that the modified screen will be displayed immediately.

```
void Output( char c )
void Output( const char *pBuf, int length = -1 )
```

These are the two routines that are used to insert new characters into the screen. The first version of the function stuffs just one character into the screen; the second sends a sequence of characters. The characters are all inserted starting at the current insertion point, using the current color.

For the most part, any given character is simply inserted in to the `m_ScreenText` array at the specified point, with `m_ScreenColor` being updated with current color. After each character, the current column is incremented, so the next character will be inserted at the following position.

When you insert characters, you modify the rule regarding incrementing the current column if the current position is at the last column in the visible screen. When this is the case, the `m_bWrap` is checked to determine the correct behavior. If the flag is true, a "\r\n" is generated, causing the current insertion point to move down one row to column 0. If the flag is false, the current insertion point is not modified.

There are exceptions to this smooth processing in Output. First, several special characters have different effects on the output window

For example, an ASCII BEL character, represented as '\a' in C++, was once used to ring a bell on mechanical teletypes. Most PCs these days don't have mechanical bells, so you just call the Windows API function `MessageBeep()` to attempt to duplicate the effect. The BEL character doesn't generate any visible display on the output screen.

The backspace character, represented as '\b' in C++, simply causes the current insertion point to back up by a single column. If the insertion point was already at column 0, nothing happens. Normally, the process of sending characters to the terminal window will follow a backspace character by a single ASCII blank, and then another backspace. The combined effect of this three-character sequence is to erase the last character typed and back up the cursor by one position.

A CR character, or '\r', causes the current insertion point to move to column 0 on the current row. More often than not, the CR character will be immediately followed by an LF, or line feed character. The LF causes the current insertion point to move down a single row without changing columns. If the current row is the last one on the visible screen, instead of moving down, the entire visible screen is scrolled up by one row, and the newly created bottom row is filled with spaces rendered in the current color.

After adding all the new characters to the screen array, `Output()` invalidates a rectangle that encloses the entire area that has been updated, causing it to be painted to the screen. Before leaving, the cursor position is updated as well.

```
void SetFont( LOGFONT LogFont )
```

Calling this routine changes fonts in the `Win32Term` window. `SetFont()` takes the LOGFONT structure that is passed in and uses it to create a new font, concurrently destroying the old font whose handle is stored in `m_hFont`. When the new font is created, you have to take into account the possibility that the screen size metrics changed. The new size characteristics of the font are stored in `m_CharSize` and `m_CharDescent`, and then the `Size()` routine is called to simulate a reszing of the screen. This forces the scrolling range to be recalculated, resulting in scroll bars either being added or removed as necessary.

```
int SetCursorPosition( int row, int col )
void GetCursorPosition( int &row, int &col )
```

These two routines revolve around the current insertion point in the text window. One function returns its present settings, and the other changes its present value.

`SetCursorPosition()` modifies the `m_Position` member, which controls the current insertion point and then calls `UpdateCursor()` just in case the cursor position has to be moved. `GetCursorPosition()` does nothing more than return the current row and column of the insertion point.

Protected code members

Protected member functions are called only from inside the `Win32Term` class. In this class, protected code members are most often called as a result of a message being sent to the window procedure, `Win32Term::WindowProc()`.

BOOL Paint()

`Paint()` is a protected routine that is called by `Dispatch()` in response to a `WM_PAINT` message. Its job is to repaint the portion of the screen that has been invalidated for some routine.

`Paint()` is one of the few truly complicated routines in the `Win32Term` class. It is called to repaint some subset of the visible window. Although it is a bit complicated, it at least operates in a very conventional fashion, looking a lot like the `Paint()` routine for any sort of generic Windows program.

The first thing `Paint()` has to do is to determine the range of rows and columns it needs to paint. The update rectangle passed in by Windows tells us the coordinates of the area that needs to be repainted. You can figure out the starting and ending rows and columns that need to be updated with just a couple of data members: `m_Offset`, which tells you how far the window has been scrolled, and `m_CharSize`, which tells us how many pixels are taken up by each character.

When the beginning and ending row and column numbers are known, the basic parameters of the paint loop are known. The outer part of the paint loop starts off something like this:

```
for ( int row = start_row ; row <= end_row ; row++ )
{
    paint_row();
```

If every character in the row to be displayed has the same background and foreground colors, you can call the Win32 API function `ExtTextOut()` to paint the entire line of text in one fell swoop. Unfortunately, every character in the line can have a different color than the one before it.

Because you want to print as many consecutive characters as you can, the inner loop tries to make as long a run of like-colored characters as possible. The inner loop proceeds much like this:

```
TextColor current_color = m_ScreenColor[ nRow ][ start_col ];
for ( int end_col = start_col ; end_col <= nEndCol ; end_col++ )
    if ( current_color != m_ScreenColor[ nRow ][ end_col ] )
```

```
            break;
end_col--;
SetTextColor(hDC, m_ScreenColor[nRow][start_col].m_Foreground);
SetBkColor(hDC, m_ScreenColor[nRow][start_col].m_Background);
SetBkMode( hDC, OPAQUE );
ExtTextOut( hDC,
            ... , // more parameters
            m_ScreenText[ nRow ].begin() + start_col,
            end_col - start_col + 1 );
```

The inner loop continues running until the column exceeds the end column of the update region.

The only remaining work to be done after the `Paint()` routine completes is to update the cursor and then exit.

void UpdateCursor()

`UpdateCursor()` is called a few different times inside the `Win32Term` class. It is called after the `Paint()` routine completes, when the window gains focus, and after one or more characters are output. All `UpdateCursor()` has to do is check to see whether the `m_bShowingCursor` flag is `true` and if it is, display the caret at the correct position on the screen. The correct position is determined by knowing the insertion row and column as stored in `m_Position`, the width and height of the character cell as stored in `m_CharSize`, and the current scrolled position of the visible screen as stored in `m_Offset`.

void SetFocus()

When the terminal window acquires the focus, its job is to draw the cursor in the correct position in the window. Because of the Win32 rules regarding the caret, you have to make sure that you do this only once. You keep track of whether the caret is already visible with the `m_bShowingCursor` member. If this member is already true, you don't redraw the cursor. Likewise, if the member is false, you draw the cursor and then set the member to be true.

void KillFocus()

When the terminal window loses focus, you have to destroy the caret. Once again, you use the `m_bShowingCursor` data member to keep track of whether the cursor has already been destroyed.

void VerticalScroll(WPARAM wParam)
void HorizontalScroll(WPARAM wParam)

The vertical and horizontal scroll routines perform exactly the same function, with one operating on the horizontal axis and the other operating on the vertical axis.

Recall from the explanation of the data members earlier in this section that the scroll bars are added to the window if you are unable to display the entire range of rows or columns for the visible window in the size window you are currently working with. If scroll bars are in use, the range defined from one end of the scroll bar to the other is held in member m_ScrollRange, and the current scrolled position of the window being displayed is found in m_Offset. Both values are in pixels.

These two routines are called when some operation is performed that causes the thumb on the scroll bar to move to a new position. This can be the result of the user moving the thumb directly, or executing one of the PageUp, PageDown, Home, or End commands. Regardless of how it is done, the type of command tells us how far to move the current position of the thumb on the scroll bar, and consequently how far to move the visible portion of the window.

After calculating how far to move the window, the Windows API function is called to actually scroll the visible portion of the window by a given number of pixels. When that is done, you update the m_Offset member to reflect the new scrolling offset of the visible window and return to the calling routine.

```
void Size( int x, int y )
```

The Size() routine is called as a result of a WM_SIZE message being sent from Windows to the Win32Term window. It is a fairly complicated routine only because it has to determine whether or not to display scroll bars, and what the scroll bar ranges ought to be if they are being displayed.

If there is plenty of room on the screen, both scroll bars are turned off by setting their range to 0. If there isn't enough room, the necessary range of the scroll bars is calculated, the values are set via calls to SetScrollRange(), and the necessary data members are updated. (Note that the amount of space can shift up or down as calculations are made that either include or remove scroll bars.) That includes m_ScrollRange, m_Offset, and m_VisibleSize. After all this is done, the window is invalidated so that it will be repainted with its new configuration in place.

```
virtual LRESULT Dispatch( HWND hwnd,
                          UINT uMsg,
                          WPARAM wParam,
                          LPARAM lParam );
```

This is the class equivalent of the Windows procedure. It takes care of invoking the appropriate handler for each window message. In `Win32Term`, the following messages are properly handled by `Dispatch()`:

Message	Handler
WM_VSCROLL	VerticalScroll()
WM_HSCROLL	HorizontalScroll()
WM_SIZE	Size()
WM_PAINT	Paint()
WM_CHAR	Output(char c)
WM_SETFOCUS	SetFocus()
WM_KILLFOCUS	KillFocus()
WM_MOUSEACTIVATE	Handled inside Dispatch()
WM_DESTROY	Handled inside Dispatch()

```
static LRESULT CALLBACK WindowProc( HWND hwnd,
                                    UINT uMsg,
                                    WPARAM wParam,
                                    LPARAM lParam )
```

This is the routine that is defined to be the Windows procedure for `Win32Term` windows. As you saw earlier in this section, under normal circumstances, this routine just acquires a pointer to the correct C++ object by calling `GetWindowLong()` and then passes control to member function `Dispatch()`.

There is one exception to this behavior, and that is when the Window is first being created. When this is the case, data won't be available from `GetWindowLong()`, but that's okay because you are being passed a pointer to the C++ object as part of the special `CreateData` package. When that happens, you take care of adding the pointer to the Window storage area so that all future messages can be passed to `Dispatch()` when they are received.

Integrating Win32Term with AnsiTerm

Just by itself, the Win32Term class doesn't give us a terminal emulator. All it does is provide a class that can be used to put colored text on the screen. Integrating it into a Terminal Emulation program requires just a little bit more glue.

As you might recall from Chapter 8, the classes that perform terminal emulation are all derived from class Terminal. Terminal is actually an abstract base class that provides a few simple functions and defines an interface for a programmer to use when writing a terminal emulator. In Chapter 8, the derived class AnsiTerminal was used as an example of a fleshed-out terminal class.

If you look at the code used in AnsiTerminal, you'll see that it uses an abstract base class to perform all the output to whatever device it is expecting to use as a window. The interface to this device is defined by yet another abstract base class: BaseWindow. So if you want to use Win32Term as the output device for a terminal emulator, you have to somehow present it to the AnsiTerminal object as a BaseWindow.

BaseWindow has the following pure virtual member functions that must be implemented before you have a usable class:

```
virtual BaseWindow &operator<<( char c );
virtual BaseWindow &operator<<( char *pStr );
virtual void Clear( void );
virtual void Goto( void );
virtual void SetAttribute( int a );
virtual int SetPosition( int row, int col );
virtual void GetPosition( int &rol, int &col );
virtual void GetDimensions( int &width, int &height );
```

This doesn't look like too formidable a list; it seems reasonable to expect to be able to implement these functions using Win32Term. But you have a little bit of a logistical problem. The constructor for class AnsiTerm requires two reference arguments. The first is an object of type RS232, and the second is an object of type BaseWindow. Because Win32Term isn't derived from BaseWindow, you can't instantiate it directly and pass it to the AnsiTerm constructor. So what I do instead is create a utility class that ties lots of loose ends together for me: class AnsiWinTerm.

Class AnsiWinTerm

This class is tightly bound to three other classes in very important ways. First of all, AnsiWinTerm is derived from two other classes Win32Term and BaseWindow. This is important for two reasons. First, because AnsiWinTerm is directly derived from Win32Term, when you create an instance of this object, you now have a working window that has all the functionality of `Win32Term`, meaning it can do the things you need a terminal window to do.

Second, because `AnsiWinTerm` is derived from `BaseWindow`, as far as the constructor for `AnsiTerm` is concerned, it is a `BaseWindow`. This means that you can safely pass a reference to an `AnsiWinTerm` to the `AnsiTerm` constructor, and it will be happy.

However, you have to do more than simply derive a class from `BaseWindow`. Now you are saddled with the responsibility for implementing all the pure virtual functions that were present in the class. If you try to instantiate an object of type `AnsiWinTerm` without defining all eight of the pure virtual functions, the compiler will give us an error. So the first task is to define and create those eight functions.

For the most part, mapping those functions to `Win32Term` functions is trivial. All eight functions are three lines or less and they are all defined in the header file. The only function that required a little bit of thought was `SetAttribute()`. The base window class supports the 16 foreground and background color attributes defined by IBM for the ANSI.SYS driver. You need to map those attributes onto RGB values. To do so easily, I created an array of RGB values that you can index into to convert the byte attributes into RGB values.

To see the actual implementation of these eight functions, see the listing for `AnsiWinTerm.h` in this section.

AnsiWinTerm and class Win32Port

Because I already have a class set up to help communicate between other library classes, it seemed like a convenient place to go to for some additional glue logic. As you probably recall from Chapter 12, using notification with class `Win32Port` requires two things: First, a customized class derived from `Win32Port` that knows how to perform notification within the frameword of your program. Second, you need a class or window in your app that can receive the notification messages and take the appropriate action they merit.

To meet the first requirement, I created a derived class called `MyWin32Port` that is derived from `Win32Port`, and extends it in just two places. First, its constructor is passed a handle to a window that expects to receive RX notification messages from the port. The handle is saved in a private data member. Second, `MyWin32Port` overrides the virtual `RxNotify()` function so that it can send a message whenever a batch of new characters arrive:

```
void MyWin32Port::RxNotify( int byte_count )
{
  ::PostMessage( m_hNotifyWindow,
                 WM_SERIAL_RX_NOTIFY,
                 byte_count,
                 0 );
}
```

How does this fit in with class `AnsiWinTerm`? I decided to make `AnsiWinTerm` the owner of the port. So it has a pointer to a `MyWin32Port` object, plus an `Open()` and `Close()` routine to open and close the port. Naturally, the `Open()` routine has to call the constructor for `MyWin32Port` with a pointer to the window handle created when the base class `Win32Term` object was created:

```
bool AnsiWinTerm::OpenPort( const string &name )
{
  m_pPort = new MyWin32Port( name, m_hWnd );
  if ( m_pPort->ErrorStatus() < 0 ) {
    ::MessageBox( m_hWnd,
                  m_pPort->ErrorName( m_pPort->ErrorStatus() ),
                  "Error opening COM Port",
                  MB_OK );
    delete m_pPort;
    m_pPort = 0;
    return false;
  }
  m_pTerminal = new AnsiTerminal( *m_pPort, *this );
  return true;
}
```

AnsiWinTerm RX notification

You can see that, in the `Open()` function in the preceding listing, you pass a copy of the window handle to the `RS232` object. It will send a proprietary `WM_SERIAL_RX_NOTIFY` message to the terminal window whenever new characters arrive on the port. This is always the best way to handle character reception, because you don't have to poll the port; instead, you wait for something interesting to happen before doing anything.

However, there appears to be a problem with this approach. The message loop for class `Win32Term` has already been written, and it certainly won't know what to do with a `WM_SERIAL_RX_NOTIFY` when one arrives. At first glance, it might appear that you have to go in and modify the source code for the base class so that it can do something useful when the message arrives.

Fortunately, C++ inheritance comes to the rescue here. If you look back at the class definition for `Win32Term`, you will see that all messages except `WM_CREATE` are routed through the `Dispatch()` function. As it happens, `Dispatch()` is a virtual function that you can override in this derived class. By writing a short version of `Dispatch()` for class `AnsiWinTerm`, you can catch the incoming RX notification messages while still depending on `Win32Term` to handle all the other stuff.

As it turns out, you need a version of `Dispatch()` for more than handling RX notification messages. Being the glue class for terminal emulation means that

Chapter 13: Win32 Terminal Emulation

AnsiWinTerm needs to handle incoming keystrokes as well, which come in by way of WM_CHAR and WM_KEYDOWN messages. The final version of Dispatch() ends up looking something like this:

```
LRESULT AnsiWinTerm::Dispatch( HWND hWnd,
                               UINT uMsg,
                               WPARAM wParam,
                               LPARAM lParam )
{
  switch( uMsg ) {
  case WM_KEYDOWN :
    {
      int key;
      switch (wParam ) {
        case VK_UP    : key = UP;    break;
        case VK_DOWN  : key = DOWN;  break;
        case VK_LEFT  : key = LEFT;  break;
        case VK_RIGHT : key = RIGHT; break;
        case VK_PRIOR : key = PGUP;  break;
        case VK_NEXT  : key = PGDN;  break;
        case VK_END   : key = END;   break;
        case VK_HOME  : key = HOME;  break;
        default       : return -1;
      }
      int count = lParam & 0xffff;
      if ( m_pTerminal )
        for ( int i = 0 ; i < count ; i++ )
          m_pTerminal->WriteKey( key );
    }
    break;
  case WM_CHAR:
    if ( m_pTerminal )
      m_pTerminal->WriteKey( (char) wParam );
    break;
  case WM_SERIAL_RX_NOTIFY :
    {
      for ( ; ; ) {
        int c = m_pTerminal->ReadPort();
        if ( c >= 0 )
          m_pTerminal->Display( c );
        else
          break;
      }
    }
```

```
    break;
  default:
    return Win32Term::Dispatch( hWnd, uMsg, wParam, lParam );
  }
  return 0L;
}
```

Notice that the version of `Dispatch()` shown here handles three messages only. If the message is something other than the three you expect, it gets passed up to the `Win32Term` version of `Dispatch()`.

AnsiWinTerm and class AnsiTerm

As you can see from the preceding code in the `OpenPort()` function, `AnsiWinTerm` proves to be a convenient owner of the `AnsiTerminal` object as well. After you have succeeded in opening the RS-232 port, you go ahead and open the terminal object that goes with it as well.

Although you might think that I have fallen victim to a kitchen-sink mentality, things do really work out well with this one class providing the focal point for all the others to link to. For one thing, you can enable three important classes, `AnsiTerminal`, `Win32Port`, and `Win32Term` to do their jobs in this program with no awareness of the other's existence. None of the important classes have to be modified to work together.

Even better, the user of these three classes gets to do it all by simply instantiating a single object of class `AnsiWinTerm`. So you maintain simplicity in your interface to the user of these classes, and you maintain the sanctity of the classes doing all the work. You do all this by creating a simple class that holds them all together.

AnsiWinTerm listings

The next section of this chapter is going to put all of these classes together into a Win32 Terminal Emulation program that is really remarkably simple. Because most of the work is offloaded into the worker classes, the main program is quite compact. The two source files for class `AnsiWinTerm` are shown in Listings 13-1 and 13-2 so you can familiarize yourself with them before diving into the sample program.

Listing 13-1: AnsiWinTerm.h — The Class Declaration

```
//
//   AnsiWinTerm.h
//
//   Source code from:
//
//   Serial Communications: Developer's Guide, 2nd Edition
//   by Mark Nelson, IDG Books, 1999
```

```
//
//   Please see the book for information on usage.
//
// This file contains the declarations for class AnsiWinTerm,
// the glue class that holds together all the pieces needed to
// create a Win32 terminal emulator. This class is used in the
// example program for Chapter 13.
//

#ifndef _ANSI_WIN_TERM_DOT_H
#define _ANSI_WIN_TERM_DOT_H

#include "AnsiTerm.h"
#include "Win32Port.h"
#include "Win32Term.h"

//
// To use notification with class Win32Port, you need to
// create a derived class that overrides all of the notification
// functions that you plan on using. This class, MyWin32Port,
// does just that, overriding the RxNotify() function so that
// you can be notified every time new data comes in.
//
// The notification function is as simple as can be, it just
// sends a proprietary message to the window that was specified
// in the constructor. It's then up to that window to decide
// what to do.
//
// This is a stripped down port class, it uses a fixed baud
// rate, only allowing you to specify the actual port to be
// opened. The steps that you need to beef up the class
// to production quality should be pretty straightforward.
//
// Fortunately, if you need to modify the baud rate or any
// other parameters you can do so immediately after opening
// the port.
//

const int WM_SERIAL_RX_NOTIFY              = WM_USER + 0x1000;

class MyWin32Port : public Win32Port
{
public:
    MyWin32Port( const string &name, HWND notify_window )
```

```cpp
            : Win32Port( name, 19200, 'N', 8, 1 ),
              m_hNotifyWindow( notify_window )
    {}
    virtual ~MyWin32Port(){}
protected :
    void RxNotify( int byte_count )
    {
        ::PostMessage( m_hNotifyWindow,
                       WM_SERIAL_RX_NOTIFY,
                       byte_count,
                       0 );
    }
    const HWND m_hNotifyWindow;
};

//
// Class AnsiWinTerm is the only class in the entire book
// that uses multiple inheritance. This class inherits all
// the attributes of Win32Term, which is capable of
// keeping a console-style text window up on the screen.
// To work with the Emulator classes, it also has to support
// the abstract interface defined for BaseWindow, so it
// derives itself from that as well. It then has to implement
// the eight pure virtual functions defined for class
// BaseWindow. Fortunately, all of those functions turn out
// to be trivially simple.
//
class AnsiWinTerm : public Win32Term, public BaseWindow
{
public:
    //
    // The parameters you need to construct the window are
    // actually only used by the base class. You pass all the
    // arguments up to the Win32Term constructor without
    // any changes. All you do with your data is to make sure
    // the two members are set to null pointers so that you don't
    // inadvertently treat them as if they were instantiated.
    //
    AnsiWinTerm( HWND hParent,
                 const char *window_name,
                 int rows,
                 int cols ) : Win32Term( hParent,
                                         window_name,
                                         rows,
```

```cpp
                                  cols )
    {
        m_pPort = 0;
        m_pTerminal = 0;
    }
    //
    // Upon destruction, you need to be sure that you
    // destroy your two member objects.
    //
    virtual ~AnsiWinTerm()
    {
        if ( m_pTerminal )
            delete m_pTerminal;
        if ( m_pPort )
            delete m_pPort;
    }

public:
    bool OpenPort( const string &name );
    void ClosePort();
    //
    // The eight pure virtual functions from
    // class BaseWindow. Each of them is implemented
    // as a simple inline function.
    //
    virtual BaseWindow &operator<<( char c )
    {
        Output( c );
        return *this;
    }
    virtual BaseWindow &operator<<( char *pStr )
    {
        Output( pStr );
        return *this;
    }
    virtual void Clear( void )
    {
        Win32Term::Clear();
    }
    virtual void Goto( void )
    {
        ::SetFocus( m_hWnd );
    }
    virtual void AnsiWinTerm::SetAttribute( int att )
```

```
    {
      attribute = (DisplayAttribute) att;
      SetForegroundColor( ForegroundPalette[ att & 0xf ] );
      SetBackgroundColor( BackgroundPalette[ (att > 4) & 0x7 ] );
    }
    virtual int SetPosition( int row, int col )
    {
        return Win32Term::SetCursorPosition( row, col );
    }
    virtual void GetPosition( int &row, int &col )
    {
        Win32Term::GetCursorPosition( row, col );
    }
    virtual void GetDimensions( int &width, int &height )
    {
        width = m_ScreenText[ 0 ].size();
        height = m_ScreenText.size();
    }
    static const COLORREF ForegroundPalette[ 16 ];
    static const COLORREF BackgroundPalette[ 8 ];

protected :
    //
    // This is the dispatcher for all window messages
    // that are sent to the terminal emulator window.
    // You intercept the RX notification messages and
    // any keystroke messages, but pass everything else
    // up to the base class for handling.
    //
    virtual LRESULT Dispatch( HWND hwnd,
                              UINT uMsg,
                              WPARAM wParam,
                              LPARAM lParam );
protected :
    //
    // The two data members used here, an RS232 port and
    // a terminal emulator. Add in the window that this
    // class implements and you have all the components
    // needed for a terminal emulation program.
    //
    MyWin32Port *   m_pPort;
    AnsiTerminal *  m_pTerminal;
};
```

```
#endif //#ifndef _ANSI_WIN_TERM_DOT_H
```

Listing 13-2: AnsiWinTerm.cpp — Member Function Implementation

```
//
//   AnsiWinTerm.cpp
//
//   Source code from:
//
//   Serial Communications: Developer's Guide, 2nd Edition
//   by Mark Nelson, IDG Books, 1999
//
//   Please see the book for information on usage.
//
// This file contains the implementation for much of class
// AnsiWinTerm, the glue class that holds together all the
// pieces needed to create a Win32 terminal emulator. This
// class is used in the example program for Chapter 13.
//

#include "AnsiWinTerm.h"

//
// Class AnsiWinTerm is derived from Win32Term, which provides
// basic support for fixed width colored characters on a screen.
// Most of what you need in terms of window message processing
// is done by that class, but there are a few messages that you
// need to intercept and handle yourself. You do that by
// overriding the Dispatch() member of that class, giving us
// first crack at all the messages. Note that at the bottom of
// this routine, if you haven't handled the message, you gladly
// pass it on to Win32Term::Dispatch(). If it has anything to
// do with painting, scrolling, or sizing, that is undoubtedly
// where it needs to be handled.
//

LRESULT AnsiWinTerm::Dispatch( HWND hWnd,
                               UINT uMsg,
                               WPARAM wParam,
                               LPARAM lParam )
{
    switch( uMsg ) {
    //
    // There are two types of keyboard messages
    // in Windows. Normal ASCII keys are sent in
```

```cpp
// via WM_CHAR, but extended/function keys
// arrive via WM_KEYDOWN. You have to do some
// interpretation here to convert windows
// scan codes into key codes that the terminal
// emulation classes know how to deal with.
//
// This handling of incoming keys is a bit
// incomplete. I don't do anything in response
// to control or shift keys in combination with
// function keys. Implementing complete support
// for all possible states isn't particularly
// hard, but the listing would be quite long.
//
// When you do finally figure out what key has
// been pressed, and converted it to a value
// that the emulation classes understand, we
// have to call the WriteKey() member of the
// AnsiTerminal class. It takes care of all the
// processing and translation needed.
//
case WM_KEYDOWN :
    {
        int key;
        switch (wParam ) {
        case VK_UP    : key = UP;    break;
        case VK_DOWN  : key = DOWN;  break;
        case VK_LEFT  : key = LEFT;  break;
        case VK_RIGHT : key = RIGHT; break;
        case VK_PRIOR : key = PGUP;  break;
        case VK_NEXT  : key = PGDN;  break;
        case VK_END   : key = END;   break;
        case VK_HOME  : key = HOME;  break;

        default :
            return -1;
        }
        bool control = (GetKeyState( VK_CONTROL ) & ~1) != 0;
        bool shift = ( GetKeyState( VK_SHIFT )& ~1 ) != 0;
        int count = lParam & 0xffff;
        if ( m_pTerminal )
            for ( int i = 0 ; i < count ; i++ )
                m_pTerminal->WriteKey( key );
    }
    break;
```

```
    //
    // WM_CHAR has the same responsibilties as WM_KEYDOWN,
    // but no translation is necessary, the ASCII value
    // passed in here is just what you expect it to be.
    //
    case WM_CHAR:
        if ( m_pTerminal )
            m_pTerminal->WriteKey( (char) wParam );
        break;
    //
    // When you get notification that RX characters have
    // arrived, you simply read in as many as you can and
    // send them off to the emulator object via the
    // member function Display()
    //
    case WM_SERIAL_RX_NOTIFY :
        {
            for ( ; ; ) {
                int c = m_pTerminal->ReadPort();
                if ( c >= 0 )
                    m_pTerminal->Display( c );
                else
                    break;
            }
        }
        break;
    //
    // Any message that you didn't handle gets routed up
    // to our base class, Win32Term. It is responsible for
    // painting the window, handling scroll bars, etc.
    //
    default:
        return Win32Term::Dispatch( hWnd, uMsg, wParam, lParam );
    }
    return 0L;
}

//
// The owner of this object is usually going to
// be the main window of an emulation program. Instead of
// letting the main window own the RS232 port, you pull it
// into this class. You don't let the outside world manipulate
// the port directly, so if anyone wants to open it or close
```

```
// it they have to go through member functions of this class.
//
// This open function is a little anemic, I don't have any
// options for baud rate, parity, etc. They could easily be
// added one by one to the list of arguments, then passed
// directly to the call to create the Win32Port object.
//
// If you are successful when it comes to opening the port,
// you also create the emulation object, which will handle
// all of the incoming characters from the port.
//
bool AnsiWinTerm::OpenPort( const string &name )
{
    m_pPort = new MyWin32Port( name, m_hWnd );
    if ( m_pPort->ErrorStatus() < 0 ) {
       ::MessageBox( m_hWnd,
                     m_pPort->ErrorName(m_pPort->ErrorStatus()),
                     "Error opening COM Port",
                     MB_OK );
        delete m_pPort;
        m_pPort = 0;
        return false;
    }
    m_pTerminal = new AnsiTerminal( *m_pPort, *this );
    return true;
}


//
// Closing the port translates into destroying two
// objects: the terminal emulator and the port itself.
//
void AnsiWinTerm::ClosePort()
{
    delete m_pTerminal;
    m_pTerminal = 0;
    delete m_pPort;
    m_pPort = 0;
}


//
// These two static arrays provide the translation
// from the display attribute values to RGB values needed
// by Win32Term. Note that this emulator skips out on
// some of the more difficult attributes, such as blinking.
```

```
// These are the simple colors used in the original EGA
// display and supported by the ANSI.SYS driver from
// MS-DOS.
//
const COLORREF AnsiWinTerm::ForegroundPalette[ 16 ] =
{
    RGB( 0, 0, 0 ),             // Black
    RGB( 128, 0, 0 ),           // Red
    RGB( 0, 128, 0 ),           // Green
    RGB( 128, 128, 0 ),         // Yellow
    RGB( 0, 0, 128 ),           // Blue
    RGB( 128, 0, 128 ),         // Magenta
    RGB( 0, 128, 128 ),         // Cyan
    RGB( 210, 210, 210 ),       // White
    RGB( 0, 0, 0 ),             // Black
    RGB( 255, 0, 0 ),           // Bold Red
    RGB( 0, 255, 0 ),           // Bold Green
    RGB( 255, 255, 0 ),         // Bold Yellow
    RGB( 0, 0, 255 ),           // Bold Blue
    RGB( 255, 0, 255 ),         // Bold Magenta
    RGB( 0, 255, 255 ),         // Bold Cyan
    RGB( 255, 255, 255 )        // Bold White
};

const COLORREF AnsiWinTerm::BackgroundPalette[ 8 ] =
{
    RGB( 0, 0, 0 ),             // Black
    RGB( 128, 0, 0 ),           // Red
    RGB( 0, 128, 0 ),           // Green
    RGB( 128, 128, 0 ),         // Yellow
    RGB( 0, 0, 128 ),           // Blue
    RGB( 128, 0, 128 ),         // Magenta
    RGB( 0, 128, 128 ),         // Cyan
    RGB( 255, 255, 255 )        // White
};
```

The Chapter 13 Demo Program

The sample program to demonstrate Win32 terminal emulation, CHAPT13.EXE, is relatively simple as far as Windows programs go. Roughly 200 lines of code, no MFC or other framework, and just a menu in the RC file are all that make up the program. 200 lines might sound like a not-so-small program, but for a full-fledged WinApp, that isn't really too bad.

In a nutshell, the main program of CHAPT13.EXE creates a simple framing window with a fairly brief menu. The framing window creates an instance of an AnsiTermWin window as a child window, and keeps the child window sized to fill the entire client area of its frame. Figure 13-3 shows the program in action (with a menu pulled down) before a port has been opened:

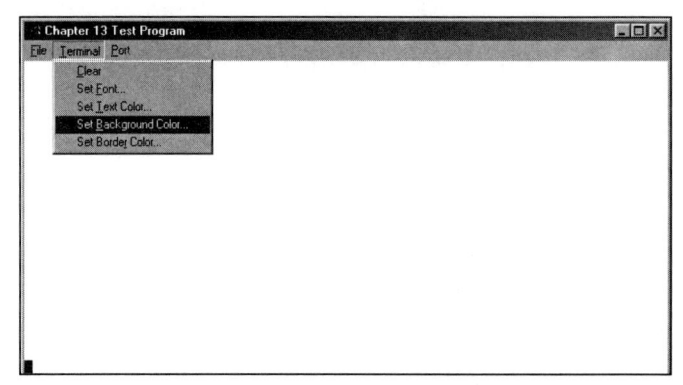

Figure 13-3: CHAPT13.EXE before a port has been opened

Menu commands

Most of the code in CHAPT13.CPP is concerned with handling the menu commands that come from the menu attached to the frame window. A quick description of the menu commands is given here:

File | Exit

The handler for this command simply posts a WM_CLOSE message to itself. This sets Windows down the path of destroying the frame window and all of its children. Both the terminal window and the frame window will receive WM_DESTROY messages to let them know that the O/S is closing them down.

Terminal | Clear

This command calls member function Clear() on the terminal object, which should give the predictable result of erasing all the text in the window. You can try executing this command immediately after changing the background color to verify that the Clear() member uses the current color definitions.

Terminal | Set Font

This command handler first brings up a ChooseFont dialog box (shown in Figure 13-4), allowing the user to select a font of his or her choice. If the user selects a font and exits the dialog by way of the OK button, the `SetFont()` member of the terminal object is called with the new font. `SetFont()` should create the new font, recalculate the system metrics, and update the display to use the new font.

Note that the ChooseFont dialog in this sample program insists on using fixed-width fonts. `Win32Term` expects any font you send to be fixed-width; any attempt to use a variable pitch font will end badly.

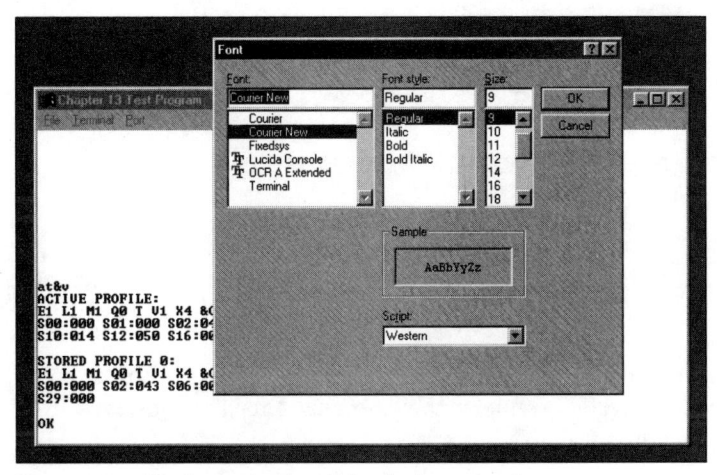

Figure 13-4: The font selection dialog is shown in place.

```
Terminal | Set Text Color
Terminal | Set Background Color
Terminal | Set Border Color
```

These three commands all pull up a color selection dialog (shown in Figure 13-5) that allows the user to choose any color for the given attribute. If the user exits the dialog by pressing OK, the appropriate member function is then called to either set the text attribute or border color.

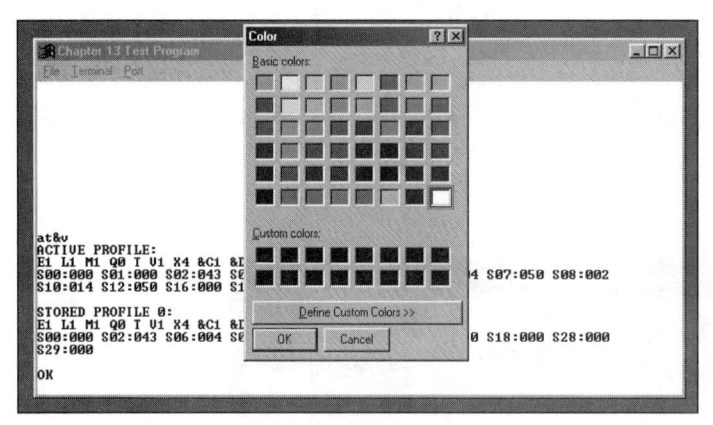

Figure 13-5: The color selection dialog

When the text attribute is changed, you won't see an immediate difference. However, all characters entered after the change will be rendered in the newly chosen color.

Changing the border color will cause an immediate change in the border color, as this member function invalidates the window, forcing a repaint. However, if no border is visible you might not notice a change.

Port | Open COMx

There are four different Open port commands for ports COM1 through COM4. When the program starts, these menu selections are enabled, and the `Close Port` menu item is disabled.

When the user opens a port, the four menu items that open ports are disabled, and the `Close Port` item is then enabled.

When one of the `Open COMx` menu items is selected, the `Open()` member of the terminal window is called, which should open the port and create the terminal emulation object. From that point on, incoming keystrokes will be routed to the terminal emulation object, as will incoming RX data from the COM port.

Figure 13-6 shows the emulator in action after it has opened the port and used it to dial a remote system using a modem.

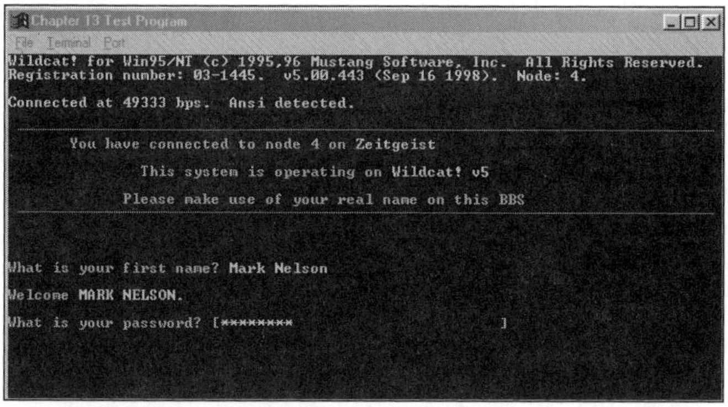

Figure 13-6: CHAPT13.EXE in action

Port | Close Port

This menu item is disabled when the program is first started up. When a port is opened, it is enabled while the four `Open COMx` menu items are disabled. Selecting this menu item invokes the `Close()` member function on the `AnsiWinTerm` object, closing the open port and stopping terminal emulation. When the member returns, the menu item is disabled, and the four `Open COMx` menu items are reenabled.

The source code

The complete listing for the source files that make up CHAPT13.EXE follow in Listings 13-3, 13-4, and 13-5. The core of the program is seen in CHAPT13.CPP, which you find in Listing 13-3. It is relatively short for a complete Windows program, which is a result of the fact that most of the hard work is done in the classes described in this chapter.

Listing 13-3: CHAPT13.CPP

```
//
//  CHAPT13.CPP
//
//  Source code from:
//
//  Serial Communications: Developer's Guide, 2nd Edition
//  by Mark Nelson, IDG Books, 1999
//
//  Please see the book for information on usage.
//
// This file contains the source code for the Chapter 13
// demo program. To build this file, use the Visual C++
// project file included in the same directory as the
```

```c
// sample code.
//

#include <windows.h>

#include "AnsiWinTerm.h"
#include "resource.h"


LRESULT CALLBACK WinProc( HWND hwnd,
                          UINT message,
                          WPARAM wParam,
                          LPARAM lParam );

//
// The WinMain() function for this program looks
// very generic. It has to register the class you
// will create for this demo program, being sure
// to include our menu and WinProc. After the class
// is registered, you can just create the window and
// let it do all the rest of the work. From that
// point on, all you have to do in this routine is
// run the message loop until somebody decides it's
// time to exit.
//

int WINAPI WinMain( HINSTANCE hInstance,
                    HINSTANCE /* hPrevInstance */,
                    LPSTR     /* lpCmdLine */,
                    int       nShowCmd )
{
    //
    // Note that you store enough space extra in our class
    // to hold a single pointer. You keep a pointer to our
    // child window in that extra space, allowing us to
    // avoid the bad taste associated with global variables.
    //
    WNDCLASS wc = { 0 };
    wc.lpfnWndProc     = WinProc;
    wc.hInstance       = hInstance;
    wc.lpszMenuName    = MAKEINTRESOURCE( IDR_MENU );
    wc.hbrBackground   = (HBRUSH) ( COLOR_WINDOW + 1 );
    wc.lpszClassName   = "Chapter13Class";
    wc.cbWndExtra      = sizeof( Win32Term * );
```

```
    if ( !RegisterClass( &wc ) ) {
        MessageBox( NULL,
                    "Could not register Chapter 13 class!",
                    NULL,
                    MB_OK );
        return 0;
    }
    HWND hwnd = CreateWindow( "Chapter13Class",
                              "Chapter 13 Test Program",
                              WS_OVERLAPPEDWINDOW
                                  | WS_CLIPCHILDREN,
                              CW_USEDEFAULT,
                              CW_USEDEFAULT,
                              647, // hand picked size to create
                              347, // just the right size frame
                              NULL,
                              NULL,
                              hInstance,
                              NULL );

    if ( hwnd == NULL ) {
        MessageBox( NULL,
                    "Chapter13.exe couldn't start!",
                    NULL,
                    MB_OK );
        return 0;
    }
    ShowWindow( hwnd, nShowCmd );
    UpdateWindow( hwnd );

    MSG msg;
    while ( GetMessage( &msg, NULL, 0, 0 ) )
    {
        TranslateMessage( &msg ) ;
        DispatchMessage( &msg ) ;
    }
    return 1;
}

//
// Each time I open or close the port I have to
// change the enabled status of five menu items.
// Namely, the four Open COMx entries and the one
// Close Port entry. This routine does the work,
```

```cpp
// and does it properly regardless of whether you
// just opened or just closed a port.
//
void UpdateMenu( HWND hwnd, bool port_open )
{
    HMENU menu = ::GetMenu( hwnd );
    if ( menu ) {
        ::EnableMenuItem( menu,
                          ID_PORT_OPEN_COM1,
                          port_open ? MF_GRAYED  : MF_ENABLED );
        ::EnableMenuItem( menu,
                          ID_PORT_OPEN_COM2,
                          port_open ? MF_GRAYED  : MF_ENABLED );
        ::EnableMenuItem( menu,
                          ID_PORT_OPEN_COM3,
                          port_open ? MF_GRAYED  : MF_ENABLED );
        ::EnableMenuItem( menu,
                          ID_PORT_OPEN_COM4,
                          port_open ? MF_GRAYED  : MF_ENABLED );
        ::EnableMenuItem( menu,
                          ID_PORT_CLOSE,
                          port_open ? MF_ENABLED : MF_GRAYED  );
    }
}


//
// This is the WinProc for the sample program. Fortunately for
// the sake of clarity, all of the things that have to do with
// terminal emulation are being handled by the Window Procedures
// in the terminal emulation window. All you have to handle in
// this procedure are menu commands and a few administrative
// details.
//
// Note that the pointer to the Terminal Emulation window is
// stored as a Window Long word. Each time I enter the loop,
// I extract that pointer for use in all the various message
// handlers in this routine.
//

LRESULT CALLBACK WinProc( HWND hWnd,
                          UINT message,
                          WPARAM wParam,
                          LPARAM lParam )
{
```

```
//
// The custom color array is here so that I can support
// the custom colors in my ChooseColor dialog.
//
static COLORREF custom_colors[ 16 ] = { 0 };
AnsiWinTerm *pTerm = (AnsiWinTerm *)::GetWindowLong(hWnd,0);
switch ( message )
{
    //
    // When my window is first created, I immediately
    // create the terminal window as a child window. I
    // get the pointer to the C++ object and store it as
    // a window long word, giving me access to it whenever
    // I need it without using a global variable.
    //
    case WM_CREATE:
        pTerm = new AnsiWinTerm(hWnd,"AnsiTerm Window",25,80);
        SetWindowLong( hWnd, 0, (LONG) pTerm );
        if ( pTerm->m_hWnd == NULL )
            MessageBox( hWnd,
                        "Can't open child window",
                        "Chapter 13",
                        MB_OK );
        SetFocus( hWnd );
        break;
    //
    // When I am being destroyed, I take it upon myself to
    // destroy the terminal object as well. Note that simply
    // calling the C++ destructor like I'm doing here isn't
    // necessarily enough to destory the window itself, but
    // because it is a child window the O/S will do that in
    // good time.
    //
    case WM_DESTROY:
        delete pTerm;
        pTerm = 0;
        PostQuitMessage( 0 );
        break;
    //
    // Just for the sake of esthetics, I respond to this
    // message with a minimum size large enough to prevent
    // somebody from resizing me down to the point of
    // ridiculousness.
    //
```

```
case WM_GETMINMAXINFO:
    {
        LPMINMAXINFO lp = (LPMINMAXINFO) lParam;
        POINT ptTemp = {
            lp->ptMinTrackSize.x,
            GetSystemMetrics( SM_CYMENU )      +
                GetSystemMetrics( SM_CYCAPTION ) +
                2 * GetSystemMetrics( SM_CYFRAME )
        };
        lp->ptMinTrackSize = ptTemp;
    }
    break;

//
// When the frame window is resized, I immediately
// resize the terminal window. Size the terminal window
// is supposed to completely fill my client area. I
// can figure out what size it is supposed to be by
// simply getting the size of my client RECT. When
// the terminal window processes this command it will
// potentially add scroll bars and offset the display.
//
case WM_SIZE:
    {
        RECT rc;
        ::GetClientRect( hWnd, &rc );
        if ( lParam != 0 )
        ::MoveWindow( pTerm->m_hWnd,
                      0, 0,
                      rc.right - rc.left + 1,
                      rc.bottom - rc.top + 1,
                      TRUE );
    }
    break;
//
// I don't want the framing window to get the focus,
// so whenever I get it, I immediately foist it upon
// the terminal window.
//
case WM_SETFOCUS :
    SetFocus( pTerm->m_hWnd );
    return 0;
//
// The rest of the code in the message loop
```

```
//  is the set of command handlers for menu
//  items.
//
case WM_COMMAND:
    switch ( LOWORD( wParam ) ) {
    //
    // Clearing the temrinal window is simply a
    // matter of calling one member function
    //
    case ID_TERMINAL_CLEAR :
        pTerm->Clear();
        break;
    //
    // Telling a window to close itself is a fast way
    // of shutting the program down.
    //
    case ID_FILE_EXIT :
        PostMessage( hWnd, WM_CLOSE, 0, 0 );
        break;
    //
    // The four Open COMx routines all do essentially
    // the same thing: attempt to open the port, and
    // if succesful, modify the menu a bit. Note that
    // the port is actually being opened inside the
    // terminal object, you're calling a wrapper routine
    // here.
    //
    case ID_PORT_OPEN_COM1 :
        if ( pTerm->OpenPort( "COM1" ) )
            UpdateMenu( hWnd, true );
        break;
    case ID_PORT_OPEN_COM2 :
        if ( pTerm->OpenPort( "COM2" ) )
            UpdateMenu( hWnd, true );
        break;
    case ID_PORT_OPEN_COM3 :
        if ( pTerm->OpenPort( "COM3" ) )
            UpdateMenu( hWnd, true );
        break;
    case ID_PORT_OPEN_COM4 :
        if ( pTerm->OpenPort( "COM4" ) )
            UpdateMenu( hWnd, true );
        break;
    //
```

```cpp
            // Closing the port is another one of those one
            // line of code things. Note that you assume that
            // you will never get this command unless the port
            // is already open. You believe that is the case
            // because you never enable the Close item on the
            // menu while the port is closed.
            //
            case ID_PORT_CLOSE :
                pTerm->ClosePort();
                UpdateMenu( hWnd, false );
                break;
            //
            // The Set Font command is really pretty simple, it's
            // just a little longer because it has to do a bit of
            // setup work to call the ChooseFont() dialog. You can
            // see in this routine that if the person presses the
            // OK button in the font dialog, the SetFont() member
            // of the terminal emulator will be called with a copy
            // of the new LOGFONT settings.
            //
            case ID_TERMINAL_SET_FONT:
                {
                    CHOOSEFONT cf = {0};
                    LOGFONT lf = pTerm->GetLogFont();
                    cf.lStructSize = sizeof( CHOOSEFONT );
                    cf.hwndOwner = hWnd;
                    cf.lpLogFont = &lf;
                    cf.Flags = CF_INITTOLOGFONTSTRUCT |
                               CF_SCREENFONTS         |
                               CF_FIXEDPITCHONLY;
                    if ( !ChooseFont( &cf ) )
                        break;
                    pTerm->SetFont( lf );
                    break;
                }
            //
            // The three remaining routines are all pretty
            // much the same. They choose a color, then pass
            // it to the terminal emulator via a function call.
            // Note that the two text routines won't have an
            // immediate noticeable effect, that doesn't happen
            // until more text arrives. Setting the border color
            // on the other hand, will cause an immediate change
            // to appear.
```

```
            //
            case ID_TERMINAL_SET_TEXT_COLOR :
                {
                    CHOOSECOLOR cc = { 0 };
                    cc.lStructSize = sizeof( CHOOSECOLOR );
                    cc.hwndOwner = hWnd;
                    cc.rgbResult = pTerm->GetForegroundColor();
                    cc.Flags = CC_ANYCOLOR | CC_RGBINIT;
                    cc.lpCustColors = custom_colors;
                    if ( ChooseColor( &cc ) )
                        pTerm->SetForegroundColor( cc.rgbResult );
                }
                break;
            case ID_TERMINAL_SET_BACKGROUND_COLOR :
                {
                    CHOOSECOLOR cc = { 0 };
                    cc.lStructSize = sizeof( CHOOSECOLOR );
                    cc.hwndOwner = hWnd;
                    cc.rgbResult = pTerm->GetBackgroundColor();
                    cc.Flags = CC_ANYCOLOR | CC_RGBINIT;
                    cc.lpCustColors = custom_colors;
                    if ( ChooseColor( &cc ) )
                        pTerm->SetBackgroundColor( cc.rgbResult );
                }
                break;
            case ID_TERMINAL_SET_BORDER_COLOR :
                {
                    CHOOSECOLOR cc = { 0 };
                    cc.lStructSize = sizeof( CHOOSECOLOR );
                    cc.hwndOwner = hWnd;
                    cc.rgbResult = pTerm->GetBorderColor();
                    cc.Flags = CC_ANYCOLOR | CC_RGBINIT;
                    cc.lpCustColors = custom_colors;
                    if ( ChooseColor( &cc ) )
                        pTerm->SetBorderColor( cc.rgbResult );
                }
                break;
            }

        default:
            return DefWindowProc( hWnd, message, wParam, lParam );
    }
    return 0L;
}
```

```
// End of CHAPT13.CPP
```

> **NOTE:** Listing 13-4 was edited for readability. Visual Studio keeps a lot of information in the RC file that is suitable for machine consumption but isn't particularly useful for our purposes.

The sample program stores its menu definition in an RC file, which is shown in Listing 13-4.

Listing 13-4: CHAPT13.RC

```
IDR_MENU MENU DISCARDABLE
BEGIN
 POPUP "&File"
 BEGIN
  MENUITEM "E&xit\tAlt-X",              ID_FILE_EXIT
 END
 POPUP "&Terminal"
 BEGIN
  MENUITEM "&Clear",              ID_TERMINAL_CLEAR
  MENUITEM "Set &Font...",        ID_TERMINAL_SET_FONT
  MENUITEM "Set &Text Color...",  ID_TERMINAL_SET_TEXT_COLOR
  MENUITEM "Set &Back Color...",  ID_TERMINAL_SET_BACKGROUND_COLOR
  MENUITEM "Set Borde&r Color...",ID_TERMINAL_SET_BORDER_COLOR
 END
 POPUP "&Port"
 BEGIN
  MENUITEM "Open COM&1",              ID_PORT_OPEN_COM1
  MENUITEM "Open COM&2",              ID_PORT_OPEN_COM2
  MENUITEM "Open COM&3",              ID_PORT_OPEN_COM3
  MENUITEM "Open COM&4",              ID_PORT_OPEN_COM4
  MENUITEM "&Close Port",             ID_PORT_CLOSE, GRAYED
 END
END
```

> **NOTE:** Listing 13-5 was edited for readability. Visual Studio keeps a lot of information in the header file that is suitable for machine consumption but isn't particularly useful for our purposes.

The identifiers that are used in the menu are stored in the header file shown in Listing 13-5. The identifiers are inserted in the file automatically by the Visual C++ IDE.

Listing 13-5: RESOURCE.H

```
#define IDR_MENU                          101
#define ID_TERMINAL_SET_FONT              1010
#define ID_FILE_EXIT                      40001
#define ID_TERMINAL_CLEAR                 40008
#define ID_TERMINAL_SET_BACKGROUND_COLOR  40021
#define ID_TERMINAL_SET_TEXT_COLOR        40022
#define ID_TERMINAL_SET_BORDER_COLOR      40023
#define ID_PORT_OPEN_COM1                 40024
#define ID_PORT_OPEN_COM2                 40025
#define ID_PORT_OPEN_COM3                 40026
#define ID_PORT_OPEN_COM4                 40027
#define ID_PORT_CLOSE                     40028
```

Suggested Improvements

Developing a terminal emulation support class under Windows takes considerably more time and effort than the equivalent task under MS-DOS. Quite a few enhancements are appropriate for this class that don't fit in the space devoted to this topic. Some features that are very desirable for a full-featured terminal emulator include:

- Cut and Paste capability
- Support for Blink, Underline, and Standout text
- A Scrollback capability
- A debugging facility

Listing 13-6 shows the header file Win32Term.h, which contains the declarations for class Win32Term. A few inline functions are defined in the header file as well, which should lead to a more efficient implementation.

The majority of the class is defined in Win32Term.cpp, which follows in Listing 13-7.

Listing 13-6: Win32Term.h — Class Win32Term

```
//
//   WIN32TERM.H
```

```cpp
//
//  Source code from:
//
//  Serial Communications Developer's Guide, 2nd Edition
//  by Mark Nelson, IDG Books, 1999
//
//  Please see the book for information on usage.
//
// This header file contains the declarations for
// class Win32Term. This class creates a window that
// can be used as part of a Win32 terminal emulator.
//

#include <windows.h>
#include <vector>
using namespace std;

//
// The vector<vector<> > variables in this class
// end up with incredibly long expanded names. This
// pragma disables the associated warnings
//
#pragma warning( disable : 4786 )


class Win32Term
{
public :
    //
    // This nested class is used to hold the background
    // and foreground colors for a single character
    // on the screen. Packaging the two together into
    // a class makes a few things a little easier in
    // some of the members.
    //
    struct TextColor
    {
        TextColor( COLORREF f = 0, COLORREF b = 0 )
            :   m_Foreground( f ),
                m_Background( b ) {}
        bool operator!=( const TextColor &that )
        {
            if ( m_Foreground != that.m_Foreground )
                return true;
```

```cpp
        return m_Background != that.m_Background;
    }
    COLORREF m_Foreground;
    COLORREF m_Background;
};
//
// This little class is used in a bunch of different
// places in the class where you hold both an x and a
// y value for something, like size, scrolling range,
// offset, etc. It's another convenience class, mostly
// here for clarity.
//
struct Pair
{
    Pair( int i = 0, int j = 0 )
    {
        x = i;
        y = j;
    }
    int x;
    int y;
};
//
// This is the structure that you have to use to
// pass data to the WinProc on a WM_CREATE
//
struct CreateData {
    SHORT size;
    Win32Term *pTerm;
};
Win32Term( HWND hParent,
           const char *window_name,
           int rows,
           int cols );
virtual ~Win32Term()
{
    if ( m_hWnd )
        SetWindowLong( m_hWnd, 0, 0 );
    if ( m_hFont )
        DeleteObject( m_hFont );
}
void SetForegroundColor( COLORREF color )
{
    m_CurrentColor.m_Foreground = color;
```

```cpp
            }
            void SetBackgroundColor( COLORREF color )
            {
                m_CurrentColor.m_Background = color;
            }
            COLORREF GetForegroundColor()
            {
                return m_CurrentColor.m_Foreground;
            }
            COLORREF GetBackgroundColor()
            {
                return m_CurrentColor.m_Background;
            }
            COLORREF GetBorderColor()
            {
                return m_BorderColor;
            }
            LOGFONT GetLogFont()
            {
                return m_lfFont;
            }
            void SetBorderColor( COLORREF color );
            virtual void Clear();
            void Output( char c );
            void Output( const char *pBuf, int length = -1 );
            void SetFont( LOGFONT LogFont );
            int SetCursorPosition( int row, int col );
            void GetCursorPosition( int &row, int &col );

    protected :
            BOOL Paint();
            void UpdateCursor();
            void SetFocus();
            void KillFocus();
            void VerticalScroll( WPARAM wParam );
            void HorizontalScroll( WPARAM wParam );
            void Size( int x, int y );
            virtual LRESULT Dispatch( HWND hwnd,
                                      UINT uMsg,
                                      WPARAM wParam,
                                      LPARAM lParam );
    public :
            HWND                    m_hWnd;
```

```
protected:
    HWND                        m_hParent;
    TextColor                   m_CurrentColor;
    vector< vector<char> >      m_ScreenText;
    vector< vector<TextColor> > m_ScreenColor;
    bool                        m_bWrap;
    bool                        m_bShowingCursor;
    HFONT                       m_hFont;
    LOGFONT                     m_lfFont;
    Pair                        m_VisibleSize;
    const Pair                  m_VirtualSize;
    Pair                        m_ScrollRange;
    Pair                        m_Offset;
    Pair                        m_Position;
    Pair                        m_CharSize;
    int                         m_iCharDescent;
    COLORREF                    m_BorderColor;

protected:
    static bool                 m_bClassRegistered;

protected:
    static LRESULT CALLBACK WindowProc( HWND hwnd,
                                        UINT uMsg,
                                        WPARAM wParam,
                                        LPARAM lParam );

};

//EOF Win32Term.h
```

Listing 13-7: Win32Term.cpp

```
//
//  WIN32TERM.CPP
//
//  Source code from:
//
//  Serial Communications: Developer's Guide, 2nd Edition
//  by Mark Nelson, IDG Books, 1999
//
//  Please see the book for information on usage.
//
// This header file contains the implementation of
// class Win32Term. This class creates a window that
```

```cpp
// can be used as part of a Win32 terminal emulator.
//

#include "Win32Term.h"
#include <algorithm>
#include <iostream>
#include <iomanip>
#include <sstream>
#include <cstring>

//
// With Visual Studio 5.0 SP3, min and max
// quit working when used in conjunction with
// class vector<T>! This code is required to
// fix the strange problem.
//
#undef max
#undef min

inline int max( int a, int b )
{
    if ( a > b )
        return a;
    else
        return b;
}

inline int min( int a, int b )
{
    if ( a < b )
        return a;
    else
        return b;
}

//
// Static variable to make sure you
// register this class with Windows once only.
//
bool Win32Term::m_bClassRegistered = false;

//
// The constructor for a Win32 object has to
// pull double duty. It has to create all the
```

```cpp
// data structures and so on that will be used
// in the class, then it has to create the
// window as well. After this is done, the window
// has been created, the message loop is running,
// and the whole thing is ready to use.
//
// Note that the number of rows and columns in
// the virtual screen is decided here in the
// constructor, and can't be changed after the
// window is constructed. The values are stored
// in a const Pair, so no amount of coding is
// going to let them be modified.
//
Win32Term::Win32Term( HWND hParent,
                      const char *window_name,
                      int rows,
                      int cols ) : m_VirtualSize( cols, rows )
{
    //
    // This code sets the two dimensional arrays to the
    // correct size, and copies default data into
    // every cell. Much less code here than the equivalent
    // that would be needed for standard C 2-D arrays.
    //
    m_ScreenText.resize( rows, vector<char>( cols ) );
    m_ScreenColor.resize( rows, vector<TextColor>( cols ) );
    m_hParent          = 0;
    m_hWnd             = 0;
    m_bShowingCursor   = false;
    m_bWrap            = true;
    m_VisibleSize      = Pair( 0, 0 );
    m_ScrollRange      = Pair( 0, 0 );
    m_Position         = Pair( 0, rows - 1 );
    //
    // setup default font information
    //
    m_lfFont.lfHeight      =    12 ;
    m_lfFont.lfWidth       =    0 ;
    m_lfFont.lfEscapement  =    0 ;
    m_lfFont.lfOrientation =    0 ;
    m_lfFont.lfWeight      =    0 ;
    m_lfFont.lfItalic      =    0 ;
    m_lfFont.lfUnderline   =    0 ;
    m_lfFont.lfStrikeOut   =    0 ;
```

```
           m_lfFont.lfCharSet =          OEM_CHARSET ;
           m_lfFont.lfOutPrecision =     OUT_DEFAULT_PRECIS ;
           m_lfFont.lfClipPrecision =    CLIP_DEFAULT_PRECIS ;
           m_lfFont.lfQuality =          DEFAULT_QUALITY ;
           m_lfFont.lfPitchAndFamily = FIXED_PITCH | FF_MODERN ;
           strcpy( m_lfFont.lfFaceName, "FixedSys" ) ;
           SetFont( m_lfFont );
           SetForegroundColor( RGB( 0, 0, 0 ) );
           SetBackgroundColor( RGB( 255, 255, 255 ) );
           Clear();
           //
           // Now I create the actual window
           //
           if ( !m_bClassRegistered ) {
            WNDCLASS wc = { 0 };
            wc.lpfnWndProc     = WindowProc;
            wc.hInstance       = GetModuleHandle( NULL );
            wc.hCursor         = LoadCursor( NULL, IDC_IBEAM );
            wc.hbrBackground   = CreateSolidBrush( RGB( 255, 255, 255 ) );
            wc.lpszClassName   = "Win32TermClass";
            wc.lpszMenuName    = NULL;
            wc.hIcon           = NULL;
            wc.cbWndExtra      = sizeof( Win32Term * );
            RegisterClass( &wc );
            m_bClassRegistered = true;
           }
           m_BorderColor = RGB( 255, 255, 255 );
           m_hParent = hParent;
           //
           // I have to pass a pointer to myself to the window
           // so that it can store the pointer in the window long
           // word. Data that is going to be passed to a
           // WM_CREATE handler has to go in this funny structure.
           //
           CreateData data = { sizeof( Win32Term * ),
                               this
                             };
           CreateWindow( "Win32TermClass",
                         window_name,
                         WS_CHILD | WS_VISIBLE | WS_VSCROLL | WS_HSCROLL,
                         0,0,
                         0,0,
                         m_hParent,
                         0,
                         GetModuleHandle( NULL ),
```

```
                        &data );
}

//
// If the user manages to pass me a good
// LOGFONT, this should all go fairly
// smoothly. The old font is deleted, the
// new one is created, you get some info
// about it, then you redo the screen size,
// offsets, scroll ranges, etc. Finally,
// you do an invalidate to force the whole
// thing to be redrawn.
//
void Win32Term::SetFont( LOGFONT LogFont )
{
    TEXTMETRIC tm;
    HDC   hDC;
    if ( m_hFont )
        DeleteObject( m_hFont );

    m_lfFont = LogFont;
    m_hFont = CreateFontIndirect( &m_lfFont );

    hDC = GetDC( m_hParent ) ;
    SelectObject( hDC, m_hFont ) ;
    GetTextMetrics( hDC, &tm ) ;
    ReleaseDC( m_hParent, hDC ) ;

    m_CharSize.x = tm.tmAveCharWidth;
    m_CharSize.y = tm.tmHeight + tm.tmExternalLeading;
    m_iCharDescent = tm.tmDescent;

    m_Offset.x = 0 ;
    m_Offset.y = m_CharSize.y * m_Position.y;
    Size( m_VisibleSize.x, m_VisibleSize.y );
    ::InvalidateRect( m_hWnd, NULL, TRUE );
    if ( m_hWnd ) {
        KillFocus();
        SetFocus();
    }
}

//
// The routine has a lot to do. Please be sure
```

```cpp
// to refer to the explanation in the book for
// a comprehensive discussion of this routine.
// You really need to understand the member
// variables that are used in this routine to
// follow the code.
//
BOOL Win32Term::Paint()
{
  PAINTSTRUCT  ps;

  HDC hDC = BeginPaint( m_hWnd, &ps ) ;
  HFONT hOldFont = SelectObject( hDC, m_hFont ) ;
  //
  // The first thing you do is figure out the
  // minimum and maximum row in the update
  // rectangle, along with the minimum and
  // maximum column. You aren't going to try
  // to display any characters outside of that
  // cell, because there wouldn't be any point.
  // This makes the routine quite a bit more
  // efficient.
  RECT rect = ps.rcPaint;
  int nRow = min( m_VirtualSize.y - 1,
                  max( 0,
                       (rect.top + m_Offset.y ) / m_CharSize.y
                     )
                );
  int nEndRow = min(m_VirtualSize.y - 1,
                    ((rect.bottom+m_Offset.y-1) / m_CharSize.y )
                   );
  int nCol = min( m_VirtualSize.x - 1,
                  max( 0,
                       ( rect.left + m_Offset.x ) / m_CharSize.x
                     )
                );
  int nEndCol = min(m_VirtualSize.x - 1,
                    ((rect.right+m_Offset.x-1)/m_CharSize.x)
                   );
  //
  // Given that info, you now enter a big for loop
  // that is going to update the display of one row
  // at a time. You print each row in blocks of text
  // that are all the same color. Printing out a
  // string of characters is much more efficient
```

```cpp
    // than just doing a single character at a time,
    // so it's worth it to do the work of figuring out
    // which ones can be done in a single shot.
    //
    for ( ; nRow <= nEndRow; nRow++ )
    {
      int nVertPos = (nRow * m_CharSize.y ) - m_Offset.y;
      //
      // For each row, you perform an ExtTextOut() for each of
      // the contiguous blocks of the same color.
      //
      for ( int start_col = nCol; start_col <= nEndCol ; ) {
          TextColor current_color = m_ScreenColor[nRow][start_col];
          int end_col;
          for (end_col = start_col ; end_col <= nEndCol ; end_col++)
            if ( current_color != m_ScreenColor[ nRow ][ end_col ] )
               break;
          end_col--;
          //
          // At this point I can print all the columns between
          // start_col and end_col using the same color
          //
          int count = end_col - start_col + 1;
          int nHorzPos = (start_col * m_CharSize.x ) - m_Offset.x;
          rect.top = nVertPos ;
          rect.bottom = nVertPos + m_CharSize.y;
          rect.left = nHorzPos;
          rect.right = nHorzPos + m_CharSize.x * count;
          SetTextColor(hDC,
                     m_ScreenColor[nRow][start_col].m_Foreground);
          SetBkColor(hDC,
                     m_ScreenColor[nRow][start_col].m_Background);
          SetBkMode( hDC, OPAQUE );
          ExtTextOut( hDC,
                     nHorzPos,
                     nVertPos,
                     ETO_OPAQUE | ETO_CLIPPED,
                     &rect,
                     (LPSTR)(m_ScreenText[nRow].begin()+start_col),
                     count,
                     NULL );
          start_col = end_col + 1;
       }
    }
    SelectObject( hDC, hOldFont );
```

```cpp
      EndPaint( m_hWnd, &ps );
      UpdateCursor();
      return TRUE;
}

//
// If you currently have the focus, you'll update
// the position of the cursor when this is called.
// If it is called when you don't have the focus,
// you won't try to move the caret. That would
// cause a lot of trouble.
//
void Win32Term::UpdateCursor()
{
   if ( m_bShowingCursor )
      SetCaretPos(
                  ( m_Position.x * m_CharSize.x ) - m_Offset.x,
                  ( m_Position.y * m_CharSize.y ) - m_Offset.y
                 );

}

//
// This is the handler that is called when this
// window gets the focus. If you didn't already
// have the cursor up, you put it up here.
//
void Win32Term::SetFocus()
{
   if ( !m_bShowingCursor )
   {
      CreateCaret( m_hWnd, NULL, m_CharSize.x, m_CharSize.y ) ;
      ShowCaret( m_hWnd ) ;
      m_bShowingCursor = true;
   }
   UpdateCursor();
}

//
// When you lose the focus you have to destroy
// the cursor. There is only one caret per
// system, hogging it is very bad.
//
void Win32Term::KillFocus()
```

```cpp
{
   if ( m_bShowingCursor )
   {
      HideCaret( m_hWnd );
      DestroyCaret() ;
      m_bShowingCursor = false;
   }
}


//
// The two output routines are nearly identical. The
// string output routine simply sits in a loop
// repeating the code in the character routine over
// and over until the string is gone.
//
void Win32Term::Output( char c )
{
    switch ( c ) {
    //
    // The alert or BEL character gets special
    // handling. In this case, special means
    // that you play a beep sound to annoy the
    // user.
    //
    case '\a' :
        MessageBeep( 0 ) ;
        break ;

    //
    // The backspace key doesn't display anything
    // on the screen, it just backs up the cursor
    // by one cell if possible.
    //
    case '\b' :
        if ( m_Position.x > 0 )
            m_Position.x-- ;
        break ;

    //
    // The Carriage Return doesn't do anything
    // to the contents of the screen either. It
    // just returns the cursor to the first column.
    // This is usually matched up with a line feed
```

```
// immediately following.
//
case '\r' :
    m_Position.x = 0 ;
    break;

//
// The line feed character causes the cursor to
// go to the next row.  Normally this is not a
// big deal, but if you were already on the last
// row of the screen, you have to scroll the whole
// thing up, which is a big deal.
//
case '\n' :
    if ( m_Position.y++ == ( m_VirtualSize.y - 1 ) )
    {
        for (int j = 0 ; j < ( m_VirtualSize.y - 1 ) ; j++ ) {
            m_ScreenText[ j ] = m_ScreenText[ j + 1 ];
            m_ScreenColor[ j ] = m_ScreenColor[ j + 1 ];
        }
        fill( m_ScreenText.back().begin(),
            m_ScreenText.back().end(),
            ' ' );
        fill( m_ScreenColor.back().begin(),
            m_ScreenColor.back().end(),
            m_CurrentColor );
        InvalidateRect( m_hWnd, NULL, FALSE );
        m_Position.y--;
    }
    break;

//
// Normal character processing is straightforward.
// You stuff the character and its color into the
// screen at the current insertion point, then update
// the cursor position.  You also invalidate the tiny
// bit of the screen that you just modified so that it
// will get repainted.
//
default:
 {
  RECT rect;
  m_ScreenText[ m_Position.y ][ m_Position.x ] = c;
  m_ScreenColor[m_Position.y][m_Position.x ] = m_CurrentColor;
```

```
            rect.left = ( m_Position.x * m_CharSize.x ) - m_Offset.x;
            rect.right = rect.left + m_CharSize.x;
            rect.top = ( m_Position.y * m_CharSize.y ) - m_Offset.y;
            rect.bottom = rect.top + m_CharSize.y;
            InvalidateRect( m_hWnd, &rect, FALSE ) ;
            //
            // If you reach the end of the line, you
            // might have to wrap to the next line.
            //
            if ( m_Position.x < ( m_VirtualSize.x - 1)  )
                m_Position.x++;
            else if ( m_bWrap )
                Output( "\r\n" ) ;
break;
        }
    }
    UpdateCursor();
}

//
// See the previous routine for docs, it is nearly
// identical.
//
void Win32Term::Output(const char *pBuf, int length /*= 1*/)
{
  if ( length == -1 )
    length = strlen( pBuf );
  for ( int i = 0 ; i < length ; i++ ) {
    switch ( pBuf[ i ] ) {
    case '\a' :
      MessageBeep( 0 ) ;
      break ;

    case '\b' :
      if ( m_Position.x > 0 )
        m_Position.x-- ;
      break ;

    case '\r' :
      m_Position.x = 0 ;
      break;

    case '\n' :
      if ( m_Position.y++ == ( m_VirtualSize.y - 1 ) )
```

```
        {
          for ( int j = 0 ; j < ( m_VirtualSize.y - 1 ) ; j++ ) {
            m_ScreenText[ j ] = m_ScreenText[ j + 1 ];
            m_ScreenColor[ j ] = m_ScreenColor[ j + 1 ];
          }
          fill( m_ScreenText.back().begin(),
                m_ScreenText.back().end(),
                ' ' );
          fill( m_ScreenColor.back().begin(),
                m_ScreenColor.back().end(),
                m_CurrentColor );
          InvalidateRect( m_hWnd, NULL, FALSE );
          m_Position.y--;
        }
        break;

      default:
        {
          RECT rect;
          m_ScreenText[ m_Position.y ][ m_Position.x ] = pBuf[ i ];
          m_ScreenColor[m_Position.y][m_Position.x]=m_CurrentColor;
          rect.left = ( m_Position.x * m_CharSize.x ) - m_Offset.x;
          rect.right = rect.left + m_CharSize.x;
          rect.top = ( m_Position.y * m_CharSize.y ) - m_Offset.y;
          rect.bottom = rect.top + m_CharSize.y;
          ::InvalidateRect( m_hWnd, &rect, FALSE ) ;
          //
          // Check to see whether you wrapped
          //
          if ( m_Position.x < ( m_VirtualSize.x - 1) )
            m_Position.x++ ;
          else if ( m_bWrap )
            Output( "\r\n", 2 ) ;
          break;
        }
    }
  }
  UpdateCursor();
}

//
// There are a big bunch of possible messages that
// you can get from the scroll bars. All you have to
// do in the handler is determine how far to scroll
```

```
//  the screen based on the input you receive in the
//  form of a message. Note that the total span of
//  the scroll bar is stored in m_ScrollRange.
//
void Win32Term::VerticalScroll( WPARAM wParam )
{
    int ScrollCommand = LOWORD( wParam );
    int ScrollPosition = HIWORD( wParam );
    int  nScrollAmt;

    switch (  ScrollCommand )
    {
        case SB_TOP :
            nScrollAmt = -m_Offset.y;
            break;

        case SB_BOTTOM :
            nScrollAmt = m_ScrollRange.y - m_Offset.y;
            break;

        case SB_PAGEUP :
            nScrollAmt = -m_VisibleSize.y;
            break;

        case SB_PAGEDOWN :
            nScrollAmt = m_VisibleSize.y;
            break;

        case SB_LINEUP:
            nScrollAmt = -m_CharSize.y;
            break;

        case SB_LINEDOWN:
            nScrollAmt = m_CharSize.y;
            break;

        case SB_THUMBPOSITION:
            nScrollAmt = ScrollPosition - m_Offset.y;
            break;

        default:
            return;
    }
```

```cpp
        if ( ( m_Offset.y + nScrollAmt ) > m_ScrollRange.y )
            nScrollAmt = m_ScrollRange.y - m_Offset.y;
        if ( ( m_Offset.y + nScrollAmt ) < 0 )
            nScrollAmt = -m_Offset.y;
        ::ScrollWindowEx( m_hWnd,
                          0,
                          -nScrollAmt,
                          NULL,
                          NULL,
                          NULL,
                          NULL,
                          SW_INVALIDATE | SW_ERASE );

    m_Offset.y += nScrollAmt;
    SetScrollPos( m_hWnd, SB_VERT, m_Offset.y, TRUE ) ;
}

void Win32Term::HorizontalScroll( WPARAM wParam )
{
    int ScrollCommand = LOWORD( wParam );
    int ScrollPosition = HIWORD( wParam );
    int nScrollAmt;

    switch ( ScrollCommand )
    {
        case SB_TOP:
            nScrollAmt = -m_Offset.x;
            break;

        case SB_BOTTOM:
            nScrollAmt = m_ScrollRange.x - m_Offset.x;
            break ;

        case SB_PAGEUP:
            nScrollAmt = -m_VisibleSize.x;
            break;

        case SB_PAGEDOWN:
            nScrollAmt = m_VisibleSize.x;
            break ;

        case SB_LINEUP:
            nScrollAmt = -m_CharSize.x;
            break ;
```

```cpp
        case SB_LINEDOWN:
            nScrollAmt = m_CharSize.x;
            break;

        case SB_THUMBPOSITION:
            nScrollAmt = ScrollPosition - m_Offset.x;
            break;

        default:
            return;
    }
    if ( ( m_Offset.x + nScrollAmt ) > m_ScrollRange.x )
        nScrollAmt = m_ScrollRange.x - m_Offset.x;
    if ( ( m_Offset.x + nScrollAmt ) < 0 )
        nScrollAmt = -m_Offset.x;
    ScrollWindowEx( m_hWnd,
                    -nScrollAmt,
                    0,
                    NULL,
                    NULL,
                    NULL,
                    NULL,
                    SW_INVALIDATE | SW_ERASE );
    m_Offset.x = m_Offset.x + nScrollAmt;
    ::SetScrollPos( m_hWnd, SB_HORZ, m_Offset.x, TRUE );
}

//
// See the text in the book for details on the Size()
// message handler. In principle this routine should
// not be too tricky, but it is complicated by the
// fact that scroll bars can pop up or disappear as
// things change.
//
void Win32Term::Size( int x, int y )
{
    //
    // First, you will try to do everything with no scroll bars.
    // If there are scroll bars, you're going to give their space
    // back, at least temporarily
    //
    long style = ::GetWindowLong( m_hWnd, GWL_STYLE );
    if ( style & WS_VSCROLL )
```

```
        x += ::GetSystemMetrics( SM_CXVSCROLL );
if ( style & WS_HSCROLL )
    y += ::GetSystemMetrics( SM_CYHSCROLL );
//
// adjust vertical settings
//
m_VisibleSize.y = y;
m_ScrollRange.y = max( 0,
                    ( m_VirtualSize.y * m_CharSize.y ) +
                        m_iCharDescent - m_VisibleSize.y
                    );
int nScrollAmt = min(m_ScrollRange.y,m_Offset.y)-m_Offset.y;
m_Offset.y = m_Offset.y + nScrollAmt;

//
// adjust horz settings
//
m_VisibleSize.x = x;
m_ScrollRange.x = max( 0,
                    (m_VirtualSize.x * m_CharSize.x ) -
                        m_VisibleSize.x
                    );
nScrollAmt = min( m_ScrollRange.x, m_Offset.x ) - m_Offset.x;
m_Offset.x = m_Offset.x + nScrollAmt;
//
// If you created a vertical scrollbar, you need to go back
// and adjust the horizontal scrollbar.
//
if ( m_ScrollRange.y > 0 ) {
    m_VisibleSize.x = x - ::GetSystemMetrics( SM_CXVSCROLL );
    m_ScrollRange.x = max( 0,
                        (m_VirtualSize.x*m_CharSize.x ) -
                            m_VisibleSize.x
                        );
    nScrollAmt = min(m_ScrollRange.x,m_Offset.x)-m_Offset.x;
    m_Offset.x = m_Offset.x + nScrollAmt;
}
//
// If you created a horzontal scrollbar, you need to go back
// and adjust the vertical scrollbar
//
if ( m_ScrollRange.x > 0 ) {
    m_VisibleSize.y = y - ::GetSystemMetrics( SM_CYHSCROLL );
    m_ScrollRange.y = max( 0,
```

```
                            (m_VirtualSize.y * m_CharSize.y ) +
                            m_iCharDescent - m_VisibleSize.y
                        );
        int nScrollAmt = min( m_ScrollRange.y, m_Offset.y ) -
                        m_Offset.y;
        m_Offset.y = m_Offset.y + nScrollAmt;
        //
        // And it's actually still possible that you need to
        // readjust the X scrollbar
        //
        m_VisibleSize.x = x - ::GetSystemMetrics( SM_CXVSCROLL );
        m_ScrollRange.x = max( 0,
                            (m_VirtualSize.x * m_CharSize.x )
                                - m_VisibleSize.x
                        );
        nScrollAmt = min( m_ScrollRange.x, m_Offset.x ) -
                        m_Offset.x;
        m_Offset.x = m_Offset.x + nScrollAmt;
    }
    //
    // Now you do the actual scrolling. Note that at this
    // point, the number in m_ScrollRange represents the
    // difference between the pixels needed to display the
    // Virtual screen and the number of pixels in the visible
    // window.
    //
    ScrollWindow( m_hWnd, 0, -nScrollAmt, NULL, NULL );
    SetScrollRange( m_hWnd, SB_VERT, 0, m_ScrollRange.y, TRUE );
    SetScrollPos( m_hWnd, SB_VERT, m_Offset.y, FALSE );
    //
    ScrollWindow( m_hWnd, nScrollAmt, 0, NULL, NULL );
    SetScrollRange( m_hWnd, SB_HORZ, 0, m_ScrollRange.x, FALSE ) ;
    SetScrollPos( m_hWnd, SB_HORZ, m_Offset.x, TRUE ) ;

    InvalidateRect( m_hWnd, NULL, FALSE );   //redraw entire window
}

//
// This is the dispatcher for messages coming into
// this window. This is the C++ equivalent of a
// WinProc, and in fact is called by the WinProc
// for this window class.
//
```

```cpp
LRESULT Win32Term::Dispatch( HWND hWnd,
                             UINT uMsg,
                             WPARAM wParam,
                             LPARAM lParam )
{
    switch( uMsg ) {
        case WM_VSCROLL:
            VerticalScroll( wParam );
            break;

        case WM_HSCROLL:
            HorizontalScroll( wParam );
            break ;

        case WM_SIZE:
            Size( LOWORD( lParam ), HIWORD( lParam ) );
            break;

        case WM_PAINT:
            Paint();
            break;

        case WM_CHAR:
            Output( (char) wParam );
            break;

        case WM_SETFOCUS:
            SetFocus();
            break ;

        case WM_KILLFOCUS:
            KillFocus();
            break;

        case WM_MOUSEACTIVATE:
            ::SetFocus( hWnd );
            return MA_ACTIVATE;
            break;

        case WM_DESTROY :
            SetWindowLong( hWnd, 0, 0 );
            m_hWnd = 0;
            break;
```

```
            default:
                return DefWindowProc( hWnd, uMsg, wParam, lParam );
        }
        return 0L;
}

//
// The WinProc for this class is what Windows
// will call when any messages are to be dispatched.
// The only time you actually do anything in this
// routine is when the window is first created,
// because then you get a special pointer to the
// C++ object passed in. You extract that pointer
// and store it in a window long word so that all
// subsequent calls to this routine can get a pointer
// to the C++ object. Thus, all subsequent calls can
// also be handled by the C++ member function
// Dispatch().
//
// Why am I so eager to have commands handled by a
// C++ member function? Most importantly, it gives
// me the opportunity to derive new classes from
// Win32Term, and let them write their own versions
// of Dispatch, allowing them to override some or
// all of the behavior of the class. This is how the
// Chapter 13 example works.
//
LRESULT CALLBACK Win32Term::WindowProc( HWND hWnd,
                                        UINT uMsg,
                                        WPARAM wParam,
                                        LPARAM lParam )
{
    Win32Term *p = (Win32Term *) ::GetWindowLong( hWnd, 0 );
    if ( p )
        return p->Dispatch( hWnd, uMsg, wParam, lParam );
    //
    // If you haven't defined the window yet, you want to make
    // sure you don't do anything that requires the pointer
    // to the object
    //
    if ( uMsg == WM_CREATE )
    {
        CreateData UNALIGNED *pData =
          (CreateData UNALIGNED *) (lParam)->lpCreateParams;
```

```
            pData->pTerm->m_hParent = ::GetParent( hWnd );
            pData->pTerm->m_hWnd = hWnd;
            SetWindowLong( hWnd, 0, (LONG) pData->pTerm );
        }
        return DefWindowProc( hWnd, uMsg, wParam, lParam );
}

//
// Normally clearing the screen is very simple. You
// just fill the screen with blanks of a certain color.
// However, sometimes it is nice to have calibration data
// on the screen so that you can do some experimentation.
// By changing the "#if 1" to "#if 0", you can turn that
// code on. It isn't pretty, but sometimes it is very
// handy.
//
void Win32Term::Clear()
{
#if 1
    for ( int row = 0 ; row < m_VirtualSize.y ; row++ ) {
        fill( m_ScreenText[ row ].begin(),
              m_ScreenText[ row ].end(),
              ' ' );
        fill( m_ScreenColor[ row ].begin(),
              m_ScreenColor[ row ].end(),
              m_CurrentColor );
    }
#else
    TextColor bars[ 2 ] = {
      TextColor( RGB(   0,   0,   0 ), RGB( 224, 224, 224 ) ),
      TextColor( RGB( 255, 255, 255 ), RGB(   0,   0,   0 ) )
    };
    bool temp_wrap = m_bWrap;
    m_bWrap = false;
    int temp_row;
    int temp_col;
    GetCursorPosition( temp_row, temp_col );
    for ( int row = 0 ; row < m_VirtualSize.y ; row++ ) {
        fill( m_ScreenText[ row ].begin(),
              m_ScreenText[ row ].end(),
              ' ' );
        fill( m_ScreenColor[ row ].begin(),
              m_ScreenColor[ row ].end(),
              bars[ row & 1 ] );
```

```
            SetForegroundColor( bars[ row & 1 ].m_Foreground );
            SetBackgroundColor( bars[ row & 1 ].m_Background );
            ostringstream s1;
            ostringstream s2;
            s1 << "*** Row " << setw( 2 ) << row;
            s2 << "Row " << setw( 2 ) << row << " ***";
            SetCursorPosition( row, 0 );
            Output( s1.str().c_str() );
            SetCursorPosition(row,m_VirtualSize.x - s2.str().size());
            Output( s2.str().c_str() );
        }
        m_bWrap = temp_wrap;
        SetCursorPosition( temp_row, temp_col );
#endif
        ::InvalidateRect( m_hWnd, NULL, TRUE );
}

//
// The border color is truly just the background
// color for the window. When you get a new
// color in for the background, you just create
// a brush for that color and stuff it into the
// class data for this window. The rest of it
// is automatic, you never have to actually draw
// the border, it's done automatically as part
// of the paint process.
//
void Win32Term::SetBorderColor( COLORREF color )
{
    HBRUSH brush = (HBRUSH)
        ::GetClassLong( m_hWnd, GCL_HBRBACKGROUND );
    if ( brush )
        DeleteObject( brush );
    brush = ::CreateSolidBrush( color );
    ::SetClassLong( m_hWnd, GCL_HBRBACKGROUND, (LONG) brush );
    m_BorderColor = color;
    ::InvalidateRect( m_hWnd, NULL, TRUE );
}

//
// Done just as you might think, with a bit
// of error checking
//
int Win32Term::SetCursorPosition( int row, int col )
```

```
{
    if ( row < 0 || col < 0 )
        return 0;
    if ( row >= m_VirtualSize.y )
        return 0;
    if ( col >= m_VirtualSize.x )
        return 0;
    m_Position.x = col;
    m_Position.y = row;
    UpdateCursor();
    return 1;
}

void Win32Term::GetCursorPosition( int &row, int &col )
{
    row = m_Position.y;
    col = m_Position.x;
}

//EOF Win32Term.cpp
```

Summary

Chapter 8 gave you a good overview of terminal emulation, and presented a framework for how a terminal emulation class might be integrated into an MS-DOS program. This chapter adds to that knowledge base by integrating the same classes into a Win32 program.

This chapter uses the same `AnsiTerminal` class demonstrated in Chapter 8, and finds it suitable to the task without change. Most of the code you've seen in this chapter focused on developing a display class that works in the GUI environment of Win32. Class `Win32Term` is integrated with the `Win32Port` class and the `AnsiTerm` class to create a working sample program, `CHAPT13.EXE`. With three powerful classes to do all the hard work, you can create `CHAPTE13.EXE` with a surprisingly small amount of source code.

Chapter 14

Using Modems Under MS-DOS

IN THIS CHAPTER

- ◆ The conflicts within the standards
- ◆ Modem capabilities
- ◆ A test program

MODEMS ARE DIFFICULT to work with, but they are an essential part of long distance communications over RS-232 links. Sophisticated operating systems such as Windows 95 provide drivers that insulate you from some (but far from all) of the problems with modems. This chapter shows you how to deal with modems when you have little or no operating system support, such as under MS-DOS. The next chapter shows you how to use TAPI (Telephony Application Programming Interface) to make modem programming a bit more palatable.

Dr. Jekyll and Mr. Modem

Probably nothing has been more of a hindrance to public acceptance of communications software than the ordinary desktop modem. This may seem contradictory; after all, what would communications software be *without* modems?

Although it is true that modems are absolutely crucial to desktop communications, it is also true that the lack of standardization between various brands and models of modems has led to a virtual Tower of Babel for end users. In principle, it ought to be simple to buy a modem and a software package, install both of them, and immediately be able to communicate with distant modems.

In practice, nothing could be farther from the truth. Most first time users realize they are in trouble when their installation software gives them a prompt that looks like this:

```
Modem setup string? _
```

This seemingly simple question usually causes the first in a never-ending series of research sessions devoted to the investigation of DIP switch settings and the "AT" command set. Eventually, most users thrash out a configuration that works for them, but even the slightest disturbance will break it, leading to yet another frustrating investigation.

In the communications industry, evolving standards are usually in a state of dynamic tension with innovation. To achieve mass acceptance, both hardware and software have to achieve a certain amount of uniformity, usually by adherence to official or de facto standards. This has proven to be true of computers, peripherals, operating systems, and even applications. Where, then, did modem manufacturers go wrong?

The hardware standards

When it comes to hardware, modem manufacturers have done pretty well. The past 30 years have seen a steady progression of modem standards, from the AT&T standards of the 1960s and 1970s to the ITU (formerly CCITT) standards in effect today.

As this book is written, virtually every modem sold to desktop users adheres to one of two standards:

V.34:   This inexpensive workhorse provides 33.6Kbps communications. The chipsets to make these modems are so inexpensive that virtually every desktop system or notebook today has a V.34 modem included.

V.90:   V.90 modems can receive data at 53 or 56Kbps in one direction, and transmit at V.34 speeds in the other direction. The 56 Kbps speed can only be achieved when one end is connected to the phone system using digital trunks, such as ISDN Primary Rate or T1 lines. This is a typical setup for an Internet Service Provider or other service bureau.

The notable thing about these modems is that virtually all the modems produced today are able to communicate with one another. Regardless of the manufacturer and the hardware used to build the modem, one V.34 or V.90 modem is able to connect to another without much trouble. This is a tribute to the standardization process.

At times, manufacturers have achieved limited success selling nonstandard modems. U.S. Robotics, Lucent, and Rockwell went through a period in the late 1990s when three different types of nonstandard 56Kbps modems were competing with one another. Consumers were purchasing these modems at a prodigious rate. However, this situation quickly settled back to business as usual, with all manufactures shifting to the newly adopted V.90 standard. There are two important facts to note about these renegade modems:

- ♦ The nonstandard modems were often created in an attempt to break new ground in throughput. Modems such as the USR X2 and the Rockwell 56K were sending data faster than their contemporary standards permitted.

After the standards caught up with technology, the nonstandard modems were replaced with conforming ones.

◆ The nonstandard modems could always fall back to slower speeds and talk to other modems that were adhering to existing standards. So, even though these modems deviated from the norm, they still offered a "safety net" to their owners.

In general, it seems that nonstandard modems are only viable as pioneers of new technologies. The rest of the time, nearly all modems sold will adhere to ITU standards.

The software standards

Today's modems are almost universally smart modems. This means that the modem has an on board microprocessor, and communicates with the computer when offline via the RS-232 interface or via a direct connection to the PC bus. The "language" used to control the modem is usually referred to as the *AT command set*.

The AT command set comes to us thanks to the pioneer of desktop modems, Hayes. To say that Hayes was an overnight success might be an exaggeration, but after the introduction of the Smartmodem 300, Hayes quickly moved to a position of industry dominance. (Sadly, after two bankruptcy proceedings only scattered remnants of Hayes remain.)

The AT command set, as introduced with the Smartmodem 300, provided a simple and convenient way for the modem to make phone calls. Before the introduction of smart modems, a user would typically make a dial up connection by picking up the telephone and dialing the number for a remote modem. When the remote end picked up the call and began sending its answer tone, the user would put the handset into an acoustic coupler, whereupon the user's modem would respond to the answer tone, leading to a connection.

You can imagine how enjoyable this would be when repeated dozens of times a day, or when trying to get through to a perpetually busy number. When the unfortunate user of a dumb modem upgraded to the Hayes Smartmodem 300, making the phone call meant just typing in the characters ATDT 555-1212, followed by a carriage return. The modem would automatically go off hook, dial the remote end, and wait for a carrier.

Even better was the fact that the entire dialing process could be automated. If a dial-up number was perpetually busy, it was a simple matter to write a dialer program that could try it once very 15 seconds. The possibilities were endless, even showing up in the movie *War Games*.

All this was accomplished using the AT command set. The "AT" in the name refers to the fact that every command starts with the two characters A and T. This is commonly referred to as the attention sequence, although it isn't clear whether the name came before or after the use of the two letters.

Every AT command sent to the modem consists of the two letters followed by a string of alphanumeric characters that ends in a carriage return character. The original

Smartmodem had a relatively small roster of commands that the user could employ. Over succeeding generations, the command set grew, leading to what I consider to be the benchmark, which is the command set for the Smartmodem 2400.

Although the name doesn't carry the cachet it once did, even today modems claim to be "Hayes compatible." They are "Hayes compatible" as long as the extent of Hayes compatibility means having a set of commands that all start with AT. In point of fact, no modem manufacturer can resist tinkering with the command set. Usually this means adding a few new commands as an extension to the set. It often means modifying a few of the existing commands, and maybe even leaving out a few that aren't frequently used.

If this sounds chaotic, it is. But fortunately, it *is* possible to identify a core set of commands that will work with every modem, and as long as you don't deviate from those, you can write software that works with every "Hayes compatible" modem. You learn later in this chapter that individual modems require unique configuration and setup commands.

THE SMARTMODEM 2400 COMMAND SET

All of the commands in this set start with the characters AT and are terminated with a carriage return character, \r, with one exception. In general, commands can be strung together by simply concatenating the command characters (minus the leading AT). For example, the three commands ATZ, ATE1, and ATV1 could be combined and sent to the modem as ATZE1V1. You can expect all modems to accept at least 40 characters per command, although most accept more.

The exception to the AT prefix rule is the Repeat command. By sending the unadorned string A/ to the modem, with no trailing carriage return, the modem repeats the last command.

Many of the commands presented in the following list are somewhat irrelevant in the desktop context this book addresses. See the specifics on each command for a discussion of the usefulness of individual commands.

ATA	The Answer command. This causes the modem to go off-hook and begin emitting the answer tone. This is usually done in response to an incoming ring detect.
ATBn	If n is set to 0, this command selects the CCITT V.22 standard for 1200bps communications. A setting of 1 selects Bell 212A. The default for modems sold in the U.S. is usually 1. Very few modems in use today use 1200bps communications, so this setting is not particularly useful.
ATDs	This is the dial command. The s stands for a dialing string. The dialing string consists of a string of digits to dial, mixed with dial string modifiers. The dialing modifiers are as follows:
	P Dial in Pulse mode. Pulse mode is usually the default setting for dialing.

Chapter 14: Using Modems Under MS-DOS 653

T	Dial in Tone mode. Because most people prefer to dial in tone mode, dialing strings typically start with ATDT.
,	Pause during dialing. The length of the pause is determined by the contents of S register 8 (more about that later), and usually defaults to 2 seconds.
!	Perform a hook flash. This is often necessary on PBX systems to access special phone system features.
W	Wait for dial tone. Most PBX systems require you to dial a trunk access code, such as 9, and then wait for a second dial tone before dialing. The W dialing code gives you that capability.
@	Wait for silence. Some systems don't provide an access tone when you connect to them. When you specify that you want to wait for silence, it means the remote end should stop ringing and be silent for 5 seconds before dialing continues.
;	Return to command mode after dialing. Normally the modem will wait for a connection after dialing. If the ; is used to terminate the dialing string, the modem dials and then returns to command mode while the call is being processed.
S=n	The value n can be a number from 0 to 3. It refers to one of four dialing strings that have been stored in the modem. Because most modem dialing is done under program control, this feature is not particularly useful today. A communications program typically has access to a dialing directory containing hundreds of numbers
ATEn	This command controls the echoing of characters in command mode. A value for n of 0 disables echoing, 1 enables. Normally there is no reason to change the default, which is to echo characters.
ATHn	A value of 0 causes the modem go hang up. A value of 1 tells the modem to go off hook. You use the ATH0 command in this chapter's Modem class to break a connection.
ATIn	The different values of n produce various product ID codes, firmware checksums, and so forth. These are relatively useless for your purposes. They might be useful for debugging a suspected hardware problem in conjunction with the manufacturer's technical support department.
ATLn	This command adjusts the speaker's volume level, with an n value of 0 being the lowest volume and 3 being the highest. Some modems require volume adjustment to be done via an external potentiometer, so this command is not always effective.

ATM*n*   The Smartmodem 2400 has four different operating modes for the speaker:

0   The speaker is *always* off.

1   The speaker is on during dialing, and turns off when carrier is detected. This is the default setting. It is useful to be able to hear the modem during the dialing stage.

2   The speaker is *always* on. This can be quite noisy after carrier is attained.

3   The speaker is off during dialing, on while waiting for carrier, and off when carrier is attained.

ATO*n*   This command is used to return the modem to the online state when it is in command mode. The default value of *n*, 0, just returns the modem to the online state. A value of 1 causes the modem to go reinitiate the equalization retraining process.

ATQ*n*   The ATQ command is used to enable or disable result codes. The normal result codes, such as OK and RING are returned by default, or when *n*=0. ATQ1 disables result codes. The Modem class developed in this chapter, always depends on result codes being sent.

ATS*r*=*n*   The S registers are used to control various facets of the modem's behavior, such as the ring to answer on, the backspace character, escape character. The pertinent S registers will be discussed later in this chapter. This command is used to set register *r* to the value *n*.

ATS*r*?   This command is used to display the value of register *r*.

ATV*n*   The modem has the ability to display result codes in numeric form or verbose form. Verbose responses are the traditional English form, such as CONNECT, OK, and so on. Numeric codes are simple numbers, which are somewhat harder to translate. Although they are somewhat more difficult for a program to deal with, verbose codes are used by the Modem class.

ATX*n*   This is yet another command that modifies the result code set. When *n*=0, the only message returned when a connection occurs is CONNECT. With higher values of *n*, messages such as CONNECT 48000 are returned. Unfortunately, the array of different message possibilities that can be returned with the various values of *n* is staggering. To avoid confusion as much as possible, I stick with the default value of *n*=4.

ATY*n*   The default value of 0 disables the long break disconnect. A value of 1 enables this disconnect type. When a break of greater than 1.6 seconds is received and disconnect is enabled, the modem disconnects.

Chapter 14: Using Modems Under MS-DOS   655

ATZ*n* The `ATZ` command performs a software reset of the modem. Optionally, a value of *n* can be passed to specify one of several profiles to set the modem to. The original Hayes Smartmodem had two profiles that could be called up: *n*=0 and *n*=1.

AT&C*n* By default, the Hayes Smartmodem kept the CD line high at all times. This is probably a bad thing for software that is trying to work effectively with the modem, because it makes it much more difficult to determine if and when a connection is actually present, and when it is broken. The `Modem` class in this chapter uses this command with *n*=1 to cause CD to accurately track the state of the carrier; *n*=0 restores the default setting and keeps CD high at all times.

AT&D*n* This command determines what action the modem takes when DTR drops from high to low. The default setting of *n*=0 causes the modem to ignore DTR; *n*=1 causes the modem to enter command mode when DTR drops; *n*=2 causes the modem to hang up and enter command mode when DTR drops. The most drastic action is taken when *n*=3 — the modem hangs up, resets all of its operating parameters, and enters command mode when DTR drops.

AT&F This command restores the factory settings of the modem. This command is particularly useful, as it is really the only way to put the modem in a known state.

AT&G*n* This command selects one of several optional guard tones. It is typically not used in the U.S.

AT&J*n* Some of the Hayes Smartmodems used this command to select different types of telephone line jacks. Very few manufacturers currently support this command.

AT&P*n* The make/break ratio in pulse dialing varies slightly between various countries. The United States uses the default value specified by *n*=0. The United Kingdom uses *n*=1.

AT&Q*n* Some modems support synchronous operation, which can be selected with values of *n* other than the default of 0. Although not commonly used, it is necessary for some users with specific hardware requirements.

AT&R*n* This option determines how the modem uses the RTS line. Under the default value of *n*=0, CTS will track RTS. With *n*=1, CTS will always be high.

AT&S*n* With the default parameter of *n*=0, the modem keeps DSR high at all times. With *n*=1, DSR is low when in command mode and high when online.

AT&T*n* This option is used to initiate one of many test procedures.

Although this list of options may seem rather long, it is by no means comprehensive. However, it provides a good basis to start from, because most new modems support this command set.

In addition to the AT commands, there are two command sequences that don't start with AT and aren't terminated with a carriage return:

A\   Repeat the last command. This is the sole command that doesn't have an AT prefix or a carriage return terminator. This command is handy when it can be used to avoid reentering a long dialing string. It is not particularly useful when writing programs to control the modem.

+++   The escape sequence. An online modem can be commanded to drop back to command mode if it sees three consecutive occurrences of the escape sequence in the data stream. Note that Hayes requires a guard time of 1 second before and after a sequence in which no other data is sent. This capability is part of the notorious Heatherington '302 patent held by Hayes, which most modem manufacturers seem to be willing to pay royalties for the privilege of using.

THE S REGISTERS

The Hayes modem maintains a bank of internal status registers, or S registers, that determine how many of the modem's functions operate. Like the AT command set, the set of S registers has been highly customized by various manufacturers. However, the basic set used by the Hayes Smartmodem 2400 has remained more or less inviolate.

The contents of the S register can be examined with the ATSr? command and modified with the ATSr=n command. The S register definitions are described in Table 14-1.

TABLE 14-1 THE S REGISTER DEFINITIONS

Register	Range	Default	Meaning
S0	0 – 255	0	Ring to answer on. A value of 0 disables the auto answer capability of the modem.
S1	0 – 255	N/A	Ring count. This is a count of the number of incoming rings on the line.
S2	7 bit ASCII characters	0x2B, '+'	The escape character used to take the modem to command mode when it is online.

Register	Range	Default	Meaning
S3	7 bit ASCII characters	0x0D, CR	The character used by the modem as a carriage return in command mode.
S4	7 bit ASCII characters	0x0A, LF	The character used by the modem as a line feed in command mode.
S5	Nonprinting ASCII control characters	0x08, BS	The character used by the modem as a backspace in command mode.
S6	0 – 255	2	The number of seconds to wait before dialing, if blind dialing is enabled.
S7	0–255	30	The number of seconds to wait for carrier after dialing is complete.
S8	0 – 255	2	The number of seconds to pause when a comma is found in the dialing string.
S9	0 – 255	6	The number of 100-millisecond units that the carrier must be active before being recognized as valid.
S10	0 – 255	14	The number of 100-millisecond units that carrier must be low before the modem disconnects.
S11	50 – 255	70	The DTMF dialing duration in milliseconds.
S12	20 – 255	50	The escape code guard time in 20 millisecond units. A valid escape code (+++) must be surrounded by this much idle line time to be considered valid.

Today's modems

The modems sold to users today generally follow the hardware and software standards shown above. However, today's modems have capabilities that far surpass those of the Smartmodem 2400, and you need to take those into account as well.

Figures 14-1 and 14-2 show a couple of representative examples of modems in use today: the 3COM Courier V.Everything 56K V.90 intelligent modem and the Diamond Multimedia SupraMax 56K internal modem.

The 3COM modem is a good example of a top end modem. In addition to supporting standard V.90 56K modulation, it is backward compatible with seemingly every modem ranging down to ancient 2400bps modems. It supports both MNP and CCITT error correction and data compression, allowing for fast and reliable connections. In addition, it has built-in Group 3 FAX capabilities, allowing the modem to both send and receive FAXes.

Figure 14-1: The 3COM Courier V.Everything 56 Kbps modem is a top-of-the-line modem.

Diamond Multimedia has a complete line of inexpensive modems that support PC and Mac interfaces, internal and external, as well as a USB interface. The SupraMax unit shown in Figure 14-2 is a very affordable unit that supports 56 Kbps data connections and is also capable of sending and receiving faxes.

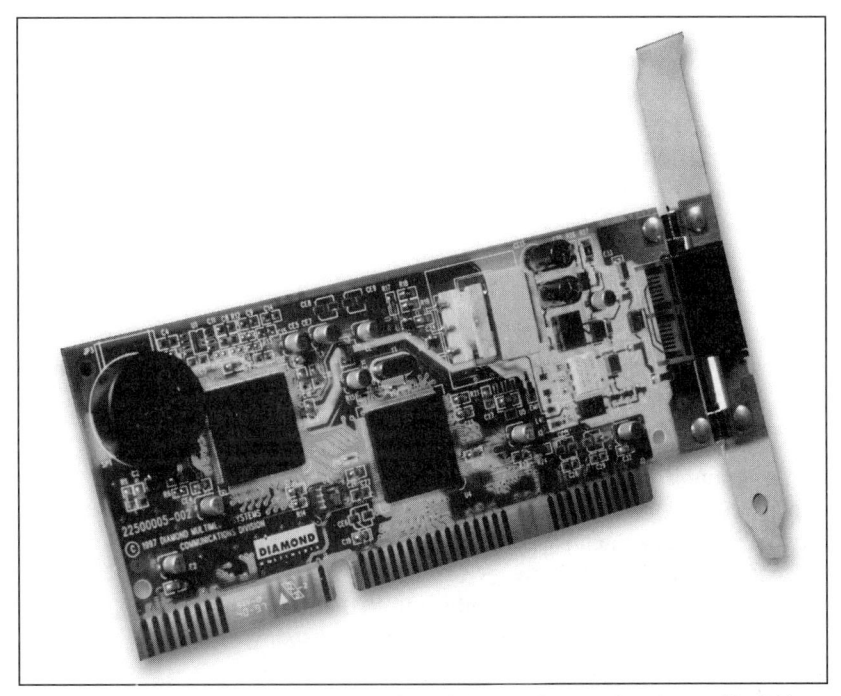

Figure 14-2: The Diamond Multimedia SupraMax 56 Kbps modem is an affordable modem.

Modem Capabilities

The first step toward writing a useful modem class is to define a set of capabilities that can be worked with in a uniform way. For any given modem, a standard setup, a list of capabilities, and a way to recognize appropriate responses from the modem needs to be defined.

The Modem class defined in this chapter keeps this information about modems in a ModemCapabilities structure. This structure contains all the information you need to write useful software that can interact with the modem:

```
struct ModemCapabilities {
    char *name;
    char *initialization_string
    char *fail_strings;
    char *compression_strings;
    char *protocol_strings;
    long initial_baud_rate;
    int locked_baud_rate;
    int handshaking;
};
```

A typical entry follows. This is for a Practical Peripherals modem, which has a feature set similar to the two pictured earlier in this chapter. This entry describes everything the Modem class needs to know about the modem to work with it.

```
{ "Practical Peripherals V.34",
  "AT &F0 &C1 &D2 S95=44",
  "NO CARRIER\0ERROR\0NO DIALTONE\0BUSY\0NO ANSWER\0\0",
  "CLASS 5\0V.42BIS\0\0",
  "LAP-M\0ALT\0\0",
  57600L,
  1,
  1
}
```

The test program in this chapter has three different modems defined in its ModemCapabilities database. When writing programs to use the Modem class, you might have to define only one or two modem types that are in use by your users. A commercial application, however, needs to develop a more comprehensive list of modems. Unfortunately, there isn't a handy source that contains the programming information for all the different modems on the market today.

The various entries in the structure are defined here.

char *name

This is simply the name of the modem type being defined. In a typical application, a user would be able to pick a particular modem off a list composed of all the name entries available.

char *initialization_string

This is a simple string used to initialize the modem. The initialization string should put the modem into a well-defined state that allows it to work properly with the Modem class. The characteristics of the modem after initialization should include:

- ◆ The modem should give verbose responses to commands. These help the user as much as they help the programmer. This should include the type of lengthy CONNECT messages typically produced using ATX4 or greater.

- ◆ The modem should disconnect if DTR drops.

- ◆ The CD line from the modem should accurately reflect whether the modem is connected to another modem.

- ◆ If available, the modem should use whatever error correcting protocols are available to it, including MNP-4 and V.42 (LAP-M).

- If available, the modem should also use whatever data compression protocols are available to it, including MNP-5 and V.42*bis*.

- The modem should have RTS/CTS handshaking enabled, if available.

- The modem should have a baud rate locked at a high rate, if available. If the baud rate isn't locked at a level considerably above that of the carrier, data compression won't be particularly useful.

char *fail_strings

This string is a list of response strings that indicate a failure to connect to a remote end. '\0' characters separate the strings, with the final string being empty. These strings contain messages such as NO CARRIER and BUSY. This enables the Modem class to compensate for unusual messages that may be issued by various modems when trying to connect.

char *compression_strings

This string is a list of response strings indicating that a connection was made using data compression. Most modems issue a connect message that looks similar to this when data compression is being used:

    CONNECT /MNP

Because many modems support various sorts of data compression, they can potentially have more than one string indicating that compression takes place. This list of strings can handle as many as each modem can issue.

char *protocol_strings

Just as with data compression, each modem has the potential to handle several sorts of error-correcting protocols. This string gives the substrings to scan for when a connect message occurs. If any of substring is matched, it can be assumed that the connection has an error-correcting protocol in place.

long initial_baud_rate

This is the baud rate that the Modem class should use to communicate with the modem initially. This value should be set as high as the modem can accommodate.

int locked_baud_rate

This boolean flag is used to indicate that the modem is configured to have a locked baud rate. This means that the modem will continue to communicate with the PC at a fixed baud rate, regardless of the speed of the connection. This is the normal state of affairs for any modem that supports either data compression or error-correcting protocols. It also implies that the modem must support handshaking.

`int handshaking`

This boolean flag indicates that the modem support RTS/CTS handshaking. Most modems today use this to support advanced communications features.

Creating a capability entry

Most modems come with a 30- to 40-page booklet that describes the various programming options available to the end user. (Unfortunately, this is becoming less common as time goes on; frequently, documentation must be ordered or downloaded separately.) It might seem like a rather difficult job to come up with a new entry for each modem. Fortunately, most modems have some features in common that can be taken advantage of.

Nearly every modem sold today supports the `AT&F` option. This option is used to restore all modem settings to their factory defaults. The factory defaults are designed to mimic the Hayes standard as best as possible. From there, it is simply a matter of scanning each option and determining whether a deviation from the default value is necessary.

Two variations that are usually needed are the two that make DTR and CD into useful control lines. These are usually accomplished with the `&C1` and `&D2` options.

By default, most modems have their protocol and error-compression capabilities enabled, which implies both hardware handshaking and a locked baud rate.

Finally, you will want to issue as much information as possible during negotiations and connection. The ATX commands are generally where this takes place.

The Modem class

Taking advantage of all this information requires the use of the `Modem` class. This class is not particularly complex, but it does take care of the tasks that most communications programs need including:

- Initializing the modem and the port-line parameters.
- Dialing out and waiting for a connection. After the connection is made, determining the parameters of the connection.
- Alternatively, answering an incoming call and waiting for a connection.
- Disconnecting when the call is complete.

The `Modem` class accomplishes all these tasks by using features that are offered by virtually every modem on the market today.

Chapter 14: Using Modems Under MS-DOS 663

Listing 14-1 shows a listing of MODEM.H, the header file that contains the class definition for the Modem class. Any program wanting to take advantage of the class needs to include this file. The public interface to the class consists of 14 member functions and a constructor.

Listing 14-1: MODEM.H

```
// ******************* START OF MODEM.H *******************
// This header file has all of the definitions and prototypes
// needed to use the Modem class.  This file should be included
// by any module that uses the Modem class.

#ifndef _MODEM_DOT_H
#define _MODEM_DOT_H

#include "rs232.h"

enum ModemError {    MODEM_SUCCESS             = 0,
                     MODEM_NO_RESPONSE         = -100,
                     MODEM_NO_CONNECTION       = -101,
                     MODEM_DISCONNECT_FAILED   = -102,
                     MODEM_USER_ABORT          = -103 };

// This structure defines the layout of the modem capability
// database elements.  At present, all the definitions that
// can be used to define a particular brand or type of modem
// are stored in a static array in MODEM.CPP.  A commercial
// application might store these offline in a database.

struct ModemCapabilities {
    char *name;
    char *initialization_string;
    char *fail_strings;
    char *compression_strings;
    char *protocol_strings;
    long initial_baud_rate;
    int locked_baud_rate;
    int handshaking;
};

// The Modem class definition

class Modem {
protected :
    RS232 *port;
    ModemCapabilities *modem_data;
```

```
        long local_baud_rate;
        int tone_dial;
        int protocol;
        int compressing;
        ModemError wait_for_response( void );
        ModemError wait_for_connection( void );
        long carrier_timeout;
        virtual void echo( char c ) { cout << c; }
        void read_line( char *buffer, int buf_size );

public :
        Modem( RS232 &rs232_port, char *modem_name );
        ModemError Initialize( void );
        ModemError Answer( void );
        ModemError Dial( char *number );
        ModemError Disconnect( void );
        ModemError SendCommand( char * );
        int ReadRegister( int reg );
        virtual ModemError UserAbort( void );
        void PulseDial( void ){ tone_dial = 0; }
        void ToneDial( void ){ tone_dial = 1; }
        void SetCarrierTimeout( long length )
        {
            carrier_timeout = length;
        }
        char *ErrorName( ModemError status );
        virtual void DumpState( void );
        int Protocol( void ){ return protocol; }
        int Compressing( void ){ return compressing; }
};

#endif // #ifdef _MODEM_DOT_H

// ****************** END OF MODEM.H ******************
```

The public interface

The 14 functions and constructor that define the public interface are all relatively straightforward. Use the descriptions in this section to illuminate the code listing shown in Listing 14-2, which follows these descriptions.

`Modem( RS232 &rs232_port, char *modem_name )`

The constructor for an object of class Modem takes two arguments. First, it needs a reference to an RS232 port that is actually attached to the modem. Second, it needs the name of the type of modem that is being used. The name would normally be pulled out of a configuration file or picked from a list of entries in a database.

The constructor initializes a couple of private data members, but doesn't actually manipulate the port or the modem. This is done when the program decides it is time in the next member function, Initialize().

ModemError Initialize(void)

This function has the job of initializing both the modem and the serial port. Initializing the modem consists of just sending the initialization string down and waiting for the appropriate response, usually an OK message. This function also turns on RTS/CTS handshaking, if the modem supports it, and sets the baud rate to the initial rate specified in the ModemCapabilities database entry.

ModemError Answer(void)

An incoming ring on the modem can be detected in one of two ways. First, the actual RING message can be read in on the serial port. This is probably the most reliable way to detect the ring. Second, the RI line from the UART can be monitored using calls to RS232::Ri().

After the ring is detected, this function can be called to cause the modem to go off hook and attempt to answer the call. It will take care of sending the message and waiting for the appropriate CONNECT or NO CARRIER message to be read in. It will also detect whether the call established an error-correcting protocol, and whether it is using data compression.

If the modem doesn't support locked baud rates, the baud rate reported by the modem as part of the CONNECT message will be applied to the port using the RS232::Set() function so that communications can begin immediately.

If the call was properly answered, MODEM_SUCCESS is returned from the function. Otherwise, one of the ModemError status codes is returned.

ModemError Dial(char *number)

This function is almost the same as the Answer() function. Instead of going off hook in response to an incoming ring, however, this function initiates the process by causing the modem to dial a digit string of the programmer's selection. It then goes through the same verification procedure while waiting for a response, and returns the same ModemError status codes.

ModemError Disconnect(void)

This function is called to break down a call in progress. Because the Initialize() function is supposed to set the modem up properly, all it should take to hang up is to drop the DTR line for a second. This function does that first, then checks to see whether the modem has responded by disconnecting.

If the modem failed to disconnect when DTR was dropped (which may be the case for some modems that don't allow software control of this feature), the +++ escape sequence is sent, followed by the ATH0 command. If this fails to disconnect the modem, about the only choice left is the power switch.

This modem returns either MODEM_SUCCESS or one of the other ModemError codes.

```
ModemError SendCommand( char * )
```

This function is provided to give the programmer the ability to send strings to the modem and monitor for the proper receipt of the OK response code.

```
int ReadRegister( int reg )
```

This function sends the ATSr? command to the modem, requesting that the modem provide the current contents of one of its status registers. The response is then read back from the modem and returned to the calling routine. If the value is less than zero, it indicates that an error occurred, and the return value should be translated to be of type ModemErrror for interpretation.

```
virtual ModemError UserAbort( void )
```

Many of the modem functions can take a long time. Functions such as Modem::Dial() may take 60 seconds or more to finish to completion. This virtual function is called periodically to check for a user-initiated abort. The base class definition just checks for incoming keystrokes and aborts if the user has hit a key. Derived classes are free to implement their own abort procedures.

```
void PulseDial( void )
void ToneDial( void )
```

These two functions are used to set the default dialing type. They act by just modifying the tone_dial member to be either true or false.

```
void SetCarrierTimeout( long length )
```

By default, the Dial() and Answer() functions will wait 60 seconds for a connection to be established before timing out and returning a failure. This function allows the programmer to modify this time. The single parameter is the new time value, in milliseconds.

Chapter 14: Using Modems Under MS-DOS

```
char *ErrorName( ModemError status )
```

This function translates `ModemError` status codes to ASCII strings, suitable for display to end users.

```
virtual void DumpState( void )
```

This function is used to print out the current status of the `Modem` object. It isn't as sophisticated as the status function used in the `RS-232` class. The function is defined as virtual to allow for derived class improvements.

```
int Protocol( void )
int Compressing( void )
```

These two functions are simply access functions that provide read-only access to protected member functions. The first is used to determine whether an error-correcting protocol is in use in the current connection. The second indicates whether data compression is in effect.

Protected members

The `Modem` class has a few protected data members and functions that are used internally to support various features of the class.

```
RS232 *port
```

This is a pointer to the port that the modem is attached to. The `Modem` class doesn't need to be a friend to the `RS232` class because it only uses the publicly available functions. However, it does need to keep a pointer to the port so that it can access the various functions and members assigned to the port.

```
ModemCapabilities *modem_data
```

This is a pointer to the capability structure passed using the constructor. It is referred to at various points by many of the member functions.

```
long local_baud_rate
```

The local baud rate is the rate that the modem changes to when either the `Dial()` or `Answer()` functions connect to another modem. If the modem is using a locked rate, this rate will be the same as the initial baud rate. Otherwise, it is at the rate that the modem indicated it was using in the CONNECT message.

```
int tone_dial
```

This member is a boolean flag that indicates whether the modem should always dial using tone mode.

`int protocol`

When a connection is made, this boolean flag is set or cleared to indicate whether an error-correcting protocol is in use.

`int compressing`

This boolean flag is used to indicate whether a data compression protocol is in effect for the current call.

`ModemError wait_for_response( void )`

Most modem functions require sending a command to the modem, then waiting for an OK response from the modem. This internal protected function is called to wait for that OK message. This is used whenever a command is sent to the modem to ensure that the modem actually received the message and responded to it.

`ModemError wait_for_connection( void );`

This function is called by both the `Dial()` and `Answer()` functions. It waits for the modem to indicate either that it has successfully answered an incoming call or that it has failed to establish carrier. This function also scans all of the strings issued by the modem to check for the presence of data compression and error-correcting protocols.

`long carrier_timeout`

The amount of time, in milliseconds, that the modem waits for a carrier when either dialing or answering.

`virtual void echo( char c )`

During any modem activity, there is normally a lot of data being sent back and forth between the modem and the computer. An echo routine is provided to enable the user to see what is happening. By default, the base class defines the echo routine as just a simple output to `std::cout`. Derived classes are free to extend or replace this as they wish.

`void read_line( char *buffer, int buf_size )`

This function is used internally to read in lines of response from the modem. It operates somewhat differently from the `RS232::Read()` function, in that it will time-

Chapter 14: Using Modems Under MS-DOS

out quickly if no data is coming in. As long as characters continue coming in at least once every half second, it will keep reading until an entire line has been assembled.

This function also echoes the input characters as they are read.

Listing 14-2: MODEM.CPP

```
// ******************* START OF MODEM.CPP *******************

// This file contains all of the code for the Modem class.  It
// should be compiled and linked with any program wanting to use
// the class.

#include <iostream.h>
#include <conio.h>
#include <string.h>
#include <stdlib.h>
#include <stdio.h>
#include <ctype.h>
#include "rs232.h"
#include "modem.h"

// The modem capability database is used to define all the
// attributes used by a particular brand of modem.  These are
// stored in the application, which is practical when just a few
// are defined.  A bigger database might have to be moved into a
// conventional file.

ModemCapabilities ModemDataBase[] = {
{ "Hayes Compatible",
  "AT &F &C1 &D2",
  "NO CARRIER\0ERROR\0NO DIALTONE\0BUSY\0NO ANSWER\0\0",
  "",
  "",
  2400L,
  0,
  0
},
{ "Practical Peripherals V.34",
  "AT &F0 &C1 &D2 S95=44",
  "NO CARRIER\0ERROR\0NO DIALTONE\0BUSY\0NO ANSWER\0\0",
  "CLASS 5\0V.42BIS\0\0",
  "LAP-M\0ALT\0\0",
  57600L,
  1,
  1
},
```

```
    { "Intel SatisFAXtion 400e",
      "AT &F",
      "NO CARRIER\0ERROR\0NO DIALTONE\0BUSY\0NO ANSWER\0\0",
      "COMP\0\0",
      "LAPM\0MNP\0REL\0\0",
      57600L,
      1,
      1
    },
    { ""
    }
};

// The modem constructor sets up the capability database for the
// modem of the particular name, but doesn't do much else.  If the
// brand-name mode is not found via an exact match, the generic
// Hayes-compatible definition is used.

Modem::Modem( RS232 &rs232_port, char *modem_name )
{
    int i;

    port = &rs232_port;
    modem_data = &ModemDataBase[ 0 ];
    for ( i = 0 ; *ModemDataBase[ i ].name != '\0' ; i++ ) {
        if (strcmp( modem_name, ModemDataBase[ i ].name ) == 0)
        {
            modem_data = &ModemDataBase[ i ];
            break;
        }
    }
    tone_dial = 1;
    carrier_timeout = 60000L;
}

// The usual translation routine is used to print out the error
// names in more descriptive form.

char *Modem::ErrorName( ModemError status )
{
    switch ( status ) {
        case MODEM_SUCCESS          : return "Success";
        case MODEM_NO_RESPONSE      : return "No Response";
        case MODEM_NO_CONNECTION    : return "No Connection";
        case MODEM_DISCONNECT_FAILED : return "Disconnect failed";
```

```
            case MODEM_USER_ABORT        : return "User abort";
            default                      : return "Unknown Error";
        }
    }

    // The initialization routine just has to send out the
    // initialization string and then wait for a response. It
    // inserts an extra one-second delay in this routine
    // because some modems need a little extra time
    // to handle initialization.

    ModemError Modem::Initialize( void )
    {
        long delay_time;

        port->Set( modem_data->initial_baud_rate );
        port->RtsCtsHandshaking( modem_data->handshaking );
        port->Write( '\r' );
        delay_time = ReadTime() + 1000;
        while ( ReadTime() < delay_time )
            port->IdleFunction();
        port->Write( modem_data->initialization_string );
        port->Write( '\r' );
        return wait_for_response();
    }


    // This protected routine is used to read lines of data back from
    // the modem, generally after a response to a command.  It reads
    // the characters in, echoes them using the echo routine, and tries
    // to assemble a complete line.  A '\n' character is used to
    // terminate the line or a timeout.

    void Modem::read_line( char *buffer, int buf_size )
    {
        int c;

        for ( ; ; ) {
            c = port->Read( 500 );
            if ( c < 0 )
                break;
            echo( (char) c );
            *buffer++ = (char) c;
            if ( --buf_size <= 1 )
                break;
            if ( c == '\n' )
                break;
```

```
    }
    *buffer = '\0';
}

// This protected routine is used to wait for an OK message
// after a modem command is sent.  If it doesn't get the message
// within 2 seconds, an error is returned.  Most commands going
// to the  modem can expect an OK response. The two notable
// exceptions are the dialing and answer commands.

ModemError Modem::wait_for_response( void )
{
    long timeout;
    char buffer[ 81 ];
    ModemError status;

    timeout = ReadTime() + 2000;

    while ( ReadTime() < timeout ) {
        read_line( buffer, 81 );
        if ( strncmp( buffer, "OK", 2 ) == 0 )
            return MODEM_SUCCESS;
        if ( ( status = UserAbort() ) != MODEM_SUCCESS )
            return status;
    }
    return MODEM_NO_RESPONSE;
}


// During dialing, the Dial routine has to scan the input stream
// for lots of different strings that can indicate various things
// about protocols, data compression, and connections. This
// command is used to scan for a list of strings stored in the
// format used by the modem capability database.

char *scan_strings( char *buffer, char *strings )
{
    char *p;

    while ( *strings ) {
        if ( ( p = strstr( buffer, strings ) ) != 0 )
            return p;
        strings += strlen( strings ) + 1;
    }
    return p;
}
```

```
// This routine is called by both the Answer and Dial routines.
// It has to scan the incoming lines of data, not just for the
// "CONNECT" message but also for the protocol and compression
// strings.  Additionally, if the baud rate is not locked,
// it has to detect the new baud rate on connection.

ModemError Modem::wait_for_connection( void )
{
    long timeout;
    char *connect;
    char buffer[ 81 ];
    ModemError status;

    compressing = 0;
    protocol = 0;
    timeout = ReadTime() + carrier_timeout;
    while ( ReadTime() < timeout ) {
        read_line( buffer, 81 );
        if ( scan_strings( buffer, modem_data->fail_strings ) )
            return MODEM_NO_CONNECTION;
        if (scan_strings(buffer,modem_data->compression_strings))
            compressing = 1;
        if (scan_strings(buffer, modem_data->protocol_strings))
            protocol = 1;
        if ( ( connect = strstr( buffer, "CONNECT" ) ) != 0 ) {
            if ( !modem_data->locked_baud_rate ) {
                local_baud_rate = atol( connect + 8 );
                if ( local_baud_rate !=0 )
                    port->Set( local_baud_rate );
            } else
                local_baud_rate = modem_data->initial_baud_rate;
            return MODEM_SUCCESS;
        }
        if ( ( status = UserAbort() ) != MODEM_SUCCESS )
            return status;
    }
    return MODEM_NO_CONNECTION;
}

// This routine dials and then has another routine do the hard
// work of waiting for a response.

ModemError Modem::Dial( char *dial_string )
{
```

```
    port->Write( "ATD" );
    if ( tone_dial )
        port->Write( 'T' );
    else
        port->Write( 'P' );
    port->Write( dial_string );
    port->Write( '\r' );
    return wait_for_connection();
}

// This routine sends the answer command and then lets the other
// routine wait for success or failure.

ModemError Modem::Answer( void )
{
    port->Write( "ATA\r" );
    return wait_for_connection();
}

// Although all the modems in the database are supposed to be
// set up so that dropping DTR causes a disconnect, some may slip
// through the net. If dropping DTR doesn't cause a disconnect,
// the escape sequence is sent, followed by a Hangup message.

ModemError Modem::Disconnect( void )
{
    long delay_time;

    port->Dtr( 0 );
    delay_time = ReadTime() + 1250;
    while ( ReadTime() < delay_time )
        port->IdleFunction();
    port->Dtr( 1 );
    port->Write( "AT\r" );
    if ( wait_for_response() == MODEM_SUCCESS ) {
        port->Set( modem_data->initial_baud_rate );
        return MODEM_SUCCESS;
    }
    port->Write( "+++" );
    delay_time = ReadTime() + 1250;
    wait_for_response();
    port->Write( "ATH0\r" );
    if ( wait_for_response() == MODEM_SUCCESS ) {
        port->Set( modem_data->initial_baud_rate );
```

```
        return MODEM_SUCCESS;
    }
    return MODEM_DISCONNECT_FAILED;
}

// This routine gives the user an opportunity to abort during long
// sequences, such as dialing.

ModemError Modem::UserAbort( void )
{
    if ( !kbhit() )
        return MODEM_SUCCESS;
    getch();
    return MODEM_USER_ABORT;

}

// ReadRegister() not only asks for the register value but also
// scans it in and converts it from ASCII to binary so that it can
// be used by the program.

int Modem::ReadRegister( int reg )
{
    char buffer[ 81 ];
    long timeout;
    int value;
    ModemError status;

    sprintf( buffer, "ATS%d?\r", reg );
    port->Write( buffer );
    timeout = ReadTime() + 3000;
    value = (int) MODEM_NO_RESPONSE;
    while ( timeout > ReadTime() ) {
        read_line( buffer, 80 );
        if ( strncmp( buffer, "OK", 2 ) == 0 )
            break;
        if ( ( status = UserAbort() ) != MODEM_SUCCESS )
            return status;
        if ( isdigit( *buffer ) )
            value = atoi( buffer );
    }
    return value;
}

// This is the generic routine to send a command of your choice.
```

```cpp
// It assumes that the command will get an OK message in return.

ModemError Modem::SendCommand( char *command )
{
    port->Write( command );
    port->Write( '\r' );
    return wait_for_response();
}

// This routine is generally useful only during debugging. It
// dumps the state of the Modem structure out to the screen.

void Modem::DumpState( void )
{
    char *p;

    cout << "\nModem Status:\n\n"
         << "Name:                "
         << modem_data->name << '\n';
    cout << "Init string:         "
         << modem_data->initialization_string << '\n';
    cout << "Fail strings:        ";
    p = modem_data->fail_strings;
    while ( *p ) {
        cout << p;
        p += strlen( p ) + 1;
        if ( *p )
            cout << ", ";
    }
    cout << '\n';
    cout << "Compression strings: ";
    p = modem_data->compression_strings;
    while ( *p ) {
        cout << p;
        p += strlen( p ) + 1;
        if ( *p )
            cout << ", ";
    }
    cout << '\n';
    cout << "Protocol strings:    ";
    p = modem_data->protocol_strings;
    while ( *p ) {
        cout << p;
        p += strlen( p ) + 1;
        if ( *p )
```

```
                cout << ", ";
        }
        cout << '\n';
        cout << "Initial baud rate:    "
             << modem_data->initial_baud_rate << '\n';
        cout << "Baud rate locked:     "
             << ((modem_data->locked_baud_rate) ? 'Y' : 'N') << '\n';
        cout << "Hardware handshaking: "
             << (( modem_data->handshaking ) ? 'Y' : 'N') << '\n';
        cout << "Dialing method:       "
             << (( tone_dial ) ? "Tone" : "Pulse" ) << '\n';
        cout << "Carrier timeout:      " << carrier_timeout << '\n';
        cout << "Connected:            "
             << (( port->Cd() ) ? 'Y' : 'N' ) << '\n';
        if ( !port->Cd() )
            return;
        cout << "Local baud rate:      " << local_baud_rate << '\n';
        cout << "Compressing:          "
             << (( compressing ) ? 'Y' : 'N' ) << '\n';
        cout << "Protocol:             "
             << (( protocol ) ? 'Y' : 'N' ) << '\n';
}

// ******************** END OF MODEM.CPP ********************
```

A Test Program

Listing 14-3 is a listing for a short program, TSTMODEM.CPP, which is used to test some modem functions. It is just a small terminal emulator that has a special menu that exercises a few of the modem functions. Preceding the listing is a reproduction of the screen shot showing the program in progress.

The menu for the test program can be accessed at any time by pressing Esc. The eight functions available from the menu provide the capability to exercise most of the functions in class Modem:

Answer: This function is used to invoke the Answer() command. It waits for the amount of time specified in the carrier_timeout variable before giving up. The function prints out the results when it returns, either with a successful acquisition of carrier or a timeout.

Exit: Quit TSTMODEM and return to the O/S.

Dial: This invokes the Dial() function, which dials out to the hard coded number specified in TSTMODEM.CPP. The result returned from the function is printed out afterward. Remember that the default abort function lets you quit by pressing any key.

Hangup: The `Hangup()` function is invoked by the this menu selection.

Initialize: This menu selection executes the `Initialize()` function. This function is also automatically called when the program starts up.

Product-Id: This menu selection calls the `SendCommand()` function with `ATI0` as the command string. This causes the modem to spit out a product ID code, which is not usually very meaningful. It just provides a way to test the `SendCommand()` member function with your modem.

Read-regs: This menu selection uses the `ReadRegister()` command to read the contents of the first 10 S registers of the modem. It then prints them out.

Status: This command invokes the `DumpState()` member function, providing a snapshot of the state of the `Modem` objects. The following is the output produced immediately after this menu item was invoked.

```
First Name? Mark Nelson

Answer Exit Dial Hangup Initialize Product-ID Read-regs Status

Enter command: S

Modem Status:

Name:                   Practical Peripherals V.34
Init string:            AT &F0 &C1 &D2 S95=44
Fail strings:           NO CARRIER, ERROR, NO DIALTONE, BUSY, NO ANSWER
Compression strings:    CLASS 5, V.42BIS
Protocol strings:       LAP-M, ALT
Initial baud rate:      57600
Baud rate locked:       Y
Hardware handshaking:   Y
Dialing method:         Tone
Carrier timeout:        60000
Connected:              Y
Local baud rate:        57600
Compressing:            Y
Protocol:               Y

NO CARRIER
```

Listing 14-3: TSTMODEM.CPP

```cpp
// ****************** START OF TSTMODEM.CPP ******************
// This short program is used to test the Modem class.  It is a
// very simple terminal emulator that can accept just a few
// commands.

#include <iostream.h>
#include <ctype.h>
#include "rs232.h"
#include "pc8250.h"
#include "modem.h"

int handle_command( Modem &modem );

// The main routine just acts as a terminal emulator.  It invokes
// a command handler if the escape key is pressed.

int main()
{
    int c;
    PC8250 port( COM1, 19200 );
    Modem modem( port, "Practical Peripherals V.34" );
    ModemError init;

    init = modem.Initialize();
    cout << "\nInitialization returned: "
         << modem.ErrorName( init )
         << '\n';
    for ( ; ; ) {
        if ( kbhit() ) {
            c = getch();
            if ( c == 27 ) {
                if ( handle_command( modem ) )
                    break;
            } else
                port.Write( c );
        }
        if ( ( c = port.Read() ) > 0 )
            cout << (char) c;
        cout.flush(); // Needed by Zortech and Microsoft
    }
    return 0;
}
```

```cpp
// The command handler is used to send various commands to the
// modem via the normal modem class.  It prints a help prompt so
// that you will know exactly what your choice of commands is.

int handle_command( Modem &modem )
{
    int c;
    int i;
    ModemError status;
    char *command;
    int registers[ 11 ];

    cout << "\nAnswer Exit Dial Hangup Initialize "
            "Product-ID Read-regs Status\n\nEnter command: ";
    cout.flush(); // Needed by Zortech and Microsoft
    c = getch();
    cout << (char) c << '\n';
    switch ( toupper( c ) ) {
        case 'A' :
            command = "Answer";
            status = modem.Answer();
            break;
        case 'D' :
            command = "Dial";
            status = modem.Dial( "1-214-555-1212" );
            break;
        case 'E' :
            return 1;
        case 'H' :
            command = "Hangup";
            status = modem.Disconnect();
            break;
        case 'I' :
            command = "Initialize";
            status = modem.Initialize();
            break;
        case 'P' :
            command = "Product ID code";
            status = modem.SendCommand( "ATI0" );
            break;
        case 'R' :
            for ( i = 1 ; i < 11 ; i++ )
```

```
                registers[ i ] = modem.ReadRegister( i );
            for ( i = 1 ; i < 11 ; i++ ) {
                cout << "Register " << i << " = ";
                cout << registers[ i ] << '\n';
            }
            return 0;
        case 'S' :
            modem.DumpState();
            return 0;
        default :
            cout << (char) 7; return 0;
    }
    cout << command
         << " returned: "
         << modem.ErrorName( status )
         << '\n';
    return 0;
}

// ****************** END OF TSTMODEM.CPP ******************
```

Making TSTMODEM.CPP

Listing 14-4 is a sample make file that is used to build the test program. If you want to use a different type of RS-232 object, modify the source code for TSTMODEM.CPP and then modify the FILES listing in the make file.

Listing 14-4: TSTMODEM.MAK

```
#CC = tcc -w
#CC = bcc -w
#CC = ztc -b
CC = cl /W4 /AL

FILES = pc8250.obj pcirq.obj queue.obj isr_8250.obj

.cpp.obj:
  $(CC) -c $<

tstmodem.exe : tstmodem.obj rs232.obj msdos.obj modem.obj $(FILES)
        $(CC) tstmodem.obj rs232.obj msdos.obj modem.obj $(FILES)
```

Summary

When the operating system doesn't provide any support, dealing with modems can be a difficult task. This Chapter showed you how to use the AT command set to control modems, but left you with on fairly onerous task: determine the proper commands to send to your particular modem.

In Chapter 15, you'll see how much easier it is when the operating system (OS) helps work with modems. The Windows Telephony API (TAPI) makes writing software that works with modems considerably easier.

Chapter 15

Using Modems Under Win32 – TAPI

IN THIS CHAPTER

- ◆ A review of TAPI's history
- ◆ A TAPI overview
- ◆ TAPI functions used in this chapter
- ◆ The SimpleTapi class
- ◆ The CHAPT15.EXE demo program

MICROSOFT PROVIDES an API for controlling phones, modems, PBXs, and other devices associated with video or audio communications. The whole world of the Telephony API (TAPI) is enormous, but in this chapter you are concerned only with the subset of TAPI devoted to modem control.

This chapter shows how to use TAPI to set up and make calls using modems. TAPI makes it easy to use modems without knowing the first thing about AT commands, special dialing commands, or even COM ports. TAPI makes your life quite a bit easier.

The History of TAPI

One of the primary duties of an operating system is to shield programmers from hardware. By providing device drivers and system APIs, a good operating system lets programmers code to a single interface that works with a wide variety of supported hardware.

When it came to device support, a primitive operating system such as MS-DOS barely lived up to the name. Programmers writing MS-DOS apps typically had to write directly to the hardware interface for all video and graphics, printer I/O, and, of course, serial and modem-based communications. This made the lives of application developers unpleasant.

Early versions of Windows added full-featured support for video displays and printers. This type of support not only made things easier for programmers but also encouraged competition among hardware vendors.

Windows didn't originally offer a specific API for dealing with modems, but its creators soon saw the light and introduced TAPI 1.*x* for 16-bit Windows. TAPI provided a high-level interface to various devices that interface to phone systems; in this book, however, the TAPI discussion is limited to modems.

The 1.*x* release of TAPI dealt specifically with what is referred to as *first-party call control*. This type of control means that programs using TAPI are able to control calls that originate from or terminate at the PC in question. First-party call control is perfect for setting up calls with a modem or for using specialized hardware to make the PC act as a telephone.

Microsoft's second major release of TAPI gave TAPI the capability to perform *third-party call control*. In this case, the TAPI application talks directly to a PBX or other phone system, becoming an active participant in a call involving two other parties. This type of control allowed TAPI to be used in call centers as a part of an ACD (Automated Call Distribution) system.

TAPI 3.0 is currently under development and is scheduled for release with Windows 2000. TAPI 3.0 adds control of media streams to the API, which will be important for the routing of voice and video over networks.

Serial communications programmers don't really get anything out of TAPI 2 or 3, so they aren't discussed at all in this chapter. What RS-232 programmers do care about are the call control features offered with the first release of TAPI. The first major release of TAPI went through several refinements that finished with release 1.4, and that is as much of the standard asthis chapter covers.

An Overview of TAPI

TAPI 2.*x* has a fairly large API for programmers to deal with. The specifications list more than 40 function calls, with a correspondingly large number of data structures, constant definitions, and so on. For your purposes, however, a subset of a dozen or so functions will give you the capability to use TAPI to place and answer calls over a modem.

TAPI notification methods

TAPI, like Windows in general, needs to be capable of dealing with events that occur at unpredictable times. Just as a user might move his or her mouse or strike a key at any time, an incoming call can occur at any time. TAPI also can encounter long periods of waiting for a remote modem to answer and finish its training sequence.

This type of programming requires some sort of method by which the operating system can notify an application program when things happen. At one time, Windows did virtually all of its notification by sending messages to windows. TAPI can do this as well, but it offers a couple of other options that might make your life easier.

TAPI 1.*x* did all notification via a mechanism referred to as the *hidden window* approach. Under this system, TAPI creates a hidden window in the context of your application and posts all messages to that window. The *WndProc* for that hidden window responds to the message by calling a user callback function.

TAPI 2.*x* added two additional notification methods: event handles and completion ports. This chapter discusses using only the hidden window callback mechanism, but you should consider using these other alternatives if they work better with your application.

Synchronous vs. asynchronous functions

Some TAPI functions can quickly do their requested job and return to the caller with a reasonable result. With others, this efficiency just isn't possible. For example, when you call `lineMakeCall()` to connect to another modem, several minutes may elapse before you know whether the function worked.

Tying up a program for protracted periods of time is definitely not a good thing in the Windows world. If the program is single threaded, the user interface will be completely unresponsive during that time, leading to user anxiety.

TAPI deals with this problem by dividing functions into two different types: *synchronous* and *asynchronous*. Synchronous functions, such as `lineInitialize()` and `lineGetDevConfig()`, return a result to the call immediately. Asynchronous functions, such as `lineAnswer()`, might return an answer immediately, but more often they return a value of 0, which means that they have no result to report.

When an asynchronous function returns a 0, indicating that it will take a bit to respond, it also returns a request id. The calling program then has to wait for a `LINE_REPLY` message to show up in its callback function with that particular ID. It's a nice, simple mechanism that is relatively easy to deal with.

If the asynchronous response delivery system is not to your liking, in many cases, you can ignore it. For example, when you place a call, rather than wait for a `LINE_REPLY` response, you can just monitor the call state as it changes. The call state will eventually go to the connected state or degrade to the idle state; in either case, you will know how the call turned out.

TAPI objects

For the purposes of this chapter, TAPI creates and uses three important objects. (Not objects in the C++ sense, but Windows objects that are referred to by a handle.) One or more of these handles is used in every TAPI call.

`HLINEAPP`—The TAPI Usage Handle

Any program that uses TAPI has to start with a call to the `lineInitialize()` or `lineInitializeEx()`. These two functions load and initialize the TAPI system, and establish the callback to the user's application. Both functions return a TAPI usage handle to the caller.

The TAPI usage handle is then used as an argument to a large number of TAPI functions. In particular, functions that don't apply to a specific device or call nearly always have an `HLINEAPP` as the first argument to the function.

HLINE—The Line Device Handle

Using TAPI to make phone calls will always mean opening up a line device with a call to `lineOpen()`. When you open a device with this function call, TAPI returns an `HLINE` handle, which is thereafter used to refer to the device. The handle is valid until it is passed to the `lineClose()` function call.

The line device handle is used in TAPI calls that address a specific line device, such as a modem, without actually having an active call, such as `lineMakeCall()`.

HCALL—The Call Handle

A call handle is used to denote an active call. It can be created by `lineMakeCall()`, or can be passed in to the callback routine when the an incoming call is detected. The handle is valid for the duration of the call. The handle is destroyed via a call to `lineDeallocateCall()`.

TAPI annoyances

Like much of the Windows API, TAPI is full of functions that fill in data structures. TAPI 1.*x* adopted a convention that is working its way into more and more of the Win32 API. Many of the data structures receive a variable number of bytes when filled in. When calling a function in this situation, you are expected to call the function once to determine how many bytes are expected, and then call it a second time with a properly allocated structure.

Microsoft already is clearly guilty of making its API function calls tremendously laborintensive; this double-calling sequence only makes things worse. For the sample class in this chapter, I frequently subvert the requirements by just calling the function once, with a ridiculously large memory allocation. However, for a production-quality program, this approach is not acceptable.

TAPI Functions Used in This Chapter

A complete discussion of TAPI is just not possible in one book chapter. Because of that, I've restricted the view of TAPI to the calls you need to make and answer with a modem. For applications that are using serial communications, these types of calls are primarily what makes TAPI interesting.

The functions described in the following sections are presented in logical groups similar to the ones that Microsoft uses to document them. I don't document all the arguments and possible return values; you should refer to your online documentation for that information.

TAPI initialization and shutdown

The two functions discussed are needed at the very start and very end of a session with a modem, whether it is in the context of an inbound or an outbound call.

```
LONG lineInitialize(   HLINEAPP lphLineApp,
                       HINSTANCE hInstance,
                       LINECALLBACK lpfnCallback,
                       LPCSTR lpszAppName,
                       LPDWORD lpdwNumDevs )
```

The TAPI documentation states that this function is obsolete, but that documentation somewhat misstates the case. In TAPI 2.0, this function is superseded by the slightly more capable lineInitializeEx() function. However, the sample program in this chapter sticks with the 1.*x* function, and it does so because you may still encounter situations in which you need to use older versions of TAPI.

This function is called to initialize TAPI and register your callback function. The first parameter, lphLineApp, is where TAPI returns a handle that it creates for your application. This Line App handle will be used in several other function calls that you use to access TAPI.

The instance handle should be the instance that your application was created with. The lpfnCallback argument contains a pointer to your callback function. This is the function that TAPI calls for all asynchronous call state and function return information. The exact duties of this function are described a bit later in this section.

The lpszAppName argument is strictly for debugging and trace help. TAPI was designed to enable several applications to share responsibilities in the communications process. When an application is dealing with an open call, it can call lineGet CallInfo(), which returns a LINE_CALLINFO structure. This structure will have a copy of the name of the application that originally called lineInitialize(), which might be useful for debugging.

The final argument is in place to enable TAPI to return a count of line devices to the calling application. In the sample TAPI class, this count is used to iterate through all possible line devices, getting information that can be used to select devices for the app to use.

TAPI applications universally return a negative number in case of an error, and this function is no exception. The error codes are defined in TAPI.H, the standard Windows include file; they start with 0x80000001 LINEERR_ALLOCATED, and continue from there. TAPI defines such a vast list of error codes that it is futile to try to enumerate all the codes that could be returned from a given function. (TAPI 1.*x* alone has more than 80 function error codes.) When the function succeeds, it returns a 0.

After calling lineInitialize(), TAPI is up and running and ready to use. You need to hang on to the HLINEAPP argument returned by TAPI; you will need it for quite a few function calls. When you're done with TAPI, you need to call line Shutdown() to shut down, unload the system DLLs, and return any resources they were using.

```
LONG lineShutdown( HLINEAPP hLineApp )
```

lineShutdown() is the counterpart to lineInitialize(). After your app is completely done using TAPI services, it calls this function with the Line Application Handle that it received from the initial call to lineInitialize().

This function has the nice characteristic of automatically shutting down any calls that you had in progress and breaking any ownership links that you had with line devices.

The function returns a zero on success and a negative number in case of a failure.

Line control

The three objects used with TAPI are the application handle, the line handle, and the call handle. This set of functions in this section deals with lines via the line handle. To TAPI, the line handle refers to a device that is connected to a phone line. This device can be many things, including a telephone, but for this chapter's purposes, it will always be a modem.

```
LONG lineConfigDialog(  DWORD dwDeviceID,
                        HWND hwndOwner,
                        LPCSTR lpszDeviceClass )
```

For a communications programmer, this is one of the really wonderful function calls that TAPI provides. It brings up a tabbed dialog box that should provide for a complete set of configuration options for a given device. Two views of this dialog box are shown in Figures 15-1 and 15-2.

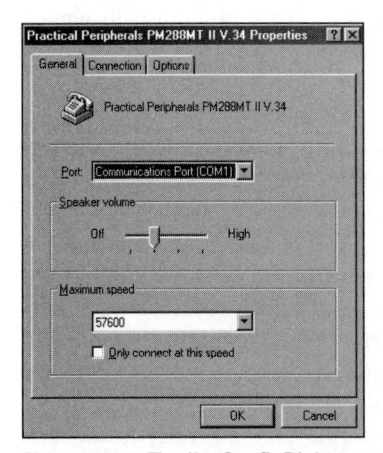

Figure 15-1: The lineConfigDialog configuration dialog box

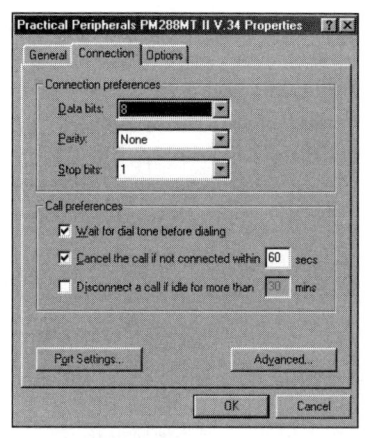

Figure 15-2: Another view of the lineConfigDialog dialog box

The dialog box that you see when you make this function provides a thorough and complete set of configuration options for the modem. This saves you days of work and guarantees that you'll have a configuration dialog box for any type of modem that Windows supports. This is truly a wonderful thing.

Setting up the parameters for this function call is simple. The dwDeviceId argument is simply the zero-based device id. (The total number of available devices is returned from the call to lineInitialize() made to initialize TAPI.) The window handle is the handle of the window you want to be the owner of the dialog box. This will typically be the handle of the main window in your app.

The final argument, lpszDeviceClass, is used to restrict the configuration elements that are shown for the given device. To show the maximum level of configuration information, you would use a class name of tapi/line. The SimpleTapi class in this chapter uses a class name of comm/datamodem, which restricts the configuration to the items one normally associates with a modem.

This is a synchronous function that returns its result immediately. A negative number is an error that should match one of the codes in TAPI.H; a return value of 0 indicates that no error occurred.

```
LONG lineGetDevCaps(   HLINEAPP hLineApp,
                       DWORD dwDeviceID,
                       DWORD dwAPIVersion,
                       DWORD dwExtVersion,
                       LPLINEDEVCAPS lpLineDevCaps )
```

The purpose of this function is to fill in a LINEDEVCAPS structure with information about the device on a given line. This is a truly hideous structure, with more than 50 defined members plus limitless extensions. It is an awful mess, and mastering it could be your life's work.

However, unpleasant as it may be, the `LINEDEVCAPS` structure has a lot of useful information, so you need to be able to read it in. This function does just that, with the following argument definitions:

`HLineApp`	The handle of the TAPI application, which was returned when your program called `lineInitialize()`.
`dwDeviceID`	The device ID for the given line. This is a zero-based integer. The number of devices is returned when you call `lineInitialize()`.
`dwAPIVersion`	TAPI allows for a certain amount of negotiation on the part of a user as to which version of the API should be used. This DWORD has the major version number of the API in the upper 16 bits and the minor version number in the lower 16 bits. Because the `SimpleTapi` class used in this book uses only features of TAPI 1.4, this parameter is set to 0x00010004.
`dwExtVersion`	In addition to filling in the defined areas of the `LINEDEVCAPS` structure, `lineGetDevCaps()` can also return extended information that the service provider makes available. This argument is used to indicate to the service provider which version of extensions is desired. This argument is not used in the `SimpleTapi` demo class from this chapter.
`lpLineDevCaps`	This is a pointer to a `LINEDEVCAPS` structure, which is going to be filled in by this function call.

This function appends a variable number of bytes to the `LINEDEVCAPS` structure. These extension bytes hold Provider Information, Switch Information, and the line name; they also hold several other fields, all of which have offsets defined in the main body of the structure.

When calling `lineGetDevCaps()`, you have to specify how much space is available in your structure by initializing the dwSize member of the structure. Upon return from the function call, you can see how much space is actually needed by checking the dwNeededSize member. If it turns out that dwNeededSize is larger than what you passed in dwSize, you need to allocate more space and call the function a second time.

In the `SimpleTapi` class, this convoluted calling system is avoided by making the buffer 4096 bytes to start with, which I confidently assume is far larger than any structure that `lineGetDevCaps()` will ever need. (Famous last words.)

`SimpleTapi` uses this function only to retrieve the name of the device, but a production program could use this data to determine pertinent items such as support baud rates, dialing capabilities, tone generation and detection capabilities, and a host of other pertinent pieces of data.

Chapter 15: Using Modems Under Win32 — TAPI

When this function succeeds (even if it failed to fill in all the extension bytes owing to lack of space), it will return a 0. A negative number should correspond to one of the error codes found in TAPI.H.

```
LONG lineOpen(   HLINEAPP hLineApp,
                 DWORD dwDeviceID,
                 LPHLINE lphLine,
                 DWORD dwApiVersion,
                 DWORD dwExtVersion,
                 DWORD dwCallBackInstance,
                 DWORD dwPrivileges,
                 DWORD dwMediaModes,
                 LPLINECALLPARAMS lpCallParams )
```

This is the function that opens a line device and makes it available for use by the application program. You need to open a line before you can make or answer a phone call, although not before you can configure a line.

This function has a hefty argument list but is actually quite manageable. Many of these arguments are identical to those described in the previous description of lineGetDevCaps():

hLineApp	The handle of the TAPI application, which was returned when your program called lineInitialize().
dwDeviceID	The zero-based device ID. This selects the line you are actually going to open.
lphLine	A pointer to the HLINE handle that will be filled in by the function call. If lineOpen() succeeds, this HLINE handle will be what you pass to most of the call control functions.
dwApiVersion	The TAPI API version you want to use, as described in the previous function. The SimpleTapi class used here will always pass 0x00010004 as this argument.
dwExtVersion	The extension version number you are requesting from the service provider. SimpleTapi will always pass a 0 here, as it doesn't attempt to make use of any extended functionality from the service provider.
dwCallbackInstance	As you might recall, TAPI does notification via a callback function. Whenever the callback function is invoked by TAPI, a copy of this dwCallbackInstance parameter is passed to it. SimpleTapi always passes a copy of *this* in this parameter, which means the callback function then has access to all the data and functionality of the class.

dwPrivileges	Because TAPI lines and calls can be passed from task to task, it is important to know exactly what you can and cannot do with a given line. This argument specifies the privileges you want with the line. Class `SimpleTapi` passes `LINECALLPRIVILEGE_OWNER` here, which means you want to be able to own both inbound and outbound calls.
dwMediaModes	The type of calls that you want to be able to perform using this line. This includes everything from voice calls to faxes to TDD calls. `SimpleTapi` specifies that it wants to use the line for modem calls by passing `LINEMEDIAMODE_DATAMODEM`.
lpCallParams	In the event that you don't know which device you want to use to make your call, you can pass the special constant `LINEMAPPER` for the device id usually given as the first argument to this call. When this is the case, you are asking TAPI to make the best possible selection for a device. To help TAPI choose the best device, fill in this argument with information about the type of capabilities that you want to have. TAPI will use that information to help pick the best device for you. If you aren't using `LINEMAPPER`, this argument should be set to NULL, which is what class `SimpleTapi` uses.

`lineOpen()` is a synchronous function call that follows the conventions of all the TAPI calls you've seen so far in this chapter, meaning that it returns 0 upon success and a negative number in case of error.

After opening a line with this call, you are responsible for eventually closing it with a call to `lineClose()`. If you don't close it, it will be shut down when your program exits or you call `lineShutDown()` to terminate TAPI services.

```
LONG lineClose( HLINE hLine )
```

This function closes the line specified by the `hLine` parameter. After this call, the line handle is invalid and should not be used. This closes the line as well as shutting down any active calls on the line.

This is a synchronous call that returns its result immediately. As always, a value of zero indicates success, and a value less than zero corresponds to one of the error codes from `TAPI.H`.

Call configuration

The functions listed in this section are all concerned with the configuration of various parameters used for setting up, tearing down, or otherwise controlling a call.

Chapter 15: Using Modems Under Win32 — TAPI

```
LONG lineTranslateDialog(  HLINEAPP hLineApp,
                           DWORD dwDeviceID,
                           DWORD dwApiVersion,
                           HWND hwndOwner,
                           LPCSTR lpszAddressIn )
```

This function pops up a dialog box that enables a user to set up the configuration of an outbound phone call. This includes items such as configuring your home area code, entering prefixes needed to dial an outside line or disable call waiting, credit card numbers, and so on.

The presence of this dialog box in the TAPI function set is another great boon to programmers. Recreating this dialog box each time you developed a communications program would be tedious and fraught with potential error. Having it built into the operating system is a big plus.

The first three parameters have already appeared several times in this chapter, as they are used in many other functions, and have exactly the same meaning as here.

The `hwndOwner` parameter simply refers to the window that will be the owner of the dialog box. This is a modal dialog, so user interaction with the owner is disabled while the dialog box is up.

The final parameter here is the address or the phone number to be dialed.

This is a synchronous function, which returns its result immediately. A negative number is an error that should match one of the codes in TAPI.H, a return value of 0 indicates that no error occurred.

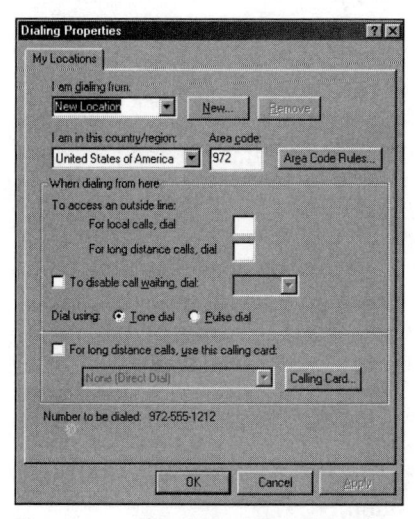

Figure 15-3: The Address Translation dialog box

```
lineTranslateAddress(   HLINEAPP hLineApp,
                        DWORD dwDeviceID,
                        DWORD dwAPIVersion,
                        LPCSTR lpszAddressIn,
                        DWORD dwCard,
                        DWORD dwTranslateOptions,
                        LPLINETRANSLATEOUT lpTranslateOut )
```

Just because you know the phone number for a remote modem doesn't mean that you are able to successfully make a call. There are quite a few factors that affect how you dial, such as whether to use tone or pulse dialing, whether to disable call waiting, and whether to dial 1 before the digits. It's a long list of things to think about.

Fortunately, TAPI has provided us with a comprehensive function that is capable of accounting for all these things, producing a dialing string that has been mangled to the appropriate degree. In the SimpleTapi class, this function is called in method MakeCall() immediately before calling TAPI function lineMakeCall().

In the simplest case, this translation might be as simple as changing 800-555-1212 to T800-555-1212. Additional options simply add addition dialing information to the string:

- hLineApp: The handle of the TAPI application, which was returned when your program called lineInitialize().

- dwDeviceID: The zero-based device id. This selects the line you are actually going to use to make the phone call.

- dwApiVersion: The TAPI API version that you want to use, as described in the previous function. The SimpleTapi class used here will always pass 0x00010004 as this argument.

- lpszAddressIn: A null-terminated string that contains the number you are planning to dial.

- dwCard: The number of the calling/credit card that will be used for dialing. This number is valid only if the CARDOVERRIDE bit is set in the next parameter. If that bit is set, this id refers to a card id stored in the registry under the TAPI setting Telephony/Cards. (The calling/credit card data is modifiable in the Telephony section of the Control Panel.)

- dwTranslateOptions: A variety of options, including credit card selection, call waiting disable, and the capability to force a local or a long distance call. See the SDK documents for more information on the flags used here. Class SimpleTapi passes a 0 in this position.

- lpTranslateOut: This structure receives the contents of the translated string. You can allocate as much space as you like for this structure, setting the dwSize member to indicate how much space is available for the function to return its translation. If you don't allocate enough space, you are supposed to detect the error and examine the `dwNeededSize` member on return. You then allocate the additional space that you need and recall the function. (`SimpleTapi` avoids this by allocating a ridiculously large buffer to begin with.)

To see this function in action, see `SimpleTapi::MakeCall()`. This is a synchronous function, which returns its result immediately. A negative number is an error that should match one of the codes in `TAPI.H`; a return value of 0 indicates that no error occurred.

Call control

These functions are the ones that are used to initiate, terminate, or manage calls. This group includes the asynchronous functions that don't return a result immediately. Accurately determining the result of these calls requires a bit of coordination with the callback function, which is discussed immediately after this group.

```
LONG lineMakeCall(  HLINE hLine,
                    LPHCALL lphCall,
                    LPCSTR lpszDestAddress,
                    DWORD dwCountryCode,
                    LPLINECALLPARAMS const lpCallParams )
```

This is the function that is used to make an outbound call. It is used in class `SimpleTapi` in the `MakeCall()` member function. The arguments to this function are described here:

- `hLine`: This is an active line handle. The line should have been opened earlier in the program with the `lineOpen()` function.

- `hCall`: A pointer to a call handle. `lineMakeCall()` returns a handle immediately, but you cannot use the handle until this function completes. This function usually operates in asynchronous mode, so you can't use the call handle until the appropriate `LINE_REPLY` message is received by the callback routine.

- `lpszDestAddress`: The actual phone number you are going to dial. This number is often processed by the `lineTranslateAddress()` function, which inserts additional commands and tones in the digit string, but it could be a number that you entered directly.

- `dwCountryCode`: The country code of the called party. `SimpleTapi` always passes a zero for this, in which case the call goes out without adding a country code.

- lpCallParams: **Parameters that give specific information about how the call should be set up.** For modem calls, you will set up a LINECALLPARAMS structure to have a dwBearerMode of LINEBEARERMODE_VOICE and a dwMediaMode of LINEMEDIAMODE_DATAMODEM. SimpleTapi sets up dwCallParamFlags to LINECALLPARAMFLAGS_IDLE, which indicates that the call should be placed on an idle line.

- The LINECALLPARAMS structure is a bulky, complex structure, but for simple modem calls on standard voice lines, it can be ignored.

When you make this function call, there are three different types of return values. A return value of less than zero indicates an error, with the code defined in TAPI.H. A return value of 0 means that the call was successful. The most likely return value from a call to this function is a positive request identifier. After you have this request identifier, you can wait for a LINE_REPLY message with a dwParam1 that matches the id to be sent to the callback function.

```
LONG lineAnswer(  HCALL hCall,
                  LPCSTR lpsUserInfo,
                  DWORD dwSize )
```

This call is made in response to an incoming call offering. When the callback function receives a LINE_CALLSTATE message with a call state of LINECALL-STATE_OFFERING, it means that an incoming call is being received by your modem. The callback function receives a call handle for this call in the hDevice parameter, which is then use to pass back to lineAnswer(). An example of this can be seen in SimpleTapi's static member function Callback().

The arguments to lineAnswer() are described here.

hCall	The call to lineAnswer() requires a valid call handle. This handle is passed in to the callback function in the hDevice argument. In SimpleTapi, the handle passed to lineAnswer() is the handle passed into the callback function when the line goes into the offering state. The handle is then stored in the SimpleTapi structure, and is valid until the call is dropped.
lpsUserInfo	This is a pointer to a string containing user information that is sent to the remote end after the call is completed. This field won't be used when making modem to modem calls over standard voice calls, so a NULL is normally passed here.
dwSize	The size of the string passed in lpsUserInfo.

Like the previous call, this function can return a negative number in case of an immediate error, or a zero in the case of immediate success. Normally, it returns a positive number denoting a request ID. The calling program then waits for a LINE_REPLY message to be sent to its callback function with the appropriate request id.

```
LONG lineDrop(  HCALL hCall,
                LPCSTR lpsUserInfo,
                DWORD dwSize )
```

This call is made to disconnect an active call. The call handle passed in should be one that was stored when a call was established. This function call kicks off the disconnect process, which may take some time to complete. The arguments to lineDrop() are described here

- hCall: The call to lineDrop() requires a valid call handle. In SimpleTapi, the call handle is stored when the call is created either by lineCallAnswer() or lineMakeCall().

- lpsUserInfo: This is a pointer to a string containing user information that is sent to the remote end during the call teardown. This field won't be used when making modem to modem calls over standard voice calls, so a NULL is normally passed here.

- dwSize: The size of the string passed in lpsUserInfo.

This is another asynchronous function call. It returns a negative number in case of an error, a 0 in case of immediate success, and a positive number if the function will proceed asynchronously. That positive number is a request id, which the calling program can then watch for as part of a LINE_REPLY callback message.

```
LONG lineDeallocateCall( HCALL hCall )
```

This function call gives up ownership of the call handle. It should be called only when the call goes idle or is disconnected. After this function call completes, the call handle is no longer valid and should be discarded.

This function returns immediately, with a 0 for success and a negative number for failure.

```
LONG lineGetID(  HLINE hLine,
                 DWORD dwAddressID,
                 HCALL hCall,
                 DWORD dwSelect,
                 LPVARSTRING lpDeviceID,
                 LPCSTR lpszDeviceClass )
```

This function is used to retrieve a device identifier associated with a line, address, or call. For the purposes of modem communications, only the identifier associated with a call is of interest.

When you call this function with the correct parameters, you get back a device identifier associated with your call. This device identifier can be treated as if it were a open port handle, meaning that it can be use to read or write bytes from the open modem port. After retrieving this device ID from class `SimpleTapi`, you can construct a `Win32Port` object with it and have full access to the port.

This is exactly what is done in the Chapter 15 demo program, which uses `SimpleTapi` to make a phone call and connect to a distant port, and then creates a `Win32Port` from the resulting TAPI session.

- `hLine`: A handle of an active call. You don't use this in `SimpleTapi`, because you are interested in getting the device identifier associated only with a call, not a line or device.

- `dwAddressID`: An address on the specified line. This is set to 0 in `SimpleTapi`.

- `hCall`: A pointer to a valid call handle. This should be the call handle that was returned from a call to `lineMakeCall()` or passed in with a new call arriving in the offering state.

- `dwSelect`: Because this function can return a device identifier based on several criteria, some way is needed to tell TAPI what is wanted. TAPI is told by passing one of three possible constants in this argument: `LINECALLSELECT_LINE`, `LINECALLSELECT_ADDRESS`, or `LINECALLSELECT_CALL`. The latter one is what is used in `SimpleTapi`.

- `lpDeviceID`: A pointer to a `VARSTRING` structure that is going to receive the returned result. In the normal manner of TAPI, this is a structure that has to be set up with to receive an argument of unspecified size, meaning that you normally guess at how much space might be needed, then deal with failure if it occurs.

- Every possible device can return different lengths and types of information in this parameter. When you call the function from `SimpleTapi` to retrieve the device identifier for a call handle, you are simply getting back another 32-bit port handle, so you don't really need to too much space.

- The actual data in the `VARSTRING` structure upon return is at the offset denoted by the dwStringOffset member of `VARSTRING`. (Needless to say, a string isn't being returned when this function is used.)

- `lpszDeviceClass`: The name of the device class. For modems, this is `comm/datamodem`.

The function returns 0 on success and a negative number on failure.

The callback function

All asynchronous notification returned by TAPI is sent to the program via a call to a callback function that is specified in the initial call to lineInitialize() or lineInitializeEx().The callback function is one you create in your program, and it should have the following function prototype:

```
VOID FAR PASCAL Callback(   DWORD hDevice,
                            DWORD dwMsg,
                            DWORD dwCallbackInstance,
                            DWORD dwParam1,
                            DWORD dwParam2,
                            DWORD dwParam3 );
```

This function has these argument definitions:

- hDevice: The handle of either the line or call associated with the specific message.

- dwMsg: A line or device message. This can be a myriad of different messages, but in SimpleTapi, you watch for only two messages: LINE_REPLY and LINE_CALLSTATE. The LINE_REPLY message is used to return the result of an asynchronous function call. LINE_CALLSTATE lets you track the progress of your call. LINE_CALLSTATE also notifies you of incoming asynchronous events, such as an incoming call or an externally generated disconnect.

- dwCallbackInstance: When you make the call to lineInitialize(), you can pass a 32-bit value that you want to always be included in calls to your callback function. This can be any sort of value you want, but in SimpleTapi, it is useful to pass a pointer to your SimpleTapi object here. That way, the callback function can operate directly on members of the object rather than rely on global pointers or other messy workarounds.

- dwParam1: The three parameters have different meanings depending on the type of message. When the message being passed in is a LINE_REPLY message (indicating the return value from an asynchronous function), dwParam1 is a request id. (The request id was returned when the asynchronous function was called.) This lets you match the LINE_REPLY message with a specific function call.

- When the message being processed is a LINE_CALLSTATE message, dwParam1 is the new state the given call or line is moving to.

- dwParam2: Like the other parameters, this value has different meanings depending on the message being passed to the callback routine. When the message is LINE_REPLY, dwParam2 is the actual return value from the function. In most cases, you want this to be 0 for success. A value less than 0 will denote one of the error codes from `TAPI.H`. In the case of a `LINE_REPLY` message, you want to convert the return code in `dwParam2` to a text message that can be displayed in the user interface.

- `dwParam3`: This is another parameter that has differing meanings depending on the message being passed. In the `SimpleTapi` callback function, the only time this value is important is when a `LINE_CALLSTATE` message is being processed and `dwParam3` is nonzero. In this case, `dwParam3` is used as a boolean flag that informs you of the change in privilege state of a given line.

The SimpleTapi Class

As usual, rather than using the Windows API directly it is much easier to wrap the API with a class, in this case, a class called `SimpleTapi`. The class shields you from some of the difficult mechanics in the API, such as repeatedly looking up constant definitions from the list of hundreds used by TAPI.

Better yet, a C++ class can be defined so that you don't ever have to change your TAPI interface code. In any given program, you will have to deal with notification issues, such as how to tell your program that it is receiving an incoming call. A good class defines the notification functions as virtual, so that simply creating a derived class can customize them. The demo program in this chapter does this using a class called `MySimpleTapi`.

Class `SimpleTapi` is designed to let you use a modem to make a data connection, then use the resulting connection for RS-232 communications. It doesn't even come close to using a full complement of TAPI, just the portions that apply to pure data calls on modems over standard phone lines.

`SimpleTapi` has seven virtual functions that must be defined by a derived class before it can be used. Five of those functions notify you of important changes in the state of the TAPI device or call. One provides a mechanism for your program to handle TAPI errors, and the seventh function provides a way for your application to give TAPI the handle of your main window.

> **NOTE:** All of the functions in this class that take an `index` argument treat it as an index in the list of TAPI devices created in the `SimpleTapi` constructor. The index is always converted to a device id before it is passed to any TAPI functions.

Class management and status

This section discusses the member functions of class `SimpleTapi` concerned with overall management of the TAPI session. For the most part, they are not directly related to making calls or configuring modems.

`SimpleTapi()`

The TAPI constructor doesn't actually open a line or try to initiate a call, but it does do a significant amount of work. It initializes most of the internal members of the class to their idle states. For example, the internal line handle and call handle variables are both set to 0. The TAPI version variable is set to 0x00010004, which is used for all function calls that request a TAPI version.

The constructor then loads the TAPI DLLs and gets things working by calling `lineInitialize()`. This function returns the `HLINEAPP` handle, which is stored in `m_hLineApp` and is used in quite a few function calls.

The constructor then builds a list of data modem devices, storing the name and device number for each. The device number has to be stored because the list of TAPI devices may well include other video, telephony, or audio devices. The calling program can access those device names later and enable the user to select the one the user wants to use when opening a line.

`~SimpleTapi()`

The destructor calls `lineShutdown()`, which releases any TAPI resources still in use. This will also shut down any calls in progress, so don't worry about whether the `m_hLine` or `m_hCall` variables are nonzero.

`bool IsOpen()`

This status function checks to see whether a TAPI device has been opened. It does this by checking whether a member variable `m_hLine` is nonzero. This is a protected member, so this accessor function is needed to determine whether the line is open.

`bool CallActive`

This function, much like `IsOpen()`, checks whether a call is active by testing protected member `m_hCall`. If the member has a nonzero value, a call is in progress and a value of true is returned.

`int GetDeviceCount()`

This member returns a count of data modem devices that are located in the constructor.

`string GetDeviceName( int index )`

Every data modem device located in the constructor is added to the `m_Devices` vector. This function returns the name of the device stored in that vector. These names might be used to populate a list box, enabling a user to select a TAPI device if more than one is available. (The sample program in this chapter doesn't offer a choice.)

`HWND GetWindow()`

There are two function calls in class `SimpleTapi` that display a dialog box. These functions need to get the handle of a window so that it can be designated as the dialog box's parent, enabling it to operate modally. This function is called internally by `ConfigureDevice()` and `ConfigureCall()` to acquire the parent window handle. That window handle is then passed in the corresponding call to the TAPI configuration functions.

This is a pure virtual function, which means that it is not defined in class `SimpleTapi`. You must define this in the derived class that you create in your application.

`static string TranslateTapiError( LONG code )`
`static string TranslateCallState( LONG code )`

These two functions translate TAPI status codes and call states. Numeric values are passed to user code via the pure virtual notification routines, and it may be desirable to translate them to readable strings. These two functions translate them to readable strings for you, providing a human-readable translation of the numeric codes.

Call and line management/configuration

This section describes the functions that are directly concerned with the use of the phone call, including making and tearing down phone calls.

`void ConfigureDevice( int index )`

This function provides a small wrapper around the TAPI function `lineConfigDialog()`. The single parameter to this call, `index`, is an index into the `m_Devices` vector initialized in the `SimpleTapi` constructor. `ConfigureDevice` converts the `index` parameter to the appropriate device id, fills in the other arguments with appropriate values, and calls `lineConfigDialog()`. This dialog box is shown earlier in this chapter in Figures 15-1 and 15-2.

ConfigureDevice() also checks the return value and calls the virtual Error() routine if one is detected. Error() is a virtual routine that has to be implemented in a derived class. This means you can customize it to work properly with the user interface in your program.

```
Void ConfigureCall( int index,
                    const string &number )
```

Like the previous function, ConfigureCall() is a wrapper around the lineTranslateDialog() TAPI function. It converts the index that is passed to a TAPI device id, fills in the other argument values, and calls the TAPI configuration function. Like the previous function, errors are passed to the virtual Error() function.

```
int OpenLine( int index )
```

This function calls the TAPI lineOpen() function with the appropriate list of arguments, which is fairly long and confusing. It needs to pass the current application handle that was created in the constructor, plus various flag constants. Most important, it passes TAPI a copy of this, a pointer to itself. The value of this is passed to the callback function whenever TAPI has any information to report regarding the state of the open line. That dwInstance value will be used by the callback function to properly access the members of *this*.

lineOpen() is also passed a pointer to the member variable m_hLine, which is assigned a value by the TAPI function. That variable is subsequently used in many of the TAPI calls that act on the open line.

```
int CloseLine()
```

This call closes the line that was opened using a call to OpenLine(). It makes a call to TAPI function lineClose(), passing in the m_hLine member. It checks for an error return; if one is found, it is passed back to the calling program via a call to virtual function Error().

After this function is called, m_hLine is set to 0, which means subsequent calls to IsOpen() will return false.

```
void MakeCall( const string &number )
Note: asynchronous function
```

This function is a wrapper around TAPI function lineMakeCall(), but thinking of it as a wrapper function tends to overlook the amount of work it has to do. Before it can call lineMakeCall(), it first calls lineTranslateAddress(), which converts the ASCII dialing digits into a modified string suitable for the modem. As discussed in the TAPI documentation, lineTranslateAddress() takes into account many different factors when creating the dial string, such as whether to use the area code, use tone or pulse dialing, disable call waiting, and so on.

After creating a usable string of dialed digits, `MakeCall()` has to set up the `LINECALLPARAMS` structure to pass to `lineMakeCall()`. When that is done, the TAPI function can be invoked.

`lineMakeCall()` normally operates in asynchronous mode. When you call the function, you save the request code in member `m_dwPendingReplyCode` and note the type of pending return in `m_eReplyAction`. (Although there is nothing in TAPI that prevents an application from having multiple pending requests, `SimpleTapi` handles only one asynchronous function call at a time.)

When a `LINE_REPLY` message is sent to the callback function, the reply code is checked against the one expected. If it is the same, a call is made to member function `HandleAnswerResult()`, a virtual pure function. This function is defined in the derived class, taking action appropriate to the application that is using it.

```
void DropCall()
Note: asynchronous function
```

Like `MakeCall()`, this is an asynchronous function call. However, unlike `MakeCall()`, this one is very easy to deal with. To begin, it calls `lineDrop()` with the stored call handle. If `lineDrop()` returns a positive response code, the stored response code is stored and the type of request you are waiting on is stored in `m_eReplyAction`.

When the appropriate `LINE_REPLY` message is detected in the callback function, a call is made to virtual function `HandleDropResult()`, which should know how the application wants to deal with the response.

For both this function and `MakeCall()` there is at least a theoretical possibility that the function returns with a successful result immediately. In the unlikely event that this happens, the `HandleDropResult()` function is called immediately.

```
HANDLE GetPortHandle()
```

This function looks simple enough. You call it when you have completed a call and are connected to the modem on the remote end. The call returns a handle that can then be used to read and write data to the port. The function internally calls `lineGetID()` to make this happen. Seems simple, doesn't it?

In a way, it is. The function is used in the demo program for this chapter to retrieve the handle when the notification routine `ConnectedEvent()` is called. It is then passed as a constructor to `Win32Port()` and terminal emulation is started.

The one important thing to remember about this function is that after you get a port handle, you are responsible for closing it. As long as your application has the port handle, you will prevent others from opening the port. So, it is important to close the handle using the Win32 API call `CloseHandle()` when you are complete. (The `Win32Port` destructor automatically does this.)

Notification functions

The nature of serial communications means that external events have to be reported to applications that are using phone lines or serial ports. The `SimpleTapi` class performs notification via these member functions.

All the notification functions in class `SimpleTapi` are declared as pure virtual. This means that you must write your own versions of these functions as part of a derived class tailored for your application.

```
void MakeCallResult( bool result )
void DropCallResult( bool result )
```

These two functions are the way the application program is notified that TAPI has finally returned the result from an asynchronous function call. The functions are both defined as pure virtual, which means that you must define them in a derived class before you can create an object.

Both functions return the actual result of the function as a single argument. In the Chapter 15 demo program, neither of these functions do anything important; they just dump the result code to the trace window. In a production program, you would want to check the result codes and display some notification to the user if an error occurred.

```
void ConnectedEvent()
void DisconnectedEvent()
```

These are the two notification functions that are called when a connection is either made or broken. These are pure virtual functions that have to be defined in your derived class. The sample program that comes with this chapter uses the `ConnectedEvent()` routine to get the port handle, open the port, then start the terminal emulator. The `DisconnectedEvent()` closes the port, returning the port handle to TAPI control.

```
void NotifyCallStateChange( long new_state )
```

This program is used to provide notification each time the TAPI state changes. The state is passed as the sole argument to the function. This function is defined as pure virtual in `SimpleTapi`, which means that you must create a derived class that implements this function.

The sample program in this chapter doesn't do anything with this function other than to print a diagnostic message. However, you can effectively use this single notification function to do the same work as `ConnectedEvent()` and `DisconnectedEvent()`, by simply watching for state `LINECALLSTATE_CONNECTED` for the connected event and either `LINECALLSTATE_IDLE` or `LINE_CALLSTATE_DISCONNECTED` for the connected event.

```
void Error( const char *msg, LONG code )
```

This pure virtual function is provided for notification of TAPI error messages. A derived class can use this function to pop up a message box, add a line to a log file, or to do nothing.

In the event that you use this to create a dialog box, it is desirable to translate the error code into a human-readable string with a call to `TranslateTapiError()`.

Important internals

The functions described in this section are internal functions that are used inside class `SimpleTapi`. Even though you won't call these functions directly, it is good to understand a little bit about what they do and how they do it.

```
void HandleMakeCallResult( DWORD result )
void HandleDropResult( DWORD result )
void HandleAnswerResult( DWORD result )
```

These member functions are called internally when a `LINE_REPLY` message is seen by the callback function. Every time one of these messages comes in, it is checked against the stored reply code in `m_dwPendingReplyCode`. In the event of a match, the `m_ReplyAction` member is checked, and one of these three functions is called.

The three functions all do some bookkeeping. In some cases, they call virtual notification functions so that the user application can be made aware of the result. Remember that you can write your program to ignore these asynchronous result codes and to just take action on changed call states.

```
void Callback( DWORD hDevice,
               DWORD dMsg,
               DWORD dwCallbackInstance,
               DWORD dwParam1,
               DWORD dwParam2,
               DWORD dwParam3 )
```

The callback routine is called from TAPI when various significant events occur. The ones to pay attention to in this class are the `LINE_REPLY` messages and `LINE_CALLSTATE` messages.

When a `LINE_REPLY` message is received, it is compared to the response code in `dwParam1` to the saved code in `m_dwPendingReplyCode`. If it is a match, it means it is a result code from an asynchronous function call. `Callback()` checks the contents of `m_ReplyAction` and calls either `HandleMakeCallResult()`, `HandleDropResult()`, or `HandleAnswerResult()`. These are all members of the base class, but the Drop and Make Call handlers will also call notification routines defined in the derived class.

If the message sent to `Callback()` is a `LINE_CALLSTATE` message, a call is first made to the `NotifyCallStateChange()` function with the value of the new state. This function is pure virtual in the base class, which means the function is defined in the derived class.

After calling the notification routine, the routine then takes action if one of four pertinent call states is entered. The first call state, `LINECALLSTATE_CONNECTED`, simply generates a call to notification routine `ConnectedEvent()`. This is another pure virtual function, which means that a notification routine defined in the derived class is being called.

The next two important events are `LINECALLSTATE_IDLE` and `LINECALLSTATE_DISCONNECTED`. They actually share one set of code, which first calls the notification routine `DisconnectedEvent()`, which is a pure virtual function in the base class that must be defined in your derived class. After calling the notification routine, `lineDeallocateCall()` is called with the `m_hCall` member as an argument. This lets TAPI know that you are done with all the resources associated with the call, allowing it to clean things up.

The final state that generates activity inside `Callback()` is the `LINECALLSTATE_OFFERING` event. This means that an incoming call is being received. `SimpleTapi` deals with this in a simple fashion, by automatically attempting to answer by calling `lineAnswer()`. Naturally, this is an asynchronous call, so nothing happens right away, but the response code is saved and a note is made that you are waiting for the response.

All other call states passed to `Callback()` are ignored and do nothing after the call to the notification routine.

`vector<TapiDevice> m_Devices`

This data member contains a list of all the data modem devices that were enumerated by TAPI when the `SimpleTapi` constructor ran. Each device has a device name and an id number, which are collectively stored in a `TapiDevice` structure defined specifically for use with this class. The user can access the names for the entries by calling `GetDeviceName()`. The TAPI device numbers are never needed by the end user, so there is no accessor for them.

`HLINEAPP m_hLineApp`

The line application handle created when TAPI is initialized in the `SimpleTapi` constructor. This handle is passed in to many different TAPI functions, such as `lineGetDevCaps()` and `lineShutdown()`.

`HCALL m_hCall`

The handle for the current call. This handle is loaded when the call is first created, which is either when `MakeCall()` is called or when an incoming offering is detected in the `Callback()` routine. It is set to 0 when the call is disconnected.

```
HLINE m_hLine
```

The handle for the current line. This handle is created when the line is opened, and is set to 0 when the line is closed.

```
LONG m_lCallState
```

The current call state. This is updated each time the callback routine gets a new call state notification from TAPI.

Debugging notes

`SimpleTapi` has some built in debugging that can help a bit in tracing its activity. I created a utility class called `ConStream` that is used to print trace messages at various points in the library, such as call state changes.

`ConStream` provides a C++ output stream that can be directed to a console window under Win32. If your program is running under the Windows GUI, `ConStream` can open a text mode window and use it for debug output. The `ConStream` static member is called `m_Trace` and has public access. You can create the window by calling the `Open()` member of this object and destroy it by calling `Close()`. The demo program in this chapter uses this debug window and enables you to open it and close it from the main menu of the program. An example of the type of output you can expect from this program is shown in Figure 15-4.

Figure 15-4: The trace window available from SimpleTapi

Room for improvement – a shortcoming

Right now, `SimpleTapi` will automatically answer any phone call that comes in while the line is active. A useful improvement to this class would be to provide a mechanism that notifies the calling program when an incoming call arrives in the offering state, allowing the calling program to make the decision as to whether or not to answer. After that decision is made, an additional notification function could be added to return the asynchronous result of the `lineAnswer()` call, probably named `AnswerResult()`.

Class Tapi32Port — the final detail

I mention earlier that you could open a `Win32Port` object given the port handle for an active TAPI call. This isn't quite true. The port that you open is actually of class `Tapi32Port`, which is derived from `Win32Port`. The only new function defined in `Tapi32Port` is a constructor. The `Tapi32Port` constructor is identical to that for `Win32Port` except that it doesn't attempt to do any initialization of the port parameters. That's because all of the pertinent parameters, such as the baud rate, handshaking, and so on, were already set to the desired values by TAPI.

All functions other than the constructor are still defined in the base class, `Win32Port`.

The Chapter 15 Demo Program

The Chapter 15 demo program is a Win32 program that provides a bare-bones implementation of TAPI features. It is built on a framework that is nearly identical to the Win32 terminal emulation program. It is a simple terminal emulator that uses TAPI to make and accept calls. After TAPI has connected, the program opens the port, using the handle provided by TAPI, and operates as a terminal emulator.

The program just has a set of commands available from a menu that let you exercise the TAPI functions. Typically, the sequence of events needed to make a call is as follows:

1. Create the TAPI object.
2. Open the line.
3. Set the phone number that you wish to dial.
4. Place the call.

To receive a call, you need to execute only Steps 1 and 2. After the line is open, the incoming call is answered automatically. The program in action is shown in Figure 15-5.

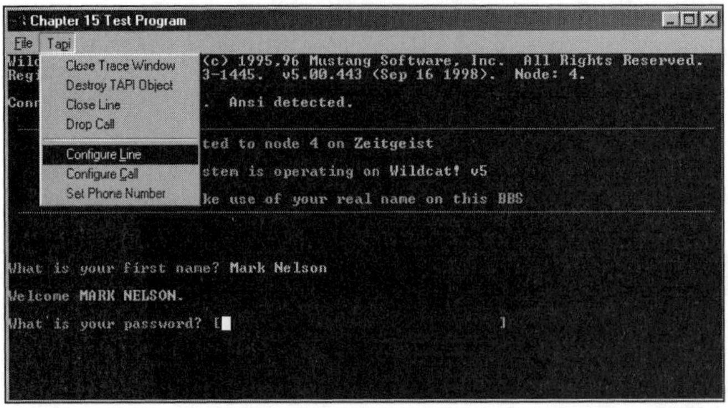

Figure 15-5: CHAPT15.EXE in action

SimpleTapi integration

Getting the `SimpleTapi` class to work with any application is always done the same way: creation of a derived class with customized virtual functions. The virtual functions deal with notification issues in a way that works with the specialized needs of the application.

In CHAPT15.EXE, the Chapter 15 demo program, a class called `MySimpleTapi` is derived from `SimpleTapi`. The glue code needed to customize `SimpleTapi` is short enough that you can fit all the code in the header file, inline with the class definition. The virtual functions that are customized for the `MySimpleTapi` are the following:

- `GetWindow`
- `ConnectedEvent`
- `DisconnectedEvent`
- `NotifyCallStateChange`
- `Error`
- `MakeCallResult`
- `DropCallResult`

Class `MySimpleTapi` also has a customized constructor whose sole purpose is to save the value of a window handle that will be used by `MySimpleTapi` to send notification messages.

You can examine the source file `MySimpleTapi.h` to see the details of these implementations. In a nutshell, the only significant functions are `ConnectedEvent()` and `DisconnectEvent()`, which are used to open and close the `Win32Port` used by the terminal emulator.

In addition to opening and closing the port, these notification handlers also send Windows messages to the main window of CHAPT15.EXE, which enables it to update menu options.

The source code

The listings for CHAPT15.EXE follow. This is a simple Win32 program that does not rely on MFC or any other framework. Make files for this program are included on the CD that ships with the book.

In addition to the derived classes described above, one additional glue class is needed: AnsiTapiTerm. This class is nearly identical to the previous terminal emulation classes described in this book, except that it opens a Tapi32Port rather than a Win32Port.

Listing 15-1 contains the C++ source for the main body of the example program.

Listing 15-1: Chapter15.cpp

```
//
//   CHAPT15.CPP
//
//   Source code from:
//
//   Serial Communications: Developer's Guide, 2nd Edition
//   by Mark Nelson, IDG Books, 1999
//
//   Please see the book for information on usage.
//
// This file contains the source code for the Chapter 15
// demo program. To build this file, use the Visual C++
// project file included in the same directory as the
// sample code. CHAPT15.CPP shows how you can use TAPI
// to manage modems in a communications
// program. The terminal emulation portion of this program
// is essentially identical to that of Chapter 13.
// It differs in the use of TAPI to set up the connection
// to a distant modem.
//

#include <windows.h>
#include "resource.h"

#include "AnsiTapiTerm.h"
#include "MySimpleTapi.h"

//
// A couple of forward references needed throughout the
```

```c
// program.
//

LRESULT CALLBACK WinProc( HWND hwnd,
                          UINT message,
                          WPARAM wParam,
                          LPARAM lParam );
BOOL CALLBACK DlgProc( HWND hWnd,
                       UINT uMsg,
                       WPARAM wParam,
                       LPARAM lParam );

//
// The WinMain() function for this program looks
// very generic. It has to register the class you
// will create for this demo program, as well as be sure
// to include your menu and WinProc. After the class
// is registered, you can create the window and
// let it do the rest of the work. From that
// point on, all you have to do is
// run the message loop until someone decides it's
// time to exit.
//

int WINAPI WinMain( HINSTANCE hInstance,
                    HINSTANCE /* hPrevInstance */,
                    LPSTR     /* lpCmdLine */,
                    int       nShowCmd )
{
    //
    // Note that you store enough extra space in the class
    // to hold two pointers. The two pointers
    // are a pointer to
    // the Terminal Emulation object and another to the
    // Tapi object.
    //
    WNDCLASS wc = { 0 };
    wc.lpfnWndProc     = WinProc;
     wc.hInstance      = hInstance;
    wc.lpszMenuName    = MAKEINTRESOURCE( IDR_MENU );
    wc.hbrBackground   = (HBRUSH) ( COLOR_WINDOW + 1 );
    wc.lpszClassName   = "Chapter15Class";
    wc.cbWndExtra      = sizeof( Win32Term * ) +
                         sizeof( MySimpleTapi * );
    if ( !RegisterClass( &wc ) ) {
```

```
        MessageBox( NULL,
                    "Could not register Chapter 15 class!",
                    NULL,
                    MB_OK );
        return 0;
    }
    HWND hwnd = CreateWindow( "Chapter15Class",
                              "Chapter 15 Test Program",
                              WS_OVERLAPPEDWINDOW |
                                  WS_CLIPCHILDREN,
                              CW_USEDEFAULT,
                              CW_USEDEFAULT,
                              647, // hand picked size
                              347,
                              NULL,
                              NULL,
                              hInstance,
                              NULL );

    if ( hwnd == NULL ) {
        MessageBox( NULL,
                    "Chapter15.exe couldn't start!",
                    NULL,
                    MB_OK );
        return 0;
    }
    ShowWindow( hwnd, nShowCmd );
    UpdateWindow( hwnd );

    MSG msg;
    while ( GetMessage( &msg, NULL, 0, 0 ) )
    {
        TranslateMessage( &msg ) ;
        DispatchMessage( &msg ) ;
    }
    return 1;
}

//
// To make the user interface a bit easier to follow, the
// TAPI menu has quite a few entries that can be enabled or
// disabled. In many cases, the entries have two different
// meanings. For example, the menu entry ID_TAPI_PLACE_CALL is set
// to have a string of "Place Call" when the there is no
// active call, and "Drop Call" when there is an active
```

```cpp
        // call. Likewise, the menu item is grayed/disabled when
        // the TAPI line is closed, and enabled when the TAPI line
        // is open.
        //
        // This routine is called to fix all the various TAPI
        // menu options whenever anything happens that might require
        // a change. Clearly it is a bit of overkill to redo all the
        // menu options when maybe just one thing changes, but it
        // is easier to do it this way.
        //

        void UpdateMenu( HWND hwnd,
                         MySimpleTapi *pTapi )
        {
            HMENU menu = GetSubMenu( GetMenu( hwnd ), 1 );
            //
            // The Open Trace Window item is always enabled.
            // You just have to determine what the appropriate text
            // should be based on the state of the trace window.
            //
            if ( SimpleTapi::m_Trace.IsOpen() )
                ModifyMenu( menu,
                            ID_TAPI_OPEN_TRACE_WINDOW,
                            MF_BYCOMMAND | MF_STRING,
                            ID_TAPI_OPEN_TRACE_WINDOW,
                            "Close Trace Window" );
            else
                ModifyMenu( menu,
                            ID_TAPI_OPEN_TRACE_WINDOW,
                            MF_BYCOMMAND | MF_STRING,
                            ID_TAPI_OPEN_TRACE_WINDOW,
                            "Open Trace Window" );
            //
            // Likewise, the second menu item, Create TAPI Object,
            // is always be enabled. The menu text is set
            // to either Create or Destroy the TAPI object.
            //
            if ( pTapi )
                ModifyMenu( menu,
                            ID_TAPI_CREATE_TAPI_OBJECT,
                            MF_BYCOMMAND | MF_STRING,
                            ID_TAPI_CREATE_TAPI_OBJECT,
                            "Destroy TAPI Object" );
            else
                ModifyMenu( menu,
```

```
                        ID_TAPI_CREATE_TAPI_OBJECT,
                        MF_BYCOMMAND | MF_STRING,
                        ID_TAPI_CREATE_TAPI_OBJECT,
                        "Create TAPI Object" );
//
// The Open Line menu item should be disabled unless
// a TAPI object exists. If a TAPI object exists,
// the text depends strictly on whether a line
// is open or not.
//
if ( pTapi && pTapi->IsOpen() )
    ModifyMenu( menu,
                ID_TAPI_OPEN_LINE,
                MF_BYCOMMAND | MF_STRING,
                ID_TAPI_OPEN_LINE,
                "Close Line" );
else
    ModifyMenu( menu,
                ID_TAPI_OPEN_LINE,
                MF_BYCOMMAND | MF_STRING,
                ID_TAPI_OPEN_LINE,
                "Open Line" );
if ( pTapi )
    EnableMenuItem( menu,
                    ID_TAPI_OPEN_LINE,
                    MF_BYCOMMAND | MF_ENABLED );
else
    EnableMenuItem( menu,
                    ID_TAPI_OPEN_LINE,
                    MF_BYCOMMAND | MF_GRAYED );
//
// The Place Call menu item has text that alternates
// between Place Call and Drop Call,
// depending on whether a call is active. It should
// be enabled only if a line is open.
//
if ( pTapi && pTapi->IsOpen() && pTapi->CallActive() )
    ModifyMenu( menu,
                ID_TAPI_PLACE_CALL,
                MF_BYCOMMAND | MF_STRING,
                ID_TAPI_PLACE_CALL,
                "Drop Call" );
else
    ModifyMenu( menu,
                ID_TAPI_PLACE_CALL,
```

```
                        MF_BYCOMMAND | MF_STRING,
                        ID_TAPI_PLACE_CALL,
                        "Place Call" );
    if ( pTapi && pTapi->IsOpen() )
        EnableMenuItem( menu,
                        ID_TAPI_PLACE_CALL,
                        MF_BYCOMMAND | MF_ENABLED );
    else
        EnableMenuItem( menu,
                        ID_TAPI_PLACE_CALL,
                        MF_BYCOMMAND | MF_GRAYED );
    //
    // The three configuration menu items are all enabled
    // if the TAPI object is alive, and disabled if it is not.
    // Their text never changes.
    //
    if ( pTapi )
        EnableMenuItem( menu,
                        ID_TAPI_CONFIGURE_LINE,
                        MF_BYCOMMAND | MF_ENABLED );
    else
        EnableMenuItem( menu,
                        ID_TAPI_CONFIGURE_LINE,
                        MF_BYCOMMAND | MF_GRAYED );
    if ( pTapi )
        EnableMenuItem( menu,
                        ID_TAPI_CONFIGURE_CALL,
                        MF_BYCOMMAND | MF_ENABLED );
    else
        EnableMenuItem( menu,
                        ID_TAPI_CONFIGURE_CALL,
                        MF_BYCOMMAND | MF_GRAYED );
    if ( pTapi )
        EnableMenuItem( menu,
                        ID_TAPI_SET_PHONE_NUMBER,
                        MF_BYCOMMAND | MF_ENABLED );
    else
        EnableMenuItem( menu,
                        ID_TAPI_SET_PHONE_NUMBER,
                        MF_BYCOMMAND | MF_GRAYED );
}


//
// The WinProc given here starts with the same core message
```

```
// handlers that were seen in Chapter 13. The main window has
// a single child window that acts as a terminal emulator when
// the port is open. The message handlers for WM_CREATE,
// WM_DESTROY, WM_GETMINMAXINFO, WM_SIZE, and WM_SETFOCUS
// all deal with issues related to that child window.
// The commands that dealt with the fonts, colors,
// and so on for the child window were removed, but they could
// easily be restored by using cut and paste.
//
// The remaining message handlers for this window all
// deal with issues related to TAPI. All but two of the
// handlers are called as a result of making selections from
// the main menu, and are under the WM_COMMAND handler. The
// other two are messages sent from the TAPI notification
// routines.
//
// Details on exactly what these message handlers do are
// found inline with the code. In general, the way to use
// this program is to:
//
// 1) Open the trace window for help with debugging.
// 2) Create a TAPI object.
// 3) Open a line.
// 4) Wait for an incoming call.
//    -- or --
// 4) Set the outbound phone number.
// 5) Place a call.
//
//   The goal is to wait for the
//   modem to connect to another modem. When that happens,
//   the port is opened and you are operating a
//   terminal emulator.
//
LRESULT CALLBACK WinProc( HWND hWnd,
                          UINT message,
                          WPARAM wParam,
                          LPARAM lParam )
{
    //
    // These two pointers reference objects that are stored
    // in the excess storage area for this window. The
    // pointers are used far and wide among various message
    // handlers, so they are set up here for anyone who wants
    // to use them. After the window has been
    // created, pTerm should always point to a valid terminal
```

```
    // emulator window, but pTapi may or may not be null
    //
    AnsiTapiTerm *pTerm;
    MySimpleTapi *pTapi;
    pTerm = (AnsiTapiTerm *) GetWindowLong( hWnd, 0 );
    pTapi = (MySimpleTapi *) GetWindowLong( hWnd, 4 );

    switch ( message )
    {
        //
        // When the window is first created, you should
        // immediately create the terminal window as a child
        // window. Get the pointer to the C++ object and store it
        // as a window long-word, giving access to it whenever
        // it is needed without using a global variable.
        //
        case WM_CREATE:
            pTerm = new AnsiTapiTerm( hWnd,
                                      "AnsiTerm Window",
                                      25, 80 );
            SetWindowLong( hWnd, 0, (LONG) pTerm );
            if ( pTerm->m_hWnd == NULL )
                MessageBox( hWnd,
                            "Can't open child window",
                            "Chapter 15",
                            MB_OK );
            SetFocus( hWnd );
            break;
        //
        // When I am being destroyed, I take it upon myself
        // to destroy both the terminal object and the TAPI
        // object, if one exists.
        //
        case WM_DESTROY:
            delete pTerm;
            pTerm = 0;
            if ( pTapi ) {
                delete pTapi;
                pTapi = 0;
            }
            PostQuitMessage( 0 );
            break;
        //
        // Just for the sake of esthetics, I respond to this message
        // with a minimum size large enough to prevent somebody from
```

```
    // resizing me down to the point of ridiculousness.
    //
        case WM_GETMINMAXINFO:
            {
                LPMINMAXINFO lp = (LPMINMAXINFO) lParam;
                POINT ptTemp = {
                    lp->ptMinTrackSize.x,
                    GetSystemMetrics( SM_CYMENU )      +
                        GetSystemMetrics( SM_CYCAPTION ) +
                        2 * GetSystemMetrics( SM_CYFRAME )
                };
                lp->ptMinTrackSize = ptTemp;
            }
            break;

    //
    // When the frame window is resized, I immediately
    // resize the terminal window. Becaise the terminal window
    // is supposed to completely fill my client area, you
    // can figure out what size it is supposed to be by
    // simply getting the size of your client rect. When
    // the terminal window processes this command, it will
    // potentially add scroll bars and offset the display.
    //
        case WM_SIZE:
            {
                RECT rc;
                ::GetClientRect( hWnd, &rc );
                if ( lParam != 0 )
                ::MoveWindow( pTerm->m_hWnd,
                              0, 0,
                              rc.right - rc.left + 1,
                              rc.bottom - rc.top + 1,
                              TRUE );
            }
            break;
    //
    // To prevent the framing window from getting out of
    // focus, immediately foist it on
    // the terminal window.
    //
        case WM_SETFOCUS :
            SetFocus( pTerm->m_hWnd );
            return 0;
    //
```

```
// The rest of the code in the message loop
// is the set of command handlers for menu
// items.
//
case WM_COMMAND:
    switch ( LOWORD( wParam ) ) {
    //
    // Telling a window to close itself is a fast way
    // of shutting the program down, so that's how
    // to deal with the File|Exit menu item.
    //
    case ID_FILE_EXIT :
        PostMessage( hWnd, WM_CLOSE, 0, 0 );
        break;
    //
    // The base class, SimpleTapi, has a trace object
    // that receives various messages as the object
    // does its TAPI stuff. This trace window can be
    // open or closed. This command toggles it back
    // and forth between these two states. Because the
    // trace object is static, you don't need to
    // use a pointer to the TAPI object. When the
    // object is opened, a completely separate
    // console window is opened to receive trace
    // information.
    //
    case ID_TAPI_OPEN_TRACE_WINDOW :
        if ( SimpleTapi::m_Trace.IsOpen() )
            SimpleTapi::m_Trace.Close();
        else
            SimpleTapi::m_Trace.Open();
        UpdateMenu( hWnd, pTapi );
        break;
    //
    // You can't do much of anything interesting
    // with this program until the SimpleTapi
    // object is created. This command handler
    // will either create or destroy the object,
    // depending on whether it currently
    // exists. The value of the pTapi after the
    // operation has to be stuffed in the window
    // storage area so that it will persist past the
    // end of this command processing.
    //
    case ID_TAPI_CREATE_TAPI_OBJECT :
```

```cpp
            if ( pTapi ) {
                delete pTapi;
                pTapi = 0;
            } else
                pTapi = new MySimpleTapi( hWnd );
            SetWindowLong( hWnd, 4, (LONG) pTapi );
            UpdateMenu( hWnd, pTapi );
            break;
//
// This menu object should be grayed out unless
// the pTapi object has been created. If it has,
// you can either open or close the line. Note
// that this call is hard coded to open the first
// TAPI line. A better program would let you
// select from among the available lines via
// some sort of selection dialog. The
// two functions called here both return
// immediately, so there is no wait for a
// delayed response.
//
        case ID_TAPI_OPEN_LINE :
            if ( pTapi->IsOpen() )
                pTapi->CloseLine();
            else
                pTapi->OpenLine( 0 );
            UpdateMenu( hWnd, pTapi );
            break;
//
// This menu item should be enabled only if a
// line has been opened. It will then either
// place a call or drop a call, depending on
// whether a call is active. This is a little
// bit tricky because
// both of these calls don't return
// an immediate result
//
        case ID_TAPI_PLACE_CALL :
            if ( pTapi->CallActive() )
                pTapi->DropCall();
            else
                pTapi->MakeCall( pTapi->m_NumberToDial );
            break;
//
// The following three menu items are enabled as
// long as a TAPI object is alive. All three are
```

```
                    // used to configure the parameters surrounding
                    // a TAPI call. The first two just invoke the
                    // standard dialogs supplied by TAPI to configure
                    // modems and the way they place calls. The third
                    // pops up a dialog that optionally
                    // modifies the current outbound phone number.
                    //
                    case ID_TAPI_CONFIGURE_LINE :
                        pTapi->ConfigureDevice( 0 );
                        break;
                    case ID_TAPI_CONFIGURE_CALL :
                        pTapi->ConfigureCall( 0, pTapi->m_NumberToDial );
                        break;
                    case ID_TAPI_SET_PHONE_NUMBER :
                        DialogBox( GetModuleHandle( NULL ),
                                   MAKEINTRESOURCE(IDD_GET_PHONE_NUMBER),
                                   hWnd,
                                   (DLGPROC) DlgProc );
                        break;

                }
                break;
            //
            // My specialized class derived from SimpleTapi
            // is called MySimpleTapi. I've configured it to
            // send the following Windows messages to a specific
            // window as part of its notification process. I use
            // the notification event to update the UI, mostly
            // by printing a message on the terminal screen.
            //
            case WM_TAPI_CONNECTED_NOTIFY :
                *pTerm << "\r\nConnected\r\n";
                UpdateMenu( hWnd, pTapi );
                break;
            case WM_TAPI_DISCONNECTED_NOTIFY :
                *pTerm << "\r\nDisconnected\r\n";
                UpdateMenu( hWnd, pTapi );
                break;
            case WM_TAPI_STATE_CHANGE_NOTIFY :
                UpdateMenu( hWnd, pTapi );
                break;
            default:
                return DefWindowProc( hWnd, message, wParam, lParam );
        }
        return 0L;
```

```
}

//
// This program was written without the use of MFC or any
// other application framework, which means that using a
// dialog box to get a text string is a bit of trouble. The
// sole use of a dialog box in this program is to get the
// phone number that is to be dialed on selection of the
// Place Call menu item.
//
// This dialog box assumes that its parent is the Chapter 15
// main window. Because of that, it can extract a pointer to
// the TAPI object from the storage area associated with that
// window. The phone number is stored in that structure,
// which means the text box can be preloaded with the number,
// and the structure updated with the new value if the user
// clicks on the OK box to exit.
//

BOOL CALLBACK DlgProc( HWND hWnd,
                       UINT uMsg,
                       WPARAM wParam,
                       LPARAM lParam )
{
    HWND hParent = GetParent( hWnd );
    MySimpleTapi *pTapi;
    pTapi = (MySimpleTapi *) GetWindowLong( hParent, 4 );

    switch ( uMsg ) {

    //
    // When the dialog is first created,
    // the edit text box is preloaded with a copy of the phone
    // number currently loaded into the text box.
    //
    case WM_INITDIALOG :
        SetDlgItemText( hWnd,
                        IDC_PHONE_NUMBER,
                        pTapi->m_NumberToDial.c_str() );
        return TRUE;

    case WM_COMMAND :
        switch ( LOWORD( wParam ) ) {
        //
        // If the user clicks on the cancel button, the program
```

```
            // exits without updating any data.
            //
            case IDCANCEL :
                EndDialog( hWnd, 0 );
                return TRUE;
            //
            // If the user clicks OK, the phone number
            // field in the TAPI object is updated with whatever was
            // typed in the field. No checks are made to ensure that
            // it is a legal number.
            //
            case IDOK :
                {
                    char number[ 25 ];
                    ::GetDlgItemText( hWnd,
                                      IDC_PHONE_NUMBER,
                                      number,
                                      24 );
                    pTapi->m_NumberToDial = number;
                    EndDialog( hWnd, 0 );
                }
                return TRUE;
        }
    }
    return FALSE;
}

// End of CHAPT15.CPP
```

Listing 15-2: SimpleTapi.h

Listing 15-2 contains the header file, which has the declaration of class `SimpleTapi`. You include this header file in any module of your program that uses the class.

```
#if !defined _SIMPLE_TAPI_H
#define _SIMPLE_TAPI_H

//
// SimpleTapi.h
//
// Source code from:
//
// Serial Communications: Developer's Guide, 2nd
// Edition by Mark Nelson, IDG Books, 1999
//
```

```cpp
//   Please see the book for information on usage.
//
// This file contains the complete declaration of
// the SimpleTapi class. SimpleTapi wraps up a limited
// subset of TAPI 1.4, using the SDK only for its modem
// control and call setup capabilities. This class
// contains several pure virtual functions that are needed
// for notification. Before you can use SimpleTapi, you
// need to create a derived class that implements those
// functions. A simple example used in the book is
// MySimpleTapi, which is used in the Chapter 15 demo.
//

#include <string>
#include <vector>
using namespace std;

//
// TAPI 1.4 contains everything you need to perform first-
// party call control, which means setting up and tearing down
// calls on your local modem.
//
#define TAPI_CURRENT_VERSION 0x00010004
#include <tapi.h>

#include "ConStream.h"
#include "resource.h"


//
// This baby class is used to hold the definitions
// of modems in the m_Devices vector in SimpleTapi. Each
// modem has a text name and a device ID. Creating this
// structure lets you easily hold them in the vector.
//
struct TapiDevice {
    int m_iDeviceNumber;
    string m_sName;
};

class SimpleTapi {
public :
    SimpleTapi();
    virtual ~SimpleTapi();
    //
```

```cpp
        // Informational
        //
        bool IsOpen(){ return m_hLine != 0; }
        bool CallActive(){ return m_hCall != 0; }
        int GetDeviceCount()
        {
            return m_Devices.size();
        }
        string GetDeviceName( int i )
        {
            return m_Devices[ i ].m_sName;
        }
        //
        // Configuration/setup
        //
        void ConfigureDevice( int index );
        void ConfigureCall( int index, const string &number );
        //
        //  The four big calls used for call progress
        //
        int OpenLine( int index );
        int CloseLine();
        void MakeCall( const string &number );   //asynchronous
        void DropCall();                         //asynchronous
        //
        // Access the com port
        //
        HANDLE GetPortHandle();
        //
        // Debug
        //
        static ConStream m_Trace;
    protected :
        void HandleMakeCallResult( DWORD result );
        void HandleDropResult( DWORD result );
        void HandleAnswerResult( DWORD result );
        //
        // All of the data members are protected and should
        // only be used internally.
        //
    protected :
        vector< TapiDevice > m_Devices;
        HLINEAPP m_hLineApp;
        HCALL m_hCall;
        bool m_bCallHandleValid;
```

```
        HLINE m_hLine;
        LONG m_lCallState;
        DWORD m_dwPendingReplyCode;
        string m_sNumber;
        enum {
            NOTHING,
            HANDLE_MAKE_CALL_RESULT,
            HANDLE_DROP_RESULT,
            HANDLE_ANSWER_RESULT
        } m_ReplyAction;
        int m_iDeviceId;
        //
        // Two general purpose functions for translating codes
        // into human-readable strings.
        //
    protected :
        static string TranslateTapiError( LONG code );
        static string TranslateCallState( LONG state );
        //
        // The static callback function is where all TAPI
        // asyncrhonous message processing takes place. That
        // means it is responsible for determining when calls
        // are initiated, completed, and dropped.
        //
    private :
        static void PASCAL Callback( DWORD hDevice,
                                     DWORD dwMsg,
                                     DWORD dwCallbackInstace,
                                     DWORD dwParam1,
                                     DWORD dwParam2,
                                     DWORD dwParam3 );
        //
        // The remaining functions in the definition are all
        // pure virtual, which means that they must be defined in
        // a derived class before a SimpleTapi object can be
        // instantiated. Nearly all of them are concerned with
        // notification messages being sent to the owner of the
        // SimpleTapi object.
        //
    protected :
        //
        // The two asynchronous functions return results via
        // a event handler.
        //
        virtual void MakeCallResult( bool result ) = 0;
```

```
            virtual void DropCallResult( bool result ) = 0;
            //
            // Two events that happen asynchronously are the making
            // and breaking of calls. You always signal these via
            // the IdleEvent()and ConnectedEvent() function calls
            //
            virtual void ConnectedEvent() = 0;
            virtual void DisconnectedEvent() = 0;

            //
            // The NotifyCallStateChange() function call
            // enables you to track the state of a call with annoyingly
            // fine precision.
            //
            virtual void NotifyCallStateChange( long new_state ) = 0;
            //
            //
            virtual void Error( const char *msg, LONG code ) = 0;
            //
            // GetWindow() isn't a notification function, but it
            // provides a way to tell SimpleTapi what the
            // handle is of the window that will be the parent of
            // the configure line/call dialogs.
            //
            virtual HWND GetWindow() = 0;

};

#endif //#if !defined _SIMPLE_TAPI_H
```

Listing 15-3 contains the source code that implements class `SimpleTapi`. You include this source file in your project; it provides the base class functionality.

Listing 15-3: SimpleTapi.cpp

```
//
//  SimpleTapi.cpp
//
//  Source code from:
//
//  Serial Communications: Developer's Guide, 2nd
//  Edition by Mark Nelson, IDG Books, 1999
//
//  Please see the book for information on usage.
//
```

Chapter 15: Using Modems Under Win32 — TAPI

```cpp
// This file contains the complete implementation of
// the SimpleTapi class. SimpleTapi wraps up a limited
// subset of TAPI 1.4 using the SDK only for its modem
// control and call setup capabilities. This class
// contains several pure virtual functions that are needed
// for notification. Before you can use SimpleTapi, you will
// need to create a derived class that implements those
// functions. A simple example used in the book is
// MySimpleTapi, used in the Chapter 15 demo.
//
#include "SimpleTapi.h"

//
// The static m_Trace object is shared by all extant
// SimpleTapi devices. It provides a way to display trace
// messages. Calling the Open() and Close() methods of this
// object opens and closes a console window that displays
// messages.
//

ConStream SimpleTapi::m_Trace;

//
// The SimpleTapi constructor has to do a couple of obvious
// things, such as clearing the internal handles and setting
// up other variables. One of the things it does that isn't
// quite as obvious is to enumerate a list of modems that
// can be used with this class. That list is stored in the
// m_Devices vector, which is suitable for insertion into
// a drop-down list for selection by a user.
//

SimpleTapi::SimpleTapi()
{
    //
    // No line is active, no call is up
    //
    m_hLine = 0;
    m_hCall = 0;
    m_bCallHandleValid = false;
    DWORD version = TAPI_CURRENT_VERSION;
    //
    // Microsoft categorizes this as an obsolete
    // function, but for a class such as this, which is
    // using TAPI only for first-party call control (setting up
```

```
    // and tearing down your own calls), it is entirely
    // adequate. It registers your application and gets an
    // application handle in m_hLineApp, and it lets TAPI know
    // that you expect to see all notifications returned via your
    // static function SimpleTapi::CallBack().
    //
    DWORD device_count;
    LONG result = lineInitialize( &m_hLineApp,
                                  GetModuleHandle( NULL ),
                                  Callback,
                                  "TAPI Application",
                                  &device_count );
    m_Trace << "SimpleTapi::SimpleTapi() "
            << "lineInitialize() returned "
            << hex << result
            << dec << "\n";
    //
    if ( result != 0 ) {
        device_count = 0;
        m_hLineApp = NULL;
    }
    //
    // You are going to add all data modems to the list of
    // useful devices. That list is a vector that contains
    // object of type TapiDevices, a little class used here
    // to hold a device name and TAPI id.
    //
    // One thing seen in the call to lineGetDevCaps()
    // is a recurrent them in Microsoft SDKs. Instead of
    // just telling you how much space you will need to get the
    // information, you are expected to make one call just
    // to find out how much space is needed, then another call
    // to get the actual data. You can buck the system in this
    // case by grossly overestimating the space needed and
    // attempting to do it all in one call.
    //
    m_Devices.resize( device_count );
    int j = 0;
    for ( int i = 0 ; i < (int) device_count ; i++ ) {
        char temp[ 4096 ];
        LINEDEVCAPS *dev_caps = (LINEDEVCAPS *) temp;
        dev_caps->dwTotalSize  = 4096;
        result = lineGetDevCaps( m_hLineApp,
                                 i,
                                 version,
```

Chapter 15: Using Modems Under Win32 — TAPI

```cpp
                            0,
                            dev_caps );
        m_Trace << "SimpleTapi::SimpleTapi() "
                << "lineGetDevCaps("
                << i
                << ") returned "
                << hex
                << result
                << dec
                << "\n";
        //
        // To qualify as a useful device, you have to get
        // a successful return from lineGetDevCaps(), the
        // device has to be a data modem, and you have to have
        // a valid device name, as denoted by
        // dwLineNameOffset. If those conditions are met, you can
        // add the device to the list of devices.
        // The name is stored as a text string that may not
        // be null terminated. Fortunately, there is a string
        // constructor that easily accommodates this.
        //
        if ( result == 0 &&
             dev_caps->dwLineNameOffset != 0 &&
             (dev_caps->dwMediaModes & LINEMEDIAMODE_DATAMODEM ))
        {
            m_Devices[ j ].m_sName
                = string( temp + dev_caps->dwLineNameOffset,
                          dev_caps->dwLineNameSize );
            m_Trace << "Device name = "
                    << m_Devices[ j ].m_sName
                    << "\n";
            m_Devices[ j++ ].m_iDeviceNumber = i;
        }
    }
    m_Devices.resize( j );
    m_ReplyAction = NOTHING;
    m_dwPendingReplyCode = -1;
}

//
// The destructor shuts down TAPI by calling lineShutdown
// and passing the application handle. At that point, the TAPI DLL
// may be unloaded and its internal resources given back to the
// system.
//
```

```cpp
SimpleTapi::~SimpleTapi()
{
    LONG result = -1;
    if ( m_hLineApp != NULL )
        result = lineShutdown( m_hLineApp );
    m_Trace << "lineShutdown() result = "
            << hex
            << result
            << dec
            << "\n";
}

//
// Many of the things that TAPI is asked to do take a long
// time to accomplish. When you kick off one of these
// asynchronous events, your call to TAPI normally returns
// immediately. Later, as TAPI makes progress on your
// request, it sends notification to you via this callback
// function.
//
// Unfortunately for C++ programmers, callback functions
// in Windows are C functions with no concept of a this
// pointer. This means that the callback function has to
// be a static C++ member function. The good news is that
// TAPI makes provision for the callback function to carry
// around an untyped pointer that the user provides. In your
// case, that pointer is to a SimpleTapi object, giving you
// immediate access to the SimpleTapi object that is actually
// the source or target of the action.
//
void PASCAL SimpleTapi::Callback( DWORD hDevice,
                                  DWORD dwMsg,
                                  DWORD dwCallbackInstance,
                                  DWORD dwParam1,
                                  DWORD dwParam2,
                                  DWORD dwParam3 )
{
    SimpleTapi *tapi = (SimpleTapi *) dwCallbackInstance;
    //
    // Like most Windows callbacks, you have to examine the
    // message type to decide what to do. SimpleTapi
    // responds to only two message types: LINE_REPLY
    // and LINE_CALLSTATE. LINE_REPLY sends responses to
    // any of the three asynchronous commands: Make Call,
    // Drop Call, and Answer. LINE_CALLSTATE keeps
```

```
            // up with the changes in a call state. It is where you
            // get the the connected and disconnected events used in the
            // Chapter 15 demo program.
            //
            switch ( dwMsg )
            {
            case LINE_REPLY :
                m_Trace << "LINE_REPLY, request = "
                        << hex
                        << dwParam1
                        << ", result = "
                        << dwParam2
                        << dec
                        << "\n";
                //
                // If the user of this class made one of the three
                // asynchronous function calls, it is presumably
                // hanging around and waiting for an answer.
                // The answer is supplied by calling one of the three
                // notification functions. These three notification
                // functions aren't defined in the base class; they
                // have to be implemented in a derived class that
                // is designed to work with a specific application.
                //
                // For this section of code to
                // work, you need to be waiting for just one pending
                // action at a time. The pending action is stored
                // in the m_ReplyAction member of the object at the
                // time the asynchronous request is made, using an
                // enumerated type defined specifically in this
                // class. Nothing is done with the result code
                // that TAPI passes here; it is just passed along
                // to whoever is at the other end of the notification
                // call.
                //
                if ( dwParam1 == tapi->m_dwPendingReplyCode ) {
                    switch ( tapi->m_ReplyAction ) {
                    case NOTHING:
                        break;
                    case HANDLE_MAKE_CALL_RESULT :
                        tapi->HandleMakeCallResult( dwParam2 );
                        break;
                    case HANDLE_DROP_RESULT       :
                        tapi->HandleDropResult( dwParam2 );
                        break;
```

```
                case HANDLE_ANSWER_RESULT    :
                    tapi->HandleAnswerResult( dwParam2 );
                    break;
            }
            tapi->m_ReplyAction = NOTHING;
        }
        break;
    //
    // The only time things are really interesting in TAPI is
    // while a call is in progress. When that is the case,
    // TAPI gives periodic updates telling you how things are
    // going. As you progress through these actions, you
    // generate notification function calls that allow the
    // owner of the TAPI object to do the appropriate things.
    // There is a general notification function that always
    // gets called, then specific notification routines for
    // the all-important connected and disconnected events.
    //
    case LINE_CALLSTATE :
        tapi->NotifyCallStateChange( dwParam1 );
        //
        // if dwParam3 is nonzero for the LINE_CALLSATE
        // event, it is being used to inform you of your
        // privilege state for the given line. For the type
        // of call control you are performing here, you should
        // always be the owner of the call.
        //
        switch ( dwParam3 ) {
            case LINECALLPRIVILEGE_OWNER :
              m_Trace << "SimpleTapi is now the owner of handle = "
                      << hex << hDevice
                      << dec << "\n";
              break;
        }
        //
        // When the LINE_CALLSTATE message is received,
        // dwParam1 contains the new state of the call.
        // A few of these states are particularly exciting,
        // and lead to notification messages. Most of those
        // cases should be pretty obvious. The TAPI docs
        // show a few more states than are shown here, and
        // a full-featured class might implement more
        // notification messages to deal with them. The ones
        // used here are adequate for a simple dialing and
        // connecting app.
```

```
//
switch ( dwParam1 ) {
    //
    // A connected state can occur after either side
    // decides to answer a call. The host application
    // surely needs to be notified by this callback
    // routine.
    //
case LINECALLSTATE_CONNECTED:
    tapi->ConnectedEvent();
    break;
case LINECALLSTATE_IDLE:
case LINECALLSTATE_DISCONNECTED:
    //
    // When the call is dropped I call
    // TAPI to free up the m_hCall handle that was
    // associated with this call way back when it
    // was first initiated.
    //
    if ( tapi->m_hCall ) {
        HCALL temp_hcall = tapi->m_hCall;
        tapi->m_hCall = 0;
        tapi->DisconnectedEvent();
        m_Trace << "Call was dropped\n";
        lineDeallocateCall( temp_hcall );
        tapi->m_bCallHandleValid = 0;
        if ( tapi->m_ReplyAction == HANDLE_DROP_RESULT ) {
            tapi->HandleDropResult( 0 );
            tapi->m_ReplyAction = NOTHING;
        }
    }
    break;
    //
    // In SimpleTapi, you always answer an
    // incoming call that is being offered if the
    // line is open. So if you don't want to answer
    // an incoming call, don't open the line.
    // This creates the m_hCall handle, which
    // will be used for the duration of the call.
    // The call to lineAnswer() will almost always
    // be given asynchronously, with a result code
    // of > 0.
    //
case LINECALLSTATE_OFFERING :
    {
```

```
                    tapi->m_hCall = (HCALL) hDevice;
                    LONG result = lineAnswer( tapi->m_hCall,
                                              NULL,
                                              0 );
                    if ( result < 0 ) {
                      tapi->Error("Error returned from lineAnswer : ",
                              result );
                    } else if ( result == 0 ) {
                        m_Trace << "lineAnswer returned : "
                                << result
                                << "\n";
                       tapi->HandleAnswerResult( 0 );
                    } else {
                        tapi->m_ReplyAction = HANDLE_ANSWER_RESULT;
                        tapi->m_dwPendingReplyCode = result;
                    }
                }
                break;
            }
            tapi->m_lCallState = dwParam1;
        }
    }

    //
    // This static member function simply translates one of the
    // seemingly infinite TAPI error status codes to a string.
    // This makes the trace information easier to read.
    //
    string SimpleTapi::TranslateTapiError( LONG code )
    {
        switch (code ) {
        case LINEERR_ALLOCATED :
            return "LINEERR_ALLOCATED";
        case LINEERR_BADDEVICEID :
            return "LINEERR_BADDEVICEID";
        case LINEERR_BEARERMODEUNAVAIL:
            return "LINEERR_BEARERMODEUNAVAIL";
        case LINEERR_CALLUNAVAIL:
            return "LINEERR_CALLUNAVAIL";
        case LINEERR_COMPLETIONOVERRUN:
            return "LINEERR_COMPLETIONOVERRUN";
        case LINEERR_CONFERENCEFULL:
            return "LINEERR_CONFERENCEFULL";
        case LINEERR_DIALBILLING:
            return "LINEERR_DIALBILLING";
```

```
            case LINEERR_DIALDIALTONE:
                return "LINEERR_DIALDIALTONE";
            case LINEERR_DIALPROMPT:
                return "LINEERR_DIALPROMPT";
            case LINEERR_DIALQUIET:
                return "LINEERR_DIALQUIET";
            case LINEERR_INCOMPATIBLEAPIVERSION:
                return "LINEERR_INCOMPATIBLEAPIVERSION";
            case LINEERR_INCOMPATIBLEEXTVERSION:
                return "LINEERR_INCOMPATIBLEEXTVERSION";
            case LINEERR_INIFILECORRUPT:
                return "LINEERR_INIFILECORRUPT";
            case LINEERR_INUSE:
                return "LINEERR_INUSE";
            case LINEERR_INVALADDRESS:
                return "LINEERR_INVALADDRESS";
            case LINEERR_INVALADDRESSID:
                return "LINEERR_INVALADDRESSID";
            case LINEERR_INVALADDRESSMODE:
                return "LINEERR_INVALADDRESSMODE";
            case LINEERR_INVALADDRESSSTATE:
                return "LINEERR_INVALADDRESSSTATE";
            case LINEERR_INVALAPPHANDLE:
                return "LINEERR_INVALAPPHANDLE";
            case LINEERR_INVALAPPNAME:
                return "LINEERR_INVALAPPNAME";
            case LINEERR_INVALBEARERMODE:
                return "LINEERR_INVALBEARERMODE";
            case LINEERR_INVALCALLCOMPLMODE:
                return "LINEERR_INVALCALLCOMPLMODE";
            case LINEERR_INVALCALLHANDLE:
                return "LINEERR_INVALCALLHANDLE";
            case LINEERR_INVALCALLPARAMS:
                return "LINEERR_INVALCALLPARAMS";
            case LINEERR_INVALCALLPRIVILEGE:
                return "LINEERR_INVALCALLPRIVILEGE";
            case LINEERR_INVALCALLSELECT:
                return "LINEERR_INVALCALLSELECT";
            case LINEERR_INVALCALLSTATE:
                return "LINEERR_INVALCALLSTATE";
            case LINEERR_INVALCALLSTATELIST:
                return "LINEERR_INVALCALLSTATELIST";
            case LINEERR_INVALCARD:
                return "LINEERR_INVALCARD";
            case LINEERR_INVALCOMPLETIONID:
```

```
        return "LINEERR_INVALCOMPLETIONID";
case LINEERR_INVALCONFCALLHANDLE:
        return "LINEERR_INVALCONFCALLHANDLE";
case LINEERR_INVALCONSULTCALLHANDLE:
        return "LINEERR_INVALCONSULTCALLHANDLE";
case LINEERR_INVALCOUNTRYCODE:
        return "LINEERR_INVALCOUNTRYCODE";
case LINEERR_INVALDEVICECLASS:
        return "LINEERR_INVALDEVICECLASS";
case LINEERR_INVALDEVICEHANDLE:
        return "LINEERR_INVALDEVICEHANDLE";
case LINEERR_INVALDIALPARAMS:
        return "LINEERR_INVALDIALPARAMS";
case LINEERR_INVALDIGITLIST:
        return "LINEERR_INVALDIGITLIST";
case LINEERR_INVALDIGITMODE:
        return "LINEERR_INVALDIGITMODE";
case LINEERR_INVALDIGITS:
        return "LINEERR_INVALDIGITS";
case LINEERR_INVALEXTVERSION:
        return "LINEERR_INVALEXTVERSION";
case LINEERR_INVALGROUPID:
        return "LINEERR_INVALGROUPID";
case LINEERR_INVALLINEHANDLE:
        return "LINEERR_INVALLINEHANDLE";
case LINEERR_INVALLINESTATE:
        return "LINEERR_INVALLINESTATE";
case LINEERR_INVALLOCATION:
        return "LINEERR_INVALLOCATION";
case LINEERR_INVALMEDIALIST:
        return "LINEERR_INVALMEDIALIST";
case LINEERR_INVALMEDIAMODE:
        return "LINEERR_INVALMEDIAMODE";
case LINEERR_INVALMESSAGEID:
        return "LINEERR_INVALMESSAGEID";
case LINEERR_INVALPARAM:
        return "LINEERR_INVALPARAM";
case LINEERR_INVALPARKID:
        return "LINEERR_INVALPARKID";
case LINEERR_INVALPARKMODE:
        return "LINEERR_INVALPARKMODE";
case LINEERR_INVALPOINTER:
        return "LINEERR_INVALPOINTER";
case LINEERR_INVALPRIVSELECT:
        return "LINEERR_INVALPRIVSELECT";
```

```
case LINEERR_INVALRATE:
    return "LINEERR_INVALRATE";
case LINEERR_INVALREQUESTMODE:
    return "LINEERR_INVALREQUESTMODE";
case LINEERR_INVALTERMINALID:
    return "LINEERR_INVALTERMINALID";
case LINEERR_INVALTERMINALMODE:
    return "LINEERR_INVALTERMINALMODE";
case LINEERR_INVALTIMEOUT:
    return "LINEERR_INVALTIMEOUT";
case LINEERR_INVALTONE:
    return "LINEERR_INVALTONE";
case LINEERR_INVALTONELIST:
    return "LINEERR_INVALTONELIST";
case LINEERR_INVALTONEMODE:
    return "LINEERR_INVALTONEMODE";
case LINEERR_INVALTRANSFERMODE:
    return "LINEERR_INVALTRANSFERMODE";
case LINEERR_LINEMAPPERFAILED:
    return "LINEERR_LINEMAPPERFAILED";
case LINEERR_NOCONFERENCE:
    return "LINEERR_NOCONFERENCE";
case LINEERR_NODEVICE:
    return "LINEERR_NODEVICE";
case LINEERR_NODRIVER:
    return "LINEERR_NODRIVER";
case LINEERR_NOMEM:
    return "LINEERR_NOMEM";
case LINEERR_NOREQUEST:
    return "LINEERR_NOREQUEST";
case LINEERR_NOTOWNER:
    return "LINEERR_NOTOWNER";
case LINEERR_NOTREGISTERED:
    return "LINEERR_NOTREGISTERED";
case LINEERR_OPERATIONFAILED:
    return "LINEERR_OPERATIONFAILED";
case LINEERR_OPERATIONUNAVAIL:
    return "LINEERR_OPERATIONUNAVAIL";
case LINEERR_RATEUNAVAIL:
    return "LINEERR_RATEUNAVAIL";
case LINEERR_RESOURCEUNAVAIL:
    return "LINEERR_RESOURCEUNAVAIL";
case LINEERR_REQUESTOVERRUN:
    return "LINEERR_REQUESTOVERRUN";
case LINEERR_STRUCTURETOOSMALL:
```

```
                    return "LINEERR_STRUCTURETOOSMALL";
            case LINEERR_TARGETNOTFOUND:
                    return "LINEERR_TARGETNOTFOUND";
            case LINEERR_TARGETSELF:
                    return "LINEERR_TARGETSELF";
            case LINEERR_UNINITIALIZED:
                    return "LINEERR_UNINITIALIZED";
            case LINEERR_USERUSERINFOTOOBIG:
                    return "LINEERR_USERUSERINFOTOOBIG";
            case LINEERR_REINIT:
                    return "LINEERR_REINIT";
            case LINEERR_ADDRESSBLOCKED:
                    return "LINEERR_ADDRESSBLOCKED";
            case LINEERR_BILLINGREJECTED:
                    return "LINEERR_BILLINGREJECTED";
            case LINEERR_INVALFEATURE:
                    return "LINEERR_INVALFEATURE";
            case LINEERR_NOMULTIPLEINSTANCE:
                    return "LINEERR_NOMULTIPLEINSTANCE";
            }
            char buf[ 128 ];
            wsprintf( buf, "Unknown error code: %08lx", code );
            return buf;
    }

    //
    // This static member function simply translates one of the
    // TAPI call state codes to a string. This makes the trace
    // information easier to read.
    //
    string SimpleTapi::TranslateCallState( LONG state )
    {
        switch ( state ) {
        case LINECALLSTATE_IDLE:
            return "LINECALLSTATE_IDLE";
        case LINECALLSTATE_OFFERING:
            return "LINECALLSTATE_OFFERING";
        case LINECALLSTATE_ACCEPTED:
            return "LINECALLSTATE_ACCEPTED";
        case LINECALLSTATE_DIALTONE:
            return "LINECALLSTATE_DIALTONE";
        case LINECALLSTATE_DIALING:
            return "LINECALLSTATE_DIALING";
        case LINECALLSTATE_RINGBACK:
            return "LINECALLSTATE_RINGBACK";
```

```
        case LINECALLSTATE_BUSY:
            return "LINECALLSTATE_BUSY";
        case LINECALLSTATE_SPECIALINFO:
            return "LINECALLSTATE_SPECIALINFO";
        case LINECALLSTATE_CONNECTED:
            return "LINECALLSTATE_CONNECTED";
        case LINECALLSTATE_PROCEEDING:
            return "LINECALLSTATE_PROCEEDING";
        case LINECALLSTATE_ONHOLD:
            return "LINECALLSTATE_ONHOLD";
        case LINECALLSTATE_CONFERENCED:
            return "LINECALLSTATE_CONFERENCED";
        case LINECALLSTATE_ONHOLDPENDCONF:
            return "LINECALLSTATE_ONHOLDPENDCONF";
        case LINECALLSTATE_ONHOLDPENDTRANSFER:
            return "LINECALLSTATE_ONHOLDPENDTRANSFER";
        case LINECALLSTATE_DISCONNECTED:
            return "LINECALLSTATE_DISCONNECTED";
        case LINECALLSTATE_UNKNOWN:
            return "LINECALLSTATE_UNKNOWN";
        case -1:
            return "";
        }
        char buf[ 128 ];
        wsprintf( buf, "Unknown call state: %08lx", state );
        return buf;
}


//
// TAPI is kind enough to provide a thorough configuration
// dialog for the devices it supports, relieving programmers
// of the horrible prospect of writing customized dialogs
// for any device a user might care to employ. All you have
// to do to invoke this id is to provide a device id
// number and a parent window handle.
//
void SimpleTapi::ConfigureDevice( int index )
{
    int dev_id = m_Devices[ index ].m_iDeviceNumber;
    LONG result = lineConfigDialog( dev_id,
                                    GetWindow(),
                                    "comm/datamodem" );
    if ( result != 0 )
        ::MessageBox( GetWindow(),
                      "Something bad happened",
```

```cpp
                            "SimpleTapi Message",
                            MB_OK );
}

//
// Configuring phone calls is another fairly difficult task
// that TAPI takes on for you. All you have to do is pass in
// the id of the device and the phone number to be called.
// TAPI then creates a dialog that takes care of thinking
// about all sorts of dialing issues.
//
void SimpleTapi::ConfigureCall( int index, const string &number )
{
    int dev_id = m_Devices[ index ].m_iDeviceNumber;
    LONG result = lineTranslateDialog( m_hLineApp,
                                       dev_id,
                                       TAPI_CURRENT_VERSION,
                                       GetWindow(),
                                       number.c_str() );
    if ( result != 0 )
        Error( "Error returned from lineTranslateDialog : ",
               result );
}

//
// If a line is open and doesn't have a call in progress, you
// can use this routine to initiate a call. Looking into
// the call, you can see that you need to have a valid m_hLine
// handle to make the call, along with a number and a device
// id. The first part of the function calls
// lineTranslateAddress()to mangle the digit string into
// something that can be used to make the call. It needs the
// device id and the phone number to do that.
//
// After the phone number has been properly mangled,
// a LINECALLPARMS structure is set up and a call is made to
// lineMakeCall. That function can do one of three things: it
// might fail with an error; it might return immediately with a
// valid result; or, most likely, it will tell you that it doesn't
// have a result yet and you'll just have to wait. When that
// happens, set up the m_ReplyAction so that you know that
// something is expected and return.
//
// When you call this function or the other
// asynchronous functions in SimpleTapi, you never get
```

Chapter 15: Using Modems Under Win32 — TAPI

```cpp
// anything useful back, which is why these functions are all of
// type void. You wait for a response to come back from the
// callback notification routines.
//

void SimpleTapi::MakeCall( const string &number )
{
    //
    // This first call is another call with an
    // indeterminate requirement for the size of the
    // data structure. The Redmond way is to call it twice,
    // the first time you will fail but find out how much
    // space you need. The second time you call it with the
    // correct amount of space. This strategy is thwarted by
    // allocating a hugely excessive amount of space so
    // that it will never fail--probably.
    //
    char buf[ 4096 ];
    LINETRANSLATEOUTPUT *lto = (LINETRANSLATEOUTPUT *) buf;
    lto->dwTotalSize = 4096;
    LONG result = lineTranslateAddress( m_hLineApp,
                                        m_iDeviceId,
                                        TAPI_CURRENT_VERSION,
                                        number.c_str(),
                                        0,
                                        0,
                                        lto );
    if ( result != 0 ) {
        Error( "Error returned from lineTranslateAddress : ",
               result );
        return;
    }
    m_sNumber = string( buf + lto->dwDialableStringOffset,
                        lto->dwDialableStringSize );
    m_Trace << "Dial number = "
            << m_sNumber
            << "\n";
    LINECALLPARAMS lcp;
    memset( &lcp, 0, sizeof( LINECALLPARAMS ) );
    lcp.dwTotalSize = sizeof( LINECALLPARAMS );
    lcp.dwBearerMode = LINEBEARERMODE_VOICE;
    lcp.dwMediaMode = LINEMEDIAMODE_DATAMODEM;
    lcp.dwCallParamFlags = LINECALLPARAMFLAGS_IDLE;
    lcp.dwAddressMode = LINEADDRESSMODE_ADDRESSID;
```

```
            result = lineMakeCall( m_hLine,
                                   &m_hCall,
                                   m_sNumber.c_str(),
                                   0,
                                   &lcp );

        if ( result < 0 ) {
            Error( "Error returned from lineMakeCall : ", result );
            return;
        } else if ( result == 0 ) {
            m_Trace << "lineMakeCall returned : "
                    << TranslateTapiError( result )
                    << "\n";
            HandleMakeCallResult( 0 );
        } else {
            m_ReplyAction = HANDLE_MAKE_CALL_RESULT;
            m_dwPendingReplyCode = result;
        }
    }

    //
    // Dropping a call is easier than making one, but it still
    // has to be dealt with asynchronously. All you need to
    // get the whole thing going is a call handle, which you
    // pass to lineDrop(). It might generate an error or an
    // immediate response, but most likely it will let you
    // know that it will get back to you later via notification
    // Make a note of that by setting the m_ReplyAction
    // enumerated value to signify that you are waiting for a
    // drop result.
    //
    void SimpleTapi::DropCall()
    {
        LONG result = lineDrop( m_hCall,
                                NULL,
                                0 );
        if ( result < 0 ) {
            Error( "Error returned from lineDrop : ", result );
            return;
        } else if ( result == 0 ) {
            m_Trace << "lineDrop returned : "
                    << dec << result
                    << "\n";
            HandleDropResult( 0 );
        } else {
```

```
            m_ReplyAction = HANDLE_DROP_RESULT;
            m_dwPendingReplyCode = result;
        }
    }

//
// These three functions are all fundamentally the same.
// Each is called when a delayed response comes
// in to a previous action, which is either a request to
// make a call, answer a call, or drop a call.
//
// Each function does a small amount of internal
// class maintenance. Two of the functions then call a
// user notification function. The two notification functions
// are pure virtual, so they must be defined in a derived
// class.
//
// Why doesn't the Answer handler have a notification
// routine? SimpleTapi doesn't have an Answer call that the
// user of the class can call. Instead, it automatically
// answers any incoming call. The user doesn't ever have
// to worry about a response to an Answer call. A more
// complete TAPI class wouldn't automatically answer calls;
// it would notify users of incoming offering states and
// let the user make some sort of answer response.
//
void SimpleTapi::HandleMakeCallResult( DWORD result )
{
    m_Trace << "lineMakeCall returned (delayed) : "
            << TranslateTapiError( result )
            << "\n";
    if ( result == 0 )
        m_bCallHandleValid = true;
    else {
        Error( "Delayed error returned from lineMakeCall : ",
               result );
        m_bCallHandleValid = false;
    }
    MakeCallResult( m_bCallHandleValid );
}

void SimpleTapi::HandleAnswerResult( DWORD result )
{
    m_Trace << "lineAnswer returned (delayed) : "
            << result
```

```
                    << "\n";
    if ( result == 0 )
        m_bCallHandleValid = true;
    else {
        Error( "Delayed error returned from lineAnswer : ",
                result );
        m_bCallHandleValid = false;
    }
}

void SimpleTapi::HandleDropResult( DWORD result )
{
    m_Trace << "lineDrop returned (delayed) : "
            << result
            << "\n";
    if ( result != 0 )
        Error( "Delayed error returned from lineDrop : ",
                result );
    DropCallResult( result == 0 );
}

//
// After creating the TAPI object, the user has to open a
// line to do anything useful. This is done with a
// call to lineOpen(). That call expects a valid device
// id, which the caller provides, and an application handle,
// which was created when the object was first built.
//
// The device id is retrieved from the m_Devices[] vector,
// which received copies of all device names and ids when you
// iterated through the list at creation time.
//
// If you open the line successfully, the m_hLine member will
// have a valid handle and you will be ready to make and
// accept calls.
//
int SimpleTapi::OpenLine( int index )
{
    m_iDeviceId = m_Devices[ index ].m_iDeviceNumber;
    LONG result = lineOpen( m_hLineApp,
                            m_iDeviceId,
                            &m_hLine,
                            TAPI_CURRENT_VERSION,
                            0,
                            (DWORD) this,
```

```
                            LINECALLPRIVILEGE_OWNER,
                            LINEMEDIAMODE_DATAMODEM,
                            NULL );
    if ( result != 0 )
        Error( "Error returned in WaitFoprCall from lineOpen : ",
               result );
    else
        NotifyCallStateChange( LINECALLSTATE_IDLE );
    return result;
}


//
// Before shutting down, you need to close the line.
// This is also a good way to make sure that you don't
// accidentally answer any incoming calls. TAPI function
// lineClose() takes care of this immediately.
//
int SimpleTapi::CloseLine()
{
    LONG result = lineClose( m_hLine );
    m_hLine = 0;
    if ( result < 0 )
        Error( "Error returned from lineClose : ", result );
    else {
        m_Trace << "lineClose returned : "
                << result
                << "\n";
        NotifyCallStateChange( -1 );
    }
    return result;
}


//
// This function is a little deceptive. After a call is put
// through to the connected state, you can take the resulting
// handle and treat it as a port handle, using it for normal
// serial port functions. In the Chapter 15 demo, you took
// the resulting port handle and turned it into a Win32Port,
// proceeding to use it as a terminal emulator.
//
// When you get this port handle, you bear a certain measure
// of responsibility for it. When you are done using it, you
// have to specifically close it with a call to
// CloseHandle(), or the books in the OS won't balance.
//
```

```
HANDLE SimpleTapi::GetPortHandle()
{
    //
    // This is another one of those calls that take an
    // unknown number of bytes. If you drastically overestimate
    // the amount needed, you may not have to deal with the
    // possibility of failure.
    //
    char temp[ 4096 ];
    VARSTRING *vs = (VARSTRING *) temp;
    vs->dwTotalSize = 4096;

    LONG result = lineGetID( 0,                      //hLine
                             0,                      //dwAddressID
                             m_hCall,                //hCall
                             LINECALLSELECT_CALL,    //dwSelect
                             vs,
                             "comm/datamodem" );
    if ( result < 0 ) {
        Error( "Error returned from lineGetID : ", result );
        return 0;
    }
    HANDLE *p = (HANDLE *) ((LPSTR) vs + vs->dwStringOffset);
    return *p;
}
//EOF SimpleTapi.cpp
```

Listing 15-4 contains the declaration for class MySimpleTapi. A program using class SimpleTapi has to create a derived class that creates specific versions of the virtual functions defined in the base class.

Listing 15-4: MySimpleTapi.h

```
//
//   MySimpleTapi.h
//
//   Source code from:
//
//   Serial Communications: Developer's Guide, 2nd
//   Edition by Mark Nelson, IDG Books, 1999
//
//   Please see the book for information on usage.
//
// This class contains the entire definition and
// implementation of MySimpleTapi. This is a concrete class
```

```
// that is derived from SimpleTapi, and implements all of
// the virtual functions needed to implement the class.
// The implementations here provide notification that is
// specific to the Chapter 15 demo program and will
// probably need to be modified to work with your program.
//
// This class performs all notification by sending Windows
// messages to a notification window. That window is passed
// in as an argument to the constructor and is stored in
// member m_hNotificationWindow.
//
// A second member is used to hold the phone number that is
// going to be dialed. In the Chapter 15 demo program,
// this member is modified by a dialog box invoked from the
// main window's menu.
//

#ifndef _MY_SIMPLE_TAPI_H
#define _MY_SIMPLE_TAPI_H

#include "SimpleTapi.h"

//
// These are the three windows messages that are sent to the
// notification window.
//
const int WM_TAPI_CONNECTED_NOTIFY      = WM_USER + 0x1002;
const int WM_TAPI_DISCONNECTED_NOTIFY   = WM_USER + 0x1003;
const int WM_TAPI_STATE_CHANGE_NOTIFY   = WM_USER + 0x1004;

class MySimpleTapi : public SimpleTapi
{
public :
    //
    // The constructor gets a copy of the handle of the
    // notification window. That is where all messages
    // are sent.
    //
    MySimpleTapi( HWND hwnd )
    {
        m_hNotificationWindow = hwnd;
    }
    //
    // This is a handy place to keep track of the number
    // that will be used to dial out.
```

```
        //
        string m_NumberToDial;

protected :
        HWND m_hNotificationWindow;
        //
        // The base class uses this virtual function when
        // it creates the configuration dialog. GetWindow() is
        // supposed to return the window that should be the parent
        // window of the dialogs. In this particular
        // implementation, it is assumed that the notification window
        // will be the same as the parent window for these
        // dialogs.
        //
        virtual HWND GetWindow()
        {
            return m_hNotificationWindow;
        }
        //
        // This event is called by the base class when a
        // connection is completed, whether it is from an
        // incoming or outgoing call. When the connection is
        // made, the important step of getting the
        // handle and using it to open the port used by the
        // terminal emulator is taken. After that port is opened, you
        // are in business and will actually pass characters in and
        // out from the communications port.
        //
        // In addition to doing this work, you also
        // send a notification message to the window associated
        // with this object. In the case of the Chapter 15 demo
        // program, that takes care of updating the menu and
        // displaying a message indicating that you are now
        // connected.
        //
        void ConnectedEvent()
        {
            AnsiTapiTerm *pTerm;
            pTerm = (AnsiTapiTerm *)
                        GetWindowLong( m_hNotificationWindow, 0 );
            HANDLE h = GetPortHandle();
            if ( h )
                pTerm->OpenPort( h );
            SendMessage( m_hNotificationWindow,
                        WM_TAPI_CONNECTED_NOTIFY,
```

```
                            0,
                            0 );
}
//
// This is the other important routine that is called
// by the base class. This routine is called when a connection
// is dropped for whatever reason, including the
// possibility that you initiated a disconnect. When
// this happens you have to immediately close the port being
// used by the terminal emulator. The Tapi32Port
// takes care of actually closing the handle that was
// used when the port was opened.
//
// In addition to doing this work, you also
// send a notification message to the window associated
// with this object. In the case of the Chapter 15 demo
// program, that takes care of updating the menu and
// displaying a message indicating that you are now
// disconnected.
//
void DisconnectedEvent()
{
    AnsiTapiTerm *pTerm;
    pTerm = (AnsiTapiTerm *)
            GetWindowLong( m_hNotificationWindow, 0 );
    pTerm->ClosePort();
    SendMessage( m_hNotificationWindow,
                 WM_TAPI_DISCONNECTED_NOTIFY,
                 0,
                 0 );
}
//
// The base class calls this routine whenever the TAPI
// state of the line changes. An informative
// trace print is performed and a notification message is sent
// to the main window of the application. That call should
// take care of updating UI features, such as the menu,
// that need to be dealt with in the new state.
//
void NotifyCallStateChange( long new_state )
{
    m_Trace << "Changing to state "
            << TranslateCallState( new_state )
            << endl;
    SendMessage( m_hNotificationWindow,
```

```cpp
                            WM_TAPI_STATE_CHANGE_NOTIFY,
                            0,
                            0 );
    }
    //
    // At this time, error messages just get a printout in
    // the trace window. Because they are pretty rare, a message
    // box might be a better choice than the trace window.
    //
    void Error( const char *msg, LONG code )
    {
        m_Trace << "ERROR: "
                << msg
                << TranslateTapiError( code )
                << endl;
    }
    //
    // When a call is made to MakeCall() with a phone number,
    // immediate results aren't had. Instead, some things
    // happen, TAPI waits a while, and eventually
    // the result is known. When that happens, this
    // notification routine is called, and the main application
    // then knows what is going on. There is nothing in
    // the main task that needs this information, so the info is
    // just dumped to the trace window.
    //
    void MakeCallResult( bool result )
    {
        m_Trace << "MakeCall() returned "
                << TranslateTapiError( result )
                << endl;
    }
    //
    // Exactly the same comments apply here as in the previous
    // function.
    //
    void DropCallResult( bool result )
    {
        m_Trace << "DropCall() returned "
                << TranslateTapiError( result )
                << endl;
    }
};

#endif //#ifndef _MY_SIMPLE_TAPI_H
```

Class `Win32Port` is nearly perfect for this application, but it does need a couple of minor adjustments. These are dealt with by deriving a class called `Tapi32Port` from `Win32Port`. The derived class's only differing behavior is in the manner in which the port is constructed. Unlike `Win32Port`, this class doesn't want to set up most of the port parameters in its construct. Things such as baud rate, handshaking, and so forth have already been set up by TAPI, so the constructor has to leave most of the port parameters unchanged.

Listings 15-5 and 15-6 have the declarations and definitions for this class.

Listing 15-5: Tapi32Port.h

```
//
// Tapi32Port.h
//
// Source code from:
//
// Serial Communications: Developer's Guide, 2nd
// Edition by Mark Nelson, IDG Books, 1999
//
// Please see the book for information on usage.
//
// This file contains the declaration for class Tapi32Port.
// This class is derived from Win32Port and uses nearly
// every bit of code from the base class with one notable
// exception. The normal constructor for Win32Port expects
// to open a port by name. When you are using TAPI, you don't
// get to open the port by name. Instead, TAPI gets the port
// all set up and ready to use, and then hands you a handle to
// the port. Tapi32Port() has an alternative constructor that
// takes that handle and inserts it into the Win32 object,
// without trying to open a port with a call to CreateFile(),
// which is inapporpriate for TAPI.
//

#ifndef _TAPI32_PORT_H
#define _TAPI32_PORT_H

#include "Win32Port.h"

class Tapi32Port : public Win32Port
{
public :
```

```
        Tapi32Port( HANDLE h );

};

#endif // #ifndef _TAPI32_PORT_H
```

Listing 15-6: Tapi32Port.cpp

```
//
//  Tapi32Port.cpp
//
//  Source code from:
//
//  Serial Communications: Developer's Guide, 2nd
//  Edition by Mark Nelson, IDG Books, 1999
//
//  Please see the book for information on usage.
//
// This file contains the complete implementation of
// class Tapi32Port. This class is derived from Win32Port
// and it uses nearly every bit of code from the base class
// with one notable exception. The normal constructor for
// Win32Port expects to open a port by name. When you are
// using TAPI, you don't get to open the port by name. Instead,
// TAPI gets the port all set up and ready to use, and then hands
// you a handle to the port. The constructor defined for this
// class takes that handle and inserts it in the Win32
// object without trying to open a port with a call to
// CreateFile(), which is inappropriate for TAPI.
//

#include <process.h>
#include "Tapi32Port.h"

Tapi32Port::Tapi32Port( HANDLE handle )
: Win32Port()
{
//
// Win32Port has to share the debug output with the parent class.
// To determine where your first line starts, call the
// FormatDebugOutput() function from your parent class.
//
    first_debug_output_line = RS232::FormatDebugOutput();
    debug_line_count = FormatDebugOutput();
    port_name = (RS232PortName) -1;
    m_hPort = handle;
```

```
    m_dwErrors = 0;           //Clear cumulative line status errors
    m_iBreakDuration = 0;     //No break in progress, initialize to 0
    SetLastError( 0 );        //Clear any Win32 error from this thread
    read_settings();          //Read and save current port settings
    saved_settings = settings; // Needed only because the base class
                              //dumps the saved settings in debug
                              //output
    //Init timeouts to ensure your overlapped reads work
    COMMTIMEOUTS timeouts = { 0x01, 0, 0, 0, 0 };
    SetCommTimeouts( m_hPort, &timeouts );
    SetupComm( m_hPort, 500, 500 ); //set buffer sizes
    error_status = RS232_SUCCESS;    //clear current class error
    //
    // Because the port opened properly, you're ready to start the
    // input and output threads. Before they start, create the
    // five Win32 events that will be used to pass requests to
    // the threads. The only argument passed to the
    // thread initialization is a pointer to this. The thread
    // needs that to find all of the data in the Win32Port
    // object that it will be manipulating.
    //
    m_hKillInputThreadEvent = CreateEvent(NULL,FALSE,FALSE,NULL);
    m_hKillOutputThreadEvent = CreateEvent(NULL,FALSE,FALSE,NULL);
    m_hWriteRequestEvent = CreateEvent( NULL, FALSE, FALSE, NULL );
    m_hReadRequestEvent = CreateEvent( NULL, FALSE, FALSE, NULL );
    m_hBreakRequestEvent = CreateEvent( NULL, FALSE, FALSE, NULL );
    m_hInputThread = _beginthread(InputThread, 0, (void *) this);
    m_hOutputThread = _beginthread(OutputThread, 0, (void *) this);
}

//EOF Tapi32Port.cpp
```

Listings 15-7 and 15-8 provide the declarations and definition of the `ConStream` debugging class.

Listing 15-7: ConStream.h

```
//
// ConStream.h: interface for the ConStream class.
//
//    Source code from:
//
//    Serial Communications: Developer's Guide, 2nd
//    Edition by Mark Nelson, IDG Books, 1999
//
// The ConStream class creates a C++ ostream object that can
```

```cpp
// be used in Win32 C++ programs to write to a console window,
// often for debugging purposes. This utility code is included
// as is with no further documentation.
//

//
// This header file defines the entire interface to the ConStream
// class. ConStream is a class that works like a standard
// iostream and writes to a console window when created in a
// Win32 application. You can have only one console window
// open at a time, so only one ConStream class is ordinarily
// created in an application.
//

#if !defined( _CONSTREAM_H )
#define _CONSTREAM_H

//
// ConStream uses the standard C++ libraries that ship
// with Visual C++ 5.0 and later, not the older libraries with the
// .h suffix. The library requires modification to work
// with the older libraries.
//
#include <windows.h>

#include <iostream>
#include <fstream>

using namespace std;

//
// The ConStream class is derived from what is normally thought of
// as ostream, which means you can use standard insertion
// operators to write to it. Of course, this includes insertion
// operators for user-defined classes. At all times, a ConStream
// object is either writing out to to a FILE  object attached to
// the NUL device, or a FILE object attached to a console
// created using the Win32 API. Which of the two is in use depends
// on whether the ConStream object has had its Open() or
// Close() method called.
//
class ConStream
   : public basic_ostream<char>
{
public :
```

```
    ConStream();
    virtual ~ConStream();
    void Open();
    void Close();
    bool IsOpen(){
        return m_hConsole != INVALID_HANDLE_VALUE;
    }
protected :
    HANDLE m_hConsole;
    basic_filebuf<char> *m_FileBuf;
    basic_filebuf<char> m_Nul;
    FILE *m_fNul;
    FILE *m_fConsole;
};

#endif // !defined( _CONSTREAM_H )
```

Listing 15-8: ConStream.cpp

```
//
// ConStream.cpp: implementation of the ConStream class.
//
//   Source code from:
//
//   Serial Communications: Developer's Guide, 2nd
//   Edition by Mark Nelson, IDG Books, 1999
//
// The ConStream class creates a C++ ostream object that can
// be used in Win32 C++ programs to write to a console window
// for debugging purposes. This utility code is included
// as is with no further documentation.

//
// Implementation of this class requires that you link in the IO.H
// and FCNTL.H header files from the standard C library. You
// should be able to substitute <cio> and <cfcnt> for these two
// includes. stdafx.h is here because the code is being used in an
// MFC application.
//

#include <io.h>
#include <fcntl.h>

#include "ConStream.h"

//
```

```
// The ConStream constructor initializes the object to point to
// the NUL device. It does this by calling two consecutive
// constructors. First, the member variable m_Nul is initialized
// with a FILE object created by opening device "nul", the bit
// bucket. Second, the base class constructor is called with a
// reference to m_Nul, which is an ofstream object. This sets up
// ConStream so that it will direct its output to the given file.
//

ConStream::ConStream() : m_Nul( m_fNul = fopen( "nul", "w" ) ),
                         basic_ostream<char>( &m_Nul )
{
    m_FileBuf = 0;
    m_hConsole = INVALID_HANDLE_VALUE;
}

//
// The ConStream destructor always has to close the m_fNul file
// object, which was created in the constructor. Even if the
// Open() method is called and the bit bucket isn't being used,
// the file object is still using memory and a system file handle.
//
// If the ConStream object was opened with a call to member
// function Open(), you have to call the Win32 API function
// FreeConsole() to close the console window. If the console
// window was open, you also call the C fclose() function on the
// m_fConsole member.
//
ConStream::~ConStream()
{
    delete m_FileBuf;
    if ( m_hConsole != INVALID_HANDLE_VALUE ) {
        FreeConsole();
        fclose( m_fConsole );
    }
    fclose( m_fNul );
}

//
// Opening the stream means doing these things:
//    1) Opening a Win32 console using the Win32 API.
//    2) Getting an OS handle to the console.
//    3) Converting the OS handle to a C stdio file handle.
//    4) Converting the C stdio file handler to a C FILE object.
//    5) Attaching the C FILE object to a C++ filebuf.
```

```
//   6) Attaching the filebuf object to this.
//   7) Disabling buffering so that you see your output in real
//      time.
//
void ConStream::Open()
{
    if ( m_hConsole == INVALID_HANDLE_VALUE ) {
      AllocConsole();
      m_hConsole = GetStdHandle( STD_OUTPUT_HANDLE );
      int handle = _open_osfhandle( (long) m_hConsole, _O_TEXT );
      m_fConsole = _fdopen( handle, "w" );
#ifdef _UNICODE
      m_FileBuf = new basic_filebuf<wchar_t>( m_fConsole );
#else
      m_FileBuf = new basic_filebuf<char>( m_fConsole );
#endif
      init( m_FileBuf );
      setf(ios::unitbuf);
    }
};

//
// Closing the ConStream is considerably simpler. Just use the
// init() call to attach the following to the NUL file stream
// and then close the console descriptors.
//
void ConStream::Close()
{
    if ( m_hConsole != INVALID_HANDLE_VALUE ) {
        init( &m_Nul );
        FreeConsole();
        fclose( m_fConsole );
        m_hConsole = INVALID_HANDLE_VALUE;
    }
};

// EOF ConStream.cpp
```

Listing 15-9 contains the resource definitions for the sample program.

Listing 15-9: Chapt15.rc

```
#include "resource.h"

#define APSTUDIO_READONLY_SYMBOLS
```

```
/////////////////////////////////////////////////////////////////
/////////
//
// Generated from the TEXTINCLUDE 2 resource.
//
#include <Windows.h>
/////////////////////////////////////////////////////////////////
/////////
#undef APSTUDIO_READONLY_SYMBOLS

/////////////////////////////////////////////////////////////////
/////////
// English (U.S.) resources

#if !defined(AFX_RESOURCE_DLL) || defined(AFX_TARG_ENU)
#ifdef _WIN32
LANGUAGE LANG_ENGLISH, SUBLANG_ENGLISH_US
#pragma code_page(1252)
#endif //_WIN32


/////////////////////////////////////////////////////////////////
/////////
//
// Menu
//

IDR_MENU MENU DISCARDABLE
BEGIN
    POPUP "&File"
    BEGIN
      MENUITEM "E&xit\tAlt-X",          ID_FILE_EXIT
    END
    POPUP "Ta&pi"
    BEGIN
      MENUITEM "Open Trace &Window",    ID_TAPI_OPEN_TRACE_WINDOW
      MENUITEM "Create &Tapi Object",   ID_TAPI_CREATE_TAPI_OBJECT
      MENUITEM "Open Line",             ID_TAPI_OPEN_LINE, GRAYED
      MENUITEM "&Place Call",           ID_TAPI_PLACE_CALL, GRAYED
      MENUITEM SEPARATOR
      MENUITEM "Configure &Line",       ID_TAPI_CONFIGURE_LINE,
                                        GRAYED
      MENUITEM "Configure &Call",       ID_TAPI_CONFIGURE_CALL,
                                        GRAYED
      MENUITEM "Set Phone Number",      ID_TAPI_SET_PHONE_NUMBER,
                                        GRAYED
```

```
        END
END


#ifdef APSTUDIO_INVOKED
/////////////////////////////////////////////////////////////////
/////////
//
// TEXTINCLUDE
//

1 TEXTINCLUDE DISCARDABLE
BEGIN
    "resource.h\0"
END

2 TEXTINCLUDE DISCARDABLE
BEGIN
    "#include <Windows.h>\0"
END

3 TEXTINCLUDE DISCARDABLE
BEGIN
    "\r\n"
    "\0"
END

#endif    // APSTUDIO_INVOKED


/////////////////////////////////////////////////////////////////
/////////
//
// Dialog
//

IDD_GET_PHONE_NUMBER DIALOG DISCARDABLE  0, 0, 186, 63
STYLE DS_MODALFRAME | WS_POPUP | WS_CAPTION
CAPTION "Set Phone Number"
FONT 8, "MS Sans Serif"
BEGIN
    DEFPUSHBUTTON       "OK",IDOK,34,42,50,14
    PUSHBUTTON          "Cancel",IDCANCEL,102,42,50,14
    EDITTEXT            IDC_PHONE_NUMBER,71,15,108,12,ES_AUTOHSCROLL
    LTEXT               "Phone Number:",IDC_STATIC,7,16,57,11
```

```
END


///////////////////////////////////////////////////////////////
/////////
//
// DESIGNINFO
//

#ifdef APSTUDIO_INVOKED
GUIDELINES DESIGNINFO DISCARDABLE
BEGIN
    IDD_GET_PHONE_NUMBER, DIALOG
    BEGIN
        LEFTMARGIN, 7
        RIGHTMARGIN, 179
        TOPMARGIN, 7
        BOTTOMMARGIN, 56
    END
END
#endif    // APSTUDIO_INVOKED

#endif    // English (U.S.) resources
///////////////////////////////////////////////////////////////
/////////



#ifndef APSTUDIO_INVOKED
///////////////////////////////////////////////////////////////
/////////
//
// Generated from the TEXTINCLUDE 3 resource.
//


///////////////////////////////////////////////////////////////
/////////
#endif    // not APSTUDIO_INVOKED
```

> `AnsiTapiTerm.cpp` and `AnsiTapiTerm.h` are substantially identical to `AnsiWinTerm.cpp` and `AnsiWinTerm.h` from Chapter 13, so they are not being reproduced here. They are present in the Chapter 15 directory on the CD that accompanies this book.

Summary

Working with modems can be quite difficult without good support from the operating system. While Microsoft was selling MS-DOS, it didn't offer any OS help to programmers. Fortunately, with the advent of Windows, Microsoft saw fit to provide TAPI, the Telephony API. TAPI insulates programmers from many of the details relating to modem setup, control, and call management.

This chapter creates a class called `SimpleTapi` that goes a step further by insulating you from some of the more difficult aspect of TAPI function calls and notification. A simple demo program built with TAPI demonstrates a final result that is actually a very comprehensive dialing and terminal program.

Chapter 16

File Transfers and ZMODEM

IN THIS CHAPTER

- The history of the protocols
- An overview of ZMODEM
- A file transfer and the FileTransfer class defined
- The Zmodem class defined
- A test program
- The CRC classes
- The source code

PROGRAMMERS WHO DEVELOP RS-232-based applications will sooner or later want to transfer files between computers. This chapter looks at how that is accomplished by using a typical file transfer protocol. The ZMODEM protocol implemented here was at one time the most popular way to send files back and forth between electronic BBS systems. You may well still find it useful in your applications.

Protocol History

In years past, the primary function of modems and communications software was to perform file transfers. At one time, the amount of new software transferred every day from BBS systems and information services was stupendous. Hobbyists today are still preoccupied with sampling as many files as possible, but the World Wide Web and ftp sites are probably the primary vehicles for that.

But there are still plenty of times when you will want to transfer files via an RS-232 connection, and the Web isn't always there when you need it. At those times, *file transfer protocols* will be your best friends.

In the late 1970s, modems were just beginning to break into the newly emerging desktop computer market. In response to a lack of established standards for transferring files, Ward Christensen developed what came to be known as the XMODEM file transfer protocol. Enhancements to XMODEM came quickly, resulting in a whole family of protocols, including YMODEM and XMODEM-1K.

The existence of standard protocols that could be used to move files around easily helped fuel the growth of telecommunications, and helped to create the world of distributed computing that we are now comfortably living in.

XMODEM was not a carefully designed protocol, resulting from intensive research and experimentation. It was much closer to being a weekend project meant as a personal utility. Given this original purpose it has held up as well over time. While it is certainly capable, XMODEM does have a few serious limitations, including:

- Protocol control characters aren't wrapped up in packets, making the protocol vulnerable to noise and single character errors. The *ACK* and *NAK* characters that are sent as responses to blocks aren't surrounded by framing and check characters, so a spurious ACK or EOT at the right time could lead a sender to falsely conclude that a successful transfer occurred.

- XMODEM requires a completely clear 8-bit channel. The channel needs to pass all control characters, including XON, XOFF, CR, and so on. Many older timesharing systems (such as some UNIX systems) are not able to meet this requirement. Their device drivers cause certain protocol characters to disappear.

- BL:The short packet lengths used by the XMODEM family, either 128 or 1024 bytes, result in inefficient use of the channel because each packet has to be acknowledged before the next one is sent. This is particularly a problem over packet switched networks, which are often used as a backbone for RS-232 data.

Enter ZMODEM

In 1986, the packet-switched network-provider Telenet commissioned Chuck Forsberg of Omen Technology to develop a new file transfer program that could be used effectively over its network. The result was ZMODEM, which consisted of both a public domain program and a new protocol. The name ZMODEM might imply that it was a lineal descendant from XMODEM and YMODEM, but this is not really the case. ZMODEM was a completely new protocol that had very little in common with either of those earlier systems.

ZMODEM has several important characteristics that make it superior to other popular protocols:

- All transactions are protected by either a 16-bit or 32-bit CRC, which greatly reduces the possibility of false ACKs and NAKs.

- The protocol works properly over communications links that absorb some or all control characters, although an 8-bit channel is still required.

- Data is sent in a continuous stream of packets, without waiting for acknowledgments. The protocol only stops sending when the receiver interrupts to report an error. Sending data in a continuous stream drastically improves transmission throughput on packet switched networks or buffered modems.

- ZMODEM labels data packets uniquely to assist in error recovery. The receiver always knows where a block of data is supposed to be stored in a file. This labeling also helps in file transfer recovery, which allows a user to restart an aborted transfer at the place where it was interrupted.

Because of these superior characteristics, ZMODEM has become a very popular protocol choice today. This popularity makes ZMODEM the natural choice to use as an illustrative example in this book.

Why ZMODEM?

Given a finite amount of available space to discuss file transfer protocols, ZMODEM is the natural choice to make. XMODEM and YMODEM are considerably simpler, and should be relatively easy for a programmer to develop using the tools presented elsewhere in this book. They have been well documented in various magazines and books before, so this book wouldn't be breaking any new ground covering them.

ZMODEM is somewhat more of a challenge to implement because it is a much more complex protocol. However, it is not only clearly superior to other protocols, it also is available nearly universally. Many UNIX and other timesharing machines that don't have XMODEM software available are capable of supporting ZMODEM.

When Chuck Forsberg developed the ZMODEM program for Telenet, he published a set of programs that were placed in the public domain. These programs, commonly referred to as RZ and SZ, were capable of transferring files using ZMODEM on a number of UNIX hosts, and were later adapted to VMS. This public domain code has been adapted here to work under MS-DOS, and has been converted to a more object-oriented architecture. While my implementation may look very different from the original RZ/SZ source, it is still driven by core code that is fundamentally identical to that originally published by Chuck Forsberg. (Forsberg copyrighted later versions of these programs and those later versions are in wide circulation.)

Omen Technology (www.omen.com) later released versions of RZ and SZ that incorporate proprietary ZMODEM enhancements, such as Run Length Encoding and Variable Length Headers. These extensions are not supported here, although ambitious programmers could certainly add them to the Zmodem class without too much difficulty.

Omen Technology additionally sells many different communications programs targeted for various platforms. Professional-YAM is a package that is a consistent leader in efficient, albeit terse, communications software. Professional-YAM is supported for a variety of host machines and operating systems. DSZ is a ubiquitous MS-DOS shareware program that performs ZMODEM file transfers. The release of this program by Omen Technology allowed BBS operators whose software did not work with ZMODEM to begin using the protocol via external protocol hooks.

Both the complete specification for ZMODEM and the RZ/SZ programs are included with the source code for this book. Versions of both that are more current are available from Omen Technology.

An Overview of ZMODEM

ZMODEM differs from XMODEM in that *all* information transferred between the sender and receiver is contained in packets, referred to in ZMODEM as *frames*. Even simple protocol messages, such as acknowledgments, are bundled in packets, giving ZMODEM good protection against accidental protocol signals.

A ZMODEM frame has two components. Each frame starts with a *header*, which identifies the frame type, and carries up to 4 bytes of information. The 4 bytes are arbitrarily referred to as ZF0 through ZF3 (at positions 3 through 0, respectively!). A stream of *data subpackets*, which are blocks of unadorned data, can optionally follow a header.

Data subpackets can each contain up to 1024 bytes of data, and are followed by a CRC value for authentication. There is no limit to the number of data subpackets that can be attached to a header, which means all of the data for a file can be sent in a single frame.

The 18 frame types defined for ZMODEM are defined in the next section. Following those definitions is an explanation of the methods and options used to encode and send the various frame types.

ZMODEM frame types

ZMODEM supports quite a variety of frame types. Not all of these frame types are required for a simple implementation of ZMODEM; some are used for more sophisticated error recovery and transfer mechanisms. The complete list is given here.

ZRQINIT=0   This frame is sent by the ZMODEM sender when it starts up. It is a request for the receiver to send its *ZRINIT* frame, which will start the file transfer. The *ZRQINIT* frame header can be used to trigger an auto download in a receiving program. This capability is demonstrated in the example program for this chapter.

ZRQINIT frames do not transmit any data subpackets. The header byte ZF0 contains the constant *ZCOMMAND* if the

	sender is attempting to send a command to the receiver (this feature is not supported in the `Zmodem` class developed here); otherwise, it contains a 0.
ZRINIT=1	This frame is sent by the receiver to indicate that it is ready to receive files from the sender. It can either be sent spontaneously, or in response to a ZRQINIT frame. This frame has four bytes of capability information packed into the header. `ZF0` and `ZF1` have the following bits that can be set or cleared depending on the capabilities of the receiver:
CANFDX=1	The receiver is capable of true full duplex operation, meaning it can send and receive data simultaneously. This capability is taken for granted in the desktop world, but it is by no means universal.
CANOVIO=2	The receiver can receive data while writing to the disk. This capability is needed to take full advantage of ZMODEM's streaming nature.
CANBRK=4	The receiver can send a break signal.
CANRLE=8	The receiver can decode RLE frames. This capability is not supported in the `Zmodem` class used here. (Note that Omen Technology may consider this to be a proprietary extension to ZMODEM.)
CANLZW=16	The receiver can uncompress data sent in the UNIX *compress* format. This capability is not supported in the `Zmodem` class used here.
CANFC32=32	The receiver can accept 32-bit CRCs.
ESCCTL=64	The receiver needs to see all control cha-racters escaped, instead of just `XON`, `XOFF`, and a few others.
	`ZF2` and `ZF3` contain the size of the receiver's input buffer. If this value is nonzero, it means the receiver can't work in full streaming mode. It will, instead, need to stop receiving while it writes data to disk.
ZSINIT=2	This frame can be optionally sent to the receiver by the sender after the ZRINIT frame is processed. It provides the receiver with some information regarding the sender's capabilities. Two bits are packed into `ZF0`:
TESCCTL=64	This bit is used to indicate that the transmitter expects *all* control characters to be escaped.

TESC8=128   This bit is used to indicate that the transmitter expects the eighth bit be escaped. This capability is not fully implemented by ZMODEM but is included in the specification for future enhancements.

A single data subpacket follows the ZSINIT header. This subpacket contains a null-terminated attention string of no more than 32 bytes. This attention string is used to awaken the sender when an error occurs.

ZACK=3   This frame type is used to acknowledge ZSINIT and ZCHALLENGE frames, as well as data subpackets followed by the ZCRCQ or ZCRCW terminators. If the response is to a ZCHALLENGE frame, the four header-flag bytes are filled with a copy of the four header bytes sent with the ZCHALLENGE header.

ZFILE=4   This is the frame type used to initiate the actual transfer of a file. This frame consists of a header followed by a single data subpacket. The subpacket contains the file information. The four header bytes are packed with various flags relating to the file about to be transferred. ZF0 contains the file conversion option; ZF1 contains an optional management option; ZF2 has the transport option; and ZF3 contains extended options.

This frame has the greatest number of options to consider, and requires the longest explanation. Most of the options here are idiosyncratic and rarely used. For our purposes, the important items transmitted in the ZFILE frame are the file name, length, and, optionally, the date. The rest of the options are detailed here for completeness.

ZF0 CONVERSION OPTIONS

ZF0 is set to one of the following values, which dictate the conversion method used when storing the file data:

ZCBIN=1   A binary transfer, data is stored with no conversion.

ZCNL=2   Convert the received end of line to use the local conventions. This option can be useful when sending ASCII files between UNIX and MS-DOS systems.

ZCRECOV=3   Recover from an interrupted file transfer. The receiver checks to see if the destination file is shorter than the file to be sent. If it is, the file transfer can be resumed at the point where it was aborted.

ZF1 MANAGEMENT OPTION

ZF1 is set to one of these values:

Chapter 16: File Tranfers and ZMODEM

ZMNEWL=1   Overwrite the destination file only if the source is newer or longer.

ZMCRC=2   Compare the CRC values of the source and destination. If the values are different, transfer the file; otherwise, skip the transfer.

ZMAPND=3   Append the source file to the destination.

ZMCLOB=4   Unconditionally write over the destination file if it exists.

ZMNEW=5   If the destination file exists, only overwrite it if the source is newer.

ZMDIFF=6   If the destination file exists, only overwrite it if the files have different lengths or dates.

ZMPROT=7   This option is the opposite of ZMCLOB. It tells the receiver to only transfer the file if the destination file does not exits.

ZF2 TRANSPORT OPTION

ZF2 is set to one of these options:

ZTLZW=1   The data being sent has been processed via the UNIX *compress* program. This option is not supported in the Zmodem class.

ZTRLE=3   The data has been compressed using Run Length Encoding. This part of the specification was superseded in later versions of ZMODEM by the creation of proprietary RLE frames.

The missing option 2 belongs to ZCRYPT, an encryption option that was defined in the original ZMODEM specification, but was never implemented.

ZF3 EXTENDED OPTIONS

ZF3 is a bitmap with extended options conditionally set. The only option defined in the ZMODEM specification is the ZTSPARS option, which allows for special processing of "sparse files." This option is defined in the ZMODEM specification, but is rarely, if ever, supported.

THE DATA SUBPACKET

The data subpacket that follows the ZFILE header contains information about the file about to be transferred. The following fields are found consecutively in the data frame:

Filename: The filename is a null terminated string.

Length: The length of the file, given as the ASCII representation in decimal

Date:	The date and time in UNIX format. This means the number is a count of the current time measured in seconds since January 1, 1970. A value of 0 is used to indicate that the date is unknown. The number is given is given as the ASCII representation in octal.
Mode:	The file mode bits expressed in UNIX format, once again as an octal number represented in ASCII. The mode is set to 0 for files sent from MS-DOS systems.
S/N:	A serial number for the transmitting program.
Files left:	The number of files remaining to be sent.
Bytes left:	The total number for bytes left for the transfer.

Every field following the file name is optional. Most implementations support the file length and date, but generally no more. The separators used in this field are bit quirky. The file name is terminated by a '\0' character, the remaining fields are separated by spaces.

ZSKIP=5	This is a nice simple frame. It is sent when the receiver elects to not receive a file that the sender has specified in a ZFILE frame. It has no data stored in the four header bytes, and doesn't send any data subpackets.
ZNAK=6	This is used to indicate that the last header was invalid for any number of reasons.
ZABORT=7	The receiver sends this frame to indicate that the session should be aborted. This frame is usually sent in response to a user-initiated cancellation.
ZFIN=8	This frame is sent when the sender has no more files to transmit. The receiver responds with a ZFIN frame of its own before exiting. An oddity of the ZMODEM specification has the sender issue the two characters — OO — after receiving the ZFIN sent by the receiver.
ZRPOS=9	This frame can be sent at any time by the receiving program. A 4-byte offset is packed into the four bytes of header information. The offset is a request to the receiver to start sending data from that particular position in the file. This can be sent at the start of the file transfer if a recovery is being attempted, or during a transfer if an error is detected in the incoming data stream.
ZDATA=10	The four header bytes of this frame contains the file offset of the data to follow. Any number of data subpackets can follow.
ZEOF=11	This indicates that all of the file data has been sent. The four header bytes contain the offset of the EOF mark. This option adds reliability to the protocol, protecting against the possibility of a premature EOF on the destination file.

ZFERR=12	The sender or receiver can send this if a read/write error occurs while accessing the file. Receiving this frame type causes the session to abort.
ZCRC=13	This frame is sent by the receiver to request the 32-bit CRC for the file that has been indicated with the ZFILE frame. The sender sends a ZCRC frame with the CRC-32 packed into the four header bytes.
ZCHALLENGE=14	This frame is used by the sender to test challenge the receiver. A random number is packed into the four data bytes of the header. The receiver is then responsible for echoing the same four digits back in another ZCHALLENGE frame. This frame type is used to help prevent malicious downloading of files to a system without the consent of the receiver.
ZCOMPL=15	This frame is sent by the receiver when a ZCOMMAND request has been fulfilled. The four header bytes contain a status code returned from the command.
ZFREECNT=17	The sender can request a count from the receiver of free space available on the default volume. The receiver responds with a ZACK frame with the free space in bytes packed into the four header bytes.
ZCOMMAND=18	This frame gives the sender the ability to send a command to the receiving system. If ZF0 is set to a 0, the receiver executes the command and returns a ZCOMPL frame when done. If ZF0 is set to ZCACK1, the receiver returns a ZCOMPL packet immediately.

Header formats

In principle, if you know the definitions for all of the frame types, and how they interact, you have enough know-how to perform ZMODEM file transfers. In practice, this doesn't give you quite enough information. You also need to know the low-level format used to create headers and data subpackets, as well as the techniques used to encode various control characters.

A ZMODEM frame is composed of a header, optionally followed by a stream of data subpackets. The header itself is relatively simple. It has four basic components:

- ◆ A header-type byte that indicates which of the three possible header types is being used.

- ◆ A frame-type byte that indicates which of the 18 possible frame types is being encoded.

- The four data bytes.
- The header CRC.

Unfortunately for ZMODEM implementers, headers come in three different varieties. A ZMODEM header can be encoded as:

- A hexadecimal header, which is encoded using only printable ASCII characters. If data subpackets follow this header, they are sent in binary, not hex.
- A 16-bit CRC binary header. The data subpackets following this header are also be sent in straight binary for more efficient use of bandwidth.
- A 32-bit CRC binary header. Data subpackets are also sent in binary, using a 32-bit CRC for reliability.

ZMODEM software would be considerably easier to implement if there was only a single header type to contend with, and it isn't entirely clear that these three types offer much more flexibility. But it's too late to change the specification, so there are three different routines for sending a header instead of just one.

HEX HEADERS

Hex headers are sent using printable ASCII characters, with the single exception of the ZDLE character (Control X, CAN, or ASCII 23). The format is:

```
ZPAD ZPAD ZDLE B frame-type ZF3 ZF2 ZF1 ZF0 CRC-1 CRC-2 CR LF XON
```

The leading ZPAD character is defined as the '*'. To detect the start of a frame, the receiver uses the ZPAD ZPAD ZDLE sequence. The character B is used to identify a hex header. After the B character, all of the characters until the trailing CR/LF/XON sequence are hex encoded, meaning a two-character printable value is used for each byte instead of the pure binary values.

The receiver uses hex headers exclusively when responding to the sender. The sender also uses hex headers for any frame that doesn't have any data subpackets that follow the header. The two forms of binary headers are normally used when data subpackets are included in the frame. However, even in that case, the sender can use hex headers if desired, at some small expense of efficiency.

When a remote sender starts a ZMODEM transfer, it first sends a ZRQINIT frame to the receiver, asking for a ZRINIT frame. On an IBM-PC, this header looks something like this:

```
**↑B00000000000000
```

The up-arrow is actually the ZDLE character as displayed using the IBM-PC character set. Not visible are the three trailing characters: a carriage return, line feed, and XON character. The XON character protects the remote end against being shut down by a spurious XOFF generated by noise. This string is the one used by terminal programs to autodetect the start of a ZMODEM file transfer. The 16-bit CRC applies to just the frame type and the four flag bytes.

16- AND 32-BIT CRC BINARY HEADERS

Hex headers aren't the most efficient way to send your data. To package information more efficiently, ZMODEM senders use *binary headers*. In binary headers, the information is packaged as single binary characters instead of hex characters, subject to ZMODEM control character encoding.

The format for the two headers are shown below:

```
16 bit: ZPAD ZDLE A frame-type ZF3 ZF2 ZF1 ZF0 CRC-1 CRC-2

32 bit: ZPAD ZDLE C frame-type ZF3 ZF2 ZF1 ZF0 CRC-1 CRC-2 CRC-3 CRC-4
```

The 32-bit CRC offers slightly higher reliability at the expense of some efficiency. When data subpackets follow the header, the format of the subpackets is determined by the format of the header. Data subpackets following 16-bit binary headers (or, optionally, the hex headers) will use 16-bit CRC checking. Data subpackets following 32-bit binary headers will use 32-bit CRC checking. 32-bit CRC headers can only be used if the receiver sent the *CANFC32* bit in the ZRINIT header. The 16- or 32-bit CRC values apply to the frame type and the position flags.

Data subpacket formats

ZMODEM gains some of its greatest efficiency by virtue of the way it sends data subpackets. Immediately following the header, the ZMODEM sender can send as many data subpackets as it wishes. A data subpacket consists of up to 1024 binary data characters, with some control characters encoded, followed by a ZDLE and a subpacket termination character.

There are four different subpacket termination characters, each of which has a slightly different purpose. All of them indicate that a 16- or 32-bit CRC value will immediately follow. The four different characters also have additional meanings:

ZCRCE (h)   This character signals the end of the data subpacket, and the end of the frame. When the receiver sees this at the end of a subpacket, it knows that it needs to start looking for a header next. This subpacket is typically used at the end of a file.

ZCRCG (i)   This character terminates the current subpacket, but indicates that there will be at least another subpacket to follow. The receiver needs to check the CRC value that follows and then start receiving a new subpacket.

ZCRCQ (j)   This character terminates the current subpacket, but not the frame. Unlike ZCRCE, however, the receiver has to do more than just verify the checksum of the subpacket. In addition, the receiver needs to send a ZACK frame to indicate that the subpacket was received successfully. This is typically sent periodically by the sender to force a response from the receiver. This helps detect a lost connection.

ZCRCW (k)   This character terminates both the subpacket and the frame. After verifying the CRC, the receiver can expect a new header to start the next frame. This termination character also indicates that the receiver needs to send a ZACK to verify the receipt of the subpacket and the frame.

During normal file transfer, a ZMODEM sender could just send the entire file contents in a series of data subpackets, using ZCRCG to terminate every subpacket except the last. The last subpacket could be terminated with a ZCRCE, which would cause the receiver to acknowledge correct receipt of the entire frame. After receiving a ZACK, the sender would be assured that all of the data was properly received.

Under many circumstances, however, the sender may want to elicit ZACK frames on a more regular basis. One example is when the sender is transmitting through a sophisticated modem with a large internal buffer. Some of these modems can buffer up as much as 20K worth of data. If the data subpackets are all being sent through a modem like this, the sender can load up the modem and get far out of sync with the receiver. If an error occurs, and the receiver issues a ZNAK, it may have to wade through 20K of data before getting caught back up with the sender. This leads to inefficient error recovery.

To solve this problem, the ZMODEM sender can use a predefined window size to regulate the synchronization between the sender and receiver. By issuing a ZCRCQ terminator once every 4K bytes or so, the sender can then wait for an acknowledgment before advancing to the next 4K window.

Encoding

When sending binary data, either as part of a header or a data subpacket, ZMODEM needs to encode certain characters that act as control characters to the transmission medium. The characters encoded this way are:

```
CAN (ZDLE)
DLE          DLE + 0x80
XON          XON + 0x80
XOFF         XOFF + 0x80
```

In addition, ZMODEM accommodates a special Telenet escape sequence, @-CR-@, by escaping CR and CR + 0x80 if the previous character was an @. Finally, if the receiver needs it, *all* control characters can be escaped if the `TESCCTL` bit is set in the `ZRINIT` frame.

Escaped characters will all be specially encoded by sending first a ZDLE, then the character ORed with 0x40, converting them to printable characters. The ZMODEM receiver can then just check for incoming ZDLE characters, and if the following character is between 0x40 and 0x5f, it converts it to its original character for by clearing the 0x40 bit.

If the character following the ZDLE is greater than 0x5f, it is normally one of the four subpacket termination characters. However, ZMODEM also has special encoding for the noncontrol `DEL` character, ASCII 0x7f. Because the terminal interface on many operating systems treats `DEL` as a backspace character, ZMODEM can encode both 0x7f and 0xff using a ZDLE escape sequence. In these cases, 0x7f is encoded as ZDLE followed by 'l' (the numeral 1,) and 0xff is encoded as ZDLE followed by 'm'. Our `Zmodem` class doesn't have to encode these characters this way, but it does have to decode them if they are encountered in the input stream.

Finally, when reading data, ZMODEM ignores incoming `XON` and `XOFF` characters, because they can't occur naturally in the incoming data stream.

The ZDLE escape encoding used by ZMODEM can exact a heavy performance penalty on file transfers and represents perhaps the weakest point of the protocol. A file that contains data that must be heavily escaped can take substantially longer to transfer using ZMODEM as compared to another streaming protocol such as YMODEM-G.

Odds and ends

ZMODEM has a couple of loose ends that don't fit naturally into the frame/header/subpacket hierarchy. One of the first oddities is that ZMODEM senders typically send a single ASCII test line ahead of their ZRQINIT frame. The text of this line is `rz\r`. On a system using a command-line interface this line has the potential to start the RZ program if it has not already been invoked. While this is certainly not a good general-purpose way to awaken a receiver, it doesn't do any harm so most implementations leave it in.

An even stranger convention is that of sending the `OO` string after the ZFIN frame is seen from the ZMODEM receiver. The ZMODEM specification says these characters stand for *Over and Out*. The exact purpose of this Dick Tracy reference is never made clear, but once again, because it does no harm most implementations leave it in place.

Finally, it is possible to abort a ZMODEM transfer with a simple string of five consecutive `CAN` characters. While this is not a legitimate ZMODEM frame, it does make sense to have it as an option. First, if a ZMODEM sender or receiver already thinks it is in the middle of receiving a data subpacket, it may ignore a ZABORT or ZFIN frame. However, it will recognize the five consecutive CAN characters, regardless of the state of its present input. Second, this is an easy sequence to type from the keyboard, allowing a manual abort of a ZMODEM transfer. Finally, the same sequence can be used to abort an XMODEM or YMODEM file transfer in progress, which gives it a nice universal touch.

A File Transfer

All these frames are put together in a relatively straightforward manner to perform a file transfer. Despite the complexity of ZMODEM at the lowest level, it has an appealing simplicity from a high level point of view. To send a single file requires just nine frames. Each additional file adds just another four frames to the total.

The following table shows the steps that are necessary to perform the most minimal possible file transfer. This might be exactly how you would want ZMODEM to operate for two computers that were directly connected and didn't have to contend with high error rates, and large buffer sizes.

The simplest ZMODEM file transfers are shown as follows:

Sender	Receiver	Frame Type
The sender requests that the receiver send its initialization parameters.		ZRQINIT
	The receiver responds with a frame that gives most of its capabilities.	ZRINIT
The sender provides the name of the file to be transferred, along with some optional data regarding its length, date, and so on.		ZFILE
	The receiver requests the file data starting at a certain location. For a new file this would normally be location 0.	ZPOS
A single data frame containing all of the file's contents is sent. All data subpackets are terminated with ZCRCG except the last, which is terminated with ZCRCE.		ZDATA

Sender	Receiver	Frame Type	Once
all of the data has been sent, the end of file is indicated.		ZEOF	
	The receiver indicates it is ready to start over with a new file.	ZRINIT	
The sender indicates that it wants to terminate the session. If the sender had more files to send, it would send another ZFILE frame.		ZFIN	
	The receiver agrees and the connection is broken.	ZFIN	

ZMODEM transfers that occur using modems in somewhat noisy environments will be modified somewhat from this simple model. The place where the major change takes place is in the way the data subpackets are sent in the ZDATA frame. Instead of terminating every data subpacket with ZCRCG, a subpacket is terminated with ZCRCQ every 4Kbytes or so.

Terminating subpackets with ZCRCQ provokes a ZACK response from the receiver. The sender can use this response to pace itself, insuring that it doesn't get too far ahead of the receiver by simply waiting for a ZACK before it sends another subpacket terminated with ZCRCQ.

Additional frames are sent in the event that a CRC error occurs while reading a data subpacket. When an error occurs, the receiver issues a ZRPOS frame with an offset indicating where it would like the sender to resume. After sending the ZRPOS frame, the receiver then has to wait while data stacked up in the buffers is flushed. Eventually, a new ZDATA frame will start and its position should match that most recently requested.

With the large number of frame types available in the ZMODEM specification, there are quite a large number of possible interactions in the model. Most of them are not explicitly defined in the specification, which means that they are defined by default by the operation of the RZ and SZ programs. Fortunately, most programs that use ZMODEM for file transfers don't attempt to do much more than what is shown in the simplest transaction in the above table.

The FileTransfer Class

While this book only has source code for a single file transfer protocol, it still makes sense to try and leave room for more possibilities in the high-level design. I left room for such possibilities by defining a high-level virtual base called `FileTransfer`. This base class defines most of the elements needed by all file transfers and leaves the specific definitions to the derived classes.

```
class FileTransfer {
    protected :
        virtual void error( char *fmt, ... );
        virtual void status( char *fmt, ... );
        RS232 *port;
        FILE *file;
        long file_length;
        long byte_count;
        int file_count;
        char file_name[ 128 ];
        char buffer[ 1025 ];
    public :
        virtual int Send( char *files[] ) = 0;
        virtual int Receive( char *file ) = 0;
};
```

The public interface to the `FileTransfer` class is nice and simple. It has a single function called to send files and another to receive files. The `Send()` function takes an array of file names as an argument, making it possible for file transfer protocols to send multiple files. Some protocols, such as XMODEM, will be capable of sending only a single file, but they will still be capable of using the filename array as an acceptable way to get the name. The `Receive()` function also takes a filename, enabling it to receive a file using protocols such as XMODEM or perhaps an ASCII Capture mode. Protocols such as ZMODEM or Kermit that transfer file names along with data simply ignore this argument.

The protected members of this class contain data elements and functions that are needed by virtually every protocol that could be derived from these classes.

```
virtual void error( char *fmt, ... )
virtual void status( char *fmt, ... )
```

The derived class that is to provide status information to the user uses these two functions. The status routine should be called periodically, enabling an application program to update any progress information that is maintained for the file transfer. The error routine is called whenever some anomalous event takes place. The presumption here is that the application program will probably want to handle these two things differently.

Both of these functions are expected to be able to handle a variable number of arguments, which will be formatted by one of the functions in the *printf* family.

```
RS232 *port
```

This is a pointer to the port where the file transfer will take place. The `Zmodem` constructor takes this port as its only argument.

```
FILE *file
```

This is a pointer to the handle for the file currently being transferred, whether for input or output.

```
long file_length
```

This is the expected length of the file being transferred. In some cases, such as with an XMODEM receiver, the file transfer routines may not know what the expected file length is. In these cases, the length should be set to -1.

```
long byte_count
```

This is the current count of bytes that have been transferred.

```
int file_count
```

This is a count of the number of files that have been transferred so far.

```
char file_name[ 128 ]
```

This buffer contains a copy of the name of the file presently being transferred.

```
char buffer[ 1025 ]
```

This buffer holds a block of data that has either been read from the file in preparation for sending, or is being accumulated in preparation for being written to the file. None of the protocols being used here have a need for a buffer longer than this, although many can get by with less. It may be preferable to design the class so that this is a void pointer, and the actual size is determined when the constructor executes. Doing it this way just makes the class somewhat simpler.

The Zmodem Class

The Zmodem class is directly derived from the FileTransfer class. It makes use of all the protected elements in the base class and has its own virtual functions to implement the Send() and Receive() routines. It has a single constructor, which takes an RS-232 port object as its only argument.

Using the Zmodem class is very simple. After opening a port, the Zmodem object can be constructed at any time. Once it exists, a simple call to Send() can be made by creating an array of file names to send, and the transfer routine takes over. Receive() is called with a nominal argument of 0, because the file name is transferred with each file.

The virtual status() and error() routines, as defined in this class, send their output directly to stdout. A production-quality program would want to create derived versions of these functions that use a windowed interface to present the information in a more friendly fashion.

The Test Program

The test program for this class, TESTZM.CPP, creates a simple PC8250 object that should work with most PC communications ports and then acts as a simple terminal emulator. A short menu can be accessed with the Esc key, offering you the option to send files, receive files, or exit. The program also will autodetect the start of a Zmodem download, so you can normally start your receive by just starting the download from the remote end. This test program is shown in Listing 16-1.

Listing 16-1: The ZMODEM Test Program

```
// ********************* START OF TESTZM.CPP *********************
//
// This is the test program for the Zmodem file transfer class.
// It is a simple terminal emulator that has a menu accessed via
// the Escape key. The Send function just sends a couple of
// predefined files. The Receive function will accept whatever
// the remote end sends.
//
#include <stdio.h>
#include <string.h>
#include <ctype.h>
#include "rs232.h"
#include "pc8250.h"
#include "zmodem.h"
#include "ascii.h"

int main()
```

```c
{
    int c;
    char *files[] = { "TESTZM.EXE", "ZMODEM.H", 0 };
    PC8250 port( COM1, 38400L, 'N', 8, 1 );
    Zmodem *zmodem;

    port.XonXoffHandshaking( 1 );
    zmodem = new Zmodem( &port );
    setbuf( stdout, 0 );
    for ( ; ; ) {
        if ( kbhit() ) {
            c = getch();
            if ( c == 27 ) {
                printf( "\n(Escape Receive Send) Command: " );
                c = getch();
                printf( "\n" );
                switch( toupper( c ) ) {
                    case 'R' :
                        printf( "Starting to receive...\n" );
                        zmodem->Receive( 0 );
                        printf( "\nReceive complete\n" );
                        break;
                    case 'S' :
                        printf( "Starting to send...\n" );
                        zmodem->Send( files );
                        printf( "\nSend complete\n" );
                        break;
                }
                if ( c == 27 || toupper( c ) == 'E' )
                    break;
            } else
                port.Write( c );
        }
        c = port.Read();
        if ( c == CAN ) {
            char buf[ 21 ];
            port.Read( buf, 20, 500 );
            if ( strnicmp( buf, "B00000000000000\r\n", 17 ) == 0 )
                zmodem->Receive( 0 );
            else {
                putc( CAN, stdout );
                for ( int i = 0 ; buf[ i ] ; i++ )
                    putc( buf[ i ], stdout );
            }
        } else if ( c > 0 )
```

```
            putc( c, stdout );
    }
    return 0;
}

// ********************* END OF TESTZM.CPP *********************
```

Listing 16-2 shows the make file to use to build this program. As with all the other make files, you need to be sure that the compiler line you will use in the first four lines of the file has the leading '#' removed. When you've accomplished that, you can build the file by typing:

```
make -f testzm.mak
```

If you are using Microsoft C++, enter:

```
nmake -f testzm.mak
```

Listing 16-2: TESTZM.MAK — The Make File for Testing ZMODEM

```
# ********************* START OF TESTZM.MAK *********************
#
# This is the make file use to create TESTZM.EXE.
# To create the executable, just type:
#
#              make -f testzm.mak
#
#CC = tcc -w
CC = bcc -w
#CC = ztc -b
#CC = cl /W4 /AL

FILES = pc8250.obj isr_8250.obj queue.obj pcirq.obj

.cpp.obj:
  $(CC) -c $<

testzm.exe : testzm.obj zmodem.obj crc.obj rs232.obj msdos.obj
$(FILES)
             $(CC) testzm.obj zmodem.obj crc.obj rs232.obj msdos.obj
$(FILES)

# ********************* END OF TESTZM.MAK *********************
```

The CRC Classes

This chapter touched very lightly the subject of CRC calculations. Rather than go into a detailed discussion of the techniques needed to develop CRC values, I instead present source code that supports both the 16-bit and 32-bit CRCs used by ZMODEM. Incidentally, the 16-bit CRC calculation used here is identical to the one used for XMODEM and YMODEM, so this code may be useful elsewhere.

Listing 16-3 shows the header file for the two `CRC` classes, `Crc16` and `Crc32`. Each class has a single constructor, which sets the `CRC` to an initial value. Each class has two other public functions: `update()`, which updates the `CRC` to account for a new data byte, and `value()`, which returns the current CRC value. The `update()` function takes advantage of the inline function capability of C++. Because the `update()` function is normally called repeatedly in a tight loop, it is an excellent candidate for inlining.

Listing 16-3 is on the CD-ROM.

The CRC functions here use a table lookup method, which should be relatively efficient. The coefficient tables used to calculate the CRC values are initialized when the first CRC object is created and are left in place for the duration of the program.

Listing 16-3: CRC.H

```
// ********************* START OF CRC.H *********************
//
// This header file contains the definitions for the two CRC
// classes, Crc16 and Crc32.
//

#ifndef _CRC_DOT_H
#define _CRC_DOT_H

// The two CRC objects create 16- and 32-bit CRC values using the
// polynomials used by ZMODEM. The calculations are table driven,
// with the table being initialized by the constructor at
// run-time. The constructor assigns an initial value to the CRC,
// and then it is updated character by character.

class Crc32 {
    private :
```

```
            static unsigned long table[ 256 ];
            static int initialized;
            unsigned long crc;
        public :
            Crc32( unsigned long init_value );
            void update( int c );
            unsigned long value( void ){ return crc; }
};

inline void Crc32::update( int c )
{
    crc = table[ ( (int) crc ^ ( c & 0xff ) ) & 0xff ] ^
          ( ( crc > 8 ) & 0x00FFFFFFL );
}

class Crc16 {
    private :
        static unsigned short table[ 256 ];
        static int initialized;
        unsigned short crc;
    public :
        Crc16( unsigned short init_value );
        void update( int c );
        unsigned short value( void ){ return crc; }
};

inline void Crc16::update( int c )
{
    crc = (unsigned short)
            ( table[ (( crc > 8 ) & 0xff ) ] ^
              ( crc << 8 ) ^ ( c & 0xff ) );
}

#endif // #ifndef _CRC_DOT_H

// *********************** END OF CRC.H ***********************
```

Listing 16-4 contains the main body of the code for both the `Crc16` and `Crc32` classes. This module has to be added to any project that uses these classes.

Listing 16-4: CRC.CPP — Supporting Code for the CRC Classes

```
// ********************* START OF CRC.CPP *********************
//
// This file contains the supporting code for the two CRC classes,
```

```cpp
// Crc16 and Crc32.
//

#include "crc.h"

unsigned long Crc32::table[ 256 ];
int Crc32::initialized = 0;

Crc32::Crc32( unsigned long init_value )
{
    if ( !initialized ) {
        int i;
        int j;
        unsigned long coeff;

        for ( i = 0; i < 256 ; i++ ) {
            coeff = i;
            for ( j = 0; j < 8; j++ ) {
                if ( coeff & 1 )
                    coeff = ( coeff > 1 ) ^ 0xEDB88320L;
                else
                    coeff >= 1;
            }
            table[ i ] = coeff;
        }
        initialized = 1;
    }
    crc = init_value;
}

unsigned short Crc16::table[ 256 ];
int Crc16::initialized = 0;

Crc16::Crc16( unsigned short init_value )
{
    if ( !initialized ) {
        int i;
        int j;
        int k;
        int crc;

        for ( i = 0 ; i < 256 ; i++ ) {
            k = i << 8;
            crc = 0;
```

```
                for ( j = 0 ; j < 8 ; j++ ) {
                    if ( ( crc ^ k ) & 0x8000 )
                        crc = ( crc << 1 ) ^ 0x1021;
                    else
                        crc <<= 1;
                    k <<= 1;
                }
                table[ i ] = (unsigned short) crc;
            }
            initialized = 1;
        }
        crc = init_value;
    }

    // ********************* END OF CRC.CPP *********************
```

Source Code

The Zmodem source code is shown in Listings 16-5 through 16-7. The three files listed are ZMODEM.H, _ZMODEM.H, and ZMODEM.CPP. The first header file is the public definitions file, which needs to be included in any module that creates a Zmodem object. The second header file contains constants and definitions used internally. Finally, the C++ file contains all of the code to implement the Zmodem class.

ON THE CD The three above-noted files are on the accompanying CD-ROM.

Listing 16-5: ZMODEM.H

```
// ********************* START OF ZMODEM.H *********************

// This header file has the class definitions needed for an
// application program to perform Zmodem file transfers.
// The Zmodem class is derived from the virtual base class
// FileTransfer. The public interface to the Zmodem class
// consists of just three functions: a constructor and
// functions to send and receive files.

#ifndef _ZMODEM_DOT_H
#define _ZMODEM_DOT_H
```

```cpp
class FileTransfer {
    protected :
        virtual void error( char *fmt, ... );
        virtual void status( char *fmt, ... );
        RS232 *port;
        FILE *file;
        long file_length;
        long byte_count;
        int file_count;
        char file_name[ 128 ];
        char buffer[ 1025 ];

    public :
        virtual int Send( char *files[] ) = 0;
        virtual int Receive( char *file ) = 0;
};

const int ZMAXHLEN = 16;    // Max header information length
const int ZATTNLEN = 32;    // Max length of attention string

class Zmodem : public FileTransfer {
private :
    int WakeUpSender( void );
    int ReceiveFiles( void );
    int ReceiveSingleFile( void );
    void SendHexHeader( int len, int type, char *hdr );
    void SendBinaryHeader( int length, int type, char * header );
    int ReadHeader( char *header );
    int ReadDataFrame( char *buf, int length );
    int ReadDataFrameCRC32( char *buf, int length );
    int ReadDataFrameCRC16( char *buf, int length );
    void SendAttentionString( void );
    void AckZFIN( void );
    int OpenInputFile( char *data );
    void PackLongIntoHeader( long header_data );
    long UnpackHeaderIntoLong( char *header );
    void SendHexEncodedChar( int c );
    void SendEncodedChar( int c );
    void SendChar( int c ) { port->Write( (char) c, 30000L ); }
    void SendZFIN( void );
    int ReadHexHeaderCRC16( char *header );
    int ReadBinaryHeaderCRC16( char *header );
    int ReadBinaryHeaderCRC32( char *header );
```

```
        int ReadEncodedByte( void );
        int ReadUnencodedByte( void );
        int ReadHexByte( void );
        int ReadChar( long timeout );
        int GetRinitHeader( void );
        int SendSingleFile( char *name );
        int SendFileContents( void );
        void SendDataFrame( char *buffer, int length, int frameend );
        int SyncWithReceiver( int flag );
        int receiver_wants_crc32;
        int current_frame_uses_crc32;
        long received_file_position;
        long transmitted_file_position;
        long last_sync_position;
        long last_reported_position;
        unsigned int receiver_buffer_length;
        int file_at_eof;
        int wake_up_sender_header_type;
        int Rxcount;
        char received_header[ ZMAXHLEN ];
        char transmitted_header[ ZMAXHLEN ];
        char attention_string[ ZATTNLEN + 1 ];
        int last_char_sent;

public :
        Zmodem( RS232 *rs232_port );
        int Send( char *files[] );
        int Receive( char *file );
};

#endif // #ifdef _ZMODEM_DOT_H

// ********************** END OF ZMODEM.H **********************
```

Listing 16-6: _ZMODEM.H

```
// ******************* START OF _ZMODEM.H *********************

// This header file has various constants used by the
// Zmodem class.

#ifndef __ZMODEM_DOT_H
#define __ZMODEM_DOT_H

const int ZPAD       = '*';  // ZPAD starts every header
```

Chapter 16: File Tranfers and ZMODEM

```
const int ZDLE       = 24;    // The general purpose escape code
const int ZBIN       = 'A';   // Starts a binary CRC16 frame
const int ZHEX       = 'B';   // Starts a hex CRC16 frame
const int ZBIN32     = 'C';   // Starts a binary CRC32 frame
const int ZMAXSPLEN  = 1024;  // Max subpacket length

// These constants define all the various frame types

const int ZRQINIT    = 0;     // Request for receiver init frame
const int ZRINIT     = 1;     // A receiver init frame
const int ZSINIT     = 2;     // A sender init frame
const int ZACK       = 3;     // General purpose Acknowledge frame
const int ZFILE      = 4;     // File name and data
const int ZSKIP      = 5;     // Skip the incoming file
const int ZNAK       = 6;     // General purpose Not Acknowledge
const int ZABORT     = 7;     // Abort session
const int ZFIN       = 8;     // Session is complete
const int ZRPOS      = 9;     // Request to start sending from
                              // a specific address
const int ZDATA      = 10;    // Start of a data frame
const int ZEOF       = 11;    // End of file
const int ZFERR      = 12;    // Fatal Read or Write error D
const int ZCRC       = 13;    // Request for CRC value of a file
const int ZCHALLENGE = 14;    // Challenge frame
const int ZCOMPL     = 15;    // Request is complete
const int ZCAN       = 16;    // Remote end canceled
const int ZFREECNT   = 17;    // Request for free bytes
                              // available on the target file system
const int ZCOMMAND   = 18;    // Command from sending program
const int ZSTDERR    = 19;    // Output to stderr data follows

// Escape sequences in binary data

const int ZCRCE      = 'h';   // CRC next, frame ends, header
                              // follows
const int ZCRCG      = 'i';   // CRC next, frame continues nonstop
const int ZCRCQ      = 'j';   // CRC next, frame conts., expect ZACK
const int ZCRCW      = 'k';   // CRC next, ZACK expected,
                              // end of frame
const int ZRUB0      = 'l';   // Translate to rubout, 0x7f
const int ZRUB1      = 'm';   // Translate to rubout, 0xff

// ReadDataFrame() return values
```

```
const int GOTFLAG     = 0x100;
const int GOTCRCE     = ZCRCE | GOTFLAG;  // ZDLE-ZCRCE received
const int GOTCRCG     = ZCRCG | GOTFLAG;  // ZDLE-ZCRCG received
const int GOTCRCQ     = ZCRCQ | GOTFLAG;  // ZDLE-ZCRCQ received
const int GOTCRCW     = ZCRCW | GOTFLAG;  // ZDLE-ZCRCW received
const int GOTCAN      = CAN   | GOTFLAG;  // CAN*5 seen

// Byte positions within header array

const int ZF0         = 3;          // Position 0 in the flags array
const int ZF1         = 2;
const int ZF2         = 1;
const int ZF3         = 0;
const int ZP0         = 0;          // Low order 8 bits of position
const int ZP1         = 1;
const int ZP2         = 2;
const int ZP3         = 3;

// Bit Masks for ZRINIT flags byte ZF0

const int CANFDX      = 0x01; // Rx can send and receive true
                              // full duplex
const int CANOVIO     = 0x02; // Rx can receive data during disk I/O
const int CANBRK      = 0x04; // Rx can send a break signal
const int CANRLE      = 0x08; // Receiver can decode RLE
const int CANLZW      = 0x10; // Receiver can uncompress
const int CANFC32     = 0x20; // Receiver can use 32-bit CRC
const int ESCCTL      = 0x40; // Receiver expects ctl chars
                              // to be escaped
const int ESC8        = 0x80; // Receiver expects 8th bit
                              // to be escaped

// Miscellaneous constants

const int OK              =  0;
const int ERROR           = -1;
const int TIMEOUT         = -2;
const int GARBAGE_COUNT   = -3;

#endif // #ifdef __ZMODEM_DOT_H

// ********************* END OF _ZMODEM.H *********************
```

Chapter 16: File Tranfers and ZMODEM   793

Listing 16-7: ZMODEM.CPP

```cpp
// ********************* START OF ZMODEM.CPP *********************

// This file contains all of the source code needed to support
// Zmodem file transfers. This code is directly derived from the
// public domain code released by Chuck Forsberg and Omen
// Technology. The Zmodem enhancements published by Omen
// Technology, including variable headers and run length encoding,
// are not supported here. The Omen Technology code is available
// with the source code for this book for the curious.

#include <stdio.h>
#include <stdlib.h>
#include <string.h>
#include <stdarg.h>
#include "rs232.h"
#include "crc.h"
#include "ascii.h"
#include "zmodem.h"
#include "_zmodem.h"

// The two notification routines belong to the base class. There
// isn't any reason to override them in a derived class such as
// Zmodem, but a specific application may want to develop its own
// virtual functions to replace these.

void FileTransfer::error( char *fmt, ... )
{
   va_list argptr;

   va_start( argptr, fmt );
   vprintf( fmt, argptr );
   putc( '\n', stdout );
   va_end( argptr );
}

void FileTransfer::status( char *fmt, ... )
{
   va_list argptr;

   va_start( argptr, fmt );
   vprintf( fmt, argptr );
   putc( '\n', stdout );
   va_end( argptr );
```

```
}

// The Zmodem constructor only has to initialize a few variables.

Zmodem::Zmodem( RS232 *rs232_port )
{
    port = rs232_port;
    file_count = 0;
    file_name[ 0 ] = '\0';
    file_length = -1L;
    file = 0;
    receiver_buffer_length = 16384;
    wake_up_sender_header_type = ZRINIT;
}

// The public Send function sends a batch of files one at a time
// via the SendSingleFile function. When a normal completion
// occurs, it is flagged with a ZFIN frame.

int Zmodem::Send( char *files[] )
{
    PackLongIntoHeader( 0L );
    SendHexHeader(4, ZRQINIT, transmitted_header);
    GetRinitHeader();
    byte_count = -1;
    while ( *files ) {
        if ( SendSingleFile( *files ) == ERROR )
                return ERROR;
        files++;
    }
    SendZFIN();
    return OK;
}

// This function is used *everywhere*, and benefits from being
// declared as inline.

inline int Zmodem::ReadChar( long timeout )
{
    int c = port->Read( timeout );
    return ( c < 0 ) ? TIMEOUT : c;
}

// This is the worker routine that transmits a single file.
```

```
int Zmodem::SendSingleFile( char *name )
{
    int c;
    unsigned long crc_value;
    long lastcrcrq = -1;
    int length;

    file = fopen( name, "rb" );
    if ( file == NULL) {
        error( "Failed to open %s", name );
        return OK;
    }
    file_at_eof = 0;
    fseek( file, 0, SEEK_END );
    file_length = ftell( file );
    fseek( file, 0, SEEK_SET );
    length = sprintf( buffer,
                      "%s%c%u 0 0 0 0",
                      name,
                      0,
                      file_length );

    for ( ; ; ) {
        PackLongIntoHeader( 0L );
        SendBinaryHeader( 4, ZFILE, transmitted_header );
        SendDataFrame( buffer, length, ZCRCW );
again:
        c = ReadHeader( received_header );
        switch ( c ) {
            case ZRINIT:
                while ( ( c = ReadChar( 5000L ) ) > 0 )
                    if ( c == ZPAD )
                        goto again;
            /* **** FALL THRU TO **** */
            default:
                continue;
            case ZCAN:
            case TIMEOUT:
            case ZABORT:
            case ZFIN:
                return ERROR;
            case ZCRC:
                if ( received_file_position != lastcrcrq ) {
                    Crc32 crc( 0xFFFFFFFFL );
```

```
                        lastcrcrq = received_file_position;
                        fseek( file, 0L, SEEK_SET );
                        while ( ( ( c = getc( file ) ) != EOF )
                                  && --lastcrcrq )
                            crc.update(c );
                        crc_value = ~crc.value();
                        fseek( file, 0L, SEEK_SET );
                        lastcrcrq = received_file_position;
                    }
                    PackLongIntoHeader( crc_value );
                    SendBinaryHeader( 4, ZCRC, transmitted_header );
                    goto again;
                case ZSKIP:
                    fclose( file );
                    return OK;
                case ZRPOS:
                    if (fseek(file,received_file_position,SEEK_SET))
                       return ERROR;
                    last_sync_position=
                      (byte_count=transmitted_file_position=
                      last_reported_position=
                      received_file_position) - 1;
                    return SendFileContents();
            }
        }
    }

    int Zmodem::SendFileContents( void )
    {
        int c;
        int e;
        int n;
        int junkcount;
        int newcnt;

        junkcount = 0;

start_read:
        newcnt = receiver_buffer_length;
        PackLongIntoHeader( transmitted_file_position );
        SendBinaryHeader( 4, ZDATA, transmitted_header );
        do {
            n = fread( buffer, 1, 1024, file );
            if ( n < 1024 )
```

Chapter 16: File Tranfers and ZMODEM

```
            file_at_eof = 1;

    if ( file_at_eof )
        e = ZCRCE;
    else if ( junkcount > 3 )
        e = ZCRCW;
    else if ( byte_count == last_sync_position )
        e = ZCRCW;
    else if ( receiver_buffer_length && ( newcnt -= n ) <= 0 )
        e = ZCRCW;
    else
        e = ZCRCG;
    SendDataFrame( buffer, n, e );
    byte_count = transmitted_file_position += n;
    if ( e == ZCRCW )
        goto waitack;
    while ( port->RXSpaceUsed() ) {
        switch ( ReadChar( 100 ) ) {
            case CAN:
            case ZPAD:
                c = SyncWithReceiver( 1 );
                if ( c == ZACK )
                    break;
                SendDataFrame( buffer, 0, ZCRCE );
                goto gotack;
            case XOFF:
            case XOFF | 0x80 :
                ReadChar( 10000L );
            default:
                junkcount++;
        }
    }
} while ( !file_at_eof );
for ( ; ; ) {
    PackLongIntoHeader( transmitted_file_position );
    SendBinaryHeader( 4, ZEOF, transmitted_header );
    switch ( SyncWithReceiver( 0 ) ) {
        case ZACK:
            continue;
        case ZRPOS:
            goto start_read;
        case ZRINIT:
            return OK;
        case ZSKIP:
```

```
                fclose( file );
                return c;
            default:
                fclose( file );
                return ERROR;
        }
    }

//Backchannel processing

waitack:
    junkcount = 0;
    c = SyncWithReceiver( 0 );
gotack:
    switch ( c ) {
        default:
        case ZCAN:
            fclose( file );
            return ERROR;
        case ZSKIP:
            fclose( file );
            return c;
        case ZACK:
        case ZRPOS:
            break;
        case ZRINIT:
            return OK;
    }
    while ( port->RXSpaceUsed() ) {
        switch ( ReadChar( 100 ) ) {
            case CAN:
            case ZPAD:
                c = SyncWithReceiver( 1 );
                goto gotack;
            case XOFF :
            case XOFF | 0x80 :
                ReadChar( 10000L );
        }
    }
    goto start_read;
}

// If all goes well, the public receive function just calls
// WakeUpSender() followed by ReceiveFiles(). If both of those
```

```
// do what they are supposed to do, a batch of files will
// have been properly transferred.

int Zmodem::Receive( char *)
{
    static char CancelString[] = {
        CAN, CAN, CAN, CAN, CAN, CAN, CAN, CAN, CAN, CAN,
        BS,  BS,  BS,  BS,  BS,  BS,  BS,  BS,  BS,  BS };

    switch ( WakeUpSender() ) {
        case 0     :
        case ZCOMPL : return OK;
        case ERROR  : break;
        default     : if ( ReceiveFiles() == OK )
                         return OK;
    }
    port->Write( CancelString, sizeof CancelString, 30000L );
    if ( file )
        fclose( file );
    return ERROR;
}

// This is the general-purpose receiver function. It calls the
// ReceiveSingleFile function repeatedly as long as the wakeup
// function keeps receiving ZFILE frames.

int Zmodem::ReceiveFiles( void )
{
    int return_status ;

    for ( ; ; ) {
        switch ( return_status = ReceiveSingleFile() ) {
            case ZEOF:
            case ZSKIP:
                switch ( WakeUpSender() ) {
                    case ZCOMPL:
                        return OK;
                    default:
                        return ERROR;
                    case ZFILE:
                        break;
                }
                continue;
            default:
```

```
                    return return_status;
                case ERROR:
                    return ERROR;
            }
        }
}

// Some data used various places in the class

static char *Zendnames[] = { "ZCRCE", "ZCRCG", "ZCRCQ", "ZCRCW"};

static char *frametypes[] = {
    "No Response to Error Correction Request",
    "No Carrier Detect",
    "TIMEOUT",
    "ERROR",
    "ZRQINIT",  "ZRINIT",   "ZSINIT",   "ZACK",     "ZFILE",
    "ZSKIP",    "ZNAK",     "ZABORT",   "ZFIN",     "ZRPOS",
    "ZDATA",    "ZEOF",     "ZFERR",    "ZCRC",     "ZCHALLENGE",
    "ZCOMPL",   "ZCAN",     "ZFREECNT", "ZCOMMAND", "ZSTDERR"
};

// This function is used when receiving files. It sends out the
// initial frame and waits for a response from the sender. If
// things go properly, it will get the file data subpacket and
// return ZFILE. If the sender has no more files, it will send a
// ZFIN, which is handled here.

int Zmodem::WakeUpSender( void )
{
    int c;
    int n;

    for ( n = 0 ; n < 16 ; n++ ) {
        PackLongIntoHeader( 0L );
        transmitted_header[ZF0] = CANFC32|CANFDX|CANOVIO|CANBRK;
        SendHexHeader( 4,
                       wake_up_sender_header_type,
                       transmitted_header );
        if ( wake_up_sender_header_type == ZSKIP )
            wake_up_sender_header_type = ZRINIT;
        for ( int try_again = 1 ; try_again ;  ) {
            switch ( ReadHeader( received_header ) ) {
                case ZRQINIT :
```

```
                    case ZEOF    :
                    case TIMEOUT :
                    default      :
                        try_again = 0;
                        break;
                    case ZFILE   :
                        wake_up_sender_header_type = ZRINIT;
                        c = ReadDataFrame( buffer, 1024 );
                        if ( c == GOTCRCW )
                            return ZFILE;
                        SendHexHeader( 4, ZNAK, transmitted_header );
                        break;
                    case ZSINIT  :
                        if (ReadDataFrame(attention_string,ZATTNLEN)
                                == GOTCRCW ) {
                            PackLongIntoHeader( 1L );
                            SendHexHeader(4,ZACK,transmitted_header);
                        } else
                            SendHexHeader(4,ZNAK,transmitted_header);
                        break;
                    case ZCOMPL  :
                        break;
                    case ZFIN    :
                        AckZFIN();
                        return ZCOMPL;
                    case ZCAN    :
                        return ERROR;
                }
            }
        }
        return 0;
}

// This is the workhorse routine that reads a single file from the
// sender. It reads in headers until it gets a ZDATA header, and
// then it switches over to reading data subpackets until it gets
// one of the end subpacket codes.

int Zmodem::ReceiveSingleFile( void )
{
    int c;
    int error_count;
    long rxbytes;
```

```c
        if ( OpenInputFile( buffer ) == ERROR )
            return wake_up_sender_header_type = ZSKIP;
    error_count = 0;
    rxbytes = 0L;
    for ( ; ; ) {
        PackLongIntoHeader( rxbytes );
        SendHexHeader( 4, ZRPOS, transmitted_header );
nxthdr:
        switch ( c = ReadHeader( received_header ) ) {
            default:
              error( "ReceiveSingleFile: ReadHeader returned %d",
                    c );
              return ERROR;
            case ZNAK:
            case TIMEOUT:
              if ( ++error_count >= 20 ) {
                error("ReceiveSingleFile: ReadHeader returned %d",
                      c );
                return ERROR;
              }
            case ZFILE:
                ReadDataFrame( buffer, 1024 );
                continue;
            case ZEOF:
              if (UnpackHeaderIntoLong(received_header)!=rxbytes)
                goto nxthdr;
              if ( fclose( file ) != 0 ) {
                wake_up_sender_header_type = ZFERR;
                error( "ReceiveSingleFile: fclose() "
                        "returned error" );
                return ERROR;
              }
              return c;
            case ERROR:
                if ( ++error_count >= 20 ) {
                    error( "ReceiveSingleFile: ReadHeader "
                            "returned %d", c );
                    return ERROR;
                }
                SendAttentionString();
                continue;
            case ZSKIP:
                fclose( file );
                status("ReceiveSingleFile: Sender SKIPPED file");
```

```
              return c;
          case ZDATA:
            if (UnpackHeaderIntoLong(received_header)!=rxbytes)
            {
              if ( ++error_count >= 20 )
                return ERROR;
              SendAttentionString();
              continue;
            }
moredata:
            switch ( c = ReadDataFrame( buffer, 1024 ) ) {
              case ZCAN:
                error("ReceiveSingleFile: ReadData returned %d",
                      c );
                return ERROR;
              case ERROR:
                if ( ++error_count >= 20 ) {
                  error( "ReceiveSingleFile: ReadData "
                         "returned %d", c );
                  return ERROR;
                }
                SendAttentionString();
                continue;
              case TIMEOUT:
                if ( ++error_count >= 20 ) {
                  error( "ReceiveSingleFile: ReadData "
                         "returned %d", c );
                  return ERROR;
                }
                continue;
              case GOTCRCW:
                error_count = 0;
                fwrite( buffer, 1, Rxcount, file );
                rxbytes += Rxcount;
                PackLongIntoHeader( rxbytes );
                SendHexHeader( 4, ZACK, transmitted_header );
                SendChar( XON );
                goto nxthdr;
              case GOTCRCQ:
                error_count = 0;
                fwrite( buffer, 1, Rxcount, file );
                rxbytes += Rxcount;
                PackLongIntoHeader( rxbytes );
                SendHexHeader( 4, ZACK, transmitted_header );
```

```
                    goto moredata;
                case GOTCRCG:
                    error_count = 0;
                    fwrite( buffer, 1, Rxcount, file );
                    rxbytes += Rxcount;
                    goto moredata;
                case GOTCRCE:
                    error_count = 0;
                    fwrite( buffer, 1, Rxcount, file );
                    rxbytes += Rxcount;
                    goto nxthdr;
                }
        }
    }
#ifdef _MSC_VER
    return 0;   // MSC 7.0 generates an error without this line,
                // although it can never be reached!
#endif
}

// This routine just has to decide whether to send the binary
// header using CRC16 or CRC32. After that it just spits out
// the data.

void Zmodem::SendBinaryHeader( int length,
                               int type,
                               char *header )
{
    int i;
    Crc32 crc32( 0xFFFFFFFFL );
    unsigned long crc32val;
    Crc16 crc16( 0 );

    status( "SendBinaryHeader: %d %s %lx",
            length,
            frametypes[ type + 4 ],
            UnpackHeaderIntoLong( header ) );
    SendChar( ZPAD );
    SendChar( ZDLE );
    if ( receiver_wants_crc32 ) {
        SendChar( ZBIN32 );
        SendEncodedChar( type );
        crc32.update( type );
        for ( i = 0; i < length; i++ ) {
```

```
            crc32.update( 0xff & header[ i ] );
            SendEncodedChar( header[ i ] );
        }
        crc32val = ~crc32.value();
        for ( i = 0 ; i < 4 ; i++ ) {
            SendEncodedChar( (int) crc32val );
            crc32val >= 8;
        }
    } else {
        SendChar( ZBIN );
        SendEncodedChar( type );
        crc16.update( type );
        for ( i = 0 ; i < length ; i++ ) {
            SendEncodedChar( header[ i ] );
            crc16.update( header[ i ] & 0xff );
        }
        crc16.update( 0 );
        crc16.update( 0 );
        SendEncodedChar( crc16.value() > 8 );
        SendEncodedChar( crc16.value() );
    }
}

// Sending the hex header involves no decisions whatsoever.

void Zmodem::SendHexHeader( int len, int type, char *header )
{
    int n;
    Crc16 crc( 0 );

    status( "SendHexHeader: %d %s %lx", len,
            frametypes[type+4], UnpackHeaderIntoLong( header ) );
    SendChar( ZPAD );
    SendChar( ZPAD );
    SendChar( ZDLE );
    SendChar( ZHEX );
    SendHexEncodedChar( type );
    crc.update( type );
    for ( n = 0 ; n < len ; n++ ) {
        SendHexEncodedChar( header[ n ] );
        crc.update( 0xff & header[ n ] );
    }
    crc.update( 0 );
    crc.update( 0 );
```

```
        SendHexEncodedChar( crc.value() > 8 );
        SendHexEncodedChar( crc.value() );
        SendChar( CR );
        SendChar( LF | 0x80 );
        if ( type != ZFIN && type != ZACK )
            SendChar( XON );
}

// Reading in headers and data subpackets is a
// difficult job. The next four routines combine to read in
// headers. The first routine dispatches one of the next three,
// depending on what the header type is.

int Zmodem::ReadHeader( char *header )
{
    int c;
    int n;
    int cancount;
    Settings settings;

    port->ReadSettings( settings );
    n = 1400;
    n += ( settings.BaudRate > 19200L ) ?
            19200 : (int) settings.BaudRate;

startover:
    cancount = 0;
again:
    switch ( c = ReadChar( 10000L ) ) {
        case TIMEOUT:
            goto finished;
        case CAN:
gotcan:
            if ( ++cancount >= 5 ) {
                c = ZCAN;
                goto finished;
            }
            switch ( c = ReadChar( 100 ) ) {
                case TIMEOUT:
                    goto again;
                case ZCRCW:
                    switch ( ReadChar( 100 ) ) {
                        case TIMEOUT:
                            c = ERROR;
```

```
                        goto finished;
                    default:
                        goto agn2;
                }
                default:
                    break;
                case CAN:
                    if ( ++cancount >= 5 ) {
                        c = ZCAN;
                        goto finished;
                    }
                    goto again;
            }
            default:
agn2:
            if ( --n == 0 ) {
                c = GARBAGE_COUNT;
                goto finished;
            }
            goto startover;
        case ZPAD | 0x80:        /* This is what we want. */
        case ZPAD:
            break;
    }
    cancount = 0;
splat:
    switch ( c = ReadUnencodedByte() ) {
        case ZPAD:
            goto splat;
        case TIMEOUT:
            goto finished;
        default:
            goto agn2;
        case ZDLE:        /* This is what we want. */
            break;
    }

    c = ReadUnencodedByte();
    switch ( c ) {
        case ZBIN32:
            current_frame_uses_crc32 = 1;
            c = ReadBinaryHeaderCRC32( header );
            break;
        case TIMEOUT:
```

```
                    goto finished;
            case ZBIN:
                    current_frame_uses_crc32 = 0;
                    c = ReadBinaryHeaderCRC16( header );
                    break;
            case ZHEX:
                    current_frame_uses_crc32 = 0;
                    c = ReadHexHeaderCRC16( header );
                    break;
            case CAN:
                    goto gotcan;
            default:
                    goto agn2;
        }
        received_file_position = header[ ZP3 ] & 0xff;
        received_file_position <<= 8;
        received_file_position += header[ ZP2 ] & 0xff;
        received_file_position <<= 8;
        received_file_position += header[ ZP1 ] & 0xff;
        received_file_position <<= 8;
        received_file_position += header[ ZP0 ] & 0xff;
finished:
        switch ( c ) {
            case GOTCAN:
                    c = ZCAN;
            /* **** FALL THRU TO **** */
            case ZNAK:
            case ZCAN:
            case ERROR:
            case TIMEOUT:
            case GARBAGE_COUNT:
                    error( "Got %s", frametypes[ c + 4 ] );
            /* **** FALL THRU TO **** */
            default:
                    if ( c >= -4 && c <= 22 )
                            error( "ReadHeader: %s %lx",
                                    frametypes[ c + 4 ],
                                    received_file_position );
                    else
                            error( "ReadHeader: %d %lx",
                                    c,
                                    received_file_position );
        }
        return c;
```

}

```
// At this point most of the hard work is done. The next
// three routines just read in the type of header and the data
// associated with it, and then check whether the CRC is correct.

int Zmodem::ReadBinaryHeaderCRC16( char *header )
{
    int c;
    int i;
    Crc16 crc( 0 );
    int header_type;

    if ( ( c = ReadEncodedByte() ) & ~0xff )
        return c;
    header_type = c;
    crc.update( c );

    for ( i = 0 ; i < 4 ; i++ ) {
        if ( ( c = ReadEncodedByte() ) & ~0xff )
            return c;
        crc.update( c );
        header[ i ] = (char) c;
    }
    if ( ( c = ReadEncodedByte() ) & ~0xff )
        return c;
    crc.update( c );
    if ( ( c = ReadEncodedByte() ) & ~0xff )
        return c;
    crc.update( c );
    if ( crc.value() & 0xFFFF ) {
        error( "Bad CRC" );
        return ERROR;
    }
    return header_type;
}

int Zmodem::ReadBinaryHeaderCRC32( char *header )
{
    int c;
    int i;
    Crc32 crc( 0xFFFFFFFFL );
    int header_type;
```

```
        if ( ( c = ReadEncodedByte() ) & ~0xff )
            return c;
        header_type = c;
        crc.update( c );

        for ( i = 0 ; i < 4 ; i++ ) {
            if ( ( c = ReadEncodedByte() ) & ~0xff )
                return c;
            crc.update( c );
            header[ i ] = (char) c;
        }
        for ( i = 0; i < 4 ; i++ ) {
            if ( ( c = ReadEncodedByte() ) & ~0xff )
                return c;
            crc.update( c );
        }
        if ( crc.value() != 0xDEBB20E3L ) {
            error( "Bad CRC" );
            return ERROR;
        }
        return header_type;
}

int Zmodem::ReadHexHeaderCRC16( char *header )
{
    int c;
    Crc16 crc( 0 );
    int i;
    int header_type;

    if ( ( c = ReadHexByte() ) < 0 )
        return c;
    header_type = c;
    crc.update( c );

    for ( i = 0 ; i < 4 ; i++ ) {
        if ( ( c = ReadHexByte() ) < 0 )
            return c;
        crc.update( c );
        header[ i ] = (char) c;
    }
    if ( ( c = ReadHexByte() ) < 0 )
        return c;
    crc.update( c );
```

```
        if ( ( c = ReadHexByte() ) < 0 )
            return c;
        crc.update( c );
        if ( crc.value() & 0xFFFF ) {
            error( "Bad CRC" );
            return ERROR;
        }
        switch ( c = ReadChar( 100 ) ) {
            case CR :
            case CR | 0x80 :
                ReadChar( 100 );
        }
        return header_type;
}

// The next three routines are used to read in binary data
// subpackets. This code is somewhat simpler than the code
// used to read in a header, mostly because there are fewer
// things that can go wrong.

int Zmodem::ReadDataFrame( char *buffer, int length )
{
    if ( current_frame_uses_crc32 )
        return ReadDataFrameCRC32( buffer, length );
    else
        return ReadDataFrameCRC16( buffer, length );
}

int Zmodem::ReadDataFrameCRC32( char *buffer, int length )
{
    int c;
    Crc32 crc( 0xFFFFFFFFL );
    char *end;
    int d;

    Rxcount = 0;
    end = buffer + length;
    while ( buffer <= end ) {
        if ( ( c = ReadEncodedByte() ) & ~0xff ) {
crcfoo:
            switch ( c ) {
                case GOTCRCE:
                case GOTCRCG:
                case GOTCRCQ:
```

```
                    case GOTCRCW:
                        d = c;
                        c &= 0xff;
                        crc.update( c );
                        if ( ( c = ReadEncodedByte() ) & ~0xff )
                            goto crcfoo;
                        crc.update( c );
                        if ( ( c = ReadEncodedByte() ) & ~0xff )
                            goto crcfoo;
                        crc.update( c );
                        if ( ( c = ReadEncodedByte() ) & ~0xff )
                            goto crcfoo;
                        crc.update( c );
                        if ( ( c = ReadEncodedByte() ) & ~0xff )
                            goto crcfoo;
                        crc.update( c );
                        if ( crc.value() != 0xDEBB20E3L ) {
                            error( "Bad CRC" );
                            return ERROR;
                        }
                        Rxcount = (int) ( length - (end - buffer) );
                        error( "ReadDataFrameCRC32: %d %s",
                                Rxcount,
                                Zendnames[ d - GOTCRCE & 3 ] );
                        return d;
                    case GOTCAN:
                        error( "Sender Canceled" );
                        return ZCAN;
                    case TIMEOUT:
                        error( "TIMEOUT" );
                        return c;
                    default:
                        error( "Garbled data subpacket" );
                        return c;
                }
            }
            *buffer++ = (char) c;
            crc.update( c );
        }
        error( "Data subpacket too long" );
        return ERROR;
    }

    int Zmodem::ReadDataFrameCRC16( char *buffer, int length )
```

```c
{
    int c;
    Crc16 crc( 0 );
    char *end;
    int d;

    Rxcount = 0;
    end = buffer + length;
    while ( buffer <= end ) {
        if ( ( c = ReadEncodedByte() ) & ~0xff ) {
crcfoo:
            switch ( c ) {
                case GOTCRCE:
                case GOTCRCG:
                case GOTCRCQ:
                case GOTCRCW:
                    crc.update( (d = c) & 0xff );
                    if ( ( c = ReadEncodedByte()) & ~0xff )
                        goto crcfoo;
                    crc.update( c );
                    if ( ( c = ReadEncodedByte() ) & ~0xff )
                        goto crcfoo;
                    crc.update( c );
                    if ( crc.value() & 0xFFFF ) {
                        error( "Bad CRC");
                        return ERROR;
                    }
                    Rxcount = (int) ( length - ( end - buffer ) );
                    error( "ReadDataFrame: %d   %s",
                        Rxcount,
                        Zendnames[ d - GOTCRCE & 3 ] );
                    return d;
                case GOTCAN:
                    error( "Sender Canceled" );
                    return ZCAN;
                case TIMEOUT:
                    error( "TIMEOUT" );
                    return c;
                default:
                    error( "Garbled data subpacket" );
                    return c;
            }
        }
        *buffer++ = (char) c;
```

```
            crc.update( c );
    }
    error( "Data subpacket too long" );
    return ERROR;
}

// The attention string processor has to process a couple of
// special characters used to sleep and send breaks.

void Zmodem::SendAttentionString()
{
    int i = 0;
    int c;
    long timer;

    while ( port->TXSpaceUsed() > 0 )
        port->IdleFunction();
    while ( ( c = attention_string[ i++ ] ) != 0 ) {
        switch ( c ) {
            case 0xde :
                timer = ReadTime() + 1000L;
                while ( ReadTime() < timer )
                    port->IdleFunction();
                break;
            case 0xdd :
                port->Break();
                break;
            default:
                SendChar( c );
        }
    }
}

// The receiver calls this function before exiting.

void Zmodem::AckZFIN( void )
{
    int n;

    status( "AckZFIN" );
    PackLongIntoHeader( 0L );
    for ( n = 0 ; n < 4 ; n++ ) {
        port->FlushRXBuffer();
        SendHexHeader( 4, ZFIN, transmitted_header );
```

```
            switch ( ReadChar( 10000L ) ) {
                case '0':
                    ReadChar( 120 );     /* Discard 2nd '0' */
                    status( "AckZFIN complete" );
                    return;
                case TIMEOUT:
                default:
                    break;
            }
        }
}

// This utility routine has to scan the incoming data subpacket
// for the file name and length.

int Zmodem::OpenInputFile( char *data )
{
    strcpy( file_name, data );
    if ( sscanf(data+strlen(data)+1, "%ld", &file_length ) < 1 )
        file_length = -1L;
    file = fopen( file_name, "wb" );
    if ( !file)
        return ERROR;
    return OK;
}

// File position values are longs packed into a 4-byte header.
// The following two routines are responsible for packing and
// unpacking the data.

void Zmodem::PackLongIntoHeader( long header_data )
{
    transmitted_header[ ZP0 ] = (char) header_data;
    transmitted_header[ ZP1 ] = (char) ( header_data > 8 );
    transmitted_header[ ZP2 ] = (char) ( header_data > 16 );
    transmitted_header[ ZP3 ] = (char) ( header_data > 24 );
}

long Zmodem::UnpackHeaderIntoLong( char *header )
{
    long l;

    l = header[ ZP3 ] & 0xff;
    l = ( l << 8 ) | ( header[ ZP2 ] & 0xff );
```

```
    l = ( l << 8 ) | ( header[ ZP1 ] & 0xff );
    l = ( l << 8 ) | ( header[ ZP0 ] & 0xff );
    return l;
}

// Hex headers need to send data in hex format.

void Zmodem::SendHexEncodedChar( int c )
{
    static char *digits = "0123456789abcdef";

    SendChar( digits[ ( c & 0xF0 ) > 4 ] );
    SendChar( digits[ c & 0xF ] );
}

// This routine handles all the escape sequences necessary to send
// control characters.

void Zmodem::SendEncodedChar( int c )
{
    if ( c & 0x60 )
        SendChar( last_char_sent = c );
    else {
        switch ( c &= 0xff ) {
            case CR :
            case CR | 0x80 :
                if ( ( last_char_sent & 0x7f ) != '@' ) {
                    SendChar( last_char_sent = c );
                    break;
                } // else fall through
            case ZDLE :
            case DLE :
            case XON :
            case XOFF :
            case DLE | 0x80 :
            case XON | 0x80 :
            case XOFF | 0x80 :
                SendChar( ZDLE );
                c ^= 0x40;
                SendChar( last_char_sent = c );
                break;
            default:
                SendChar( last_char_sent = c );
        }
```

            }
    }

    // Reading a byte, accounting for escape sequences, and checking
    // for the 5*CAN abort sequence.

    int Zmodem::ReadEncodedByte(void)
    {
        int c;

        for (; ;) {
            c = ReadChar(10000L);
            if (c == ZDLE)
                break;
            switch (c) {
                case XON :
                case XON | 0x80 :
                case XOFF :
                case XOFF | 0x80 :
                    break;
                default:
                    return c;
            }
        }
        for (; ;) {
            if ((c = ReadChar(10000L)) < 0)
                return c;
            if (c == CAN && (c = ReadChar(10000L)) < 0)
                return c;
            if (c == CAN && (c = ReadChar(10000L)) < 0)
                return c;
            if (c == CAN && (c = ReadChar(10000L)) < 0)
                return c;
            switch (c) {
                case CAN:
                    return GOTCAN;
                case ZCRCE:
                case ZCRCG:
                case ZCRCQ:
                case ZCRCW:
                    return c | GOTFLAG;
                case ZRUB0:
                    return 0x7f;
                case ZRUB1:

```
                    return 0xff;
            case XOFF :
            case XOFF | 0x80 :
            case XON :
            case XON | 0x80 :
                break;
            default:
                if ( ( c & 0x60 ) ==  0x40 )
                    return ( c ^ 0x40 );
                else
                    return ERROR;
        }
    }
}

// This routine reads a raw data byte, throws out the parity bit,
// and ignores handshaking characters.

int Zmodem::ReadUnencodedByte( void )
{
    int c;

    for ( ; ; ) {
        if ( ( c = ReadChar( 10000L ) ) < 0 )
            return c;
        switch ( c &= 0x7f ) {
            case XON:
            case XOFF:
                continue;
            default:
                return c;
        }
    }
}

// To read hex headers hex values need to be converted to a
// usable format.

int Zmodem::ReadHexByte( void )
{
    int c;
    int n;

    if ( ( c = ReadUnencodedByte() ) < 0 )
```

Chapter 16: File Tranfers and ZMODEM 819

```
        return c;
    n = c - '0';
    if ( n > 9 )
        n -= ( 'a' - ':' );
    if ( n & ~0xF )
        return ERROR;
    if ( ( c = ReadUnencodedByte( )) < 0 )
        return c;
    c -= '0';
    if ( c > 9 )
        c -= ( 'a' - ':' );
    if ( c & ~0xF )
        return ERROR;
    c += ( n << 4 );
    return c;
}

// The sender needs to get the RINIT frame before it can start
// sending the file. This routine takes care of that.

int Zmodem::GetRinitHeader( void )
{
  int i;

  for ( i = 0 ; i < 10 ; i++ ) {
    switch ( ReadHeader( received_header ) ) {
      case ZCHALLENGE:  //Echo receiver's challenge number
        PackLongIntoHeader( received_file_position );
        SendHexHeader( 4, ZACK, transmitted_header );
        continue;
      case ZCOMMAND:    // They didn't see our ZRQINIT
        PackLongIntoHeader( 0L );
        SendHexHeader( 4, ZRQINIT, transmitted_header );
        continue;
      case ZRINIT:
        receiver_wants_crc32 = received_header[ ZF0 ] & CANFC32;
        receiver_buffer_length =
                ( received_header[ ZP0 ] & 0xff ) +
                ( ( received_header[ ZP1 ] & 0xff ) << 8 );
        return OK;
      case ZCAN:
      case TIMEOUT:
        return ERROR;
      case ZRQINIT:
```

```
                if ( received_header[ ZF0 ] == ZCOMMAND )
                    continue;
            default:
                SendHexHeader( 4, ZNAK, transmitted_header );
                continue;
            }
        }
        return ERROR;
    }

    // This routine sends a data subpacket, which is used here to send
    // file names and file data.

    void Zmodem::SendDataFrame( char *buffer, int length, int frameend )
    {
        Crc32 crc32( 0xFFFFFFFFL );
        unsigned long crc32val;
        Crc16 crc16( 0 );
        int i;

        status( "SendDataFrame: %d %s",
                length, Zendnames[ frameend - ZCRCE & 3 ] );
        if ( receiver_wants_crc32 ) {
            for ( i = 0 ; i < length ; i++ ) {
                SendEncodedChar( buffer[ i ] );
                crc32.update( buffer[ i ] & 0xff );
            }
            SendChar( ZDLE );
            SendChar( frameend );
            crc32.update( frameend );
            crc32val = ~crc32.value();
            for ( i = 0 ; i < 4 ; i++ ) {
                SendEncodedChar( (int) crc32val );
                crc32val >= 8;
            }
        } else {
            for ( i = 0 ; i < length ; i++ ) {
                SendEncodedChar( buffer[ i ] );
                crc16.update( buffer[ i ] & 0xff );
            }
            SendChar( ZDLE);
            SendChar( frameend);
            crc16.update( frameend );
            crc16.update( 0 );
```

```
            crc16.update( 0 );
            SendEncodedChar( crc16.value() > 8 );
            SendEncodedChar( crc16.value() );
        }
        if ( frameend == ZCRCW )
            SendChar( XON );
}

// The sender sends a ZFIN frame just before exiting.

void Zmodem::SendZFIN( void )
{
    for ( ; ; ) {
        PackLongIntoHeader( 0L );
        SendHexHeader( 4, ZFIN, transmitted_header );
        switch ( ReadHeader( received_header ) ) {
            case ZFIN:
                SendChar( 'O');
                SendChar( 'O');
            case ZCAN:
            case TIMEOUT:
                return;
        }
    }
}

int Zmodem::SyncWithReceiver( int flag )
{
  int c;

  for ( ; ; ) {
    c = ReadHeader( received_header );
    switch ( c ) {
      case ZCAN:
      case ZABORT:
      case ZFIN:
      case TIMEOUT:
        return ERROR;
      case ZRPOS:
        if ( fseek( file, received_file_position, SEEK_SET ) )
          return ERROR;
        file_at_eof = 0;
        byte_count = last_reported_position
            = transmitted_file_position = received_file_position;
```

```
          last_sync_position = received_file_position;
          return c;
        case ZACK:
          last_reported_position = received_file_position;
          if ( flag || transmitted_file_position ==
                          received_file_position )
            return ZACK;
          continue;
        case ZRINIT:
        case ZSKIP:
          fclose( file );
          return c;
        case ERROR:
        default:
          SendBinaryHeader( 4, ZNAK, transmitted_header );
          continue;
      }
    }
}

// ********************* END OF ZMODEM.CPP *********************
```

Summary

In this chapter, you were introduced to a popular file transfer protocol called ZMODEM. You saw how with the use of this protocol, the Zmodem class encapsulates engines which both send and receive files. A short sample program ties the file transfer class together with the RS232 classes and provides a complete program that can interchange ASCII and binary files with a remote system of any type.

Appendix

What's on the CD-ROM?

THE CD-ROM THAT ACCOMPANIES this book contains the source code for all the sample programs and classes covered in each chapter. These programs are organized into the directories listed in the following table. The directories are named after the chapters. For example, you can find the programs for Chapter 4 in the CHAPT04 directory, the programs for Chapter 5 in the CHAPT05 directory, and so on.

File Name	Description
CHAPT03\CHAPT03.CPP	16-Bit test program for class PC8250
CHAPT03\CHAPT03.EXE	16-Bit executable of the test program
CHAPT03\CHAPT03.MAK	A makefile for Borland or Microsoft C++
CHAPT04\CHAPT04.CPP	16-Bit test program for the Digi Classic board
CHAPT04\CHAPT04.EXE	16-Bit executable of the test program
CHAPT04\CHAPT04.MAK	A makefile for Borland or Microsoft C++
CHAPT04\CLASSIC.CPP	Implementation of the ClassicHandler class
CHAPT04\CLASSIC.H	Declaration of the ClassicHandler class
CHAPT05\CHAPT05.CPP	16-Bit test program for the initelligent Digi board.
CHAPT05\CHAPT05.EXE	16-Bit executable of the test program
CHAPT05\CHAPT05.MAK	A makefile for Borland or Microsoft C++
CHAPT05\DIGI.CPP	Implementation of the Digiboard class
CHAPT05\DIGI.H	Declaration of the Digiboard class
CHAPT06\CHAPT06.CPP	16-Bit test program for the BiosPort class
CHAPT06\CHAPT06.EXE	16-Bit executable of the test program
CHAPT06\CHAPT06.MAK	A makefile for Borland or Microsoft C++
CHAPT06\BIOSPORT.CPP	Implementation of the BiosPort class
CHAPT06\BIOSPORT.H	Declaration of the BiosPort class

Continued

(Continued)

File Name	Description
CHAPT07\CHAPT07.CPP	16-Bit test program for the Fossil class
CHAPT07\CHAPT07.EXE	16-Bit executable of the test program.
CHAPT07\CHAPT07.MAK	A makefile for Borland or Microsoft C++
CHAPT07\BIOSPORT.CPP	A copy of the file from Chapter 6
CHAPT07\BIOSPORT.H	A copy of the file from Chapter 6
CHAPT07\FOSSIL.CPP	Implementation of the Fossil class
CHAPT07\FOSSIL.H	Declaration of the Fossile class
CHAPT08\TESTTERM.CPP	16-Bit test program for the terminal emulation classes
CHAPT08\TESTTERM.EXE	16-Bit executable of the test program
CHAPT08\TESTTERM.MAK	A makefile for Borland or Microsoft C++
CHAPT09\TERMW16.CPP	16-Bit test program for the Win16Port class
CHAPT09\TERMW16.DEF	A file needed by the linker for this program
CHAPT09\TERMW16.EXE	16-Bit exeuctable of the test program
CHAPT09\TERMW16B.MAK	A makefile for Borland C++
CHAPT09\TERMW16M.MAK	A makefile for Microsoft C++
CHAPT12\Chapt12.cpp	Part of the 32-bit test progrma for the Win32Port class
CHAPT12\Chapt12.dsp	The Visual C++ project file for the program
CHAPT12\Chapt12.dsw	The Visual C++ workspace file for the program
CHAPT12\Chapt12.h	The header file for the app's application class
CHAPT12\Chapt12.ico	The icon used in Chapt12.exe
CHAPT12\Chapt12.rc	The resource file use in the test program
CHAPT12\Chapt12Dlg.cpp	The implementation of the dialog class
CHAPT12\Chapt12Dlg.h	The declarations of the dialog class
CHAPT12\MyWin32Port.h	Definition for a class derived from Win32Port
CHAPT12\resource.h	The resource IDs
CHAPT12\Debug\Chapt12.exe	The 32-bit executable for the test program
CHAPT13\AnsiWinTerm.cpp	Class used in Win32 terminal emulation

File Name	Description
CHAPT13\AnsiWinTerm.h	Header file for the AnsiWinTerm class
CHAPT13\Chapt13.cpp	32-bit test program of terminal emulation
CHAPT13\Chapt13.dsp	Visual C++ project file
CHAPT13\Chapt13.dsw	Visual C++ workspace file
CHAPT13\Chapt13.rc	The resource file used in the test program
CHAPT13\resource.h	IDs defined in the resource file
CHAPT13\Win32Term.cpp	The Win32 general purpose terminal class
CHAPT13\Win32Term.h	Definition of the class
CHAPT13\Debug\Chapt13.exe	32-bit executable of the test program.
CHAPT14\MODEM.CPP	Implementation of the Modem class
CHAPT14\MODEM.H	Declarations of the Modem class
CHAPT14\TSTMODEM.CPP	16-bit test program for the Modem class
CHAPT14\TSTMODEM.EXE	16-bit executable of the test program
CHAPT14\TSTMODEM.MAK	Make file for use with Borland or Microsoft C++
CHAPT15\Chapt15.cpp	The TAPI test program
CHAPT15\Chapt15.dsp	Microsoft Visual C++ project file
CHAPT15\chapt15.dsw	Microsoft Visual C++ workspace file
CHAPT15\Chapt15.rc	Resources used in the TAPI test program
CHAPT15\resource.h	IDs of the resources
CHAPT15\AnsiTapiTerm.cpp	A derived class used to implement TAPI here
CHAPT15\AnsiTapiTerm.h	The declaration of the derived class
CHAPT15\ConStream.cpp	A class used to print debug output to the console
CHAPT15\ConStream.h	Declaration of the class
CHAPT15\MySimpleTapi.h	A derived class used to implement TAPI here
CHAPT15\SimpleTapi.cpp	Implementation of the TAPI class
CHAPT15\SimpleTapi.h	Declarations of the TAPI class
CHAPT15\Tapi32Port.cpp	Derived class used in this program

Continued

(Continued)

File Name	Description
CHAPT15\Tapi32Port.h	Declaration of the derived class
CHAPT15\Win32Term.cpp	Copy of the class definition from Chapter 13
CHAPT15\Win32Term.h	Copy of the class declaration from Chapter 13
CHAPT15\Debug\Chapt15.exe	32-bit executable for this chapter
CHAPT16\CRC.CPP	The CRC class definition used by the Zmodem class
CHAPT16\CRC.H	The CRC class declaration
CHAPT16\RZSZ0308.ZIP	An early versoin of Chuck Forsberg's rz/sz programs
CHAPT16\TESTZM.CPP	The 16-bit ZMODEM test program's source
CHAPT16\TESTZM.EXE	The 16-bit ZMODEM test program's executable
CHAPT16\TESTZM.MAK	A make file for Borland or Microsoft C++
CHAPT16\ZMODEM.CPP	The implemenation of the Zmodem class
CHAPT16\ZMODEM.H	The declaration of the Zmodem class
CHAPT16_ZMODEM.H	An internal header file for the Zmodem class
CHAPT16\ZMODEM.DOC	An early version of the Zmodem spec by Forsberg.
COMMON\ANSITERM.CPP	Implementation of the AnsiTerm class
COMMON\ANSITERM.H	Declaration fo the AnsiTerm class
COMMON\ASCII.H	Defintions of commonly used ASCII control characters
COMMON\BASEWIND.H	The base class for a window used in terminal emulation
COMMON\RS232.CPP	The RS232 class definition
COMMON\RS232.H	The RS232 class declaration
COMMON\TERMINAL.H	Base class used in terminal emulation
COMMON16\ISR_8250.CPP	Code implementing a generic interrupt handler
COMMON16\MSDOS.CPP	A few routines specific to 16 bit MS-DOS
COMMON16\PC8250.CPP	The PC8250 16-bit class definition
COMMON16\PC8250.H	The PC8250 16-bit class declaration
COMMON16\PCIRQ.CPP	Code used in conjunction with the interrupt handler

File Name	Description
COMMON16\PCIRQ.H	Declarations used with the 16-bit interrupt handler
COMMON16\QUEUE.CPP	A generic queue class used by class PC8250
COMMON16\QUEUE.H	Declarations of the queue class
COMMON16\Textwind.cpp	A generic 16 bit text-mode windowing class
COMMON16\Textwind.h	Declarations for the text-mode windowing class
COMMON16\WIN16.CPP	Definition of the Win16Port class
COMMON16\WIN16.H	Declaration of the Win16Port class
COMMON16_8250.H	Hardware definitions
COMMON16_PC8250.H	Hardware definitions
COMMON32\Dcb32.cpp	Implemenation of a wrapper classed used by Win32Port
COMMON32\Dcb32.h	Declaration of the class
COMMON32\MTDeque.h	A deque<> class with multithreading protection
COMMON32\Win32Port.cpp	The 32 bit Win32Port class defintion
COMMON32\Win32Port.h	The class declaration

In addition to the source code, each 32-bit and 16-bit sample program on the CD-ROM includes make files suitable for use by Visual C++. The 16-bit programs also include make files suitable for us by Borland C++. The 16-bit programs can be created by using the compiler's `make` command from the command line. The 32-bit projects can be opened using Visual Studio and built interactively. The 16-bit programs can be built with Borland C++ 4.0 or 4.5 or Microsoft Visual C++ 1.52. The 32-bit programs can be built with Microsoft Visual C++ 5 or 6.

> **NOTE:** All CD-ROM files are read-only. Therfore, if you open a file from the CD-ROM and make any changes to it, you need to save it to your hard drive. Also, if you copy a file from the CD-ROM to your hard drive, the file retains its read-only attribute. To change this attribute after copying a file, right-click the file name or icon and select Properties from the shortcut menu. In the Properties dialog box, click the General tab and remove the checkmark from the Read-only checkbox.

Glossary

abstract base class This is a class whose member functions are all pure virtual. The abstract base class cannot be instantiated by itself. Only those classes derived from the abstract base class can be created and used to perform useful work. This terminology is not part of the C++ standard; it is part of the jargon that has grown around the language.

American National Standards Institute (ANSI) The primary technical standards body in the United States.

American Standard Code for Information Interchange (ASCII) This standard is officially defined as ANSI Standard X3.4. This seven-bit specification has become the universally accepted standard way of exchanging text data.

ANSI Standard for C Programming Language (ANSI C) This standard was published in February 1990, as Standard X3.159-1989.

bits per second (bps) A commonly used measure of signaling speed. Usually this figure is used to indicate total throughput capability of a medium.

carrier detect (CD) The commonly used name for the Received Line Signal Detect (RLSD) signal used in RS-232 communications. A data communications equipment (DCE) asserts the RLSD line when it establishes a connection with another modem, indicating the circuit is ready to use.

data communications equipment (DCE) The original RS-232 specification had a worldview where every piece of data communications equipment was either a DTE (data terminal equipment) or a DCE (data communications equipment). In the simplest terms, a DCE device is a modem and a DTE device is a terminal.

data set ready (DSR) An RS-232 signal generated by a data communications equipment (DCE). DSR is generally used to indicate that a modem is powered up and ready to receive and send data. It is infrequently used as a handshaking line in conjunction with data terminal ready (DTR).

data terminal equipment (DTE) This designation is part of the RS-232 specification. A DTE is a device that connects to a data communications equipment (DCE) and uses it to communicate with a DTE at some remote location. A DTE is usually a terminal or a PC acting as a terminal via terminal emulation software. (See data communications equipment.)

data terminal ready (DTR) An RS-232 signal generated by a data terminal equipment (DTE). DTR is usually used to indicate that a terminal is powered up and ready to send and receive data. It is infrequently used as a handshaking line in conjunction with data set ready (DSR).

digiBoard A multiport board made by Digi International, Inc. This company makes many different varieties of boards. Some come with on-board processors and are referred to as "Intelligent Boards."

Electronic Industries Association (EIA) A group composed of companies involved in the electronics industry. While the EIA is involved in many activities, it is mentioned in this book because of its sponsorship of the RS-232 standard. The EIA can be reached at the following address:

> Electronic Industries Association
> 2001 Eye Street NW
> Washington, DC 20006

flow control See "handshaking."

FOSSIL FOSSIL is an acronym for "Fido/Opus/Seadog Standard Interface Layer." FOSSIL drivers were developed to provide a device independent programming standard BBS programmers could use to access communications hardware.

full duplex A full duplex communications channel allows simultaneous communications in both directions. This is the predominant type of communications channel in use by desktop machines today.

half duplex A half duplex channel allows communications to go in either direction, but not simultaneously. This requires the two modems at either end of the line to cooperate using some sort of protocol to determine who is allowed to transmit at any given time.

handshaking In general, handshaking can be the exchange of signals between communicating entities. In this book, I use the term handshaking to mean the process by which a receiver throttles a transmitter to avoid buffer overflow.

hardware handshaking Hardware handshaking consists of using the RTS/CTS or DTR/DSR signal pairs to throttle transmission. A receiver can block transmission of additional characters by dropping a control line until the receiver buffer has been emptied down to a predetermined point.

high water mark When using software or hardware handshaking, the high water mark refers to a specific point in the input buffer. When the input buffer fills up past this point, the RS-232 driver will attempt to block any further incoming data through the use of handshaking.

International Standards Organization (ISO) The ISO is another standards body sanctioned by the United Nations.

International Telecommunications Union (ITU) The International Telecommunications Union, once known as the CCITT. An international standards body chartered by the United Nations. The ITU is primarily concerned with standards in the area of telecommunications, and is the dominant body that sets standards for today's generation of modems.

link access protocol for modems (LAPM) V.42 modems use LAPM as their preferred method of error control.

low water mark When using software or hardware handshaking, the low water mark refers to a specific point in the input buffer. When the input buffer is emptied below this point, the RS-232 driver will remove any blocking that has prevented the reception of incoming data.

marking Digital communications lines are historically referred to as being in either a "marking" or "spacing" state, dating back to the days of telegraphy. A 1 bit is referred to as a marking bit, and a 0 is a spacing bit.

MNP-4/MNP-5 MNP stands for Microcom Network Protocol. Microcom, Inc., is a company that established a set or proprietary protocols for their modems. MNP-4 and MNP-5 are the two best known protocols, and are widely licensed by other modem manufacturers. MNP-4 is used to provide an error-free connection between two modems. MNP-5 is used to perform data compression on the transmitted data stream. V.42 and V.42bis will probably supercede these standards.

modem In general, a modem (short for modulator/demodulator) is a device that converts serial data to a format that can be transmitted over dialup or leased phone lines, and converts data received from the phone lines back to serial data.

multiport board RS-232 multiport boards are boards equipped with multiple RS-232 ports. In the desktop PC world, these boards usually have 4, 8, or 16 ports. These boards are divided into two categories. Intelligent boards have an on-board processor and memory to move much of the processing off the PC motherboard. Non-intelligent boards just have Universal Asynchronous Receiver/Transmitters (UARTs) and glue circuitry, which means the PC has to handle interrupts for all the UARTs.

Null modem cable A Null modem cable is a special cable used to connect two DTE devices together directly without a modem. It routes RS-232 signals properly so that both devices have inputs connected to outputs and outputs connected to inputs.

overrun error A hardware error caused when the UART receives another incoming byte before the CPU has read the last one.

parity bit A parity bit is an extra bit that is added to a data byte being transmitted. Usually the parity bit is set to a 0 or 1 in order to force the data byte to have an odd or even number of set data bits, hence the terms "odd parity" and "even parity." This extra bit allows the receiver to detect any single bit error.

pure virtual function In C++, a pure virtual function is a function defined as 0 in a base class. The presence of a pure function in a class means that the class cannot be instantiated. In this book, class RS232 has several pure virtual functions. This means that only classes derived from RS232 can be instantiated.

Received Line Signal Detect (RLSD) See carrier detect (CD).

request to send (RTS) One of the six modem control lines supported on the IBM PC standard communications port. RTS is generally paired up with clear to send (CTS) to provide RTS/CTS hardware handshaking.

RS-232-C The best known Electronic Industries Association (EIA) standard relating to low-speed asynchronous communications.

software handshaking Software handshaking refers to the process of using the XON/XOFF character pairs to disable then reenable the transmission of characters from a transmitter. The receiver issues an XOFF when it is in danger of having its buffer overflow. It issues an XON to resume transmission after the buffer is emptied.

spacing Digital communications lines are historically referred to as being in either a "marking" or "spacing" state, dating back to the days of telegraphy. A 1 bit is referred to as a marking bit, and a 0 is a spacing bit.

start bit This is the first bit issued when a Universal Asynchronous Receiver/Transmitter (UART) wants to send a data byte. The start bit will unambiguously tell the receiver that a set of data bits is to follow. This is normally a space, or 0 bit.

stop bit This bit is normally issued by a Universal Asynchronous Receiver/Transmitter (UART) to follow the data byte. This bit is usually a mark, or 1 bit, and is used to separate consecutive characters and to help with resynchronization.

Unicode Unicode is a recently approved standard that replaces traditional 7-bit ASCII with a 16-bit standard for character transmission, storage, and display. Unicode gives good coverage to most international alphabets, including Asian languages, and is expected to come into wide use rapidly.

Universal Asynchronous Receiver/Transmitter (UART) A UART is normally a single chip dedicated to converting bytes to and from a serial data stream that can travel on RS-232 data lines.

V.22, V.22bis These International Telecommunications Union (ITU) standards specify the format for 1200 and 2400 bps modems used over dialup telephone lines. At one time, V.22*bis* modems represented the majority of installed modems in the field. However, they were displaced by faster models some years ago.

V.24 This International Telecommunications Standard (ITU) is the sister standard to the Electronic Industries Association (EIA's) RS-232-C. Although it defines a few additional circuits above and beyond the 25 defined by RS-232-C, they are essentially identical.

V.32, V.32bis These International Telecommunications Union (ITU) standards specify the formats for 9600 and 14,400 bps modems used over dialup telephone lines. Like their V.22 siblings, modems that use these standards were once the predominant desktop modems. They were bypassed by faster equipment.

V.34 This International Telecommunications Union (ITU) specification dictates the protocol used to provide 33.6 Kbps communications. These modems were the standard for desktop users until the late 1990s when the V.90 modems ascended to supremacy.

V.42
This International Telecommunications Union (ITU) specification dictates the protocol used to provide an error free connection between two modems. V.42 implicitly supports MNP-4 when necessary, although its normal mode of operation is Link Access Protocol for Modems (LAPM).

V.42bis This is the Link Access Protocol for Modems (ITU) specification for data compression for modems. V.42*bis* represents a substantial improvement over its predecessor, MNP-5, in that it can compress up to 4:1 and can disable compression when necessary.

V.90 The V.90 standard dictates how the current crop of so-called 56K modems communicate. This standard ended a fierce struggle between US Robotics (now 3COM) and Rockwell over who would define what may be the final generation of dialup voice line modems.

virtual functions In C++, a virtual function is a function that is called by way of a function pointer. Virtual functions in a base class will point to different functions, depending on which derived class is used to instantiate the base class.

XON/XOFF XON/XOFF handshaking is a form of software handshaking. The name comes from the fact that the XOFF character is used to throttle transmission and the XON character is used to restart it.

ZMODEM ZMODEM is a widely used file transfer protocol that improves on many of the deficiencies found in XMODEM and YMODEM.

Index

3COM modems
  missing DR bit, 125
  V.90, 657-658
9-pin connector
  9- to 25-pin adapter, 17-18
  PC-to-modem cable, 15
  pinouts, 7
  RS-232 signal assignments, 7
16-bit CRC binary headers
  (ZMODEM, 774, 775
16-bit serial transmission, 5. *See also* Unicode
  O/S-dependent functions, WIN16.CPP for, 421
  PC8250 class for, 105
25-pin connector
  9- to 25-pin adapter, 17-18
  PC-to-modem cable, 14
  pinouts, 7
  RS-232 signal assignments, 7
32-bit CRC binary headers
  (ZMODEM], 774, 775
32-bit programs, PC8250 class with, 105
8088 PCs, Interrupt Request/Interrupt Acknowledge pins, 127
8250 UART chip family, 21, 22-24, 106. *See also* PC8250 class
  8250 register set, 106-107
  with I/O bus, 106-107
  IER (Interrupt Enable Register), 109-112
  IIR (Interrupt ID Register), 112-113
  LCR (Line Control Register), 113-116
  LSR (Line Status Register), 118-119
  MCR (Modem Control Register), 116-118
  MSR (Modem Status Register), 119-120
  RBR (Receive Buffer Register), 108-109
  THR (Transmit Holding Register), 109
  16550 FCR (FIFO Control Register), 120-122
  16650/16750 chip extensions, 120-122

bugs
  false modem status interrupt, 124
  interrupt pulsing, 123
  missing DR bit, 125
  motherboard timing, 124-125
  TX interrupt jump starts, 123-124
interrupts, 110-112
RS232 class implementation, 69, 105
_8250.H (PC8250/ISR), 143-144
8259 PIC (Programmable Interrupt Controller), 127-128
16550 UART chip family, 22, 24-25
  16550 FCR (FIFO Control Register), 120-122
16560/16570 UART chip family, 22, 25
16650/16750 UART chips, 122
56kbs modems, 657-658

A

adapters, 45-46
  gender changer, 18
  9- to 25-pin adapter, 17-18
  null modem adapter, 18
AddPort() function
  ClassicHandler class, 211-212
  Handler class, 207
Adjust() function (RS232 Settings), code for, 102
AL register field definitions
  BIOS interface, 270-271
  Digi driver INT 14H interface, 225
alternate status check function (Digi driver INT 14H interface), 232
American National Standard Institute (ANSI), escape sequences specification (ANSI X3.64), 329-330
ANSI C, function pointers, 51-53
ANSI X3.64 standard (escape sequences), 329
  listing of, 332-333
Ansi_parms[] array (AnsiTerminal class), 342, 345, 346

ANSI.SYS driver, 329-330
  command syntax, 331
  keyboard escape sequences, 335-337
AnsiTapiTerm class, with SimpleTapi test program, 711-724
ANSITERM.CPP (AnsiTerminal class), 347-359
AnsiTerminal class
  class descriptor source code, 341-342
  debugging macros for, 360-361
  implementation source code, 347-359
  integrating with Win32Term class, 596-597
  keyboard translations, 335-337
  ownership by AnsiWinTerm class, 600
  functions
    AnsiTerminal() constructor, 346
    ~AnsiTerminal() destructor, 346
    cursor_move(), 344
    cursor_position_report(), 344
    Display(), 346
    erase_in_display(), 345
    erase_in_line(), 345
    parse(), 343
    parse_ansi_string(), 343-344
    position_cursor(), 344
    ReadPort(), 343
    restore_position(), 345
    save_position(), 345
    set_color(), 345
    set_mode(), 346
    WriteKey(), 346-347
  members
    ansi_parms[] array, 342
    extended_keys[] array, 342-343
    keys[] array, 342-343
    parm_count index, 342
    saved_col, 342
    saved_row, 342
  test program source code, 339-341
ANSITRM.H (AnsiTerminal class), 341-342

836 Index

AnsiWinTerm classclass descriptor
  source code, 600-605
  class implementation source
    code, 605-609
  creating, 596-597
  ownership of AnsiTerminal
    object, 600
  protected members
    Close(), 613
    Open(), 612
  public functions
    Dispatch(), 598-600
    SetFont(), 611
  test program
    identifiers file, 623
    menu commands, 609-613
    RC file code, 622
    source code, 613-622
ANSIWINTERM.CPP (Win32Term
  class), 605-609
ANSIWINTERM.H (Win32Term
  class), 600-605
Answer() function (Modem class),
  665, 667, 668
  testing, 677
AnswerResult() function (SimpleTapi
  class), 709
AntiTerminal class, BaseWindow
  class functions for, 367
ASCII standard
  display terminals, ANSI X3.64
    standard for, 329-330
  ESC (Escape) character, 329
  limitations, 5
  standard character set, 4
  ZMODEM test line, 777
ASCII.H (PC8250/ISR source code),
  144-145
asynchronous functions
  SimpleTapi class, 703
  TAPI, 685, 699-700
asynchronous transmissions, 10
AT command set, 651-652
  creating capability entries using,
    662
  SmartModem 2400
    [+++], 656
    A[\], 656
    ATA, 652-656
    ATBn, 652
    AT&Cn, 655
    AT&Dn, 655
    ATDs, 652-653
    ATEn, 653
    AT&F, 655, 662
    AT&Gn, 655

ATHn, 653
ATIn, 653
AT&Jn, 655
ATLn, 653
ATMn, 654
ATOn, 654
AT&Pn, 655
AT&Qn, 655
ATQn, 654
AT&Rn, 655
AT&Sn, 655
ATSr=n, 654, 656. *See also*
  SmartModem 2400
AT&Tn, 655
ATVn, 654
ATXn, 654
ATYn, 654
ATZn, 655

B

BASEWIND.H (BaseWindow class),
  362-365
BaseWindow class
  converting Win32Term class to,
    596
  creating AnsiWinTerm class
    from, 596-597
  functions
    BaseWindow() constructor,
      365
    ~BaseWindow() destructor,
      365
    Clear(), 345, 346, 366
    GetAttribute(), 346, 365-366
    GetDimension(), 345, 367
    GetPosition(), 344, 345, 367
    Goto(), 346, 366
    SetAttribute(), 346, 366
    SetPosition(), 344, 345,
      366-367
    SetWrap() function, 346,
      365
  insertion operators, 366
  source code for, 362-365
  with Terminal base class, 338
  virtual functions in, 360-361
baud, defined, 10
Baud Rate combo box (Win32Port
  test program), 511
BBS system software, 39-40
  FOSSIL interface, 299-300
Bell 103 modems, 29
Bel!' 212 modems, 29
binary data transfers (ZMODEM, 5
  data subpack formats, 775-776

encoding, 776-777
header file formats, 774-775
BIOS interface functions
  initialize port (function 0),
    270-271
  input single character (function
    2), 272
  limitations, 275
  output single character
    (function 1), 271
  read line, modem status
    (function 2), 272
BIOS, standard, 225, 265-267
BIOSPort class, 269-270
  class descriptor source code,
    277-279
  EBIOSPort class inheritance
    from, 276-277
  implementation source code,
    279-290
  interface limitations, 275
  testing program source, 295-297
  unsupported functions, 276
BIOSPORT.CPP (BIOSPort class),
  279-290
BIOSPORT.CPP (EBIOSPort class),
  279-295
BIOSPORT.H (BIOSPort
  class/EBIOSPort class),
  277-279
  in FOSSIL.H, 323
bit maps
  16550 FCR (FIFO Control
    Register), 121
  Digi driver AL register, 225
  IER (Interrupt Enable Register),
    110
  LCR (Line Control Register), 113
  LSR (Line Status Register),
    118-119
  MCR (Modem Control Register),
    117
  MSR (Modem Status Register),
    119-120
bits per second, 10
blink feature, adding to
  Win32TermClass, 623
blocked data member (PC8250
  class/ISR), 134
blocking data member (PC8250
  class/ISR), 134
BNU FOSSIL driver (Nugent), 309
Borland 16-bit compiler, 105
  Win 16 test program make file for,
    430

Index   837

break control function, FOSSIL
  driver, 308
Break Detect bit (8250 LSR), 119
Break Duration edit control
  (Win32Port test program),
  513
Break() function
  EBIOSPort class, 276
  PC8250 class, 178
  RS232 class, 78, 100
BreakDetect() function
  PC8250 class, 179-180
  RS232 class, 71-72
BreakDetectNotify() function
  (Win32Port class), 499
breakout boxes, 41-43
buffer[] buffer (FileTransfer class),
  781
buffering
  double-buffering, 108-109
  on-chip buffering, 109
bugs, 8250 UART chip family
  false modem status interrupt,
    124
  interrupt pulsing, 123
  missing DR bit, 125
  motherboard timing, 124-125
  TX interrupt jump starts,
    123-124
BuildComm DCB() function
  Win16 comm API, 391-392
  Win32 serial API, 445-446
BuildCommDCBAndTimeouts()
  function (Win32 serial API),
  446
buses, intelligent multiport boards,
  220
byte counts, in function returns, 60
byte_count data member
  (FileTransfer class), 781
ByteCount data member (RS232
  class), 60, 67-68
  with Peek() function, 76
  with Read() functions, 73-74
  with Write() functions, 74-75

C

C programming language
  function pointers, 51-53
  libraries for, 40-41
  maintenance requirements,
    50-51
C++ programming language
  advantages of, 49, 53–54
  C++ compilers

accessing Digi API func-
  tions, 224
error-checking by, 53-55
C++ objects, pointers to in Win
  API, 576
function return values, 58-59
inheritance
  with AnsiWinTerm class,
    598
  from EBIOSPort class,
    276-277
  integrating WIN APIs with,
    574-577
  libraries for, 40-41
  new classes, deriving, 54-55
  protected members, accessing,
    63
  virtual functions, 49, 362
cabling
  homemade cables, 20, 44-45
  Macintosh systems, 19
  PC-to-modem, 14
  PC-to-PC (null modem cable),
    15-17
Caldera Systems, DR-DOS, 217
call control functions (TAPI),
  695-698
Call Handle (TAPI), 686
CallActive() function (SimpleTapi
  class), 701
Callback() function (TAPI), 696,
  699-700, 706-708
callback functions
  TAPI 2.x, 696, 699-700, 706-708
  in Windows programming, 575
Carrier Detect (CD) line, 8, 12
carrier_timeout member (Modem
  class), 668
CD (Carrier Detetct) line, 8, 12
CD edit control (Win32Port test
  program), 513
Cd() function (PC8250 class), 179
CdNotify() function (Win32Port
  class), 499
CHAPT04.CPP (ClassicHandler test
  program), 213-216
CHAPT05.CPP (DigiBoard test
  program), 265-267
CHAPT06.MAK (BIOSPort/EBIOPort
  classes), 295-297
CHAPT07.EXE (Fossil test program),
  323-324
CHAPT12.EXE (Win32Port class
  program), 509-516
CHAPT15.CPP (SimpleTapi test
  program), 711-724

CHAPT15.EXE (SimpleTapi test
  program), 710-711
Chapt15.rc (SimpleTapi test
  program), 759-763
check_modem_status() function
  (Win32Port class), 481-482,
  495-496
check_rx_handshaking() function
  (PC8250 class), 174
check_uart() function (PC8250
  class), 174
Citadel BBS system, 40
classes
  AnsiTapiTerm class, 711
  AnsiTerminal class, integrating
    with Win32Term class,
    596-597
  AnsiWinTerm class
    class descriptor source code,
      600-605
    creating, 596-597
    implementation source
      code, 605-609
    notification functions,
      598-600
  Base Window class, class
    descriptor source code,
    362-365
  in C++
    design conventions, 58
    new classes, deriving, 54-55
    RS232 base class code,
      55-57, 86-90
  ClassicHandler class
    constructor source code,
      208-209
    destructor source code,
      211-212
    implementation source
      code, 209-211
  ConStream debugging class, 708
    class descriptor source code,
      755-757
    implementation source
      code, 757-759
  Crc16/Crc32 classes
    class descriptor source code,
      785-786
    implementation source
      code, 786-788
  DCB helper class
    class descriptor source code,
      559-560
    implementation source
      code, 560-565

Continued

838   Index

classes, DCB helper class *(continued)*
FileTransfer class
functions, 780
protected members, 780-781
Fossil class
class descriptor source code, 310-312
implementation source code, 312-323
for MNP modems, 31-32
Modem class
class descriptor source code, 663-664
implementation source code, 669-677
public functions, 664-667
test program source code, 677-681
MTDeque helper class, 503-504
MySimpleTapi, source code, 748-752
MyWin32Port derived class, 516-517
with AnsiWinTerm class, 598
notification routines, 482-483
PC8250 class, ISR (Interrupt Service Routine), 129-133
SimpleTapi class
call/line management functions, 702-704
class descriptor source code, 724-728
implementation source code, 728-748
internal functions, 706-708
notification routines, 705-706, 707
resource definitions source code, 759-763
session management functions, 701-702
test program source code, 711-724
Tapi32Port class
class descriptor source code, 753-754
implementation source code, 754-755
Terminal base class, source code, 337-339
TextWindow class
class descriptor source code, 367-370
implementation source code, 370-386
Win16Port class
class descriptor source code, 402-404
implementation source code, 404-421
test program source code, 423-429
Win32Port class
class descriptor source code, 517-521
constants, 499-500
implementation source code, 521-559
input thread, 477-482
MTDeque helper class source code, 565-570
notification routines, 482-484
output thread, 472-477
protected member functions, 492-497
public member functions, 485-492
threading in, 471-482
Win32Term class
basic structure, 578-579
class descriptor source code, 623-627
CreateData, 581
data members, 581-587
implementation source code, 627-648
integrating with AnsiTerminal class, 596-597
protected functions, 592-595
public functions, 587-592
TextColor, 580-581
Zmodem class
class descriptor source code, 788-790
constants definition file source code, 790-792
implementation source code, 792-822
test program source code, 782-784
Classic multiport board (Digi International), 204-205
configuring, 205-206
test program, 213-216
classic_isr(), 212
CLASSIC.H (ClassicHandler source code), 208-211
ClassicHandler class
constructor implementation, 209-211
constructor source code, 208-209
destructor source code, 211-212
test program source code, 213-216
Clear() function
AnsiWinTerm class, 610
Base Window class, 345, 346, 366
BaseWindow class, 338
MTDeque helper class, 503
PC8250 Queue support class, 188
Win32Term class, 589, 590
clear port buffers function (Digi driver INT 14H interface), 232-233
clear RX buffer function (Digi driver INT 14H interface), 236-237
Clear to Send (CTS) line, 8, 11
clear TX buffer function (Digi driver INT 14H interface), 237
clear_error() function (Win32Port class), 481-482, 495
notification routines, 483
ClearCommBreak() function, 459
Win16 API, 392, 395-396
Win32 serial API, 446-447
ClearCommError() function (Win32Port class), 483, 496-497
Close() function (AnsiWinTerm class), 613
close port function (FOSSIL driver), 303-304
CloseComm() function (Win16 API), 392
CloseHandle() function (Win32 serial API), 447
with SimpleTapi class, 704
CloseLine() function (SimpleTapi class), 703
CLRBREAK function (Win32 serial API), 451
CLRDTR function (Win32 serial API), 451
CLRRTS function (Win32 serial API), 451
clrscr() function, 16-bit version, 328
code portability

Index 839

C++ and, 49-50, 57
  reusing PC8250 class, 203
COM cards (IBM-compatible), 125-128
  with laptops, 126
comm ports
  as devices, 434
  Win16 versus Win32 systems, 433-434
COMMCONFIG structure (Win32 serial API), 449-450, 452, 456, 460, 463
  members listing, 439-440
CommConfigDialog() function (Win32 serial API), 439, 448-450, 460
COMMPROP structure (Win32 serial API), 463
  members listing, 440-443
COMMTIMEOUTS structure (Win32 serial API), 462
  members listing, 438-439
communications (COM) cards
  with laptops, 126
  standard, IBM-compatible, 125-126
communications programming
  breakout boxes, 41-43
  frame buffer clearing, 327-328
  ISR (Interrupt Service Routine) writing, 126
  line monitors, 43-44
  modem hardware, 650-651
  MS-Windows, 389-390
  software, 39-41
  Win16 system, 389-390
  Win32 systems, 433-434
compilers
  16-bit, 105
  C++
    accessing Digi API functions, 224
    error-checking by, 53-55
    TERMW16 make files for, 430-431
  MS-DOS, accessing Digi API functions, 224
compressing member (Modem class), 668
*compression_strings member (ModemCapabilities structure), 661
computer-to-computer connections, 6

COMSTAT structure API function, 400-401, 496-497
configuration functions (TAPI), 692-695
ConfigureCall() function (SimpleTapi class), 702, 703
ConfigureDevice() function (SimpleTapi class), 702-703, 702-703
configuring intelligent multiport boards, 243-244
ConnectedEvent() function (SimpleTapi class), 704, 705, 707
connectors, 6. *See also* cabling
ConnectToIRQ () function (PC8250/Interrupt Manager), 188, 197, 207
ConStream debugging class, 708
  class descriptor source code, 755-757
  implementation source code, 757-759
ConStream.cpp (ConStream debugging class), 757-759
ConStream.h (ConStream debugging class), 755-757
constructors
  absence of in RS232 class, 61-62
  AnsiTerminal class, 346
  ClassicHandler class, 208-209
  PC8250 class, 172
control blocks
  intelligent multiport board interfaces, 222-223
  reading/writing code, 223
control DTR function (FOSSIL driver), 304
control lines
  directionality, 9
  listing of, 8-9
  logic levels, 11
  subsets, 11-12
  voltage conventions, 10
control programs, multiport board CPUs, 222
control registers (8250 UARTs), 23
conversion options (ZF0) (ZMODEM), 770
CPUs in intelligent multiport boards, 221-222
CRC calculations
  CRC binary headers (ZMODEM), 774-775

Crc16/Crc32 classes, 785-788
Crc16/Crc32 classes
  class descriptor source code, 785-786
  implementation source code, 786-788
CRC.CCP (Crc16/Crc32 classes), 786-788
CRC.H (Crc16/Crc32 classes), 785-786
CreateData private class (Win32Term class), 581
CreateFile() function (Win 32 serial API), 447-448, 452, 453, 454, 455, 456, 500
  opening ports using, 434
  in Win32Port class, 471
CreateWindow() function (Win32 API), 577
  with Win32Term class, 588
CTS (Clear To Send) line, 8, 11
CTS edit control (Win32Port test program), 513
Cts() function (PC8250 class), 179
CtsNotify() function (Win32Port class), 499
Cursor Down escape sequence (ANSI.SYS), 332
Cursor Left escape sequence (ANSI.SYS), 332
Cursor Position escape sequence (ANSI.SYS), 332
Cursor Right escape sequence (ANSI.SYS), 332
Cursor Up escape sequence (ANSI.SYS), 332
cursor_move() function (AnsiTerminal class), 344
cursor_position_report() function (AnsiTerminal class), 344
cut and paste
  adding to Win32TermClass, 623
CXDOS5.SYS device driver, 224

D

D-Subminiature 9-pin connector (IBM), 3
D-Subminiature 25-pin connector, 3
Data Communications Equipment (DCE), RS-232 standard interface, 2
data communications lines
  directionality, 9
  listing of, 8

Continued

840 Index

data communications lines *(continued)*
   marking state, 10
   spacing, 10
   voltage conventions, 10
Data Ready bit (8250 LSR), 118
Data Ready (DR) bit (8250 LSR) problems with, 125
data reception flow rates, 8250 UARTs, 108-109
Data Set Ready (DSR) line, 8, 12
data structures
   Modem class, ModemCapabilities, 659-662
   TAPI 2.x
      LINE_CALLINFO, 687
      LINECALLPARAMS, 696
      LINEDEVCAPS, 689-691
   Win32 DCB structure
      API functions for, 445-446, 455
      Win16 comm API, 391-394, 398-400, 398-400, 402
      Win32 serial API, 435-438
   Win32 serial API, 460
      COMMCONFIG, 439-440, 449-450, 452, 456, 463
      COMMPROP, 440-443, 463
      COMMTIMEOUTS, 438-439, 462
      COMSTAT, 496-497
      DCB, 455
      MODEMSETTINGS, 460, 463
      OVERLAPPED, 444, 457, 458-459, 478
   Win32Term class, LOGFONT, 590
data subpackets (ZMODEM), 771
   ZCRCE format, 775
   ZCRCG format, 775
   ZCRCQ (j) format, 776, 779
   ZCRCW (k) format, 776
Data Terminal Equipment (DTE), RS-232 standard interface, 2
Data Terminal Ready (DTR) line, 8, 12
data transmission rates, 8250 chip systems, 109
DCB (Device Control Blocks) structure
   API functions for, 445-446, 455
   Win16 comm API, 391-394, 398-400, 398-400, 402
   Win32 serial API, 435-438

DCB helper class (Win32Port class), 504-505
   class descriptor source code, 559-560
   dequeue implementation source code, 565-570
   implementation source code, 560-565
DCB.CPP (Win32Port class), 560-565
DCB.H (Win32Port class), 559-560
DCE (Data Communications Equipment)
   modems as, 5-6
   RS-232 standard interface for, 2
DEBUG macro (AnsiTerminal class), 360-361
debug_line_count member (RS232 class), 66
debug_line_counter member (RS232 class), 84
debugging. *See also* errors, error handling
   code for
      SimpleTapi class, 708
      Win32TermClass, 623
   terminal emulation code, 360-361
DebugLineCount() function (RS232 class), 76
DEC VT-220 terminal, escape sequences, 329-330
DEC VT-52, escape sequences, 328-329
DeleteObject() function (Win32 API), 589
DeletePort() function
   ClassicHandler class, 212
   Handler class, 207
dequeuing, in Win32Port class, 503-504
derived classes, 54-55
Device Control Blocks (DCB), API functions for, 391-394, 398-400
device drivers
   frame buffers, 327-328
   intelligent multiport boards
      Digi API for, 224
      MS-DOS device driver, 243
      PC8250, ISR (Interrupt Service Routine), 129-133
      Window APIs for, 390
Device Status request escape sequence (ANSI.SYS), 332
devices, comm ports as, 434

Dial() function (Modem class), 665, 667, 668
   testing, 677
dialog boxes
   AnsiWinTerm class
      color selections, 611
      font selection, 610-611
   CHAPT12.EXE Win32 test program, 510-516
   CommConfig, 450
   TAPI 2.x
      address translations, 693
      modem configuration options, 688-689
      outbound call configurations, 693
Diamond Multimedia modems, 657-658
Digi driver functions, accessing, 224
Digi INT14 driver functions
   alternate status check (function 8), 232
   clear port buffers (function 9), 232-233
   clear RX buffer (function 0x10), 236-237
   clear TX buffer (function 0x11), 237
   drop handshaking lines (function 0x0B), 233
   enable/disable BIOS pacing (function 0x20), 240-241
   extended port control (function 5), 229
   extended port initialization (function 4), 227-229
   get board information (function 6; subfunction 2), 230-231
   get buffer counts (function 0xFD), 241
   get buffer sizes, watermarks count (function 0x1B), 238-239
   get driver information (function 6; subfunction 1), 230
   get driver name (function 6; subfunction 0xff), 231
   get pointer to character ready flag (function 0x0D), 235
   get port name (function 6;subfunction 0), 229-230
   get RX buffer space count (function 0x15), 238
   get TX buffer free space count (function 0x12), 237

Index 841

initialize port (function 0), 225-226
input buffer count (function 0x0A), 233
input single character (function 2), 227
output single character (function 1), 226
peek at character (function 0x14), 238
raise port handshake lines (function 0x13), 237-238
read a buffer (function 0x0F), 236
read line/modem status (function 3), 227
read operating port parameters (function 0x0C), 234-235
send break (function 7), 232
set handshaking type (function 0x1EC), 240
set handshaking watermarks count (function 0x1C), 239
write a buffer (function 0x0E), 236
Digi International
    intelligent multiport boards, 220
        configuring, 243-244
        device driver API, 224
    non-intelligent multiport boards (Classic), 204
DigiBoard class
    character-ready flag pointer, 235
    class descriptor source code, 246-248
    implementation source code, 249-265
    read_buffer() function, 236
    testing program (CHAPT05.EXE), 265-267
    write_buffer() function, 236
DIGI.CPP (Digiboard class), 249-265
DIGI.H (Digiboard class), 246-248
DIGIMAP.EXE, multiport configuration assistance, 243
Disconnect() function (Modem class), 665-666
DisconnectedEvent() function (SimpleTapi class), 705
DisconnectFromIRQ () function (PC8250/Interrupt Manager), 188, 197
Dispatch() function

AnsiWinTerm class, 598-600
frame buffers, 327-328
Win32Term class, 594-595
Display() function
    AnsiTerminal class, 346
    Terminal base class, 339
door programs, 300
DOS support (Digi device driver), 229
DR (Data Ready) bit (8250 UARTs), problems with, 125
DR-DOS (Caldera), 217
drop handshaking lines function (Digi driver INT 14H interface), 233
DropCall() function (SimpleTAPI class), 704
DropCallResult() function (SimpleTapi class), 705
DSR (Data Set Ready) line, 8, 12
DSR edit control (Win32Port test program), 513
Dsr() function (PC8250 class), 179
DsrNotify() function (Win32Port class), 499
DSZ.COM (Forsberg), 300
DTE (Data Terminal Equipment), RS-232 standard interface, 2
DTE/DCE communications, 5-6
    local flow control, 36
    problems with, 5-6
DTR check box (Win32Port test program), 512
DTR (Data Terminal Ready) line, 8, 12
    8250 chip systems, 116-118
Dtr() function
    EBIOSPort class, 276
    PC8250 class, 181-182
    RS232 class, 61, 79, 101
DtrDsrHandshaking() function (Win32Port class), 487
DtrHandshaking() function
    PC8250 class, 181
    RS232 class, 78-79, 101
DTS/DSR check box (Win32Port test program), 512
dual port RAM, 220
"dumb" modems, 31
dumb terminals, 329
Dump Status button (Win32Port test program), 514
DumpState() function (Modem class), 667
    testing, 678

E

EBIOS
    Digi driver emulation, 225
    FOSSIL driver incompatibility with, 308
    interface functions, 265-267
        extended port initialization (function 4), 272-273
        limitations, 275
        read modem control register (function 5, subfunction 0), 274
        write modem control register (function 5, subfunction 1), 274
EBIOSPort class, 269-270
    class descriptor source code, 277-279
    implementation source code, 279-295
    inheritance from BIOSPort class, 276-277
    interface limitations, 275
    testing (CHAPT06.MAK), 295-297
    write_settings(), 276-277
echo() function (Modem class), 668
edge-triggered interrupts, 127
EIA (Electronic Industries Alliance)
    EIA-232-C RS-232 standard, 2
    EIA-232-F RS-232 standard, 2
ElapsedTime member (RS232 class), 60-61, 67-68
    with Read() functions, 73-74
    with Write() functions, 74-75
electrical lines (signal-ground), 13. I/O voltage
Electronic Industries Alliance (EIA), RS-232 standards, 2
element names, conventions for, 58
enable/disable BIOS pacing function (Digi driver INT 14H interface), 240-241
EnableCommNotification function (Win16 API), 392
end-to-end flow control, 36
Erase Screen escape sequence (ANSI.SYS), 332
Erase to End of Line escape sequence, 332-333
erase_in_display function (AnsiTerminal class), 345
erase_in_line function (AnsiTerminal class), 345

Error() function
  File Transfer class, 780-781
  SimpleTapi class, 703, 706
error_status member
  RS232 class, 60, 65-66
    OpenComm() API function with, 394-395
  Win32Port class, 477
ErrorName() function, 58
  Modem class, 667
  PC8250 class, 183-184
  RS232 class, 81-83, 92-93
  Win32Port class, 492
errors, error-handling. *See also* notification routines
  8250 data transmission errors, 118-119
  in C applications, 50-51
  Classic board error handler, 211
  by C++ compilers, 53-55
  hardware overruns, FIFO for, 120-122
  modem error functions, 665-666
  in RS232, 71-72
  RS232 class error codes, 59-60
  in Win32 input thread, 480-482
  Win32Port class, 482-483
ErrorStatus() function (RS232 class), 65-66, 76
escape sequences, 329
  ANSI.SYS
    command syntax, 330-331
    development of, 329-330
    keyboard control sequences, 335-337
    terminal control sequences, 331-334
  UNIX termcap file, 329
  ZMODEM, 776-777
EscapeCommFunction()
  Win16 comm API, 392-393
  Win32 serial API, 450-451
event-driven programming, 390
event masks, in Win16Port class, 396-397
events, UNIX termcap files, 179
Exit() function (Modem class), testing, 677
Exit (Win32Port test program), 516
extended options (ZF3) (ZMODEM), 771
extended port control function (Digi driver INT 14H interface), 227-229
extended port initialization function

Digi driver EBIOS interface, 272-273
Digi driver INT 14H interface), 227-229
extended_keys array [] (AntiTerminal class), 342-343
external protocols, 300
Extract() functions (MTDeque class), 503

F

*fail_strings (ModemCapabilities structure), 661
fatal errors, RS232 class, 59. *See also* errors, error-handling
FCR (FIFO Control Register), 120-122
female connectors, 6
Fido-Opus-Seadog Standard Interface Layer .*See* FOSSIL driver
FIFO Control Register (FCR), 120-122
FIFO (first in, first out) buffer, 16550 chips, 120-122
fifo_setting data member (PC8250 class), 135
*file pointer (FileTransfer class), 781
file transfer protocols, 36-37. *See also* modems
  Kermit, 39-40
  XMODEM, 37, 765-766
  YMODEM, 37, 766
  ZMODEM, 38
    aborting transfers, 777-778
    data subpacket formats, 775-776
    frame types, 768-775
    header formats, 773-775
    history, 767-768, 767-768
    simplest, chart overview, 778-779
    Zmodem class source code, 788-822
file_count data member (FileTransfer class), 781
file_length data member (FileTransfer class), 781
file_name[] buffer (FileTransfer class), 781
File|Exit command (AnsiWinTerm test program), 610
FileTransfer class
  functions, Send(), 780

protected members
  *file, 781
  *port, 781
  buffer[], 781
  byte_count, 781
  error(), 780-781
  file_count, 781
  file_length, 781
  file_name[], 781
  status(), 780-781
  uses for, 780
first-party call control (TAPI), 684
first_debug_output_line data member
  PC8250 class, 135
  RS232 class, 84
  Win32Port class, 500
flow control
  end-to-end, 36
  local, 36
  RTS/CTS, 33-35
  XON/XOFF, 35
Flush RX button (Win32Port test program), 515
Flush TX button
  FOSSIL driver, 304-305
  Win32Port test program, 515
FlushComm() function (Win16 API), 293
FlushRXBuffer() function
  PC8250 class, 176-177
  Win32Port class, 491-492
FlushTXBuffer() function
  PC8250 class, 182
  RS232 class, 80-81, 80-81, 91
  Win32Port class, 492
foreign language characters, ASCII for, 5
FormatDebugOutput() function
  PC8250 class, 182-183
  RS232 class, 66, 83-86, 93-94
  Win32Port class, 487-491, 500
FormatDebugString() function (Win32Port class), 496
Fossil class, 309
  class descriptor source code, 310-312
  implementation source code, 312-323
  test program source code, 323-324
FOSSIL driver, 269
  availability, 300-301
  break control (function 0x1A), 308

Index   843

close port (function 5), 303-304
control DTR (function 6), 304
EBIOS incompatibility, 308
flush TX buffer (function 8), 304-305
get FOSSIL driver information (function 0x1B), 308-309
get received byte (function 2), 302
history, 299-301
initialize port (function 0), 301
open serial port (function 4), 303
purge input buffer (function 9), 305
purge output buffer (function 0x0A), 305
read a buffer (function 0x18), 307
read status registers (function 3), 302-303
select flow control (function 0x0F), 306-307
single character peek (function 0x0C), 306
sources for, 309
transmit single byte (function 1), 302
transmit with no wait (function 0x0B), 306
write a buffer (function 0x19), 308
fossil_struct() function (FOSSIL driver), 309
FOSSIL.CPP (Fossil class), 312-323
FOSSIL.H (Fossil class), 310-312
  BIOSPORT.H in, 323
frame buffers, 327-328
frame headers (ZMODEM)
  16-bit/32-bit CRC, 774, 775
  hexadecimal, 774-775
frame types (ZMODEM)
  ZABORT, 772
  ZACK, 769-770
  ZCHALLENGE, 772
  ZCOMMAND, 772
  ZCOMPL, 772
  ZCRC, 772
  ZDATA, 772, 778
  ZEOF, 779
  ZFERR, 772
  ZFILE, 778
  ZFIN, 772, 779
  ZFREECNT, 772
  ZNAK, 772

ZRINIT, 769, 778-779
ZRPOS, 772, 778, 779
ZRQINIT, 768-769, 777, 778
ZSINIT, 769-770
ZSKIP, 772
frames (ZMODEM)
  components
    conversion options, 770
    data subpacket, 771
    extended options, 771
    frame types, 769-770, 771-772
    frametypes, 768-770
    header formats, 773-775
    management options, 770-771
    transport options, 771
Framing Error bit (8250 LSR), 119
Framing Error Count edit control (Win32Port test program), 513
FramingError() function
  PC8250 class, 179-180
  RS232 class, 71-72
FramingErrorNotify() function (Win32Port class), 499
FreeCount() function
  Queue support class, 178, 188
function names, conventions for, 58
function pointers (C programming language), 51-53
functions
  idle, redefining in MS-Window systems, 421
  mandatory versus optional, 62, 68-69
  return values, 58-59
    byte counts, 60
    error codes, 59-60
  virtual functions, 66-67
    Base Window class, 362
    C++, 49, 362
    MyWin32Port derived class, 516-517
    optional, 62
    RS232 class, 77
    Win32Port class, notification routines, 482-484

G

gender changers, 18
get board information function (Digi driver INT 14H interface), 230-231

get buffer counts function (Digi driver INT 14H interface), 241
get buffer sizes, watermarks function (Digi driver INT 14H interface), 238-239
get driver information function (Digi driver INT 14H interface), 230
get driver name function (Digi driver INT 14H interface), 231
get FOSSIL driver information function (FOSSIL driver), 308-309
get pointer to character ready flag function (Digi driver INT 14H interface), 235
get port name function (Digi driver INT 14H interface), 227-229
get received byte function (FOSSIL driver), 302
get RX buffer space counte function (Digi driver INT 14H interface), 238
get TX buffer free space count function (Digi driver INT 14H interface), 237
GetAttribute() function (Base Window class), 346, 365-366
GetBackgroundColor() function (Win32Term class), 590
GetBorderColor() function (Win32Term class), 590
GetCommConfig() function (Win32 serial API), 451-452, 460
GetCommError() function (Win16 API), 293-294, 395, 396
  with COMSTAT structure API function, 400-401
  with Win16Port class, 402
GetCommEventMask() function (Win16 API), 394
GetCommMask() function (Win32 serial API), 452-453
GetCommModemStatus() function (Win32 serial API), 453-454
GetCommProperties() function (Win32 serial API), 440, 454, 463
GetCommState() function
  Win 16 comm API, 394
  Win32 serial API, 454-455, 462

GetCommTimeout() (Win32 serial API), 438, 455
GetCursorPosition() function (Win32Term class), 591-592
GetDefaultCommConfig() (Win32 serial API), 455-456
GetDeviceCount() function (SimpleTapi class), 701-702
GetDeviceName() function (SimpleTapi class), 702
GetDimension() function (Base Window class), 345, 367
GetForegroundColor() function (Win32Term class), 590
GetLastError() function (Win32 serial API), 497
  with CloseHandle() function, 447
  with GetCommModem Status() function, 454,
  with GetCommTimeouts() function, 456
  with PurgeComm() function, 457
  with ReadFile() function, 459
  with WriteFile() function, 466, 497
GetLogFont() (Win32Term class), 590
GetModemStatus() function (win32Port class), 495
GetOverlappedResults() function (Win32 serial API), 456-457,
  with ReadFile() function, 458-459,
  with WaitCommEvent() function, 465, 466-467
  with Win32Port class, 477, 479, 481-482.
GetPortHandle() (SimpleTapi class), 704
GetPosition() function (Base Window class), 344, 345, 367
GetWindow() function (SimpleTapi class), 702
GetWindowLong() function (Win32 API), 576-577
Goto() function (Base Window class), 338, 346, 366

H

half-duplex modems, 11, 28
HandleAnswerResult() function (SimpleTapi class), 706

HandleDropResult() function (SimpleTapi class), 704, 706
HandleMakeCallResult() function (SimpleTapi class), 706
Handler class (ClassicHandler), 207
  class descriptor source code, 208-209
  class destructor code, 211-212
  implementation source code, 209-211
handshaking
  DTR/DSR, 12
  locked DTE communications, 33
  ModemCapabilities structure, 662
  PC8250/ISR data members, 134
  RTS/CTS, 11
Hangup() function (Modem test program), testing, 678
hardware
  adapters, 45-46
  breakout boxes, 41-43
  cable-making equipment, 44-45
  IBM-compatible PCs, COM card interrupts, 127-128
  line monitors, 43-44
  modems, standard versus nonstandard, 649-651
  multiport boards, 203-204
  configuring, 220-222
  portability, 2
  voltmeters, 46
hardware flow control (RTS/CTS), 33-35
HardwareOverrunError() function
  PC8250 class, 179-180
  RS232 class, 71-72
  Win16Port class, 402
HardwareOverrunErrorNotify() function (Win32Port class), 499
Hayes Smartmodem. *See* SmartModem 2400
Head() function (Queue support class), 188
hex (hexadecimal) headers (ZMODEM), 774-775
hidden window notification (TAPI), 684-685
high-speed modems, 13
HortizontalScroll() (Win32Term class), 593-594
HW Overrun Error Count edit control, 513
HWND object (in Windows), 575

I

I/O bus, with 8250 register set, 106-107
IBM-compatible PCs
  COM card configurations, 125-128
  MCA (Micro Channel Architecture), 128
IBM DOS Technical Reference Manual, ANSI.SYS definitions, 329-330
idle function, in MS-Windows systems, 505-506
  redefining, 421
IdleFunction() function
  RS232 class, 73, 83
  Win32Port class, 505-506
IER (Interrupt Enable Register), 109-112
IIR (Interrupt ID Register), 112-113
inheritance. *See also* portability
  AnsiWinTerm class, 598
  EBIOSPort class, 276-277
initial_baud_rate member (ModemCapabilities structure), 661
*initialization_string member (ModemCapabilties structure), 659-662
Initialize() function (Modem class), 665
  testing, 678
initialize port function
  BIOS interface, 270-271
  Digi driver INT 14H interface, 225-226
  FOSSIL driver, 301
input buffer count function (Digi driver INT 14H interface), 233
input single character function
  BIOS interface, 272
  Digi driver INT 14H interface, 227
input thread, Win32Port class, 477-482
inputs, undefined, 8
InputThread() function (Win32Port class), 477-482
Insert() function
  MTDeque helper class, 503
  Queue helper class, 187
insertion operators, Base Window class, 366

Index

INT 14H driver functions (Digi APIs)
  alternate status check (function 8), 232
  clear port buffers (function 9), 232-233
  clear RX buffer (function 0x10), 236-237
  clear TX buffer (function 0x11), 237
  drop handshaking lines (function 0x0B), 233
  enable/disable BIOS pacing (function 0x20), 240-241
  extended port control (function 5), 229
  extended port initialization (function 4), 227-229
  get board information (function 6;subfunction 2), 230-231
  get buffer counts (function 0xFD), 241
  get buffer sizes, watermarks count (function 0x1B), 238-239
  get driver information (function 6;subfunction 1), 230
  get driver name (function 6;subfunction 0xff), 231
  get pointer to character ready flag (function 0x0D), 235
  get port name (function 6;subfunction 0), 229-230
  get RX buffer space count (function 0x15), 238
  get TX buffer free space count (function 0x12), 237
  initialize port (function 0), 225
  input buffer count (function 0x0A), 233
  input single character (function 2), 227
  output single character (function 1), 226
  peek at character (function 0x14), 238
  raise port handshake lines (function 0x13), 237-238
  read a buffer (function 0x0F), 236
  read line/modem status (function 3), 227
  read operating port parameters (function 0x0C), 234-235
  send break (function 7), 232
  set handshaking type (function 0x1EC), 240
  set handshaking watermarks count (function 0x1C), 239
  write a buffer (function 0x0E), 236
int86()/int86x() functions, 224
INTA (Interrupt Acknowledge) pins (8088 PCs), 127
intelligent multiport boards, 26-28
  configuring, 219-222, 243-244
  software interface, 222-223
interfaces. *See also* handshaking
  graphical (MS-Windows), 390
  intelligent multiport board control blocks, 222-223
  Windows NT/9X-PC8520 class, 105
  wrapper classes as, 69
internal functions (SimpleTapi class), 706-708
International Organization for Standardization (ISO), Unicode standard, 5
Interrupt Acknowledge (INTA) pins (8088 PCs), 127
Interrupt Enable Register (IER), 109-112
interrupt functions
  8250 UART chip family, 23-24, 110-112
  bugs/problems, 123-124
  handler code, 145-148
  IBM-compatible PCs
    edge-triggered, 127
    hardware, 127-128
    open collector configuration, 127-128
  with multiport boards, 207
Interrupt ID Register (IID), 112-113
interrupt lines
  handler management of, 207
  multiport board sharing of, 204-205
Interrupt Manager package (PC8250 class)
  ConnectToIRQ() function, 188, 197
  DisconnectFromIRQ() function, 188, 197
  source code (PCIRQ.CPP), 189-197
  source code (PCIRQ.H), 189
interrupt pulsing problems (8250 UARTs), 123
Interrupt Request (INTR) pins (8088 PCs), 127
Interrupt Service Routine (ISR), PC8250 class, 112
  class description/class definitions (PC8250.H), 129-133
  isr_data members listing, 133-136
  source code (_8250.H), 143-144
  source code (_PC8250.H), 142
  source code (ASCII.H), 144-145
  source code (ISR_8250.CPP), 136-142
  writing, 126
interrupt_number data member (PC8250 class), 135
INTR (Interrupt request) pins (8088 PCs), 127
InUseCount() function (Queue support class), 178, 188
irq data member (PC8250 class), 135
ISO (International Organization for Standardization), Unicode standard, 5
IsOpen() function (SimpleTapi), 701
ISR (Interrupt Service Routine)
  ClassicHandler class, classic_isr(), 212
  Digi multiboards, 205
  PC8250 class
    class description/class definitions (PC8250.H), 205
    isr_data members listing, 133-136
    source code (_8250.H), 143-144
    source code (_PC8250.H), 142
    source code (ASCII.H), 144-145
    source code (ISR_8250.CPP), 136-142
    writing, 126
isr_8250() function, 136
  with Handler class, 207
ISR_8250.CCP (PC8250 ISR source code), 136-142
isr_data structures (PC8150 class/ISR), 133-136
ITU Recommendation V.24, 2

K

Kermit protocol (file transfers), 39-40
Keyboard Key Reassignment escape sequence (ANSI.SYS), 334

846 Index

KEYBOARD_FAKE macro (AnsiTerminal class), 360-361
keys[] array (AnsiTerminal class), 342-343
keystrokes, keyboard sequences, ANSITerminal class keyboard translations, 335-337
KillFocus() function (Win32Term class), 593

L

laptop computers, COM cards with, 126
LCR (Line Control Register), 113-116
libraries, C/C++, 40-41
Line Control Register (LCR), 113-116
Line Device Handle (TAPI), 686
    lineOpen() function, 691-692
line errors, detecting in Win32 input thread, 480-482
Line Handle object (TAPI)
    lineConfigDialog() function, 688-689
    lineGetDevCaps() function, 689-691
line monitors, 43-44
Line Status interrupt (PC8250 driver), 111, 112-113
    handler code, 147-148
Line Status Register (LSR), 118-119
LINE_CALLINFO structure (TAPI), 687
line_status data member
    PC8250 class ISR, 134
    Win16Port class, 402
lineAnswer() function (TAPI), 685, 696-697
lineCallAnswer() function (TAPI), 697
LINECALLPARAMS structure (TAPI), 696
lineClose() function (TAPI), 692, 703
lineConfigDialog() function (TAPI), 688-689, 702
lineDeallocateCall() function (TAPI), 686, 697-698
LINEDEVCAPS structure (TAPI), 689-691
lineDrop() function (TAPI), 697, 704
lineGetDevCaps() function (TAPI), 689-691
lineGetDevConfig() function (TAPI), 685

lineGetID() function (SimpleTapi class), 704
lineInitialize() function (TAPI), 685, 687, 690
lineInitializeEx() function (TAPI), 685, 687
lineMakeCall() function (TAPI), 685, 686, 695-696
    with CloseLine() function, 703-704
    with lineAnswer() function 697
    with lineDeallocateCall() function, 698
    with MakeCall() function, 694
lineOpen() function (TAPI), 686, 691-692, 703
lineShutdown() function (TAPI), 687-688, 692
lineTranslateAddress() function (TAPI), 693-695
lineTranslateDialog() function (TAPI), 693, 703
local flow control, 36
local_baud_rate member (Modem class), 667
locked DTE communications, flow control, 33
locked_baud_rate member (ModemCapabilities structure), 661-662
LOGFONT structure (Win32Term class), 590
logic levels, 10
ls_int_count data member (PC8250 class/ISR), 133
LSR (Line Status Register), 118-119

M

m_bClassRegistered data member (Win32Term class), 587
m_bInputThreadReading data member (Win32Port class), 500-501
m_BorderColor data member (Win32Term class), 586
m_bShowingCursor data member (Win32Term class), 583-584
m_bWrap data member (Win32Term class), 583
m_CharSize data member (Win32Term class), 586
m_CurrentColor data member (Win32Term class), 582
m_Dcb data member (Win32Port class), 501

m_Devices data member (SimpleTapi clas), 707
m_dwErrors data member (Win32Port class), 501-502
m_dwModemStatus data member (Win32Port class), 502
m_dwWindowsError data member (Win32Port class), 501
m_hBreakRequest data member (Win32Port class), 502
m_hCall (SimpleTapi class), 707
m_hFont data member (Win32Term class), 584
m_hInputThread data member (Win32Port class), 501
m_hKillInputThreadEvent data memebr (Win32Port class), 502
m_hKillOutputThreadEvent data member (Win32Port class), 502
m_hLine (SimpleTapi class), 708
m_hLineApp (SimpleTapi class), 707
m_hOutputThread data member (Win32Port class), 501
m_hParent data member (Win32Term class), 582
m_hPort data member (Win32Port class), 500
m_hReadRequestEvent data member (Win32Port class), 502
m_hWnd data member (Win32Term class), 581-582
m_hWriteRequestEvent data memebr (Win32Port class), 502
m_iBreakDuration data member (Win32Port class), 500
m_iCharDescent data member (Win32Term class), 586
m_lCallState (SimpleTapi class), 708
m_lfFont data member (Win32Term class), 584
m_Offset data member (Win32Term class), 585-586
m_Position data member (Win32Term class), 586
m_RxQueue data member (Win32Port class), 501
m_ScreenText data member (Win32Term class), 582-583
m_ScrollRange data member (Win32Term class), 585
m_Trace member (ConStream class), 708

Index

m_TxQueue data member
(Win32Port class), 501
m_VirtualSize data member
(Win32Term class), 585
m_VisibleSize data member
(Win32Term class), 584-585
Macintosh systems, cabling for, 19
macros, terminal emulation
debuggers, 360-361
make files
BIOSPort/EBIOSPort classes test
file, 295-297
Modem class test program, 681
PC8250 class test program,
modifying, 201
terminal emulation classes test
files, 386-387
Win16 terminal test program,
430-431
ZMODEM test program, 784
MakeCall() function (SimpleTapi
class), 694, 695, 703-704
MakeCallResult() function
(SimpleTapi class), 705
male connectors, 324
management options (ZF1)
(ZMODEM), 770-771
mapping, 8250 register offsets, 107
marking state, defined, 10
MCA (Micro Channel Architecture),
128
MCR (Modem Control Register),
116-118
menu commands (AnsiTermWin test
program)
File|Exit, 610
Port|Close Port, 613
Port|Open COMx, 612
Terminal|Clear, 610
Terminal|Set Background Color,
611-612
Terminal|Set Border Color,
611-612
Terminal|Set Font, 610-611
Terminal|Set Text Color,
611-612
MessageBeep(), in Win32Term class,
591
MFC programs (Win32Port test
program), 509-516
Microsoft 16-bit compiler, 105, 430
milliseconds parameter (Rs232
class), 61
MNP-4 modems, 430-431
MNP-5 modems, 32

Modem class
class descriptor source code,
663-664
class implementation source
code, 669-677
features, 662-663
protected members
carrier_timeout, 668
echo(), 668
*local_baud_rate, 667
*modem_data, 667
*port, 667
protocol, 668
read_line(), 668-669
tone_dial, 667-668
wait_for_connection(), 668
wait_for_response(), 668
public functions
Answer(), 665, 667, 668
Dial(), 665, 667, 668
Disconnect(), 665-666
DumpState(), 667
*ErrorName(), 667
Initialize(), 664-665
Modem() constructor,
664-665
PulseDial(), 666
ReadRegister(), 666
SendCommand(), 666
SetCarrierTimeout(),
666-667
ToneDial(), 666
UserAbort(), 666
structures, ModemCapabilities,
659-662
test program source code,
677-681
Modem() constructor function
(Modem class), 664-665
Modem Control Register (MCR),
116-118
*modem_data pointer (Modem
class), 667
modem status, evaluating in Win32
input thread, 480-482
Modem Status interrupt (PC8250
drivers), 111, 112-113
handler code, 145-146
problems/bugs, 124
Modem Status Register (MSR),
119-120
modem_status data member
(PC8250 class/ISR), 134
modem_status_register pointer
(Win16Port class), 402

ModemCapabilities structure
(Modem class), 659-662
MODEM.CPP (Modem class),
669-677
MODEM.H (Modem class), 663-664
modems, 684. *See also* file transfer
protocols; Modem class;
SimpleTapi class
56k, 657-658
AT command set, 651-652
Smartmodem 2400, listing
of, 652-656
data rate changes, 28-30
defining in Modem class,
659-662
Diamond Multimedia,
657-658
DTE communications, 5-6
error functions (Modem class),
665-666
factory defaults, creating
capability entries using, 662
half-duplex, 11
handshaking, 11
hardware standards, 649-651
intelligence features, 31-33
inter-communication, 650
Macintosh system cabling, 19
MS-DOS systems, testing
connections, 677-681
nonstandard, 651
remote echoing, 28
S register definition list,
656-657
smart, 651
speed limits, 28
status events, tracking, 179
TAPI 2.x
call configuration functions,
692-695
call control functions,
695-698
callback function, 699-700
history, 683-684
initialization/shutdown
functions, 686-688
overview, 684-686
3COM
missing DR bit, 125
V.90, 657-658
MODEMSETTINGS structure (Win32
serial API), 460, 463
modular connectors, 45
motherboard timing problems (8250
UARTs), 124-125

848 Index

MS-DOS systems
  ANSI.SYS escape sequences, 331-334
  intelligent multiport boards for, 27-28
  MODE command, in Windows NT/9X programs, 445-446
  modems, hardware standards, 649-651
  MS-DOS compilers, accessing Digi API functions, 53-55
  multitasking approaches, 217
MS-Windows systems. *See also* Win32 systems
  16-bit O/S-dependent functions, 421
  classes, 69
  device driver APIs, 390
  event driven programming for, 390
  graphical user interface, 390
  idle function, redefining, 421
  integrating Win APIs with C++, 574-577
  RS-232 APIs, 69
  subclassing, 422
  Win32 Telephony API (TAPI), 683-684
  Windows comm API functions, 390
  Windows NT/9X programs
    MODE command equivalent, 445-446
    PC8250 class with, 105
ms_int_count data member (PC8250 class/ISR), 133
MSDOS.CPP code file, O/S-specific routines, 103
MSR (Modem Status Register), 119-120
MTDeque helper class (Win32Port class), 503-504
MTDEQUE.H (Win32Port class), 565-570
MTTTY.C (MultiThreaded TTY Program), 469-470
multiline edit control (Win16 API), 422
multiport boards
  configuring, 243-244
  CXDOS5.SYS device driver, 224
  dual port RAM, 220
  handler class for, 203
  intelligent, 26-28, 219-223
  interrupt line sharing, 204-205
  MS-DOS multitasking, 217

nonintelligent, 204, 212
shared interrupt multiport boards, 25-26
status registers
  configuring, 205-206
  variable features, 207
multitasking, MS-DOS systems, 217
MySimpleTapi class, 710-711
  class descriptor source code, 748-752
  functions, 710
  with SimpleTapi class, 711
MySimpleTapi.h (MySimpleTapi class), 748-752
MyWin32Port class, 483
  with AnsiWinTerm class, 598
  virtual functions, 516-517

N

*name member (ModemCapabilities structure), 660
naming conventions, C++ classes, 58
nonintelligent multiport boards, 204
  status registers, 212
nonstandard modems, 651
Notification check box (Win32Port test program), 512
notification routines
  SimpleTapi class, 705-706, 707, 708-709
  Win32Port class, 482-484, 597-598
NotifyCallStateChange() function (SimpleTapi class), 705, 707
null modem cable, 6, 15-19
  rational version, 16-17

O

offsets, 8250 family registers, 107
OnRiNotify() function (Win32Port class), 483
Open/Close button (Win32Port test program), 516
open collector configuration, 127-128
Open() function (AnsiWinTerm class), 612
OpenComm() function (Win16 API), 392, 394-395
  with DBC structure function, 398-400
OpenLine() function (SimpleTapi class), 703
Opus BBS system, 40

OUT1 line/OUT2 line (8250 UARTs), 116-118
Output() function (Win32Term class), 589, 590-591
output lines, 8250 chip systems, 116-118
output, screen (TextWindow class), 367
output single character function
  BIOS interface, 270-271
  Digi driver INT 14H interface, 226
output_worker function (Win32Port class), 474-475
OutputThread() function (Win32Port class), 473-477
overflow data member (PC8250 class/ISR), 133
overlapped I/O, Win32 serial communications, 434
OVERLAPPED structure (Win32 serial API), 457, 458-459, 478
  members listing, 444
Overrun Error bit (8250 LSR), 119

P

Paint() function (Win32Term class), 580, 592-593
Pair private class (Win32Term class), 581
parity bit field (LCR), 115
Parity Combo box (Win32Port test program), 511
Parity Error bit (8250 LSR), 119
Parity Error Count edit control (Win32Port test program), 513
parity settings (Set() function), 70
ParityError() function
  PC8250 class, 179-180
  RS232 class, 71-72
ParityErrorNotify() function (Win32Port class), 499
parm_count index (AntiTerminal class), 342
parse() function (AnsiTerminal class), 343
parse_ansi_string function() (AnsiTerminal class), 343-344
PBX devices, distinctive ring feature, 13
PC Comm ports, multiport board interface, 224

Index 849

PC-to-modem cabling, 14-15
PC-to-PC connections, null modem cabling, 15-17
PC8250 class
    constructor, 172
        Handler class implementation, 206
    functions
        BreakDetect(), 179-180
        Dtr(), 181-182
        DtrHandshaking(), 181
        ErrorName(), 183-184
        FormatDebugOutput(), 182-183
        FramingError(), 179-180
        HardwareOverrunError(), 179-180
        ParityError(), 179-180
        PeekBuffer(), 182
        Rts(), 181-182
        RtsCtsHandshaking(), 181
        RXSpaceFree(), 178
        RXSpaceUsed(), 178
        SoftwareOverrunError(), 180
        TXSpaceFree(), 178
        TXSpaceUsed(), 178
        XonXoffHandshaking(), 180-181
    implementation source code, 148-172
    Interrupt Manager package
        ConnectToIRQ() function, 188, 197
        descriptor source code, 189
        DisconnectFromIRQ() function, 188, 197
        implementation source code, 189-197
    ISR (Interrupt Service Routine)
        descriptor source code (8250 UART interface), 142
        descriptor source code (ASCII definitions) 144-145
        descriptor source code (PC8250 class), 129-133
        descriptor source code (registers), 143-144
        implementation source code, 136-142
    limitations, 105
PC8250 object, creating using Zmodem class, 782-784
Queue support class
    Clear() function, 188

descriptor source code, 184-186
FreeCount() function, 188
Head() function, 188
implementation source code, 187
Insert() function, 187
InUseCount() function, 188
Peek() function, 188
Queue() function, 187
Remove() function, 188
Tail() function, 188
reusing in handler class, 203
test program source code, 197-200
PC8250() constructor function (PC8250 class), 172-173
PC8250.H (PC8250 class/ISR), 129-133
_PC8250.H (PC8250/ISR), 142
PCIRQ.CPP (PC8250 support), 189-197
PCIRQ.H (PC8250 support), 189
PCs (IBM compatible), COM card configurations, 125-128
peek at character function (Digi driver INT 14H interface), 238
Peek Buffer button (Win32Port test program), 515
Peek() function
    implementing in Windows, 401
    MTDeque helper class, 503
    PC8250 Queue support class, 182
    RS232 class, 75-76, 79-80, 91-92, 102
    Win32Port class, 491
PeekBuffer() function (PC8250 class), 182
PeekMesage() function (16-bit MS-Windows), 421
performance, RS-232-C specification limits, 13
PIC (Programmable Interrupt Controller), 127-128
Plug and Play, with Classic multiboard, 206
Port Combo box (Win32Port test program), 510
port-name member (RS232 class), 64-65
Port|Close Port command (AnsiWinTerm test program), 613

Port|Open COMx command (AnsiWinTerm test program), 612
portability. *See also* inheritance
    C++ for, 49-50, 57
    standards and, 2-3
*port pointer
    FileTransfer class, 781
    Modem class, 667
ports
    adding using multiport boards, 25-26
    configuring for Digi multiport board, 244-246
    Win16 versus Win32 systems, 433-434
position_cursor() function (AnsiTerminal class), 344
Product-Id function (Modem test program), 678
Programmable Interrupt Controller (PIC), 127-128. *See also* 8259 PIC
protected members
    RS232 class, 63-67
    Win32Port class, 492-497
protocol member (Modem class), 668
protocols
    BBS systems, 300
    file transfers
        Kermit, 39-40
        XMODEM, 37, 765-766
        YMODEM, 37, 766
        ZMODEM, 38, 767-778
*protocol_strings member (ModemCapabilities structure), 661
PulseDial() function (Modem class), 666
purge input buffer function (FOSSIL driver), 305
purge output buffer function (FOSSIL driver), 305
PurgeComm() function (Win32 serial API), 457-458

Q

Queue() function (Queue support class), 187
Queue support class (PC8250 class)
    Clear() function, 188
    descriptor source code, 187
    FreeCount() function, 188

Continued

850   Index

Queue support class *(continued)*
　functions, 178
　Head() function, 188
　implementation source code
　　(QUEUE.H), 184-186
　Insert() function, 187
　InUseCount() function, 188
　Peek() function, 182, 188
　Queue() function, 187
　Remove() function, 188
　Tail() function, 188
QUEUE.CPP (Queue support class),
　187
QUEUE.H (Queue support class),
　184-186

R

raise port handshake lines function
　(Digi driver INT 14H
　interface), 237-238
RAM, dual port, 220
rational null modem cable, 16-17
RBR (Receive Buffer Register),
　108-109
RC file (Win16 programs),
　423-429
RD (Received Data) line, 8
　asynchronous transmissions, 10
RDA (Receive Data Available)
　interrupt (8250 UARTs), 110,
　112-113
read a buffer function
　Digi driver INT 14H interface,
　　236
　FOSSIL driver, 307
Read Bytes drop-down list
　(Win32Port test program),
　512
Read Char button (Win32Port test
　program), 515
Read() function
　in C applications, 50-53
　in C++ applications, 49
　RS232 class, 60, 66, 68, 72-74,
　　95-96, 338
　with RXSpaceUsed() function, 70
　timed version, 505
read line/modem status function,
　BIOS interface, 272
　Digi driver INT 14H interface,
　　227
read modem control register (EBIOS
　interface), 274

read operating port parameters
　function (Digi driver INT
　14H interface), 234-235
Read-regs function (Modem test
　program), 678
read status registers function
　(FOSSIL driver), 302-303
read_buffer() function
　DigiBoard class, 236
　PC8250 class, 175-176
　Win32Port class, 492-493
read_byte() function
　PC8250 class, 175
　RS232 class, 67
　Win32Port class, 493
read_line() function (Modem class),
　668-669
read_settings() function
　EBIOSPort class, 276
　PC8250 class, 177
　Win32Port class, 494-495
　WindowsPort class, 394
ReadBuffer() function (RS232 class),
　66-67, 98-100
ReadComm() function (Win16 API),
　395, 434
ReadFile() function (Win32 serial
　API), 434, 457-459, 465,
　478-479, 502
ReadKey() function (TextWindow
　class), 367
ReadPort() function
　AnsiTerminal class, 343
　Terminal base class, 338-339
ReadRegister() function (Modem
　class), 666
　testing, 678
ReadSettings() function (RS232
　class), 65, 76
ReadTime() function (16-bit MS-
　Windows), 422
Receive Buffer Register (RBR),
　108-109
Receive Data Available (RDA)
　interrupt (8250 UARTs), 110,
　112-113
Receive interrupt (PC8250 driver),
　handler code, 146-147
Received Data (RD) line, 8
　asynchronous transmissions, 10
register sets (8250 UARTs), 106-107
　16550 FCR (FIFO Control
　　Register), 120-122
　Digi API systems, 225-241

IER (Interrupt Enable Register),
　109-112
IIR (Interrupt ID Register),
　112-113
LCR (Line Control Register),
　113-116
LSR (Line Status Register),
　118-119
MCR (Modem Control Register),
　116-118
MSR (Modem Status Register),
　119-120
RBR (Receive Buffer Register),
　108-109
THR (Transmit Holding
　Register), 109
remote echoing, 28
Remove() function (PC8250/Queue
　class), 188
Request To Send (RTS) line, 8, 11
Reset Mode escape sequence
　(ANSI.SYS), 334
resource definitions (SimpleTapi test
　program), 759-763
response times
　8250 receivers, 108-109
　8250 transmitters, 109
Restore Cursor Position escape
　sequence (ANSI.SYS), 332
restore_position function
　(AnsiTerminal class), 345
RI edit control (Win32Port test
　program), 513
Ri() function (PC8250 class), 179
RI (Ring Indicator) line, 9, 13
RiNotify() function (Win32 Port
　class), 499
RLSD (Received Line Signal Detect).
　See CD (Carrier Detect)
RS-232 connections, 6
　25-pin/9-pin connectors, 7
　9- to 25-pin adapter, 17-18
　data transmissions, 5
　directionality of, 9
　duplication in standards, 3
　electrical characteristics, 8
　PC-to-modem cables, 14-15
　PC-to-PC (null modem cable),
　　15-17
　standards for, 2-3, 2-3, 6
　　DTE/DCE connections, 2
　　omissions, 3
　　RS-232-C specification lim-
　　　its, 13
　　versions, 2

UART for, 10
Win16 comm API functions for, 390
Windows APIs for, 69
RS-232 Data Line Analyzer, 44
RS-422 connections (Macintosh systems), 19
RS232 class, 49, 182-183
   ByteCount element, 60
   class definition code files, 54-57, 86
   constructor, absence of, 57, 61-62
   default parameters, 61-62
   ElapsedTime member, 60-61
   error codes, 59
      with Win32Port class, 477
   error_status member, 60
   mandatory functions, 62
      BreakDetect(), 71-72
      FramingError(), 71-72
      HardwareOverrunError(), 71-72
      ParityError(), 71-72
      RXSpaceUsed(), 70-71
      Set(), 69-70
      TXSpaceFree(), 70
   mandatory versus optional functions, 62
   member functions
      read_buffer(), 66-67
      read_byte(), 67
      write_buffer(), 67
      write_byte(), 67
   nonvirtual functions, 72-76
      DebugLineCount() function, 76
      ErrorStatus() function, 76
      Peek() function, 75-76
      Read() functions, 72-74
      ReadSettings() function, 76
      Write() functions, 74-75
   optional functions, 77-86
      Break(), 78
      destructor, 77
      Dtr() function, 79
      DtrDsrHandshaking() function, 78-79
      ErrorName() function, 81-83
      FlushRXBuffer() function, 80-81
      FlushTXBuffer() function, 80-81
      FormatDebugOutput() function, 83-86
      IdleFunction() function, 83
      Peek() function, 79-80
      Rts() function, 79
      RtsCtsHandshaking() function, 78-79
      RXSpaceFree() function, 80
      SoftwareOverrunError(), 78
      TXSpaceUsed() function, 80
      XonXoffHandshaking() function, 78-79
   parameter setting, 61-62
   protected members, 63-68
   public data members, 67-68
   public functions, 68-72
   return values, function, 58-60
   using mandatory/nonvirtual functions, 76-77
   viritual destructor, 77
   Win32Port class, relationship to, 484
RS232.CPP (RS232 class), 91-102
RS232Error class (RS232 class), 65-66
   ErrorStatus() function, 76
RS232.H code file (RS232 class), 86-90
RS232PortName class @index H:(RS232 class), 63-64
RS232_SUCCESS error code, 59-60
RS232_TIMEOUT error, 61
RTS check box (Win32Port test program), 512
RTS/CTS checkbox (Win32Port test program), 512
RTS/CTS flow control, 33-35
   advantages of, 36
RTS (Request To Send) line, 8, 11
   8250 chip systems, 116-118
Rts() function
   EBIOSPort class, 276
   PC8250 class, 181-182
   RS232 class, 61, 79, 102
RtsCtsHandshaking() function
   PC8250 class, 181
   RS232 class, 78-79, 101
   Win32Port class, 487
RX FIFO, 120-122
rx_int_count data member (PC8250 class/ISR), 133
RxNotify() function (Win32Port class), 483, 497-498
RXQueue data member (PC8250 class/ISR), 135
RXSpaceFree() function
   PC8250 class, 178
   RS232 class, 80, 101
   Win32Port class, 486-487
RXSpaceUsed() function
   PC8250 class, 178
   RS232 class, 70-71
   Win32Port class, 486-487

S

S registers, definition list, 656-657
Save Cursor position escape sequence (ANSI.SYS), 332
save_position() function (AnsiTerminal class), 345
saved_col member (AnsiTerminal class), 342, 345
saved_row member (AnsiTerminal class), 342, 345
saved_settings member (RS232 class), 64-65
screen output
   TextWindow class, 367
   Win32 terminal, 609
screens (terminals)
   clr_scr() function for, 327-328
   terminal control (escape) sequences, 328
scrollback capability
   adding to Win32TermClass, 623
select flow control function (FOSSIL driver), 306-307
Send Break button (Win32Port test program), 514
send break function (Digi driver INT 14H interface), 232
Send Buffer button (Win32Port test program), 513-514
Send() function (FileTransfer class), 780
send_handshake_char data member (PC8250 class/ISR), 134
SendCommand() function (Modem class), 666
   testing, 678
serial connections, electrical characteristics, 8
Set Colors escape sequence (ANSI.SYS), 333
Set() function
   PC8250 class, 178
   RS232 class, 61, 69-70
set handshaking type function (Digi driver INT 14H interface), 240

852   Index

set handshaking watermarks function (Digi driver INT 14H interface), 239
Set Mode escape sequence (ANSI.SYS), 333-334
set_color() function (AnsiTerminal class), 345-346
set_mode() function (AnsiTerminal class), 346
set_uart_address_and_irq priate member (PC8250 class), 173-174
SetAttribute() function (BaseWindow class), 346, 366
SetBackgroundColor() function (Win32Term class), 589
SetBorderColor function (Win32Term class), 589
SETBREAK function (Win32 serial API), 451
SetCarrierTimeout() function (Modem class), 666-667
SetCommBreak() function
   Win16 comm API, 392, 395-396
   Win32 serial API, 447, 459, 502
SetCommConfig() function (Win32 serial API), 452, 459-460
SetCommEventMask() function (Windows com), 396-397
SetCommMask() function (Win32 serial API), 460-461
SetCommState() function
   with DCB, 435
   Win16 comm API, 397
   Win32 serial API, 392, 460, 461-462, 501
SetCommTimeouts() function (Win32 serial API), 438, 462
SetCursorPosition() function (Win32Term class), 591-592
SetDefaultCommConfig() function (Win32 serial API), 462-463
SETDTR function (Win32 serial API), 451
SetFocus() function (Win32Term class), 593
SetFont() function
   AnsiWinTerm class, 611
   Win32Term class, 591
SetForegroundColor() function (Win32Term class), 589
SetParity() function (Dcb class), 505
SetPosition() function (BaseWindow class), 338, 344, 345, 366-367

SETRTS function (Win32 serial API), 451
Settings class (RS232 class), 64-65
   Adjust() function code, 102
settings member, Win32Port class, 494
SetupComm() function (Win32 serial API), 463-464
SetWindowLong() function (Win32 API), 576-577
SetWrap() function (BaseWindow class), 346, 365
SETXOFF function (Win32 serial API), 451
SETXON function (Win32 serial API), 451
shared interrupt multiport boards, 25-28
signal ground lines, 9, 13
SimpleTapi class
   accessing Win32Port class, 698
   Callback() function in, 699-700
   class descriptor source code, 724-728
   class name, 689
   connecting with Win32 Port, 704
   debugging features, 708
   demo program components, 710-711
   functions
      AnswerResult(), 709
      CallActive(), 701
      Callback(), 696, 706-708
      CloseLine() function, 703
      ConfigureCall(), 702, 703
      ConfigureDevice(), 702-703, 702-703
      ConnectedEvent(), 704, 705, 707
      DisconnectedEvent(), 705
      DropCall(), 704
      DropCallResult(), 705
      Error(), 703, 706
      GetDeviceCount(), 701-702
      GetDeviceName(), 702
      GetPortHandle(), 704
      GetWindow() function, 702
      HandleAnswerResult(), 706
      HandleDropResult(), 704, 706
      HandleMakeCallResult(), 706
      IsOpen(), 701
      lineConfigDialog(), 702
      MakeCall(), 694, 695,

        703-704
      MakeCallResult(), 705
      NotifyCallStateChange(), 705, 707
      OpenLine(), 703
      SimpleTapi() constructor, 701
      ~SimpleTapi() destructor, 701
      TranslateCallState(), 702
      TranslateTapiError(), 702
   implementation source code, 728-748
   integrating into applications, 710-711
   lineOpen() with, 691-692
   members
      m_Devices, 707
      m_hCall, 707
      m_hLine, 708
      m_hLineApp, 707
      m_lCallState, 708
   TAPI 1.4 in, 687, 690
   test program, resource definitions, 759-763
   uses for, 700
SimpleTapi() constructor function (SimpleTapi), 701
SimpleTapi.cpp (SimpleTapi class), 728-748
SimpleTapi.h (SimpleTapi class), 724-728
Simtel file repository, FOSSIL drivers, 309
single character peek function (FOSSIL driver), 306
Size() function (Win32Term class), 594
smart modems, 31, 651
smart terminals, 329
Smartmodem 2400, AT command set listing, 652-656
software
   8250 UART family support, 106
   BBS systems, 39-40
   communications packages, 39
   intelligent multiport board control blocks, 222-223
   multiport boards, CPU control programs, 222
   portability, standards and, 2
   programming libraries, 40
software flow control (XON/XOFF), 33-35
SoftwareOverrunError() function

Index 853

PC8250 class, 180
RS232 class, 78, 101
SoftwareOverrunErrorNotify()
    function (Win32Port class),
    499
source code
    AnsiTerminal class
        ANSITERM.CPP, 347-359
        ANSITERM.H, 341-342
    AnsiWinTerm class
        ANSIWINTERM.CPP,
            605-609
        ANSIWINTERM.H, 600-605
        CHAPT13.CPP, 613-622
        CHAPT13.RC, 622
        RESOURCE.H, 622
    Base Window class
        BASEWIND.H, 362-365
    BIOSPort class
        BIOSPORT.CPP, 279-290
        BIOSPORT.H, 277-279
    ClassicHandler class
        CHAPT04.CPP, 213-216
        CLASSIC.CPP, 209-211
        CLASSIC.H, 208-209
        destructor, 211-212
    ConStream debugging class
        Constream.cpp, 757-759
        Constream.h, 755-757
    Crc16/Crc32 classes
        CRC.CPP, 786-788
        CRC.H, 785-786
    DCB helper class
        DCB.CPP, 560-565
        DCB.H, 559-560
    DigiBoard class
        DIGI.CPP, 249-265
        DIGI.H, 246-248
    EBIOSPort class
        BIOSPORT.CPP, 279-295
        BIOSPORT.H, 277-279
    Fossil class
        FOSSIL.CPP, 312-323
        FOSSIL.H, 310-312
    Modem class
        MODEM.CPP, 669-677
        MODEM.H, 663-664
        TSTMODEM.CPP, 679-681
        TSTMODEM.MAK, 681
    MySimpleTapi
        MySimpleTapi.h, 748-752
    PC8250 class
        PC8250.CPP, 148-172
    PC8250 class ISR
        _8250.H, 143-144

_PC8250.H, 142
ASCII.H, 144-145
ISR_8250.CCP, 136-142
PC8250.H, 129-133
Queue support class
    QUEUE.CPP, 187
    QUEUE.H, 184-186
SimpleTapi class
    CHAPT15.CPP, 711-724
    Chapt15.rc, 759-763
    SimpleTapi.cpp, 728-748
    SimpleTapi.h, 724-728
Tapi32Port class
    Tapi32Port.cpp, 754-755
    Tapi32Port.h, 753-754
Terminal base class
    TERMINAL.H, 337-338
TextWindow class
    TEXTWIND.CPP, 370-386
    TEXTWIND.H, 367-370
TMTDeque helper class
    MTDEQUE.H, 565-570
Win16Port class
    TERMW16.CPP, 423-429
    WIN16.CPP, 404-421
    WIN16.H, 402-404
Win32Port class
    WIN32PORT.CPP, 521-559
    WIN32PORT.H, 517-521
Win32Term class
    WIN32TERM.CPP, 627-648
    WIN32TERM.H, 623-627
Zmodem class
    ZMODEM.CPP, 792-822
    ZMODEM.H, 788-790
    _ZMODEM.H, 790-792
SpaceFree() function (MTDeque
    class), 503
SpaceUsed() function (MTDeque
    class), 503
spacing, defined, 10
specifications, FOSSIL driver,
    301-309
standards
    ASCII text standard, 3
    C++, 2
    ITU Recommendation V.24, 2
    modem hardware, 650-651
    RS-232 connections, 6
        DTE/DCE connections, 2
        omissions, 3
        RS-232-C specification limits, 13
        versions, 2
    Unicode text standard, 5

standout text feature, adding to
    Win32TermClass, 623
start bits, 10
Start Spew/Stop Spew button
    (Win32Port test program),
    514
status() function (FileTransfer class),
    780-781
status registers (8250 UARTs), 23
    ClassicHandler class, 212
    formats, 207
    multiboards
        configuring, 205-206
        Digi system, 205
Statys function (Modem test
    program), 678
stop bits, 10
Stop Bits combo box (Win32Port
    test program), 511
string terminators, 62
subclassing (MS-Windows systems),
    422
SW Overrun Error Count edit
    control (Win32Port test
    program), 513
synchronous functions (TAPI 2.x),
    685
    lineConfigDialog(), 688-689
    lineOpen(), 692
syntax. *See also* source code
    ANSI.SYS commands, 331
    AT command set, 652
    RS232 function/element names,
        58

T

Tail() function (Queue support class),
    188
TAPI 1.4, in SimpleTapi class, 687,
    690
TAPI 2.x, 692
    functions
        Callback(), 699-700
        lineAnswer(), 696-697
        lineCallAnswer(), 697
        lineClose(), 692, 703
        lineConfigDialog(), 688-689
        lineDeallocateCall(), 686,
            697-698
        lineDrop(), 697, 704
        lineGetDevCaps(), 689-691
        lineInitialize(), 687, 690
        lineInitializeEx(), 685, 687

Continued

Index

TAPI 2.x, functions *(continued)*
   lineMakeCall(), 685, 686,
      694, 695-696, 697, 698,
      703-704
   lineOpen(), 686, 691-692,
      703
   lineShutdown(), 687-688,
      692
   lineTranslateAddress(),
      693-695
   lineTranslateDialog(), 693,
      703
  history/versions, 683-684
  notification methods, 684-685
  notification routines, 684-686
  objects
   Call Handle, 686
   Line Device Handle, 686
   Usage Handle, 685-686
  structures
   LINE_CALLINFO, 687
   LINECALLPARAMS, 696
   LINEDEVCAPS, 689-691
  synchronous vs. asynchronous
    functions, 685
TAPI 3, 684
Tapi32Port class
  class descriptor source code,
    753-754
  implementation source code
    (Tapi32Port.cpp), 754-755
  opening in AnsiTapiTerm class,
    711
  Win32Port class in, 753-755
Tapi32Port.cpp (Tapi32Port class),
  754-755
Tapi32Port.h (Tapi32Port class)0,
  753-754
TD (Transmitted Data) line, 8
  asynchronous transmissions, 10
Telephony API. *See* TAPI 2.x
Telnet escape sequence (ZMODEM),
  776
termcap file (UNIX systems), 329
Terminal base class, 337
  class descriptor source code,
    337-338
  constructor function, 338
  Display() function, 339
  ReadPort() function, 338-339
  uses for, 337
  WriteKey() function, 339
terminal control sequences, 328-329
terminal emulation, 323
  AnsiTerminal class, 337,
    341-359

    integrating with Win32Term
      class, 596-597
  AnsiTermWin class
   identifiers file source code,
    623
   RC file source code, 622
   test programs source code,
    609, 613-622
  Base Window class, 362-367
  debugging, 360-361
  Terminal base class, 337-339
  TestWindow class, 367-386
   test program make file,
    386-387
  Win32Term class, 573-574
   basic structure, 578-579
   improvements to, 622-648
Terminal|Clear command
  (AnsiWinTerm test
  program), 610
Terminal|Set Background Color
  command (AnsiWinTerm
  test program), 611-612
Terminal|Set Border Color command
  (AnsiWinTerm test
  program), 611-612
Terminal|Set Font command
  (AnsiWinTerm test
  program), 610-611
Terminal|Set Text Color command
  (AnsiWinTerm test
  program), 611-612
TERMINAL.H (Terminal base class),
  337-338
terminals
  ANSI.SYS escape sequences,
    331-334
  DCE communications, 5-6
  dumb versus smart, 329
  sending commands to, 327-329
terminators, for Read()/Write()
  routines, 62
TERMW16B.MAK (Win16Port class),
  430
TERMW16.CPP (Win16Port class),
  422-429
TERMW16M.MAK (Win16Port
  class), 430-431
TERMW.DEF file (Win16Port class),
  429-430
CHAPT03.CPP (PC8250 class),
  197-200
  limitations for Windows
    programs, 422
TEST232W.EXE (PC8250 class), DEF
  file code, 423-429

testing programs
  AnsiTerminal class
   debugging macros, 360-361
   TESTTERM.CPP, 339-341
  AnsiTermWin class
   CHAP13.EXE, 609-622
   CHAPT13.RC, 622
   RESOURCE.H, 623
  BIOSPort/EBIOSPort classes
   CHAPT06.MAK, 295-297
  ClassicHandler class
   CHAPT04.CPP, 213-216
  DigiBoard class
   CHAPT05.EXE, 265-267
  Fossil class
   CHAPT07.EXE, 323-324
  Modem class
   TSTMODEM.CPP, 677-681
  PC8250 class
   TEST232.CPP, 197-200
  SimpleTapi class
   CHAPT15.CPP, 711-724
   CHAPT15.EXE, 710-711
   Chapt15.rc, 759-763
  terminal emulation classes
   TESTTERM.MAK, 386-387
  Win16Port class
   TEST232W.EXE, 429-430
   TERMW16.CPP, 422-429
  Win32Port class, console-based
    screen
   CHAPT12.CPP, 509-516
  Zmodem class
   TESTZM.CPP, 782-784
   TESTZM.MAK, 784
TESTTERM.CPP (AnsiTerminal
  class), 339-341
TESTTERM.MAK (terminal
  emulation test), 386-387
TESTZM.CPP (Zmodem test
  program), 782-784
TESTZM.MAK (Zmodem test
  program), 784
Texas Instruments, UART
  datasheets, 123
text-based information
  ASCII standard for, 3-4
  foreign characters, 5
  Unicode standard for, 5
text window (Win 32 terminal
  emulation), basic
  requirements, 574
TextColor private class (Win32Term
  class), 580-581
TEXTWIND.CPP (TextWindow class
  descriptor), 370-386

Index

TEXTWIND.H (TextWindow class implementation), 367-370
TextWindow class
  as BaseWindow, 367
  class descriptor source code, 367-370
  implementation file source code, 370-386
  ReadKey() function, 367
  with Terminal base class, 338
third-party call control (TAPI), 684
THR (Transmit Holding Register), 109
THRE (Transmit Holding Register Empty) interrupt, 111, 112-113
threading
  MTTTY.C program example, 469-470
  in Win32 serial communications, 434
  Win32Port class, 471-472
    input thread, 477-482
    output thread, 472-477
  3COM modems
    missing DR bit, 125
    V.90, 657-658
time, elapsed, calculating, 60-61
time parameters, RS232 class functions, 60-61
timing problems (8250 UARTs), 124-125
tone_dial member (Modem class), 667-668
ToneDial() function (Modem class), 666
trace window (SimpleTapi), 708
translate_error() function (Win32Port class), 477
translate_last_error() function (Win32Port class), 497
TranslateCallState() function (SimpleTapi class), 702
TranslateTapiError() function (SimpleTapi class), 702
transmission speeds, history, 28-30
Transmit Holding Register Empty [THRE], 111, 112-113, 119
Transmit Holding Register (THR), 109
transmit single byte function (FOSSIL driver), 302
transmit with no wait function (FOSSIL driver), 306
TransmitCommChar() function
  Win16 comm API, 397

Win32 serial API, 464, 466
Transmitted Data (TD) line, 8
  asynchronous transmissions, 10
Transmitter Empty bit (8250 LSR), 119
transport options (ZF2) (ZMODEM), 771
trigger level bits, 16550 FCR (FIFO Control Register), 121
TSTMODEM.CPP (Modem class), 677-681
TSTMODEM.MAK (Modem test program), 681
TX Empty Count edit control (Win32Port test program), 513
TX interrupt (PC8250 drivers) bugs/problems, 123-124
  handler code, 146
tx_int_count data member (PC8250 class/ISR), 133
tx_running data member (PC8250 class/ISR), 133
TxNotify() function (Win32Port class), 475, 483-484, 498-499
TXQueue data member (PC8250 class/ISR), 134
TXSpaceFree() function
  PC8250 class, 178
  RS232 class, 70, 101
  Win32Port class, 486-487
TXSpaceUsed() function
  PC8250 class, 178
  RS232 class, 80
  Win32Port class, 486-487

U

uart data member (PC8250 class ISR), 133
UART systems
  8250 clones, 21, 22-24
  16450 chips, 22
  16550 chips, 22, 24-25
  16560/16570 chips, 22, 25
  functions of, 20
  multiport boards, 207, 220-222
  RS-232 interface using, 10
uart_type data member (PC8250 class/ISR), 8, 133
underline feature, adding to Win32TermClass, 623
UngetCommChar() function (Win16 API), 397
  using for Peek() function, 401

Unicode standard, 5
UNIX systems
  intelligent multiport boards for, 27-28
  termcap file escape sequences, 329
Update button (Win32Port test program), 511
UpdateCursor() function (Win32Term class), 591-592, 593
U.S. Robotics. *See* 3COM
Usage Handle object (TAPI), 685-686
UserAbort() function (Modem class), 666

V

V.22 modems, 29
V.22*bis* modems, 29
V.32 modems, 29
V.32*bis* modems, 30
V.34 modems, 30, 650
V.42/V.42*bis* modems, 32-33
V.90 modems, 30, 657-658
  as hardware standard, 650
VerticalScroll() (Win32Term class), 593-594
ViewComm (Greenleaf Software), 44
virtual functions. *See also* functions *and individual classes*
  Base Window class, 362
  C++, 49, 362
  MyWin32Port derived class, 516-517
  RS232 class, 77
  Win32Port class, notification routines, 482-484
voltage
  communications versus control lines, 10
  serial communications, 8
voltmeters, 46

W

wait_for_connection() function, 668
wait_for_response() function (Modem class), 668
WaitCommEvent() function (Win32 serial API), 464-465
  with SetCommMask() function 460,
  with Win32Port class, 478, 481, 496, 501-502

856 Index

WaitForMultipleEvents() function (Win32Port class), 502
WaitForMultipleObjects() function (Win32Port class), 479
warning errors, RS232 class, 59. *See also* errors, error handling
Web sites
   Digi International hardware, 204
   FOSSIL drivers, 309
   RS-232 standard (EIA), 2
   UART datasheets, 123
Win16 comm API
   data structures
      COMSTAT, 400-401
      DBC, 398-400
      DCB, 402
   functions
      BuildCommDCB(), 391-392
      ClearCommBreak(), 392, 395-396
      CloseComm(), 392
      EnableCommNotification(), 392
      EscapeCommFunction(), 292-393
      FlushComm(), 293
      GetCommError(), 293-294, 395, 396
      GetCommEventMask(), 394
      GetCommState(), 394
      OpenComm(), 392, 394-395, 398-400
      Peek() function equivalent, 401
      PeekMessage(), 421
      ReadComm(), 395, 433
      SetCommBreak(), 392, 395-396
      SetCommEventMask(), 396-397
      SetCommState(), 392, 397
      TransmitCommChar(), 397
      UngetCommChar(), 397
      WriteComm(), 397-398, 433
   ReadTime() with, 422
Win16 multiline edit control, 422
Win16 systems. *See also* Win16Port class
   communications APIs for, 390-401
   programming for, 389-390
   RC files, 423-429
   Win32 programming comparisons, 433-444
WIN16.CPP (Win16Port class), 404-421
WIN16.H (Win16Port class), 402-404
Win16Port class, 390
   class descriptor source code (WIN16.H), 402-404
   DCB structures, 402
   event masks, use of, 396-397
   GetCommError() API function with, 402
   HardwareOverrunError() functions with, 402
   implementation file source code (WIN16.H), 404-421
   line_status element, 402
   modem_status_register, 402
   public members, 484-492
   test program (TERMW!6.CPP), 422-429
Win32 serial API, 598, 693-695, 765-766
   BuildCommDB() function, 445-446, 445-446
   CommConfigDialog() function, 439
   data structures
      COMMCONFIG, 439-440, 449-450, 452, 456, 460, 463
      COMMPROP, 440-443, 463
      COMMTIMEOUTS, 438-439, 462
      COMSTAT, 496-497
      DCB, 435-438, 445-446, 455
      MODEMSETTINGS, 460, 463
      OVERLAPPED, 444, 457, 458-459, 478
   documentation limits, 469
   functions
      BuildCommDCBandTimeouts(), 446
      ClearCommBreak(), 446-447, 459
      CloseHandle(), 447
      CommConfigDialog(), 448-450, 460
      CreateFile(), 434, 447-448, 452, 453, 454, 455, 457, 500
      CreateWindow(), 577
      EscapeCommFunction(), 450-451
      GetCommConfig(), 451-452, 460
      GetCommMask(), 452-453
      GetCommModemStatus(), 453-454
      GetCommProperties(), 440, 454, 463
      GetCommState(), 454-455, 462
      GetCommTimeouts(), 438, 455
      GetDefaultCommConfig(), 455-456
      GetLastError(), 447, 454, 456, 457, 459, 466, 477, 497
      GetOverlappedResult(), 456-457, 458-459, 465, 466-467, 477, 481
      GetWindowLong(), 576-577
      PurgeComm(), 457-458
      ReadFile(), 434, 457, 458-459, 465, 478-479, 502
      SetCommBreak(), 447, 459, 502
      SetCommConfig(), 452, 459-460
      SetCommMask(), 460-461
      SetCommState(), 460, 461-462, 501
      SetCommTimeouts(), 438, 462
      SetDefaultCommConfig(), 462-463
      SetupComm(), 463-464
      SetWindowLong, 576-577
      TransmitCommChar(), 464, 466
      WaitCommEvent(), 481, 496, 501-502
      WaitForCommEvent(), 460, 464-465, 478
      WriteFile(), 434, 457, 466-467, 475-477
   MTTTY.C program example, 469-470
Win32 systems. *See also* MS-Windows systems
   intelligent multiport boards for, 27-28
   programming for, 433-434
   SimpleTapi class implementation, 709-711
   TAPI for
   threading, 434
   Win32 programming comparisons, 433-444

Index

Win32Port class, 469
  accessing from SimpleTapi, 698
  API functions for, 444-467
  class descriptor source code (WIN32PORT.H), 517-521
  clear_error() function, 481
  ClearCommError() function, 483, 496-497
  console-based test program (CHAPT12.CPP), 509-516
  constants, 499-500
  data members, 499
    first_debug_output_line, 500
    m_bInputThreadReading, 500-501
    m_Dcb, 501
    m_dwErrors, 501-502
    m_dwModemStatus, 502
    m_dwWindowsError, 501
    m_hInputThread, 501
    m_hKillInputThreadEvent, 502
    m_hKillOutputThreadEvent, 502
    m_hOutputThread, 501
    m_hPort, 500
    m_iBreakDuration, 500
    m_RxQueue, 501
    m_TxQueue, 501
  DCB helper class, 504-505
    class description (DCB.H), 559-560
    implementation file (DCB.CPP), 560-565
  DCB structure members in, 435
  error_status member, 477
  FormatDebugString() function, 496
  GetModemStatus() function, 495
  IdleFunction() function, 505-506
  implementation file (WIN32PORT.CPP), 521-559
  MTDeque helper class, 503-504
    header/implementation file (MTDEQUE.H), 565-570
  notification functions
    BreakDetectNotify(), 499
    CdNotify(), 499
    CtsNotify(), 499
    DsrNotify(), 499
    FramingErrorNotify(), 499
    HardwareOverrunErrorNotify(), 499
    ParityErrorNotify(), 499
    RiNotify(), 499
    RxNotify(), 483, 497-498
    SoftwareOverrunErrorNotify(), 499
    TxNotify() function, 483-484
  notification routines, 482-484, 597-598
    TxNotify(), 498-499
  OnRiNotify() function, 483
  output_worker function, 474-475
  protected functions, 492
    check_modem_status(), 481-482, 495-496
    clear_error(), 483
    clear_error() function, 495
    read_buffer(), 492-493
    read_byte(), 493
    read_settings(), 494-495
    translate_last_error(), 497
    write_buffer(), 493
    write_byte(), 493-494
    write_settings(), 494
  public functions
    constructor function, 484-485
    destructor function, 486
    DtrDsrHandshaking(), 487
    ErrorName(), 492
    FlushRXBuffer(), 491-492
    FlushTXBuffer(), 492
    FormatDebugOutput(), 487-491, 500
    Peek(), 491
    RtsCtsHandshaking(), 487
    RXSpace Free(), 486-487
    RXSpace Used(), 486-487
    TXSpace Used(), 486-487
    TXSpaceFree(), 486-487
    Win32Port() constructor, 484-485
    ~Win32Port() destructor, 486
    XonXoffHandshaking(), 487
  RS232 class, relationship to, 484
  in Tapi32Port class, 753-755
  threading in, 471-472, 471-472
    InputThread() function, 477-482
    OutputThread() function, 472-477
  translate_error() function, 477
  TxNotify() function, 475
  WaitForMultipleEvents() function, 502
  WriteFile() function with, 475-477
Win32Port() constructor (Win32Port class, 484-485
  with SimpleTapi class, 704
WIN32PORT.CPP (Win32Port class), 521-559
WIN32PORT.H (Win32Port class), 517-521
Win32Term class, 573-574
  basic structure, 578-579
  class descriptor source code, 623-627
  converting to BaseWindow class, 596
  creating AnsiWinTerm class from, 596-597
  data members
    m_bClassRegistered, 587
    m_BorderColor, 586
    m_bShowingCursor, 583-584
    m_bWrap, 583
    m_CharSize, 586
    m_CurrentColor, 582
    m_hFont, 584
    m_hParent, 582
    m_hWnd, 581-582
    m_iCharDescent, 586
    m_lfFont, 584
    m_Offset, 585-586
    m_Position, 586
    m_ScreenText, 582-583
    m_ScrollRange, 585
    m_VirtualSize, 585
    m_VisibleSize, 584-585
  data structures, LOGFONT, 590
  implementation source code, 627-648
  integrating with AnsiTerminal class, 596-597
  member functions
    Dispatch(), 594-595
    HorizontalScroll(), 593-594
    KillFocus(), 593
    Paint(), 580, 592-593
    SetFocus(), 593
    Size(), 594
    UpdateCursor(), 593
    VerticalScroll(), 593-594
    WindowProc(), 588, 595
  private classes
    CreateData, 581
    Pair, 581
    TextColor, 580-581

Continued

Win32Term class *(continued)*
  public functions
    Clear(), 590
    GetBackgroundColor(), 590
    GetBorderColor() function, 590
    GetCursorPosition(), 591-592
    GetForegroundColor(), 590
    GetLogFont(), 590
    Output(), 590-591
    SetBackgroundColor(), 589
    SetBorderColor(), 589
    SetCursorPosition(), 591-592
    SetFont(), 591
    SetForegroundColor(), 589
    Win32Term() constructor, 587-588
    ~Win32Term() destructor, 588-589
WIN32TERM.CPP (Win32Term class), 627-648
WIN32TERM.H (Win32Term class), 623-627
window handles, in Windows programming, 575
WindowProc() function (Win32Term class), 588, 595
Windows (Microsoft). *See* MS-Windows; Win32 systems
WindowsPort class, GetCommState() API function, 394
WinProc
  for HWND callbacks, 575, 577
  TAPI hidden window, 685
wired OR. *See* open collector configuration
word length bit field (LCR), 575-576
Word Size combo box (Win32Port test program), 511
wrapper classes, defined, 69
write a buffer function
  Digi driver INT 14H interface, 236
  FOSSIL driver, 308
Write() functions (RS232 class), 62, 66, 74-75, 96-97
  timed version, 505
write modem control register, EBIOS interface, 274
write_buffer() function
  DigiBoard class, 236
  PC8250 class, 176
  RS232 class, 67

with TransmitCommChar() API function, 397
Win32Port class, 493
write_byte() function
  PC8250 class, 175
  RS232 class, 67
  with TransmitCommChar() API function, 397
  Win32Port class, 493-494
write_settings() function
  EBIOSPort class, 276
  PC8250 class, 177
  with SetCommState() API function, 397
  Win32Port class, 494
WriteComm() function (Win16 API), 397-398, 433
WriteFile() function, 457, 466-467
  Win16Port class, 475-477
  Win32 serial API, 433
WriteKey() function
  AnsiTerminal class, 346-347
  Terminal base class, 339

X

X00.SYS (Gwinn) Fossil driver, 309
XEMCFG.EXE, multiport configuration file, 243
XEMDOS5.SYS
  DigiBoard class interface descriptor source code, 249-265
  implementation source code, 246-248
  multiport board driver, 244-246
XMODEM protocol (file transfers), 37, 765-766
XON/XOFF check box (Win32Port test program), 512
XON/XOFF flow control, 35
XonXoffHandshaking() function
  PC8250 class, 180-181
  RS232 class, 61, 78-79, 101
  Win32Port class, 487

Y

YMODEM protocol (file transfers), 37, 766

Z

ZABORT frame type (ZMODEM), 772
ZACK frame type (ZMODEM), 769-770

ZCHALLENGE frame type (ZMODEM), 772
ZCOMMAND frame type (ZMODEM), 772
ZCOMPL frame type (ZMODEM), 772
ZCR frame type (ZMODEM), 772
ZCRCE data packet format (ZMODEM), 775
ZCRCG data packet format (ZMODEM), 775
ZCRCQ (j) data packet format (ZMODEM), 776, 779
ZCRCW (k) data packet format (ZMODEM), 776
ZDATA frame type (ZMODEM), 772, 778
ZDLE characters (ZMODEM), 777
ZEOF frame type (ZMODEM), 779
ZFERR frame type (ZMODEM), 772
ZFILE frame type (ZMODEM), 778
ZFIN frame type (ZMODEM), 772
ZFIN frame type (ZMODEM), 779
ZFREECNT frame type (ZMODEM), 772
_ZMODEM.CPP (Zmodem class), 792-822
_ZMODEM.H (Zmodem class), 790-792
Zmodem class
  class descriptor source code, 788-790
  constants definition file, 790-792
  FileTransfer class relationship, 782
  implementation source code, 792-822
ZMODEM file transfer protocol, 38
  conversion options (ZF0), 770
  CRC calculations (Crc16/Crc32 classes), 785-788
  data subpack formats
    ZCRCE, 775
    ZCRCG, 775
    ZCRCG (j), 779
    ZCRCQ (j), 776
    ZCRCW (k), 776
  data subpacket, 771-772
  encoding binary data, 776-777
  extended options (ZF3), 771
  frame types
    ZABORT, 772
    ZACK, 770
    ZCHALLENGE, 773

Index

ZCOMMAND, 773
ZCOMPL, 773
ZCRC, 773
ZDATA, 772, 778
ZEOF, 779
ZFERR, 773
ZFILE, 778
ZFIN, 772, 779
ZFREECNT, 773
ZNAK, 772
ZRINIT, 769, 778-779
ZRPOS, 772, 778, 779
ZRQINIT, 768-769, 777, 778
ZSINIT, 769-770
ZSKIP, 772
frame components, 768
header formats, 773-774
    hex (hexadecimal) headers, 774-775
    16-bit/32-bit CRC, 774, 775
history, 767-768
management options (ZF1), 770-771
transport options (ZF2), 771

_ZMODEM.CPP (Zmodem class), 792-822
ZMODEM.H (Zmodem class), 788-790
_ZMODEM.H (Zmodem class), 790-792
ZNAK frame type (ZMODEM), 772
ZRINIT frame type (ZMODEM), 769, 778-779
ZRPOS frame type (ZMODEM), 772, 778, 779
ZRQINIT frame type (ZMODEM), 768-769, 778
    ASCII test line, 777
ZSINIT frame type (ZMODEM), 769-770
ZSKIP frame type (ZMODEM), 772

IDG Books Worldwide, Inc. End-User License Agreement

READ THIS. You should carefully read these terms and conditions before opening the software packet(s) included with this book ("Book"). This is a license agreement ("Agreement") between you and IDG Books Worldwide, Inc. ("IDGB"). By opening the accompanying software packet(s), you acknowledge that you have read and accept the following terms and conditions. If you do not agree and do not want to be bound by such terms and conditions, promptly return the Book and the unopened software packet(s) to the place you obtained them for a full refund.

1. **License Grant**. IDGB grants to you (either an individual or entity) a nonexclusive license to use one copy of the enclosed software program(s) (collectively, the "Software") solely for your own personal or business purposes on a single computer (whether a standard computer or a workstation component of a multiuser network). The Software is in use on a computer when it is loaded into temporary memory (RAM) or installed into permanent memory (hard disk, CD-ROM, or other storage device). IDGB reserves all rights not expressly granted herein.

2. **Ownership**. IDGB is the owner of all right, title, and interest, including copyright, in and to the compilation of the Software recorded on the disk(s) or CD-ROM ("Software Media"). Copyright to the individual programs recorded on the Software Media is owned by the author or other authorized copyright owner of each program. Ownership of the Software and all proprietary rights relating thereto remain with IDGB and its licensers.

3. **Restrictions On Use and Transfer**.

   (a) You may only (i) make one copy of the Software for backup or archival purposes, or (ii) transfer the Software to a single hard disk, provided that you keep the original for backup or archival purposes. You may not (i) rent or lease the Software, (ii) copy or reproduce the Software through a LAN or other network system or through any computer subscriber system or bulletin-board system, or (iii) modify, adapt, or create derivative works based on the Software.

   (b) You may not reverse engineer, decompile, or disassemble the Software. You may transfer the Software and user documentation on a permanent basis, provided that the transferee agrees to accept the terms and conditions of this Agreement and you retain no copies. If the Software is an update or has been updated, any transfer must include the most recent update and all prior versions.

4. **Restrictions on Use of Individual Programs.** You must follow the individual requirements and restrictions detailed for each individual program in the *What's on the CD-ROM?* Appendix in the back of this Book. These limitations are also contained in the individual license agreements recorded on the Software Media. These limitations may include a requirement that after using the program for a specified period of time, the user must pay a registration fee or discontinue use. By opening the Software packet(s), you will be agreeing to abide by the licenses and restrictions for these individual programs that are detailed in the Appendix and on the Software Media. None of the material on this Software Media or listed in this Book may ever be redistributed, in original or modified form, for commercial purposes.

5. **Limited Warranty.**

   (a) IDGB warrants that the Software and Software Media are free from defects in materials and workmanship under normal use for a period of sixty (60) days from the date of purchase of this Book. If IDGB receives notification within the warranty period of defects in materials or workmanship, IDGB will replace the defective Software Media.

   (b) IDGB AND THE AUTHOR OF THE BOOK DISCLAIM ALL OTHER WARRANTIES, EXPRESS OR IMPLIED, INCLUDING WITHOUT LIMITATION IMPLIED WARRANTIES OF MERCHANTABILITY AND FITNESS FOR A PARTICULAR PURPOSE, WITH RESPECT TO THE SOFTWARE, THE PROGRAMS, THE SOURCE CODE CONTAINED THEREIN, AND/OR THE TECHNIQUES DESCRIBED IN THIS BOOK. IDGB DOES NOT WARRANT THAT THE FUNCTIONS CONTAINED IN THE SOFTWARE WILL MEET YOUR REQUIREMENTS OR THAT THE OPERATION OF THE SOFTWARE WILL BE ERROR FREE.

   (c) This limited warranty gives you specific legal rights, and you may have other rights that vary from jurisdiction to jurisdiction.

6. **Remedies.**

   (a) IDGB's entire liability and your exclusive remedy for defects in materials and workmanship shall be limited to replacement of the Software Media, which may be returned to IDGB with a copy of your receipt at the following address: Software Media Fulfillment Department, Attn.: *Serial Communications Developer's Guide, Second Edition*, IDG Books Worldwide, Inc., 7260 Shadeland Station, Ste. 100, Indianapolis, IN 46256, or call 1-800-762-2974. Please allow three to four weeks for delivery. This Limited Warranty is void if failure of the Software Media has resulted from accident, abuse, or misapplication. Any replacement Software Media will be warranted for the remainder of the original warranty period or thirty (30) days, whichever is longer.

(b) In no event shall IDGB or the author be liable for any damages whatsoever (including without limitation damages for loss of business profits, business interruption, loss of business information, or any other pecuniary loss) arising from the use of or inability to use the Book or the Software, even if IDGB has been advised of the possibility of such damages.

(c) Because some jurisdictions do not allow the exclusion or limitation of liability for consequential or incidental damages, the above limitation or exclusion may not apply to you.

7. <u>U.S. Government Restricted Rights</u>. Use, duplication, or disclosure of the Software by the U.S. Government is subject to restrictions stated in paragraph (c)(1)(ii) of the Rights in Technical Data and Computer Software clause of DFARS 252.227-7013, and in subparagraphs (a) through (d) of the Commercial Computer – Restricted Rights clause at FAR 52.227-19, and in similar clauses in the NASA FAR supplement, when applicable.

8. <u>General</u>. This Agreement constitutes the entire understanding of the parties and revokes and supersedes all prior agreements, oral or written, between them and may not be modified or amended except in a writing signed by both parties hereto that specifically refers to this Agreement. This Agreement shall take precedence over any other documents that may be in conflict herewith. If any one or more provisions contained in this Agreement are held by any court or tribunal to be invalid, illegal, or otherwise unenforceable, each and every other provision shall remain in full force and effect.

my2cents.idgbooks.com

Register This Book — And Win!

Visit **http://my2cents.idgbooks.com** to register this book and we'll automatically enter you in our fantastic monthly prize giveaway. It's also your opportunity to give us feedback: let us know what you thought of this book and how you would like to see other topics covered.

Discover IDG Books Online!

The IDG Books Online Web site is your online resource for tackling technology — at home and at the office. Frequently updated, the IDG Books Online Web site features exclusive software, insider information, online books, and live events!

10 Productive & Career-Enhancing Things You Can Do at www.idgbooks.com

- Nab source code for your own programming projects.
- Download software.
- Read Web exclusives: special articles and book excerpts by IDG Books Worldwide authors.
- Take advantage of resources to help you advance your career as a Novell or Microsoft professional.
- Buy IDG Books Worldwide titles or find a convenient bookstore that carries them.
- Register your book and win a prize.
- Chat live online with authors.
- Sign up for regular e-mail updates about our latest books.
- Suggest a book you'd like to read or write.
- Give us your 2¢ about our books and about our Web site.

You say you're not on the Web yet? It's easy to get started with IDG Books' *Discover the Internet,* available at local retailers everywhere.

CD-ROM Installation Instructions

The CD-ROM that accompanies this book includes all the source code presented in the chapters. To use this code on your PC, simply copy the directory structure to the location of your choice on your PC. You can do this by using XCOPY from the command line:

```
C:\>
C:\> MD CODE
C:\CODE> XCOPY D:\*.* . /S
```

Another alternative is to use Windows Explorer to copy the root directory of the CD-ROM. You can then paste it into the directory of your choice.

The sample programs from each chapter are found in a directory named after the respective chapter. This directory also includes the suitable make files for the programs.